The Scientific Study of Peace and War: A Text Reader

The Scientific Study of Peace and War

A Text Reader

John A. Vasquez
Marie T. Henehan

Lexington Books
An Imprint of Macmillan, Inc.
New York

Maxwell Macmillan Canada
Toronto

Maxwell Macmillan International
New York   Oxford   Singapore   Sydney

This book is published as part of the Issues in World Politics Series, James N. Rosenau and William C. Potter, consulting editors.

Library of Congress Cataloging-in-Publication Data

The Scientific study of peace and war: a text reader / edited by John A. Vasquez, Marie T. Henehan.
    p.   cm.—(Issues in world politics series)
    Includes bibliographical references and index.
    ISBN 0-669-20104-9 (case : alk. paper).—ISBN 0-669-20105-7 (pbk. : alk. paper)
    1. Peace—Research—Methodology. 2. War—Research—Methodology. I. Vasquez, John A., 1945–   . II. Henehan, Marie T. III. Series.
JX1904.5.S35 1992
327.1'72'072—dc20   91-12169
                                                                     CIP

Lexington Books
An Imprint of Macmillan, Inc.
866 Third Avenue, New York, N.Y. 10022

Macmillan, Inc. is part of the Maxwell Communication Group of Companies.

Printed in the United States of America

printing number
1 2 3 4 5 6 7 8 9 10

To Elyse Henehan Vasquez
Our most important collaboration

Contents

II The Expansion of War

III Peace and the Global Institutional Context

IV The Termination and Impact of War

V Conclusion

Appendix   Applying the Scientific Method to the Study of War

Methodological Contents

Introduction to the Scientific Method

Percentages and Probabilities

Two-by-Two Contingency Tables (Yule's Q and phi)

Rank-Order Correlation (tau b), Percentages, and Probability Models (Poisson Process Model)

Statistical Significance

Correlational Analysis (Pearson's r and Multiple Regression)

Time-Series Analysis (Forecasting)

Impact Assessment Technique (Box-Tiao)

Modeling

Formal Theory

Inductive Theory Construction

Preface

This book is meant to serve two purposes: to introduce students to the scientific study of peace and war and to provide general readers with an overview of current scientific knowledge about war. Both of us have taught courses concerned with questions of war and peace for some time. What amazes us is how little of the scientific work on war and peace has found its way into undergraduate classrooms. Many popular textbooks written while much of the scientific study of war was in its infancy continue to be used in subsequent editions without much attempt by their authors to incorporate recent scientific evidence or thinking about war. Too many students, in our view, are being educated about the causes of war with simplistic theories and with little regard for scientific evidence or the best scholarly thinking on the subject.

There are several reasons for this paucity of scientific education. One is that so few scientific studies are available for undergraduate use. Most are published in journals, and books devoted to the subject are hardbacks aimed at a scholarly audience. We hope to correct this situation by bringing together in a single volume the best and most important research on war and peace in the last twenty-five years. Although Francis Beer's fine textbook, *Peace against War,* provides an overview of this research up to 1981, it does not reprint articles. Like many other college instructors, we believe it is essential that students read actual research, not just summaries of it.

Nevertheless, scientific studies of war and peace can be difficult to read, and most undergraduates have not been taught how to read quantitative articles. Indeed, one of the reasons scientific research on war has not been available for the classroom is the feeling that students cannot read it. This was brought home to us a few years ago when one of us went on leave for a semester and was replaced by a promising doctoral student, who proceeded to replace most of the quantitative studies in an upper-level course on the causes of war with simpler material. When asked why he did this, he replied "that quantitative material is too difficult for students to understand." This is often true, but what is so disappointing is that it never seemed to occur to him that one of the purposes of college courses is to teach students how to read and analyze material that they might not have been able to read before they took the course. That is precisely what we try to accomplish in this text reader.

One of our main objectives in this book is to teach students how to read scientific studies of peace and war, or what is sometimes called peace research. In the appendix (chapter 15), we have provided a learning package designed to help students learn how to read scientific research by having them conduct an elementary data analysis. Our experience has been that much of the complexity of scientific research disappears as students actually attempt to go about conducting their own research. Faced with problems of marshaling data and making inferences, they find that abstract concepts and methodological concerns become more relevant, and hence easier to understand.

Parts I–IV of the book reprint some of the most important research on war and peace. There is a brief introduction to each article, and following each is commentary highlighting and interpreting the main findings. We carefully take readers through the methodological assumptions and techniques used in the analysis. Each reprinted article contains a variety of methodological issues that could be addressed, but in a collection of fourteen articles, such exhaustive treatment would be cumbersome. Instead, we have chosen to treat one or two issues in depth for each piece. For example, although statistical significance is important for nearly all statistical studies, it is treated in depth only in the commentary on the Wallace article in chapter 3. In this way, each commentary is one lesson in methodology. The commentary also introduces readers to a number of terms (printed in **boldface**) that will aid them in their comprehension of the scientific approach. Those who are very new to the scientific method may want to read the commentary first, while more advanced students can go right to the article that is reprinted.

Within each part, the chapters have been arranged so that the easiest techniques, like comparisons using percentages, are introduced first. Each reprinted article serves as a lesson not only for what the research can impart about war but for providing students with the skills necessary to read and evaluate scientific research on war and peace. We hope that this book will help reduce scientific illiteracy among liberal arts majors and introduce them to the norms of scientific inquiry.

Another reason that scientific studies on war and peace have not been used in the classroom or had a wide readership has been the sentiment of many traditional and now neotraditional scholars that such studies have not generated much knowledge. For some, this reflects a deeper philosophical position that politics, history, and war cannot be studied scientifically. This view was expressed early on (Bull 1966) just as a few scholars were attempting to learn and apply the scientific approach. Ultimately, this is an empirical question; either the scientific study of war and peace will be able to identify and corroborate a body of generalizations, or it will fail to do so.

This book seeks to address this question by furnishing an interim report of what we know about war in the form of a compendium of the best work to date. Although we are still far from a general scientific theory of war, we have a body of evidence, derived mostly from the 1816–1965 period, about some of the factors that appear to be associated with the onset and spread of war in the modern era. In addition, we have evidence about who wins wars, patterns of recovery, and the impact of war on global and domestic political systems.

The book is organized so as to bring that body of research and findings into a coherent whole, making what we have learned clearer. In this sense, this book is meant to be one statement in the emerging scholarly debate about how research might cumulate in knowledge and serve as a basis for constructing a scientific theory of war and peace. More important, this book is meant to provide general readers, particularly those unfamiliar with contemporary academic international relations inquiry, with an overview and guide to the scientific study of war. Many practicing scientists, medical doctors, and psychologists who have been concerned about nuclear weapons and the danger their proliferation poses even in a post–Cold War era have felt the need for such an overview, and we hope this volume helps meet the need. We also think that many who are responsible for the diplomacy and military policy of their states will find this volume worthwhile, not because it provides specific advice but because much of the research raises serious questions about the adequacy of popular beliefs about what causes war and how peace can be maintained.

Any collaborative work involves some division of labor. Our differing interests and skills led us naturally to assume responsibility for different tasks associated with this project. John Vasquez has written the Major Findings section of each commentary and is responsible for the interpretations presented in those sections. Marie Henehan has written the Methodological Notes and taken responsibility for explaining the methodological concepts and statistical techniques used in the reprinted articles. Each of us, however, read and commented on the other's work, and we share equally in the design and thrust of the book.

This book can be used in two ways. For those interested primarily in knowledge about war and peace, the chapters can be read in order, except that the appendix (chapter 15), which presents the learning package, should be used fairly early on by those who lack an extensive background in social science data analysis. We assume that in many international relations courses, the book will be used in this manner. For those interested primarily in the methods and in quantitative analysis, we have classified the reprinted articles according to the main statistical techniques they employ and suggest that they be read according to the difficulty of the statistical analysis. To facilitate this second use of the book, we have provided a methodological table of contents following the main table of contents.

All of the articles are reprinted in their original form, complete and unabridged, with the exceptions of those by Leng (one table has been deleted), Organski and Kugler, and Vasquez, and the excerpt from Bueno de Mesquita's book, *The War Trap.*

Several people have generously provided their time to read all or parts of the manuscript. Our special thanks go to Paul Diehl and Randolph Siverson, who reviewed the entire manuscript and provided several important suggestions on the book as a whole and our commentary. Thanks are also due to William Potter and James Rosenau, the series editors, for their efforts, and especially to Jim Rosenau who provided some important ideas about the organization and format of the book. We are particularly indebted to Jack Levy, J. David Singer, Michael Wallace, Russell Leng, Bruce Bueno de Mesquita, Frank Wayman, Manus Midlarsky, Peter Wallensteen, A. F. K. Organski, Jacek Kugler, Karen Rasler, William Thompson, and Stuart Bremer for reading our commentary on their work and responding to it. We would also like to express our appreciation to Bruce Russett for permission to reprint material from his edited book, *Peace, War, and Numbers,* and for his editing of *The Journal of Conflict Resolution,* which we found indispensable in our search for the best articles in the field and from which we have reprinted several pieces. Trying to develop an innovative reader is not an easy or speedy process, and we are grateful we have had the opportunity to work closely with Paul O'Connell, Jaime Welch Donohue, and the editorial staff at Lexington Books. Our gratitude also goes to our undergraduates, whose views on these and several other articles aided us greatly in making our final selection.

Although we have benefited from the advice and comments we have received, the final responsibility for the contents of this volume remains with us. Finally, this book is dedicated to our daughter, Elyse, who we hope will grow up in a more peaceful world than we have.

M.T.H.
J.V.

Block Island
January 1991

Introduction:
Studying War Scientifically

John A. Vasquez

The Nature of Science

Through the ages, many have written about war, and a considerable amount of this effort has been devoted to understanding why people kill each other. Those of us committed to the scientific study of war believe that part of the reason so little progress has been made in understanding is that social inquiry has not followed a sufficiently rigorous method. Philosophical analyses of the physical world, for example, even when conducted by such a brilliant thinker as Aristotle, did not produce a cumulative body of knowledge. A substantial advancement in our understanding came only with the development and application of the scientific method. Only through the use of controlled observation, the collection of evidence, careful inferences, and the belief that hypotheses must always be tested before being accepted was progress made. This same kind of rigor and commitment to the truth—no matter which privileged theories are challenged—will be necessary before any real knowledge about war and peace is acquired.

Lewis F. Richardson, one of the first to study war scientifically, expressed these kinds of concerns when he decided to apply scientific methods to this problem. He felt there were many vehemently held opinions about war, its causes, and ways to prevent it, but little attempt to subject those opinions to systematic testing to see if they were accurate. In letters to Quincy Wright, he lamented:

> There is in the world a great deal of brilliant, witty political discussion which leads to no settled convictions. My aim has been different: namely to examine a few notions by quantitative techniques in the hope of reaching a reliable answer.

> I notice that many of those who are considered to be experts on foreign affairs do not base their opinions on historical facts, but on some sort of instinctive reasoning. (Richardson 1960b: v)

Unfortunately, many people who discuss politics seem more interested in persuading others of the rightness of their cause than in understanding. As a result, few take the time to carefully study the world in an empirical fashion.

Richardson's statement should make it clear that science is primarily an **empirical** method of inquiry that can be used to study how the world works. The scientific method cannot tell us what is *good* or what values *should* be pursued. Once we have an understanding of how the world works, we may be in a position to make changes so that humans can do things—fly, for example—that they were unable to do before. Pure science can produce an applied science of engineering, and clearly many of the early peace researchers hoped that a scientific study of war would help control and prevent war.

In this way, the **normative**—what we value or the way we believe people ought to behave—informs the empirical. The normative determines the uses to which we might put knowledge, as well as shaping what we study and how we define problems, but it should not blind us to the way the world actually works. Nor should our values and beliefs so shape our observations and the way we make inferences that evidence is ignored or consciously manipulated. Because the normative plays such a large role in shaping inquiry, it is important to remember that when we speak of scientific **objectivity**, we mean simply that scholars should not distort their evidence to fit their beliefs; that is, they should be honest and truthful. We do not mean that science is neutral in terms of the values its research is used to support. Science has had a tremendous impact on how we live, what we believe, and how we think. All of these things have normative implications, but science itself is not a method for telling us whether these things are good or bad. For that we must look to other discourses.

At the start, it is important to keep in mind the purpose of science. A scientific approach aims to uncover general patterns, not the unique. It seeks to uncover the **nomothetic** (from the Greek, *nomos*, meaning "lawlike") rather than the **idiographic** ("the particular"), which falls within the domain of historical description. A scientific study does not attempt to delineate the particular causes of a specific war, but examines a large number of wars to identify the conditions associated with war as a general social phenomenon.

The earliest stages of a science are usually devoted to identifying generalizations. One way to identify these generalizations is to come up with a verbal statement that describes a general pattern—for example, "alliances bring about war, not peace." Such a statement might be refined, qualified, and made more precise; with some reflection and study, it eventually becomes a working **hypothesis** about one of the factors associated with the onset of war. Such statements need not always be verbal; they can also be mathematical, with symbols representing concepts.

The crucial point for the scientifically oriented, however, is that the hypothesis be tested against the evidence before being accepted. Ransacking history for anecdotes that support an argument is no substitute for a systematic review of all the relevant evidence. In this regard, those who take a scientific approach do not object to careful historical analyses of particular wars; indeed they usually read a great number of them. Nor do they object to case studies or even theoretical history. Their objection is to attempting to establish generalizations through an overreliance on argumentation and armchair philosophizing, as was often done in the 1950s and 1960s. Science outlines a set of criteria for determining which statements will be accepted and which will be rejected. It is a self-imposed system for determining beliefs and knowledge about the empirical world.

Science insists on sifting through the evidence, and this usually involves counting—if for no other purpose, at least to count those instances that support a generalization and compare them with those instances that do not. Much of the research in the early stages of a science, and hence in this book, is confined to just that: seeing how many cases support or fail to support a hypothesis.

Counting, of course, involves statistics, and there is a popular prejudice against statistics. Some even argue that anything can be proved with statistics or that statistics lie. Of course, statistics do not lie; people lie, and they can use either statistics or words to do so. What separates the sophisticated from the statistically illiterate is that the former can read and tell when statistics are being misused and the latter cannot. Those who are illiterate tend to reject or accept blindly any statistical argument because they are unable to evaluate it or even understand others' evaluations. This book aims to give you the skills necessary to examine the evidence yourself. It progresses from the simple use of percentages to more complicated techniques, teaching you how to read tables and interpret statistics so that you can evaluate an author's interpretation and conclusion.

Once some generalizations are established, the next step in scientific inquiry is to try to construct an explanation of these patterns. An **explanation** answers the question "why?" and often takes the form of a causal analysis. While explanation logically follows discovery of patterns, the two often go hand in hand, with theoretical hunches suggesting patterns and empirical observation informing theoretical explanations. Although the two go together, it is important to understand that the practices that lead to discovery and theory construction are analytically distinct from the philosophical justifications and rules used for accepting or rejecting a hypothesis or explanation as accurate or true. The **logic of discovery** is not the same as the **logic of confirmation**. Discovery may occur for a variety of reasons—because of a correct view of the world or by serendipity, for example. Confirmation, however, involves following specific procedures to test a hypothesis and assess its adequacy in light of the evidence.

The best way to learn about scientific research, in our view, is to actually do it. To this end, we have reprinted a learning package developed by Stuart A. Bremer and colleagues and adapted by Marie Henehan. It is in the appendix, leaving to the discretion of the instructor or the reader when to use it. Readers who are unfamiliar with contemporary social science data analysis might want to begin with the learning package. Part I of the learning package provides a brief history of the scientific study of peace and war. For those new to the use of quantitative techniques, the completion of parts II and III will make comprehension of the articles in this book considerably easier. Part IV, which shows how to develop and test a hypothesis on the onset of war, can be equally useful as an introductory exercise at the beginning of a course or as a capstone project at the end. With some or all of the learning package as background, readers will be ready to tackle scientific studies on war. We hope that the articles presented in this book will serve as useful illustrations of the merits and promise of the scientific approach.

Factors Related to the Onset of War

What do we know about war? How much confidence do we have about our knowledge? These questions guide our inquiry throughout this book. The two questions go together because the scientific approach assumes that we can never be sure that what we think is true actually is true. Science is an open-ended process; it is a way of thinking about empirical truth and searching for it rather than an end or body of knowledge that, once established, is beyond refutation. What we establish today we might have to reject tomorrow because of new tests or evidence. When we use the word *true*, we must always be tentative. What we really mean is that a hypothesis has passed empirical tests and has not been falsified by the evidence or is consistent with the evidence. Because of this aspect of science, some scholars prefer not to use terms like *true* and *false*, substituting *accurate* and *erroneous*, *adequate* and *inadequate*, or *accept* and *reject*. While these terms indicate the tentative nature of empirical truth, they tend to become functional equivalents of *true* and, as such, can be seen as intellectual euphemisms. For this reason, we will not always shy away from using *true* and *false*, but readers should be aware of the tentative way in which we employ these terms.

These caveats made, it should be clear that more appropriate questions than "What do we know about war?" are "What have we learned about war?" and "How accurate are our beliefs about war and peace in light of the evidence?" The past twenty-five years have seen the testing of a number of popular beliefs about the causes of war, and that process has helped refine thinking about war and raised serious questions about existing explanations of war. Most of these tests, however, have been confined to mapping what J. David Singer has called the *correlates* of war. In other words, the research has not attempted to delineate the causes of war but simply to identify all of the factors that seem to coappear with war. Discovering which of these factors associated with war act as causes and which are simply correlates or

epiphenomena is something that will require making difficult inferences and is best done once the mapping of correlates is more complete.

Nevertheless, the articles reprinted in part I have uncovered some interesting patterns with important theoretical implications for explaining why war occurs. Jack Levy (chapter 1) examines the role that alliances play in war and peace by looking at great power alliances from the sixteenth to the twentieth centuries. His evidence shows that, contrary to some beliefs, alliances do not prevent war, but instead are usually followed by war within five years of their formation. The major exception to this pattern is the nineteenth century where alliances are not generally followed by war.

Many scholars think alliances might be associated with peace because they are the typical device by which a balance of power is maintained, which many of these scholars believe is the real factor maintaining peace. Since Levy's analysis shows that alliances are not followed by peace, but by war, this raises questions about the adequacy of the belief that the balance of power is associated with peace. Nevertheless, supporters of the balance of power would reject this implication by arguing that only a fluid alliance structure is associated with peace, while permanent alliances may be associated with war if they undermine the balancing process. While the absence of an association between alliance making and peace is disappointing, supporters of the balance of power argue that a more critical test would be a direct examination of the relationship between balancing and war. J. David Singer, Stuart Bremer, and John Stuckey (chapter 2) provide evidence on this hypothesis.

Notions that differences in the distribution of power are important for the onset of war are as old as Thucydides (1954:25), who asserted that the growth of Athenian power and the fear this caused in Sparta made the Peloponnesian War inevitable. In eighteenth-century Europe, the belief that war is associated with the increase of power of one state led to the idea that a relative balance of power among nations would reduce the prospect of war. Singer, Bremer, and Stuckey provide a systematic test of the idea that certain distributions of capability within the major state system are associated with peace and others with war. In a rather surprising result, they find that parity (or relative balance) in the system is associated with less war in the nineteenth century but more war in the twentieth century. A close analysis of this study suggests that the different distributions of capability in the two centuries produce different types of war, with the implication that differences in capability do not bring about war or maintain peace. Differences in capability might affect the kind of warfare that results but not whether war occurs or is avoided.

Although hardly definitive, both the Levy and the Singer, Bremer, and Stuckey findings raise questions about a balance-of-power explanation of war. Neither provides any evidence to support this explanation, and each reports associations that are contrary to what would be expected if the balance-of-power explanation were accurate. Such contrary evidence can be explained away, but at some point a balance-of-power explanation must be able to pass important tests, and this has not yet happened, despite extensive research.

Further evidence refuting a power politics logic is provided by Michael Wallace's study in chapter 3. In examining the characteristics distinguishing crises that escalate to war from the many that do not, he identifies the presence of an ongoing arms race as a critical factor. Conversely, a peace-through-strength model is unable to differentiate between the crises that go to war and those that do not, indicating that being stronger than the other will not prevent war. Instead, an arms race resulting from the attempt to increase strength may fuel tensions, which increase hostility and the probability of war.

Paul Diehl (chapter 4) has criticized Wallace's arms race studies and has eliminated the relationship between arms races and dispute escalation by employing a new index of "military buildups" and a new sample. In a response to Diehl, Wallace (1990) employs Diehl's index and still finds a statistically significant relationship, but the measure of association drops considerably. Nevertheless, the frequency distribution (in Wallace 1990) shows that disputes that occur in the absence of arms races rarely escalate, while about half of the "mutual military buildups" escalate to war.

Levy's and Wallace's studies suggest a possible pattern: states fearing war enter alliances and build up their military, and these practices increase the likelihood of war instead of producing peace. Most wars are not preceded by alliances and arms races, however, indicating that these practices may be associated with only certain types of wars—probably wars between major states that are relatively equal in capability.

Russell Leng's analysis in chapter 5 provides some insights as to why some of the disputes with ongoing military buildups may not escalate. He shows that the first crisis between two states is not likely to escalate to war, but, as the crises repeat and persist, they are characterized by a pattern of bargaining that makes them escalate to war, usually by the third crisis. Leng shows that crisis escalation to war is associated with attempts to show resolve by increasingly escalating realpolitik tactics from one crisis to the next while ignoring realist counsels of prudence.

Another factor that may prevent disputes with ongoing military buildups (like that between the United States and the Soviet Union) from escalating is the absence of territorial contiguity. Several pieces of research show that territorial contiguity is an important characteristic of disputes that escalate to war. Gochman and Leng (1983) find that disputes that involve a physical threat to vital territorial issues are more likely to escalate to war than disputes over other issues. More impressively, Diehl (1985b) finds that about one-fourth (twelve of fifty) of the disputes involving territorial contiguity escalate, whereas only one of fifty-four noncontiguous disputes escalate (about 2 percent). Finally, Bremer (forthcoming) shows that of several variables associated with the onset of war, contiguity is the most potent.

Bruce Bueno de Mesquita (chapter 6) attempts to identify some of the necessary conditions for the initiation of war and hence the escalation of crisis to war. He finds that wars are initiated by the side that has a greater capability after geographical distance and alliance commitments are factored in. The side with a greater "expected utility" for war will tend to be the initiator. Bueno de Mesquita's analysis tells us something about the kinds of factors that affect the initiation and timing of war once leaders have already decided that war is necessary.

The findings produced by the studies in part I suggest a pattern that can be pieced together to provide a more coherent explanation of the onset of war. War between relative equals seems to result from a series of steps, each associated with the onset of war. Alliances appear to be a way of preparing for war and usually result in such. More dangerous are arms races. Crises that occur in the absence of some form of military buildup rarely escalate to war, but crises that do occur in the presence of military buildups frequently escalate, especially if they involve disputes over territory that is contiguous to one of the parties. The first crisis is not likely to escalate, but if they persist, the probability of escalation goes up, with the third crisis very likely to end in war.

These factors imply that after each step is taken, it becomes more difficult to avoid war because of increased tension and hostility. The hostility is most likely a function of the failure to resolve the issue underlying the dispute. Unable to come to some accommodation, one or both sides try to impose a settlement through confrontation. Both sides prepare for the worse. Alliances tighten, and arms races are fueled. In such an atmosphere, another crisis is likely to emerge. Bargaining takes on a harder line, and preventing crisis escalation becomes increasingly problematic as crises persist. Eventually one emerges that escalates to war. The side that initiates the war is likely to be the stronger side as measured by Bueno de Mesquita's expected utility score.

It must be emphasized that such an explanation is an interpretation of the findings presented in part I. Other interpretations are possible, and we will not have a sense of which explanations are the most acceptable until they have been tested by further research. Recent research has found alliances, arms races, certain kinds of bargaining techniques, and repeated crises associated with the onset of some kinds of war. Why these factors bring about war, how they are connected, and what initially produces them remain matters needing investigation. Further discussion of the meaning of this pattern for constructing an explanation of war is provided in the concluding part of the book.

The Expansion of War

Most wars are fought between two parties; only a few spread to become world wars. Why do some wars spread, while others do not? The selections in part II address this question.

Randolph Siverson and Joel King (chapter 7) posit that alliances may be the main culprit in spreading war. They find that a major factor associated with large wars is the presence of prewar alliances. The more typical dyadic (two-party) war tends to be fought by states without prewar alliances.

If Siverson and King are correct, then it would be expected that a system with extensive alliances would be more likely to have large wars than a system with few alliances. Alliances would not necessarily cause these wars, but if war broke out in that context, it would be likely to draw in nonbelligerents because of their entangling alliances.

Frank Wayman provides evidence in chapter 8 that something like this may be operating in the twentieth century. He finds that when alliances polarize the system into two hostile blocs, this is correlated with large wars. When the system has not recently (bi)polarized, wars are of lesser magnitude.

In addition to the question of alliance polarization, Wayman investigates the effect of bipolar and multipolar distributions of power. A bipolar distribution of power occurs when capabilities (usually measured by population, economic production, and military personnel) are concentrated in the hands of two states, as with the United States and the Soviet Union in the 1950s and early 1960s. A multipolar system has capabilities spread out to three to five or more states, as was the case in the early twentieth century. Wayman finds that prior to the two world wars, a multipolar distribution of power existed. He shows that a multipolar distribution of power is associated with wars of very high magnitude, while wars of low magnitude are associated with a bipolar distribution of power.

Wayman's findings imply that a precondition of world wars is a multipolar distribution of power that a system of alliances has harnessed into two polarized blocs. World wars are associated with the presence of several major states that are brought together into two separate blocs. Such a statistical finding seems to fit the historical situation that emerged in the World War I and World War II periods.

As John Vasquez notes in chapter 14, to this pattern we can add Singer, Bremer, and Stuckey's finding that wars of high magnitude in the twentieth century are associated with relative parity. This probably means that when alliances polarized the system into two blocs, it did so in a manner that made each bloc relatively equal to the other. This suggests a new hypothesis: the necessary conditions for a large war, like a world war, are (1) a multipolar distribution of capability, that is (2) polarized into two hostile blocs that (3) are relatively equal in the sense that one bloc does not have a preponderance of power. These factors do not cause war, but if a war should break out in these conditions, then it is apt to spread to become a large war.

Alliances obviously play the key role in converting a multipolar distribution of capability into a structure that will make world war possible. From this perspective, alliances are pernicious because they have the unanticipated consequence of bringing about the necessary conditions of world war. Not only are world wars devastating, but they seem to come about without anyone really wanting or desiring them. Again, these conclusions, derived from statistical analyses, correspond to what we know historically about World War I and World War II. Although several leaders were willing to risk war, no one, including Adolf Hitler, wanted a general world war. All of the initiators were counting on keeping the war limited in terms of the number of participants or its goals so they could win it militarily or through a negotiated victory.

Manus Midlarsky's study (chapter 9) offers additional clues about how world wars are brought about. In a detailed analysis of the period prior to World War I, he finds that the number of disputes accumulates and makes the system unstable. The period prior to 1893 lacks this characteristic. Here crises and disputes occur, but as new disputes arise, others are removed from the global political agenda, thereby keeping the number of ongoing disputes relatively constant.

For Midlarsky, world war is associated with the inability of the system to handle disputes. Why do disputes pile up instead of being resolved? Through a number of tests, Midlarsky discovers that so long as disputes between major states are kept separate from disputes between minor states, the system will be stable. However, when the disputes of major states are combined with disputes involving major and minor states, the system is unstable and eventually breaks down, resulting in war.

One of the ways in which these two sets of disputes are combined is through alliances. Thus, Midlarsky provides further, albeit indirect, evidence that alliances may bring about a structure that favors world war.

The readings in this part of the book illustrate how scientific studies, even when conducted independently of each other, can be used to build on one another. Moreover, the findings in this part are related to those in part I. Levy shows that great power alliances are more likely to result in war than other alliances. Wallace's relationship on arms races appears to hold more for world wars than other wars. Leng's findings on how behavior in one crisis affects behavior on the next are certainly relevant to Midlarsky's conclusions. Although far from complete, a picture of wars between relative equals is emerging.

Peace

The studies in parts I and II tell us something about war, but they do not explicitly tell us a great deal about what prevents it. Here, Peter Wallensteen's research, reprinted in chapter 10, is very important, for he helps identify the factors that appear to be associated with peace. Wallensteen finds that periods of peace in the post-Napoleonic era all seem to be associated with major states' agreeing on certain basic "rules of the game" and avoiding unilateral acts. Periods resulting in war, by contrast, find major states trying to resolve issues by acting on their own. This suggests that when states can come up with a way to resolve issues on the basis of some agreed-upon principles, even simple rules of deference, they might be able to avoid war among themselves. When they are not able to do this, it is not surprising that Wallensteen finds that they engage in alliance making and a buildup of armaments, precisely the kind of behavior we find associated with war in the studies reprinted in part I.

Wallensteen's analysis provides support for the view that war is a way of making decisions and that it will persist until acceptable alternative ways of making decisions are adopted. Nevertheless, Wallensteen's analysis provides a basis for optimism; he demonstrates empirically that at times states have been successful in implementing alternative ways of making decisions. He shows that peace is possible and provides a guide as to how it might be constructed.

The Termination and Impact of War

The scientific study of war has been concerned not only with the causes of war and the conditions of peace but also with how wars end and their impact on the future. The work reprinted in part IV highlights some of the best research in this area.

Steven Rosen (chapter 11) is primarily concerned with who wins wars. His analysis establishes the fact that wars are usually won by the side that has access to more revenue and has lost a lower percentage of its population. His careful comparison of cases shows that, of these two factors, greater revenue appears to be more critical.

A.F.K. Organski and Jacek Kugler (chapter 12) examine recovery from war. They hypothesize the existence of a "phoenix factor." (The phoenix is an Egyptian mythological bird that lives for five hundred to six hundred years, consumes itself by fire, and then rises from its own ashes renewed and youthful.) Organski and Kugler find that fifteen to twenty years after a major war, the losers catch up with the winners economically and surpass them in power. They provide evidence to show that this was the case in both World War I and World War II. On the basis of this evidence, they argue that war cannot fundamentally change long-term economic growth and shifts in power. This raises questions about the extent to which war can serve the purposes of a global struggle for power.

Karen Rasler and William Thompson (chapter 13) consider the domestic political effects of wars. They find that most interstate wars do not have a permanent effect on the domestic political economy of states but that large global wars do have an important impact: they result in a permanent increase in domestic taxes and expenditures. The additional revenues and expenditures brought about by the global war do not return to prewar levels after the war is concluded. Their work provides empirical support for arguments that certain kinds of war increase the power and centralization of the state apparatus.

The readings in part IV show how many ideas about war can be best addressed by analyzing careful and precise measures. Part V returns to questions of explanation and the contribution of the scientific study of war to our understanding.

Interpreting the Findings

The concluding article (chapter 14) reviews the major scientific project studying war—the Correlates of War. It is an attempt to piece together the various findings that have been produced into a coherent set of explanations about why war occurs and spreads. In addition, it provides a brief review of some of the less extensive research on conditions of peace. Most of the other articles reprinted in this book are discussed in this analysis and are placed within the context of findings from numerous other studies. Vasquez attempts to show that some findings are stronger than others and that progress had indeed been made in the cumulation of knowledge. Following this review is the appendix, which contains the learning package on the scientific study of war.

I
Factors in the Onset of War

1

Alliance Formation and War Behavior: An Analysis of the Great Powers, 1495–1975

Jack S. Levy

Editors' Introduction

The role that alliances play in the onset of war and the maintenance of peace has long been a subject of discussion and debate.
Many have thought that alliances might be a way of preventing
war; others have argued that alliances are a way of preparing for
war. In this article, Jack Levy explores the relationship between
alliances and great power war. He empirically examines alliance
and war data he has collected to see whether alliances involving
the most powerful states in the system are followed by war or
peace. One of the contributions of his project is that he has collected data for a 500-year period (1495–1975), a significant advance over most other data-based studies of war, which begin
with 1816.

Theories of Alliances and War

One important aspect of international alliance behavior concerns the relationship between alliances and war. Much of the theorizing about this relationship is essentially a debate between those who believe that alliances
are stabilizing and contribute to peace and those who believe that alliances
are destabilizing and conducive to war. Each side advances a variety of

Jack S. Levy, "Alliance Formation and War Behavior: An Analysis of the Great Powers, 1495–
1975," *Journal of Conflict Resolution*, Vol. 25, No. 4 (December 1981), pp. 581–613. Copyright © 1981 by Sage Publications, Inc. Reprinted by permission of Sage Publications, Inc. and
the author.

Author's note: I wish to thank Clif Morgan for assistance with much of the data analysis, and
the University of Texas Research Institute for financial support.

plausible theoretical arguments, derived from several different conceptual frameworks and supported by numerous historical examples. After reviewing the nature of these theoretical generalizations, we shall attempt to help resolve this debate through an empirical analysis of the alliance-war relationship over the last five centuries.

One of the oldest and most common arguments linking alliances to peace, advanced by statesmen as well as scholars, is that alliances deter war by enhancing the credibility of military intervention in support of the victims of aggression and by clarifying the precise nature of the military coalition that would confront any aggressor. A more generalized argument is that alliance commitments reduce the level of uncertainty in the international system and thus minimize the likelihood of a war generated by misperception and miscalculations (Singer et al. 1972:23). Others claim that concrete alliance commitments minimize the chance of a major shift in the alliance configuration and its potentially destabilizing consequences (Osgood 1967: 86). Many balance of power theorists assert that alliances are an indispensable means of maintaining an equilibrium and preserving a balance of power, and hence keeping the peace (Gulick 1955: 61–62; Holsti et al. 1973: 31–32). Alliances may also contribute to stability when a more moderate member uses the alliance to constrain a revisionist alliance partner (Liska 1968: 34–36). In addition, there exist numerous indirect theoretical linkages through which alliances may contribute to peace; for example, alliance with a respected power may enhance the prestige (and hence the domestic authority and stability) of a regime whose collapse might be destabilizing for the international system (Liska 1968: 37–40).

Perhaps even more widely accepted are the opposing arguments, strongly influenced by the experiences of the early twentieth century, that alliances are destabilizing and conducive to war. One major line of argument is that alliances tend to generate counteralliances, which generate further mistrust and tensions, leading to arms races and the further polarization of the alliance structure and ultimately to war (Kaplan 1957: 24; Holsti et al. 1973: 33; Wright 1965: 774).

Exacerbating this dynamic of escalation is the inherent tendency of an existing alliance to generate its own policy imperatives, so that the alliance comes to be perceived as an end in itself, transcending the more concrete national security interests for which it was initially created (Holsti et al. 1973: 34–35). Political decision makers come to believe that support for one's allies, regardless of its consequences, is essential to their national prestige, and that the failure to provide support would ultimately result in their diplomatic isolation in a hostile and threatening world. This symbolic significance of an alliance commitment may also become linked with public opinion (for example, "national honor") and the domestic security of elites, thus further increasing the importance of alliance solidarity. It is for these reasons that the policies and precipitous actions of secondary states often drag their Great

Power protectors into war. Thus alliances may contribute not only to the incidence of war but also to the scope of war, by spreading it to additional states and geographical areas (Scott 1967: 117; Fay 1928: 34).

Balance of power theorists make an implicit but critical distinction between ad hoc alliances and permanent alliances. Ad hoc alliances, formed for the specific purpose of counterbalancing a dangerous shift in relative power capabilities, are necessary for checking any aggressive state (Wright 1965: 773). Permanent alliances, on the other hand, are destabilizing precisely because they interfere with the flexibility of the international system to generate the ad hoc alliances necessary in order to maintain a stable equilibrium. Alliance commitments reduce the number of possible coalitions which could conceivably form against any aggressor, and are therefore conducive to war (Morgenthau 1967: 335). In addition, permanent alliances facilitate war by reducing the number of states which can play the role of the "balancer"—an unaligned state which constantly shifts its political support to the side of the weaker coalition, with the ultimate threat of military intervention (Claude 1962: 47–48; Gulick 1955: 65–67). This accounts for the concern of balance of power theorists for "flexible" alliance configurations. It is also argued that the uncertainty concerning the nature of the defensive coalition that might form serves itself as a deterrent, so that permanent alliances contribute to war by reducing the uncertainty and hence simplifying the calculations of the aggressor (Morgenthau 1967: 335; Bueno de Mesquita 1975: 190). From a different theoretical perspective, Deutsch and Singer (1964: 317–381) argue that pluralist cross-cutting pressures minimize the likelihood of mutually reinforcing antagonisms which lead to war and that alliance commitments contribute to war by limiting these cross-cutting pressures. Thus a polarized alliance structure, characterized by the absence of cross-cutting ties, may lead to war because of the rigidities which prevent the formation of certain counterbalancing coalitions (Singer and Small 1968: 251; Wallace, 1973a). Nonpolarized alliance systems, on the other hand, facilitate the formation of countervailing ad hoc alliances and are conducive to peace.

Recently, there have been a number of efforts to subject some of these theoretical propositions to rigorous empirical test. Most of these empirical studies are based on the war and alliance data generated by Singer and his colleagues on the Correlates of War Project, covering the period 1816–1965 (Singer and Small 1966b, 1972). Singer and Small (1966c) find that national alliance commitments are strongly associated with national war behavior. At the systemic level, they find that alliances are associated with relative peace in the nineteenth century but with relatively high levels of war in the twentieth century, so that over the entire period there is a low association between alliance formation and the amount of war (Singer and Small 1967). This relationship holds both for indicators of the number of alliances and the degree of bipolarity of the alliance configuration. Wallace (1973a) finds a nonlinear relationship between alliance polarization and war, in which very high or very low levels of polarization predict war. Using some different indicators of polarization, Bueno de Mesquita (1975, 1978) finds that the "tightness" of the alliance structure is unrelated to war but that changes toward increasing tightness are correlated with higher levels of war, while "discrete" alliances are associated with relatively low levels of war. In addition, there are several studies of whether alliance commitments lead to military intervention in an ongoing war, and hence to the expansion of that war. Singer and Small (1966b) find that alliance commitments do in fact increase the likelihood of intervention in support of one's ally. Sabrosky (1980) finds that alliance commitments predict to wartime reliability in the nineteenth century but not in the twentieth, and that defensive alliances are more reliable than neutrality pacts. Siverson and King (1980) demonstrate that the empirical linkages between alliance commitments and wartime support of allies are a function of various characteristics of the alliance.

There are clearly a variety of plausible theoretical linkages between alliances and war (or peace). Recent empirical studies have yet to demonstrate conclusively, however, which of these complex linkages is most important, in conjunction with which other factors, and under which conditions. Nor do we have an answer to the basic question of the aggregate impact of these linkages; given that some of the complex linkages between alliances and war are stabilizing and others are destabilizing, the question is whether the vector sum of these tendencies points toward peace or toward war. It is this basic question which is the focus of this study. It is an important question in itself, and the process of answering will ultimately contribute to the development of an explanatory theory.

In approaching this question, we shall focus on the alliance and war behavior of the Great Powers. One problem with the empirical studies noted above is that they include all states in the international system. Yet many of our theories of alliances and war, particularly those derived from a balance of power framework, refer primarily to Great Power behavior, given their overriding importance as the dominant actors in the system. By including all states in the analysis, there is a risk of drowning potentially significant patterns of Great Power behavior in a sea of noise generated by smaller states operating in a more restricted temporal or geographical setting. For the purpose of analyzing the alliance and war behavior of the Great Powers, however, the nineteenth and twentieth centuries do not provide an adequate data base. This period does not include a sufficient number of cases of wars involving Great Powers to permit generalizations concerning the relationship between Great Power alliance formation and war behavior. It also precludes the investigation of some important theoretical questions or the analysis of long-term historical changes in the alliance-war relationship. A more extended temporal domain would increase the number of cases and, by increasing the variation in underlying international conditions (and the randomness of their effects), facilitate a comparative historical analysis. It is to this task that we now turn.

Research Design

In order to answer the general question of whether alliances are associated more with war or with peace, we shall investigate the following interrelated and more specific questions, which provide different operational slants on the general theoretical question: Are periods of high levels of alliance formation also characterized by high frequencies and amounts of war? Are alliances generally followed by war? Are wars generally preceded by alliances? Are there differences depending on the nature of the alliance, the types of wars, and the historical period? After conceptualizing, operationalizing, and measuring the dependent and independent variables, we shall utilize several different methods to analyze their empirical relationships.

I have defined and identified the Great Powers elsewhere (Levy 1983: ch. 2), so only a brief summary is necessary here. A Great Power is defined as a state which plays a major role in international politics with respect to security-related issues. Operational indicators of Great Power status include the following: possession of a high level of power capabilities; participation in international congresses and conferences; de facto identification as a Great Power by an international conference or organization; admission to a formal or informal organization of powers (such as the Concert of Europe); participation in Great Power guarantees, territorial compensations, or partitions; and generally treatment as a relative equal by other Great Powers, in terms of protocol, alliances, and so on. The Great Power system began in 1495, which marks the fusion of several separate historical processes: the internal centralization of power within territorial states, the decline of the universal secular authority of the Pope and Holy Roman Emperor, the coalescence of the major territorial states of Europe into an interdependent system of power relations, and the emergence of a global world economy centered in Europe and sustained by sea power.[1] The theoretical criteria noted above are applied to the historical literature (Levy 1983: ch. 2), and the resulting Great Power system emerges as shown in table 1–1.

The Dependent Variable: International War

Our focus here is on interstate wars involving at least one Great Power; civil, imperial, and colonial wars are excluded. None of the existing compilations of war data is entirely adequate for our purpose here, so I have generated a new data set by systematically combining some of the existing data (for details, see Levy 1983: ch. 3). Prior to 1815, wars are included if

---

[1] This argument draws considerable support from the historical literature (Petrie 1947:1–2, 11; Mowat 1928:7, 28; Hill 1914:2:209; Albrecht-Carrié 1975:6:1081–1082; Mattingly 1955: 124–125; Oman 1936:16; Dehio 1962:23; Howard 1976:20; Wallerstein 1976; Modelski 1978).

Table 1–1
Composition of the Modern Great Power System

France	1495–1975
England/Great Britain	1495–1975
Austrian Hapsburgs/Austria/Austria-Hungary	1495–1519; 1556–1918
Spain	1495–1519; 1556–1808
Ottoman Empire	1495–1699
United Hapsburgs	1519–1556
The Netherlands	1609–1713
Sweden	1617–1721
Russia/Soviet Union	1721–1975
Prussia/Germany/West Germany	1740–1975
Italy	1861–1943
United States	1898–1975
Japan	1905–1945
China	1949–1975

and only if they were included in at least two of the following compilations: Wright's *A Study of War* (1965); Sorokin's *Social and Cultural Dynamics, Volume III: Fluctuation of Social Relationships, War, and Revolution* (1937); and Woods and Baltzly's *Is War Diminishing?* (1915). After 1815 the Singer-Small data are used. Excluded from the above are wars not involving at least one Power, civil and imperial wars, and wars not meeting Singer's 1000 battle deaths criterion. There were 119 interstate wars involving the Great Powers, and of these, 64 are particularly serious in that they involve Great Powers on both sides of the conflict.

The measurement of war is based on the Singer-Small conceptualization (1972), with a few modifications. The dimensions include frequency, duration (elapsed time), extent (number of participating Great Powers), magnitude (nation-years), severity, intensity (deaths per million European population), and concentration (fatalities per nation-year). Each of the wars is measured along each of these dimensions; a more thorough treatment, together with a discussion of analytical and methodological problems, can be found in Levy (1983: ch. 4).

The Independent Variable: International Alliances

The concern here is with international military alliances, the most useful definition of which has been provided by Russett (1971: 262): "A formal agreement among a limited number of countries concerning the conditions under which they will or will not employ military force." There are a number of analytical problems involved, however, in refining this concept for empirical analysis.

The best conceptualization and compilation for empirical analysis is that done by Singer and Small (1966b) for the post-Vienna period. They focus on formal military alliances and classify them (on the basis of the written treaty) as follows: "(I) Defense Pact: Intervene militarily on the side of any treaty partner that is attacked militarily; (II) Neutrality and Non-Aggression Pact: Remain militarily neutral if any cosignatory is attacked . . . ; (III) Entente: Consult and/or cooperate in a crisis, including armed attack." They exclude wartime alliances, those concluded within three months of (and therefore assumed to be in anticipation of) war, collective security agreements, treaties of guarantee involving all relevant powers, agreements concerning general rules of behavior and unilateral guarantees (Singer and Small 1966c: 136).

While the Singer-Small conceptualization has served as a sound framework for a plethora of alliance studies, it is not without its analytical problems. One is the classification of the rather vague "nonaggression" pact along with the neutrality pact as a "Type II" alliance. Whereas the neutrality pact generally obligates each signatory to remain militarily neutral in the event of an attack on the other, and may even designate specific aggressors to which the alliance is applicable, the more sweeping non-aggression pact is simply an assurance that neither will use force against the other. The credibility of such a guarantee may be questionable, however, for it may be in situations of greatest suspicion and mistrust that some form of generalized reassurance is sought. Consider the renunciation of force agreement between the Soviet Union and the Federal Republic of Germany in 1970; surely we would not want to consider these states as "allies." The non-aggression pact is fundamentally different from the more specific and more credible neutrality pact, and perhaps ought to be classified as "agreements limited to general rules of behavior" (for example, Kellogg-Briand Pact), which Singer and Small (1966c: 136) exclude from their compilation.[2] In addition, "entente" pacts, involving "consultation" and "cooperation," do not formally specify the conditions under which force will or will not be employed, and should not be treated as formal military alliances (an example is the 1938 Franco-German entente pact). Similarly, treaties of "friendship" or "amity" will not be considered military alliances.[3]

---

[2] As a result, some class II pacts may involve lower levels of commitment than class III pacts, as confirmed by Sabrosky's (1980) empirical study of wartime reliability. Consequently, the Singer-Small classification may not be a genuine ordinal scale of measurement, and the various studies which used ordinal statistical measures (Wallace 1973a; Bueno de Mesquita, 1975) may technically be in error.

[3] It is necessary to make further modifications of the Singer-Small conceptualization. Since unilateral guarantees impose formal obligations for the use of force under certain conditions, they will be included here. (There is no a priori reason to believe that formal unilateral guarantees have less influence on subsequent behavior than do mutual defense or neutrality pacts. Certainly not all alliances impose identical obligations upon all signatories, and a unilateral guarantee can be considered an important form of the larger class of asymmetrical alliance treaties. Unilateral guarantees are truly unilateral, of course, only on the military level, and often involve a variety of political or economic tradeoffs—for example, the English-Russian Subsidy Treaty of 1755.)

Our aim here is to compile a list of all defensive and neutrality alliances (involving at least one Great Power) satisfying the above criteria. Given the impracticability of examining the texts of all conceivable alliance treaties over the last five centuries, some approximations must be made. For the period 1815–1965, the Singer-Small alliance data (1967) are used, with the modifications outlined above. Three additional compilations serve as the data base for the decade since 1965 (Keesing's 1974; Grenville 1974; Rohn 1974). The pre-1815 period presents more of a problem. Given the selectivity of secondary historical analyses, several sources must be used to guarantee comprehensiveness and also to provide enough information on each alliance in order to ascertain whether it satisfies our analytical criteria (particularly its "defensive" character). Consequently, we examine several leading historical sources (Albrecht-Carrié 1975; Mowat 1928; Hill 1914; Petrie 1947; Langer 1968; Mostecky 1965; Parry and Hopkins 1970) and include in this compilation any alliance which is identified by at least two of these sources, once it meets the criteria established above.[4]

Also included are multilateral guarantees (excluded by Singer and Small) of territorial frontiers or peace settlements, as long as they formally specify military sanction (such as the Barrier Treaties of Utrecht). Collective security agreements involving the members of an international organization (for example, UN Charter) are excluded, however, because such "universal alliances" are not specific in terms of either the nature of the act sufficient to trigger a response or the commitment to use military force. Formal military alliances between a Great Power and a subnational (or transnational) political entity within another state (excluded by Singer and Small) are included here; while historically rare, they may be no less important than an alliance with a weak European state and equally capable of generating an internationalized civil war (for example, England and the French Huguenots in the sixteenth century). Formal agreements for the provision of mercenaries by one state to another in the event of war are included, for they imply at least neutrality. For the same reasons we include subsidy treaties, where a state formally agrees in advance to pay a cash subsidy for another's participation in a future war (which should be distinguished from a wartime subsidy), or to provide a certain number of troops for a cash subsidy. Formal agreements establishing a demilitarized zone—in which two states agree to respect the neutrality of a third state in the event of a war—impose no obligations regarding the use of force against each other and hence are excluded, as are agreements prohibiting the use of particular weapons. Pacts regarding the denial of military facilities to the enemy or restricted passage of troops or ships, or free use or passage of the same by allies, are more ambiguous but are included because of the strong implication of neutrality. Royal marriage pacts involving two states are included only if accompanied by provisions regarding the use of force against each other in wartime.

[4] Given the possible lack of independence between the Mostecky and Parry/Hopkins indexes, these sources alone are not considered sufficient for inclusion.

There are numerous analytical problems involved in the identification of these alliances. One is whether renewals of existing alliances and bilateral treaties supplementing multilateral pacts should be identified as separate alliances. The main criterion here is whether the second alliance increases significantly the existing degree of commitment, either in terms of a less neutral or more offensive character (for example, the bilateral treaties between the Soviet Union and its East European allies supplementing the multilateral Warsaw Pact; see Rohn 1974:124). Another problem is whether multilateral pacts should be aggregated or disaggregated (such as The Triple Alliance of 1887, or separate Italo-German and Italo-Austrian pacts supplementing the Triple Alliance of 1882). Fortunately, problems of this kind arise relatively infrequently and are handled on a case-by-case basis.

Table 1–2
Number of Alliances Over Time

	Century					
	16th	*17th*	*18th*	*19th*	*20th*	*16th–20th*
Number of alliances	5	9	15	25	65	119
Number of Great Power alliances	4	5	14	14	10	47
Great Power alliances/ Number of alliances	80%	56%	93%	56%	15%	39%

The resulting compilation of alliances is presented in Levy (1983: ch. 4). A theoretically important subset of this compilation consists of alliances involving two or more Great Powers, which will be referred to as "Great Power Alliances." It is very difficult to determine the termination dates of alliances, particularly given our reliance on secondary sources, for which the termination of an alliance is generally of less significance than its inception. Consequently, for the present time, termination dates are given only for the period since 1815, based on the Singer-Small data.

The Nature of Alliances: Quantitative Description

Before turning to the alliance-war relationship, let us first consider the nature of the alliances themselves and their change over time. First—and this is not revealed by our compilation of alliances but is clearly evident from the process of their generation—there appears to be a fundamental difference in the character of alliances before and after the Congress of Vienna. Prior to 1815, the vast majority of earlier peacetime alliances were offensive in nature, in that the initiation of military action was explicitly called for in the treaty and not conditional upon an external military attack. Since 1815, the offensive alliance has become an extremely rare phenomenon; in nearly all modern treaties, the action triggering the alliance commitment is a military attack against one of the allies.[5]

Also interesting is the fact that the frequency of alliance formation (at least of defensive or neutrality pacts) has increased noticeably over time. This is demonstrated in table 1–2, where the number of alliances, Great Power alliances, and their ratio is indicated for each century. The observed increase results largely from the increasing participation of secondary states

---

[5] We have not explicitly identified all offensive alliances, for several reasons: (1) our main theoretical concern is with defensive alliances, (2) offensive alliances are more reflections than causes of instability and war, and (3) their empirical identification involves some difficult methodological problems due to their secret nature.

in alliances with Great Powers (due in part to the expanding number of such states in the international system). The frequency of Great Power alliances, however, has been relatively constant over the last three centuries. The meaning underlying these trends will become clear in a later section.

Alliances and War: An Empirical Analysis

As noted earlier, we shall examine a number of more narrowly defined operational problems in order to deal with the more general question of the relationship between alliances and war. Let us first examine the simple correlation between alliance formation and war, using the frequency and amount indicators per 10-year period.[6] The resulting ordinal-level correlations (Kendall's tau-b) between alliances and war and between Great Power alliances and Great Power war are given in table 1–3.[7]

Regardless of whether we focus on alliances and war involving the Great Powers, or Great Power alliances and wars between the Powers, these results tend to contradict the popular hypothesis that the greater the number of alliances, the greater the amount of war. The empirical evidence points in the opposite direction: historically, periods of high alliance formation have been characterized by relatively infrequent wars, of short duration, low magnitude, severity and intensity, and average concentration.[8]

---

[6] These dimensions are not entirely independent, of course; the total severity and other dimensions of war in a given period of time are functions of its frequency. The product-moment correlation coefficients between frequency and the other war indicators (aggregated by 10-year periods) are as follows: duration, .54; extent, .82; magnitude, .42; severity, .32; intensity, .33; concentration, .29.

[7] This rank-order correlation coefficient is used in order to avoid the distortion resulting from the disproportionate effect of a few extreme cases (periods of very high levels of war) on the Pearson product-moment coefficient, and also to minimize the impact of measurement error; there is some imprecision in the quantitative data, but not enough to disrupt any ordinal rankings. A 10-year period is the optimum period of temporal aggregation for our purposes here. With five-year periods, the average time between alliance formation and war within each period is too short to capture the full causal impact of many alliances. With 25-year periods, however, alliances and wars separated by nearly a quarter-century could be included within one period.

Here we are using the correlations for descriptive rather than inferential purposes, and do not include significance levels. Since we are dealing with the population of all alliances and wars meeting our criteria, rather than samples from those populations, there is no sampling distribution, no sampling error, and hence no basis for determining the statistical significance of a sample statistic. For those interested, however, I note that all but five of the tau-b's in table 1–3 are significant at $p = .05$ or less.

[8] It might be objected that the possibility of serial correlation in the war and alliance time series may pose problems for this analysis. A Durbin-Watson test indicates that there does appear to be significant autocorrelation in the alliance frequency indicator (10-year periods), but none in the frequency of Great Power alliances or number of Powers in at least one alliance each period; analysis based on the separate pre- and post-1815 periods shows no significant autocorrelation in any of the alliance indicators. Regarding the war indicators: For Great Power wars, only the

Table 1–3
Rank-Order Correlations (Kendall's tau-b) between Number of Alliances and War Indicators

War Indicator	Alliances and War	GP Alliances and GP War
Frequency	−.12	−.20
Duration	−.32	−.31
Extent	−.15	−.17
Magnitude	−.32	−.28
Severity	−.16	−.16
Intensity	−.19	−.18
Concentration	−.01	−.07

Note: n = 47; 10-year periods.

Another measure of alliance formation, reflecting the plausible view that the number of alliances a state is involved in may be less important than the fact that it has any at all, is the number of Great Powers in (or forming) alliances in any given period. The rank-order correlations between the number of Powers forming alliances in a given period and the amount of war are given in table 1–4. The correlations involving Great Power war are not significantly different and need not be included here. We see that the differences between table 1–3 and 1–4 are not substantially significant.[9]

Table 1–4
Rank-Order Correlations: Number of Powers Forming Alliances and Amount of War

War Indicator	Kendall's tau-b
Frequency	−.13
Duration	−.30
Extent	−.14
Magnitude	−.26
Severity	−.14
Intensity	−.16
Concentration	−.04

Note: n = 47; 10-year periods.

duration and possibly the magnitude indicators show signs of autocorrelation; for interstate wars involving the powers, only the extent and concentration indicators demonstrate autocorrelation. These potential problems are not serious here, however, for several reasons. First, rank-order correlation analysis is much less sensitive to serial correlation than is classical regression analysis. Second, autocorrelation does *not* result in biased population estimators; the fact that the variance of the parameters is underestimated is of little concern to us, since we are dealing with the population rather than a sample and do not rely on significance tests (Johnston 1972:214–221, 246–249; Goldberger 1964:238–241). Finally, given the very general nature of the question under consideration (is the empirical association positive or negative?), the lack of precision necessary to establish this relationship, and the consistency of the

Table 1–5
Rank-Order Correlations (Kendall's tau-b):
Alliance Indicators and Characteristics of the
Average War

War Indicator	Number of Alliances	Number of Powers Forming Alliances
Duration	−.38	−.33
Extent	−.19	−.15
Magnitude	−.33	−.28
Severity	−.14	−.12
Intensity	−.19	−.15
Concentration	.00	−.02

Note: n = 47; 10-year periods.

Whether we focus on the number of new alliances or the number of Powers forming alliances, on treaties and wars involving the Powers or between the Powers, the conclusion remains the same: Alliance formation is associated with relatively low levels of war.

The preceding analysis (and nearly all of the quantitative studies of war) focuses on the total amount of war (along each of our dimensions) in a given period. Equally important (depending on the precise question under consideration) are the characteristics of the average war (given that war occurs). By normalizing the war indicators with respect to frequency, we can compare the characteristics of the average war in periods of high and low alliance formation. The resulting rank-order correlations are presented in table 1–5. Again we find no positive correlations. Wars that occur in periods characterized by high levels of alliance formation are generally lower in duration, extent, magnitude, severity, and intensity (and equal in concentration) than those in periods of low alliance activity. These results reinforce our earlier findings—that alliance formation is *not* associated with higher levels of war; if anything, it tends to be associated with lower levels of war. The fact that these results hold true for a variety of different measures of alliances and war greatly enhances our confidence in their validity.

It is possible, of course, that this relationship is not consistent over the entire five-century span of the modern Great Power system; the relationship may vary over time. Singer and Small have given us good reason to believe that the twentieth century is different from the nineteenth in this regard, and

results across all indicators (whether characterized by autocorrelation or not), we can be fairly certain that the application of highly sophisticated statistical techniques to remove autoregressive tendencies would not have an appreciable impact on the results of this analysis.

[9] This is not surprising, given the following moderately high correlations (tau-b) between the various alliance indicators (for 10-year periods of aggregation): number of alliances and number of Great Power alliances, .55; number of alliances and number of Great Powers entering alliances per period, .66; number of Great Power alliances and number of Great Powers entering alliances, .80.

it is conventional to regard the Congress of Vienna as a significant turning point for the international system. We can test the hypothesis that the alliance-war relationship varies over time by analyzing the correlations separately for each of the historical periods defined above. The resulting rank-order correlations (tau-b), using the number of alliance pacts per 10-year periods,[10] are given in table 1–6.

Table 1–6 indicates that the absence of a positive relationship between alliances and war that we found for the system as a whole seems to hold for its distinct periods, though there may be a slight (but statistically insignificant) positive relationship between the number of alliances and the number of Powers engaged in war. The relationships between alliances and war are nonexistent in the sixteenth to eighteenth centuries, somewhat negative in the nineteenth century (except for the magnitude of the average war), and more strongly negative in the twentieth century;[11] the difference is greatest for the fatality-based indicators of the total amount of war and all dimensions of the average war.

While the preceding correlational analysis does contribute to our understanding of the alliance-war relationship, it fails to reveal certain crucial aspects of that relationship and hence fails to recognize some significant changes over time. More particularly, it fails to distinguish between necessary and sufficient conditions for war (that is, if alliance formation were a necessary condition for war, then historically all wars would be preceded by alliances, whereas if alliances were a sufficient condition for war, then all alliances would be followed by war). A correlational analysis cannot differentiate, for example, between a situation in which most alliances are followed by war while few wars are preceded by alliance formation, and one in which few alliances are followed by wars while most wars are preceded

---

[10] The results are substantially the same if we focus on the number of new Great Power alliances or on the number of Powers entering alliances.

[11] These negative correlations for the twentieth century appear to be at odds with the Singer-Small (1967) findings. There are several explanations for this discrepancy. First, while Singer and Small include all interstate alliances and wars (including the numerous small state alliances of the 1930s), we exclude all those not involving a Great Power. Second, they use an indicator of existing alliances, while we focus on alliance formation (for reasons discussed earlier); we do get more positive correlations using existing alliances, though in the nineteenth century we get more strongly negative correlations. (In previous centuries this distinction is less relevant, given the ad hoc and transient character of most alliances and the frequency with which they were soon followed by war.) In addition, we use a longer period of temporal aggression (10 years) for alliances and war; a five-year period would generate correlations close to zero for all indicators except extent and magnitude (about −.13). Finally, and of considerable importance, while we use a rank-order measure of association (tau-b), Singer and Small use Pearson's r. This gives disproportionate influence to extreme cases, and—in conjunction with their inclusion of the numerous small power pacts prior to the wars of the 1930s—accounts for much of the positive correlations (as well as their discrepancy with the negative nineteenth-century correlations). The use of r with our data would generate positive correlations above .22 for all but the extent and magnitude indicators.

Table 1–6
Rank-Order Correlations (Kendall's tau-b): Alliance Formation and War Behavior, by Century*

War Indicator	Century		
	16th–18th	19th	20th
Amount of war per period			
Frequency	.09	−.35	−.10
Duration	−.14	−.16	−.05
Extent	.20	−.22	−.25
Magnitude	−.07	−.13	−.25
Severity	.06	−.06	−.15
Intensity	.05	−.06	−.25
Concentration	.13	−.06	−.25
Characteristics of			
the average war			
Duration	−.23	.06	−.25
Extent	.18	−.13	−.41
Magnitude	−.08	.19	−.15
Severity	.04	−.06	−.35
Intensity	.01	−.06	−.35
Concentration	.10	−.06	−.25

* Number of alliances involving the Great Powers, by 10-year periods.

by alliance formation. The distinction is of considerable importance, however, particularly for the ultimate task of developing causal theory. In order to investigate this aspect of the alliance-war relationship, therefore, we shall consider the questions of the extent to which alliance formation has historically been followed by war, and the extent to which wars have historically been preceded by alliance formation.

For the purposes of this empirical analysis, a five-year time lag will be used as an operational criterion of inclusion and exclusion, so that only war following alliances within five years will be considered. No temporal criterion can reflect causality, of course, but in an aggregate data analysis of this kind it allows us to make some reasonable approximations. A shorter period would not be sufficient to encompass the causal effects of underlying structural factors like alliances, while longer periods would exaggerate the duration of these causal effects. In addition, it is necessary to determine which wars within this period are to be counted—that is, all interstate wars involving Great Powers, all Great Power wars, only wars involving a member of the alliance in question, or only wars involving two or more alliance members. The proper measure depends on the hypothesis under consideration. For balance of power theory, for example, all wars would presumably be relevant because of the flexibility of the alliance system. However, if the concern is with one ally dragging another into war because of their formal commitments, perhaps wars involving two or more allies would be a better indicator. In addition, alliances of two or more Powers may have different effects from alliances involving only one Power. Given the variety of theoretical general-

Table 1–7
Proportion of Alliances Followed by War within Five Years

Type of Alliance and War	Proportion of Alliances Followed by War within Five Years (Century)					
	16th	17th	18th	19th	20th	16th–20th
All neutrality and defensive alliances	n = 5	n = 9	n = 15	n = 25	n = 63	n = 117
Any war involving a Great Power	1.0	.89	.73	.44	.81	.73
Great Power war	.8	.78	.67	.16	.22	.33
War involving an ally	1.0	.56	.67	.28	.87	.40
War involving 2 or more allies	.6	.56	.47	.00	.08	.17
Great Power alliances	n = 4	n = 5	n = 14	n = 14	n = 9	n = 46
Any war involving a Great Power	1.0	1.0	.71	.29	1.0	.7
Great Power war	.75	1.0	.71	.0	.56	.5
War involving an ally	1.0	.8	.71	.07	.67	.54
War involving 2 or more allies	.75	.8	.5	.0	.44	.39

izations regarding alliances and war, the analysis will be conducted for each of these various indicators, for each provides a slightly different operational perspective on the overall theoretical relationship. In addition, by examining more restricted types of alliance, we can reduce the likelihood that our results are simply the result of random chance (a point to which we shall return later).

For each of the last five centuries, we compute the proportion of alliances followed by war within five years and the proportion of wars preceded by alliances within five years. For each analysis, we differentiate between wars in general and Great Power wars and between alliances in general, Great Power alliances, alliances involving a war participant, and alliances involving two or more war participants. The results are presented in tables 1–7 and 1–8, respectively. Given the various conceptual and methodological problems raised previously, these figures should not be interpreted as anything more than rough approximations.

Tables 1–7 and 1–8 present a different view of the alliance-war relationship than our earlier correlation analysis, and indicate some rather significant variations over time. Table 1–7 suggests that, except for the nineteenth century, the vast majority of alliances (from 56% to 100%, depending on the particular indicator and time period) have been followed by wars involving at least one ally, and many of these wars were Great Power wars involving two or more allies. Great Power alliances have been even more likely to be followed by war.[12] All Great Power alliances of the sixteenth, seventeenth, and twentieth centuries have been followed by a war involving a Great Power

---

[12] The fact that the proportions do not drop significantly as we become more discriminating, by moving from wars in general to Great Power wars and finally to wars involving two or more allies, suggests that these empirical associations are not simply the random outcome of a large number of wars.

Table 1–8
Proportion of Wars Preceded by Alliance Formation within Five Years

Type of War and Alliance	Proportion of Wars Preceded by Alliance Formation within Five Years (Century)					
	16th	17th	18th	19th	20th	16th–20th
All wars involving a Great Power	n = 34	n = 29	n = 17	n = 20	n = 15	n = 115
Any alliance involving a Great Power	.18	.41	.53	.50	.80	.43
Great Power alliances	.15	.24	.41	.10	.47	.24
Alliances involving a war participant	.18	.14	.35	.25	.60	.26
Alliance of 2 or more war participants	.06	.14	.29	.00	.13	.11
Great Powers wars	n = 26	n = 17	n = 10	n = 5	n = 5	n = 63
Any alliance involving a Great Power	.19	.35	.50	.60	.60	.35
Great Power alliances	.15	.29	.50	.00	.60	.27
Alliance involving a war participant	.19	.24	.50	.40	.60	.30
Alliance of 2 or more war participants	.08	.24	.50	.00	.40	.21

within five years; 72% of these wars were Great Power wars, 78% were wars involving an ally, and 61% involved two or more allies. These general relationships were strongest in the sixteenth and seventeenth centuries,[13] followed by the eighteenth and twentieth centuries; for the twentieth century, however, only Great Power alliances have often been followed by Great Power war. This rather striking and consistent pattern does not hold, however, for the nineteenth century. A very small proportion of nineteenth-century alliances are followed by Great Power wars involving one or two allies; of the 14 Great Power alliances, none was followed by Great Power war involving two of the allies, and only one by a war involving one of the allies. With the exception of the nineteenth century, then, we can conclude that defensive and neutrality alliances, when they have occurred, have been excellent predictors of wars involving (or between) the Great Powers, appearing thus to have nearly constituted sufficient conditions for war in some periods.[14]

We get a different view of the alliance-war relationship, however, if we look at the proportion of wars preceded by alliances. Wars are preceded by alliances less than a fifth of the time in the sixteenth century, less than a third of the time in the seventeenth century, and less than half the time in the eighteenth century. For the most part, this is basically true, regardless of the type of alliance or war. The results for the nineteenth and twentieth centuries are more sensitive to the particular war and alliance indicators and are more likely to reflect the random occurrence of the large number of alliances in those periods. Only two of the 20 wars (and none of the Great Power wars) of the nineteenth century are preceded by Great Power alliances. The twentieth century is much like the eighteenth, in that roughly half of the Great Power wars are preceded by Great Power alliances (involving two or more war participants). With so few wars (except perhaps for Great Power wars of the eighteenth and twentieth centuries) being preceded by alliances, we can conclude that alliance formation has not been a factor involved in the processes leading to most wars, and that other variables have generally been more important as causes of war.

This analysis of the relative numbers of alliances followed by wars and wars preceded by alliances has been useful in a descriptive sense, but we must recognize that it exaggerates the true empirical relationship between alliances and war. Even in the absence of a relationship between alliances and war, we would expect a certain number of wars (particularly in the

---

[13] The fact that the highest proportions occur in periods with the smallest number of cases may raise some questions regarding their significance, but these are dispelled somewhat by the analysis based on a probability model in table 1–9.

[14] Here "condition" should not be equated with cause; for this, it would be necessary to demonstrate nonspuriousness (the absence of other causal agents).

most warlike centuries) to fall randomly into the five-year periods following alliance formation, and a certain number of alliances to fall randomly into the five-year periods preceding wars. Our question, then is whether the proportion of alliances followed by wars and the number of wars preceded by alliances is significantly different than we would expect on the basis of chance.

The proportion (or number) of periods characterized by the occurrence of a random event can be predicted from a Poisson process model.[15] If λ is the average number of wars per five-year period (for example, for the sixteenth century with 34 wars, λ = 34 wars/20 five-year periods = 1.7 wars/period), then the proportion of periods with r wars is given by

$$P\ (r) = \frac{\lambda^r e^{-\lambda}}{r!}$$

The proportion of periods characterized by the absence of war is then $P(0) = e^{-\lambda}$, and thus the proportions of periods characterized by war is simply $(1 - e^{-\lambda})$. This expected value, based on the null hypothesis of no alliance-war relationship and the random occurrence of wars, can then be compared to the observed value by taking percentage differences [$(P_o - P_e)/P_e$ where P_e = expected proportion and P_o = observed proportion]. The same procedure can also be used to compare the observed and expected number of periods characterized by alliance formation. Here we differentiate only between wars and Great Power wars, alliances and Great Power alliances; the average values for the other indicators cannot be calculated. The calculations are done for each century, since the preceding empirical analysis suggested some significant differences across centuries. The resulting percentage differences between observed and expected values are given in table 1–9.

These results reinforce and clarify our earlier analysis. In the sixteenth, seventeenth, and eighteenth centuries, the proportion of alliances followed by war is greater (by an average of one-third) than would be expected on the basis of a null alliance-war relationship and random distribution of each. What is particularly striking is the fact that these proportions are uniformly positive for the four different categories of alliances and wars. In the nine-

---

[15] The necessary assumption for the application of the Poisson distribution—that the data consist of independent observations—is satisfied. As noted earlier, a Durbin-Watson test on each of the time series for the sixteenth–eighteenth centuries and nineteenth–twentieth centuries indicates the absence of serial correlation in the frequency of war, frequency of Great Power war, frequency of alliance formation, and frequency of Great Power alliance formation (For the two alliance indicators for the nineteenth century the observed Durbin-Watson coefficients [1.51 and 1.45] are far above d_L [1.05], the critical upper value for positive autocorrelation, and fall within the inconclusive region but very close to d_u [1.54], the critical value for the assertion of independent observations; see Ostrom 1978: 33–34; Goldberger 1964: 244.) This is sufficient, I think, to justify the use of the Poisson probability model.

Table 1–9
Empirical Associations between Alliances and Wars: Percentage
Differences, Observed vs. Expected*

	Century				
	16th	17th	18th	19th	20th
Alliances followed by war	.22	.16	.29	−.30	.23
Alliances followed by Great Power war	.08	.37	.69	−.27	−.26
Great Power alliances followed by war	.21	.28	.25	−.55	.53
Great Power alliances followed by Great Power war	.03	.72	.82	−1.00	.85
Wars preceded by alliances	−.20	.15	.00	−.31	−.19
Wars preceded by Great Power alliances	−.18	.09	−.18	−.80	−.10
Great Power wars preceded by alliances	−.12	−.02	−.06	−.17	−.39
Great Power wars preceded by Great Power wars	−.15	.35	.00	−1.00	.25

* Positive values indicate more wars or alliances than expected on the basis of the null hypothesis and random distributions. Proportions rather than percentages are listed.

teenth century, on the other hand, alliances were followed by war much *less* frequently (by an average of about 40%) than expected by chance, with Great Power alliances being particularly unlikely to be followed by war. The positive relationship returns in the twentieth century (with one interesting exception). If we switch our focus to the likelihood of wars being preceded by alliances, we get further support for our earlier findings. We find that disproportionately few wars are preceded by periods of alliance formation in the sixteenth, nineteenth, and twentieth centuries (with one important exception). The relationships for the seventeenth and eighteenth centuries are more sensitive to the different types of alliances and wars but are generally null or positive for the seventeenth century and null or slightly negative for the eighteenth century.

These results tend to reinforce our earlier findings. A disproportionately high number of alliances are followed by war, except in the nineteenth century, with Great Power alliances being particularly destabilizing. Disproportionately few wars, on the other hand, are preceded by alliances, except that Great Power wars are often preceded by Great Power alliances in the seventeenth and twentieth centuries.

The preceding analyses have been conducted at the systemic level, dealing with the aggregate numbers of alliances and wars in the system, though some effort has been made to identify particular participants in both alliances and wars. It would be useful now to shift to the national level of analysis and determine for each state the proportion of its alliances followed by a war in which it is involved, and the proportion of its wars preceded by alliances. Separate analyses are conducted for the sixteenth–eighteenth, nineteenth, and twentieth centuries (since our previous analyses suggest that similar patterns exist within the first group). The resulting proportions for each state, in each category, and for each period are then classified as low

Table 1–10
National Alliance Formation and War Behavior

	Number of Great Powers with Proportions of Alliances and Wars of Each Type, by Century								
	16th–18th			19th			20th		
Type of Alliance and War	Lo	Med	Hi	Lo	Med	Hi	Lo	Med	Hi
% alliances followed by war	1	2	5	5	1	0	2	3	2
% alliances followed by Great Power war	1	2	5	6	0	0	4	2	1
% Great Power alliances followed by Great Power war	1	2	5	6	0	0	1	3	3
% wars preceded by alliances	7	1	0	3	3	0	4	4	1
% wars preceded by Great Power alliances	7	1	0	6	0	0	5	4	0
% Great Power wars preceded by Great Power alliances	6	2	0	6	0	0	5	3	1

(below one-third), medium (between one- and two-thirds), and high (over two-thirds). The number of Great Powers with low, medium, and high proportions of alliances followed by war and wars preceded by alliances is given in table 1–10.

The results from table 1–10 are consistent with our earlier systemic-level findings. Prior to the nineteenth century a state's conclusion of a treaty of alliance was generally followed by its involvement in war. This was true over two-thirds of the time for two-thirds of the Great Powers.[16] On the other hand, it was relatively infrequent that a state's wars were preceded by alliance pacts (for no Power did this proportion exceed two-thirds). The patterns for the nineteenth century are particularly clear, as demonstrated in table 1–10: Alliances were rarely followed by war, and wars were rarely preceded by alliances. There have been much greater variations in state behavior in the twentieth century, and the evidence is more ambiguous: The proportion of alliances followed by war range from low to high. For only one Power, however, is war most often preceded by alliance formation. It should be noted that for the most part the above findings are relatively insensitive to the particular indicators of alliances and wars. It should also be noted that this national-level analysis confirms, among other things, the previously observed differences between the nineteenth and twentieth centuries.

---

[16] Significantly, it was only Sweden, geographically removed from Europe's central core, whose alliances were rarely followed by war. The Ottoman Empire, with only one formal alliance, has been excluded from the analysis.

Interpretation of the Findings

The use of multiple indicators and methods has revealed some rather interesting patterns in the alliance-war relationship. It is evident that the empirical relationship between alliance formation and war behavior has changed over time. Within certain well-defined periods, however, some fairly clear and consistent patterns develop. Let us now attempt to explain these patterns.

First let us consider the period prior to the nineteenth century. While peacetime alliance formation was relatively infrequent in the early years of the system, we have found that a disproportionately large number of these alliances (both in percentage terms and relative to our expectations based on chance) were followed by war within five years of their inception. Thus, early alliance formation, when it occurred, was associated with war rather than peace.[17] Particularly striking is the fact that nearly 80% of the Great Power alliances were followed by Great Power war. We cannot infer from this empirical association, however, a causal relationship between alliances and war, for there is good reason to believe that the correlation may be spurious. That is, alliances may be generated by the same underlying processes that were independently leading to war. In fact, nearly all alliances are motivated by the fear that there exists some probability of war, and this was particularly true in earlier times. Osgood's interpretation (1967:71–75) of eighteenth-century alliance formation applies to the two previous centuries as well: The motivation for alliances was fundamentally offensive rather than defensive in nature. Alliances were generally formed in anticipation of war.[18] Given the nature of warfare in this era, extensive preparations for war were not necessary, so that defensive alliances for the protection against surprise attack were not an important consideration. Of course, even if the processes leading to war had other underlying causes, it is quite possible that the ad hoc and secretive nature of these alliances contributed further to the unstable conditions by generating mistrust, suspicions, and subsequent tensions leading to war, and that the existence of alliances increased the importance of image and prestige considerations, which may be highly destabilizing. Further evidence is necessary, however, if this hypothesis is to be confirmed, if the independent causal effects of alliances and other variables are to be disentangled.

The limited independent impact of alliances on pre-nineteenth-century

---

[17] The fact that we have excluded from this analysis wartime alliances and offensive alliances designed for the explicit purpose (that is, as formally stated in the text of the treaty) of launching a war renders these results all the more striking.

[18] This observation demonstrates the utility of the extended temporal domain of this study—by providing a broadened historical perspective and facilitating a controlled and comparative analysis, we can resolve questions of this nature.

wars is demonstrated, from a different perspective, by the fact that those wars were rarely preceded (within five years) by alliance formation; in the sixteenth and eighteenth centuries, this was even less than we might expect on the basis of chance alone. This constitutes rather convincing evidence that wars during this period were rarely caused by alliance formation, that wars generally had causes unrelated to alliances, and that these other causes were generally more important.

The nature of the alliance-war relationship changes noticeably after the Congress of Vienna, and then again at the end of the nineteenth century. Whereas a disproportionately high number of earlier alliances were followed by war within five years, the opposite was true of nineteenth-century alliance formation; of the 14 Great Power alliances, none was followed by Great Power war and only one was followed by a war involving an ally. Thus alliances, when they occurred, were not a destabilizing force in the nineteenth century. Furthermore, few of the wars of the nineteenth century were even preceded by alliance formation (none of the five Great Power wars was preceded by Great Power alliances). This implies that formal alliances were rarely involved in the processes leading to war in the nineteenth century, and thus we must look elsewhere for the causes of war. How are we to explain this change from previous centuries, where alliances were associated with war rather than peace?

Whereas previously alliances were generally ad hoc in nature and formed deliberately as a prelude to war (even if not explicitly stated in the text of the alliance treaty), the nineteenth century was characterized by more permanent alliances formed in peacetime for the purposes of maintaining the status quo and enhancing deterrence. One reason for this was the rise of a modified concept of collective security, as applied in the Concert of Europe, to guarantee the provisions of the Congress of Vienna. Perhaps even more important, particularly by the sixth decade of the nineteenth century, was the changing nature of military technology and warfare. The development of the railroad, use of conscription, and development of the general staff system all contributed to the increasing speed of military operations and greater importance of military preparedness (Langer 1931:6; Osgood 1967:81–82). In order to protect themselves against the threat of surprise attack and rapid defeat, states formed more permanent defensive coalitions in peacetime. Also important was Bismarck's conception and use of alliances as a means of diffusing serious conflicts of interest by entangling the rival powers in a complex network of formal agreements and providing incentives for their mutual cooperation (for example, the Dual Alliance, Three Emperors' League, Triple Alliance, and Reinsurance Treaty, which served to modify the Austro-Russian conflicts in the Balkans). This hypothesis—that nineteenth-century alliances were not made in anticipation of an imminent war but rather as a means of maintaining the status quo, restraining one's allies, and providing for deterrence and defense against a rapid offensive—implies that nineteenth-century alliances were formed under less unfavorable (or more stable) conditions than those in earlier periods. The explanation for the positive association between alliances and war in the sixteenth to eighteenth centuries, and the negative association in the nineteenth century, lies primarily with the differing diplomatic, technological, and political conditions under which these alliances were formed.

It is more difficult to explain the patterns of alliance formation and war behavior in the twentieth century, where, as in the sixteenth to eighteenth centuries, alliances have been followed by war disproportionately often but where wars have been preceded by alliances relatively infrequently. How do we explain this change from the nineteenth century?

In many respects the nature of the alliances themselves did not change significantly. As in the nineteenth century, there have been few offensive alliances in peacetime, in which two states jointly agree to initiate military action. Nor has the pre-nineteenth-century pattern been common, in which alliances are formed primarily in anticipation of an imminent war and for the purposes of enhancing the prospects of victory in that war (with some exceptions, such as the Nazi-Soviet Pact). Instead, most alliances, like those of the nineteenth century, were defensive or deterrent in nature, designed to supplement one's military power, deter aggression, and aid in defense in the event that deterrence failed. As in the nineteenth century, military preparedness and planning in advance were absolutely vital to the successful conduct of war, so that allies and a coordinated allied military strategy were sought as guarantees against the threat of surprise attack and war in an age of offensive dominance in military technology. The Franco-Russian alliance of 1932 was not fundamentally different in nature from that of 1892. Nor were the French alliances with Eastern European and Balkan states in the interwar period fundamentally different from the Austrian, German, or Italian alliances with the Balkan states in the 1880s. The collective security arrangements of the League of Nations after World War I were no different in principle (though perhaps more formalized) from those of the Concert of Europe after the Napoleonic Wars.

There are some respects, however, in which twentieth-century alliances differ from those of the nineteenth century. Unlike many of the alliances of the Bismarckian period, few (if any) alliances in the twentieth century have been consciously motivated by the concern to restrain one's allies as well as to deter one's enemies. Much more evidence would be necessary, however, before it could be demonstrated that these restraining alliances were in fact the primary reason for the nonconflictual consequences of war in the nineteenth century, and that the absence of this idiosyncratic factor was a main reason for the violent consequences of alliances in the twentieth century. Nor can these differences be explained by the decline of the balance of power system, as some have hypothesized (Holsti et al. 1973:37). If the alliance–war association were negative in the nineteenth century because of the existence of a balance of power system with the hypothesized stabilizing role of alliances, then we might expect an even more negative relationship in the eighteenth century, when the "assumptions" of balance of power theory were satisfied to an even greater extent; Morgenthau (1967:182–183) refers to this as the "golden age" of the balance of power. The positive association between alliances and war in the eighteenth century would seem sufficient reason to reject this hypothesis.

Related to the general notion of a balance of power system is the more specific distinction between polarized and nonpolarized (or flexible) alliance configurations. As noted earlier, it is widely believed that the former are war-prone while the latter are stabilizing. Perhaps it is the absence of polarized alliance systems in the nineteenth century and their presence during part of the twentieth century that accounts for the differences in the observed alliance-war associations. This explanation cannot be accepted without further investigations, however, because the hypothesized relationship between alliance polarization and war behavior has yet to be confirmed by empirical analysis; the studies cited earlier (Singer and Small 1967; Wallace 1973a; Bueno de Mesquita 1975, 1978) have generated rather mixed results. These derive in part from some difficult analytical problems, which we might briefly consider.

A highly polarized alliance structure is one in which there exist two well-defined clusters of states with many alliance bonds within each cluster but no bonds across clusters and no shifting of alliance partners (for example, the Cold War alliance system.) A nonpolarized alliance structure, on the other hand, is generally conceived as a configuration characterized by a number of alliance ties, the absence of two well-defined clusters of states, and either (1) a series of cross-cutting alliance bonds (as in the Bismarckian system) and/or (2) rapidly shifting alliance partners (such as the Diplomatic Revolution" of the mid-eighteenth century). While it is possible to distinguish between these polar types of alliances at any given point in time, we must recognize their dynamic nature and the fact that nearly all polarized alliance configurations evolve out of nonpolarized ones; shifting coalitions in pursuit of viable allies suddenly become crystallized into opposing camps as these new alliance relationships become formalized and institutionalized as war approaches. If war follows, it may be the result of (1) the existing polarized alliance system, (2) the destabilizing impact of the rapidly shifting coalitions occurring earlier, (3) the change from a flexible system to a more polarized one (as Bueno de Mesquita 1975 discovers), or (4) a spurious correlation involving antecedent conditions and processes.

It is possible to find examples of highly polarized alliance systems, but their consequences are far from obvious. The polarized alliance system centered on NATO and the Warsaw Pact have thus far avoided war, whereas that centered on the League of Augsburg (against Louis XIV) failed to deter war—although in each case perhaps more important factors were operating.

Even more ambiguous is the pre–World War I alliance system, which may have contributed to peace for decades (Osgood 1967:86), yet was a major factor in the escalation from crisis to war in 1914 (Fay 1928). The hypothesis that polarized alliance systems are associated with war can be neither confirmed nor rejected on the basis of this limited evidence.

We can also find several clear examples of periods of nonpolarized alliance configurations. A historical analysis will demonstrate, however, that contrary to the standard balance of power hypothesis, nearly all periods of the most highly flexible alliance systems have been followed by relatively high levels of war.[19] The apparent fact that the flexible alliance systems of earlier periods did not have a pacifying effect provides further evidence that the polarization of the alliance structure cannot explain the variation in conflict behavior in the nineteenth and twentieth centuries. It is particularly interesting to note that one of the few cases of a nonpolarized alliance system associated with peace (the Bismarckian period of 1871–1890) is characterized by a static system of pluralist cross-cutting ties, rather than a dynamic system of rapidly shifting coalitions. This suggests the hypothesis that it is the dynamic process of rapidly shifting coalitions and ad hoc alliances—and not a pluralist, cross-cutting alliance configurations of a more static nature—that tends to be associated with war.[20]

There is good reason to believe, however, that this is a spurious association, reflecting the unstable conditions under which alliances tend to be formed. It is neither polarized or nonpolarized alliances, nor the change from one to another, that lead to war. Rather, it is the underlying international and domestic conditions and events which trigger a dynamic process of escalation. This induces an anticipation of impending war by statesmen and hence their frantic search for allies, leading to rapidly shifting coalitions and ultimately to war, either directly or after the polarization of the alliance system. More static nonpolarized alliance systems (like the Bismarckian system), on the other hand, tend to arise under more favorable international conditions. This, together with the fact that the other differences between nineteenth- and twentieth-century alliances appear to be rather limited in their impact, suggests that the primary explanation for the differences in the

---

[19] Some of the most obvious periods of nonpolarized alliance systems include the following: (1) 1495–1525, the rapidly shifting coalitions of the Italian Wars and the manipulations involving the Hapsburgs, Valois, and English; (2) 1657–1677, the shifting coalitions involving the Anglo-Dutch naval rivalry and French expansion; (3) 1717–1725, the maneuverings and disintegration of the Quadruple Alliance; (4) 1740–1760, the Kaunitzian system and the "Diplomatic Revolution"; (5) 1871–1890, the Bismarckian system; (6) 1920–1941, the hectic search for allies in the Interwar system. An examination of the compilation of wars (Levy 1983:ch.3) reveals that all but one of these periods of nonpolarized alliance systems (1871–1890) are characterized by relatively high levels of war.

[20] For this reason future studies of nonpolarized or flexible alliances would profit from an explicit distinction between an alliance configuration characterized by pluralist (and state) cross-cutting ties and one involving rapidly shifting coalitions.

alliance-war relationship in the nineteenth and twentieth centuries cannot be found in the nature of the alliances themselves, but must involve the preexisting international and domestic conditions under which they arise.

Conclusions

This study can be seen as part of an ongoing tradition of research, initiated by Singer and Small and continued by Wallace, Bueno de Mesquita, Siverson and King, and others. These have all helped resolve the descriptive-empirical debate over whether alliance formation has historically been associated with war or with peace. This study goes beyond the earlier ones in several significant respects, however. First is the extension of the temporal domain of the study, from 1815 to the beginning of the modern system in the late fifteenth century. This has added a historical perspective, increased the number of cases for a statistical analysis, and facilitated a controlled comparative analysis. A second major contribution is an explicit focus on the Great Powers, given their leading role in international politics and their distinctive patterns of behavior. Finally, our recognition of the important distinctions between necessary and sufficient conditions for war and utilization of other techniques besides simple correlation analysis have facilitated a more refined analysis of the alliance-war relationship. The result has been several significant descriptive-empirical findings regarding alliance formation and war behavior among the Great Powers.

We have found that some aspects of the alliance-war relationship are consistent over time, while other aspects demonstrate some rather significant changes. First, for the period as a whole and also for each of the last five centuries, the evidence clearly contradicts the hypothesis that alliance formation is generally associated with high levels of war. To the contrary, it is more often associated with peace, particularly in the nineteenth and twentieth centuries. In addition, for none of the last five centuries have wars generally been preceded by alliances.[21] This consistent pattern leads to the important conclusion that alliances have not generally played an important part in the processes leading to most wars involving the Great Powers, and that consequently other variables must be more significant in any general theory of war.

There are some significant differences in the alliance-war relationship over time, but these derive from variations in the extent to which alliance

---

[21] It is true that many twentieth-century wars have been preceded by alliances, but this is primarily the result of the large number of twentieth-century alliances falling randomly into a prewar period. This relationship disappears with the application of a random probability model, except that Great Power wars in the twentieth and seventeenth centuries were preceded by Great Power alliances disproportionately often.

formation, when it occurs, is followed by war. In the sixteenth through eighteenth centuries, over two-thirds of the alliances were soon followed by war (with a much higher frequency that we might expect on the basis of chance). Given the fundamentally offensive nature of most alliances during this period, however, there is good reason to believe that this alliance-war association may be spurious, reflecting the search for alliances as a means of preparing for an aggressive war, or at least for a war which is perceived to be imminent. The pattern was distinctly different in the nineteenth century, in that very few alliances were followed by war; these relationships were even more strongly negative for Great Power alliances and wars. The proposition that alliances actually deterred war cannot be accepted, however, without further evidence designed to demonstrate the absence of spuriousness. The alliance-war relationship in the twentieth century is quite distinct from that in the nineteenth and much like that in the sixteenth to eighteenth centuries (though not quite as strong). Alliances have generally (and with disproportionate frequency) been followed by war, but these wars have involved states other than the allies. It is concluded that the differences between the nineteenth and twentieth centuries cannot be explained by either the decline of the balance of power system or the higher level of polarization of twentieth-century alliances, but must be traced to preexisting international or domestic conditions.

On the basis of this study, we can make a number of suggestions regarding the kinds of future research which might contribute most to the further development of our knowledge regarding alliances and war. First of all, further conceptualization of the alliance variable is necessary. The questionable inclusion of the sweeping non-aggression pact along with neutrality alliances (as well as the ambiguity of entente pacts) has already been mentioned. Even more important is the presumed distinction between offensive and defensive alliances. An offensive treaty of alliance is one in which the formal (written) commitment to use military force is not conditional upon a military attack against one of the signatories, but is made explicitly (and secretly) for the purposes of initiating a war. The inclusion of offensive alliances from the Singer-Small compilation (and our own as well) is justified, given the question they (we) choose to investigate,[22] but this must not blind us to the theoretical importance of offensive alliances.[23]

---

[22] This exclusion is (presumably) justified on the same grounds as the exclusion of wartime alliances and alliances made within three months of war: In a study of the "extent to which alliances predicted to war," it is necessary to exclude alliances made when the "probability of war had approached 'certainty,' thus contaminating the assumed independence between the two observations which were to be correlated" (Singer and Small 1966b).

[23] Offensive alliances are important for several reasons. We have seen, first of all, that in the pre-Napoleonic era the vast majority of alliances were offensive rather than defensive (or neutrality or entente) in nature. Second, offensive treaties are not entirely irrelevant to the

Even more important, we must recognize that the empirical distinction between offensive and defensive alliances is rarely very clear, and that the three-month rule is a highly arbitrary operational criterion for eliminating alliances formed with the near "certainty" of war. The critical point is that nearly *all* alliances are formed in anticipation of *some* probability of war. This fear of war is the primary motivating factor underlying nearly all alliance formation, as implied by Liska's widely accepted generalization that "alliances are against, and only derivatively for, someone or something" (1968:12). Consequently, the "contamination" of observations to be correlated can never be completely eliminated. Alliances are rarely an entirely independent predictor to war. Rather, they are generally formed when underlying international (or domestic) conditions make the perceived likelihood of war sufficiently high that statesmen search for allies (or undertake other means) in order to deter war, fight the war successfully in the event it occurs, or perhaps even to initiate war under more favorable circumstances. Thus observed alliance-war correlations might be spurious, reflecting antecedent conditions which may independently contribute to war. In terms of alliances, the critical question is the extent to which alliance formation contributes to a dynamic process of conflict escalation already underway, and the relative importance of the alliance-war linkage compared to the linkages between the antecedent conditions, resulting political tensions, and war. A multivariate analysis in which there are controls for the antecedent variables would certainly move us beyond most existing studies of the alliance-war relationship. What is ultimately necessary, however, is the conceptualization of alliances as an intervening variable in a dynamic model of conflict escalation incorporating the reciprocal interactions among antecedent conditions, political tensions, alliances, and war.

Editors' Commentary

Major Findings

Levy's analysis is a systematic examination of whether alliances are a sufficient and/or necessary condition of war. If alliances are

---

question of the causes of war, or whether alliances predict to war. Whether or not an ambitious, expansionist state elects to go to war may be greatly affected by its ability to secure the military support of key third states (as well as the neutrality of others), for calculation of third state behavior is a key variable in the decision for war (Blainey 1973:246). On the other hand, while offensive alliances may greatly increase the probability of war, they do not make war absolutely inevitable; not all offensive treaties of alliance have been followed by war. In addition, of course, offensive and wartime alliances (those concluded during the course of a war) often contribute to the escalation, extent, magnitude, and severity of the war. (Singer and Small themselves recognize that their criteria might not be appropriate for these kinds of questions; 1966c:136.)

a **sufficient condition** for war, then every time there is an alliance, it will be followed by war. If alliances are instead a **necessary condition** for war, then every war will be preceded by an alliance, though some alliances may not lead to war. Since there has been serious disagreement about the effect of alliances, Levy actually has two hypotheses that he is able to evaluate with one set of observations: (1) alliances will be followed by war and (2) alliances will be followed by peace.

Levy provides important evidence that alliances involving the strongest states in the system are generally followed by war, not peace. This information is not revealed, however, by conventional correlational analysis. The initial findings, which are weak negative correlations, suggest that alliances may be associated with peace; that is, the more alliances there are, the less war there will be. However, when he looks instead at whether there is war or peace after the formation of an alliance, it is very clear that, with the exception of the nineteenth century, most alliances are followed by war within five years of their formation.

Thus, in table 1–7, Levy reports that alliances are followed by a war involving an ally[1] 100 percent of the time in the sixteenth century, 56 percent of the time in the seventeenth century, 67 percent in the eighteenth, and 87 percent in the twentieth. (To get a percentage from the proportion, multiply by 100.) This means that no alliances are followed by five years of peace in the sixteenth century, 44 percent are followed by peace in the seventeenth, and only 33 percent and 13 percent are followed by peace in the eighteenth and twentieth centuries, respectively. Clearly alliances are more often followed by war than by peace and therefore cannot be considered a good way of ensuring the peace. Instead they appear to be a way of preparing for war.

Levy shows, in contrast, that things were very different in the nineteenth century. There, only 28 percent of the alliances were followed by a war involving an ally, which means that 72 percent were followed by at least a five-year period of peace for those making the alliance. One inference suggested by this discrepant finding is that alliances need not always result in war, but the reason that this is the case is not clear. One possibility is that there is something about the nineteenth century that is not present in the other centuries that makes alliances more associated with peace. Another is that the alliances of the nineteenth century are fundamentally different from those in other centuries. This in turn sug-

---

[1] Emphasis is placed on this particular dependent variable so as to ensure that the war following an alliance involves at least one member that made the alliance.

gests the possibility that there are different types of alliances—some associated with war and others with peace. Which of these possibilities will turn out to be correct and which are simply figments of our imagination will have to be determined by more research. Science progresses by uncovering certain findings and then raising questions about them that suggest new hypotheses.

Levy follows his analysis of sufficient conditions with an examination of necessary conditions. A necessary condition of war would be a factor that is always present before a war. In other words, a war cannot occur if that condition is absent, but it should be remembered that just because a factor is necessary does not mean that its presence will bring about a war. A necessary condition need not also be a sufficient condition. Technically the absence of a condition even in one war (or type of war) would mean that it is not a true necessary condition. To test for a necessary condition, one first examines war and then looks at the characteristics of periods that precede war to see what they all have in common. If they have nothing in common, then there are no necessary conditions of war.

In table 1–8, Levy finds that except for the twentieth century, most wars are fought without alliances' having preceded them (using the alliance-involving-a-war-participant indicator), and even in the twentieth century, 40 percent of the wars fought are not preceded by an alliance (involving a war participant). These findings show not only that alliances are not a necessary condition of war but also that something other than alliances must be causing these wars. This does not mean that alliances are not a sufficient condition of war but simply that war is probably multicausal; that is, it may be brought about by several factors.

It should be noted that Levy's analysis up to this point is based on examining the number of alliances and wars within the entire system. Not until table 1–10 does he look at whether the alliances of specific states are followed by war. When he does, the general pattern of his findings is sustained: in the sixteenth through eighteenth centuries, the alliances of individual states tend to be followed by war, whereas in the nineteenth century they are not. The findings for the twentieth century are more complex, but for the most part, alliances of individual states are followed by war.

On the basis of Levy's analysis, it can be concluded that alliances tend to be associated with war and do not bring about peace; however, it cannot be inferred from this association that alliances are a *cause* of war. Nations often enter alliances when war is perceived to be likely. In addition, alliances, as shown by the findings on the nineteenth century, need not always have a bellicose result. The exact causal effect of alliances still needs to be established, but one thing is clear: alliances generally are followed by war, not by peace. Levy's analysis is important also because it demonstrates that many wars occur without any alliances at all, meaning that other factors besides alliances may bring about war.

Methodological Notes

Levy's article is a good example of the remarkable amount of information that can be generated simply by the careful use of percentages, proportions, and ordinal level correlation. He confines his analysis to only the most powerful states in the system but looks at all alliances and wars involving these states from 1495 to 1975. One of the main contributions of his work is the observation of five centuries of data. By using such a long time span, Levy is able to establish that the nineteenth century is unique and unusually peaceful by comparison to the other four centuries.

The first test Levy runs is a rank-order correlation between the number of alliances and the incidence of war. A correlation is a statistical measurement of the extent to which two variables co-occur. A rank-order correlation uses ordinal measures of alliances and wars.

There are three different levels of measurement:

1. **Nominal** measures place each case in a category according to some characteristic, such as color, sex, shape, or political party.
2. **Ordinal** measures look at more or less of a quality and are used most frequently when cases are rank ordered from the highest to the lowest. An ordinal measure of population size provides more information than a nominal measure, like large/small, in that a rank ordering by population tells which state is the most populous, the second most, and so on.
3. An **interval** measure is even more precise. Here the actual population of states would be reported. This information would tell not only that China is larger than the United States or the Soviet Union but exactly how much larger it is.

The level of measurement is important because certain statistics are appropriate only for certain levels of measurement. In Levy's first test, tau-b, a rank-order correlation, which ranges from −1.0 to +1.0, is employed. The three most extreme outcomes of this test of whether alliances lead to war would be:

1. 1.0, a perfect **positive** relationship between alliances and war.

2. −1.0, a perfect **negative** relationship between alliances and war (meaning that alliances are correlated with peace).

3. 0.0, showing **no** relationship between alliances and war. This would mean that alliances are associated with neither war nor peace, which is sometimes referred to as a **null** finding.

It is rare to get such pure findings. More often we see numbers such as .02, −.14, or .22, which would mean essentially no relationship; −.45, .57, or −.63, which would mean a moderate relationship; or .86, −.92, which would mean a strong relationship (positive or negative, depending on the sign). Since all of the correlations reported in tables 1–3 and 1–4 are negative, Levy concludes that alliances are correlated with infrequent wars of short duration, low magnitude, severity, and intensity, and average concentration.

Table 1–5 also shows no positive relationships with the indicators of war. The findings on duration (−.38 and −.33) and magnitude (−.33 and −.28) indicate that some wars are shorter and smaller when there is much alliance formation. It should be kept in mind, however, that this is not the same as saying that alliances are associated with peace because an ordinal scale of war measures the **frequencies** of war (tables 1–3 and 1–4) or **levels** of war already under way (table 1–5) (in contrast to a nominal measure, which could measure the presence and absence of war). When the lowest score on war is zero, meaning no war, and there is a very strong negative correlation, we can say that alliances are associated with peace, but the weak negative correlations mean that alliances are associated with low frequencies of war. This implies that alliances might be associated with a certain type of war, although further research would be needed to explore this possibility. When the correlations are very low (0.0 to −.20), the appropriate conclusion is that the number of alliances is not associated with the number of wars.

Turning to the search for necessary and sufficient conditions, Levy asks whether alliances are followed by war and whether wars are preceded by alliances. The methodological implication of this shift from sufficient conditions to necessary conditions is that different techniques are appropriate to the two tasks. You can see that when you are searching for a sufficient condition of war, correlational analysis is appropriate. Scientific explanations normally specify sufficient conditions; hence, hypotheses are typically tested by looking for the presence of an **independent variable**, in this case alliances, and seeing if it is followed by the presence of the **dependent variable,** war. If a factor is sufficient to trigger war, then it will be strongly correlated with war. If, however, a factor is a necessary condition, then war cannot occur without it, but the condition may occur without war's breaking out. Such a factor would not have a very high correlation with war but would nevertheless be essential to a complete explanation. In this way, the percentages Levy employs make use of more of the information contained in his data and pave the way for a more thorough causal analysis, the possibilities for which are explored in chapter 14.

The technique Levy uses is the simplest level of statistics, percentages. Note that he uses fractions, or proportions, so that 1.0 = 100 percent; .8 = 80 percent. The use of a time lag of five years makes it possible to observe whether alliances are followed by war and whether wars are preceded by alliances. Tables 1–7 and 1–8 show that most alliances are followed by wars involving at least one ally but that wars are preceded by alliances less than half of the time.

A simple percentage, however, is only descriptive and does not adequately measure the relationship. Some alliances and wars may occur in the same time period simply by chance, or **randomly.** In order to tell whether there is a relationship between the two, we have to determine whether the number of observed cases exceeds what would occur randomly.

This is where the Poisson process model comes in. It is not necessary to understand the math behind it—merely to know that it is a way of predicting what can be expected by chance, so that we can determine how much of the alliance/war activity exceeds that amount. If we observe that war occurs 75 percent of the time when there are alliances, we do not know what that means. But if we can estimate what a "normal" amount of war would be, say 50 percent, then we can measure the difference. The Poisson formula calculates the difference between the amount of war actually observed and what would be expected randomly based on the average number of wars per five-year period (symbolized by λ, the Greek letter lambda), and expressing that as a proportion. (To convert the proportions to percentages, multiply by 100.) The differences between the average (Poisson) values and the observed values are reported in table 1–9. For example, in the sixteenth century, there are 22 percent more cases of alliances followed by war than one would expect randomly.

Finally, not content to observe the incidence of alliances and war only at the systemic level, Levy repeats his analysis for each individual state (national level), producing the findings reported in table 1–10. This is methodologically important because it allows us to infer that individual behavior is consistent with the delineated systemic patterns. In other words, when an individual state enters an alliance, there is a likelihood that it will be involved in a war within five years. To try to make that inference without examining the individual cases would be to commit what is called an **ecological fallacy**, which consists of applying a finding regarding a group or system to its individual members. For example, suppose an organization raised more money in December than in November. It would be incorrect to infer that a particular member raised more money in December than in November.

Levy's study has made a number of important contributions. The use of three different types of statistics furthers our understanding of the complex relationship between alliances and war. Several different indicators of the two variables are used, so that strong findings are rendered more robust. The unpacking of the correlations to identify necessary and sufficient conditions provides more information about the role of alliances than does correlational analysis alone. Wars generally follow alliances, but they are not necessarily preceded by alliances. Therefore, eliminating alliances will not prevent war. However, the existence of alliances is hardly benign. We will see in chapter 7, in the article by Siverson and King, that alliances serve to expand wars once they break out.

Finally, Levy's generation of data for a time span of five centuries provides the key to understanding the deviant nature of the nineteenth century. Many quantitative studies of war use data beginning with 1816, and one of the intriguing and puzzling findings produced by this body of research, as in the study by Singer Bremer and Stuckey (see chapter 2), is that different factors are associated with war in the nineteenth and twentieth centuries.

2

Capability Distribution, Uncertainty, and Major Power War, 1820–1965

J. David Singer
Stuart Bremer
John Stuckey

Editors' Introduction

Traditional wisdom about international relations suggests two broad and contradictory propositions about the effect of power on war and peace. One, associated with balance-of-power thinking, argues that when a balance of relative equality (or parity) of power is maintained among three or more major states, war is less likely. This is especially the case if the alliance structure is not rigid and major states can shift from one bloc to another so as to keep the capability distribution relatively equal. The other proposition asserts that only when there is a *preponderance* of power—one side or state has overwhelming power over others—will peace be maintained. In this article, J. David Singer, Stuart Bremer, and John Stuckey provide one of the early important tests of these two competing explanations.

Introduction

In any systematic effort to identify the immediate or remote sources of international war, one has a variety of more or less equally reasonable options. First of all, one can focus either on the behavior of the relevant governments, or on the background conditions within which such behavior

Reprinted from *Peace, War, and Numbers,* edited by Bruce M. Russett (Sage Publications, 1972), pp. 19–48. Reprinted by permission of the editor and the senior author.

Authors' Note: Comments on an earlier version of this paper by Karl Deutsch, Melvin Small, Michael Wallace, and James Ray were particularly helpful. We would also like to thank Dorothy LaBarr for her patience and thoroughness in preparing the tables and text, and to acknowledge the support of the National Science Foundation under Grant number 010058.

occurs. And if one leans toward ecologically oriented models—as we do—the choice is between the attributes of the nations themselves and the attributes of the system or sub-system within which the nations are located. Further, one may choose to focus on the structural attributes of the nations or the system or on their cultural or physical attributes.

In the Correlates of War project, we have recently begun to examine the behavioral patterns of nations in conflict, in order to ascertain whether there are recurrent patterns which consistently distinguish between those conflicts which eventuate in war and those which do not (Leng and Singer 1970). But even though we contend that no model is adequate unless it includes such behavioral and interactional phenomena, we also believe that behavior cannot be understood adequately except in its ecological context.

Hence, the first two phases of the project have been restricted to the attributes of the system and those of the nations and pairs of nations that comprise the system. In the process, we have found it necessary to allocate more energy to data generation and acquisition (not to mention data management) than to data analysis, and in addition to making these data sets available via the International Relations Archive of the Inter-University Consortium for Political Research, we have published a fair number of them (Singer and Small 1966a, 1966b; Russett, Singer, and Small 1968; Small and Singer 1969, 1970; Wallace and Singer 1970). In due course three handbooks will be published, embracing, respectively, the fluctuating and cumulative incidence of war, the changing structure of the international system since the Congress of Vienna, and the capabilities of the states which constitute that system. We prepare these volumes not only to make our data as widely available as possible, but also in order to explain why and how we construct our most important measures. That is, unlike some other social science sectors, the international politics field finds very little data of a ready-made nature, requiring those of us in that particular vineyard to first convert our concepts into operational indicators, prior to any analysis. And even though we still have some major index construction and data generation tasks before us, we have not been completely inattentive to the possibilities of some modest theoretical analyses (Singer and Small 1966c, 1968; Singer and Wallace 1970; Wallace 1971; Bremer, Singer, and Luterbacher 1973; Gleditsch and Singer 1972; and Skjelsbaek 1971). These partial and tentative analyses are, of course, essentially of a brush-clearing nature, preliminary to the testing of more complex and complete models.

The report at hand falls into that same brush-clearing category, designed to help us sort out some of the dominant regularities in the international system, and to aid in evaluating a number of equally plausible, but logically incompatible, theoretical formulations. To be quite explicit about it, we suspect that anyone who takes a given model of war (or most other international phenomena) very seriously at this stage of the game has just not looked at the referent world very carefully. Just as our colleagues in the physical and biological sciences have found that nature is full of apparent inconsistencies and paradoxes, requiring a constant interplay between theoretical schemes and empirical investigations, we believe that the complexities of war and global politics will require more than mathematical rigor and elegant logical exercises. So much, then, for the epistemological case on which we rest our research strategy. In the Conclusion, we will address ourselves to the equally important normative case, but let us turn now to the investigation at hand.

The Query and Its Rationale

Our concern here is to ascertain the extent to which the war-proneness of the major powers, from 1820 through 1965, can be attributed to certain structural properties of the sub-system which they constitute. The first of these properties is the distribution of national capabilities within it at given points in time, and the second is the direction and rate of change in that distribution between any two of those points in time.

Before presenting our measures and analyses, however, it is pertinent to ask why one might expect to find any relationship between the distribution of "power" on the one hand, and the incidence of war, on the other. Without either tracing the discussion as it has unfolded in the literature of diplomatic history and international politics, or developing a full articulation of our own line of reasoning, we may nevertheless summarize what looks to us like a fairly plausible set of considerations.

The Major Powers' Preoccupation with Relative Capability

We begin with the assumption that the foreign policy elites of all national states are, at one time or another, concerned with their nation's standing in the power and/or prestige pecking order.[1] For any given nation at any given time, certain ranking scales will be of considerably greater salience than others, as will the relative position of one or another of their neighbors. Normally, we would not expect the decision makers of Burma to worry very much about their nation's military-industrial capability vis-à-vis that of Bolivia, or find the Swedish foreign office attending to the rise in Afghanistan's diplomatic prestige. Nor would it be particularly salient to the Mexican defense ministry that Australia's preparedness level had risen sharply

---

[1] While power and prestige are far from identical, and nations may well have statuses on these two dimensions that are quite inconsistent with each other, there is usually a high correlation between the two. In this paper, we focus only on power, but will deal with prestige (or attributed diplomatic importance) in a later one; for some tentative analyses, see Midlarsky (1969), East (1969), Wallace (1971), and Wallace (1972). For more detail on the composition of the international system and its sub-systems, see Singer and Small (1966a) and Russett, Singer, and Small (1968).

over the previous half-decade. That is, the salience of a given nation's rank position on a given power or prestige dimension will only be high for the foreign policy elites of those other nations that are relatively interdependent with the first, and are "in the same league."

But we are talking here only about major powers, which—almost by definition—are highly interdependent one with the other, and clearly in the same upper strata on most of the recognized power or prestige dimensions. This becomes more evident if we indicate which states comprise the major power sub-system during the different periods of the century and a half which concerns us here. While the data introduced in a later report will indicate how valid the classification is, we emphasize that our criteria— quite intentionally—are less than operational. That is, rather than define the major power sub-system over time in terms of certain objective power and/or prestige indicators, we adhere to the rather intuitive criteria of the diplomatic historians. On the other hand, the consensus among those who have specialized in the various regions and epochs is remarkably high (especially from 1816 through 1945), and it leads to the following.

As the post-Congress period opens, we find Austria-Hungary, Prussia, Russia, France, and Britain constituting this select sub-system. Italy joins the group after unification in 1860, as does Germany as the successor state to Prussia in 1870. The two non-European newcomers are Japan in 1895, following its victory over China, and the United States, after defeating Spain in 1898. These eight continue as the sole major powers until World War I, which sees the dismemberment of the Austro-Hungarian empire, and the temporary loss of position for Germany (from 1918 to 1924) and Russia (from 1917 to 1921). World War II leads to the temporary elimination of France (from 1940 to 1944) and the permanent (i.e., at least through 1965) elimination of the Axis powers of Italy, Germany, and Japan. As the victors in that war, Britain, Russia, and the United States continue as members of the major power category, France regains membership in 1945, and China qualifies as of 1950.

It should not be difficult to argue that these states become major powers by dint of close attention to relative capability, and remain so in the same way. Of course, mere allocation of attention to their power and prestige vis-à-vis others will not suffice. They must begin with a solid territorial and demographic base, build upon that a superior industrial and/or military capability, and utilize those resources with a modicum of political competence.[2] Nor would it be difficult to argue that all of the major powers are sufficiently interdependent, directly or indirectly, to warrant treatment as a discernible sub-system. To a very considerable extent, during the epoch at

---

[2] If one accepts the propositions that successful war experience usually leads to increases in national power, and that the more powerful nations usually "win" their wars, the high war involvement and win-lose scores of the major powers offer some evidence that the majors are not only attentive to, but high on relative capabilities (Small and Singer 1970).

hand, the policies of each impinge on the fate of the others; and as Campbell (1958) has urged in another context, this condition, plus a similarity of attributes, permits us to think of them as a single social system. We could, of course, go on to construct and apply a number of indices which might reflect the similarities and the interdependence of the major powers, but such an exercise is probably not necessary here.

If, then, we can assume that the states which constitute this oligarchy (Schwarzenberger 1951) do indeed represent the most powerful members of the international system and that they are in relatively frequent interaction with one another, the next question is the extent to which they all collaborate to preserve the status quo, or conversely, vie with one another for supremacy. Our view is that neither extreme holds very often, and that the cooperative and competitive interactions among them fluctuate markedly over time. Further, as Langer (1931), Gulick (1955), Kissinger (1957), and others have demonstrated, even when they work together to impose a common peace, they keep a sharp eye on their relative capabilities. Each major foreign office is, at a given point in time, deeply concerned with the growth of some of their neighbors' strength and the decline of others'. Moreover, yesterday's allies are often tomorrow's rivals or enemies. Even as domestic political power has passed from the hands of the kings, kaisers, czars, and emperors to party bureaucrats and elected bourgeois rulers, the instability of coalitions has abated but slightly. Despite the inhibitory effects of articulated ideologies, competition for public office, and all the demagoguery which comes in the train of popular diplomacy, major power relationships continue to shift, albeit more slowly.

The Role of Uncertainty

It is, however, one thing to argue that the distribution and redistribution of relative capability will turn out to be a major factor in the behavior of national states, and quite another to predict the strength—and direction—of its relationship with war. As a matter of fact, we contend that a rather strong case can be made for two alternative, but incompatible, models. In each of these models, capability configurations represent the predictor or independent variables, and decision makers' uncertainty serves as the (unmeasured) intervening variable. By uncertainty we mean nothing more than the difficulty which foreign policy elites experience in discerning the stratifications and clusters in the system, and predicting the behavior of the other members of that system.

How does uncertainty link up with capability patterns on the one hand and with war or peace, on the other? Considering the latter connection first, those who believe that it is *un*certainty which usually makes for war will argue that most war is the result of misjudgment, erroneous perception, and poor predictions. The opposing view is that high levels of *certainty* are, on the contrary, often at the root of war, and that the major inhibitor to war is a *lack* of clarity, order, and predictability. When relative capabilities are difficult to appraise, and when coalition bonds are ambiguous, outcomes are more in doubt, and it is that very uncertainty which helps governments to draw back from the brink of war (Haas and Whiting 1956:50).

Shifting from the possible link between uncertainty and war to that between capability distributions and such uncertainty, both schools of thought tend to converge. Here, the assumption is that three different variables will affect uncertainty in the system: the extent to which capabilities are highly concentrated in the hands of a very few nations, whether the distribution is changing toward higher or lower concentration, and the rate at which relative capabilities are moving. The model, as we see it, holds that uncertainty levels will rise when: (a) capabilities are more equally distributed and not concentrated; (b) the direction of change is toward such equal distribution and away from high concentrations; and (c) when there is high fluidity, rather than stability, in capability distributions.

To summarize, we find two contending models of more or less equal plausibility. One, which we might call the "preponderance and stability" model, holds that war will *in*crease as the system moves away from a high and stable concentration of capabilities. The other, which might be called the "parity and fluidity" model, holds that war will *de*crease as the system moves away from such a high and stable concentration and toward a more ambiguous state of approximate parity, coupled with a relatively fluid movement of the nations up and down the power hierarchy.

For the moment, we will leave these models in their pre-operational and verbal form. Then, after describing the measures and the resulting data in some detail, we can return to their formal articulation and to an examination of the extent to which each fits the empirical world of the past century and a half. It should, of course, be emphasized that even if our design were flawless, our measures impeccable, and our analyses beyond reproach, the findings would nevertheless be far from conclusive. First of all, there is Popper's dictum (1959) regarding the disconfirmability, as opposed to the confirmability of empirical generalizations. Second, we must stress that the generalizations being tested here are very gross and undifferentiated. This, we believe, is as it should be in the early stages of a particular line of theoretical investigation, but we recognize at the same time that a more refined set of tests, with attention to additional variables and tighter analytical controls, is ultimately required.

The Variables and Their Measurement

Space limitations and the conventions of scientific reporting usually preclude a fully detailed description of the precise operations by which one's verbalized constructs are converted into machine-readable data. This is especially unfortunate when most of these constructs or variables are not found in ready-made operational form (such as votes) and have not yet achieved even partial acceptance as reliable and valid indices (such as gross national product). But as we noted at the outset, we have been neither bashful nor niggardly in publishing our data, and we can therefore refer to those separate studies in which our rationale, procedures, and results are presented in greater detail. Thus, we will describe and justify our measures in only the briefest fashion here, beginning with the outcome variable (war) and then moving on to our predictor variables: concentration, change in concentration, and movement.

The Incidence of War

We begin by distinguishing among inter-state, extra-systemic, and civil wars; the latter two are of no concern here, and we deal only with those of the first type in which at least one major power was an active participate and in which each side sustained at least 1,000 battle-connected fatalities. The particular index used in the analysis at hand is a reflection of the magnitude of war underway, as measured in nation months of such major power inter-state war. And since our time unit is the half-decade, we measure the warlikeness of each such period as the average annual amount of war underway during that period. The war data for each of the 29 periods from 1820 to 1965 are shown in table 2–1.[3]

National Capabilities

To this juncture, we have alluded to power, strength, and capability, but have side-stepped any definitions; that delicate chore can no longer be avoided. As one of us (Singer, 1963) emphasized some years ago, power is to political science what wealth is to economics, but not nearly as measurable. The focus there was on the influence *process,* and the range of strategies appropriate to each basic type of inter-nation influence situation; relative capabilities, or the bases of power, were by and large ignored.

Recently, several serious efforts to convert the intuitive notions of national capability or power base have appeared (German 1960; Fucks 1965), but rather than examine them or compare our approach to theirs, we will merely summarize our measures here. In a later volume we plan to discuss the several existing efforts, indicate the theoretical reasoning behind our own measures, and present our data in considerable detail.

---

[3] Despite the modest fluctuations in the size of the major power subsystem, we do not normalize the war measure. Full details of our data generation and index construction procedures, and the considerations of validity and reliability upon which the indices rest, along with extensive tabular materials, are found in our forthcoming *Wages of War* (Singer and Small 1972).

Table 2–1
Capability and War Indices

Period Beginning (T0)	CON (T0)	Average Annual ΔCON (T0→T1)	Average Annual MOVE (T0→T1)	Average Annual Nation-Months of WAR Underway (T0→T1)
1820	0.241	−0.15	0.40	(2.92)
1825	0.233	0.17	0.47	6.68
1830	0.242	0.02	0.41	0.00
1835	0.243	−0.22	0.88	0.00
1840	0.232	0.50	0.60	0.00
1845	0.257	0.06	0.28	6.40
1850	0.260	0.34	0.67	9.36
1855	0.276	0.07	0.38	17.24
1860	0.280	−0.49	0.82	16.82
1865	0.255	−0.45	1.23	12.98
1870	0.233	−0.15	0.46	5.44
1875	0.225	0.02	0.34	3.52
1880	0.226	−0.36	0.53	2.64
1885	0.208	−0.10	0.65	2.12
1890	0.203	0.39	0.55	0.00
1895	0.223	−0.41	0.67	0.00
1900	0.202	0.09	0.93	4.32
1905	0.207	0.10	0.37	3.40
1910	0.212	−0.14	0.74	8.47
1913	0.208	2.34	1.69	87.06
1920	0.371	−2.49	1.26	0.00
1925	0.247	−0.13	0.80	0.00
1930	0.241	−0.25	2.57	6.68
1935	0.228	−0.37	2.23	8.73
1938	0.217	2.50	2.82	123.97
1946	0.417	−3.10	1.88	0.00
1950	0.293	0.76	0.99	103.34
1955	0.331	−0.56	1.36	0.52
1960	(0.303)	(0.09)	(1.21)	0.44

Note: For display convenience the values of ΔCON and MOVE have been multiplied by 100. The original values were used in all computations. Figures shown in parentheses ( ) are shown for information only; they are not used in the univariate statistics of table 2–2 or in the CON LEADS models.

We begin with six separate indicators, combine them into three, and then combine those into a single power base or war potential (Knorr 1956) score for each nation every half decade. The six fall into three groupings of two dimensions each. The *demographic* dimension includes, first, the nation's total population, and second, the number of people living in cities of 20,000 or larger. The *industrial* dimension embraces both energy consumption (from 1885 on) and iron or steel production. The energy may come from many sources, but is converted into coal ton equivalents, and the iron/steel production is based on the former only until 1895, at which time we shift to steel alone. The third pair of measures are *military* expenditures and armed forces size, excluding reserves.

As to the more obvious validity questions, we carefully considered the need for separate indicators of social organization, national unity and motivation, and technical skills, but concluded that each of those was adequately reflected in one or more of the six specific indices. Closely related to the choice of indices and sub-indices is the matter of their relative contributions to a nation's power base. And while we are still experimenting with a number of weighting and interaction effect schemes, our tendency is to treat them as equally important, and additive in their effect. In line with these tentative assumptions, we first compute the total score (in people, tons, dollars, etc.) for the system, and then ascertain each nation's percentage share. This has the virtue of normalizing all of our data, reduces the computational problems associated with fluctuating currency conversion rates, avoids that of changes in purchasing power, and puts the figures into ideal form for the computation of our concentration-distribution scores, to which we will turn in a moment.

In addition, since the validity of the composite six-dimensional score is a long way from being demonstrated, we computed these percentage share scores not only for all six dimensions combined, but for the three two-dimensional indices of demographic, industrial, and military capability, and then for each of the six separately. There are, thus, ten power indices for each nation every half-decade, but only the *composite* scores are utilized in our analyses here.

The Distribution of Capabilities

In our discussion of the impact of certainty and uncertainty on the incidence of major power war, we indicated that capability distributions should exercise a strong effect on these certainty levels. How do we measure CON, or the extent to which these capabilities are concentrated or diffused among the nations which comprise the major power sub-system?

Once more, the measurement problem is sufficiently complex to warrant reference to a fuller statement elsewhere (Singer and Ray 1972). To summarize here, we have been struck with the empirical inadequacy of several measures of inequality which have been rather widely used, and have thus devised our own.[4] To operationally measure the concentration of capabilities (within the grouping of from five to eight major powers) we proceed as follows. First, we compute the standard deviation of the ob-

[4] For example, the Gini is often as sensitive to changing N as to the allocation of shares, when the N is low. And the Schutz index, because it sums the ratios of advantage of those above the equal share point, is sensitive only to their shares *as a group* and is not sensitive to the distribution *within* that group. Thus, the index would be the same (.5) for each of the following percentage distributions: 70-20-10-0-0; 70-7.5-7.5-7.5-7.5; and 70-15-15-0-0. The same holds if the index is computed on the basis of those below the equal share point. An alternative approach is that of Brams (1968), and a useful discussion is in Alker and Russett (1964).

served percentage shares. Second, we divide that figure by the *maximum* standard deviation of the percentage shares that is possible for a given N; that maximum would occur if one nation held 100 percent of the shares, and the others had none at all. The resulting index ranges from zero (reflecting perfect equality in the distribution) to 1.0 (in which case one nation holds 100 percent of that capability), and—if our interpretation of the relevant data is correct—should turn out to be high in face validity. The concentration scores are listed in table 2–1, along with the war data and the change and movement measures, to which we now turn.[5]

Movement and Change of Capability Distributions

Having dealt with the measurement of our outcome variable and the key predictor variable, we can now shift to the indices which reflect change across time in the latter. As the scores in table 2–1 make clear, the distribution of power in the major power sub-system is by no means a static thing. How do we measure such shifts?

Two rather distinct indices are employed. The first is a straightforward reflection of the extent to which the concentration index has gone up or down during the period (usually five years) between any two observations. We call it simply change in concentration, or ΔCON. The second is a bit more complex, and it reflects the number of percentage shares which have been exchanged between and among the major powers during each period, whether or not that redistribution leads to a change in the rank ordering.

We begin by comparing the percentage of capability shares held by each of the nations at the beginning and the end of the half-decade. If, for example, the top ranked nation held 30 percent of the composite capability shares at the beginning of a half-decade, and the other four held, respectively, 25, 20, 15, and 10 percent, and the distribution at the end of the period were 35, 25, 15, 15, and 10, there would have been a movement of 10 percentage shares. That is, the top nation picked up 5 percentage shares, number three lost 5, and the remaining three scores remained constant. But in order to make the movement index (called MOVE) comparable across all 30 periods in our 150 years, with the size (and composition) of the sub-system changing from time to time, it must be normalized. That normal-

---

[5] The formula for computing concentration is as follows:

$$CON = \sqrt{\frac{\sum_{i=1}^{n} (Si)^2 - \frac{1}{n}}{1 - \frac{1}{n}}}$$

where n = number of nations in system, and Si = nation i's share (from .00 to 1.00) of the system's capabilities.

ization is achieved by dividing by the *maximum possible* amount of movement or redistribution. That maximum, in turn, would occur if the lowest ranked nation picked up all the shares between the two observations, and ended up with 100 percent of them. Thus, our denominator is computed by subtracting the lowest nation's score from 100 percent and multiplying that difference by 2, since whatever it gained will have been lost by the others.[6]

It is now time to mention two irregularities that must be dealt with in computing our capability distribution and war measures. First, as already noted, the major power sub-system (as we define it) gains and loses members at several points during the century and a half under study. This not only requires us to normalize for its size when measuring capability distributions, but also to eliminate the distortions that could arise in measuring change or movement between two observations that are based on dissimilar sub-system membership. We do this by counting only the movement of shares between and among nations which were members at both observation points, and thus avoid any artifact which could arise merely because the 100 percent is divided among a smaller or larger population at the separate data points.

The second irregularity stems from the fact that we would get rather distorted indices of relative capability if we measured the military, industrial, and demographic strengths during the two world wars. Thus, in place of the 1915, 1940, and 1945 observation years, we use 1913, 1938, and 1946, respectively. But this makes several of our inter-observation intervals longer or shorter than five years. For the war measure, as mentioned earlier, we solve that problem by converting each period's total nation months of inter-state war underway into an *average annual* index. For the change in concentration and the movement measures—which are essentially rate of change measures—we merely divide all the inter-observation scores by the number of years which have elapsed between them; this again produces an average annual index.

Having now summarized, albeit briefly, the ways in which we convert our separate war and capability concepts into operational indices, we can present the resulting figures. In table 2–1, then, we list the CON, ΔCON, MOVE, and WAR indices for each of the 29 observation points embraced in the study. Bear in mind that CON is the only one of our indices which is

---

[6] The formula for computing movement is as follows:

$$MOVE = \frac{\sum_{i=1}^{n} \left| Si_{t-1} - Si_t \right|}{2(1 - Sm_t)}$$

where n = number of nations in system, Si = nation i's share of the system's capabilities, m = nation with lowest share of capabilities, and t, t − 1 = observation points.

measured at a *single* point in time; the change and movement indices reflect the average annual magnitudes during the period immediately following the CON observation, and the amount of war is also that underway during the years immediately following that observation. However, a variety of time lags and leads will be introduced when we turn to our analyses, resulting in re-alignments across the rows as we move the various columns upward and downward.

Examining the Data

Before we get to our analyses and the testing of the contending models, certain characteristics of the several data sets merit a brief discussion. Our motives are two-fold. The careful examination of one's data series, time plots, and scatter plots is, in our judgment, an important prerequisite to the conduct of statistical analyses. In addition, there are the well-known constraints which one's data distributions can impose in the selection and interpretation of the statistical analyses employed. The relevant summary statistics for our four variables are shown in table 2–2.[7]

Looking at the measures of central tendency, we note that the differences between the means and medians for our three predictor variables are quite small in all three time spans. This suggests that these variables do not have seriously skewed distributions. The same cannot be said for the war variable, however. The mean nation-months of war figure for the 20th century is 24.78, while the median value is only 3.86, indicating that the distribution is positively skewed. This condition is no doubt due to the extreme values associated with World War I, World War II, and the Korean war.

Examining the measures of dispersion (range and standard deviation), we find that, as one might expect, all of our measures vary less in the 19th century than in the 20th. With one exception these differences are not serious, and that exception is the war variable. Again we find the three large wars in our series exerting a disproportionate influence on the distributional properties of the war variable. The standard deviation of war in the 19th century is 6.08, while the comparable figure for the 20th century is 44.07. Although Chauvenet's criterion (Young 1962) might cast some doubt on the analyses associated with such outliers, we feel that the brush-clearing nature of this work suggests neither the transformation nor the elimination of these data points. We realize, however, that these values may weaken the predictive power of our models, particularly in the 20th century.

---

[7] As we move into the examination and analysis of our data, we want to acknowledge our debt to Dan Fox of The University of Michigan Statistical Research Laboratory, for the creation of a set of programs particularly suited to time series data management and analysis in the social sciences.

Table 2–2
Descriptive Statistics

	CON	ΔCON	MOVE	WAR
Entire span (N = 28)				
Mean	.250	−.0007	.0096	15.36
Median	.237	−.0012	.0071	3.92
Maximum	.417	.0250	.0282	123.97
Minimum	.202	−.0310	.0028	0.0
Standard deviation	.0504	.0105	.0069	32.33
Range	.215	.0560	.0254	123.97
Auto-correlation	.21	−.58	.63	−.15
Secular trend (beta)	.30	−.09	.66	.32
(b)	.0004	−.00002	.0001	.2501
19th century (N = 14)				
Mean	.244	−.0005	.0058	5.94
Median	.242	−.0004	.0050	4.48
Maximum	.280	.0050	.0123	17.24
Minimum	.208	−.0049	.0028	0.0
Standard deviation	.0201	.0028	.0026	6.08
Range	.072	.0099	.0095	17.24
Auto-correlation	.62	.18	.01	.72
Secular trend (beta)	−.24	−.37	.17	−.01
(b)	−.0002	−.0005	.00002	−.0042
20th century (N = 14)				
Mean	.257	−.0009	.0315	24.78
Median	.226	−.0014	.0113	3.86
Maximum	.417	.0250	.0282	123.97
Minimum	.202	−.0310	.0037	0.0
Standard deviation	.0692	.0149	.0078	44.07
Range	.215	.0560	.0245	123.97
Auto-correlation	.13	−.60	.50	−.32
Secular trend (beta)	.61	−.14	.56	.18
(b)	.0020	−.0001	.0002	.3849

Note: The auto-correlation coefficient shown is first-order only. For the separate century series, each variable was divided according to its lag-lead relationship in the ADD/CON LEADS model. Thus, the statistics shown above for the 19th century include the CON observation at 1885, ΔCON and MOVE 1885–1890, and WAR 1890–1894. The 20th century series begins with the following observation on each variable.

Two additional descriptors will also be important when we turn to our analyses. One of these is the *auto-correlation* coefficient, reflecting the extent to which each successive value of a given variable is independent of, or highly correlated with, the prior value of that same variable. For the entire time span, several of our indices show rather high auto-correlations, with ΔCON at −.58 and MOVE at .63. These turn out, however, to be quite different when we examine the centuries separately, suggesting further that these epochs are divided by more than a change in digits. Now we find that CON shows a .62 auto-correlation in the earlier epoch but only .13 in the present. The two indices of redistribution are negligibly auto-correlated in the 19th, but discernibly so ($-.60$ and $.50$) in the 20th. As to the amount of war underway in each half decade, there is a high $.72$ correlation between successive periods in the earlier century, but a low $-.32$ in this century. We will return to the implications of these in the context of our multivariate analyses, but we should point out here that the important consideration is not so much that of auto-correlation of the indices, but of the auto-correlations of the differences between the predicted and observed values (i.e., residuals) of the outcome variable.

Then there is the closely related problem of secular trends. If one's variables are steadily rising or falling during the period under study, they can produce statistical associations that are largely a consequence of such trends. Hence the widespread use of "first differences" and other techniques for de-trending in the analysis of time series data. How serious is the problem in the study at hand? If we standardize each variable and regress the resulting series on the year of observation, also standardized, we can then estimate the trend of our various series by comparing the resulting slopes (or beta weights, which of course are equal to the product-moment correlation coefficients).

For the entire time span, MOVE shows the steepest slope, with a standardized regression coefficient of $.66$; CON and WAR are moderately steep with coefficients of $.30$ and $.32$ respectively. In the 19th century, ΔCON ($-.37$) and CON ($-.24$) show downward slopes, MOVE is slightly positive ($.17$), and WAR ($-.01$) shows virtually no trend whatever. CON develops a sharp positive trend ($.61$) in the 20th century, as does MOVE ($.56$). The other variables show weak 20th century trends, $-.14$ for ΔCON and $.18$ for WAR.

Before turning to our analyses, one additional data problem requires brief attention. Important, from both the substantive and methodological viewpoints, is the extent to which the predictor variables covary with each other, and these coefficients are shown under the correlation matrices in tables 2–4, 2–5, and 2–6. For the entire span, the product-moment correlation between CON in one period and ΔCON in the next is $-.71$; that between CON and ΔCON during the preceding half-decade is $.47$. When CON is correlated with the amount of movement in the subsequent half-decade, we find a coefficient of $.21$, and it is $.50$ when correlated with the half decade preceding it. As to the top indices which reflect the durability of capability distribution, any suspicion that they might be tapping the same phenomenon is quickly dispelled; the correlation between ΔCON and MOVE is a negligible $.08$. When we turn to our multivariate analyses and discuss the problem of multi-collinearity, these correlations as well as those that obtain within the separate centuries will be examined further.

The Bivariate Analyses

With our theoretical rationale, index construction, and data summaries behind us, we can return to the query which led to the investigation in the first place: what are the effects of capability distribution and redistribution on the incidence of war involving the members of the major power sub-system? We approach the question in two stages, the first of which is a series of bivariate analyses. These are employed not only because it seems useful to know as much as possible about such relationships prior to the examination of more complex models, but also because the theoretical argument suggests that CON, ΔCON, and MOVE should exercise independent—as well as combined—effects on decision maker uncertainty and on war. From there, we will move on to a number of multivariate analyses, in which we compare the war fluctuation patterns *predicted* by several additive and multiplicative models against the patterns which were actually *observed*.

We begin in a direct fashion and ask whether there is any discernible association between our several measures of capability distribution on the one hand, and fluctuations in the incidence of war, on the other. Bear in mind that: (a) CON is measured as of the first day (more or less) of every fifth year (except for the 1913, 1938, and 1946 substitutions noted earlier); (b) ΔCON and MOVE are measured between two successive readings of CON; and (c) WAR is measured during the period immediately following either the observation of CON or the second of the two observations on which ΔCON and MOVE are based. (A typical set of observations would be: ΔCON and MOVE from 1 January 1840 to 1 January 1845; CON at 1 January 1840; and WAR from 1 January 1845 through 31 December 1849.) The working assumption here is that whatever independent effects each of the predictor variables will have upon the incidence of war will be felt within the subsequent half-decade. In the multivariate analyses, we will experiment with these time lags and leads, and in a follow-up study (when our annual data are in) we will further explore the effects of different, and more precisely measured, time lags and leads.

Turning, then, to the product-moment correlations between these predictor variables and major power inter-state war, we examine the coefficients reported in table 2–3. If those who view high concentration, upward change in concentration, and low movement as conducive to decisional certainty (and thus to low levels of war) are correct, we should find negative correlations for the CON-WAR and ΔCON-WAR association and positive ones for the MOVE-WAR association. Conversely, if the world is closer to the model articulated by those who see low concentration, downward change in concentration, and high movement as conducive to uncertainty (and thus to low levels of war), the signs would be just the opposite. What do we find?

Table 2–3

Bivariate Correlation Coefficients (r) and Coefficients of Determination between Capability Indices and WAR in Succeeding Time Period

	Average Annual Nation-Months of War Underway $_{t_1 \rightarrow t_2}$					
	Total Span (N=28)		19th Century (N=14)		20th Century (N=14)	
	r	r^2	r	r^2	r	r^2
CON_{t_0}	−.10	.01	.81	.66	−.23	.05
$\Delta CON_{t_0 \rightarrow t_1}$	−.38	.14	.19	.04	−.41	.17
$MOVE_{t_0 \rightarrow t_1}$	.34	.12	−.01	.00	.24	.06

Examining the total century and a half first, it looks as if the preponderance and stability school has the better of the predictive models. While correlation coefficients of −.10, −.38, and .34 are not impressively high, all three are in the direction predicted by that particular model.[8] But as we have already intimated, there seem to be intuitive as well as empirical grounds for treating the centuries separately. Not only have many historians noted the transitional role of the 1890's, but several of our own analyses to date (Singer and Small 1966c, 1968) reinforce that impression.[9] Our suspicions are further reinforced when we compute the correlations for the centuries separately. We now find that those who recommend high concentration and low movement in order to reduce the incidence of war do not do quite so well. In the 20th century, the signs are all in the direction predicted by their model, while for the 19th century (or more precisely, the period ending with the 1890–1895 observations), the signs are reversed.[10]

Before leaving the bivariate analyses, however, a brief digression is in order that we might check for the presence and effect of cross-lag correlations. Here the search is not for the impact of the predictor variable on the outcome at subsequent observations, but for the impact of the "outcome" variable on chronologically subsequent values of the putative "predictor"

---

[8] Throughout this paper we employ standardized measures of association (correlation coefficients and standardized regression coefficients). Our objective is to evaluate the relative contribution of variables rather than to establish empirical laws, and in this regard we have adopted what Blalock (1961) has called the "quantitative" criterion for evaluating the importance of variables.

[9] In this and prior studies we have examined the effects of dividing the 150 years into three or more periods, or of using such salient years as 1871 or 1914 as our cutting point, but the clearest distinctions tend to be found when the 1890–1900 decade is used as our inter-epoch division.

[10] The scatter plots, while not reproduced here, reveal the stronger linear relationships quite clearly, and in the case of the 20th century CON-WAR association, suggest a possible curvilinear pattern; the conversion to logarithmic plots does not, however, produce a linear association. On the other hand, a rank order (rho) correlation of −.53 also suggests that the CON-WAR association in the 20th century is far from negligible.

variable. In the case at hand, we expected to find a number of cross-correlations, and some did indeed turn up. That is, when we correlated the amount of war underway in any period against the concentration measure in the subsequent period, we found a coefficient of .80 for the full 150 years, .52 for the 19th century, and .81 for the 20th. Similarly, for the impact of prior war on ΔCON, the coefficients were − .66, − .51, and − .68; and for its effect on MOVE, they were .30, .46, and .17. Most of these are sufficiently strong to suggest the need for re-examining the extent to which our capability indices predict to subsequent war when the effects of *prior* war have been removed. Hence, we predicted the CON, ΔCON, and MOVE measures from preceding levels of war; the variance in those measures which could *not* be so explained (i.e., residual variance) was then used as a relatively less biased predictor of war in the following half-decade.

For the entire period, the residual correlation between CON and WAR is a negligible .01, the effect on the 19th century coefficient is to reduce it from .81 to .65, and for the 20th, the association drops from − .23 to − .03. As to the relationship between the residuals of ΔCON and WAR, the coefficients drop from − .29 to − .01, from .18 to − .03, and − .34 to − .06, for the full and the separate epochs, respectively. The impact on the predictive power of MOVE, however, is to strengthen rather than reduce it. The full span's coefficient rises from .34 to .45, and those for the 19th century rise from − .01 to − .17, and from .23 to .41, respectively.[11]

Having emphasized the importance of such a cross-lag correlation check, however, we would now back off and argue that residuals should *not* be used in either the bivariate analyses at hand or in the multivariate ones which follow in the next section. That is, our theoretical concern here is exclusively with the effect of the concentration and redistribution of capabilities upon the incidence of war in the following period, regardless of what produced those capability configurations. Thus, while the war-to-capability association must be kept in mind, it is of minor consequence in the analyses at hand. We will, however, return to it in later reports, in which a number of feedback models will be put to the test.

Thus we conclude this section on the associations between capability concentrations and major power inter-state war by noting that the evidence is, for the moment, quite divided. While high concentration and changes toward it do—as the preponderance and stability school suggests—tend to reduce the incidence of war in the current century, such is clearly not the

---

[11] Given the fact that most of the changes in the size of the major power sub-system occur as the result of high magnitude wars, we also examined the extent to which such changes themselves might be affecting the value of CON. It turns out—not surprisingly—that whatever decrease is found in the predictive power of CON vis-à-vis subsequent war is already accounted for by prior war; thus there is no need to control for the effects of both prior war *and* change in system size.

case in the previous century. Those patterns are much closer to what is predicted by the peace-through-parity-and-fluidity model. Let us turn, then, to a more detailed and complex scrutiny of the question.

The Multivariate Analyses

With the bivariate analyses and some very tentative conclusions behind us, we can now turn to the multivariate models and consider the possible *joint* effects of capability configurations on the incidence of major power war. We do this via the consideration of four different versions of our model, reflecting those of an additive and those of a multiplicative type, and distinguishing between those in which we measure CON before ΔCON or MOVE and those in which CON follows ΔCON and MOVE chronologically. Before examining the several models and the extent to which they match the historical realities, we consider the rationale behind each type.

Looking at the additive-multiplicative distinctions first, let us think of our three predictor variables as if they were merely binary in nature, with 1 reflecting a high value of each and 0 reflecting a low value. Let us assume, further, that war will result if the variables, singly or in combination, reach a threshold of 1 or more. If their effects are additive, it is clear that we will have wars as long as *any one* of them is equal to 1. On the other hand, if their effects are *multiplicative, all* of them must equal 1, since a 0 value on any one of them will give us a product of 0. Another way to look at this distinction is to think of the road to war as having either fixed or flexible exits. In the multiplicative case, there are several exits, since we only need to have a low value (i.e., 0), for *any* one of them to avoid war; hence the flexibility of exits from the road to war. In the additive case, however, the exits are quite fixed; unless *every* one of the predictors is low (i.e., 0), war will result. We might also think of the additive version as a "marginal" one, in that the magnitude of each variable can only exercise a marginal effect on the probability of war, whereas the magnitude of each in the multiplicative case can be determining, at least in the negative sense.[12]

In addition to considering additive and multiplicative versions of the basic model, we need to consider the chronological sequence in which the variables are combined in accounting for the incidence of war. In the bivariate analyses, since the effects of each predictor variable upon war were measured separately, this was no problem. But here, especially since we already know that there is some interdependence among the three predictors, that sequence becomes critical. Unless we want to assume that the

---

[12] For an illuminating discussion of the statistical treatment of multiplicative and other interactive models, see Blalock (1965).

capability configurations could exercise their impact later than five years after being observed—which we do not—there are two major options. In one, we measure CON at 1870 (for example), ΔCON and MOVE between 1870 and 1875, and WAR from 1875 through 1879; we call this the CON LEADS version. In the other, we measure CON at 1875, with ΔCON and MOVE observed between 1870 and 1875, and WAR again measured during the 1875–1879 period; this is the CON LAGS version.

Thus, the basic model can be represented in four different forms:

ADD/CON LEADS:
$$WAR_{t_1 \to 2} = \alpha + \beta_1(CON_{t_0}) + \beta_2(\Delta CON_{t_0 \to 1}) + \beta_3(MOVE_{t_0 \to 1}) + \epsilon$$

ADD/CON LAGS:
$$WAR_{t_1 \to 2} = \alpha + \beta_1(\Delta CON_{t_0 \to 1}) + \beta_2(MOVE_{t_0 \to 1}) + \beta_3(CON_{t_1}) + \epsilon$$

MULT/CON LEADS:
$$WAR_{t_1 \to 2} = \alpha \times (CON_{t_0}^{\beta_1}) \times (\Delta CON_{t_0 \to 1}^{\beta_2}) \times (MOVE_{t_0 \to 1}^{\beta_3}) \times \epsilon$$

MULT/CON LAGS:
$$WAR_{t_1 \to 2} = \alpha \times (\Delta CON_{t_0 \to 1}^{\beta_1}) \times (MOVE_{t_0 \to 1}^{\beta_2}) \times (CON_{t_1}^{\beta_3}) \times \epsilon$$

where α = estimated constant term, or intercept; β = estimated regression coefficient, and ϵ = error term, or unexplained variance. How well do the several versions predict to the actual historical pattern of major power inter-state war? In table 2–4 we show the following for each version of the

Table 2–4
Predictive Power of Four Versions of the Capability-War Model, Entire Span ($N=28$)

Version	Multiples			Con		ΔCON		MOVE	
	R	R^2	$\bar{R}^2$	b	r^2	b	r^2	b	r^2
ADD/CON leads	.56	.31	.23	−.28	.04	−.61	.20	.45	.20
ADD/CON lags	.55	.30	.22	−.18	.02	−.33	.11	.46	.18
MULT/CON leads	.43	.19	.09	−.27	.04	−.57	.15	.21	.04
MULT/CON lags	.43	.18	.08	−.22	.03	−.28	.07	.24	.05

R_2 = Multiple correlation coefficient.
R^2 = Coefficient of multiple determination.
$\bar{R}^2$ = Corrected coefficient of multiple determination.
b_2 = Standardized regression coefficient.
r^2 = Squared partial correlation coefficient.
Correlations among the predictor variables:

$\Delta CON_{t_0 \to t_1}$	1.00	−.71	.47
$MOVE_{t_0 \to t_1}$	.08	.21	.50
	$\Delta CON_{t_0 \to t_1}$	CON_{t_0}	CON_{t_1}

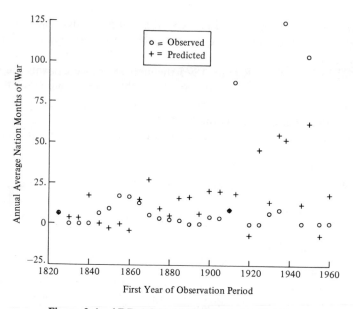

Figure 2-1. ADD / CON LEADS Model, Full Span

model: the multiple regression coefficient (R), the multiple coefficient of determination (R^2), and the corrected multiple coefficient of determination ($\bar{R}^2$), as well as the beta weights, or standardized regression coefficients (*b*), and the squared partial correlation coefficients (r^2) between each of the separate predictor variables and war, controlling for the other two.[13]

The overall impression is that all four versions of the preponderance and stability model do moderately well in predicting to the incidence of war. Every one of the signs is in the direction predicted by that model, with high con and upward Δ CON preceding low levels of war (i.e., negative correlations with war) and high movement predicting to high levels of war. But

---

[13] $\bar{R}^2$ is the coefficient of multiple determination, corrected for degrees of freedom in thefollowing way:

$$\bar{R}^2 = 1 - \left[\frac{(1 - R^2)(N - 1)}{N - k - 1} \right]$$

where N = number of observations, and k = number of predictor variables. This index thus conservatively adjusts the goodness-of-fit estimate, penalizing the researcher for a large number of predictor variables and a small number of observations. This rewards parsimony and high N/k ratios; see Ezekiel and Fox (1959, Chap. 17) and Deutsch, Singer, and Smith (1965).

The regression coefficients of the multiplicative models were estimated by means of a log$_e$ (X + C) transformation on all the variables, where C = 1.0 minus the minimum value of variable X. As Russett et al. explain (1964, pp. 311–313), *addition* of these transformed series is equivalent to the *multiplication* of their original values, and permits the researcher to isolate a unique coefficient for each variable's contribution to the combined multiplicative term. Without this transformation, only a gross coefficient for the interactive effect of the three variables could be estimated.

the direction of the signs is a relatively crude index; how close is the fit between predicted and observed war levels?

Here we see that the two additive versions of the model, accounting as they do for 31 and 30 percent of the variance, do fairly well, whereas the multiplicative versions do not do as well. But this is only true before we correct for the degrees of freedom lost or gained by the number of observations and the number of predictor variables. When we introduce those corrections, none of the versions turns out to be particularly powerful in accounting for the observed levels of war. We also note that it makes little difference whether we observe CON before or after the two redistribution indices (ΔCON and MOVE). As to the predictive power of the separate indices, the impact of CON in the additive versions is consistently less than that of ΔCON and MOVE; in the multiplicative versions, this pattern is less clear. In sum, however, it is noteworthy that a model could predict as well as this one does, given the already apparent differences between the 19th and 20th century systems. One indication of its overall predictive power is revealed in figure 2–1; the observed war values are shown as o's and those predicted by the ADD/CON LEADS version are shown as plus signs. What we see, in the distance between each pair of half-decade points, is that our fit is considerably better for the earlier than for the later epoch. More specifically, while it seems to predict fairly well to the occurrence and non-occurrence of war, it seriously underestimates the war levels generated by the two World Wars and the Korean War, for example.

Do the several versions of our model do better when we examine the two centuries separately? As tables 2–5 and 2–6 indicate, their predictive power is impressively high for the 19th century and rather low for the 20th; this disparity would account for the mixed results in the overall time span. In table 2–5, reflecting the earlier epoch, we find that the additive versions

Table 2–5
Predictive Power of Four Versions of the Capability-War Model, 19th Century (N = 14)

Version	*Multiples*			*Con*		ΔCON		*MOVE*	
	R	R^2	R^2	b	r^2	b	r^2	b	r^2
ADD/CON LEADS	.85	.73	.65	.85	.72	.29	.19	−.38	.00
ADD/CON LAGS	.85	.73	.65	.96	.71	−.31	.17	−.39	.00
MULT/CON LEADS	.72	.52	.38	.73	.52	.16	.04	−.08	.01
MULT/CON LAGS	.72	.52	.38	.83	.50	−.35	.13	−.08	.01

Correlations among the predictor variables:

$\Delta CON_{t_0 \to t_1}$	1.00	−.14	.49
$MOVE_{t_0 \to t_1}$	−.46	.19	−.12
	$\Delta CON_{t_0 \to t_1}$	CON_{t_0}	CON_{t_1}

are once again considerably more powerful than the multiplicative ones. More important, however, are the differences among the corrected coefficients of determination. This very conservative index shows that the additive versions account for at least 65 percent of the variance in our outcome variable (WAR) in the first of our two epochs.

As to the 20th century, the multiple coefficients of determination (R^2) are far from negligible, but unlike the findings for the entire period and the 19th century, here we find the multiplicative version to be more powerful than the additive one. This is not only quite consistent with our bivariate results, but is understandable in the context of our interpretation of multiplicative models. That is, the $-.23$ correlation between CON and WAR in the 20th century suggests that there is *some* association between the two, and an examination of our scatter plots showed that while most war did occur when CON was low, there were several periods in which CON was low, but *no* war occurred. To put it another way, low CON was *necessary* in order for large wars to occur, but it was far from sufficient. The multiple exit interpretation would suggest, then, that the absence of a downward change in CON (i.e., $-\Delta CON$), a high MOVE, or the effect of some unmeasured intervening variable(s) nevertheless permitted the low CON state of affairs to remain a peaceful one.

Looking at the beta weights, we find that all the signs but one are in the directions predicted by the parity-fluidity school's version of the model in the 19th century, and by the preponderance-stability version in the 20th. That exception occurs in the 19th century ADD and MULT models, when

Table 2–6

Predictive Power of Four Versions of the Capability-War Model, 20th Century (N = 14)

Version	Multiples			Con		ΔCON		MOVE	
	R	R^2	$\bar{R}^2$	b	r^2	b	r^2	b	r^2
ADD/CON LEADS	.59	.35	.15	−.50	.12	−.85	.29	.44	.19
ADD/CON LAGS	.56	.31	.10	−.31	.07	−.32	.10	.45	.17
MULT/CON LEADS	.68	.46	.30	−.81	.31	−1.11	.46	.37	.18
MULT/CON LAGS	.64	.41	.23	−.58	.24	−.24	.07	.42	.18

Correlations among the predictor variables:

$\Delta CON_{t_0 \to t_1}$ 1.00   −.75   .49

$MOVE_{t_0 \to t_1}$ .14   .16   .51

          $\Delta CON_{t_0 \to t_1}$ CON_{t_0} CON_{t_1}

R = Multiple correlation coefficient.
R^2 = Coefficient of multiple determination.
$\bar{R}^2$ = Corrected coefficient of multiple determination.
b = Standardized regression coefficient.
r^2 = Squared partial correlation coefficient.

we observe CON after ΔCON and MOVE in the unfolding of events. Whereas a change toward higher concentration makes for more war when CON itself leads, it makes for less war (as the preponderance-stability school would predict) when CON follows behind ΔCON and MOVE. This result is a consequence of the high auto-correlation (.62) in CON in the 19th century.[14]

Returning to the other beta weights, we ask which of the separate indicators exercises the strongest impact. In the 19th century, CON is by far the most potent variable in the regression equation, with all r^2 values greater than .50. This is, of course, fully consonant with the bivariate findings, as is the negligible strength of the movement index. And, as noted above, the effect of ΔCON (when we control for CON and MOVE) is a moderately strong and positive one when CON leads the redistribution measures, and almost as strong but negative when CON follows in the chronological sequence. In the 20th century, on the other hand, we find that all three predictor variables exercise approximately the same impact.[15] And whereas the additive versions give the better fit in the earlier epoch, the multiplicative ones do better in the current century. As a matter of fact, the MULT/CON LEADS version shows fairly strong predictive power, with an R^2 of .46 and partial r^2's of .31 and .46 for CON and ΔCON, respectively. Again the

---

[14] The explanation for this phenomenon is somewhat lengthy and several discussions of it may be found in Harris (ed., 1963). To put the matter briefly, suppose that the true CON measures at t_0 and t_1 were equal. ΔCON would then be positively related to the errors in CON at t_1 and negatively related to the errors in CON at t_0, since ΔCON would under these circumstances be equal to the difference between these error terms. If the simple correlation between WAR and ΔCON were positive, as we have found, then the partial relationship between WAR and ΔCON controlling for CON at t_0 would also be positive. This necessarily follows since by controlling for CON at t_0 we are controlling for its error as well; thus the partial association between WAR and ΔCON is the equivalent of the relationship between WAR and the error in CON at t_1, controlling for the error in CON at t_0. As the error in CON at t_1 increases, ΔCON will also increase, and since the relationship between ΔCON and WAR is positive, so also must the relationship between WAR and the error in CON at t_1 be positive.

However, when we control for CON at t_1, rather than at t_0, and investigate the relationship between ΔCON and WAR, we are analyzing the relationship between WAR and the error in CON at t_0, controlling for the error in CON at t_1. As the error in CON at t_0 increases, ΔCON will decrease, and since the relationship between ΔCON and WAR is positive, the relationship between WAR and the error in CON at t_0 must be negative.

Even though our ΔCON measure is not, as assumed above, simply a function of error, the error components are present and apparently responsible for the observed sign reversal. This reversal supports the positive effect of ΔCON on WAR in the 20th century, but it also points up some of the problems which may be encountered when both a variable and its first-difference derivation are used in a regression equation.

[15] Parenthetically, for those who suspect that the definition of war used here may be too broad in that it embraces *all* inter-state war involving major powers, we mention a relevant finding. That is, if we look only at those eight wars in which there is a major power on *each* side, we find that there was a decline in CON during the half decade preceding all but one of those wars. Since these are almost equally divided between the centuries, they lend some support to the peace through preponderance doctrine.

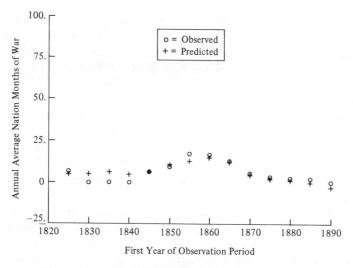

Figure 2-2. ADD/CON LEADS Model, 19th Century

bivariate and multivariate analyses point quite consistently in the same direction.[16]

An examination of figures 2–2 and 2–3 will not only reaffirm, but strengthen, the above statistical results. Plotted on the same scale as figure 2–1, these indicate the discrepancy between the levels of war predicted by the ADD/CON LEADS model and the amounts that actually occurred in each half-decade. The deviations (i.e., the distances between 0 and + for each half-decade) are remarkably small in the 19th century, but much less consistent in the 20th century plot. The parity-fluidity school is thus strongly

---

[16] We mentioned earlier the problems of multi-collinearity (high correlations among the predictor variables) and auto-correlated error terms. Because our predictor variables are highly correlated in several cases, we omitted one of them at a time and computed the predictions each of our models would have made from each pair of predictor variables, to see the effect of deleting a variable which was highly correlated with another in the equation. The coefficients from those equations were, predictably, similar in sign and strength to the predictions made from our three-variable models, although they naturally produced somewhat poorer overall results. Had we been interested in finding the "perfect" model we would not have included all three variables each time, but for the purposes of this paper, we considered it useful to present the results for each of the variables in all four variations of the multivariate model. As noted earlier, the correlations between the various predictor variables for each time period are shown beneath tables 2–4, 2–5, and 2–6, respectively.

As to the auto-correlation problem, table 2–2 shows that several of our variables do exhibit noticeable first-order auto-correlation r's: −.13 for the 150 year WAR series, and .73 and −.29 for the separate centuries. The predictions of our four models do a fair job of explaining, where it exists, the auto-correlation in the war variable. The most highly auto-correlated residual terms result from our 19th century predictions; in the case of the ADD/CON LEADS model, the coefficient of that residual series is .47, which, although sizeable, is considerably lower than the amount of auto-correlation in the original series. The coefficients for the residuals of its predictions are .27 for the 150 year span, .47 for the 19th century, and −.13 for the 20th.

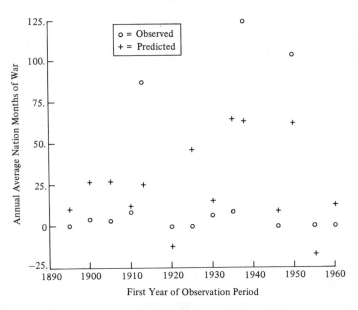

Figure 2-3. ADD/CON LEADS Model, 20th Century

vindicated in the earlier epoch, while those who look to peace-through-preponderance-and-stability have the better of the argument in the later one.

A close look at table 2–7 permits us to see more specifically wherein the amount of war predicted by the models deviates from that which actually occurred. Note, by way of introduction, that even though the same basic model is employed (i.e., ADD/CON LEADS, reflected in the first line in tables 24, 2–5, and 2–6), the difference in the predictions made by the full span model and those for the separate centuries is a result of the difference in signs, as already mentioned. That is, since the best-fitting equation for the entire span has the same signs as that which is nearly the best for the 20th century, it therefore imposes *its* predictions on the 19th century.[17]

Shifting to the columns for the war levels predicted by the parity-fluidity (19th century) and preponderance-stability (20th century) models, a number of specific discrepancies merit explicit comment. Working our way down, we first note that the model underestimates—or more accurately, lags in predicting—the amount of war in the 1820–1840 period. From there on to the end of the 19th century, the fit is fairly good, giving us our estimated standard error of 3.60, which is a function of the actual discrepancy between the predicted and the observed values.

---

[17] We say "nearly," because we actually get the best fit in the 20th century with the multiplicative version.

Table 2–7

Observed Levels of War and Levels Predicted by ADD/CON LEADS Model: Entire Time Span and Separate Centuries

| Period Beginning | Observed | *Average Annual Number of Nation-Months Underway* | | |
		Full-Span Model Predictions	19th Century Model Predictions	20th Century Model Predictions
1825	6.68	6.72	4.80	
1830	0.0	3.51	4.78	
1835	0.0	3.44	6.06	
1840	0.0	17.79	4.39	
1845	6.40	0.36	6.32	
1850	9.36	−2.54	10.23	
1855	17.24	−0.20	12.41	
1860	16.82	−4.35	15.33	
1865	12.98	14.87	12.32	
1870	5.44	27.10	5.92	
1875	3.52	9.31	2.69	
1880	2.64	5.06	1.89	
1885	2.12	16.03	−0.43	
1890	0.0	16.84	−3.51	
1895	0.0	6.35		10.16
1900	4.32	20.44		26.92
1905	3.40	20.15		27.39
1910	8.47	7.47		11.91
1913	87.06	18.96		25.62
1920	0.0	−7.29		−11.95
1925	0.0	45.64		46.28
1930	6.68	13.56		15.36
1935	8.73	54.36		64.54
1938	123.97	51.70		63.13
1936	0.0	11.83		9.12
1950	103.34	61.94		62.24
1955	0.52	−7.36		−16.90
1960	0.44	18.45		13.12

Moving into the later of our two eras, the 20th century model tends to overestimate the levels for 1925–29 and 1935–37, to underestimate the magnitudes of World War I, World War II and the Korean War, and to overestimate the final decade's warlikeness. This latter discrepancy may well be accounted for by the coding rules used for this particular study, excluding as they do the appreciable levels of *extra*-systemic war which marked that period. In general, the 20th century model spreads out the total amount of war more evenly, rather than predicting the radical fluctuations which do in fact occur; the standard error of the prediction is 40.48. For both centuries, of course, the inclusion of additional variables would have given us a better fit, but our objective was not so much to create or discover a best-fitting model as it was to test an *a priori* one.

Conclusion

Before we summarize the results of these analyses, it is important to make very explicit the tentative nature of our findings. Nor is this a mere genuflection in the direction of scientific custom. The study is preliminary in several fundamental meanings of the word.

First, there are the standard problems associated with any "first cut" investigation. Among these are: (a) the absence of any prior analyses of the same type; (b) the possibility of inaccuracies in our data, and as Morgenstern (1963) reminds us, the sources of error may indeed be considerable; and (c) the lack of any hard evidence against which the validity of our predictor variables might be measured. In this vein, our use of the composite index of capability may possibly conceal certain differences that could be revealed by each of the separate (demographic, industrial, and military) indices.

Secondly, the reliance on quinquennial observations might well account for an untoward portion of the results, in both the positive and negative sense of the word. The cutting points between the half-decades can so distribute the capability and war scores that, by accident alone, they may fall into either the "right" or "wrong" time period. Had we used a measure of the amount of war *begun* in a given period, that problem would have been even more accentuated; by measuring war underway, we minimize but do not eliminate the dangers of such an artifact. And any *annual* fluctuation in the predictor variables is concealed. In addition, the fixed interval between observations forecloses the use of briefer or longer spans in experimenting with various lag and lead relationships. In a follow-up study, when our annual capability data are available, we will have much more flexibility in our design, and will be able to ascertain whether the quinquennial time units do indeed represent a source of distortion in the results.

Third, our use of the single nation as our object of analysis may not only be an inaccurate reflection of who the "real" actors are, but produce distorted measures of capability and its distribution. Fourth, as we noted, our decision to defer the analysis of the feedback loops which connect *prior war to concentration* as well as *concentration to subsequent war* leaves our analysis of the problem far from complete. Fifth, it may well be that these findings will continue to hold as we re-examine our model's applicability to the major sub-system, but turn out to be quite inapplicable to the power and war dynamics of other sub-systems or the international system as a whole. Finally, it should be emphasized that this investigation is at the systemic level only and that no inferences can be made as to which particular nations, blocs, or dyads become involved in war resulting from the distribution or redistribution of capabilities.

With these caveats in mind, let us summarize what we have done in the investigation at hand, and what we think has been discovered. To recapitulate the theoretical argument, we have synthesized from the literature two distinct and incompatible models of the way in which the distribution and redistribution of capabilities affects the incidence of major power war. One, which we see as a formal and integrated version of the classical balance of power viewpoint (Haas 1953), predicts that there will be less war when there is: (a) approximate parity among the major nations; (b) change toward parity rather than away from it; and (c) a relatively fluid power hierarchy. The other, reflecting the hegemony view, predicts that there will be less war when there is: (a) a preponderance of power concentrated in the hands of a very few nations; (b) change, if any, toward greater concentration; and (c) a relatively stable rank order among, and intervals between, the major powers. Even though a variety of intervening variables may be introduced as the link between such capability configurations and the preservation of peace, we suggest that decisional uncertainty is a parsimonious and appropriate one, and is implied in many of the traditional analyses. While both schools agree that parity and fluidity increase that uncertainty, only the first would hold that such uncertainty makes for peace; the preponderance and stability school sees uncertainty as leading to war.

These two sets of predictions have been consolidated into a single basic model incorporating the three predictor variables (capability concentration, rate and direction of change in concentration, and the movement of capability shares among the powers) and the outcome variable (amount of interstate war involving major powers). But the classical theorizers were less than precise in their formulations, and said little in regard either to the sequence in which the variables should exercise their effects, or the way in which those effects might combine, making it necessary to construct alternative representations. Since an examination of only the most obvious version would be less than a fair test, we articulated and tested four versions: an additive and a multiplicative form with the measurement of concentration prior to the measurement of its change and movement, and an additive and multiplicative one with concentration measured after change and movement.

The first test of all four versions was for the entire century and a half since the Congress of Vienna, and it showed the preponderance and stability school's predictions to be closer to historical reality than those of the parity and fluidity school. But even though the correlations were all in the direction predicted by the preponderance school, their goodness of fit was not very impressive. Then, on the basis of prior findings, as well as a number of visual and statistical examinations of the data, we divided the century and a half into two separate eras of equal length, and re-tested the models.

This time, the predictions of the *parity and fluidity* school turned out to be correct in the direction of their associations and strong in their fit with 19th century reality. Particularly powerful was the additive form of the model with concentration measured prior to its redistribution. And, not surprisingly, given the results of the full 150 year analyses, the 20th century findings matched the predictions of the *preponderance and stability* school.

But whereas the corrected coefficient of determination ($\bar{R}^2$) for the parity model in the earlier era was .65, the best of those for the preponderance model in the contemporary era was .31.

Bearing in mind the opening paragraphs in this section, as well as the relatively clear empirical results, we conclude that the concentration of major power capabilities does indeed exercise an impact on the incidence of war and that its impact has been a radically different one in the past and present centuries. As to possible explanations for these radical differences, space limitations preclude any lengthy consideration. For the moment, though, we might speculate that uncertainty—our unmeasured intervening variable—plays a different role in the two centuries. When diplomacy was still largely in the hands of small elite groups, the uncertainty factor (allegedly resulting from an equal distribution of power, and fluidity in the rank orderings) may have been modest in both its magnitude and its effects. Schooled in the accepted norms of the game, these professionals might be uncertain as to exactly who ranked where, but nevertheless fairly confident as to general behavior patterns. The shared culture made it relatively clear what each would do in given—and familiar—situations of conflict or crisis, and their relative freedom of action made it easier to conform to such regularized expectations.

By the turn of the century, however, industrialization, urbanization, and the democratization of diplomacy may have begun to erode the rules of the game. Conventional definitions of the national interest were no longer widely accepted at home, and political oppositions and interest groups could make certain foreign policy moves difficult and costly to a regime. The increasing need to mobilize popular support as well as material resources meant that the vagaries of domestic politics would intrude more fully into a nation's diplomacy. And a grasp of other nations' domestic politics has never been a strong point in the foreign offices of the world. Hence, the normal uncertainties of the "balance of power" system were aggravated by these additional uncertainties, meaning that the probability of war could only be kept within bounds when power configurations were exceptionally clear and the pecking order was quite unambiguous. This is, of course, only one of several possible interpretations, and a highly speculative one at that.[18] In due course, then, we hope to bring more solid evidence to bear on the power-war relationships which are reported here; in that context, a number of technological, sociological and political hypotheses will receive due consideration.

Given our findings and the associated caveats, are any policy implications worth noting? On the one hand—as our critics continue to remind

---

[18] It has been alleged (e.g., Bleicher, 1971) that one abuses the scientific method by advancing alternative interpretations without supporting data. Our view is that such a practice not only enhances the quality and cumulativeness of science by suggesting possible follow-up investigations, but helps keep our discipline relevant to the real problems of war and peace in the immediate future.

us—such macro-level phenomena as the distribution of military-industrial capabilities are not exactly susceptible to short run policy control. In this, as in other of our analyses to date, the independent variables are indeed "independent" as far as immediate human intervention is concerned. They change rather slowly, and worse yet, they seldom seem to change in response to conscious and intelligent planning.

On the other hand, a fuller understanding of these structural conditions is much to be valued. Not only do they appear to exercise a powerful impact on the peacefulness of the international system, but they also constitute some of the major constraints within which men and groups act and interact. Despite the views of Rapoport (1970) and others that "there is no lack of knowledge about 'what men could do' to insure peace," we are struck with the evidence to the contrary.

Closely related is the familiar issue of how similar the world of the 1970s and 1980s is to that of the 1816–1895 or 1900–1965 periods. If the system has changed drastically on one or more occasions in this century, or is likely to do so in the near future, how relevant are the results of historical analyses? Our findings in the Correlates of War project to date suggest rather strongly that: (a) today's world *is* different from that of the 19th century, but (b) the most discernible changes occurred around the turn of the century and not with the first or second World War or with the advent of nuclear weapons and ballistic missiles. For the moment, then, all we can say is that it behooves us to treat all such alleged transformations as empirical questions, and to ascertain the extent to which such changes have affected the probability of war. We suspect, as noted above, that the 20th century system *is* a less stable and less easily understood one than the 19th, and that we *are* experiencing different types of war brought on by differing conditions. But it may also have given us the knowledge and skills that make it more tractable to us than the 19th century was for those who sought to understand and control the international politics of that era.

In saying this, however, we have no illusions that social scientific discoveries related to war (or other problems of social justice) will inevitably be utilized to better the lot of humanity (Singer 1970b). Knowledge can not only remain *un*applied; it can also be *mis*applied. But that is no justification for eschewing knowledge. Rather, our job is to ask the most important questions, seek the answers in the most efficient and rigorous fashion, publish our findings and interpretations in an expeditious fashion—and act on them in a forthright manner. As we see it, peace research—especially on the structural conditions that make for war—*is* peace action of a critical sort. Thus, as we continue to press for the policy changes that we *suspect* may improve man's chances for survival and dignity, we nevertheless continue that research which will permit us to replace mere suspicion with relatively hard knowledge.

Editors' Commentary

Major Findings

Singer, Bremer, and Stuckey not only provide significant empirical tests of the balance-of-power and the preponderance-of-power schools but also reformulate much of the contradictory and imprecise theorizing so that the propositions can be tested. Balance-of-power thinking, like all realist approaches, sees world politics as a constant struggle for power. If one state succeeds in gaining a significant degree of power over another, then it will be in a position to successfully threaten that other state in order to get what it wants. The only way the state being threatened can prevent an attack is by giving in or by securing allies that would restore a balance of power. Balance-of-power advocates are especially concerned about strong states overrunning weaker states and see alliance making as a way of undercutting the strength of a stronger state or bloc. Therefore a *system* of states where power is relatively dispersed and alliances are flexible, so that a balance can be maintained, should be more peaceful and should protect the independence of states.

The rationale behind this proposition is that states will not initiate a war unless they are pretty sure of winning it. In social science language, it is assumed that uncertainty makes states conservative and that leaders are unwilling to take great risks. In such a situation, states are not prone to start wars. Thus, uncertainty produced by a relative equality of capability is seen as producing peace. In Singer, Bremer, and Stuckey's terms, there is less war when there is approximate parity (or change toward it) and a fluid hierarchy.

The preponderance-of-power school of thought argues that relative equality does not prevent war since each side still has a fifty-fifty chance of winning. Only when the defender state has overwhelming power can it be secure, for no state would initiate a war it was certain to lose. The rationale underlying this position is that uncertainty is associated with war, since leaders are willing to take risks if they have a decent chance of success. As Singer et al. state this position, there is less war in the system when there is a concentration of capability (or change toward it) in the hands of a few states and a relatively stable rank among nation-states.

These two contradictory positions are, as Singer et al. point out, an example of traditional wisdom's not providing any real knowledge or guidance and running into a dead end because of the failure to test equally plausible but incompatible arguments through systematic empirical research. One of the major contributions of this article is that it begins to provide some of that research. Equally important is that the authors are able to reconceptualize and operationalize ambiguous terms, like *power, balance,* and *preponderance,* so that their empirical referents can be observed. Hence, they look at power only in terms of material capabilities and at balance and preponderance as the amount of concentration of such capabilities in the system.

This means that their analysis and rationale are conducted at the systemic level, not the national level. Therefore, their analysis is not intended to test directly the logic of preventing attack by balancing power. Nevertheless, a systemic test does capture the notion that periods dominated by a group of relatively equal states are more peaceful than periods when power is concentrated in one or two states.

The findings produced in this study have stirred considerable discussion, as well as spurred more research. Singer, Bremer, and Stuckey find that the effect of capability concentration in the system is different depending on whether one examines the nineteenth or the twentieth century. In the nineteenth century, they find that parity in the system, change toward parity, and fluidity make for less war. In the twentieth century, they find the opposite: preponderance (high concentration of capability) in the system, change toward concentration, and stability make for less war. The relationship in the nineteenth century is strong, with a corrected R^2 of .65 (a multiple R of .85). The relationship in the twentieth century is of moderate strength with a corrected R^2 of .30 (a multiple R of .68) (see the multiples in tables 2–5 and 2–6 respectively).

The different findings for the two centuries are somewhat problematic, since we do not normally expect a general pattern to shift radically from one century to the next without some fundamental reason. If a balance of power produces peace in one period, it should do so in another; otherwise, we begin to suspect that the relationship we have uncovered is not really generalizable and accurate.

Singer, Bremer, and Stuckey try to explain the shift by saying that there was a reason why the effect of capability did change: the international system itself changed and introduced a new variable that drastically affected the role that uncertainty played in the system. By the turn of the century, they argue, industrialization, urbanization, and the democratization of diplomacy had eroded the nineteenth-century elite and its consensus on the rules of the game. Thereafter, domestic politics intruded more. Whereas in the nineteenth century a relative balance was enough to keep an elite in check, only a clear preponderance and stable hierarchy was sufficient to keep actors operating within the mass politics of the twentieth century in check.

Because this explanation is introduced after the test results are known and one of its purposes is to save the theoretical thrust of the analysis—i.e., that capability has an effect—it can be seen as an **ad hoc explanation.** When one ad hoc explanation after another is offered in order to refine and save a theoretical approach, scientific norms are violated because too many ad hoc explanations make a proposition nonfalsifiable. Here, however, only one ad hoc explanation has been introduced, and it appears to have some plausibility. Nevertheless, it must not be forgotten that this is a hypothesis that *has yet to be tested* and assessed in the light of other explanations of the discrepant findings.

An alternative explanation of the findings is provided by Bueno de Mesquita (1981a), who argues, as have several other scholars, that the dependent variable, i.e. nation-months, used by Singer, Bremer, and Stuckey does not measure war and peace but the magnitude of war. Singer's et al. findings, then, tell us something about whether large or small wars (in terms of nation-months) are associated with parity or preponderance, but they cannot tell us whether balance or preponderance is related to the onset of war. For several scholars, one of the flaws of this study is that it *misspecifies* the dependent variable; i.e., its use of nation-months does not really capture the relationship of distribution of capabilities and the onset of war as adequately as would a dichotomous war/no war measure. Bueno de Mesquita argues that one must examine a different dependent variable—the dichotomous variable of war/no war. If this is a correct argument, then using this measure should produce different findings, and this is indeed the case. Bueno de Mesquita (1981a) finds that neither a balance nor a preponderance of capabilities is related to the onset of war. This **null** finding means that the likelihood of war's occurring is just as great when there is a balance of power as when there is a preponderance of power. This suggests that the distribution of power is not a factor in causing war, although it may be a factor in the magnitude of war (that is, how widespread war is in terms of nation-months). Additional critiques of Singer, Bremer, and Stuckey's research may be found in Thompson (1983a) and Vasquez (1986).

Regardless of the discussion this study has provoked, a close reading supports three important conclusions. First, the distribution of capability and its effects are different in the two centuries.

Second, the amount of war and the kind of warfare the two centuries experience are different. Third, because the dependent variable is the magnitude of war (as measured by nation-months of war) and not a dichotomous war/no war variable, it is not established that a parity or preponderance model is related to peace, only that they are related to differing magnitudes of war. This implies that neither a balance of power nor a preponderance of power is associated with peace. Rather, each seems to be associated with a different kind of war.

Methodological Notes

The Singer, Bremer, and Stuckey article is a good piece from which to learn a fairly large number of methodological principles. A few definitions and explanations here will allow even novices to navigate this important study.

The first issue the authors discuss is the **validity** and **reliability** of their measures. A measure is **valid** if it measures what it is supposed to measure, that is, if it actually indicates instances of the concept. In order to study something scientifically, we need to find aspects of the phenomenon that can be observed. These are called **indicators.** They do not capture all of the richness of a concept, but when we are satisfied that at least some aspects of a concept are validly measured, we can make inferences based on analyses of these indicators. It is useful to use multiple indicators, as these authors do, to tap as much of the concept as possible.

Reliability means that the operational definition and measurement procedures are clear enough so that two or more researchers working independently would produce the same data. In this way, reliability can be tested, whereas assessments of validity rely on argumentation over the meaning of a concept and can never be established as correct simply through empirical analysis.

Another matter the authors devote considerable attention to is the kind of statistical techniques they employ. This study uses multiple regression analysis, which is based on the product moment correlation coefficient, also known as Pearson's r, an interval-level statistic. The best way to see how Pearson's r is used is to look at a **scatterplot.** If you wanted to calculate a Pearson's r between interval measures of power and war initiation, each case, or nation, would have a power score (for example, number of military personnel in 10,000s) and the number of wars it initiated. A scatterplot would show where each nation fell on each measure, as shown in figure 2–4 using data from the learning package in chapter 15.

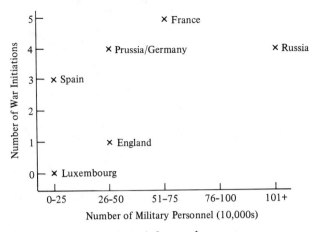

Figure 2-4. A Scatterplot

One should always examine the scatterplots before reporting a correlation to be sure that the relationship is really linear and not curvilinear, since Pearson's *r* can only describe a relationship in which a steady (linear) increase in one variable is associated with a steady increase (or decrease) in another. If the relationship is more complex, for example curvilinear, Pearson's *r* is not valid. An example of a curvilinear relationship is that between the amount one eats and one's health. Not eating at all is very unhealthy. As food consumption rises, health increases, but only to a point. When food consumption greatly exceeds the number of calories burned, health begins to decline again.

Pearson's *r* is calculated on the basis of two steps. First, a **regression line** is drawn (by hand or by the computer) such that each point is as close to it as possible (see figure 2–5). The slope of this line expresses how much of an increase (or decrease) in the dependent variable is produced by an increase in the independent variable. The formula for a line is $y = a + bx$, where y is the dependent variable, a is the constant or intercept (where the line crosses the y axis), b is the slope (the rate at which the line rises [or falls, if b is negative]), and x is the independent variable. Using the formula for a line, regression analysis describes the dependent variable as $y = a + bx + e$, with e representing measurement error.

The second step is the calculation of the correlation. Pearson's *r* tells us how closely related the two variables are to each other. Once the cases are plotted and the regression line is drawn, the average distance of the points from the line is calculated according

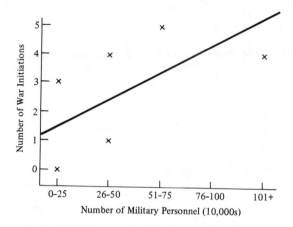

Figure 2-5. Scatterplot with Regression Line

to a formula that produces a number between −1.0 and 1.0. When there is obviously no relationship between the two variables, as in figure 2–6, there is so much distance between the points and the line that the correlation is 0.0. When the relationship is a perfect positive one, as in figure 2–7, there is no distance, and *r* = 1.0. There can also be a perfect negative relationship, as in figure 2–8, in which case the correlation would be −1.0. The Pearson's *r* for the data in figure 2–5 is .51.

The findings in this article are presented in two parts. The bivariate analyses are quite straightforward. The Pearson's *r* correlations are presented for the relationship between each of the

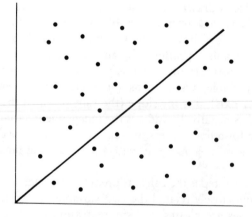

Figure 2-6. No Relationship

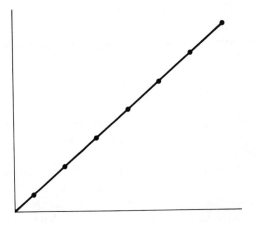

Figure 2-7. A Perfect Positive Relationship

three independent variables—concentration, change in concentration, and movement—and war. When they are used for a multiple correlation analysis, Pearson's *r*'s are referred to as partial correlation coefficients. When a correlation based on measuring the amount of variance—the distance of each point from the regression line—is used, the correlation is squared in order to get a measure of the amount of variance that is accounted for. This is called r^2. A Pearson's *r* of .50 yields an r^2 of .25, which is interpreted as meaning that 25 percent of the variance is accounted for by the independent variable. In table 2–3, only the concentration

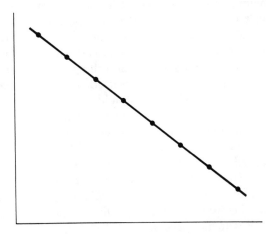

Figure 2-8. A Perfect Negative Relationship

variable accounts for more than 50 percent of the variance (.66) and only for the nineteenth century.

The authors then move to **multiple regression.** Multiple regression uses the formula for regression and adds other variables:

$$y = \alpha + \beta_1 + \beta_2 + \beta_3 + \epsilon.$$

Lower case beta (β) is the **estimated regression coefficient,** meaning that it gives the slope of the line for the relevant independent variable. Next, in tables 2–4 and 2–5, beta weights (b) are reported. These numbers give an idea of the strength of the relationship between each independent variable and the dependent variable. Then the authors report r^2 to indicate how much of the variance is accounted for by each of the independent variables.

The contribution made by multiple regression is to calculate how much of the variation in the dependent variable is accounted for by a *combination* of the independent variables. The **multiple correlation coefficient** R is similar to Pearson's r, but it measures the impact of the combination of the independent variables. R^2, the multiple coefficient of determination, measures the amount of variance in the dependent variable accounted for by the three independent variables together. Naturally, it is often the case that a combination of variables will account for more than one will. Since it would be possible to account for a great deal of the variance simply by including a very large number of independent variables, the R^2 is corrected for this possibility. The result is called corrected R^2 ($\bar{R}^2$), which provides a slightly more conservative statistic.

The major methodological contributions of this article are the measurement of concepts related to the balance of power and preponderance of power, the comparison of two competing models, the use of multiple regression to measure the combined effects of independent variables, and controlling for century to see whether different models fit different eras. The challenge of the findings is to explain why they should be different for the two centuries. The authors propose one explanation. Others, like Bueno de Mesquita (1981a), have suggested that the findings pose an anomaly that can be eliminated if the dependent variable is operationalized as war/no war. From this perspective, Singer, Bremer, and Stuckey have not found that the onset of war is related to different distributions of capabilities in the two centuries but that the distribution of capabilities in a period affects the *magnitude* of war that occurs.

3
Armaments and Escalation: Two Competing Hypotheses

Michael D. Wallace

Editors' Introduction

Just as there have been contradictory views about the role of power in the onset of war, so too have there been contradictory views about the role of military expenditures and arms races. Many have thought of arms races as increasing the probability of war because they increase insecurity and hostility. Others advocate the advice of the Roman general Vegetius: "Who would desire peace should be prepared for war." Michael Wallace tests these two popular notions about the causes of war. The peace-through-strength proposition holds that the best way a state can avoid war is to be so strong that no one will dare attack it. The armaments-tension proposition sees arms races as fueling tensions that increase the probability of war, especially if a crisis should arise. Much of what makes this article important is that it tests two competing hypotheses against each other. When this type of research design is used, the magnitude of the findings is less important than the relative performance of the two propositions.

Since classical times, scholars of statecraft and military affairs alike have asserted that strengthening their nations' military capabilities would help not only to ensure victory should war occur, but might serve as well to *prevent* the outbreak of war by intimidating or deterring an adversary. The fourth-century Roman general Vegetius put the point succinctly: "[Qui]*desiderat pacem, praeparet bellum—nemo provocare, nemo audet offendere quem intellegit superiorem esse pugnaturum.*" Hans Morgenthau,

Reprinted from *International Studies Quarterly*, 26 (March 1982), pp. 37–56. Copyright © 1982 by the International Studies Association. Reprinted by permission of ISA and the author.

whose *Politics Among Nations* has instructed several generations of statesmen and scholars, takes the point a step further:

> The political objective of military preparations of any kind is to deter other nations from using military force by making it too risky for them to do so. The political aim of military preparations is, in other words, to make the actual application of military force unnecessary by inducing the prospective enemy to desist from the use of military force. (1960:30)

It scarcely needs mention that this belief in the war-preventing character of military might is almost an article of faith among the world's elites: They have, almost without exception, hewed faithfully to its precepts by providing ever-increasing resources for their military establishments. It is surprising, therefore, that the evidence adduced to support this "peace through preparedness" doctrine is almost entirely anecdotal and idiosyncratic. Both popular and scholarly works "ransack history" for examples which purport to show how failure to maintain adequate armed forces strength has led to an aggressive war. But the reader will find little or no systematic, scientific evidence in the literature linking military preparedness with the preservation of peace.[1]

The lack of evidence is especially significant when we recall that the "military preparedness" hypothesis is flatly contradicted by a frequently articulated counterhypothesis. This asserts that increasing armed forces strength will lead, not to stability, but to a matching effort by one's adversary. The result is arms competition, and, according to this view, there is a positive interaction or synergistic effect between bilateral tensions and arms competition. Grievances and hostility lead one or both nations to begin arming, either as a threat or from an expectation of armed conflict; each military increment alarms the other side still further, increasing tensions once again, thus leading to pressure for still more armed might, and so on. The result of this positive feedback cycle is that both the motive and the means for a violent resolution of the conflict undergo simultaneous and rapid enhancement. According to this model, the likely outcome of such an "armament-tension spiral" (Singer 1958) or *arms race* is war.

In other words, if this model is accurate, the growing military might of international rivals is by no means the mere passive reflection of increasing tensions. Rather, the rapid bilateral militarization we refer to as an arms race is in and of itself an important link in the escalation process which results in the settlement of international differences by war.

---

[1] There have been, of course, a number of systematic studies linking the *distribution* of military capability with the frequency and magnitude of war. These do not, however, speak directly to the preparedness question, for several reasons: (a) they almost always adduce data at the systemic or subsystemic rather than the state level of analysis; (b) they usually involve nonmilitary as well as military forms of capability; and (c) their focus is usually on the long-term *origins* of conflict rather than on its provocation or escalation in the short run. For an excellent review of this literature and an incisive discussion of the issues involved, see Moul (1980).

Thus the "preparedness" and "arms race" hypotheses make directly opposing predictions concerning the consequences of increasing one's military might. The "preparedness" hypothesis sees this as a necessary step in preserving the peace; conversely, *failing* to increase military strength to match or exceed one's adversary is almost certain to provoke war. On the other hand, the "arms race" hypothesis sees such increases as dangerous and likely to lead to the very conflict they were designed to prevent.

This controversy has obvious and immediate relevance to current policy debates over military spending and weapons acquisition. Therefore, a systematic and comparative test of these two hypotheses is desirable to discover which, if either, fits the available data.

The Preparedness Model

Those who assert that military preparedness will deter an aggressor and thus reduce the probability of war are concerned first and foremost with the current military balance. Only military superiority "on the ground," it is asserted, will deter aggression; the mere *potential* to undertake a build-up is insufficient. Moreover, it is *relative* and not absolute military strength that is crucial; the resisting or "status quo" power must be sufficiently strong by comparison with a potential aggressor or "revisionist" power to deter an attack. Thus, in propositional form, the preparedness model asserts: *International conflict and disputes in which the distribution of military capability favors the revisionist state are more likely to result in war than those in which the balance favors the status quo state.*

Although the current military balance is its central concern, the preparedness school also focuses attention on *shifts* in the distribution of capabilities. A tenuous superiority may be of little protection if the opposing state is rapidly closing the gap. On the one hand, the perception of imminent ascendancy may stimulate aggressive ambitions. On the other hand, a power in relative decline may be tempted to initiate a preemptive war while it still possesses a "window" of overall superiority. Thus we may hypothesize: *International conflicts and disputes which are accompanied by a shift in the distribution of relative military capability in favor of a revisionist state, or to the detriment of a status quo state, are more likely to result in war than those in which such a shift does not occur.*

To test these hypotheses, it was first necessary to select a population of cases for observation. The population selected was that of serious disputes occurring between great powers from 1816 to 1965. These data were obtained from the Correlates of War Project at the University of Michigan,[2]

---

[2] The author would like to thank Professor J. David Singer for making this list of serious disputes available. The entire data set is currently being updated and "cleaned." The final version will be published in a manuscript coauthored by Charles Gochman and Zeev Maoz,

and include all instances of the use of overt threat of hostile force by one great power against another. A list of the participants in these disputes, the dates on which they occurred, their outcomes, along with the data for the indices described below, is found in appendix 3–A. Of the 99 disputes included in the list, 26 escalated into all-out interstate war, while 73 terminated short of war. The question thus becomes: Is a great power serious dispute more likely to escalate if the revisionist party to the dispute is (a) significantly stronger militarily, (b) gaining significantly in strength relative to the status quo power, or (c) both stronger and growing?

In order to answer these questions, we must make two determinations: First, which of the two disputants in each case is to be classified as revisionist, and which as status quo? Second, how can we establish their respective military capabilities?

Determining which side was which was relatively easy in most cases. For example, in 1936 Germany was clearly revisionist and Britain status quo, while in 1950 the Soviet Union was evidently revisionist and the United States status quo. There were, of course, a few cases where this determination was far less evident. In these cases, a number of standard diplomatic history references were consulted, and a preliminary judgment made. The reliability of this classification was then checked by an informal panel of colleagues and graduate students. In all cases, a "test-retest" reliability of .9 or better was achieved.

Data on military capabilities were also gleaned from the compilations produced by the Correlates of War Project; to construct the indices, I used the overall military expenditure total for each nation, converted to sterling from 1816 to 1919, and to dollars thereafter. To measure the military balance, I averaged each nation's expenditures for the three years prior to the dispute, then computed the ratio of revisionist to status quo strength. Thus, positive index values greater than unity implied a stronger revisionist power, while those less than unity meant the status quo nation was stronger.

After experimenting with different thresholds, 1.5 was selected to indicate a decisive superiority for the revisionist state. For the index to exceed this value, the revisionist side would have to have a military budget 50% greater than its status quo rival. In 28 of the 99 disputes, the challenger achieved this level of superiority, while in 71 cases it failed to do so. If this dichotomization is tabulated against war–no war outcome, we obtain the result displayed in table 3–1. There is quite clearly no evidence of a relationship between revisionist superiority prior to a crisis, and the escalation of that crisis into war.

If revisionist military superiority does not affect crisis outcome, what

---

whose efforts were chiefly responsible for its generation. Those wishing to use these data for their own purposes should therefore communicate with Singer. For more information concerning the version used here, see my earlier article (Wallace 1979).

Table 3–1

	Revisionist Superiority >50%	Revisionist Weaker or <50% Stronger
War outcome	9	17
No-war outcome	19	54

Corrected X^2 = .50, n.s.

ϕ = .09.

about the *growth* of revisionist might relative to that of the status quo power? To answer this question, I calculated a new index based upon the ratio of the rates of growth of the two powers' arms expenditures for the five years prior to the dispute, placing the growth rate of the revisionist power in the numerator, and that of the status quo power in the denominator. The resulting index would be insensitive to the absolute rates of growth of arms expenditures for the two powers, while very sensitively reflecting *relative* changes in their position. Large index values mean the revisionist power was forging ahead; small ones that the status quo power was maintaining or improving upon its position.

Of course, negative growth rates required special treatment. Where they occurred in the numerator, they were left as is; the resulting negative index value correctly reflected a revisionist "loss." When found in the denominator, the absolute value was taken prior to computation; in those few cases where this occurred, the absolute values were very small, meaning that little distortion would be generated by this procedure. Finally, where both the numerator and denominator were negative, the inverse of the ratio was used, so that, for example, a small negative value for the revisionist state combined with a large negative value for the status quo power would be correctly interpreted as a revisionist "win."

If we decide arbitrarily that a status quo power has "lost" the competition when its rate of armed forces growth is at least 50% less than that of the revisionist power over five years, then 28 of the 99 disputes were preceded by status quo losses, while in 71 cases the status quo power either held its own or improved its position. If we then separate out these cases according to whether or not the dispute escalated to war, we obtain the distribution in table 3–2. It is obvious that relative rates of growth have even less success in predicting dispute outcome.

Table 3–2

	Revisionist "Wins"	Revisionist Does Not Win
War outcome	7	19
No-War outcome	21	52

Corrected X^2 = .004, n.s.

ϕ = .03.

Table 3–3

	Revisionist Threat	No Threat
War outcome	11	15
No-war outcome	25	48

$X^2 = .25$, n.s.
$\phi = .07$.

But perhaps these simple indices may not do full justice to the preparedness hypothesis. In discussions of the major historical arms competitions (such as the Anglo-German naval race of the early 1900s or the current superpower arms race), it is the combination of revisionist strength *and* rapid growth relative to the status quo power that is perceived as threatening to peace. Thus, an index reflecting both relative military capabilities and relative growth rates would have more predictive power than indices reflecting each taken separately.

To construct such an index, the two previous indices were multiplied together. This new index thus measures the *combined* effect of revisionist strength and revisionist growth. The larger the index value, the more "threat" the revisionist state presumably poses to the status quo power.

If we use a value of unity as a threshold to dichotomize the data, and tabulate the result against dispute outcome once again, we obtain the result displayed in table 3–3.

Once again it is clear that the result is negative: Combining existing revisionist superiority with incipient superiority is no help in determining which great power disputes will escalate, and which will not. Overall, it is scarcely possible to avoid the conclusion that military preparedness, however useful it may be in achieving *other* national goals, appears to have little or no capacity to prevent serious disputes from escalating to war.

The Arms Race Model

Unlike the preparedness model, the arms race model has been the subject of a considerable amount of scientific investigation.[3] However, almost all of this extensive literature has focused on the origins, process, and outcome of the arms race itself, and not directly on the *impact* of arms races on the conflict process. In an earlier work, I discovered that periods of rapid growth in great power military expenditures were followed by sharp increases in the frequency of onset, magnitude, and severity of international wars (Wallace

---

[3] The mathematical study of arms races began over a generation ago with Richardson (1960a). This now voluminous literature is extensively summarized and reviewed in Busch (1970), Chaterjee (1975), and Hollist (1978).

1972). This seemed to dovetail closely with the implicit premise of most of the arms race literature, namely, that uncontrolled arms races increase the probability of war. This leads to the following empirical hypothesis: *International conflicts and disputes which are accompanied by arms races are much more likely to result in war than those in which an arms race does not occur.*

An important qualifying clarification must be entered here. Many writers use the term "arms race" quite loosely to include almost any situation of competitive military growth (Huntington 1958; Gray 1971). Defining an arms race in these terms, it is not surprising that these writers find the arms race–war model of war onset lacking even in intuitive plausibility; by their definition, there have been many arms races not resulting in war. But here, as elsewhere (Wallace 1976, 1979), I shall use the term arms race to refer only to very rapid, simultaneous arms growth exceeding a specific quantitative threshold to be determined below.

In an earlier article (Wallace 1979), I undertook a preliminary test of the arms hypothesis. I shall begin by summarizing the procedures and results of that test, and then go on to show how these procedures can be extended to allow a comparative test of the arms race and preparedness hypotheses.

My original test procedure began with the set of 99 great power disputes described above. Using this population, I developed an index to delineate that group preceded by arms races. Beginning once again with the Correlates of War data on annual military expenditures, I fitted a polynomial function to each national series for the period ten years prior to the onset of the dispute, in order to estimate the smoothed time rate of change (delta) for each nation immediately prior to the dispute. An arms race index was then computed by taking the *product* of the deltas for each side. This index-constructed procedure ensured that only long-term, intense, bilateral growth in arms expenditures would score high on the arms race scale.

Taking as a threshold for an arms race an average annual bilateral predispute growth rate of 10% (that is, an index value equal to or exceeding 90.0), I ascertained that 28 dispute dyads were preceded by an arms race, and 71 were not. Tabulating these against the outcome of the dispute (war–no war), I obtained the result in table 3–4. Apparently, almost all disputes accompanied by an arms race ended in war; almost all of those not

Table 3–4

	Arms Race	No Arms Race
War outcome	23	3
No-war outcome	5	68

Corrected $X^2 = 60.0$, $p < .0001$.
$\phi = .80$.

so accompanied did not escalate. The strength of the relationship is clearly indicated by computing the Yules' Q value for the table, which is .98; the more conservative φ coefficient is .80.

Such an extraordinarily powerful finding is likely to generate suspicion, and so indeed it proved. One critic (Weede 1980) pointed out that all of my observations might not be truly independent. This is because many of the dyads might not be separate conflicts, but part of the same conflict spread by contagion. This, of course, would bias the results.

It is good scientific practice to see how results would be affected if the *least* favorable situation obtains, so I began to merge all of the conflict dyads arising from a single war or dispute. However, it quickly became apparent that this procedure was too severe; it would have merged, for example, the onset of war between France and Germany in 1939 with the outbreak of hostilities between Japan and the United States in 1941, despite the consensus of historians that these two outbreaks had little to do with each other.

So a modified aggregation procedure was used: I merged all dyads in which two or more allied nations entered simultaneously into a conflict with a common foe. This procedure reduced the N from 99 to 80, and produced the results displayed in table 3–5.

The revised results, while not as striking as the original table, provide more than adequate support for the hypothesis that conflicts preceded by arms races are more likely to result in war. Of the 15 conflicts preceded by an arms race, 11 resulted in war, while only 2 out of 65 conflicts *not* preceded by an arms race ended in war, yielding 74 out of 80 correct predictions. Thus, even if we assume that a military alliance completely precludes an independent national decision regarding conflict escalation (an extreme assumption indeed), the situation is not substantially altered.

Thus, tested by itself, the arms race hypothesis seems impressively substantiated. What happens when we test the preparedness and arms race hypotheses together? Is there a joint or interaction effect among the indices which is not visible in the bivariate tables?

The Indices Combined

Is the strong observed relationship between arms races and crisis escalation affected by the military preparedness of the two sides? In other words, is an

Table 3–5

	Arms Race	No Arms Race
War outcome	11	2
No-war outcome	4	63

Corrected X^2 = 39.2, p<.001.
φ = .67.

Table 3–6
Revisionist Superior by >50%

	Arms Race	No Arms Race
War outcome	8	1
No-war outcome	2	17

arms race which is "won" by the revisionist more likely to result in escalation than an arms race which is "tied" or won by the status quo power? To test this intriguing possibility, I partitioned the bivariate arms race–war outcome table using the values of the ratio of military expenditures index. The two partial tables resulting are displayed as tables 3–6 and 3–7.[4]

It is clear from these results that the arms race–war outcome relationship is not noticeably affected by the military balance at the *end* of the arms race. In table 3–6, the preparedness hypothesis predicts war, but only 9 out of 28 cases result in war. Moreover, 17 out of the 19 incorrect predictions are accounted for by the arms race hypothesis, while of the 9 correct predictions made by the preparedness hypothesis, 8 were also correctly made by the arms race hypothesis. In other words, even if a revisionist makes a substantial relative gain prior to a dispute, war is rather unlikely (only one chance in three) unless this revisionist gain is made during an all-out bilateral arms race.

Looking at table 3–7, that is, those cases in which the preparedness hypothesis does *not* predict war, we see 54 correct predictions out of 71. But here, all but two of the incorrect predictions are successfully predicted by the arms race hypothesis, while conversely this hypothesis makes only three "errors" not made by the preparedness hypothesis. In other words, crises preceded by arms races are very likely ($p = .88$) to end in war, even if the revisionist power does not gain any substantial advantage in the race.

Table 3–7
Revisionist Weaker or <50% Stronger

	Arms Race	No Arms Race
War outcome	15	2
No-war outcome	3	51

---

[4] Summary statistics are not computed for these tables, as some of the cell values are too small for these to be meaningful.

A Cautionary Note

The relationships reported here are unusually strong and unambiguous by the standards of social science. Precisely for this reason, caution must be used in interpreting them. First, the usual disclaimers regarding the data must be entered. Both the universe of dispute cases and the military expenditure data were generated from preliminary compilations. While it is unlikely that they are wildly incorrect, a replication after final "cleaning" may well produce some changes. Even softer and less operational, of course, is the distinction between revisionist and status quo powers, for which this author is solely responsible. Conceivably, at least part of the poor relative showing the preparedness hypothesis could be accounted for by some systematic bias in this coding. Again, only replication will settle the matter one way or another.

Second, these findings do *not* mean that arms races always lead to war, or that the distribution of military capability is in no way associated with the onset of war. Here we have concerned ourselves only with the factors associated with the *escalation* of conflicts into full-scale war; we have not even considered those factors responsible for the *origins* of conflict in the first place. To prove that arms races necessarily lead to war, we would have to show that they play a key role in the initiation as well as the escalation of conflict, and no attempt has been made to do this. Moreover, there are excellent theoretical grounds for believing that arms races are *not* the sole cause of conflict; if this were so, then simultaneous military build-ups by friendly powers would lead to enmity, and we know this is seldom the case (Gray 1971).

On the other side of the coin, the fact that the military balance does not appear to affect conflict escalation in the short run does not preclude its impact in the long run. Many scientific studies (Choucri and North 1975; Singer, Bremer, and Stuckey 1972; Gochman 1975; Luterbacher 1975; Wallace 1972, 1973b) suggest quite strongly that over the long term, in conjunction with other factors, the distribution of military capability in the system is central to the origins of conflict. All that has been demonstrated here is that short-term imbalances do not of themselves promote conflict escalation.

But however carefully qualified, the findings reported here are significant. When two powers engage in acts of force or threats of violence against one another, we must assume their relationship is characterized by considerable tension. Yet, in only 3 of 71 cases did such acts lead to war when not preceded by an arms race. Conversely, when an arms race *did* precede a significant threat or act of violence, war was avoided only 5 out of 28 times. It is difficult, therefore, to avoid the conclusion that, over the 150 years from Waterloo to Vietnam, arms races are a danger to the peace of the international system.

By contrast, losing the advantage to a revisionist power has proven much less dangerous; in only 9 of 26 cases where this resulted did war occur, and 8 of those cases were accompanied by arms races. In only 2 cases was a status quo power's "loss" without an arms race to a revisionist state followed by a crisis which escalated to war.

Policy Implications

With the ever-growing capabilities of weapons of mass destruction, great power strategic policy has of necessity been directed more and more toward the prevention of a strategic exchange, with correspondingly less emphasis on military victory in the classical sense. The question was and remains, however, how best to attain this goal? From the very outset, there have been two competing views.

On the one side, the traditionalists argue that peace can only be maintained if "we" equal, surpass, or pull level with "them" in military capability, and most especially, in strategic nuclear capability. This view (certainly the majority view among decision makers of both superpowers) stresses of course the potential political advantages of superiority, and the corresponding penalties for inferiority. But its intellectual centerpiece is unquestionably some formulation of the preparedness doctrine: If we do not augment our arsenals, the enemy will be tempted to attack, and Armageddon will be upon us.

On the other side (and usually in the minority) have been those who argue that the arms race must be brought under control, and eventually reversed by arms control and disarmament measures. To some extent, this view results from a simple fear of weapons of mass destruction, but at its core is some version of the arms race hypothesis. They argue that nuclear weapons are not only dangerous of themselves, but also that the very terror they inspire intensifies the armaments-tension spiral. Unless these weapons can be controlled, they will be used, with a new and universal holocaust ensuing.

It is clear that the findings presented here tend to lend support to the minority "arms control" position rather than the majority "peace through strength" view. In particular, they reinforce with hard evidence the fears of those who argue that an intensification of the superpower arms competition could lead to a "hair-trigger" situation in which a major confrontation would be far more likely to result in all-out war. At the same time, they provide evidence against those who argue that winning (or at least not losing) the arms race is a safe and acceptable substitute for ending it.

Translated into the current policy context, the message is clear; despite the current souring of the international climate, and despite the ideological predispositions of those in leadership positions, it is vitally important both to avoid the resumption of an uncontrolled strategic arms competition and to resume efforts to achieve arms control.

Appendix 3–A:
Arms Race and Preparedness Indices for Nations in Serious Disputes, 1816–1965

Year	Revisionist State	Status Quo State	War Outcome (Y/N)	Ratio of Military Expenditures	Ratio of Expenditure Growth	Combined Superiority Index	Arms Race Index
1833	Russia	UK	N	0.92	−0.61	−0.56	2.73
1833	Russia	France	N	0.53	0.21	0.11	0.17
1836	Russia	UK	N	1.19	−1.49	−1.77	1.00
1840	France	Russia	N	1.18	0.06	0.07	12.90
1840	France	Germany	N	3.67	−0.53	−1.95	0.66
1849	Russia	UK	N	1.08	0.95	1.03	1.02
1849	Russia	France	N	0.74	1.63	1.21	36.27
1850	Germany	Austria	N	0.37	0.06	0.02	9.54
1853	Russia	UK	Y	1.56	−0.28	−0.44	0.06
1853	Russia	France	Y	1.00	−0.59	−0.59	31.74
1854	Russia	Austria	N	1.71	0.25	0.43	53.80
1859	France	Austria	Y	2.20	0.77	1.69	120.91
1861	Russia	UK	N	0.77	1.95	1.50	0.16
1866	Germany	Austria	Y	0.57	−1.77	−1.01	148.61
1866	Italy	Austria	Y	1.16	1.13	1.31	575.14
1867	France	Italy	N	1.68	−0.15	0.25	55.00
1870	Germany	France	Y	0.33	−6.19	2.04	8.91
1875	France	Germany	N	1.64	0.07	0.11	1.19
1877	Russia	UK	N	1.26	0.69	0.87	3.22
1878	Russia	UK	N	1.16	0.15	0.17	0.88
1878	Italy	Austria	N	0.82	3.05	2.50	0.48
1885	Russia	UK	N	0.91	1.46	1.33	4.93
1887	France	Germany	N	1.73	1.22	2.11	1.07
1888	France	Italy	N	2.51	−0.27	−0.68	7.17
1888	France	Austria	N	3.10	−1.71	−5.30	8.35
1888	France	England	N	1.11	−0.08	−0.09	1.63
1893	Russia	Austria	N	2.41	−6.81	−16.41	0.23
1895	Japan	Russia	N	0.42	0.49	0.21	61.53
1897	Russia	UK	N	1.03	0.36	0.37	0.17
1898	France	UK	N	1.03	0.14	0.14	0.35
1899	Germany	UK	N	0.97	−0.06	−0.06	0.39
1900	Japan	Russia	N	0.47	1.94	0.91	53.17
1902	US	Japan	N	0.97	0.52	0.50	0.15
1902	US	UK	N	0.39	0.14	0.05	0.01
1903	US	UK	N	0.36	0.27	0.10	0.07
1904	Russia	UK	N	0.50	0.43	0.21	0.07
1904	Japan	Russia	Y	0.31	1.37	0.42	221.00
1905	Germany	France	N	1.09	23.90	26.05	0.04
1911	Germany	France	N	1.25	1.61	2.01	2.48
1911	Germany	UK	N	1.04	2.70	2.81	28.07
1912	Russia	Austria	N	2.58	2.33	6.01	0.02
1912	Italy	Austria	N	0.99	6.94	6.87	0.37
1913	France	Italy	N	1.84	0.39	0.72	43.39
1914	Germany	UK	Y	1.07	1.66	1.78	133.20
1914	Germany	France	Y	1.17	1.07	1.25	231.25
1914	Germany	Russia	Y	0.96	1.02	0.98	205.35
1914	Austria	UK	Y	0.44	2.04	0.90	90.00
1914	Austria	France	Y	0.47	1.32	0.62	156.25

Year	Revisionist State	Status Quo State	War Outcome (Y/N)	Ratio of Military Expenditures	Ratio of Expenditure Growth	Combined Superiority Index	Arms Race Index
1914	Austria	Russia	Y	0.39	1.26	0.49	138.75
1915	Germany	Italy	Y	2.66	1.01	2.69	811.30
1915	Austria	Italy	Y	1.66	1.20	1.99	912.38
1917	Germany	US	Y	8.52	7.38	62.88	349.68
1923	Russia	UK	N	0.04	−0.61	−0.02	0.04
1931	Japan	US	N	0.34	1.88	0.64	0.53
1932	Japan	UK	N	0.44	−1.18	−0.52	0.85
1932	Japan	US	N	0.33	0.92	0.30	1.05
1934	Germany	Italy	N	0.90	3.02	2.72	14.58
1934	Japan	Russia	N	0.43	1.39	0.60	0.13
1935	Japan	Russia	N	0.39	0.70	0.27	106.13
1935	Italy	UK	N	0.62	−2.15	−1.33	38.21
1936	Germany	UK	N	1.62	8.34	13.51	112.68
1936	Germany	France	N	1.17	3.47	4.06	5.56
1937	Japan	Russia	N	0.20	0.47	0.09	51.47
1937	Japan	US	N	0.50	2.17	1.09	28.28
1938	Japan	Russia	N	0.27	0.95	0.26	14.96
1938	Germany	UK	N	2.41	2.18	5.25	90.06
1938	Germany	France	N	2.43	5.87	14.26	25.97
1939	Japan	France	N	1.42	2.75	3.90	11.49
1939	Japan	UK	Y	0.99	0.90	0.89	261.23
1939	Germany	France	Y	4.56	4.50	20.52	495.51
1939	Germany	UK	Y	3.19	1.48	4.72	420.08
1940	Italy	UK	Y	0.39	0.40	0.16	559.50
1940	Italy	France	Y	0.61	0.61	0.37	643.70
1940	Japan	UK	N	0.71	0.70	0.50	39.98
1940	Japan	France	N	1.11	1.07	1.19	11.49
1941	Germany	Russia	Y	1.76	1.66	2.92	221.61
1941	Germany	US	Y	6.75	1.83	12.35	536.89
1941	Italy	US	Y	0.57	0.83	0.47	543.07
1941	Japan	US	Y	0.98	1.00	0.98	314.58
1945	Japan	Russia	Y	0.48	2.03	0.97	102.93
1946	Russia	US	N	0.43	0.33	0.14	0.03
1948	Russia	US	N	0.41	0.58	0.24	0.32
1948	Russia	UK	N	1.33	0.62	0.82	0.25
1948	Russia	France	N	6.28	0.56	3.52	10.01
1953	Russia	US	N	0.56	0.47	0.26	68.72
1953	Russia	UK	N	5.49	−1.34	−7.36	41.80
1954	China	UK	N	0.79	−0.09	−0.07	22.89
1956	China	US	N	6.77	−0.17	−1.15	25.03
1956	Russia	France	N	8.43	0.95	8.01	61.89
1956	Russia	UK	N	6.22	1.06	6.59	53.05
1958	China	US	N	0.14	−14.89	−2.08	65.02
1958	Russia	UK	N	6.32	33.52	211.85	0.19
1960	Russia	US	N	0.64	1.01	0.65	6.34
1961	Russia	US	N	0.67	0.98	0.66	14.14
1962	China	US	N	0.13	0.92	0.12	103.73
1962	Russia	US	N	0.72	2.40	1.73	122.10
1964	Russia	US	N	0.82	3.32	2.72	30.70
1965	China	UK	N	1.19	0.62	0.74	81.43
1965	China	US	N	0.12	1.51	0.18	47.97

Editors' Commentary

Major Findings

Wallace finds that the peace-through-strength hypothesis is unable to predict which crises will escalate to war and which will not, whereas the arms race model is an excellent predictor. In other words, if you wanted to guess whether a particular dispute would be likely to escalate to war and all you knew was whether the two parties were engaged in an arms race, you would be able to guess fairly accurately what would happen. Conversely, if all you knew was whether the revisionist state was stronger or weaker, your success in guessing would be random; that is, knowing the strength of a disputant would produce no more accurate a prediction than guessing the outcome by flipping a coin. A strong and statistically significant association tells us that guessing the dependent variable on the basis of the independent variable will be more accurate than guessing randomly.

Wallace's findings imply that preparing for war will not ensure peace and could well increase the probability of war if an arms race results. He finds that serious disputes that occur during an arms race are much more likely to escalate to war than serious disputes that occur in the absence of arms races. He does not find, however, that arms races produce war; rather, arms races encourage serious disputes to escalate to war. How they do that, Wallace does not examine, but they probably have that effect by increasing hostility and the sense of threat between each side, while simultaneously giving each the means to fight a war. Arms races work not alone but in conjunction with other factors.

When a study produces clear findings about politically controversial claims, as Wallace's does, it can expect a great deal of scrutiny and attempts to employ alternate measures, samples, data, and test designs to see if the findings persist. No one disagrees that Wallace's findings support his conclusions; what they disagree about is whether the findings are an accurate portrayal of the world.

It should be kept in mind that the findings of any piece of statistical research, just like the observations of any experiment conducted in a laboratory, are a function of either processes in "the real world" or the measures and test design of the study, or some combination of the two. It is extremely difficult, particularly on the basis of one or two studies, to determine what produces a finding. Particularly in the early stages of a science, it is easy to reject a study's conclusions by finding some flaw in a research design, potential error in a measure, or a plausible way of conducting the study in a different manner.

Just because an alternate method of testing produces a different result, however, does not mean automatically that the new results are necessarily more accurate. The research design and measures of the alternative study must be examined with as much care as the original study. Often fault will also be found with it. When this happens, some students or nonscientists throw their hands up in despair and frustration, but this reaction is not called for. One of the beauties of the scientific method is that it is open; it is based on an analysis of the evidence and invites replication. Further research, including the collecting of more evidence, can answer questions that are raised.

Wallace's early findings were first challenged by Weede (1980), who employed a different sample. Weede finds fault with Wallace's treating as separate cases all instances of a dispute between two parties that result in a large war. For example, he objects to counting as separate cases the arms races between Germany and the United Kingdom, Germany and France, Germany and the Soviet Union, Germany and the United States, the United Kingdom and Italy, France and Italy, Japan and the United States, and Japan and the Soviet Union prior to World War II as discrete cases. Each of these dyads has a dispute that escalates to war, but the result is only one war. Treating them as multiple cases, Weede claims, inflates the number of instances supporting Wallace's arms race hypothesis.

Wallace's response to Weede, in this article, is to eliminate all cases where allies simultaneously enter the war against a common enemy but to keep cases in the sample where this condition is not met (for example, U.S. entry into World War II is treated as a separate case). When he does this, the relationship still holds but is reduced from the original phi of .80 to a phi of .67.

More serious challenges to Wallace are made by Paul Diehl in the next chapter. Diehl eliminates most of the relationship between arms races and escalation of crises to war by using new measures of what he calls military buildups and by changing the sample. Wallace's analysis has produced a spate of criticisms and research attempting to undercut his findings. While it may be discouraging to someone new to the scientific study of peace and war to find that most studies are not definitive and that scientific scholars disagree over how the findings should be interpreted, it is important to remember that criticism that gives rise to new research is what often enables knowledge eventually to cumulate.

Methodological Notes

Wallace tests his two models by employing contingency tables like those in the learning package in chapter 15. A contingency table is a visual representation of the number of cases in each combination of the values of each variable. When variables have a large number of values or there are many variables in the analysis, contingency tables become unmanageably large. However, since Wallace has only two variables with two values each, it is easy as well as useful to visually inspect how many cases have arms races and war, arms races and no war, no arms races and war, and no arms races and no war.

Wallace's cases consist of ninety-nine serious disputes, twenty-six of which escalated to war and seventy-three of which did not. The dependent variable is a dichotomous (two-value), nominal, escalation-to-war vs. no-escalation-to-war variable, which is associated with dichotomous measures of revisionist military superiority, revisionist victory–lack of victory, revisionist threat–no threat, and ongoing arms race–no arms race.

Only certain statistics are appropriate for a two-by-two contingency table, such as Yule's Q and phi. You will be able to tell just by looking at it that the data in table 3–1, for example, do not reveal a relationship. Since Yule's Q tends to be biased in the direction of exaggerating a relationship, Wallace uses a more conservative alternate nominal statistic for two-by-two tables, phi (ϕ). The phi in table 3–1 is .09, very low.

Wallace also employs a **statistical significance test**, chi square (χ^2). Whenever we have data that do not comprise the whole **universe** or **population**, we are dealing in effect with a sample. This means that we must ask whether the sample is truly representative of the universe and whether the relationship found in the sample would be likely to be found in the universe. A measure of statistical significance tells us whether to suspect that the observed finding occurred by chance and whether it is likely to hold true for other samples.

Normally, significance tests are conducted only on random samples or samples representative of the population an analyst is studying. Sometimes, however, significance tests are calculated for other kinds of samples or a population of cases within a certain time frame (as Wallace did) in order to gain some idea of how generalizable the finding on these cases might be to similar cases in another period. When this is done, the significance test is said to be of only heuristic value.

Chi square produces a value on the basis of which it can be stated the probability that the finding is just random and not due to a real relationship. When the probability that the finding is random is less than 5 in 100 ($p < .05$), we say that the finding is statistically significant. More stringent thresholds can be used, such as $p < .01$ (see the Leng article in chapter 5) or $p < .001$ (see table 3–5 in this Wallace article). The phi of .67 in table 3–5, for example, is statistically significant at the .001 level.

If there are more than 5 chances in 100 (or 1 chance in 100 or 1 chance in 1,000) that the finding is random, we say that it is statistically insignificant or nonsignificant, no matter how strong the correlation is. (In table 3–1, *nonsignificant* has been abbreviated n.s.) Usually nonsignificant findings are also weak associations, but sometimes, when there is a small number of cases (a small N), the correlation can be quite high but is nonsignificant because the sample is too small. For example, if you had just three cases and all supported your hypothesis, the correlations would be perfect but statistically nonsignificant. The nonsignificance would indicate that you could not confidently generalize from these three cases to all other cases. In sum, when $p < .05$, we can then look to the measure of association to evaluate the hypothesis and accept or reject it on the basis of its magnitude. If the finding is nonsignificant, we reject the hypothesis regardless of the magnitude of the measure of association.

Wallace now proceeds to compare the preparedness model with the arms race model. While the Singer, Bremer, and Stuckey article (chapter 2) compared two competing hypotheses by looking for positive or negative correlations for the same independent variables, Wallace uses different indicators for his two models and tests them separately. It would be unsatisfactory to test only one model and then conclude that the other is deficient. His contribution lies in assessing the utility of each. He also responds to critics such as Weede by subjecting the arms race data to very stringent tests, which reduce his findings from phi = .80 to phi = .67. The fact that the relationship still holds after such changes in the sample is impressive. Finally, not content simply to declare the arms race model superior, he explores the possibility that arms races will have a more escalatory effect when the revisionist power wins the arms race. Even this modification does not reduce the overall predictive power of the arms race model.

Wallace's analysis and the debate over it represent an excellent example of how science uses multiple tests and careful examination of evidence to try to resolve empirical disagreements. The next article, that by Paul Diehl, extends the discussion on arms races by criticizing certain aspects of Wallace's research design and then redoing that analysis to see if the findings still hold.

4

Arms Races and Escalation: A Closer Look

Paul F. Diehl

Editors' Introduction

Paul Diehl raises some serious questions about Wallace's analysis (chapter 3). He argues that there is no relationship between arms races and the escalation of serious disputes to war. He maintains that Wallace's strong findings are a function of an arms race index that is not reliable and valid and a research design that inflates the number of cases supporting the proposition. Diehl replaces the concept of arms race with mutual military buildup and shows that there is little relationship between these, as well as unilateral military buildups, and escalation to war.

Conventional wisdom has always presupposed a link between rapid military buildups and war. The old dictum "if you want peace, prepare for war" offers one perspective on the inter-relationship of military spending and the outbreak of conflict. The spiral model is indicative of a more dangerous connection between increasing weapons and war. Whether the effect is deterrence or provocation, a nation's decision to significantly increase its military capability could be an important factor in the understanding of interstate war.

Despite the central nature of military spending in national security

Reprinted from the *Journal of Peace Research*, Vol. 20, No. 3 (1983), pp. 205–212, by permission of the publisher and the author.

An earlier version of this paper was presented at the Annual Meeting of the International Studies Association-South, Atlanta, 4–6 November 1982.

The author would like to thank Michael Champion, Miroslav Nincic, Peter Wallensteen, J. David Singer, Bradley Martin, and Bruce Russett for their comments and suggestions. In addition, gratitude is expressed to Mary Macknick and Louis Erste for technical assistance in this project.

decision-making, empirical researchers have generally ignored its possible effect on the initiation of war. This void in the academic literature noted by Singer (1970c) in 1969 remains large today.

Nevertheless, some recent efforts have extended the pioneering ideas of Richardson (1960a), studying the impact of arms races and military spending decisions on the outbreak of war. The most interesting work in this area has been that of Michael Wallace. He used early Correlates of War (COW) Project compilations on major power military expenditures and serious disputes to investigate nation behavior in conflict generated situations. In a widely quoted article, Wallace (1979) concluded that the presence or absence of an arms race between two rivals correctly predicted war/no war outcomes in over 90% of the serious disputes studied. Those results are summarized in table 4–1.

A later study by the same author (Wallace 1982), using the same data base, served to reinforce this strong association between arms races and war. The general paucity of alternative investigations makes Wallace's studies the most definitive to date.

If Wallace's findings are correct, the implications for policymaking on arms limitation are clear. The START [Strategic Arms Reduction Talks] negotiations must proceed with all deliberate speed, lest a clash between the superpowers should escalate to all-out war. However, certain methodological problems cast doubt on the validity of Wallace's conclusions. It is the purpose of this paper to detail these difficulties and retest the military buildup-war relationship with a modified set of assumptions and indicators.

A Closer Look

The Correlates of War treats multi-party serious disputes (three or more disputants) as one integrated dispute. Where there was a clear informal/formal partnership among the disputants on one side and where the subject matter of the dispute was the same for each partner, the dispute classification scheme served to reflect the interconnection of events and interests for all those involved. Wallace chose to code each dispute participant dyadically

Table 4–1
Wallace's "Arms Races and Escalation"

	War	No War
Arms race	23	5
No arms race	3	68

$X^2 = 62.99$.

$\phi = .8$.

$Q = .98$.

against those nations in opposition. Thus, the original 1914 dispute which escalated to World War I is analyzed as if it were six separate disputes and consequently six individual wars. Overall, 26 distinct wars are created where only 7 or 8 integrated ones occurred.[1] As a result, the strength of the arms race–war relationship stems not from an abundance of distinct cases of dispute escalation, but merely is a function of a coding decision. Wallace's (1980) response to this problem was to re-evaluate his results using only *formal* alliance patterns to combine certain sets of disputes. This only partly solved the difficulty of numerical inflation of disputes and wars. The follow-up analysis failed to consider situations which share similar characteristics to those involving formal alliances, but merely lack a signed instrument between the parties.

A related problem is Wallace's inclusion in his population of serious disputes those cases which were not independent of ongoing wars. In some ways, this explains the fact that the two World Wars account for over 80% of the explanatory capability in his study (Weede 1980). Serious problems are inherent in studying war-related disputes in this context. Wallace's purpose was to assess whether an arms race affected the probability of a serious dispute escalating to war. However, in cases where one or both disputants are involved in a war, the probability of that war-related dispute escalating is greater than that of a dispute independent of an ongoing war. An inference about the effect of an arms race on a war-related dispute must be considered tentative at best. In Wallace's work, the arms race impact (if any) on dispute escalation is indiscernible from the effects of the ongoing war. Nevertheless, it is these cases of war-related disputes which enhance the confirmation of the hypothesis that arms races lead to war.

Wallace's results indicate the U.S.S.R.-Japan dispute of 1945 to be an instance of an arms race leading to the escalation of a dispute. Yet, it is difficult to believe that this brief war was anything but a result of the hostilities associated with World War II. To suggest that an arms race in the late 1930s exercised any influence on the outbreak of war in this dispute five years later is premature without additional research and runs contrary to accumulated historical opinion on the subject.[2]

Wallace (1979:8) justifies his choice of cases and the dyadic coding method by stating:

> In the case of those wars which involved more than two powers, each dyad is coded separately. Thus, for example, World War II is coded as an initi-

---

[1] The number of separate wars in that study is variable, depending on how the analyst would treat the interrelationship of the European and Pacific theatres in World War II.

[2] In cases which involved war-time disputes, Wallace studied the disputant's military expenditures in the nearest pre-war year instead of the year before the dispute.

ation of Franco-German and Anglo-German hostilities in 1939, an Anglo-Italian and Franco-Italian outbreak in 1940 and a Russo-German and Japanese-American conflict initiated in 1941. This was done to avoid the practical and conceptual difficulties of aggregating military capabilities of nations entering the conflict at different times.

This explanation is open to criticism as the disputes involving different actors in different years are coded as separate disputes anyway according to COW criteria. If the disputants entered the dispute in the same year (thereby determining the same data points for military expenditures—the ten years prior to that year in the Wallace study), it is irrelevant if the disputants entered the war emanating from the dispute at different times. Furthermore, Wallace's explanation provides no justification for separating a dispute (such as the 1939 Poland crisis) in which all parties entered the dispute and the war at the same time.

Wallace's method of determining an arms race is not without conceptual problems. An arms race is conventionally described as a process involving competitive interaction, manifested by rapid increases in military spending and weaponry. In Wallace's analysis, it is only determined whether or not the disputants are rapidly arming themselves; there is no determination if this spending is directed against the dispute opponent(s). More properly, the process described by Wallace is a "mutual military buildup" rather than an "arms race" per se. A determination of the latter must await the completion of a more sensitive test of military spending decisions.

Beyond the absence of definitional rigor, the mutuality of rapid spending increases cannot necessarily be deduced from Wallace's arms race index. By multiplying the products of each side's cardinal spline estimate of military spending, a unilateral buildup by one side might be defined as an arms race. For example, if country A had a score of 100 (high) and country B had a score of 1 (low), the net index would be 100 and the situation classified as a Wallace arms race. Clearly, this instance is neither a mutual military buildup nor an arms race in any reasonable definition of the two terms.

Wallace also chooses a seemingly arbitrary threshold of a 90.00 index score to distinguish between arms races and their absence. No justification is presented and experimentation with alternative thresholds is not evident. Wallace's conclusions are substantially weakened if the threshold is lowered to 50.00. Then, ten additional cases would be contrary to the escalation model, while its strength would not be enhanced by even a single case.

While Wallace's striking findings have dominated this topic area over the past few years, it seems that criticisms associated with his work are sufficient to warrant a re-examination of the relationship between rapid military buildups and war.

A Re-evaluation

In retesting Wallace's conclusions, a number of modifications are made. The temporal domain is extended five years, now 1816–1970, to reflect the most complete listing of COW serious disputes. Since Wallace used only a preliminary draft of this same compilation, the dispute populations are not identical across studies. The addition of newly discovered disputes and the correction of coding errors would suggest that the set of cases used by this replication attempt is more accurate than that employed by Wallace.

Each serious dispute is treated as an integrated whole (non-dyadically) as is consistent with the original COW coding scheme. For example, the dispute leading to the outbreak of the Crimean War is coded: Russia v. Great Britain and France. Where it was clear that partnerships existed and the partners were inexorably tied up in the disposition of the dispute, it seems reasonable to consider allies together rather than separately in the dyadic scheme. Surely, the military calculus of the opposing side must consider the joint actions of those partners. Moreover, good scientific practice requires that findings should be reanalyzed under the most conservative, yet reasonable, set of cases. If Wallace's results are conclusive, they should be able to be reproduced under the conditions outlined here.

Certain factors dictated that some of the cases be eliminated from the study. Any dispute which was related to an ongoing major power war was dropped from the population.[3] As discussed above in the critique of Wallace, the escalatory effects of the ongoing war are indistinguishable from those of arms increases. To include those cases might yield a false indication of the real effects military buildups have on the initiation of war.

It is all but impossible to accurately estimate war-time military expenditures for a nation whose whole economy is devoted to the war effort. Accordingly, COW treats expenditures during the two World Wars as missing data. Due to this data limitation and the nature of the arms race indicator, cases independent of ongoing wars from 1915–1920 and 1940–1947 are necessarily eliminated.[4] Idiosyncrasies in the data set resulted in the

---

[3] The cases dropped are mainly those which occurred after the outbreak of World War I and World War II. Other cases eliminated were those associated with the Crimean War, and the 1866 war involving Germany, Italy and Austria. The Russo-Japanese conflicts in the 1930s are included as both temporally preceded the Polish crisis and were distinct from tensions in Europe and elsewhere in Asia.

[4] The most notable absence necessitated by data unavailability is the U.S.-Japan dispute of 1941. Unlike other disputes surrounding the World War II, this dispute could justifiably be considered separate from the European War. There was also missing data for one side in two disputes: U.S.S.R.–Great Britain in 1923 and the dispute over Korea in 1950. However, calculation of a military buildup index for the side for which data were available indicated an absence of a mutual military buildup according to the criteria used in this study. Consequently, these cases remain included in the analysis. In addition, a 1948 dispute involving the Soviet Union and the three Allied Powers was not excluded despite the inclusion of only two (instead

elimination of another case.[5] Overall, the analysis here considers 86 separate disputes.[6]

A measure of mutual arms buildup must reflect significant military increases for both sides in a dispute and yet be able to detect instances where only a unilateral buildup is present. In addition, an appropriate threshold point must be chosen to differentiate between incremental spending patterns and those which are abnormally high. These two considerations were judged to be lacking in the original Wallace article.

With this in mind, an index of military growth for each side in a dispute will be constructed from the newly revised COW file on military expenditures (an earlier version was used by Wallace in his work). This index is the mean rate of change in military expenditures (expressed in common currency and controlled for price fluctuations) for each side in the three years prior to the initiation of the dispute.[7]

Only expenditures prior to the initiation of the dispute are analyzed. This precludes consideration of military spending which was reactive to the dispute itself. In this way, the index is able to isolate the effects of an arms buildup from the bias of dispute-induced spending. Dispute spending patterns tend to reflect significant spending increases whether war results or not. This is not surprising as nations seek to ensure security in a crisis situation.

Furthermore, the index measures only spending trends in the immediate past of the dispute. Military expenditures tend to show greater variation as one moves farther back in a time-series. Too often, studying a time period of five or ten years will cause an overlap into a war period or time frame in which other disputes influenced expenditure patterns. Focusing on the three years prior to the dispute allows consideration of behavior which is more perceptually important than comparable spending decisions ten years be-

---

of three) years of military expenditure data in the military buildup indicator. Missing data for the war year 1945 were responsible for this alteration.

[5] The dispute between France and Italy in 1860 is not considered. Prior to the dispute, Italy's military expenditures were coded as those only of Sardinia. With the advent of Italian unification, expenditure figures were derived from all of Italy. Consequently, an artificial jump in military spending occurs in the data set. This changeover occurs in one of the years under study for this case and to avoid misconceptions, this dispute is eliminated from the sample.

[6] Some wars which resulted from a major power serious dispute, but did not involve major power participation on both sides are included in this study. These are: the 1863 war between Denmark on one side and Germany and Austria on the other; Italy's invasion of Ethiopia in 1934; and the Sino-Indian border war of 1962.

[7] The formula for the index is:

$$\% \, \Delta \, (M_{t-2} \rightarrow M_{t-1}) \, + \, \% \, \Delta \, (M_{t-3} \rightarrow M_{t-2})/2$$

where t is the year of the dispute and $M = m_1 + m_2 \ldots m_k$; where m_i represents the military expenditures of a major power on that side of the dispute.

Table 4–2
Mutual Military Buildup and Escalation

	War	*No War*
Mutual military buildup	3	9
No mutual military buildup	10	64

$X^2 = 1.06$.
$\phi = .11$.
$Q = .36$

fore. Rapid changes in military expenditures are warning signals not only for peace researchers, but are perhaps one of the indicators used by foreign policy elites to ascertain a large scale military buildup by an opponent.

In this study, I have chosen to designate any instance of both dispute sides increasing their military expenditures at a rate of 8% or greater for the three years before the dispute as a "mutual military buildup." This threshold was chosen because it most perfectly captured the dividing line between incremental increases in military outlays and abnormal spending increases. This coding decision allows the World War I dispute to be classified as a mutual military buildup as is the concerted opinion of most historians. In no case, however, are both sides in such a buildup below a 10% threshold often cited as an indicator of high level military spending increases.[8]

The operational definitions of a "major power," "serious dispute," and "war" developed by Singer & Small (1972) and used by Wallace are retained in this study.

Results

The determination of a mutual military buildup or its absence for each dispute was combined with the outcome of that dispute and the aggregated results are presented in table 4–2.

No meaningful covariation exists here between mutual military buildups and dispute escalation. Only 25% of the disputes which were preceded by a mutual military buildup escalated to war, while almost 77% of the major power wars constituting this sample population were preceded by periods in which there was no incidence of joint and rapid spending increases by the protagonists.

Of the three disputes which fit the escalation hypothesis, one is World War I and the other two led to the Second World War. However, even these cases raise questions about the impact of mutual arms buildup on the outbreak of war. There were five other disputes prior to World War II which

---

[8] Experimentation with other thresholds did not significantly affect the results reported here.

Table 4–3
Unilateral Buildup and Escalation*

	War	No War
Unilateral buildup	3	30
No unilateral buildup	7	34

$X^2 = .997.$
$\phi = .12.$
$Q = -.35.$

* Table includes only those cases which fail to meet the criteria for a mutual military buildup.

were preceded by this type of buildup and yet did not escalate to war. This suggests that the cases which support the escalation model might only be the product of a spurious association.

Overall, it appears that most serious disputes do not involve previous dual military spending increases and most serious disputes do not escalate to war; but there does not seem to be any connection between these facts. The Yule's Q value is .36 indicating a much weaker positive relationship than Wallace reported. However, the more conservative ϕ coefficient is only .11 and the Chi-square value is not significant at any meaningful level.

It is possible that this analysis, aggregated over a two-century period, may hide a relationship that is present in only a portion of this time period. Other scholars have noted inter-century differences in studying international conflict. Therefore, the results were disaggregated, divided into 19th and 20th groups and the hypothesis retested. The findings were quite similar to the original results. Although the association was stronger in the 20th century, neither relationship was significant at the .10 level.[9] It is also important to consider the effect of an unilateral arms buildup on the outbreak of war. It may be that the absence of mutuality in arms increases causes one side or the other to consider war a more viable means of competition. In testing this possibility, cases in which there was no mutual military buildup are considered (N = 74). The proposition that a unilateral buildup (constituting a 10% or more increase in military expenditures by one and only one side using the same index construction as before) affects the probability of a dispute escalating to war is considered in table 4–3.

There seems to be no basis for concluding that a unilateral military buildup prior to a dispute increases the chances of war. A Yule's Q value of −.35 suggests a possible negative association between unilateral buildups

---

[9] The ϕ value for the 19th Century war .08 and Chi-square was a paltry .198. The 20th Century yielded a ϕ of .18 and a Chi-square value of 1.79.

and war but the Chi-square value indicates that the association is not statistically significant.

Towards a Convergence of Findings

The findings presented here are quite contrary to Wallace (1979). This lends itself to a number of possible explanations. Immediately the differences in arms indices come to mind. However, Wallace's cardinal spline function is heavily weighted toward changes in military expenditures in the three or four years prior to the dispute, much as the index used in this study. In applying the Wallace measure to the data set used in this study, similar findings can be reported where coding rules between the studies were not in conflict. Where differences did exist, the variation can be explained by reference to other factors beside index construction. Thus, I conclude that the differences in findings are not attributable to differences in the military spending indices.

Another hypothesis is that differences between the two studies' data sets led to divergent findings. Wallace's list of disputes was only in its early stages of completion when his article first appeared. The population of serious disputes used in this replication attempt represents a more recent and complete version of that list. In comparing the two versions (prior to any coding decisions), the disparities do not seem to be extraordinary, at least not to suggest radically different conclusions. The newer data set includes a few more cases of pre–World War II disputes which were preceded by dual arms increases but did not escalate to war. The Korean War, actually preceded by spending cutbacks, is another instance of a dispute not covered by Wallace. Most of the other changes in the new file are additions or deletions of "no buildup–no war" disputes. As a whole, the empirical validity of the escalation hypothesis is weakened when tested with the updated file, but the changes alone are insufficient to reject Wallace's conclusions.

Beyond simple changes in the number of cases, the new file contains some corrections. The Russo-Japanese War of 1904 had its dispute beginning in 1903 according to the latest file. This is an update from the Wallace report that the dispute began in 1904. Wallace considers spending increases in this dispute through the actual first year of the dispute (1903). It is not surprising then that he concludes that an arms race took place before the war. However, according to the corrected files, one might infer that spending in 1903 was reactive to the dispute and that the Wallace index would yield a false indication of prior military competition. Looking only at military spending patterns prior to the beginning of the dispute (pre-1903), this study finds no significant joint arms increases occurring.

Differences in military expenditure figures might account for opposite conclusions in a few cases. Wallace replaced some interpolated data points with his own estimates of military appropriations. This may explain why different results are obtained in the 1866 dispute/war between Germany, Italy and Austria.[10]

While revision of research files is to some degree a continuing process, it is presumed (pending comparison) that the data used in this study are more complete and accurate than previous compilations.

Most of the remaining conflict in the aggregate findings of the two studies can be traced to differences in coding procedures. Ten cases which were not independent of ongoing wars, yet exhibited covariation of spending increases and escalation, were eliminated in this study. In addition, the non-dyadic coding method used here resulted in the collapse of ten cases, which fit the escalation hypothesis, into three integrated disputes. In each case, the two World Wars account for almost all the instances. In effect, the strength of the arms race–war relationship cited by Wallace rests heavily on the two World Wars. The relationship seems absent in any other circumstance and gains statistical significance only through an artificial division of an integrated situation.

Conclusions

This study retested Wallace's (1979) findings that a mutual military buildup between major powers increased the probability of a serious dispute escalating to war. Using a modified set of assumptions and indicators, it was discovered that only one-fourth of the disputes preceded by mutual military buildups resulted in war, while ten of thirteen wars occurred in the absence of joint arms increases by the dispute participants. Therefore, it was concluded that mutual military buildups did not exercise any general impact on the initiation of war under the limited conditions studied. This lack of a relationship between military spending and dispute escalation remained unchanged when controls were instituted for inter-century differences and when retested to ascertain the influence of a unilateral military buildup.

In considering the differences in findings between this study and Wallace's work, the importance of assumptions, coding decisions and data manipulation techniques in empirical research should be highlighted. Apparently insignificant research choices can collectively influence results in a profound way. We owe it to our colleagues and those in policymaking circles to be explicit and reveal all relevant information that impinges on the conduct of the study. This is not to imply that academics should retreat to

---

[10] These manipulations are not apparent in any of the Wallace articles. The disclosure of these transformations was graciously made to me in a personal conversation with Professor Wallace. However, analysis of the extent and validity of these changes cannot be assessed without a copy of the Wallace data base. Professor Wallace is attempting to reconstruct that file and results as of this writing are incomplete.

merely debating semantics or methodological approaches. Rather, it means we must give greater attention to the research design of a study and consider the study and its utility in light of the validity of that design. The operative message is that creativity and rigor must coexist in research. Neither is a substitute for the other.

This paper does not in any way lay to rest the debate over the danger of rapid military spending increases. What is apparent, however, is that they do not constitute an explanation by themselves for the escalation of disputes. Future research should expand the scope of past studies to consider arms buildups in their contexts of the national attributes of the participants as well as the systemic conditions prevailing at that point in time. There is also a need to study outcomes of military buildups beyond those which end in war. Incidences of compromise and capitulation resulting from arms acquisition may be just as significant as war outcomes. The relative mix of mutual and self-stimulatory processes driving each nation's spending increases may be an important key in predicting those outcomes.

A careful examination of the relationship of the arms races and war might yet provide guidance to foreign policy elites, such that at a minimum, those decision makers can avoid mistakes which could have unintended but disastrous consequences.

Editors' Commentary

Major Findings

Diehl provides three major findings. First, changes in the measure of Wallace's index of arms races make the association Wallace found between arms races and escalation disappear. Second, most wars between major states (77 percent) are not preceded by arms competition, which means that most wars occur in the absence of arms races. Third, most of the cases supporting the armaments-tension proposition are associated with World War I and World War II, which implies that arms races may play more of a role in bringing about large global wars than in the typical **dyadic** war (one state on each side) between major states.

Diehl was able to eliminate the relationship Wallace found by changing the sample and the measure of the independent variable. Whether one accepts his conclusion depends on whether such a procedure is considered legitimate. Diehl eliminates seventeen cases associated with ongoing war (see note 3). He argues that seven or eight large wars are treated by Wallace as twenty-six dyadic wars. For Diehl, if one dispute (such as the 1914 crisis) escalates to war and then other dyads having arms races become involved in the war, this is only one case supporting the proposition, not several. Wallace, in response to Weede, is prepared to eliminate some but not all of these cases. By eliminating the cases, Diehl reduces the number of cases supporting the proposition.

Although Diehl does not make much of it, this change in the sample tells us something: namely that an arms race between two powerful rivals in the system may encourage others to become involved in arms races because of the threatening environment, thereby encouraging war, when it comes, to spread and to be severe since everyone is well prepared. In the process of eliminating the relationship, Diehl, as well as Weede, delimits the circumstances under which the relationship is strongest, albeit whether arms races are more important for the onset of war or its spreading needs to be investigated further.

In addition to dropping certain cases, Diehl also adds cases since 1965, as well as others Wallace's preliminary data may have missed. Among these new cases, many that do not escalate to war in the presence of ongoing military buildups are in the nuclear era. Since most analysts would think that disputes involving a nuclear state would not escalate even in the presence of an arms race (because of nuclear deterrence or some other inhibiting factor), this raises the question of whether the cases involving nuclear powers (including those used by Wallace) are legitimate ones on which to test this proposition. In a later article, Diehl (1985a) confines his sample to enduring rivalries from 1816 to 1980, and these include a number of disputes where one or both sides has nuclear weapons. These consist of United States–USSR (fourteen cases), United States–China (eleven cases), United Kingdom–USSR (seven cases), United Kingdom–China (three cases), France–USSR (four cases), and USSR–China (three cases). Of course, nuclear weapons may not be the only or the most important variable these cases have in common. It also turns out that all of these rivals, with the exception of the USSR–China, are not contiguous, and territorial contiguity has been found to be a critical element in the escalation of disputes (Diehl 1985b; Bremer forthcoming). This suggests that the pugnacious effect of arms races can be overridden by other variables, like nuclear weapons, or will not occur in the absence of certain variables, like territorial contiguity.

Of equal importance, Diehl employs a different index for identifying arms races, one that is simpler. Diehl was unable to replicate Wallace's index, which is difficult to calculate (see Siverson and Diehl 1989:218, 4). Wallace's (1990) response to this criticism was to apply Diehl's index to a revised set of his own cases using the same criteria he did in his response to Weede. He finds that of the fifty-nine disputes that occur without an ongoing arms race, only three escalate; but of the forty-three disputes with ongoing arms races, twenty-four escalate and nineteen do not (Wallace 1990:121). This is still a statistically significant relationship, but the phi is now reduced to a weak .30. These latest results suggest that while disputes in the absence of arms races rarely escalate, many disputes can arise during an ongoing arms race (as measured by Diehl) *without* escalating to war. This suggests that arms races may be a necessary but not a sufficient condition for escalation; in other words, disputes without arms races will tend not to escalate, but something other than just arms races is needed for disputes to escalate. This finding, however, will still have to be reconciled with Diehl's finding that almost 77 percent of the wars are not preceded by joint and rapid spending increases.

Methodologically, Diehl's index (as well as others, e.g. Altfeld 1983) is identifying arms races within ongoing disputes that do not have a tendency to escalate. This means that Wallace's findings are sensitive to changes in operational definition, a point substantiated by Houweling and Siccama (1981:176–178). Theoretically, this means that arms races may not be as pernicious as some have thought, although they clearly are dangerous under certain circumstances.

What can be concluded from the Diehl-Wallace controversy? First, an examination of Wallace's and Diehl's frequency distributions reveals that disputes that occur in the absence of arms races or mutual military buildups do not escalate to war. Second, depending on one's index and sample, half (or considerably more) of the disputes with an ongoing arms race or military buildup escalate. Rather than continuing the debate between Diehl and Wallace, the cumulation of knowledge is better served by asking what separates the military buildups that escalate disputes from those that do not. One possible factor is that disputes that do not escalate involve the presence of nuclear weapons. Another is that disputes that escalate involve territorial contiguity or rivals that are contiguous. In other articles, Diehl (1985a, 1985b) finds that twelve of thirteen wars involving enduring rivals begin with disputes concerning territorial contiguity; the only exception is the Japanese attack on Pearl Harbor. Recent research provides even more evidence on the critical role played by territorial contiguity (Bremer forthcoming; Siverson and Starr 1990).

Third, until Wallace's index is replicated, his conclusions cannot be accepted. Nevertheless, his analysis does raise the possibility that some measure of military expenditures will be able to discriminate between arms races (or buildups) that lead to dispute escalation and those that do not. For example, even Diehl (1985a), in a later study, finds that among major states that are rivals, an increase in one's defense burden can, under the right circumstances, increase the probability of a dispute's escalating to war. More important, other scholars working independently have had some success in distinguishing the kinds of arms races that lead directly to war from those that do not (Smith 1980; Morrow 1989).

Fourth, one of the reasons Wallace (1990) (using Diehl's measure) did not find that all disputes during an ongoing arms race escalate to war may be that the first crisis between two states often does not escalate to war. Frequently a series of crises must occur before war breaks out, as Leng demonstrates (reprinted in the next chapter), and Diehl (1985a:340) confirms with the finding that over 90 percent of rivalries go to war only after a series of militarized disputes. Fifth, Diehl makes the important point that the concept of military buildups may be more useful than arms races. Wallace's index may not measure mutual military buildups and not all buildups need to be mutual in order to be war producing (Diehl 1985a:338–41).

Finally, it must be emphasized that no one has challenged Wallace's findings on the peace-through-strength hypothesis. Winning an arms race does not prevent the escalation of disputes, and losing an arms race does not encourage disputes to escalate to war. Likewise Diehl (1985:343, 346) finds the peace-through-strength hypothesis deficient.

Methodological Notes

Diehl's research challenges both the reliability and the validity of Wallace's work. Siverson and Diehl (1989:211, 218) have noted that it is not surprising that the first systematic findings in an area may have errors in the analysis, but it is significant that Diehl has not been able to replicate Wallace's findings.

Diehl, however, wants to do more than conduct a replication. In addition to developing a more reliable measure, he argues that the concept of military buildups is more useful and that a reduced sample would be more valid. As a result of this different research design, Diehl finds nearly no relationship between military buildups and war. The change that accounts for the major difference in the findings is the change in the sample. By eliminating many of Wallace's cases, Diehl shows that Wallace's findings were produced largely by World War I and World War II.

Since the different findings are produced by different samples, one cannot conclude that Diehl has eliminated Wallace's relationship. Rather, it can be interpreted that both pieces of research found *something*. Clearly Wallace has found some cases of disputes in the presence of arms races' escalating to war. Whether one creates a sample in which such disputes are the majority of cases, a minority of cases, or only a couple of cases, it is important to explain why these cases escalate. Even if the cases are "only" the two world wars, these are recognized as very important cases, and an understanding of them is important in preventing a future world war.

Conversely, although Diehl finds no significant relationship between military buildups and war, his findings do not mean that these buildups are without danger. Even if only one-fourth of the disputes preceded by mutual military buildups result in war, then we need to study these cases. As noted in the previous chapter, Wallace rejects the validity of eliminating as many cases as Diehl did. Nevertheless, when in more recent work, Wallace (1990) did use Diehl's index as a measure, his finding, although reduced to .30, was statistically significant.

Although Diehl and Wallace disagree over the sample, Wallace's willingness to use Diehl's index demonstrates some of the advantages of the scientific method. Continued empirical work can lead to progress in the search for answers to apparently intractable questions, such as which index is more useful. While validity questions can be argued forever, we must remember to look at the findings and see what they tell us. Even if a sample or measure does not seem to capture the concept we have in mind, if it produces strong findings, we may still be able to draw inferences from them and perhaps even reconceptualize the variables producing them.

The debate between Wallace and Diehl raises not only theoretical and methodological questions; it also raises the question of the policy relevance of scientific research. There is a debate in the field over how appropriate it is to apply the findings of scientific work to questions of foreign policy. On the one hand, many argue that the science of studying war is in its infancy, and therefore preliminary findings are likely to be quite weak. It would be incorrect and irresponsible to urge policymakers to implement a policy on the basis of preliminary findings, even though for centuries, policymakers have been implementing theories without evidence. Also, we cannot simply tell policymakers to act on this research, because it has flaws and there are contradictions among different results. For example, do we tell policymakers to read Wallace and stop arms races—or to read Diehl and go ahead with military buildups? Finally, there are many strong reasons for those studying war to keep their distance from government, if only to preserve their intellectual independence until the field is better established.

On the other hand, some, especially J. David Singer (1979:131–132, 136–137), argue that it is time for policymakers to end their centuries-old practice of implementing speculation and turn to the social scientific community for guidance. Although some findings are tentative, many of them fly in the face of some long-held assumptions. Wallace is quite clear on his conclusion that the evidence shows that Vegetius's prescription is dangerous. If the research design suggested in the Major Findings section were carried out and the findings showed that *nuclear* arms races without a *territorial dispute* do not escalate to war but that others do, then the United States might well be more careful about assuming that deterrence against the Soviet Union (with which it had no territorial dispute) had worked and can be applied elsewhere.

The tension between these two positions is difficult to resolve. On the one hand, it is frustrating to watch national decision makers take actions that research shows are dangerous. On the other hand, it seems that when scientists get too close to government, all too often the result is that science is subordinated to the demands of policy rather than policy being informed by science. Perhaps a more appropriate avenue is to work for the dissemination of scientific knowledge so that more people will be aware of the risks of war associated with certain actions their leaders take.

5

When Will They Ever Learn?
Coercive Bargaining in Recurrent
Crises

Russell J. Leng

Editors' Introduction

Historians have long recognized that how states interact and bargain with one another in a crisis can have a direct effect on whether there is an escalation to war. What kinds of bargaining tactics increase the probability of crises' escalating to war, and what tactics might help disputants avoid war? These are some of the major concerns of Russell Leng's work. To address them, it is necessary to have detailed information on how states behave toward one another throughout a crisis. Leng has painstakingly collected data that reconstruct the coercive bargaining behavior of states in these situations. One of the major contributions of this article is that it looks at recurrent crises and the effect one crisis has on the behavior of states in a subsequent crisis.

Writing in the long afterglow of the Cuban Missile Crisis, Coral Bell (1971:116) suggested that properly managed crises of the future "may ultimately enable states to write the peace treaties without first fighting the wars." It was Bell's view that, after one or two dangerous encounters, the contending nations would develop "conventions" that would allow them to resolve future crises and restore the balance of

Russell J. Leng, "When Will They Ever Learn? Coercive Bargaining in Recurrent Crises," *Journal of Conflict Resolution*, Vol. 27 No. 3 (September 1983), pp. 379–419. Copyright © 1983 by Sage Publications, Inc. Reprinted by permission of Sage Publications, Inc. and the author.

Author's note: I would like to thank Michael Brecher, Claudio Cioffi-Revilla, Murray Dry, Charles Gochman, Noel Kaplowitz, Stephan Walker, and Oran Young for their critical readings and helpful suggestions.

power without resorting to war. Similar optimism had been expressed 10 years earlier by McClelland (1961:202–203), who predicted that an examination of the historical record of states engaged in successive disputes would show "progressively refined techniques of crisis demobilization."

It is an intriguing thesis, but is the optimism warranted? A glance at the historical record suggests that if contending states learn anything from one crisis to the next, it may be to become more belligerent with each successive encounter. The purpose of this study is to examine which of these views is more correct. We do so through an empirical investigation of the bargaining behavior of six pairs of states that found themselves embroiled in three successive crises.

We begin with the premise that there are two salient components to what policymakers are likely to learn from one dispute to the next. The first is what we will call "experiential learning"; that is, a straightforward application of the lessons learned from the outcome of one dispute to the bargaining strategy and tactics chosen in the next encounter with the same adversary. The second is the propensity to view the nature of international conflict and, consequently, appropriate strategies and tactics, from a real-politik orientation that stresses the importance of demonstrating power and resolve.

Experiential Learning

Common sense suggests that the success or failure of the bargaining strategy employed in one crisis is likely to influence the bargaining strategy chosen in the next one. Jervis (1976) offers some persuasive insights into the nature of the learning process for policymakers.

Jervis points out that policymakers learn general and superficial lessons from history, and that they are likely to draw strong analogies from previous disputes to current conflicts (1976:229–230). The analogies tend to be drawn from the larger, more dramatic components of a previous dispute, particularly the outcome. According to Jervis, a tendency to see their own state's behavior as decisive encourages policymakers to consider unsuccessful outcomes as failures of policy, so that they are likely to react by switching to a different bargaining strategy in the next encounter. By the same token, Jervis argues, a successful policy may make policymakers insensitive to changes in the situation, and cause them to apply the same bargaining strategy in the next dispute rather than undertake the major effort of devising a new bargaining strategy that is adjusted to changed circumstances (1976:280).

We argue that the propensity to draw lessons from the outcome of one dispute to guide policymaking in the next is especially strong when statesmen find that they are engaged in a second or third crisis with the same adversary. Beyond their concern about an immediate security threat, policymakers are likely to view these conflicts as critical turning points in their nation's relations with the contending power (see Young 1967:18; Bell 1971:9–11; Snyder and Diesing 1977:187–189).

A Realpolitik Conflict Orientation

The literature on conflict bargaining places heavy emphasis on the techniques of "coercive diplomacy"—in particular, the use of threats and commitments to demonstrate resolve (Schelling 1960; George et al. 1971; George and Smoke 1974). Empirical support for the theoretical emphasis on this aspect of conflict bargaining appears in recent studies demonstrating the pervasiveness of coercive bargaining across a wide range (both temporally and quantitatively) of historical crises (Snyder and Diesing 1977; Leng and Wheeler 1979).

The roots of this emphasis on the demonstration of power and resolve lie in a realpolitik tradition[1] that views interstate conflict as dictated by considerations of power politics and prescribes bargaining strategies that demonstrate power and a willingness to use it. This is not to say that a realpolitik orientation leads to unbounded belligerency. It is assumed that states will be restrained by prudence—that is, a careful calculation of the adversary's power and the costs and risks relative to the interests at stake. Bell's (1971) thesis is based on a realist orientation that stresses prudent statesmanship.

But a reputation for resolve can be a critical component of a state's interests. Consequently, the problem lies in choosing between the necessity for prudence and the admonition to provide a credible demonstration of power and resolve by acting with assertiveness when vital interests are at stake. Hans Morgenthau (1978:519), realism's principal spokesman in the post–World War II era, argued that a diplomacy that ends in war has failed in its primary objective—the promotion of the national interest by peaceful means. But Morgenthau also warned that, in a "world where power counts," it is imprudent to appear weak or irresolute lest the adversary be tempted to try to bully you into submission (1978:521). A crisis presents a test of a state's power and resolve; from the perspective of a national leader, the line between prudence and a failure of nerve (or "appeasement") is not easily

---

[1] By a "realpolitik tradition" we refer to an implicit practical consensus grounded in what Ashley (1981) describes as "practical realism," an orientation growing out of a "co-reflective self-understanding: a *tradition*" (1981:211). Ashley distinguishes between "practical realism" in which the "aim is to undertake interpretations that make possible the orientation of action within a common tradition" (1981:211), and "technical realism" which represents a "set of statements embodying assumptions and explaining laws" (1981:215), as in positivistic approaches to theory in the sciences.

drawn. Whether statesmen are correct in making this assumption is more difficult to determine. As Snyder and Diesing (1977:187) put it, "What stands out is the discrepancy between the little evidence that statesmen *do* infer an opponent's resolve from his behavior in previous cases and the massive evidence that decision makers *think* such inferences are made."

Tying this to the preceding discussion of experiential learning, we hypothesize that policymakers tend to view an unsuccessful outcome in a previous dispute with an adversary of relatively equal capability as a consequence of their own state's bargaining strategy—that is, as a failure to act with sufficient strength and resolve. Consequently, a diplomatic failure is likely to be followed by a more coercive bargaining strategy—a strategy demonstrating power and firmness through the use of threats, including the threat of war, in the next encounter. We will refer to this as the Experiential Learning-Realpolitik (ELR) model of crisis bargaining behavior.

A Caveat

Whatever the claims for the enduring strength of realpolitik, or political realism, as a guide to the thoughts and actions of statesmen (Morgenthau 1978:5), it is an oversimplification to treat states as unitary actors with a single-minded focus on power considerations in all situations. Much of the recent work on foreign policy decision-making has focused on the differences among states, whether as a result of the particular belief systems of policymakers (George 1969; Holsti 1976b; Walker 1977), the sectarian political and economic interests that they represent (Lockhart 1979; Keohane and Nye 1977), or the effects of bureaucratic politics (Allison 1971) to name a few prominent possibilities. Nevertheless, we propose that when national leaders find themselves embroiled in interstate crises where vital interests are at stake, the similarities in their behavior are more striking than the differences, and these similarities are a reflection of a realpolitik tradition that stresses the importance of demonstrating resolve. The notion that crises present situations that are uniquely suited for a realist model is also argued by Keohane and Nye (1977:29–31), whose work usually discounts this approach to contemporary international politics. Bueno de Mesquita (1981b:21–29) also makes a compelling argument for analyzing crises from the perspective of national leaders with realist orientations.

Hypotheses

Consistent with Jervis's (1976:229–230) argument that policymakers tend to make simple distinctions between success and failure according to the outcome of disputes, we have classified the dispute outcome for each party as a *diplomatic victory, diplomatic defeat, compromise,* or *war.* Thus we can specify four ELR hypotheses that relate the outcome of the previous dispute to predicted changes (if any) in state A's bargaining in the current dispute.

> *Hypothesis 1:* If the outcome of the preceding crisis with state B was a diplomatic victory for state A, then A will employ the same degree of coercion in the next crisis with B.

> *Hypothesis 2:* If the outcome of the preceding crisis with state B was a diplomatic defeat for state A, then A will employ a more coercive bargaining strategy in the next crisis with B.

Experiential learning alone predicts that the policymakers in state A are likely to repeat the same bargaining strategy when it has been associated with a successful outcome and to change it when it has been associated with a diplomatic defeat. A realpolitik orientation would lead policymakers—and the public—to view the "failure" as resulting from a bargaining strategy lacking in sufficient resolve.

A more ambiguous situation occurs when the outcome is a diplomatic compromise. All compromises are positive outcomes in one sense because war is avoided. But if one's state is forced to retreat from an important objective, a policymaker with a realist orientation is likely to see this as the consequence of a failure to demonstrate sufficient resolve—particularly if the basic issues in contention remain unsettled. Consider the Berlin crisis of 1961, which ended in a stalemate. After his Vienna meeting with Premier Khrushchev and the Soviet fait accompli represented by the Wall, President Kennedy concluded that the time might come when he would have to run "the supreme risk to convince Khrushchev that conciliation did not mean humiliation" (Schlesinger 1965:391).

Hypothesis 3 is divided into two parts to distinguish between the two types of compromise outcomes.

> *Hypothesis 3a:* If the preceding crisis resulted in a compromise that resolved the issue in contention without a significant retreat from state A's publicly stated objectives, then A will repeat the same bargaining strategy in the next crisis with B.

> *Hypothesis 3b:* If the preceding crisis resulted in a compromise that caused state A to retreat significantly from its publicly stated objectives, then A will adopt a more coercive bargaining strategy in the next crisis with B.

Our fourth and final hypothesis predicts changes in the degree of coercion in A's bargaining if the preceding crisis with B ended in war. This is a more complex situation because the lessons learned are likely to be based on the outcome of the war as well as on the outcome of the crisis that preceded it. On the one hand, the outbreak of an unwanted war represents a diplomatic failure, even in realpolitik terms. Following the logic of our ELR model, each side is likely to view its own behavior as having encouraged the other—through a lack of resolve—to attempt to achieve its ends by force. Therefore the ELR model would predict more coercive bargaining by both sides in the next crisis. Note that this hypothesis can be contrasted with the other side of the realist coin, which prescribes prudence. Prudence suggests that the lesson to be learned from the previous crisis is to act with greater caution—that is, to adopt a less coercive strategy and to avoid escalation to another unwanted war.

The emphasis on resolve in the ELR model suggests that national leaders are likely to draw similar conclusions when the outcome of the war itself is added to these considerations. A militarily victorious state would see no reason for accommodation in the next crisis. Rather it would assume that it could bully the other into submission to avoid the high costs of another military defeat. But the battlefield loser also is likely to become more determined to demonstrate *its* resolve through a tougher bargaining strategy so that the previously victorious adversary will not conclude that it can be bullied, and also because of pressure (in some instances coming from the public and in others from other members of the regime) to avoid another national humiliation—even if it means fighting another war. A war that ends in stalemate, with no real peace settlement, is little better. Neither side emerges satisfied; so each is determined to act with greater resolve in the next encounter.

An exception occurs when a new crisis follows a war in which state A launched a premeditated attack on B. The outbreak of war, in this instance, was not the result of a diplomatic failure: It was the intended outcome. In such instances the realpolitik logic in our model suggests that if A wishes to succeed (without going to war) in the next dispute with B, then A must signal to B that its intentions have changed and that compliance with its demands will enable B to avoid another war. This suggests a more accommodative bargaining strategy than in the previous dispute.

These propositions are summarized in the two parts of Hypothesis 4. Both parts assume that A wishes to avoid an unnecessary war in the current crisis. In Hypothesis 4a, state A wants to demonstrate its resolve to face another war if it is necessary to achieve its objectives; in Hypothesis 4b, A wants to avoid the misperception that it is preparing for another premeditated attack on B.

> *Hypothesis 4a:* If the preceding crisis with state B ended in a war that state A wished to avoid, then A will adopt a more coercive bargaining strategy in the next crisis with B.

Table 5–1
Hypothesized Changes in Bargaining Strategies

Hypothesis	Outcome of Preceding Crisis	Change in Coercion
1	Diplomatic Victory	No Change
2	Diplomatic Defeat	More Coercive
3a	Compromise (Satisfactory)	No Change
3b	Compromise (Unsatisfactory)	More Coercive
4a	War (Unwanted)	More Coercive
4b	War (Premeditated)	Less Coercive

Hypothesis 4b: If state A launched a premeditated attack on state B in the preceding crisis, then A will adopt a less coercive bargaining strategy in the next crisis with B.

Of the four outcomes that we have considered, a crisis preceded by one that ended in war best illustrates the tension between that side of realism stressing a demonstration of resolve and that prescribing prudence. Consider the presumably rare instance (there is none in our sample) of a war that ended in a mutually satisfactory peace settlement that is then followed by a new crisis between the two states. A *prudent* calculation of the costs and risks suggests that a more accommodative bargaining strategy might achieve the same results without risking another war. But if one begins with the assumption that a crisis represents a test of a nation's resolve, then any accommodative moves would be interpreted as a sign of weakness and only encourage more belligerent bargaining by the adversary. From this perspective, realism prescribes an essentially coercive bargaining strategy to make one's resolve credible. A choice between these two views is at the heart of the tension between prudence and resolve, between "hawks" and "doves," and between deterrence and spiral theories of conflict bargaining (see Jervis 1976:chap. 3). The four hypotheses are summarized in table 5–1.[2]

---

[2] We have used the term "model" somewhat loosely to refer to the set of ELR hypotheses obtained by combining assumptions from realpolitik with Jervis's (1976) experiential learning propositions; however, a more formal mathematical model could be constructed by converting the possible outcomes into utility functions whereby the utility (U_{i-1}) that state A obtained in the previous encounter with state B predicts the level of bargaining coercion (C_i) that A will employ in the next crisis with B. Since hypothesis 2, 3b, and 4a all say that $U_{i-1} < 0$, therefore, in the current crises $c_i > C_{i-1}$, the number of hypotheses could be reduced to four. As an extension of the analysis in this article, the four-state model could be explored as a Markov process—a suggestion for which I am indebted to Claudio Cioffi-Revilla. In the present article, we have employed a hypothesis-testing approach to retain the descriptive richness of a verbal exposition of the ELR model in the six hypothetical situations.

Data Generation

The Crises

To test the hypotheses, we have chosen 18 crises (or "militarized disputes")[3] involving six pairs of states, each in three successive crises. We selected three successive crises so that we could consider any unexpected effects that two previous crises might have on bargaining in a third. This provides a useful check on the part of our hypotheses that predicts that the *preceding* crisis outcome will exert the most influence over bargaining in the next crisis. All of the crises took place in the twentieth century. Since the hypotheses are dependent on the assumption that the states are evenly matched militarily, we included only sets of crises between states of relatively even military capabilities. Although the attributes of the states are markedly different within and among the dyads, none of the states undergoes a radical change in regimes between the crises.[4]

We began with a randomly drawn sample of 40 precoded crises occurring between 1815 and 1975. These were selected from the compilation of interstate wars in Singer and Small's *Wages of War* (1972), from an unpublished list of interstate disputes generated from Langer's *Encyclopedia of World History* (1972), and from Dupuy and Dupuy's *Encyclopedia of Military History* (1977). From this sample, we chose all those pairs of states engaged in at least two successive crises that both appear in the sample and occur in the 20th century. Then we selected all the pairs in this group that were involved in a third crisis with each other within a relatively short period of time, regardless of whether the third crisis appeared in the sample of coded crises or not. In four cases (Palestine War, Berlin Wall, Six Day War, and Bangladesh), the third dispute did not appear in the original randomly drawn sample, so it was necessary to generate new data for this study. The process represents a reasonable compromise between the benefits of pure randomness and the high costs of generating new data. (See Gamson

---

[3] The operational definition of a militarized dispute is a dispute in which at least one of the parties threatens the other with the use of force. We have used the term "crisis" because of its familiarity; however, the operational distinction we have used is based on the threat to security represented by the explicit threat to employ military force. (See Leng and Gochman 1982.)

[4] Occasionally, as in the case of Great Britain in the 1930s, or Israel and India after World War II, there are changes in prime ministers, but the same party leadership remains in control, and the key policy makers retain first-hand memories of the last crisis. The major exception to this occurs in the United States between the First and Second Berlin crises. Kennedy was not active in national government at the time of the First Berlin crisis; nevertheless, there is ample evidence that he and his advisors, who included Acheson, Harriman, and Kohler, were well aware of the "lessons" from that experience (See Schlesinger 1965:379–383). Moreover, as Jervis (1976:239) argues, events that are of great importance for the nation are likely to have a strong impact on future policy makers even if they were not politically involved in the decisions at the time. In this respect, we can think of such events as comprising the most salient components of the long-term institutional memory of policy makers (see Ward 1982a:96–99).

1975:22–24, for a very similar approach.) Because of the initial random selection of cases, we expect no systematic bias in the sample. Although this is not a large sample, it comes from a relatively small population. In a recently completed compilation of the universe of serious interstate disputes, Gochman and Maoz (1984) report 36 "enduring rivalries," including the 6 pairs in this study. The number shrinks to 24, however, when one subtracts nineteenth century disputes, states significantly uneven in military capability, and the European allies of the United States in post–World War II disputes with the Soviet Union.

Participants

In real world crises, it is often difficult to determine the primary participants. But if few international crises are purely dyadic, each participant nevertheless enters the crisis for its own reasons, so that the stakes vary from one pair of disputants to another. Deciding whether two or more actors should be considered as parts of a single coalition, or as independent participants engaged in the dispute at different levels and for different reasons, often requires difficult qualitative judgments. Britain, France, and Czechoslovakia all stood on one side of the Munich crisis, yet the stakes for Britain and France were substantially different from those facing Czechoslovakia. Moreover, Hitler's bargaining with the Czechs took on a different character from his bargaining with the British and French. It is possible, however, to treat Britain and France as a single coalition for all three of the crises in the 1930s. The drawback to this approach is that it assumes that the policymakers in both states are drawing the same lessons from previous crises with the other side. Even in the British-French combination (which is the strongest example of a working coalition in our sample) it is clear that the British perception of the issues represented by the German reoccupation of the Rhineland, for example, was different from that of the French.

Some of the divergences of interests, stakes, and perceptions of actors involved on the same side in the other crises in the sample are even greater than in the British-French disputes with Germany in the 1930s; therefore, we have limited the analysis of our disputes to the two predominant actors in each case.[5] A list of the sample of crises and participants appears in table 5–2.

---

[5] This presents no problem for the Soviet-American or Indo-Pakistani disputes. Several other actors besides the main participants are involved in the pre–World War I disputes, but with the possible exception of the 1914 crisis, it is not difficult to separate the bargaining of the dyad from that of other major powers. In the 1914 crisis it seems reasonable to relate the outcomes of the German-French experiences over Morocco and the Russian-Austrian diplomacy during the first Balkan War crisis to their behavior in 1914. In the Egyptian-Israeli cases, Egypt was not the dominant member of the Arab coalition that attacked Israel in 1948, but it is reasonable to assume that the outcome of that strategy—even if Egypt was not the author—would affect Egyptian bargaining in the next dispute with Israel. In the Suez and Six Day crises, Syria

Table 5–2
Actors, Dates, and Outcomes for the 18 Crises

Actors and Disputes	Begin-End	Dispute Outcome
France-Germany		
First Moroccan Crisis	3/31/1905–3/31/1906	French Victory
Second Moroccan Crisis	5/21/1911–11/4/1911	Compromise
Pre–World War I	6/28/1914–8/6/1914	War
Austria-Russia		
Bosnian Crisis	10/06/1908–3/31/1909	Austrian Victory
First Balkan War	8/14/1912–5/30/1913	Compromise
Pre–World War I	6/28/1914–8/6/1914	War
Britain-Germany		
Rhineland	3/7/1936–5/30/1936	German Victory
Munich Crisis	2/20/1938–9/30/1938	German Victory
Polish-Danzig	3/21/1939–9/1/1939	War
India-Pakistan		
First Kashmir	10/26/1947–12/29/1948	War[a]
Second Kashmir	1/9/1965–8/5/1965	War
Bangladesh	3/15/1971–12/3/1971	War
Egypt-Israel		
Palestine War	10/10/1947–5/15/1948	War
Suez War	7/26/1956–10/31/1956	War
Six Day War	4/7/1967–6/5/1967	War
Soviet Union–United States		
Berlin Blockade	6/7/1948–5/12/1949	U.S. Victory
Berlin Wall	6/4/1961–10/28/1961	Compromise
Cuban Missle	9/4/1962–11/20/1962	U.S. Victory

[a] See note 7.

For each of the cases appearing in table 5–2, we used the accounts of diplomatic historians to identify the primary disputants, the beginning of the dispute, and the end of the dispute. The first threat of force was identified from events data on the behavior of the disputants.

Coding Scheme

Events data tracing the behavior and interactions of the disputants in the 18 cases were generated from the accounts of journalists and diplomatic historians. Over 15,000 events from 53 sources were identified for the 18

---

and, to a lesser extent, Jordan, were involved in the conflict with Israel, but Nasser tended to treat them as junior partners. In the crisis preceding the Six Day War, Israel's interactions with these states, particularly Syria, may have led Egypt to *become* embroiled in the crisis, but it is less plausible to assume that they would have a determining effect on Nasser's bargaining once the die was cast and Egyptian forces moved into the Sinai.

cases. The *New York Times* provided a constant source for all 18 cases. This was cross-checked and augmented by the accounts of 2 or 3 diplomatic histories for each dispute. The verbal descriptions, with duplicates culled out, were placed in a chronological file and then coded using the Behavioral Correlates of War (BCOW) typology designed by Leng and Singer (1977). The coded events serve as the raw data for operational indicators of the participants' influence strategies and tactics.[6]

Indicator Construction

Dispute Outcomes

The categorization of dispute outcomes as diplomatic victories, defeats, or compromises has been based on information gathered from historical accounts and case studies. War outcomes have been based on criteria developed by Singer and Small (1972), and historical accounts.[7]

Most of the outcomes are relatively straightforward. However, for disputes that ended in diplomatic compromises, it is necessary to distinguish between mutually satisfactory compromises (Type a), and stalemates or compromises where both parties were forced into a diplomatic retreat (Type b). All three compromise outcomes in our sample happened to fall into Type b. The second Moroccan crisis "settled" the Moroccan issue but nationalists in both states regarded the settlement as a "sell-out" (Snyder and Diesing 1977:545; Lockhart 1979:40). Neither side was happy with the outcome of the first Balkan War dispute. Russia was forced to abandon publicly an initially strong stand in support of her Serbian ally; Austria was forced to accept the growing strength of Serbia and Bulgaria in the Balkans (Helmreich 1938). The Berlin crisis of 1961 ended in a stalemate.[8] It produced a sense in the Kennedy administration that it would be necessary to demonstrate greater toughness the next time. On the other side, Khrushchev re-

---

[6] The coding scheme allows us to obtain a full description of each influence attempt, including *what* is requested of the target and *how* the request is made, as well as a full description of any accompanying inducements. The description of what is requested allows us to search ahead in time to check subsequent actions by the target for compliance with the request.

[7] The first Kashmir dispute between India and Pakistan is a borderline case. Singer and Small (1972:394) "tentatively" classify the fighting as an "Imperial War" (India versus Kashmir) but not an interstate war, the grounds being that India avoided engaging Pakistani troops. Other analysts (see Burke 1974:120), however, consider this an undeclared war between India and Pakistan. For our purposes we have adopted the latter classification.

[8] It might be argued that the imposition of the Wall represents a successful fait accompli so the outcome should be considered satisfactory from the perspective of the Soviet Union. This interpretation would lead to more impressive findings for Hypothesis 3 (see table 5–7) since the Soviet bargaining strategy during the Cuban Missile Crisis then would be consistent with the hypothesis.

treated from his public "ultimatum" to negotiate a separate peace treaty with East Germany. Thus, interestingly, we find that neither side emerged with any cause for real satisfaction following any of the diplomatic compromises in our sample.

In the case of crises ending in wars, it is necessary to make a distinction between wars that both sides would have preferred to avoid and premeditated attacks. In our sample, the Indo-Pakistani and Arab-Israeli crises all end in war. The Israelis emerged victorious from a premeditated attack by the Arabs in the Palestine War of 1948. Then, in 1956, the Israelis, with the assistance of Britain and France, launched a premeditated attack on Egypt and again emerged as the military victors. We have classified the outcomes of both of the Kashmir wars as stalemates. Soviet mediation efforts did achieve a ceasefire in the second Kashmir war, but this did not lead to meaningful peace talks and the basic issues remained unresolved (see Burke 1974:189–192).

A's Bargaining Strategy

Our dependent variable is the change in state A's bargaining strategy from one dispute to the next. As an operational indicator we have used Leng and Wheeler's (1979) method of identifying the "predominant influence strategy." This approach has the advantage of yielding operational categories that are representative of the types of bargaining appearing in recent qualitative studies of conflict bargaining (see Snyder and Diesing 1977). The predominant influence strategy represents the overall plan of action each side employs to influence the behavior of the other. Each influence strategy is composed of a mix of *influence attempts*—requests accompanied by positive, negative, or "carrot-and-stick" inducements (promises, rewards, threats, punishments)—employed by state A in exchanges with state B. Influence attempts can be considered the tactical moves of an influence strategy.

For each influence attempt by A, B's responses are categorized according to the degree to which B complies with A's demands. There are five response categories: (1) to *comply* with the demand; (2) to *placate* A with an alternative promise or reward; (3) to *ignore* A's demand by inaction; (4) to *defy* A with a counterthreat or punishment; and (5) to employ a *mixed* response combining defying and placating actions. Each selection of inducements that accompany a demand by A is related to the way in which B has already responded to A's previous influence attempts. Thus, the influence strategy is an overall plan of action prescribing appropriate adjustments in A's influence attempts given B's particular types of responses. We have categorized influence strategies into four types that reflect ideal patterns of influence attempt selections associated with particular responses. In order of most to least coercive, these are *aggressive bullying, cautious bullying, re-*

ciprocating, and *appeasing.* Without going into the decision rules and range of permissible inducements associated with each of the types, we will describe the most distinctive characteristics of each.[9]

1. *Aggressive bullying.* As its label suggests, an aggressive bullying strategy is the most coercive of the four types. Inducements are composed almost solely of escalating threats and punishments, including specific compellent threats of war and the use of force. Any response short of outright compliance is met with a more severe threat or punishment, and the actor does not hesitate to demonstrate a willingness to go to war. Only very modest "pretended concessions" (Snyder and Diesing 1977:89), such as a conditional offer to negotiate, are used. These are merely pretexts for bullying or the use of force.

2. *Cautious bullying.* The threat is also the basic inducement in a cautious bullying strategy—second in our ranking of most to least coercive strategies. If B defies or ignores A's threats, the threats and punishments may escalate, but (to avoid pushing B to war) A avoids ultimata and other specific commitments to use force. State A employs physical moves such as shows of strength, military maneuvers, or alerts indicating military preparedness but stops short of being the first to initiate actions that could cause B to consider war unavoidable (such as a full-scale mobilization). *Placative* responses from B are met with carrot-and-stick inducements including conditional concessions such as offers to negotiate or promises that will not affect A's substantive goals.

3. *Reciprocating.* A reciprocating influence strategy combines "tit-for-tat" replies to B's influence attempts with occasional accommodating initiatives. Threats from B are met with firmness (counterthreats), and positive initiatives are met with offers of concessions. State A issues only deterrent threats. It does not initiate escalatory moves, but demonstrates its preparedness in the face of threats from B. A may employ the negative actions associated with an aggressive or cautious bullying strategy, but only in response to similar actions by B. Unlike the two bullying strategies, A may offer real concessions to achieve a compromise settlement.

4. *Appeasing.* Finally, the least coercive strategy is *appeasing.* State A offers exclusively positive inducements. If B responds by defying or ignoring A, A will make more accommodating moves. A avoids any threats of force except to prepare for war following aggressive bullying by B. Threats—even deterrent threats—are not initiated by A. Any positive inducement is acceptable to avoid war.

---

[9] This is a revision of a typology of influence strategies employed by Leng and Wheeler (1979). The major changes are the distinction between the two types of bullying strategies and removal of the trial-and-error type. The conceptual distinction between the two types of bullying was suggested by the discussion of coercive bargaining appearing in Snyder and Diesing (1977).

Determination of each state's predominant[10] influence strategy is based on two factors: (1) the types of inducements that it employs; and (2) any adjustments in its influence attempts following feedback from the other disputant. That is, we first ask whether the types of inducements employed by state A within a particular phase of the dispute are consistent with the range of inducements for one or more of the influence strategy types described above. Being the first to use a compellent threat of force, for example, is within the range of acceptable options for an aggressive bullying strategy, but not for a reciprocating strategy. The second step is to ask whether the tactical adjustments in each of A's inducements, following B's response to A's previous inducement, are consistent with the decision rules for one or more influence strategies. A placating response by B to a warning by A, for example, could lead to a more explicit threat by an aggressive bully, to a carrot-and-stick inducement by a cautious bully, and to different degrees of positive inducements by a state employing a reciprocating or appeasing influence strategy. A summary of the decision rules for tactical adjustments in inducements for the four types of influence strategies appears in table 5–3.

The pluses (+) and minuses (−) preceding the letter codes in table 5–3 indicate the nature of any prescribed shift in state A's choice of inducements following B's response. In the first case (row 1, column 1) for example, a positive inducement by A has produced a compliant response by B. If A is following an aggressive bullying strategy (column 2), it selects a more negative (+N) inducement for its next influence attempt, but if it is employing a cautious bullying strategy (column 3) it repeats (R) the same type and degree of inducement. In the case of a reciprocating strategy, A may repeat the same type and degree of inducement, or shift to an even more positive inducement (+P). Note that in this case, the reciprocating strategy (which rewards cooperation from the opponent) may lead to a more positive inducement than would an appeasing strategy.

Before proceeding further, it may be useful to summarize the classification procedure with an example. Consider a sequence from the Cuban Missile Crisis. On October 25 the United States instituted the blockade announced in President Kennedy's "quarantine" speech. On the next day, the United States demonstrated the seriousness of its intentions by stopping and searching a Soviet-chartered vessel. The action, which was coded as a negative inducement to back up the demand to remove the missiles, was followed by a mixed response from the Soviets (table 5–3, row 10, column 1). The next U.S. influence attempt was a carrot-and-stick inducement de-

---

[10] We say the *predominant* influence strategy because not all influence attempts are likely to be consistent with just one influence strategy; moreover, the decision rules for influence-attempt choices occasionally overlap, so that the same choice may fit two influence strategies. A discussion of this problem and operational procedures for choosing the predominant influence strategy appear in Leng and Wheeler (1979:669–70).

Table 5–3
Inducement Decision Rules for Influence Strategies

A's Last Inducement and B's Response		Aggressive Bullying	Cautious Bullying	Reciprocating	Appeasing
Positive:	Comply	+N	R	R or +P	R
	Placate	−P and +N	+N	R	+P
	Ignore	−P and +N	+N	−P	+P
	Defy	−P and +N	−P and +N	+N	+P
	Mixed	−P and +N	+N	+N	+P
Negative:	Comply	+P and +N	R	−N or +P	R
	Placate	+N	+P	−N and +P	−N and +P
	Ignore	+N	+N	R or +N	R or +P
	Defy	+N	+N	+N	+P
	Mixed	+N	+N and +P	+P	−N or +P
Carrot-Stick:	Comply	+N	R	+P	R
	Placate	−P and +N	+N	R	−N and +P
	Ignore	−P and +N	+N	R or +N	+P
	Defy	−P and +N	+N	+N	+P
	Mixed	−P and +N	+N	R	+P
None:	Comply	+N	R	+P	R
	Placate	+N	+N	+P or R	+P
	Ignore	+N	+N	+P	+P
	Defy	+N	+N	+N	+P
	Mixed	+N	+N	+P or +N	+P

Notes: R = Repeat same inducement. N = More negative or more coercive. P = More positive or cooperative.

livered by Robert Kennedy to Soviet ambassador Dobrynin on the 27th. The United States demanded that the Soviets begin dismantling the missile sites on the following day, but the inducements were accompanied by new promises to not invade Cuba and to dismantle U.S. missiles in Turkey—along with a threat to intervene militarily if the Soviets failed to comply with the demand. In this instance, the Soviets did agree to comply. Because the second U.S. influence attempt represented an increase in the severity of the threat ($+N$) over that seen in the blockade actions as well as an increase in positive inducements ($+P$) following the mixed Soviet response to the previous influence attempt, the U.S. influence strategy at this point was classified as cautious bullying (table 5–3, row 10, column 3).

Hostility as an Indicator of Degree of Coercion

Categorizing influence strategies into four basic types provides good qualitative distinctions, but it is a relatively insensitive measure of changes in the level of coercion. An actor may continue the same type of influence strategy according to our typology—but do so more coercively—and still be categorized in the same type. To obtain a more sensitive measure of the degree of hostility, we calculated daily *hostility scores*. Each act directed by one disputant to the other is assigned to a category on a friendliness-hostility continuum. The categories (developed by Rubin and Hill 1973, and modified to fit the BCOW data) yield weights ranging from −3 (most hostile) to +3 (most friendly). The weighted daily scores are summed, then divided by the number of days in the crisis phase, and finally multiplied by seven to provide weekly hostility scores for each disputant. The mean weekly hostility score is the actor's hostility score for the dispute.[11]

Although the hostility score provides a more sensitive measure of changes in the level of coercive acts, it lacks the qualitative theoretical strength of the typology of influence strategies; moreover, it tends to be particularly sensitive to any escalation in military activities. Therefore, we use the influence strategy as the basic indicator of changes in bargaining strategies except when it is impossible to determine the influence strategy being employed, or when state A employs the same influence strategy as it did in the previous dispute. In these cases we code a change in the level of coercion if there is a statistically significant ($p = .05$) change in the hostility score.

Dispute Phases

We have divided each of the disputes, and the bargaining strategies employed, into two phases: those before and those after the first threat of force (prethreat and postthreat). The division is useful for two reasons. First, we expect the postthreat phase of the dispute to best indicate changes in influence strategies. The prethreat phase is often like the early round sparring of two heavyweight boxers: There is a good deal of probing as each side attempts to get a sense of the strategy of the other. The first overt threat of force signals that the dispute has escalated to the point at which vital interests are at stake (see Leng and Gochman 1982; Snyder and Diesing 1977). The second advantage of dividing the dispute into phases is that it provides an operational means of determining which state was the first to move to significantly more coercive bargaining tactics. This becomes im-

---

[11] In some instances the change in the hostility scores may differ from changes in the predominant influence attempts. This is largely because hostility scores reflect the total number of negative acts and tend to reach greater magnitudes in rapidly escalating disputes whereas influence strategies are more representative of the overall bargaining. A good example of the distinction can be seen by comparing the second Kashmir and Bangladesh disputes. Although each side employed a reciprocating strategy in the former, military actions—largely through border clashes—escalated rapidly. The Bangladesh dispute, on the other hand, was more drawn out, but each side employed a cautious bullying strategy.

portant for judging the findings for Hypotheses 1 and 2. A listing of the first threat of force for each case appears in table 5–4.

Analysis and Findings

[The table presenting the predominant influence strategies and the hostility scores for each state in each phase of the dispute, as well as for the dispute as a whole, has been deleted.]

The findings for Hypothesis 1—that is, when the outcome of the preceding dispute was a diplomatic victory for A—are summarized in table 5–5. Table 5–5 indicates the changes, if any, in A's influence strategy (IS) and mean hostility score (Host). In cases in which the same influence strategy is pursued but with a higher mean hostility score—as in the second Moroccan and first Balkan cases—we have used a difference of means test with a confidence interval of 95% to provide a cutoff between changes which are and those which are not at a significant level.

In only two of the five cases are the influence strategy and the mean hostility score the same for both disputes. In the first Balkan dispute, previously successful Austria moved to more coercive bargaining tactics; in the Polish-Danzig dispute, Germany moved to a more assertive bargaining strategy with Britain, although its hostility score remained at approximately the same level. The U.S. bargaining in the Berlin Wall crisis provides a different

Table 5–4
First Threats of Force

Dispute	Date	Actor and Action
First Moroccan	5/22/1905	Germany: Vague threat of force
Second Moroccan	7/1/1911	Germany: Naval show of strength
Pre–World War I	7/28/1914	Russia: Partial mobilization
Bosnian	3/21/1909	Germany: Ultimatum to Russia[a]
First Balkan War	11/23/1912	Russia, then Austria: Mobilization[b]
Pre–World War I	7/26/1914	Russia: Partial mobilization
Rhineland	3/7/1936	Germany: Reoccupies Rhineland
Munich Crisis	5/20/1938	Britain: Verbal deterrent threat
Polish Crisis	3/30/1939	Britain: Verbal deterrent threat
Palestine	12/17/1947	Egypt (Arab Council): Verbal threat
Suez	10/25/1956	Israel: Mobilization
Six Day War	5/14/1967	Egypt: Show of strength; troops into D.M.Z.
First Kashmir	1/2/1948	India: Verbal threat of force
Second Kashmir	5/3/1965	India and Pakistan: Troops clash
Bangladesh	4/20/1971	India: Show of strength
Berlin Blockade	6/24/1948	USSR: Complete blockade of Berlin
Berlin Wall	8/13/1961	USSR: Begin Wall; U.S. show of strength follows
Cuban Missile	10/22/1962	U.S. Verbal threat; announce blockade

[a] Action by Germany, but on behalf of Austria.

[b] There were earlier "trial" mobilizations by Russia, but this is the first clear threat to Austria.

Table 5–5

Hypothesis 1: State A's Bargaining Following a Diplomatic Victory in the Preceding Crisis

Current Crisis	Actor	Changes in Coercion					
		Postthreat Phrase			Total Dispute		
		IS	Host	Score	IS	Host	Score
Second Moroccan	France	S	$+C^{ns}$	+	S	$+C^{n.s.}$	+
First Balkan	Austria	N	$+C^*$	−	N	$+C^*$	−
Munich	Germany	S	S	+	S	S	+
Polish	Germany	$+C$	S	−	$+C$	S	−
Second Berlin	U.S.	S	$-C$	−	$+C$	$-C$	−
Correct Predictions and Significance Level		2 − 3 (p. = n.s.)			2 − 3 (p. = n.s.)		

Notes: S = same; $+C$ = more coercive; $-C$ = less coercive; N = no identifiable influence strategy.
* Significant at p = .01; n.s. = not significant (difference of means test).

sort of deviation from the prediction. Kennedy advisors who had been present at the previous Berlin crisis (particularly Acheson) argued that the United States should follow the same bargaining strategy, particularly the airlift response, if Khrushchev should attempt to blockade the city. The same advice was offered by de Gaulle when Kennedy visited Paris at the end of May 1961 (Schlesinger 1965: 351, 379–383). But while Kennedy did employ the same type of overall bargaining strategy (reciprocating), the mean level of U.S. hostility was *lower* than in the first Berlin crisis, reflecting more vigorous U.S. efforts to achieve a negotiated settlement. Thus, while these findings do not support the hypothesis, neither do they suggest a movement to more coercive bargaining in disputes following diplomatic successes. In fact, in all five cases the first threat of force (which is our operational indicator of which party was the first to move to a more coercive bargaining strategy) came from the other disputant.

The findings offer stronger support for Hypothesis 2, which predicts more coercive bargaining by state A in those cases in which A suffered a diplomatic defeat in the preceding dispute. These are summarized in table 5–6.

In all five instances, A's bargaining became more coercive. Moreover, in each instance A was the first party to employ a threat of force. In three of the cases the same basic type of influence strategy was pursued, but significantly more coercive acts accompanied it.

Turning to Hypothesis 3, as we mentioned earlier, all of the disputes ending in a diplomatic compromise in our sample fell into type b, which predicts more coercive bargaining by both sides.

The findings in table 5–7 support the hypothesized movement by both parties to more coercive strategies. The two exceptions are Austria's actions

Table 5–6
Hypothesis 2: A's Bargaining Following a Diplomatic Defeat in the Previous Crisis

	Phases					
	Postthreat			Total Dispute		
Current Crisis: Actor	IS	Host: Level	Score	IS	Host	Score
Second Moroccan: Germany	S	+C*	+	S	+C*	+
Balkan: Russia	S	+C*	+	S	+C*	+
Munich: Britain	S	+C*	+	S	+C*	+
Polish: Britain	+C	−C	+	+C	+C	+
Berlin: USSR	+C	−C	+	+C	−C	+
Correct Predictions and Significance Level	5-0 (p = .001)			5-0 (p = .001)		

Notes: S = same influence strategy or hostility level; +C = more coercive; −C = less coercive.
* Significant at P = .01 level (difference of means test).

toward Russia in the pre–World War I crisis and the Soviet behavior in the Cuban Missile Crisis. That Austria's actions are not significantly more coercive may be related to the structure of the dispute—that is, the hostile Austrian acts were directed primarily at Russia's ally, Serbia, rather than at Russia itself. Like Germany during the Munich crisis, Austria hoped to be able to punish Serbia without bringing Russia into the fray. The Soviet behavior in the postthreat phase of the Cuban Missile Crisis appears to be more exceptional. In this dispute one party, faced with a bullying strategy by the other, adopted a more accommodative strategy presumably to avoid the risks of nuclear war.

Hypothesis 4a predicts a more coercive influence strategy for state A

Table 5–7
Hypothesis 3: A's Bargaining Following a Diplomatic Compromise in the Preceding Crisis

	Postthreat			Total Dispute		
Current Crisis: Actor	IS	Host	Score	IS	Host	Score
Pre–World War I: France	+C	+C	+	+C	+C	+
Pre–World War I: Germany	+C	+C	+	+C	+C	+
Pre–World War I: Russia	+C	+C	+	+C	−C	+
Pre–World War I: Austria	N	+C[n.s.]	−	N	+C[n.s.]	−
Cuban M.C.: U.S.	+C	+C	+	N	+C	+
Cuban M.C.: USSR	−C	+C	−	−C	+C	−
Current Predictions and Significance Level	4 − 2 (p = .01)			4 − 2 (p = .01)		

Notes: S = same influence strategy or hostility level; +C = more coercive; −C = less coercive.
* Significant at p = .01 level (difference of means test).

following a crisis that ended in an unwanted war. When war was A's objective in the preceding crisis, Hypothesis 4b predicts that A will switch to a more accommodative bargaining strategy in the subsequent crisis.

As table 5–8 indicates, Hypothesis 4a correctly predicts the change to a more coercive bargaining strategy in the postthreat phase of the dispute in all six of the cases of crises following unwanted wars. Five of the six cases also exhibit more coercive bargaining scores for the entire dispute. The exception is India's bargaining in the Bangladesh dispute, which reflects attempts to seek a diplomatic solution during the prethreat phase of the dispute. That strategy changed during the postthreat phase as the situation became economically and politically intolerable for the government of Indira Gandhi.

The Suez and Six Day War disputes each follow a premeditated war: the Arab attack that launched the Palestine war in 1948, and Israel's attack across the Sinai in 1956. Consequently, Hypothesis 4b predicts more accommodative strategies by Egypt in the Suez crisis and by Israel in the crisis preceding the Six Day War. In the Suez crisis, Egypt's postthreat behavior consisted of essentially military moves in response to those of Israel. There is no discernible influence strategy by the Egyptians in this case, although the hostility score for Egypt is higher than in the period preceding the Palestine War. The dispute preceding the Six Day War is more consistent with the hypothesis. The first threat of force comes, as predicted, from Egypt in its efforts to displace the UNEF forces in the Sinai. Israel responds to the Egyptian move with more coercive bargaining, but it does not reach the level of coercion exhibited during the Suez crisis. Israel's cautious bullying strategy still demonstrates plenty of toughness and resolve, but the door is left open—at least for a short time—for a diplomatic solution.

Table 5–8
Hypothesis 4: A's Bargaining Following a War Outcome in the Preceding Crisis

| | | Change in Degree of Coercion | | | | | |
| | | Postthreat | | | Total Dispute | | |
Current Dispute: Actor	Preceding War Type	IS	Host	Score	IS	Host	Score
Suez: Israel	A	+C	+C	+	+C	+C	+
Six Day: Egypt	A	+C	+C	+	+C	+C	+
Second Kashmir: India	A	S	+C*	+	S	+C*	+
Second Kashmir: Pakistan	A	S	+C*	+	S	+C*	+
Bangladesh: India	A	+C	−C	+	S	−C	−
Bangladesh: Pakistan	A	+C	−C	+	+C	−C	+
Suez: Egypt	B	None	+C	−	None	+C	−
Six Day: Israel	B	−C	−C	+	−C	S	+
Total Correct Predictions		7 − 1 (p = .001)			6 − 2 (p = .01)		

Notes: S = same influence strategy or hostility level; +C = more coercive; −C = less coercive.
* Significant at p = .01 (difference of means test); A = unplanned war; B = premeditated attack.

Summary of Findings

With the exception of crises following a diplomatic victory for state A, the findings are in the direction predicted by the ELR hypotheses. Even in this instance, the fact that A was never the first to issue a threat of force in the subsequent dispute suggests support for the model.

Because the sample was not drawn in a purely random manner and since the number of cases tested for each hypothesis is small, one must be cautious about drawing inferences to a larger population. Nevertheless, significance tests can provide an objective measure of whether the variables selected to test our hypotheses tell us anything about the variance across the cases beyond mere chance (Winch and Campbell 1969).

Using a binomial test with a 99% confidence interval, the results for Hypotheses 2, 3, and 4 are statistically significant. As one might expect, we do best with the least ambiguous cases: diplomatic defeats and wars. Overall, the ELR hypotheses correctly predict changes in 18 of 24 cases of repeat encounters for the individual disputants—a distribution that is significant at the $p = .001$ level.

Some Other Possibilities

Taken at face value, the findings offer support for the ELR model. But before drawing any conclusions, we should consider some alternative explanations.

Experiential Learning Alone

Does the ELR model do better than a simple experiential learning (EL) model? An EL model alone predicts simply that policymakers will change unsuccessful bargaining strategies and retain those that are successful. A stronger test is placed on the ELR model as it must predict the direction of the change. This means that with our trichotomous dependent variable, the expected agreement with the EL model (except in the five instances of diplomatic victories) is 67%, whereas it is only 33% for the ELR model.

Another way of comparing the models is by moving beyond the effects of the most recent preceding crisis to consider the full sequence of outcomes and bargaining strategies from the first to the third dispute. There are 16 possible permutations resulting from 4 types of outcomes for 2 successive crises. In fact, just 5 of the possibilities obtain in the 12 cases in the sample. These are: victory-victory (1 case), victory-compromise (3), defeat-compromise (3), defeat-defeat (1), and war-war (4). For the ELR model, taking into account the outcomes of both the first dispute and the second does not change the predicted strategy for the third dispute. With the ex-

Table 5–9
EL Model Versus ELR Model: Changes in Coercion in Third Dispute

Actor	Outcomes: Preceding Disputes	Change in Coercion: Second Dispute	Change in Coercion in Third Dispute		
			Predicted		
			EL	ELR	Actual
France	VC*	S**	CH	+C	+C
Germany	DC	+C	+C	+C	+C
Austria	VC	+C	−C	+C	S
Russia	DC	+C	+C	+C	+C
Britain	DD	+C	−C	+C	+C
Germany	VV	S	S	S	+C
Israel	WW	+C	−C	−C	−C
Egypt	WW	+C	−C	+C	+C
India	WW	+C	−C	+C	+C
Pakistan	WW	+C	−C	+C	+C
United States	VC	+C	−C	+C	+C
Soviet Union	DC	+C	+C	+C	−C

* V = diplomatic victory; C = compromise (type b); D = diplomatic defeat; W = war.
** S = same; +C = more coercive; −C = less coercive; CH = any change.

ception of the double victories, the logic of this model associates the unsatisfactory second outcome with a failure to demonstrate sufficient resolve; therefore, it predicts more coercive bargaining in the third dispute. For the EL model, however, it does make a difference. If state A moved to a more (or less) coercive strategy in the second dispute and fared no better (or worse) than in the first dispute, then the EL model should predict a switch in the *opposite* direction in the third dispute.[12] Applying this reasoning to the cases in our sample, we find that the EL model correctly predicts only 4 of the 12 possibilities, but the ELR model correctly predicts 9 of the 12 bargaining strategies. The individual cases are summarized in table 5–9.

Prudence Versus Resolve

At the outset of this article we drew a distinction between the side of realpolitik that stresses the demonstration of power and the willingness to use it, and that which calls for prudence in action. Prudence prescribes a careful calculation of costs and risks based on (1) political stakes, and (2) relative power (Morgenthau 1978:11–12, 519–521). But, as Snyder and

---

[12] To give just one example, Austria achieved a diplomatic victory in the Bosnian crisis; nevertheless, she switched to a more coercive bargaining strategy in the first Balkan dispute which ended in an unsatisfactory compromise. According to the ELR model, the Austrian policymakers would interpret the second outcome as resulting from a failure to bargain with sufficient resolve; therefore it would predict an even more coercive bargaining strategy in the third dispute. The EL model, on the other hand, would suggest a change to greater accommodation on the basis of the unsuccessful results of the change to more coercive bargaining in the previous dispute.

Diesing argue (1977:193), "a crisis occurs only when the net balance of interests and power is even enough that both sides can plausibly see some chance of winning."

We find little variance from one crisis to the next within the pairs of states in the sample, so we would not expect to find strategic shifts based on changing issues.[13]

Regarding possible changes in the relative capabilities of the adversaries from one crisis to the next, a hypothesis based on prudence would predict a change to more coercive bargaining by those states enjoying a shift in power in their favor, and to more accommodative bargaining by states finding themselves at a new disadvantage (Morgenthau 1978:520–521).

The difficulty of objectively measuring the relative power of the two adversaries (not to mention their perceptions of it) makes us reluctant to attempt a systematic analysis.[14] We can take a less formal look at the hypothesis, however, by examining instances in which there were relatively unambiguous shifts in military strength from one dispute to the next. This appears to be the case in the Egyptian-Israeli disputes in 1956 and 1967, the Indo-Pakistani dispute in 1973, and the 1961 and 1962 Soviet-American crises. In all but one of these five cases (Israel in 1967), the state whose military position improved moved to a more coercive strategy; but in only one instance (Soviet Union in 1962) does the state whose relative military position weakened move to a more accommodative bargaining strategy. In each of the other four instances, it too moved to more coercive bargaining—contrary to what prudence would prescribe. The most dramatic examples are Egypt and Pakistan: These states fought two unsuccessful wars and found themselves in a third crisis in a relatively weaker military position, but nevertheless moved to even more coercive bargaining. In sum, in those instances in which we can observe a relatively unambiguous shift in military power, the prudence hypothesis is supported only about half the time. Bargaining, however, is consistent with the ELR model in all but one instance—Soviet bargaining in the Cuban Missile Crisis.

---

[13] The territorial issues at stake between Israel and Egypt and between India and Pakistan vary somewhat, but they remain at a very high level of significance to these states' security concerns. The Balkan issues bedeviling Russia and Austria and the relationship between Germany and France remain essentially the same throughout the pre–World War I era. As in the case of the British-German disputes, they become more severe as the war approaches, but the experience of the past disputes would appear to contribute to that importance as well as the particular issues themselves. In the Cold War crises between the United States and the Soviet Union, it can be argued that Cuba was of greater importance to the United States and that Berlin was of greater importance to the Soviet Union; however, even in these cases, the seriousness of the stakes in all three disputes is more salient than differences of degree.

[14] Even with the benefit of historical hindsight, judgments can be problematic. Consider the Russo-Austrian disputes. In the first two crises in the Balkans, Russia was not ready for war. She was better prepared in 1914, but then Austria was backed solidly by a German military commitment.

Coercion Begets Coercion

While the ELR hypotheses correctly predict changes in coercion in 18 of the 24 cases, a simple prediction that any state will move to more coercive bargaining with each successive crisis is correct in 17 of the 24 cases. This raises questions about the validity of the EL notion that changes in coercion are related to the *outcomes* of previous crises. It suggests rather that coercive behavior in one crisis simply begets more coercive behavior in the next—in much the same way that it has been shown to do so within crises (see Ward 1982a; Leng and Wheeler 1979; Snyder and Diesing 1977; North et al. 1964).

In 14 of the 24 cases it is possible to make some distinctions between these two hypotheses. At first glance, the ELR hypothesis does not fare well. In the 7 instances in which the ELR hypothesis predicts either the same level of coercion for a diplomatically victorious state (table 5–5) or a more accommodative strategy by a state that launched a premeditated attack on the other (table 5–8), it appears to do no better than a hypothesis that simply predicts more coercive behavior. Each is correct in 3 of the 7 cases. But if we consider the effect that the other party's bargaining behavior within the current dispute is likely to have on state A's bargaining strategy, a different picture emerges.[15]

In those cases where the previous dispute ended in a diplomatic defeat, unsatisfactory compromise, or an unwanted and unsuccessful war for A, the ELR prediction that A would move to a more coercive bargaining strategy would not be altered by the strategy employed by B. If B should move to a more coercive strategy as well, that would intensify the perceived need for A to demonstrate resolve. If B should move to a more accommodative strategy, that would be interpreted as a sign that B's resolve was weakening and that A's more coercive strategy was working. The situation is different in those cases in which A emerged victorious from the previous dispute. Following the logic of our ELR model, we would expect A to begin with the same strategy as in the previous dispute, but to respond in kind should B switch to more coercive bargaining. Similarly, a state that launched a premeditated attack on the other party in the previous dispute would be expected to turn away from its more accommodative bargaining in the next encounter should it be faced with a shift to more coercive bargaining by the adversary. In the latter instance,

---

[15] If the experience in the preceding crisis is thought of as the most salient component of the long-term institutional memory of A's policymakers, then B's responses to A's actions within the current crisis comprise their short-term memory. The assumption is that the long-term memory leads to a historical propensity to employ a particular level of coercive behavior, but that this can be altered by interaction within the current crisis. (See Ward 1982a for a discussion of long-term versus short-term memory in interstate conflict.)

however, we would not expect the hostility score (which is our best indicator of military escalation) to rise above that of the previous dispute. A wants to demonstrate resolve in the face of a more belligerent approach by B, but it does not want to signal that B has no recourse but to prepare for war.[16]

If we take a second look at the seven cases in tables 5–5 and 5–8 in which state A either achieved a diplomatic victory or launched a premeditated attack on state B, the findings are interesting. In none of these seven instances was A the first to threaten the use of force—our operational indicator of the first party to move to more coercive bargaining. *Following* the initial threat of force from B, A does bargain more coercively in six of the seven cases. As we noted above, in three of these instances the level of coercion rises above that employed in the previous dispute. Of these cases, two follow diplomatic victories. The third case, which is represented by Egypt's military moves in the few days preceding the 1965 war, comes only after overt military threats from Israel.

In sum, the emphasis on resolve in the ELR model, as well as the findings from previous studies, lead us to expect state A to respond in kind to the predicted increase in the level of coercive bargaining by state B. But, in all seven instances in which the outcome of the preceding crisis makes it possible to hypothesize which of the two parties should be the first to initiate more coercive bargaining, the results are consistent with the predictions of the ELR model. Given the small number of cases and our relatively crude measure of which party was the first to raise the level of coercion, these findings should be treated with caution. Nevertheless, a tentative judgment favors the ELR hypothesis over a simple prediction that both sides will move to more coercive bargaining with each successive crisis.

Events Occurring between the Disputes

What about the interactions between the two disputants in the periods between the successive disputes? The ELR model is based on the proposition that the experience of the last crisis should be so salient that it exerts the most powerful influence over bargaining in the next crisis with the same adversary; however, a large number of salient events can occur between the crises to affect the diplomatic climate between the disputants. Could the patterns that we have observed have their origins in the periods between the crises? If so, we would expect to observe a pattern of growing hostility

---

[16] In the crisis preceding the 1967 war, Israel appeared to do just that. The hostility score for Israel was −36 in the Suez crisis; in the 1967 crisis, it was −33.

in the periods preceding the crises in those 17 instances in which state A moved to more coercive bargaining.

We do not have events data for these interim periods to allow us to conduct an empirical test of this possibility;[17] however, it is possible to obtain a good sense of the overall patterns from historical accounts. There is a pattern of growing hostility in Russian-Austrian relations prior to World War I and, to a lesser extent, in British-German relations prior to World War II. (It could be argued—especially in the Russian-Austrian case—that this resulted from the preceding crises between the two states.) On the other hand, German-French relations over the 10 years before World War I do *not* represent a consistent pattern of rising hostility, nor do U.S.-Soviet relations between the two Berlin crises, nor do Indo-Pakistani relations in the interim periods between their three wars. In other words, we do not find the kind of pattern that we would expect if events during the intervals between the crises were causing the shifts toward more coercive crisis bargaining. Added to this is our earlier finding: States that suffered diplomatic defeats or that were the targets of premeditated attacks in one crisis were invariably the first to threaten the use of force in the next crisis. Thus, while we cannot entirely rule out the possibility that some of the bargaining that we observed may be caused by events occurring between the crises, the evidence that we have obtained, as well as the overall interaction patterns in the interim periods, point in the other direction.

Other Variables

This, of course, does not exhaust the list of possible alternative or additional predictor variables. Some of the more prominent variables that we have not considered are types of regimes, variations in belief systems and risk-taking propensities of national leaders, differences between major and minor powers, bureaucratic politics, domestic politics, the influence of third parties, and the nature of the international system at the time of the dispute. The size of our sample and available space do not permit systematic testing or an extended discussion of all these variables, but their potential significance warns against drawing more than tentative conclusions from our findings. Nevertheless, the consistency of the findings across a sample of disputes in which these variables vary considerably is supportive of the basic model.

---

[17] A promising indicator has been developed by Allan (1982:6–8). Allan measures the "diplomatic climate" as perceived by state A vis-à-vis state B by an integral function of B's conflictual behavior toward A for the whole past to the present. The continuous function gives greater weight to more recent events, but periods of intense conflictual activity, such as a crisis, will load the memory component of the function and be "forgotten" slowly.

Conclusion

We have conducted an initial test of four hypotheses derived from two general propositions. The first is the experiential learning proposition that, when a pair of evenly matched states become engaged in successive crises, each party is likely to draw lessons from the outcome of the preceding crisis based on the relative success or failure of the bargaining strategy employed. The second is the realist proposition that policymakers view crisis bargaining as a test of a state's power and resolve, so that unsuccessful outcomes are seen as resulting from a failure to demonstrate sufficient resolve.

On the other hand, realism prescribes prudence. And prudence suggests that the management of crises is dependent on a diplomacy that can lead to mutual accommodation. This requires self-restraint and a sense of proportion in the exercise and demonstration of power. The threat of force is always present in a crisis, but its assertion can mean the end of effective negotiation and the beginning of an ultimately uncontrollable spiral of escalating conflict. Prudence suggests that a state that has suffered a recent defeat—whether through war or by being forced to submit in an escalating crisis—should act with greater caution in the next encounter with the same adversary. But our findings indicate that if states do learn from these experiences, the lesson tends to be to use more coercive bargaining the next time.

These findings were the result of a historical examination of 18 crises involving six pairs of states engaged in three successive crises each. Working from the ELR hypotheses derived from the experiential learning and realpolitik propositions summarized above, we attempted to predict shifts in the degree of coercion in bargaining strategies and levels of hostile actions for each state as it moved from one crisis to the next. The predictions were correct in 18 of the 24 cases. Although we were working with a relatively small sample, that 15 of the correct predictions were for movement to *more coercive* bargaining with each successive encounter does not encourage optimism regarding the propensity of policymakers to develop progressively refined techniques or "conventions" to manage and "demobilize" crises as they gain more experience.

We have proposed that the reason for this dismal record is tied to the pervasiveness of a realpolitik orientation to crisis bargaining that places a heavy emphasis on the importance of a reputation for resolve when vital interests are at stake. But while our findings from the actions of states embroiled in crises are consistent with this view, we cannot reach conclusions regarding motivations from actions alone. We argue only that this is a plausible explanation given the prominence of the realpolitik tradition—in particular, its strong emphasis on the demonstration of power and resolve.

We can only speculate on why statesmen appear to stress this side of realism. We suspect that it has something to do with how policymakers conceive of their roles as defenders of the national interest and the expectations that they share with the public regarding what is appropriate behavior when national security is threatened.[18] It may be rooted in a kind of folklore of international politics that venerates aggressive national leaders and views peacemakers as compromisers. Paradoxically, such a view is at odds with the most basic assumptions of realpolitik: It encourages national leaders to refuse to acknowledge the limits of their own power, especially in relation to the power and resolve of the adversary. It leads to the assumption that all is within reach if one only acts with sufficient resolve. It is a rejection of prudence in favor of "brinkmanship."

There are, of course, some exceptions to the pattern that obtains in our sample. The most dramatic is the behavior of the Soviet Union following the United States' ultimatum and blockade during the Cuban Missile Crisis. It is the one instance in which, after two preceding crises, a bullying strategy by one side resulted in a switch to a more appeasing strategy by the other. But the Cuban Missile Crisis is the exception: It is the only instance in our sample in which the third crisis did not end in war.

Editors' Commentary

Major Findings

One of the major findings of Leng's article is that as crises persist, it becomes increasingly difficult to avoid war. This is because as disputants move from one crisis to the next, the bargaining becomes more hostile and aggressive. This outcome is not something that either of the theoretical approaches Leng tests anticipates, but it makes sense from what is known generally about how people react to hostility.

Leng's study is based on an examination of states involved in repeated crises. He looks at eighteen crises involving a total of six pairs of equally matched states. He begins his analysis by seeking to investigate whether learning across crises occurs and, in particular, whether success leads to repeating behavior and failure leads to a change in strategy.

While a pure learning model might suggest a fundamental shift in strategy if it did not work, Leng finds that states that are defeated in one crisis become more coercive in the next. Moreover, a state defeated in one crisis tends to initiate the next crisis. By the

---

[18] We refer here to the normative component of role expectations that define appropriate behavior in particular situations (see Sarbin and Allen 1968:501). In this regard, there is a natural interaction between the policymaker's conception of his role as defender of the national interest and the cues that he takes from the attentive public.

third crisis, there is a tendency to continue to escalate, even if escalation in the second dispute failed.

What seems to be occurring is that leaders rely on realist folklore, which stresses demonstration of power, and attribute their loss to an insufficient use of force and resolve. At the same time, however, leaders seem unable to heed realist prescriptions on prudence (Leng 1986). This suggests that coercion begets coercion and that the next crisis will always have a higher level of coercion. Leng finds the latter to be true in seventeen of his twenty-four cases. From a pure realist perspective, "rationality" would dictate less coercion if there were a decrease in power since the last crisis. In four of five cases, the opposite happens.

The result is that war usually breaks out by the third crisis. A major exception is the 1962 Cuban missile crisis. Nevertheless, it is significant that it was in the Cuban missile crisis that the United States and the Soviet Union came closest to nuclear war. Indeed, if Khrushchev had responded to U.S. actions with a move on Berlin, as Kennedy feared, war might not have been averted.

Leng's research provides a clear idea of the bargaining tactics associated with crisis escalation and shows that such tactics are pursued after less coercive bargaining has been deemed to have failed in earlier crises. Such behavior can lead to a hostile spiral where the actions of one side lead the other to reciprocate in a more hostile manner until war results (Holsti, North, and Brody 1968).

Leng's study points out that the causes of war can be drawn out and cumulative. War often occurs through an escalation of a crisis, but most crises do not escalate to war. Other researchers have also found that a pattern of crises between two states increases the probability of war (Wallensteen 1981:74–75, 84). The main point here is that if states are unable to resolve the issue underlying their dispute, other crises will emerge, and more coercive tactics will be employed, making escalation to war more probable. Similarly, Diehl (1985a:340) has found that rivals typically have two disputes before going to war. As noted earlier, this might explain why some disputes that have ongoing mutual military buildups do not escalate to war. For some states, war occurs only after efforts just short of war have failed to bring results. For other states, as table 5–2 makes clear, war is initiated in the first crisis. The factors distinguishing the states that go to war on the first crisis from those that do not have yet to be identified by further research, but one factor evident from table 5–2 is that major states appear more cautious than minor states.

In either case, as war looms, it is likely that each side will try to time the onset of war to its advantage. In the next chapter, Bueno de Mesquita shows that states act as if they calculate their expected utility before initiating a war; that is, he finds that states with a higher expected utility for war tend to be those that initiate the war.

Methodological Notes

In Leng's article, we can see some of the advantages and disadvantages of using a **random sample**. When the entire number of cases we are interested in studying is too large, it is scientifically valid to take a sample, but the cases must be chosen randomly. If we pick and choose cases according to whether we think they will fit the theory, the sample will be biased. This is one of the major critiques that quantitative scholars lodge against traditionalists.

Even if the cases are chosen without regard for their support of the theory, as long as they are not chosen randomly, there is a strong likelihood that they will not represent the entire population. The failure to be representative is the technical meaning of **bias** in data collection. The classic "man in the street" style of collecting opinions is not scientifically valid because the people one encounters in the street do not consist of a random sample (especially if they are all actually *men*!). Although the reporter may say he or she picked people "at random," this is not the case. Certain types of people will pass certain corners at certain times. Such a sample is called a **convenience sample,** and it produces biased results. Yet when polling organizations want to measure American public opinion, they do not have to survey all adult Americans. They can get a fairly accurate picture using a sample of only 1,500 people. This is possible because of its random, and hence representative, quality.

Leng has the opposite problem of public opinion pollsters. The population, or universe, he is interested in—the total number of crises or militarized disputes between evenly matched pairs—is relatively small. Since it is, even though his sample is small (eighteen crises), the sample is likely to have the same characteristics as the population. Remember, nevertheless, that we must always be cautious in interpreting results based on small samples and small numbers of cases. In the study of a phenomenon as rare as war, that problem arises fairly frequently.

Once the sample is chosen, we might ask: How does one measure, or operationalize, these crises? We have seen that it is fairly straightforward to measure war as nation-months of war as long as the information is available in the historical record. A crisis, on the other hand, is a series of events. Measuring or coding aspects of events produces what is known as events data. This type of data has its own set of potential problems. One is whether a source is biased. The *New York Times* is often criticized because of its Western or American bias, although most of the phenomena of interest here are all Western. Leng deals with the problem of source validity by augmenting the *New York Times* with diplomatic histories of the disputes.

A second problem is that one person might perceive an event as having a crisis characteristic when another does not. This gives rise to the need for a special measure of reliability (see chapter 2) called **intercoder reliability.** The researcher must develop precise enough coding rules so that when different people do the coding, they get a very high percentage of the same answers. You can see in the section on indicator construction in this chapter how complicated the coding procedure can become (see table 5–3).

The third problem is that since such a scheme requires a great deal of research and many people to carry it out, it is difficult to generate a data set with a large number of cases. These problems are all manageable, though, and are more than compensated for by the fact that Leng has made an important contribution to the study of the actual *behavior* of decision makers. Other studies look at changes in the number of alliances, amount of war, levels of capability, and so forth and make certain assumptions about the way people behaved to produce the outcome. Leng measures and analyzes the actual behavior and interactions among nation-states. Hence his contribution to the data gathering on war is called the *Behavioral* Correlates of War.

The actual findings begin in table 5–5. Leng uses a difference-of-means test. This means that he calculates the mean of the dependent variable as observed and the mean of what the variable would be randomly and computes how different the observed value is from the expected value. On the basis of the difference, a computation is made to determine whether the difference between the observed mean and the expected mean is statistically significant (see the methodological notes in chapter 3). If $p < .01$, the difference is statistically significant, and we assume that the difference is produced by the independent variable. Although the findings based on statistical significance are important, it should not be overlooked that one of the most important findings is based on the simple proportion that seventeen of twenty-four cases showed increased coercion.

Leng's study is also an example of how research might begin as a deductive test of one or more models and then move to a more inductive search to explain unanticipated results. **Deduction** involves making a generalized statement and then testing it; **induction** entails discovering relationships and then generalizing about them. Leng's finding about increasing escalation across crises is basically an inductive finding; his theory did not anticipate it before beginning the research. By contrast, the next article illustrates a very deductive approach to research known as formal theory.

6
Excerpts from *The War Trap*

Bruce Bueno de Mesquita

Editors' Introduction

Bueno de Mesquita's analysis is an exemplary illustration of **deductive** theorizing. Unlike the other selections in this reader, which test hypotheses found in the literature or inductively investigate a problem through a systematic examination of the data, *The War Trap* attempts to use a few assumptions to derive an explanation of why states initiate wars and win them. Bueno de Mesquita employs the basic rational choice assumption that political actors behave *as if* they seek to maximize benefits and minimize costs.

Unlike many others who work in the rational choice area, Bueno de Mesquita has been particularly successful in operationalizing and testing his explanations. The selection here begins with his translating his verbal explanation into mathematical symbols. Next, he operationalizes the various components of his explanation. He concludes with three relatively straightforward tests using Yule's Q and lambda to assess the test results.

Expected Utility from a Bilateral War

In a bilateral war, success affords one the subsequent opportunity to influence the policies of the adversary, making them more consistent with one's own interests. This opportunity may range from actually manipulating the economic, social, or military policies of the defeated state so that they serve one's own interests to merely preventing the adversary from changing its policies in undesirable ways. Whatever the actual goal or gains, the differences in interests or policies that encourage the war indicate the maximum change an aggressor could expect to achieve. If U_{ii} is the utility some potential conflict initiator i attaches to his most preferred policy platform (so that $U_{ii} = 1$), then the maximum shift in the policies of nation j—i's potential opponent—that can be realized is the difference between the policies that i wants j to hold and j's policy position, or $U_{ii} - U_{ij}$, with U_{ij} (which is less than or equal to U_{ii}) being i's value for j's policy positions before the war. If i loses, then it may expect j to impose changes on it so that i's postwar posture is consistent with the desires of j. Thus the current utility of failure in the war is $U_{ij} - U_{ii}$, or the maximum amount by which i might have to change its world view to satisfy the desires of j.

In addition to i's calculation of current relations with j, it is likely that i also examines, when possible, what it perceives to be the future of its relationship with j. If i believes that relations are improving—that is, that

$$\Delta(U_{ii} - U_{ij})_{t0} \to {}_{tn} < 0$$

indicating that i believes j will move closer to the policy position i desires for j in the near future—this might mitigate some of any currently existing antagonism. Conversely, if i anticipates a deterioration in relations with j—that is, that

$$\Delta(U_{ii} - U_{ij})_{t0} \to {}_{tn} > 0$$

indicating that i believes there is something to be gained by preventing j's policies from moving away from those desired by i for j—this may aggravate or even create antagonisms.

I define nation i's expected utility from a *bilateral war* with j $[E(U_i)_b]$ in the following way:

$$E(U_i)_b = [P_i(U_{ii} - U_{ij}) + (1 - P_i)(U_{ij} - U_{ii})]_{t0}$$

$$+ P_{i_{t0}} [\Delta (U_{ii} - U_{ij})]_{t0} \to {}_{tn} + (1 - P_i)_{t0}$$

$$[\Delta(U_{ij} - U_{ij})]_{t0} \to {}_{tn}$$

$$(6.1)$$

where

$U_{ii} = i$'s utility for i's preferred view of the world. $U_{ii} = 1$ by definition.

$U_{ij} = i$'s utility for j's policies. U_{ij} can vary between 1 and -1.

$(U_{ii} - U_{ij})_{t0}$ = i's perception of what might be gained by succeeding in a bilateral conflict with j in which i can then impose new policies on j. This term reflects i's current evaluation of the difference between the policies that i currently desires j to hold and i's perception of j's current policies (hence it is evaluated at time t_0). Thus the greater perceived similarity between the policies i desires for j and j's current policies (i.e., $U_{ij} \rightarrow U_{ii}$), the less utility i expects to derive from altering j's policies.

$(U_{ij} - U_{ii})_{t0}$ = i's perception of what might be lost by failing in a bilateral contest with j in which j can then impose new policies on i. This term reflects i's current evaluation of how much j could shift i's policies away from its world view to make them more in line with j's interests as perceived by i. Like the previous term, this term is evaluated based on current policies (at t_0).

$\Delta(U_{ii} - U_{ij})_{t0} \rightarrow _{tn}$ = i's perception of anticipated change in the difference between i's world view and j's policies over the time period t_0 (the present) to some future time (t_n).

$\Delta(U_{ij} - U_{ii})_{t0} \rightarrow _{tn}$ = i's perception of anticipated change in how much j would want to alter i's policy outlook in the future compared to j's current perceived policy differences with i. Thus this term represents i's perception of anticipated future potential policy losses (over the period t_0 to the future period t_n) to j, while the previous term represents i's perception of future potential policy gains to be derived from imposing i's will on j. Both this and the previous term represent i's estimates under the assumption of no war.

P_i = i's current perception of his probability of succeeding against j in a bilateral conflict. And finally,

$1 - P_i$ = i's current perception of his probability of losing against j in a bilateral conflict.

Since $(U_{ii} - U_{ij}) + (U_{ij} - U_{ii}) = 0$, the expectation of a gain or loss in a bilateral war is solely determined by the relative strength of the attacker and its opponent. Of course, while the expectation of a gain or loss is determined by the relative strength of the two sides, the *magnitude* of those gains or losses is strongly influenced by the current and anticipated future values of U_{ii} and U_{ij}. Thus the theory treats bilateral wars as if they are viewed as situations involving pure competition. i believes it can gain as much from a bilateral conflict as i believes j must lose. This is a rather conservative viewpoint, since in reality, j—if it loses—is likely to lose more than i actually gains. Once i must consider the possibility of third parties entering the conflict, however, its viewpoint ceases to be one of pure competition. All other states beside i and j may have mixed motives, with some elements encouraging their outright support for one side or the other, and with other considerations encouraging them to try to mediate the dispute.

Expected Utility from a Multilateral War

... Whether i believes a third-party nation k will support i or j is determined, not surprisingly, by i's belief about k's relative utility for i and j. Thus whereas the expectation of gains or losses in a bilateral war depends on the relative capabilities of the attacker and defender, the expectation of support or opposition from third parties depends on utilities. The magnitude of the expected support or opposition, on the other hand, depends both on k's perceived relative utility for i and j and on k's strength across the distance from k to i and from k to j.

When the perceived expected utility of k for i is greater than zero, i believes that k would more likely support i than j. If the expected utility is less than zero, i believes that k will support j. When the expected utility equals zero, k is expected to be indifferent and hence unlikely to favor either the attacker or the defender. How much support k is likely to give, of course, depends on how much i believes that k values i's policy preferences relative to j's. The more $E(U_i)$, for k_l deviates from zero, the more the leader of i is willing to believe that k will commit himself to the war (Starr 1972; Altfeld, and Bueno de Mesquita 1979; Altfeld 1979).

When the leader of i sums the expected utility $E(U_i)$ for k_l across all third-party states k, he derives an overall estimate of the expected impact of third states. If the sum of the $E(U_i)$ for k_l is positive, then more support can be expected for i than for j; if it is negative, i believes that more support will go to j. When the sum of $E(U_i)$ for k_l, is zero, i believes that, on balance, though some may aid i and some may aid j, the effect of third states is neutralized. Of course, even if this sum is negative and the leader of i believes the effect of the other nations will be against him, this does not mean that i cannot see value in going to war. If $E(U_i)_b$ is greater than $\sum_{l=1}^{5}$ of $E(U_i)$ for k_l, then the overall expected value of the contemplated war is positive, making its consideration rational.[1]

Expected-Utility Decision Rules

The overall utility that i may expect from initiating a war against j [denoted $E(U_i)$], in the absence of uncertainty, is calculated as follows:

---

[1] Note that the computation and summation of the multilateral lotteries is not based on an interpersonal comparison of utilities because each term of $E(U_i)$ for k_l is theoretically equal to i's perception of each k's expected utility contribution. i, then, is simply comparing his estimate of the utility associated with one k to the utility associated with another k.

$$E(U_i) = E(U_i)_b + \sum_{l=1}^{5} E(U_i)_{k_l} \qquad (6.2)$$

Equation 6.2 simply indicates that i is concerned with the overall expected gains or losses from fighting a war with j, where the overall expected value of the war depends on the relative capability advantage i or j has in the bilateral war (as determined by the P_i terms) and on the likely behavior of third parties to the conflict (as determined by the terms involving k). The support of third parties is neither necessary nor sufficient for i to expect to gain from a war with j, just as the value of the P_i terms alone cannot determine i's expectations. Taken together, however, i can know the expected value of the three risky situations that may arise in war: (a) fighting on its own against its adversary; (b) fighting with the aid of some third parties; and (c) fighting in the face of opposition from some third parties. When the three lotteries . . . are combined, as in equation 6.2, then i knows whether the war is likely to yield gains or losses. In particular, if $E(U_i) > 0$, the war is expected to yield benefits, while if the expected value $E(U_i) < 0$, attacking j is irrational. When $E(U_i) = 0$, i is indifferent, so far as the material calculation is concerned, with respect to attacking or not attacking j. Of course, this calculation only reveals whether minimal, necessary conditions have been satisfied. i must still decide about a number of other considerations, including the "rightness" or "wrongness" of a war with j. War, being a brutalizing and devastating experience, rarely survives as an option once these additional considerations are introduced. For those willing to contemplate attacking another nation, however, *war logically cannot survive as a rational alternative when the value of the expected-utility calculation is less than zero.*

Equation 6.2 depicts the general expected-utility model. However, it does not reflect responses to conditions of risk or uncertainty nor the additional effects of varying levels of risk acceptance among national leaders. Several different decision rules could be specified to reflect the differences between a risk-acceptant and a risk-averse decision maker. . . .

The Independent Variables: Operationalizing Expected Utility

Measuring Probability

The expected-utility equations . . . contain six different probability terms. These are the probability of gaining or losing in a bilateral war (i.e, P_i and $1 - P_i$), the probability of gaining or losing with the aid of friendly nations (P_{ik} and $1 - P_{ik}$), and the probability of gaining or losing when opposed by nations friendly toward one's adversary ($1 - P_{jk}$ and P_{jk}). Each of these is operationalized using the composite national capabilities scores developed by the Correlates of War project. . . .

The composite-capabilities index for each nation provides the basic building block from which I construct the probability estimates required for an empirical investigation of the expected-utility theory. Before explaining how these scores are combined to yield estimates of the probable outcome of a war, however, I must digress to explain how the composite capabilities of a nation are adjusted to reflect the impact of distance.

. . . An adjustment in national capabilities to reflect the debilitating impact of distance must reflect three considerations. First, a nation's power must decline monotonically with distance. (At least, its conventional power must. Nuclear missiles, if anything, are a more powerful source of power far from home than they are close to home because of the potentially lethal effects of radioactive fallout). Second, the rate at which that decline occurs must be greater, the weaker the nation is at home. Third, the rate of decline must itself decline with major advances in technology. Boulding's suggested indicator of a nation's "loss-of-strength gradient" reflects most of these qualities. He suggests adjusting a nation's power by the number of support personnel required to maintain a combat soldier across varying distances from home (Boulding 1962). While an indicator of that sort would be quite acceptable, the necessary data are unfortunately not available. I have therefore devised an alternative indicator.

When I say that technology (or basic national power) affects the transferability of a nation's power over distance, I do not particularly mean that some people can travel a certain number of miles, while others cannot. Instead, I mean that certain nations can transfer and support some of their power, even though the lines of supply and command are stretched across several days' travel time, while others can support forces fewer days from their "home base." Consequently my indicator depends on the number of days it takes to transport a major military operation. Using estimates derived from conversations with officers in the armed forces of the United States and corroborated in my reading of military history, I have defined the transport range for the years 1816–1918 to be 250 miles per day. From 1919 through 1945 I define the range as 375 miles per day, while after 1945 it is 500 miles per day. Of course, small airlifts to anywhere in the world can be completed within one day, but major operations involving naval transport require about one day for each 500 miles traveled. It is estimated, for instance, that it would take the United States ten days to launch a full-scale operation in the Middle East, about 5,000–6,000 miles away (Kissinger 1979).

Distances between nations were computed from several sources, including *Distances between Ports* (U.S. Navy 1965), the *Official Airline Guide* (1978), and a variety of atlases. In each case, I attempted to derive the shortest distance between the locus of power of the potential attacker and the closest point of its intended victim. . . .

Once the distance from each place to each other place was ascertained, national capabilities were computed in the following manner:

Adjusted Capabilities

$$= Composite\ Capabilities^{\ \log\ [(miles/miles\ per\ day)\ +\ (10\ -\ e)]}$$

with the number of miles per day varying as indicated earlier. . . .

Measurement of Utility Values

The indicator(s) of utility must capture the congruence of interests between nations i and j, i and k, and j and k. The congruence of interests among states may be reflected by the general similarity of their behavior across a variety of dimensions. To assess the utility one state's leader has for the foreign policies of another state's leader, one might focus on . . . the similarities and dissimilarities in the alliance commitments of each pair of nations (Singer and Small 1968; Haas 1970; Wallace 1973a; Bueno de Mesquita 1975; Altfeld and Bueno de Mesquita 1979). . . .

Using military alliances as an indicator of national utilities has several merits beyond the potential sensitivity to foreign policy changes. Such alliances are explicit statements about the contingent behavior of one nation toward another in the event of war. As such, they should be particularly reflective of those factors that influence a nation's war-related utility for another nation. Furthermore, with the application of suitable distinctions between types of alliances, formal military agreements are both available and fairly comparable for virtually all pairs of nations for the entire time span under investigation. . . .

Measuring Uncertainty

. . . We should recall that the sign of the expected-utility calculation for a bilateral war depends only on the relative magnitude of the probability terms, while the sign of the two calculations concerning the likely behavior of third parties is determined by the relative value of the utility terms U_{iki} and U_{ikj}. The potential initiator of a war or other serious conflict is assumed to be confident about his estimate of his own nation's capabilities, and also about the capabilities of his potential adversary. What he may be uncertain about is the likely response of other states to the initiation of a war. It is that uncertainty that I hope to identify and measure.

The dyadic utility scores computed with tau B . . . provide a "best estimate" of the congruence of interests between nations as reflected by the similarity of their alliance commitments. Changes in those commitments have the potential to clarify or obscure the level of utility one nation has for another nation's foreign policy. Whether such changes clarify or obscure the expected behavior of potential third parties to wars depends on the context of prior expectations that had been formed. If a set of relations among nations persists unchanged for a long enough time, it should be possible for any decision maker to learn from the actions of states their true level of commitment to one another. If the set of commitments changes in such a way that most relevant relationships are being strengthened by increasing the similarity of relationships, then the leader of *i* is presumed to become more confident about his ability to estimate the likely behavior of each third party to the war he is contemplating. If commitments are shifting toward a decrease in the harmony of interests, then the decision maker may be more uncertain about the expected behavior of third parties in the event of war. . . .

. . . When the set of common interests remains unchanged or increases, it is easier for *i* to discern the likely behavior of other nations. When the set of common interests in the regional subsystem decreases, on the other hand, it is harder for *i* to anticipate the true set of utilities that each state has for others, and hence it is more difficult to anticipate the probable behavior of third parties in the event that *i* attacks *j*. This uncertainty may now be operationalized as the change in the tightness of the system's coalitions during a two-year period ending in the year when *i* is considering attacking *j*. A two-year interval is chosen because it seems long enough for meaningful changes to occur, and yet it is short enough so that the leader in *i* is not likely to have discerned fully all of the implications and meaning of the changed relationships in the system.

When the system's tightness—or the cohesiveness of coalitions— increases or remains unchanged, uncertainty is assumed to be absent, so that decisions are made under conditions of risk, but when the system's tightness declines during a two-year period, culminating in the year in which the expected-utility calculation is being made, then the key leader calculating his nation's utility is alerted to the difficulty inherent in estimating accurately the probable behavior of other states in the event that he chooses to initiate a war against nation *j*. . . .

Expected Utility and Conflict Initiation

I begin my analysis with broad brush strokes, outlining the general tendency for initiators of wars (or serious disputes) to expect to derive positive utility from their actions. Combining Gochman's data on interstate threats and interstate interventions with interstate war data from Singer and Small (which I have updated, using their coding rules, through 1974), I have data on 251 conflict initiators. Of these, 193 by my calculations possessed positive expected utility. Their opponents, on the other hand, had positive expected utility only 39 times. How meaningful is this difference? To answer that question, we must know what the general frequency of positive expected-utility scores is in the population of annual dyads.

Only 14 percent of all dyads have positive expected-utility scores, with that number going up to 38 percent if only the higher risk, regional dyads are counted. Given 251 victims, we should expect about 35 to have positive expected utility based on the worldwide average. Focusing only on regional dyads leads us to expect that about 93 victims will have positive expected utility. Of course, if national leaders do not behave as if they are expected-utility maximizers, we should expect the same frequency of positive expected utility among initiators as in the population of dyads in general. The results cited above clearly bear out the inference that positive expected-utility scores among victims are distributed as one would expect, given the frequency of such scores in the universe of dyads between 1816 and 1974 ($z = .6$, not significant), but the frequency for conflict initiators is radically different. Initiators have positive expected utility far more often than one would expect by chance ($z = 28.6$, $p < .001$).

The results just reported strongly support the proposition that positive expected utility is necessary—though not sufficient—for a leader to initiate a serious international dispute, including a war. This is all the more striking when we examine the initiators and their victims directly, rather than as a proportion of the universe of dyads. Table 6–1 shows the frequency of positive and negative expected-utility scores among war initiators and their opponents, while tables 6–2 and 6–3 present the same analysis for interstate interventions and interstate threats, respectively. In looking over these three tables we should have two expectations. First, positive expected utility should be—within the bounds of measurement error—necessary but not sufficient for states to initiate conflicts. Second, the strength of the relationship should decline as we move from conflictual strategies that involve warfare to those involving lesser levels of conflict and mere threats. After all, threatening action is not the same as taking action. More cases involving threats are likely to be bluffs than are cases involving actual combat. It is relatively easy to back down from a threat without too much loss, but it is very difficult to back down without suffering a serious loss once one has launched a military operation against another state. Consequently, leaders

Table 6–1
Interstate War Initiation and Expected Utility

Expected utility score	Initiator	Opponent
Greater than[a] or equal to zero	65	11
Less than zero	11	65

Note: Yule's $Q = .94$. $\lambda_A = .71$.
[a] Risk-averse states that are weaker than their adversaries are, of course, treated as having negative expected utility.

Table 6–2
Interstate Interventions and Expected Utility

Expected Utility Score	Initiator	Opponent
Greater than[a] or equal to zero	78	14
Less than zero	24	88

Note: Yule's $Q = .91$. $\lambda_A = .63$.

[a] Risk-averse states that are weaker than their adversaries are, of course, treated as having negative expected utility.

are probably less likely to put themselves in a combat situation from which they might have to back down than they are to elect a situation that only involves verbal assaults.

Since the theory stipulates necessary—but not sufficient—conditions for initiating war (or other serious disputes), a measure of one-way association is appropriate for ascertaining how well the data fit the theory. Yule's Q (also known as gamma) is such a measure. Q for table 6–1 is .94. It is .91 for table 6–2, and for interstate threats, Q is .82. Another way of viewing these results is to ascertain how different the distribution of initiator expected-utility scores is from the distribution of positive expected-utility scores in the population of annual dyads. Using chi-square to measure that difference in the distribution of expected-utility scores between the set of interstate war initiators and the total set of dyads reveals that positive expected utility for the war initiators is so much more prevalent than expected by chance that chi-square exceeds 334, indicating an almost infinitesimal likelihood that this difference has occurred by chance. Similarly, for interstate interventions and interstate threats, the chi-square statistics are 331 and 171, respectively. By contrast, the respective chi-square statistics for the distribution of positive expected utility scores among the victims in wars, interventions, and threats relative to the distribution of this attribute in the population of dyads, equal .01, .04, and .88. These results indicate that positive expected utility scores among victims occur about as often as one would expect by chance. In each case the data comply with the expectations derived from the theory. The results of interstate wars and interventions are in fact almost perfect.

Table 6–3
Interstate Threats and Expected Utility

Expected Utility Score	Initiator	Opponent
Greater than[a] or equal to zero	50	13
Less than zero	23	60

Note: Yule's $Q = .82$. $\lambda_A = .51$.

[a] Risk-averse states that are weaker than their adversaries are, of course, treated as having negative expected utility.

Appendix 6–A:
Interstate Wars

Year	Initiator	Opponent	$E(U_i)$	$E(U_j)$	Winner
1823	FRN	SPN	1.951	−1.951	FRN
1827	UK	TUR	1.295	−1.385	UK
1827	FRN	TUR	1.382	−1.508	FRN
1827	RUS	TUR	1.323	−1.323	RUS
1828	RUS	TUR	.379	−1.430	RUS
1846	USA	MEX	.483	−.754	USA
1848	ITA	AUH	−1.496	1.496	AUH
1848	GMY	DEN	1.883	−1.883	GMY
1849	FRN	PAP	.958	−.958	FRN
1851	BRA	ARG	.492	−.492	BRA
1853	TUR	RUS	−.756	1.347	TUR
1856	UK	IRN	1.038	−1.093	UK
1859	AUH	ITA	.583	−.583	ITA
1859	SPN	MOR	1.053	−1.053	SPN
1860	ITA	PAP	.826	−.826	ITA
1860	ITA	SIC	.337	−.337	ITA
1862	FRN	MEX	1.529	−1.989	MEX
1863	COL	ECU	.016	−.016	COL
1864	GMY	DEN	.403	−2.391	GMY
1865	SPN	CHL	.484	−1.055	CHL
1866	GMY	AUH	.000	.000	GMY
1866	GMY	BAD	.000	−.000	GMY
1866	GMY	BAV	.000	−.000	GMY
1866	GMY	SAX	.000	−.000	GMY
1866	GMY	HSE	.000	−.000	GMY
1866	GMY	HSG	.000	−.000	GMY
1866	GMY	WRT	.000	−.000	GMY
1866	GMY	HAN	.000	−.000	GMY
1870	FRN	GMY	.108	−.108	GMY
1877	RUS	TUR	1.076	−1.076	RUS
1885	GUA	SAL	.236	−.236	SAL
1897	GRC	TUR	−.866	.866	TUR
1898	USA	SPN	.620	−.964	USA
1904	JPN	RUS	.102	−.102	JPN
1906	GUA	HON	.501	−.501	GUA
1906	GUA	SAL	.424	−.424	GUA
1907	NIC	HON	−.396	.396	NIC
1907	NIC	SAL	−.510	.510	NIC
1909	SPN	MOR	2.551	−2.551	SPN
1911	ITA	TUR	1.787	−1.861	ITA
1912	YUG	TUR	−.384	.384	YUG
1913	BUL	YUG	.000	.000	YUG
1913	BUL	GRC	.000	.000	GRC
1914	AUH	YUG	2.010	−2.010	YUG
1919	RUM	HUN	.427	−.427	RUM
1919	GRC	TUR	.080	−.080	TUR
1931	JPN	CHN	.010	−.010	JPN
1932	PAR	BOL	−.318	.318	PAR
1935	ITA	ETH	.305	−.369	ITA
1937	JPN	CHN	.042	−.042	JPN
1939	JPN	USR	.029	−.029	USR
1939	JPN	MON	.998	−.953	MON
1939	GMY	POL	.306	−.306	POL
1939	USR	FIN	.842	−.842	USR

1948	EGY	ISR	1.116	−1.116	ISR
1948	IRQ	ISR	.933[a]	−.933	ISR
1948	SYR	ISR	.303	−.303	ISR
1948	LEB	ISR	.252	−.252	ISR
1948	JOR	ISR	.909	−.909	ISR
1950	PRK	ROK	−.209	.209	?[b]
1956	USR	HUN	.018	−.017	USR
1956	ISR	EGY	.013	−.013	ISR
1962	CHN	IND	.611	−.611	CHN
1962	EGY	YEM	.000	−.000	EGY
1962	EGY	SAU	.000	−.000	EGY
1965	IND	PAK	−.005	.005[a]	PAK
1965	RVN	DRV	.846	−.846	DRV
1965	USA	DRV	1.299	−1.153	DRV
1967	ISR	EGY	.312	−.312	ISR
1967	ISR	SYR	.316	−.316	ISR
1967	ISR	JOR	.366	−.366	ISR
1969	SAL	HON	.000	−.000	SAL
1971	IND	PAK	.673	−.673	IND
1973	EGY	ISR	.343	−.343	ISR
1973	SYR	ISR	.722[a]	−.722	ISR
1974	TUR	CYP	1.968	−1.968	TUR

[a] A risk-averse nation that failed to satisfy all of the decision rules for a risk-averse actor.

[b] I was unable to designate one side or the other as the winner.

List of Abbreviations used in Appendix 6-A:

ALB	Albania	GMY	Prussia before 1870;	PAN	Panama
ARG	Argentina		Germany, 1870–1945	PAP	Papal States
AUH	Austria-Hungary	GRC	Greece	PAR	Paraguay
AUL	Australia	GUA	Guatemala	POL	Poland
AUS	Austria	HAN	Hanover	POR	Portugal
BAD	Baden	HOL	Holland	PRK	People's Republic of
BAV	Bavaria	HON	Honduras		Korea (North Korea)
BEL	Belgium	HSE	Hesse Electoral	ROK	Republic of Korea
BOL	Bolivia	HSG	Hesse Gran Ducal		(South Korea)
BRA	Brazil	HUN	Hungary	RUM	Rumania
BUL	Bulgaria	IND	India	RUS	Russia before 1917
BUR	Burma	INS	Indonesia	RVN	Republic of Vietnam
CHL	Chile	IRN	Iran		(South Vietnam)
CHN	China before 1949;	IRQ	Iraq	SAL	El Salvador
	People's Republic	ISR	Israel	SAU	Saudi Arabia
	of China	ITA	Italy after 1860;	SAX	Saxony
COL	Colombia		Sardinia before 1860	SIC	The Two Sicilies
CUB	Cuba	JOR	Jordan	SPN	Spain
CYP	Cyprus	JPN	Japan	SWZ	Switzerland
CZE	Czechoslovakia	KOR	Korea before 1948	SYR	Syria
DEN	Denmark	LAT	Latvia	TAI	Taiwan
DOM	Dominican Republic	LEB	Lebanon	TUN	Tunesia
DRV	Democratic Republic	LIT	Lithuania	TUR	Turkey
	of Vietnam	MAL	Malaysia	UK	United Kingdom
ECU	Ecuador	MEX	Mexico	USA	United States of America
EGY	Egypt	MON	Mongolia	USR	Soviet Union, 1917–
EST	Estonia	MOR	Morocco		present
ETH	Ethiopia	NIC	Nicaragua	VEN	Venezuela
FIN	Finland	NOR	Norway	WRT	Wuerttemberg
FRN	France	NEW	New Zealand	YEM	Yemen
GDR	German Democratic	PAK	Pakistan	YUG	Yugoslavia
	Republic				

Editors' Commentary

Major Findings

Bueno de Mesquita has been in the forefront of applying a deductive approach to the scientific study of war. Such an approach can provide a great deal of **explanatory power.** That is, we can use the assumption that decision makers act as if they seek to maximize benefits and minimize costs to predict the choice they will make when faced with various options. Such an approach is often used to explain, after the fact, why one option was selected over another, although this kind of **post hoc** reasoning is much more prone to error and nonfalsifiability. The explanatory power of rational-choice approaches is considered to be high because, with a single basic assumption, they appear to be able to account for a variety of actions and decisions. For this reason, they have been employed to analyze a number of topics in the social sciences, most prominently in economics.

Explanatory power, however, must not be confused with accuracy. Explanatory power simply means the ability to come up with theoretical answers as to why something happened. These answers or hypotheses must then be tested. Those employing rational choice approaches have sometimes been criticized for neglecting the second part of the process, although that has not been the case with Bueno de Mesquita.

In the book excerpted here, Bueno de Mesquita's explanation and research design are intended only to look at the necessary conditions of war (or dispute) initiation. He does not argue that an expected utility for war will lead to war, only that one side must have an expected utility for war in order for war to occur. Further, he maintains that the side that initiates war or a dispute will be the one with an expected utility score favoring war.

The expected utility scores are intended to reflect the expected gains and losses of going to war. For Bueno de Mesquita, all other factors being equal, gains must exceed losses for war to be initiated. The hypothetical calculations are complex because they are first calculated to determine the net benefit or loss for a dyadic war and then recalculated to see if this outcome is changed by the intervention of third parties on one side or the other as weighted by the probability that intervention will occur.

In the seventy-six wars he looks at, he finds that in sixty-five instances, the war was initiated by the nation that had an expected utility score equal to or greater than one. Only eleven wars were initiated by nations that had an expected utility score of less than zero (table 6–1). This produces a strong association between utility scores and initiation of war: Yule's Q = .94, and the more conservative lambda = .71. The two other tests also produce strong associations, indicating that armed interventions and threat to use armed force tend to be initiated by the nation with an expected utility score greater than or equal to zero.

In each of these two other tests, however, the association goes down, and the number of exceptions increases. For example, there are 24 initiations out of 102 armed interventions that occur when a state has a negative utility (table 6–2). These are exceptions to the proposition and should not occur. Likewise, out of 73 threats, 23 are initiated by states with a negative utility (table 6–3). Although these are deviations, Bueno de Mesquita notes that the deviations increase as the risks lessen. His approach would predict more bluffing as one moves from war to armed intervention to threat. He concludes that his tests support his propositions and are important evidence of the usefulness of his approach.

A close reading of Bueno de Mesquita's operationalizations gives us a better sense of which empirical factors produce a utility for conflict initiation. First, and probably most important, wars are initiated by the side with more capability (as discounted by distance). Second, tightening alliance commitments in the system make war more likely if other factors push toward war, since tightening eliminates uncertainty. We also know from a previous study by Bueno de Mesquita (1978) that there is a correlation between the tightness of the alliance structure in the system and the onset of war, at least for the twentieth century. One of the major contributions of Bueno de Mesquita's analysis is that he provides a precise model of how leaders might calculate the relative influence of capability, geographical distance, and alliance commitments in deciding whether to initiate war. Such a model, however, must be seen as a theoretical analysis of what *in effect* leaders do and not as a historical description of their actual thought processes.

What do Bueno de Mesquita's findings mean in light of the other findings in this part of the book? Since they are findings about the necessary conditions of war, they must not be confused with the proposition that war starts because one side has a stronger capability than another. If one were to calculate the difference in capability or the expected utility for war for all dyads in the system, one would end up predicting war between most dyads. Disparity in capability does not produce wars.

Bueno de Mesquita's findings tell us something only about who is likely to initiate wars, once other factors bring about a war situation. It makes sense that once a war is likely, the side with the greater capability and commitment from allies will try to initiate it, and the side with less capability and weaker commitment from allies will try to delay the start of war. If there is going to be a war, each side would want to make last-minute calculations about the likelihood of winning and act accordingly. Bueno de Mesquita's analysis can be seen as providing important information that is relevant to the timing of wars once other factors have pushed leaders toward a decision for war.

Methodological Notes

Bueno de Mesquita's method can be distinguished from those used in the other articles in this book by the fact that he expresses his theory in mathematical terms, much like the axioms of geometry. The difference from geometry, of course, is that he is talking about the empirical world and must test his deductions. Bueno de Mesquita both produces a mathematically expressed "formal" theory and tests it statistically.

The formal part of the theory involves expressing the expected utility of a state for initiating war with another actor. All one needs to do is to get used to reading $E(U)$ as expected utility, i as the initiator nation, and j as the opponent. The mathematical relationship being explored is whether the initiator has an expected utility in initiating war that is positive (> 0) or negative (< 0). While the equations appear abstract, one needs only remember that they are statements about how a nation calculates its position relative to a rival.

Equally important is the test of the theory, and this is quite easy to comprehend. In order to test his theory, Bueno de Mesquita must operationalize his variables. Expected utility is measured in terms of a nation's military, industrial, and demographic capabilities combined into a capabilities index. Utility values are measured as military alliances, which indicate not only how similar two nations' interests are but how much a nation is willing to commit for those shared interests.

Factoring in a measure of uncertainty based on system tightness and a measure of the willingness of leaders to take risks, Bueno de Mesquita constructs an index of expected utility. When that index is greater than zero, he predicts that that side will be the initiator of the war. To test this idea, he predicts that initiators as a group will more frequently possess a positive utility score than targets. This, in fact, happens in his sample far more often than would be expected by chance, meaning that the difference between the number of initiators with positive expected utility and the number of targets with positive expected utility is statistically significant ($p < .001$). The Yule's Q of .94 and the lambda (λ) of .71 in table 6–1 show that there is a strong relationship between a positive expected utility and initiation of war. Similarly, the tendency to engage in intervention and threats is also positively linked to positive expected utility (tables 6–2 and 6–3). Finally, as indicated by chi square, these findings are statistically significant. Nations generally do not initiate a war unless they have a positive expected utility.

These are impressive associations, but one of the problems with Bueno de Mesquita's analysis has been that, while expected utility can predict the initiator for most wars, it fails to predict the victor in important cases (as in World War I and World War II). Although in the aggregate, it is generally true that those that initiate wars tend to win, this has not really held since 1911. Karl Deutsch (1980:292) reports that from 1816 to 1965, about 80 percent of all interstate wars were won by those that initiated them, but from 1911 to 1965, only about 40 percent of the war initiators were victorious, while about 60 percent lost.

One of the reasons Bueno de Mesquita's findings differ from those of Deutsch is the use of a different aggregation of time periods; a more important difference, and one of the criticisms of the research design, has been his treatment of his cases. Some wars, like the Seven Weeks' War, generate a number of dyadic cases (see appendix 6–A) that inflate the number of cases supporting his propositions. Other wars, like World War I and World War II (for technical reasons that Bueno de Mesquita [1981b:100] explains in his book), are treated as simple dyadic cases between Austria-Hungary and Serbia and between Germany and Poland (see appendix 6–A). This undercounts deviant cases but also has led some critics to argue that this procedure reflects the inability of expected utility to explain world war adequately. (For additional criticisms on the ability of expected utility to predict victory, see Maoz 1983, 1990:ch. 8; Ray and Vural 1986.)

Expected utility approaches have attracted considerable attention in the last few years. In part this is because they provide a parsimonious framework that can factor different variables, like distance, uncertainty, and risk, into a basic cost-benefit approach. Since this approach is similar to aspects of microeconomics, it also allows analysts to draw upon the theory and techniques of an older discipline to overcome problems.

The more general approach of rational choice has also been subjected to a number of criticisms. It has been argued that the assumption that states and individuals maximize benefits and minimize costs as their primary goals is unrealistic and that political actors do not actually make elaborate cost-benefit calculations. The response to such criticism is that it does not matter if these assumptions are empirically accurate; all that is important is that the theory is able to predict behavior accurately and explain it by assuming that decision makers act as if they were rational calculators (even if they are not). The problem with this defense is that it implicitly recognizes that a theory that could explain and predict as well as a rational choice theory but at the same time accurately describe the process by which decisions are made would be superior. Hence, numerous scholars are constructing historically informed explanations of foreign policymaking based on cognitive psychology or organization theory. Such explanations have not been any less successful than rational choice explanations, thereby suggesting that such unrealistic assumptions about "rationality" may not be necessary.

The criticism on assumptions has led to the charge that rational choice is not so much an empirical theory as it is a philosophy of decision making. In this sense, rational choice can be seen as a guide to how decision makers *should* behave. Clearly, if they were to behave in this way, the theory would be an accurate description and explanation of behavior. Thus, as decision makers become socialized to make decisions in this manner, rational choice theory becomes prone to a self-fulfilling prophecy. This implies that decision makers' behavior can be explained by rational choice only so long as decision makers accept the idea and philosophy of rational choice.

Recently this has led some scholars to maintain that the true function of rational choice theory, like most other theories, is to act as a social construction of reality—that is, to turn ideas into reality by making people and institutions behave in accordance with those ideas. In this sense, rational choice is seen as part of a long process by which the culture of modernity, with its emphasis on individualism and capitalist economic arrangements, has been imposed on the world by the West. From this perspective, rational choice is not the way all people behave in history, nor is it necessarily the best way or even a good way of making decisions. Rather, it is simply the preferred way modern bureaucratic culture has had for making decisions.

II
The Expansion of War

7
Alliances and the Expansion of War

Randolph M. Siverson
Joel King

Editors' Introduction

The second part of this book treats a different dependent variable, the expansion of war. The first entry, by Randolph Siverson and Joel King, explores why some wars are large while most others are fought between only two states. Richardson (1960b:249) had shown that wars are typically fought between only two states (dyadic wars); relatively few wars involve more than three states. In this article, Siverson and King are not concerned with what causes war but why war spreads once it breaks out. They find that alliances are associated with large wars and may in fact act as a contagion mechanism to help them spread. This implies that if war breaks out in a system characterized by many alliance bonds, it is more likely spread than a war that breaks out in a system where there are no alliances.

Introduction

Despite differences in data sets, several investigators of international war have reported some strikingly similar findings. One of these similarities is a

Reprinted from *To Augur Well*, edited by J. David Singer and Michael D. Wallace (Sage Publications, 1979), pp. 37–49. Reprinted by permission of the senior editor and the senior author.

Authors' note: The authors wish to express their appreciation to Ann Sturgeon King for her valuable research assistance and to Ole R. Holsti for his helpful comments. An earlier version of this chapter was presented at the Annual Meeting of the International Studies Association, Washington, D.C., February 22–25, 1978.

161

recurrent pattern in the magnitude of warfare in the international system, often observed as cyclical fluctuations in the nation-months of war within a given period. Although the precise length of the cycles differs from investigation to investigation, they have been observed by Wright (1965), Denton (1966), Moyal (1949), and Singer and Small (1972). However, relatively little has been said about the explanation of these "clusters" of warfare. Thus far research has tended to *eliminate* explanations. For example, Singer and Small (1972:188–202) demonstrate that the peaks are not associated with any secular increase in the amount of warfare, once controls are introduced for the number of nations in the international system. Similarly, Singer and Small (1972:205) and Richardson (1960b:128–132) present findings which clearly indicate that these sharp peaks in nation-months of war are not the result of many wars breaking out at the same time.

If, however, one makes a distinction between the war (as historically named) and the behavior of the units of which it is composed, some recent research points to an avenue which might profitably be taken in investigating the peaks of warfare. Davis, Duncan, and Siverson (1978), using a variety of stochastic models, demonstrate that during the period of 1815–1965 the outbreak of *dyadic* warfare has been heavily influenced by a contagious process. This means that initiation of hostilities within one dyad *increases the probability* that other dyads will begin fighting. In other words, dyadic wars may spread, and this may reach such proportions that a large war results.

However, even a cursory examination of the historical record reveals that not all wars expand. While some wars begin by attracting a large number of participants, or add them later, other wars remain limited in size, never growing beyond a small initial number of combatants. Hence, the problem is to identify the factors influencing war *contagion*. Can we construct indicators which can help in forecasting whether a potential war will remain small or become large?

Thus far, there has not been an *explicit* and systematic attempt to account for war *expansion;* rather, the research has tended to treat size as one indicator of the *occurrence* of war. The point we wish to make is that occurrence and size are very different attributes and that the process generating the size of a war may well be an *extension* of the process that starts wars rather than the same thing. If this is the case, then the indicators useful in forecasting the *occurrence* of war may not be the same as those needed to forecast the potential *size* of the war.

There are, of course, a number of variables in international politics which have been hypothesized as agents for, or early warning indicators of, the spread of war. One certainly is geography, which has received recent attention in a variety of guises. Starr and Most (1976) provide an exciting new conceptualization of the role of borders in the spread of conflict.[1] Using three data sets which provide measures of various types and levels of international conflict since 1945, they demonstrate that common borders have an impact upon the spread of war. Blainey (1973:232), although operating without hard data, evokes the venerable "heartland" geographic metaphor when he asserts that "a war was more likely to widen if it began near the hub of Europe."

The factor to which we shall direct our attention here is the network of alliance bonds among states. Unlike geography, alliances are the outcome of deliberate choices in which nations make commitments to each other. Thus, decision makers can manipulate alliances, and it is not unreasonable to believe that these manipulations indicate commitments held by decision makers. One may reasonably investigate, then, the extent to which these commitments draw nations into wars.

Several observers of alliance politics have commented upon the entangling nature of alliances. Yet by no means does there exist a consensus about the effects of alliances upon the spreading of war. While Ball and Killough (quoted in Holsti et al. 1973:274) assert that alliances "make it more probable that a localized war will spread," there are an ample number of contradictory assertions in the literature. For example, George Liska, a prominent alliance theorist, concludes that "in themselves, alliances neither limit nor expand conflicts" (Liska 1962:138). Similarly, Blainey (1973:229) observes that it is "doubtful whether it [the alliance hypothesis] fits many general wars."

If conjectural theorizing is somewhat equivocal concerning the war-spreading impact of alliances, is there any evidence relevant to this problem in the recent *empirical* studies of alliances and war? The answer here is affirmative, but, because of some important conceptual differences, the evidence, at least at this point, is both limited and circumstantial.

In an early study, Singer and Small (1968) found that in the period 1900–1945 the percentage of nations in any alliance and the percentage of nations in defense pacts produced moderate correlations (.53 and .43, respectively) with the nation-months of war.[2] For the same variables, the results from the period 1815–1899 are slightly negative ($-$ .16 each). Hence the nature and extent of this relationship is unclear. Still, the correlations for the 1900–1945 period are suggestive of a relationship between alliances and the magnitude of war.

More recently, Wallace (1973a) uncovered some strong curvilinear relationships between his measure of alliance polarity and nation-months of

---

[1] Also on borders and war participation, see Wesley (1962) and Richardson (1960b).

[2] In their research design, alliance data from year t were correlated with warfare data which were the sum of t, t + 1 and t + 3 (p. 275).

war. Wallace interpreted his findings as supporting the proposition that "war is more probable both at very low and at very high levels of polarization" (1973a:597). But since Wallace's dependent variable was not war frequency, but nation-months of war, it would appear that high and low levels of polarization increase the magnitude of war and not necessarily its frequency. Moreover, Wallace's results were strong for three of the periods he examined (i.e., 1815–1964, 1815–1944, and 1850–1964) but not for 1815–1919; in this last case the R^2 was only .15, as compared to .61, .70, and .60, respectively, for the other three. Thus, as in the Singer and Small study, the relationship between alliance and war remains clouded during the period typically described as being dominated by the balance of power. Still, the overall results appear to portray a relationship between alliance polarization and nation-months of war which cannot be neglected. With reference to the problem considered here, if one focuses on the end of the curve describing high polarization and large war, it is reasonable to speculate that the alliances constituting this polarization may not *themselves* start wars. Rather, they may be responsible for increasing the *probability* that a war will spread, thus driving up the nation-months of war for the system as a whole. The middle of the curve (moderate polarity) could be interpreted as nations with alliances being restrained from warfare by cross-cutting alliances. The low end of the polarization, war curve should, we believe, be interpreted with considerable caution since the relationship is weakest in that period (1815–1919) which probably had the lowest overall polarization.

In a later paper Singer and Small (1974:290–294) examined at least one aspect of alliances as agents of war contagion in a very direct way. Specifically, they explored the question, "does high alliance involvement on the eve of war make a nation less likely to be *drawn into that war?*" (p. 290, emphasis added). In probing this question they constructed two tables displaying the frequency with which *major* powers (1) *belonged* to alliances and then entered into war and (2) *joined* alliances and then entered into war. The Q statistic, a measure of correlation for 2 × 2 tables,[3] for these was .02 and .18, respectively. On the basis of these relationships it would appear that alliance membership has virtually no impact upon war entry and that alliance initiation has only a very slight effect. These results are certainly not supportive of the idea that alliances are related to war size, but as we will demonstrate below, there are other aspects of this relationship which require further investigation.[4]

Finally, Sabrosky's (1975) analysis of the 1908–1909 Bosnian crisis and the 1914 crisis appears to be relevant. Sabrosky's analytical purpose

---

[3] See note 8 below.

[4] In fairness to Singer and Small, it must be emphasized that they were not directly investigating the same general problem which is of interest to us. Their central goal was evaluating the accuracy of the assumptions and prescriptions of a policy document.

was to trace out the changes in European international politics which took place between these two crises, allowing the first to be contained, but precipitating the explosion of World War I in the second. One of the factors examined by Sabrosky was the changes which took place in the European alliance structure between the two crises. He concluded that "If there is a prolonged period of alliance aggregation around the same contending power centers . . . then the system may become both more crisis-prone and more war-prone." He does not, however, explicitly address the extent to which alliances had a direct impact upon the expansion of the Serbian crisis from a two-party (Serbia and Austria-Hungary) to a multiparty conflict. In fact, while noting the "consensus among diplomatic historians to the effect that, without these alliances, the initial Austria-Serbian war probably would have remained limited to those two states" Sabrosky asserted that the effect of alliances on expansion is uncertain (p. 6).

Hence existing empirical research suggests some circumstantial support for the hypothesis that alliances spread war. Two studies which indirectly link alliances to the expansion of war yield results which are at least partially consistent with the hypothesis. The other studies we have examined are at least not inconsistent with the hypothesis.

The Problem

The central concern of the analysis which follows is the relationship between alliances and expansion of war. Is it the case that alliances among nations serve as a network for spreading war and conflict? If so, then the existence of these networks may well serve as an early warning indicator of a possible large war if and when nations within the network(s) become involved in a situation of conflict. Previous research seeking to connect alliances with war has measured various attributes of alliances in each *year;* the "alliance-year" was thus the unit of analysis. It has then attempted to investigate the impact of each variable on some measure of warfare for some selected $t, t+_1, t+_2, \ldots, t+_n$. In essence, research of this type has attempted to assess the impact of alliances as causal factors in the *start* of war. Our interest is in assessing the effect of alliance membership on war involvement once a war has begun; specifically, to what extent do preexisting alliance involvements produce *larger* wars? Therefore, our unit of analysis will be the individual nation at the time of the outbreak of war in the system.

The measures of warfare characteristics in the various works mentioned above have typically been frequency, magnitude, and/or severity. From our perspective it would seem that alliances should be related to magnitude, and not frequency or severity. However, magnitude has usually been measured as the number of nation-months of war in a given year. Thus, it measures two analytically separate concepts, the *duration* of the war and the *size* of the war.[5] If alliances act as agents of infectious contagion, it is clear that alliance patterns should be related to *size* of a war; it is not clear why there should be any relationship between alliances and the *length* of a war. Our interest in the size of opposing war coalitions is intimately related to this, since by definition the size of any war is the sum of the numbers in the two opposing camps.

The Data

The data we will use in this study have been compiled by Singer's Correlates of War Project (Singer 1972). The data on national war participation are presented in great detail in Singer and Small's *The Wages of War* (1972). Basically, these data describe and measure armed conflicts having at least 1,000 fatalities which occurred between 1815 and 1965.[6] Our use of the data will be restricted to that on inter*state* wars; this limit is occasioned by the fact that in the alliance data only agreements made by states are included, so our population of war participants should be similarly limited.

The alliance data are drawn from Sabrosky's (1980) revision of Singer and Small's (1966b, 1968) earlier lists. In general, this list includes all formal alliances between national political units meeting Singer and Small's (1974:19–22) criteria for membership in the international system. The alliances collected in the data are of a politico-military nature dealing with (1) mutual defense, (2) agreements to consult, or (3) neutrality. At this point in our research we shall treat these three types of alliance as equivalent. The reasoning behind this decision is that all alliances imply some commitment between or among nations. This commitment frequently goes beyond the strict legal confines of the treaty which codifies it; alliances can grow and expand or they may decay. Our expectation, however, is that regardless of type, all alliances have *some* influence on the probability that a nation will become "entangled" in a war once it begins. It must be added that we include only alliances which existed *before* any member became involved in war. Hence, we specifically exclude any alliance formed *during* war.

Data Analysis

We begin by asking two questions about each nation existing in the international system at the time a war begins. First, did the nation participate in

---

[5] The terms alliance and coalition are frequently used as synonyms. In this chapter we will refer to prewar groups as alliances and groups emerging in the war as coalitions.

[6] To be included as participants in a war, nations were required to have had 1,000 combatants in the war area.

Table 7–1
Alliance Membership and War Participation, 1815–1965

War participants?	Alliance membership?	
	No	Yes
No	1399	974
Yes	88	100

N = 2561
Q = .24

the war? Second, did the nation have an existing alliance commitment at least three months prior to the outbreak of the war?[7] This double classification produces the cross-tabulation shown in table 7–1 The data in this table reveal a positive relationship (Q = .24), but it is not very strong.[8] In fact, it is clear from the table that having an alliance at the time a war breaks out has only a modest impact upon whether or not a nation will become involved in the war. Of the nations having alliances, 9.3 percent participated in war, while 5.9 percent of the nations *not* having alliances participated. This table shows that alliance membership does have an impact upon war participation, and that a slim majority of war participants (53.2 percent) had prewar alliances. However, it also indicates that in the vast majority of cases (974), nations having alliances at the time a war erupted did not become entangled and drawn into the war.

It should be noted that this table is somewhat similar to two used by Singer and Small in their assessment of predictors of war in history (1974:293) and briefly mentioned above. However, their data are different in two significant respects. First, their analysis is restricted to major actors only. Second, they use all nation-years between 1815 and 1965, while our analysis focuses only on the time after a war has broken out. Thus Singer and Small are addressing the question of whether alliances are associated with the *occurrence* of war rather than war contagion, even though their stated question is "does high alliance involvement on the *eve* of war make a nation less likely to be drawn into that war?" (p. 290, emphasis added). The inclusion of all years essentially avoids the question of contagion.

To return to table 7–1, it may be argued, however, that the conceptualization of the international system implied by this table is naive. The tabulation of *all* alliance members against *all* war participants implies that

---

[7] Since we are interested in each distinct war, those wars beginning in the same year were treated separately and not simply aggregated.

[8] Yule's Q is used in our analysis of 2 × 2 tables. Its use permits not only a summary measure of the strength of relationship, but also allows comparisons among tables. Although there has been some criticism of Q as a measure (Blalock 1960:298), recent work in the area of categorical data analysis indicates that the alternatives are all inferior to Q (Davis 1971; Feinberg 1977).

a war between any two nations is equally relevant to all other nations. Can we reasonably expect a war involving one alliance to have an equal impact upon *all* nations and alliances no matter how distant? For example, should we expect the war between Spain (unallied) and Peru and Bolivia (allied before and during the war) in 1879 to have drawn in the other aligned nations (United Kingdom, Germany, Austria-Hungary, and Turkey), even though none had an alliance with a belligerent? To make such an assumption for *all* nations would be inappropriate even in today's interdependent world. An alternative view of the international system, focusing upon the direct, observable linkages among nations, would lead us to reformulate our measure of the independent variable (alliance membership). Our concern is not alliance membership per se, but whether or not a nation has an alliance with one or more of the *belligerents* participating in the war.

Table 7–2 presents the relationship between war participation and this new alliance variable. From this table it is evident that having an alliance with a belligerent is a much stronger predictor of war participation than mere alliance membership. Of the 2,263 cases of nations not aligned with a belligerent, only 5 percent became involved in war, while 25.2 percent of the 298 cases in which nations had alliances with belligerents show participation. A nation having an alliance with a belligerent is five times more likely to become involved in war. The measure of association for this table is Q = .73, indicating a strong relationship.

One of the continuing problems of the research on the relationship between alliances and war has been the over time instability of the relationship between the variables. Singer and Small (1968) found a negative relationship between their variables in the nineteenth century and a positive relationship in the twentieth century, while Wallace, who was able to report strong correlations, found only a very poor fit for the model during the period 1815–1919. In view of the instability of relationship in these previous findings it could be suspected that the strong relationship in table 7–2 might be similarly altered if the data were divided into nineteenth and twentieth century subperiods. The results of such a division are shown in table 7–3. The findings for the two centuries are not only similar to each other, but also (as should then follow) to the distributions in table 7–2. This

Table 7–2
Alliance Partnership with Belligerents and War Participation, 1815–1965

War participation?	Alliance partnership with belligerent?	
	No	Yes
No	2150	233
Yes	113	75

N = 2561
Q = .73

similarity is reflected in the magnitudes of the associations in the tables. For table 7–3a (1815–1899) Q = .76 and for 7–3b (1900–1965) Q = .72. Clearly, therefore, the results do not reflect the instability of relationship which has plagued previous research.

Tables 7–1 through 7–3, but most particularly 7–2 and 7–3, indicate relationships between alliance membership and war participation which are consistent with alliances as agents of infection. Having an alliance with a belligerent on the eve of war clearly increases a nation's probability of being involved in that war. There are, however, some aspects of this which deserve further attention. While the data above are consistent with the hypothesis that alliances are agents of infection, they could *also* be interpreted as merely supporting the generalization that nations with alliances are more war-prone than nations without alliances.

To rule out this alternative interpretation, we need to examine the relationships between the size of each *wartime coalition* and the *prewar alliance* status of its members. As shown in table 7–1, some 88 nations (or 46.8 percent) of the 188 war participants had no alliance prior to their participation in war. Thus, in almost half of the cases, something other than alliances was responsible for war participation. However, if alliances increase the probability of a war coalition growing, the absence of alliances should tend to limit participation in a war coalition. Hence, it may be expected that if two nations with no alliances initiate a war, there is a lower probability of the war spreading than if two nations with allies were to begin fighting. Consequently, we may hypothesize that most of the 88 war participants without prewar allies fought without partners, while the 100 war participants with prewar alliances would probably fight within war

Table 7–3
Alliance Partnership with Belligerents and War Participation

a. 1815–1899

War Participation?	Alliance with Belligerent?	
	No	Yes
No	953	55
Yes	54	23

N = 1085
Q = .76

b. 1900–1965

War Participation?	Alliance with Belligerent?	
	No	Yes
No	1197	168
Yes	59	52

N = 1474
Q = .72

coalitions. Table 7–4 reports the number of nations participating in war with and without coalition partners according to whether or not they had alliances prior to the war. Clearly the table bears out our hypothesis. Nations without alliances account for the majority of war participation without partners, and nations with alliances account for a similar amount of participation in war as part of a coalition. The Yule's Q value of .64 indicates a moderately strong relationship.

The data contained in table 7–4 are amenable to a somewhat more sensitive analysis. While keeping the independent variable, prewar alliance membership, in categorical form, we can subcategorize the war coalition variable according to the size of the coalition and conduct a one-way analysis-of-variance (ANOVA). In this analysis we would predict a relationship between prewar alliance status and the size of the war-time coalition. Table 7–5 reports the results of the ANOVA. While the F ratio is of sufficient size ($F = 8.868$) to make the differences between the two groups significant, η, the correlation ratio (Freeman 1965:120–130) is only .213, indicating a rather weak relationship between prewar alliance status and the size of war coalition in which a nation participates. Given the apparent strength of the relationship shown in table 7–4, the greatly diminished relationship when the more sensitive dependent variable is used is, to say the least, disconcerting. To understand why this happens, a visual tabulation of the data used in table 7–5 is needed.

Table 7–6 shows such a tabulation and it is revealing. This table contains an interesting pattern; considering only the first seven categories (war coalitions having less than 11 members), the data are highly consistent with the hypothesis that alliance membership tends to produce large war coalitions. But in the last three categories, containing war coalitions of 11, 14, and 18 members, the impact of alliance upon the size of the war coalition is less in each respective case. An empirical description of the process in table 7–6 would appear to be one in which alliance has a strong impact upon the size of a war coalition up to a certain point, but as these war coalitions grow larger, the impact lessens and other factors draw in participants.

Without at this time entering into a formal analysis of these three coalitions, it may be mentioned that they are, respectively, the allied coali-

Table 7–4
Alliance Membership and War Coalition, 1815–1965

War Coalition?	Alliance Membership?	
	No	Yes
No	52	24
Yes	36	76

$$N = 188$$
$$Q = .64$$

Table 7–5
Analysis of Variance of War Coalition Size

	Average Size of War Coalition		
	No Alliance 4.08	*Pre-war Alliance* 6.5	
Source of Variation	*Σ of Squares*	*df*	*Mean Squares*
Between (alliance status)	281.07	1	281.07
Within (error)	5895.35	186	31.70

F = 8.868.
P = .0033.
η = .213.

tions of World War I, Korea, and World War II. The last two cases are somewhat complicated. In Korea many nations joined the coalition under the auspices of the United Nations. In a sense a case could be made for dropping this coalition from the analysis because of the confounding influence of the UN. However, at this point, it would appear premature to do so. In the case of World War II, the allied coalition contained a number of unwilling participants (e.g., Holland, Belgium, Norway) which were not aligned prior to the war, as well as nations which were not aligned but shared a broad sense of community with the United Kingdom (i.e., South Africa, Canada, New Zealand, Australia).

Table 7–6
Cross-tabulation of Alliance Status and War Coalition Size

Size of War Coalition	*Pre-war Alliance* *Status of Nations*		*Total*
	No Allies	*Allies*	
1	52	24	76
2	10	10	20
3	3	9	12
4	7	9	16
5	0	5	5
7	0	7	7
9	0	9	9
11	2	9	11
14	6	8	14
18	8	10	18
Total	88	100	

Summary and Conclusions

In this chapter we have attempted to explore the possibility that the process of infectious contagion which characterizes war initiation between 1815 and 1965 (Davis, Duncan, and Siverson 1978) was influenced by the prewar alliances linking war coalition members. The evidence is not conclusive, but is consistent with such an hypothesis. As we have seen above, nations with alliances are more war-prone than nations without alliances (tables 7–1 through 7–3). Nations having alliances with belligerents are more likely to participate in wars than nations not having alliances, or those having alliances but not with a belligerent. Thus there is some level of "attraction." More specifically, there is a strong relationship between the existence of a war coalition and the alliance status of the coalition members prior to the war. War participation without coalition partners tends to be characteristic of nations having no prewar allies, while war coalitions tend to be made up predominantly of prewar allies (table 7–4). However, as the final table clearly indicates, *very* large war coalitions appear to be the outcome of alliances *and* other factors.

One relevant theoretical point should be discussed briefly in conclusion. The above findings may be interpreted as indicating that large and small wars are the outcomes of related but different processes. In particular, what the analysis above seems to suggest is that *without* alliance linkages wars tend to remain small, but given these linkages, wars tend to become large. Hence the *size* of a war may be the outcome of an extension of the process producing the *occurrence* of a war. Consider the fact that in 19 of the 50 wars between 1815 and 1965 (38 percent) neither party (or parties) on either side had prewar alliances. These also tended to be very small wars, with all but three being dyadic, and the three nondyadic wars containing only three parties each. What did alliances have to do with the *start* of these wars? Our research, of course, does not focus upon this question, but it may be said that the absence of alliance partners probably helped constrain their size. We will return to a variation of this point in discussing some possible directions for further research.

There are at least two avenues that further investigation should explore. The first relates to the role of geography. Recall our earlier observation that geography may also be involved in the contagion process. Yet this variable does not appear to explain who will fight whom, but rather, at best, only who will fight at all. To put the point in the context of a historical example, consider the Franco-Prussian War and World War I. In both cases the geography was roughly the same, but the coalitions were quite different. Prior to the outbreak of war in 1870 France had no allies and fought alone, but in 1914 she had allies a'plenty. In view of this, future research examining the impact of geography may have to be recast to take account of alliance configurations.

At least one additional problem may be identified. From table 7–2 it may be seen that many nations having alliances with belligerents did not end up entering the war. Clearly, there exist limits to the influence of alliance on the "drawing in" of nations. If we are to understand fully the nature of alliances as war-spreading networks, it is of critical importance that these limits be investigated. Since the present research indicates that alliances influence the size of a war, it is not unreasonable to begin research on this subject by looking at the characteristics of the alliances themselves (e.g., the age and size of the alliance) and the alliance attributes of the various nations (e.g., did a nation have more than one alliance?) as predictors of whether or not a nation will enter a war; we are currently at work on this problem.

If progress can be made in this area, then it is possible that data on alliances can serve not only to identify the networks for the spread of war, but also to estimate the limits of that spread as well. Such a capability may be useful to decision makers engaged in crisis and conflict management. Past studies of crisis and conflict management have focused almost exclusively on limiting escalation; expansion has largely been ignored. The reason for this is probably that crisis studies have generally attempted to explain a given historical process in which the participants are known at the outset. Hence studies of the pre–World War I crisis, a classic case of escalation, have devoted almost no attention to an explicit consideration of how a local crisis and war expanded into a much larger conflagration. Decision makers charged with crisis or conflict management may consider the problem of expansion. Ultimately we hope that data on alliances or other commitments will lead to ready identification of the probable extent of crisis or conflict expansion. If the initial explosion cannot be stopped, at least an understanding of the possibilities for contagion might help decision makers avoid widening violence.

Editors' Commentary

Major Findings

Siverson and King find that alliances may play an important role in determining whether a war will be fought by two parties or a coalition. To demonstrate this, they begin their analysis by dividing wars into two categories—those fought by two parties and those fought by a coalition (table 7–4)—and then ask what separates the larger wars from dyadic wars. They predict that wars of coalition will have been preceded by alliances, whereas belligerents in dyadic wars will tend not to have had prewar alliances.

To test the hypothesis that alliances precede wars of coalition but not dyadic wars, Siverson and King identify 188 instances between 1815 and 1965 in which a state participates in war. (Note that these 188 cases are not wars. There are only 50 inter-state wars in their study, but these 50 wars involve 188 instances of a state fighting in a war). They find that when states fight alone (no war coalition), most of the participants did not have a prewar alliance (52 participants did not have a prewar alliance, and only 24 did). Conversely, when states fight in coalition, they frequently have a prewar alliance (76 participants did, while 36 did not). This distribution produces a Yule's Q of .64 (table 7–4).

These findings do not mean that every time there are alliances in the system, world wars will break out. This clearly could not be the case since there have been many alliances but only a few world wars. Rather, the findings imply that *if* war breaks out when there are many alliance bonds in the system, those that are not imme-diately involved in the war but are allied with one of the bellig-erents may be dragged into the war. Put another way, a system with extensive alliances is more likely to have wars that spread than a system with few alliances. In their conclusion, Siverson and King point out that of the nineteen wars in which neither party had a prewar alliance, all but three were fought dyadically. Fur-thermore, these three nondyadic wars remained very small, with only one additional state being dragged in.

These findings suggest that alliances may act as a contagion mechanism by which wars spread and expand. Alliances, then, not only fail to ensure peace, as Levy's (1981) evidence shows, but may actually spread war once it breaks out. Not all alliances do this, however, which means that certain kinds of alliances are more prone to spreading war than others. In a follow-up study, Siverson and King (1980) identify some of the characteristics of alliances that are dangerous.

Methodological Notes

The Siverson and King article uses Yule's Q and one-way ANalysis Of VAriance (ANOVA) to analyze the role of alliances in the expansion of war. Let us take a close look at what these statistics can tell us.

First, it is important to stress what indicators are used. Sta-tistical studies of war use a variety of indicators to measure wars, but it is important to note that Siverson and King are concerned with the size of a war, as indicated by the number of participants. While other studies take the year as the unit of analysis and code it for variables such as the amount of alliance aggregation, this study uses the nation at the time war breaks out as the unit of analysis. The data are comprised of a list of the nations that exist in the international system whenever war breaks out, meaning that a given nation can appear more than once (each time war occurs). With an average over the 1816–1965 period of about 51 nations in the system and 50 cases of interstate war, 2,561 cases of nations that exist when war breaks out are generated. Of the 2,561 cases, 188 cases are nations that participate in the war and 2,373 are nations that do not participate.

If you have completed the learning package in chapter 15, you know how to calculate Yule's Q and when to use it. As Siverson and King point out, it is arguably the best statistic for categorical (nominal level) two-by-two contingency tables. Table 7–1 reports only a weak relationship between alliances and war ($Q = .24$), but when the authors look at alliances with belligerents, the findings are much higher ($Q = .73$ in table 7–2; Q .76 and .72 in table 7–3). Since the associations are so impressive, it is appropriate to take a closer look at the cell entries in the contingency tables to discover how they affect the magnitude of Q.

While the use of Yule's Q is valid here, the statistic can be inflated when one cell (as opposed to two) is very large. This is not a factor in table 7–1; cells a and b are both very large, and the Yule's Q is quite low (.24). However, in tables 7–2 and 7–3, cell a is way out of proportion to the other cells. In other words, by far most of the nations in the system when the various wars break out are involved in neither alliances with belligerents nor wars. While this fact increases the association between alliance activity and war, the fact that so many nations are involved in neither does not tell us that much about what happens when a nation *is* involved in an alliance.

The next set of findings provides something of a response to this concern. Looking at just the 188 war participants, Siverson and King explore the hypothesis that alliances lead to wider wars. Here the findings are unambiguous: most of the dyadic wars are fought by participants that did not have prewar alliances, and most of the wars fought by coalitions had as their members nations with prewar alliances. The Yule's Q here is .64, lower than the earlier findings, but given the distribution of cases among the cells, it can be interpreted with confidence as indicating a solid moderate relationship.

For the final set of findings, the authors use one-way analysis of variance (ANOVA). *Variance* is the measure of the distance of each case from a regression line and can be analyzed only when a variable goes up and down by equal degrees, or intervals. When both variables are interval, we can use Pearson's *r* and regression, but when only one variable is interval, we use a statistic called eta (η), also known as the correlation ratio, that describes the relationship between a nominal-level independent variable and the variance in an interval-level dependent variable.

The findings in table 7–5 show that the variation is statistically significant but that the relationship between size of war coalition and alliance status is very weak (eta = .213). While the Yule's Q values are directly comparable with each other, it is not as appropriate to compare an eta with a Yule's Q since they are based on different levels of measurement and since Yule's Q tends to overstate a relationship. However, because both statistics range from 0.00 for no relationship to ±1.00 for a perfect relationship, it is clear that the .213 is much weaker than the findings in tables 7–2, 7–3, and 7–4.

Rather then let the eta stand alone, the authors present the contingency table (table 7–6), so that readers can see that there is more of a relationship than the eta captures if the three largest wartime coalitions (Korea, World War I, and World War II) are eliminated. Granted these three wars are extremely important, and no complete analysis of war can ignore them; however, if they were eliminated, the eta would be much higher. Of course, it is not legitimate to throw out deviant cases to raise correlations, but an argument can be made that the dynamics of world wars are different—that they are more likely to drag in more previously unallied participants. Also, although there are many nations without prewar alliances that became involved in these three wars (2, 6, and 8), there are more cases that did have alliances (9, 8, and 10). It is necessary to explain their behavior and explain why they are different.

This article shows that there is an important relationship between alliances with belligerents and war. Although it is not a perfect relationship, the findings indicate that there is a risk entailed in joining an alliance. One explanation that has been offered for why certain alliances are so dangerous is that they polarize the system, a proposition explored in the next article.

8

Bipolarity and War: The Role of Capability Concentration and Alliance Patterns among Major Powers, 1816–1965

Frank Whelon Wayman

Editors' Introduction

Frank Wayman's analysis provides an example of how careful measurement can clarify conceptual confusion and how research can resolve theoretical debate and advance inquiry. Since 1964 when Kenneth Waltz, on the one hand, and Karl Deutsch and J. David Singer, on the other, coincidentally published two theoretical pieces in the same year reaching opposite conclusions about the effects of bipolarity and multipolarity, there has been considerable discussion over the true effects of polarity. Wayman makes it clear that these effects will differ depending on whether one is talking about a bipolarity of capability (involving such factors as population, level of industrialization, and military strength) or a (bi)polarization of the world into two hostile alliance blocs. Obviously, these dimensions are analytically distinct, and as Wayman shows, they are uncorrelated with each other, although at times one may lead to the other, as in the early Cold War. Wayman shows that different kinds of polarity (that of capability versus that of blocs) are associated with different magnitudes of war. His analysis can be used to make inferences about the factors associated with the wars of highest magnitude—world wars.

Polarization and War

One of the great debates in the study of international conflict involves the relation between the polarization of an international system and the out-

Reprinted from the *Journal of Peace Research*, Vol. 21, No. 1 (1984), pp. 61–78, by permission of the publisher and the author.

break of war.[1] In its classic and simplest form, as articulated by Waltz (1964, 1967) and Deutsch and Singer (1964), this debate centers on whether "bipolarity" or "multipolarity" is more likely to lead to war. The present paper proposes to integrate partially the two sides in this debate through a new analytic framework. This new framework is necessary for three reasons. First, the distinction between bipolarity and multipolariy, like the distinction between liberal and conservative, is multidimensional in character; just as there are different dimensions of liberalism, so there are different dimensions of bipolarity. While this point has been made by a number of scholars, including Rapkin et al. (1979), and Snyder and Diesing (1977), the implications for the classic literature and for empirical research on war and peace have not been adequately examined; the present paper will investigate both such implications. Second, while it is not fully realized by scholars, sometimes the major power system is neither bipolar nor multipolar, but rather purely multipolar on one dimension and purely bipolar on another; the minuscule inter-dimension correlations documented below should help drive this point home and raise serious questions about much of the empirical work that has been done to test the Waltz and Deutsch-Singer hypotheses. Third, the theoretical and empirical work in the present paper increases the support for the contention that (a), contrary to the conventional wisdom, a multipolar power distribution breeds large scale wars, while (b) multipolarity on other dimensions—the "spatial" or "horizontal" dimensions of friendship and hostility patterns—may lead to peace. In the paper, correlation and regression analysis of data from the Correlates of War Project is used to explore this relationship of polarization to warfare over the period from 1815 to 1965. The data analysis, while ambiguous at points, suggests that spatial, or alignment, bipolarity increases the threat of war, while power bipolarity decreases that threat.

The Debate on Polarity

"Bipolarity" usually refers to a situation in which the international system or one of its subsystems is dominated by two superpowers, each with a supporting bloc of relatively weak allies. "Multipolarity" usually refers to an opposite condition in which more than two great powers play dominant roles in the international system. Deutsch and Singer argue that for two

[1] The author would like to thank Don Anderson, Mike Champion, Pat Dobel, Leo Hazlewood, George Liska, Cliff Morgan, Mikoninčić, Al Sabrosky, David Singer, and the anonymous reviewers from *JPR* for their comments on this paper. Special thanks are due to J. David Singer for his recommendations concerning the paper, and also for the highly collegial and cooperative atmosphere that he maintains at the Correlates of War Project. Finally, thanks are due to Mike Champion, Cliff Morgan, and Judy Nowack for helping the author in gaining efficient access to the data that are analyzed in this paper.

reasons multipolarity is more stable—i.e., more likely to remain in a steady, peaceful state—than bipolarity. First, in a bipolar world, all conflicts involve the nations of one side against those of the other, so that each side comes to regard the other as the enemy. In a multipolar world, interaction patterns increase in complexity and variety. An enemy on one issue becomes an ally on another. Cross-cutting cleavages and cross-pressures decrease the likelihood that implacable hostilities will develop (Deutsch and Singer, 1964, p. 394). Second, as the number of poles increases, each actor is forced to divide his attention among more and more poles. This divided attention makes escalating arms races of the type Richardson describes less likely (ibid., p. 399).

Waltz counters with the thesis that bipolarity is more stable than multipolarity. Selecting the Cold War between the United States and the Soviet Union as a bipolar system, he argues that the second-strike capabilities and militarily dominant position of the two superpowers (1) deterred any possible attack the one might launch on the other, and (2) allowed each to control extremists in their own camps (as, for example, the U.S. did against Britain and France when they seized the Suez Canal in 1956). The result of these two restraints was a relatively peaceful Cold War era despite high tensions. Waltz also addresses the matter of divided attention, but argues that as the number of poles increase, divided attention breeds miscalculation and thereby increases the probability of war.

Deutsch, Singer and Waltz carried on their debate about polarity in the aftermath of Kaplan's *System and Process in International Politics* (1957), which popularized the discussion of power systems in terms of the ideal types of multipolarity (the classic balance of power) and loose or tight bipolarity. It is a thesis of this paper that the balance of power and alliance polarization should not be treated in terms of such ideal types, but should rather be treated in terms of the variables used to compute the product-moment about the center of a space (Wallace, 1973a). In such an analysis, the two key variables are the weight, or power of a country, and the degree of hostility or friendship which obtains in its relations with other nation-states in the system.

Measuring Weights and Hostility

In applying this model to the real world, the weight of each state and the degree of its hostility or friendship to other states must be measured. Measuring the weight, or power, of a country has been approached in several ways. One method has been to look for concrete power-attributes, or capabilities, which can be used as measures of countries' power (Sabrosky 1975; Knorr 1956). This approach has been criticized on grounds that (1) "power" should be reserved for the ability of country A to modify the behavior of country B; (2) attributes, such as GNP and military spending, only provide certain tools or capabilities that can be converted into power, and do not represent power itself; (3) power, unlike these attributes, is variable across a limited domain and scope (Dahl 1970, p. 18); (4) the capabilities or power of a set of countries may not be additive when they form an alliance; (5) power is an extremely ambiguous, and perhaps superfluous, concept in social science analysis (Riker 1962, 1969).

A second approach to the measurement of power is to look for measures of *perceived* national power. This approach assumes that "power," in the phrase "the balance of power," means the perceived power of a country in the minds of statesmen and other attentive observers of the international system. Perceived power is thus a key factor in the minds of statesmen as they adjust their national policies and alliance patterns. This formulation assumes that statesmen and others make judgments about the power of states on a ratio scale. These judgments are conceivably recoverable through some instrument such as a questionnaire.

A third approach in the literature on national power is to look for objective attributes that predict perceived power. Alcock and Newcombe (1970), studying the perceptions of students and citizens in Canada and Latin America, concluded that GNP and military expenditures are both excellent predictors of perceived national power, with military expenditures being a better predictor if warring nations are included in the ratings. Their approach integrates the first two by demonstrating that attributes, such as GNP, are highly correlated with perceived power.

The second key variable, the degree of hostility between pairs of nations, can be measured by questionnaire administration (Klingberg 1941), analysis of alliance data (Wallace 1973a), analysis of voting in or membership in international organizations, analysis of trade data (Goldmann 1974, p. 134ff.; Wall 1972) or content analysis. Such data can then be scaled through the use of multidimensional scaling routines. Efforts based on perceptual data (Klingberg 1941) and on aggregate data (Wallace 1973a) have been productive in this way. For ease of presentation, these analyses can often be presented visually in graphs in which friendly nations cluster close together and hostile nations are distant from one another. The present paper analyzes pairs of nations in terms of the degree of hostile or friendly relations between their governments. Sometimes hostile pairs are labelled "distant" from each other, and the reader should realize that this is a spatial metaphor for hostility between the governments, *not* a description of geographic distance.

Propositions about Polarization

A model involving weight and locations suggests the following definitions and propositions about polarity.

Definition 1. A system is *power bipolar* when capabilities are so distributed that two dominant hostile powers are more powerful than other actors to a degree that gives the dominant powers autonomy in self-defense.

The second-strike capabilities of the U.S. and the Soviet Union in the 1960s would illustrate this concept.

Definition 2. A system is *power multipolar* when capabilities are more evenly distributed than in the power bipolar condition, and when hostility is still high.

Definition 3. A system is *cluster bipolar* when most or all of the states in the system are tightly packed into two political clusters, with high mutual hostility, and very few or no states play intermediate or cross-cutting roles. In the perfect form of tight cluster bipolarity, the members are all mutually closer to each other than any of them are to any member of the other cluster.

Definition 4. A system is *cluster multipolar* when the states are more evenly distributed throughout the space, with many opportunities for intermediaries and many cross-cutting loyalties to moderate hostility.

Power bipolarity and power multipolarity are mutually exclusive categories. So are cluster bipolarity and cluster multipolarity. *It is essential to realize, however, that a system that is power bipolar can be either cluster bipolar or cluster multipolar, and that a power multipolar system can likewise be either cluster multipolar or cluster bipolar.*[2] Thus, in table 8–1, starting clockwise from the upper left corner, the reader can examine how Europe has proceeded through four successive types of international system since 1919. In the period after World War I and before the rise of Hitler, the European state system, in which the United States was by now an actor, was power multipolar and cluster multipolar.

In World War II, the European system was cluster bipolar—with virtually all the key actors locked into a deadly conflict between fascist and anti-fascist coalitions—but power multipolar—with Britain, the United States, and the Soviet Union depending on each other for support against

---

[2] The splitting of "polarization" into two different dimensions, as is done here, is fundamentally different from the approach of Richard Rosecrance in his discussion of "Bi-multipolarity." He treats this concept as an "intermediate" level of a unidimensional continuum from bipolarity to multipolarity. As such, his concept mixes a discussion of power concentration with a discussion of coalition clustering without distinguishing the two. It thereby carries forward the ambiguities inherent in the Deutsch, Singer, and Waltz debate. See Rosecrance (1966).

Table 8–1
Two Dimensions of Polarization

	Coalition Configuration	
Power Concentration	*Cluster multipolarity* (Many clusters)	*Cluster bipolarity* (Two clusters)
Power multipolarity (Dispersed capabilities	European System 1919–1939	European System 1941–1945
Power bipolarity (Concentrated capabilities)	Aspects of the European System 1965–1975	European System 1948–1955

the Axis onslaught. In the Cold War of the early 1950s, Europe was power bipolar and cluster bipolar. By the early 1970s, European remained power bipolar, but had moved towards cluster multipolarity, to some extent with the partial dissolution of the tightly clustered Cold War alliance patterns, but much more as indicated by shifting trade and economic indicators of polarization.[3]

A fifth definition is useful for the development of the argument:

Definition 5. A system is *unipolar* if none of the states in the system are hostile enough to each other to induce mutual fear and aggressive designs.

Rapkin, Thompson, and Christopherson (1979) have drawn similar distinctions. Differences in terminology should not obscure these similarities. What they call "bipolarity" is here called "power bipolarity." What they call "bipolarization" is here called "cluster bipolarity." The terminology used here is simply useful for drawing out the implications of the Deutsch-Singer-Waltz debate. While Rapkin, Thompson, and Christopherson (1979) have expressed the key distinction and traced its origins in empirical studies by a host of authors, they did not trace its implications back to the Deutsch-Singer-Waltz debate or use insights gleaned from such a literature review to test the Deutsch-Singer-Waltz hypotheses about system structure and war; this effort will be undertaken in the present paper. Hence, the following set of propositions provides the theoretical rationale for emphasizing the distinction between power and spatial polarity.

Proposition 1. The greater the number of pairs of states in the system with a degree of hostility above some critical level, the greater the likelihood of war.

---

[3] Coalition configuration and power concentration have been presented as dichotomous variables to simplify discussion in the historical examples and definitions above; they will be treated as continuous variables in the measurement section of the paper.

This proposition states an obvious, but nonetheless important, relationship: hostility leads to mutual fear and a high probability of warfare. Two countries close together (again, close in the cluster analysis of friendship, not necessarily in geographic proximity) have by definition compatible interests, and tend to identify with each other to the point where war between them is unthinkable. Examples in the contemporary of world would be Denmark and Sweden, or Canada and the United States (Deutsch et al. 1957). It is when actors are extremely distant from each other along some dimension—as in the case of Israel and the P.L.O.—that the potential for violence is high.

Proposition one correctly asserts that hostility increases the likelihood of war. To fully understand proposition one, we must place it in the context of two other propositions. How the system is polarized affects the likelihood of the war becoming massive (examined in proposition two) and even the strength of the relationship between hostility and war (examined in proposition three).

> *Proposition 2.* In a system that is power bipolar, warfare if it occurs is likely to be minimal and not system-engulfing, whereas in a system that is power multipolar, warfare will be of higher magnitude if it occurs.

When the strongest powers in the system are fairly independent of support from their allies, as they are under power bipolarity, they can confidently manage a crisis in which one of their allies has taken a position of extreme hostility towards the enemy coalition. Since such a self-sufficient big power does not really need the ally in a vital sense, the ally can be left isolated until it sees the dangers of its extreme position and compromises that position. When the big powers are not self-sufficient, any member of their coalition which takes an extreme position on an issue has a chance of dragging the big power, and thence the whole alliance, into a conflagration. The classic instance of such power multipolar behavior is World War I. In 1914, the Central Powers (Germany and Austria-Hungary) were in an inferior position in terms of capabilities (Sabrosky 1975). Germany felt isolated and surrounded by enemies on two fronts. When Germany's sole European ally, Austria-Hungary, became involved in a dispute with Serbia over the assassination of Austrian Archduke Ferdinand, Germany gave Austria-Hungary a "blank check." Confident of German backing, Austria-Hungary delivered a set of unreasonable demands to Serbia, refused to accept the Serbian note capitulating to the demands, and prepared to invade Serbia. This induced Russian mobilization, which precipitated German activation of the Schlieffen plan, which in turn plunged most of European into a massive war.

A second example of power multipolarity is the outbreak of the Great Peloponnesian War (432–404 B.C.) between Athens and Sparta. In the

Greek system, both Athens and Sparta felt threatened by each other, and relied on elaborate coalitions for security. Corcyra, a friend of Athens, became involved in a dispute with Corinth, an ally of Sparta. Keeping the Corcyrean navy from falling into Corinthian hands was as critical to Athenian military defense as Corinth's wealth was to any Spartan war effort. Athens could not tolerate a Corcyrean defeat, nor could Sparta tolerate a Corinthian defeat. Despite the attempts of statesmen in Sparta and Athens to arbitrate the dispute, Athens was forced to defend Corcyra, and Corinth was able to convince Sparta and her allies to go to war against Athens (Kagan 1969).

Power bipolarity has characterized the era of thermonuclear confrontation between the United States and the Soviet Union. As Waltz noted in the articles cited above, these power relationships have forced the superpowers to treat each other with great care, to manage conflicts so as to prevent their escalation, and have allowed the superpowers to restrain the behavior of their allies. Of course, the danger of severe warfare remains if a conflict starts between the superpowers and escalates into a nuclear war. But so far the empirical results have been an era in which Soviet and American troops have avoided combat with each other and no system-wide wars have broken out.

Proposition 3. In a system that is cluster bipolar, the amount of warfare per year is likely to be large, whereas in a cluster multipolar system, warfare is likely to be of lower magnitude per unit of time.

This third proposition follows from the fact that two important conflict-reducing agents—namely, intermediary relationships and cross-cutting cleavages—exist in a multipolar setting but are eliminated in a cluster bipolar one. Intermediary relationships involve the existence of a group of actors between the two enemy camps on a single dimension of conflict. The intermediaries, or actors in the middle, have a number of peacekeeping roles to perform. First, they play face saving roles. These include (1) good offices, or the offer of a neutral meeting ground (for example, the French government made such an offer in 1968 to the U.S. and North Vietnam; both sides were able to accept Paris as a neutral meeting ground); (2) mediation, in which neutral parties propose peace solutions that would be unacceptable if they came from the enemy camp (for example, Kissinger's Middle East shuttle diplomacy); and (3) arbitration, in which neutral parties have decisive powers in resolving the dispute (and which is therefore rarely employed). In addition, the intermediaries, by simply playing their role as moderates who do not have extremely hostile relations with anyone, can set the tone of political argument in the entire system. The more numerous the intermediaries, the more moderate will be this overall tone. A similar moderating effect has been observed in the class conflict within nations: in class politics in industrial societies, the emerging new middle class has played such a moderating role (Dahrendorf 1959, p. 51).

The peacekeeping roles of intermediaries are determined by their spatial location between enemy camps. Because the intermediaries are not extremely distant from either side, they have moderately good relations with both sides. This insures that the intermediaries will have relatively tranquil relations with virtually all members of the system, in contrast to the nations on the extremes who necessarily view each other across a distance twice as great. This tranquility provides a basis from which the intermediaries can provide good offices and act as mediators and arbitrators of disputes.

The above model assumes that intermediary relationships occur along a single dimension of conflict. When conflicts are more than one-dimensional, a second conflict-reducing agent may be introduced in multipolar settings, namely, cross-cutting cleavages (Rae and Taylor 1970, pp. 85–92). Whereas the impact of intermediary relations stems from the relatively low distance (i.e., dissimilarity) between the intermediaries and the extremists, the impact of cross-cutting cleavages depends not on distance but on the hostility-reducing impact of cross-cutting alliance bonds. In the words of an ancient saying, "the enemy of my enemy is my friend." Thus, if Egypt and Saudi Arabia, which fought each other in Yemen in the 1960s, shared a common hostility towards Israel, the common hostility would act as a bond holding them closer together than they would otherwise be. If Jordan, Israel, and Saudi Arabia face a common threat from Arab extremists, they are distracted from their hostility for each other and forced to concentrate on their common threat. If Saudi Arabia and the U.S., which differ over Israel, sense a common interest in blocking radical socialism in the Arab world, this will lead them to realize that differences over Israel need not constitute an insurmountable barrier to friendship. A multitude of such cross-cutting loyalties, in which a nation's opponent on one issue becomes its ally on another, make a nation aware that it may have shared interests with all actors—including actors with which it would have been purely and diametrically opposed in a one-dimensional conflict.

As some of the examples may suggest, however, cross-cutting cleavages are not an unmixed blessing. A party that feels itself threatened along one dimension of conflict has an incentive to exacerbate tensions along another, in a way that can split the opposing coalition. Such strategies increase hostility between members of the system and increase the risk of violence. This is a rule that applies to all levels of conflict. In the example above, for instance, the Soviet Union, trying to penetrate the Arab world in the face of Arab distaste for Soviet style communism, has found favor with the militant Arabs by arming them for war against Israel. Similarly, Saudi Arabia's monarchy can reduce the threat it faces from radical Arabs by taking the forefront in financing the the struggle against Israel. A similar phenomenon occurs in American domestic politics. Since the New Deal, the Democrats have been the majority party. Furthermore, on economic issues the Democrats have enjoyed the support of the majority of the American public. Aspiring Republican politicians have therefore been tempted to exacerbate symbolic cross-cutting issues such as the Red-scares and law-and-order in order to win some of the Democratic voters over to the Republican camp. These tactics have sometimes brought success at the polls, but have embittered the political climate within the United States. Thus, cross-cutting cleavages can act to reduce hostility and distance, but they can also be exploited with the opposite effect.

Intermediary functions are the consequence of the relatively short distances from the intermediaries to the wings. Cross-cutting functions, rather than the consequence of distances, are a cause acting over time to reduce the distance that would otherwise exist between hostile pairs in a one-dimensional conflict, but sometimes inducing an increase in distance and hostility.

The Classic Debate Revisited

In their debate on polarity, Deutsch and Singer and Waltz are divided by two differences. The first is a genuine disagreement about the effect of multiple sources of stimuli. Waltz argues that multiple stimuli are confusing and dangerous, and that therefore a simple, bipolar world is safer. Deutsch and Singer argue that these multiple stimuli, by diluting attention, lessen the likelihood of a vicious cycle of increased tension and reciprocal arms build-ups. The ability to completely focus attention on one enemy pole would occur, in the language of this paper, if power were absolutely bipolar *or* if clustering were absolutely bipolar. In either case, the only important opponents would be located at one point, and attention could focus on that point. To the degree that the system becomes multipolar in *both senses*, attention can no longer be focused on just one enemy, and attention becomes diluted. With theoretical predictions leading in opposite directions, it becomes an empirical question whether multiple stimuli will either produce a more peaceful system or a more violent one.

The second disagreement is partly semantic. Waltz argues that super-power dominance makes a bipolar world stable, while Deutsch and Singer argue that cross-cutting cleavages and mediators make a multipolar world stable. Waltz's argument that power bipolarity is more stable than power multipolarity (proposition 2 above) is not fundamentally in conflict with Deutsch and Singer's contention that cluster multipolarity is more stable than cluster bipolarity (proposition 3 above). Both may simultaneously be correct.

Empirical Evidence, 1815–1965

These two propositions can be tested, in an exploratory way, with existing data. The Correlates of War Project has produced data over a long enough time series to allow variation in systemic polarization and to observe the impact of such variation on warfare (Singer and Small 1968, 1972; Singer, Bremer and Stuckey 1972). The series so far gathered do not always allow the ideal operationalization of concepts; as a result, there is the danger that hypotheses may be accepted or rejected prematurely, on the basis of inappropriate specification or operationalization. The data analysis which follows should therefore be regarded as preliminary, and not as a definitive test of the hypotheses from the theory.

To insure as much of an independent test of the theory as possible, no data were analyzed until after the theory had been constructed, circulated among colleagues, and put in final form. In this way, the hypotheses are derived from the historical examples and reasoning of the first part of this paper, and not from prior exploration of the data set.

Measurement

The test of hypotheses in the paper is based on analysis of the system of interactions among the major powers.[4] As defined by Singer and Small (1972), this major power system varied in number from four to eight members during the period from 1815 to 1965. This is an appropriate group of states to analyze for two reasons. First, a focus on the major powers insures that one will examine only states that do interact significantly with each other; it is a focus on states "which—almost by definition—are highly interdependent one with the other," and hence are guaranteed to make up a true "system" (Singer et al., 1972, p. 22). Second , the major powers were the nations with the capabilities and predilections to engage in the rivalries associated with the balance of power and the balance of terror. It is among such a group of states, competing with and observing each other, that one would expect hypotheses about polarity to be confirmed. In 1816, at the dawn of the period to be studied, these major powers were Austria-Hungary, England, France, Prussia, and Russia. The group grew to include at various times Italy, Japan, the United States, and China. Some members dropped out, so that by 1965 the major powers were again five in number.

In the analysis below, measurements will be made on the major powers at five year intervals, from 1815 to 1965. To avoid the distorting effects of the world wars, and to maintain consistency with earlier research, these intervals of measurement are thrice modified, with readings taken in 1913

---

[4] In this it differs from alliance analyses that include all members of the international system. These analyses include Bueno de Mesquita (1975) and Wallace (1973a).

rather than in 1915, in 1938 rather than 1940, and in 1946 rather than 1945.

The main index of warfare is the magnitude of war, measured in nation-months of interstate war, as reported in Singer and Small (1972) and Singer, Bremer and Stuckey (1972, p. 29). Also measured was the frequency of interstate wars fought by major powers. These war indices all cover a five-year period following the moment at which system polarization is measured; for example, if polarization is measured in January 1820, warfare is measured from January 1820 through December 1824.

Two measures of power concentration were employed in the present study. One, reported by Singer, Bremer, and Stuckey (1972), measures the inequality of the capabilities of the major powers. This index is based on the standard deviation of the capabilities of the major powers. This index is based on the standard deviation of the capabilities of the major powers; this number approaches zero when the major powers are roughly equal in capabilities. The second index, derived from the Singer-Bremer-Stuckey data set, is a computation of the percentage of major power capabilities held by the two greatest powers.[5] These two indices are highly correlated with each other (r = .90 for 1815-1965, r = .75 for the nineteenth century, and r = .93 for the twentieth century), and tend to produce very similar results in hypothesis testing. By either measure, power concentration was the lowest around the turn of the century and just before World War II (see table 8–2).

Measuring the clustering of the system is more difficult than measuring warfare or power concentration. Perhaps the ideal data would be scaling of hostility and friendship levels gleaned from content analysis of diplomatic documents. Such data are not directly available for the time span being examined. The best available data are the data on alliances.[6] While alliance data measure one aspect of cooperation between pairs of states, they are not without their problems. One difficulty is that alliances may be an interven-

---

[5] The data base, from the Correlates of War Project, is an updated version of that reported in Singer, Bremer, and Stuckey (1972).

[6] Singer and Small (1968). Trade has also been proposed as an indicator of "bipolarization" or cluster polarity. See Goldmann (1974) and Wall (1972). Goldmann and Wall demonstrate the relevance of trade, aid, and related data to measures and post–World War II polarization patterns. Trade data, however, do not exist, even for all the major powers, back to 1816, so statistical analyses of trade and international conflict have been limited to the twentieth century. Extensive C.O.W. analyses of trade volume and trade dependency have failed to detect any relationship between trade and militarized disputes or war, 1950–1976. These studies were path breaking in that they examined not only trade volume, but also the marginal utilities for imports and exports of each side (using price elasticities of supply and demand). See Huelshof and Soltvedt (1981). Their study was discouraging because of the persistent absence of statistically significant relationships between trade and disputes or war. Given this experience, given the already monumental task of treating power concentration and alliance polarization, and given the dearth of trade data over the 1815–1965 period, trade was not included in the present study.

Table 8–2
Two Measures of Power Polarization

Year	CON[a]	TWOCON[b]	Year	CON	TWOCON
1815	–	–	1895	.223	.47
1820	.241	.58	1900	.202	.44
1825	.233	.58	1905	.207	.43
1830	.242	.58	1910	.212	.45
1835	.243	.57	1913	.208	.46
1840	.232	.57	1920	.371	.61
1845	.257	.57	1925	.247	.52
1850	.260	.57	1930	.241	.48
1855	.276	.58	1935	.228	.51
1860	.280	.57	1938	.217	.48
1865	.255	.56	1946	.417	.90
1870	.233	.51	1950	.293	.65
1875	.225	.50	1955	.331	.69
1880	.226	.49	1960	.303	.66
1885	.208	.48	1965	–	–
1890	.203	.48			

[a] CON is the concentration index of major power capabilities reported in Singer, Bremer and Stuckey, "Capability Distribution, Uncertainty, and Major Power War," p. 22.
[b] TWOCON is the percentage of major power capabilities held by the two largest powers.

ing variable between more basic displays of hostility/friendship and the outbreak of war. This difficulty makes it dangerous to attribute causal significance to the correlations examined below. A second problem is that the major power alliance data are not rich enough in information to be subjected to multidimensional scaling analysis. The cluster analysis that can be performed does not allow separate measurement of the degree of inter-mediation and the degree of cross-cutting in the system.

On the basis of the alliance data, a polarization index was con-structed. To do this, a "bloc" was defined as a set of nations each of which had a defense pact with each of the others; for example, in 1955, France, the United States, and the United Kingdom formed a bloc. The number of "poles" in the system is equal to the number of blocs plus the number of non-bloc major powers. Cluster bipolarity would exist if there were only two poles. The maximum number of potential poles in any year is of course identical to the number of major powers. The formation of blocs, by reducing the number of poles, cuts down on the potential for cross-cutting cleavages and intermediary roles. The ratio of actual poles to potential poles was used as a measure of alliance polarization. The ratio would reach 1.0 under maximum cluster multipolarity, when there are no blocs; it would approach 0.0 under cluster bipolarity (or, as in the unique case of the Holy Alliance of 1820, unipolarity). This index is presented in table 8–3.

The main periods of bipolarity, when the index is at its lowest values, were just before World War I, and during the Cold War.

Table 8–3
Alliance Polarization

Year	Alliance Polarization[a]	Year	Alliance Polarization
1815	.40	1895	.56
1820	.20	1900	.62
	(UNIPOLAR)	1905	.50
1825	.80	1910	.50
1830	.80	1913	.50
1835	.60	1920	.80
1840	.40	1925	1.00
1845	.60	1930	1.00
1850	.80	1935	.86
1855	.80	1938	.86
1860	.83	1946	1.00
1865	.83	1950	.40
1870	1.00	1955	.40
1875	.83	1960	.40
1880	.83	1965	.60
1885	.67		
1890	.67		

[a] A value of 1.0 represents maximum alliance multipolarity. Low values represent clustering of the system into blocs, thereby tending toward alliance bipolarity.

Correlations and Hypothesis Testing

With the indices constructed, it was possible to test several of the theoretical claims from the first section of the paper. One of the important findings of the data analysis is that power polarity and cluster polarization are in fact separate dimensions. Indeed, using the measures developed for this study, the two concepts are almost totally uncorrelated with each other. Over the period 1815–1965, the alliance polarization index correlates 0.01 with the measure of bipolar power concentration (TWOCON) and 0.12 with the Singer-Bremer-Stuckey measure of power concentration (CON). In the nineteenth century, the alliance polarization measure correlates—0.28 with TWOCON and 0.13 with CON. In the twentieth century, these correlations are 0.10 and 0.16, respectively. None of these correlations are statistically significant at the .05 level.[7]

This complete lack of association between measures of power concentration and alliance polarization has implications both for the polarization

---

[7] Within a specific historic period, cluster polarity and power polarity may be more highly correlated. Such a correlation is suggested by the findings of Rapkin, Thompson, and Christopherson (1979). Their study of the 1948–1973 era, published as the bulk of the present research was being completed, is based on COPDAB event data. While Rapkin, Thompson, and Christopherson arrive at their findings with radically different operationalizations, there are clear parallels between their concept of "polarity" and the concept of "power polarity" in the present study, as well as between their concept of "polarization" and the concept of "cluster polarity" in the present study.

literature already discussed and for the theoretical work of Snyder and Diesing (1977, pp. 419–470). Of course, as noted at the outset, if the two aspects of "bipolarity" are not even statistically assoicated with each other, then the early literature that classified all international systems as either "bipolar" or "multipolar" needs to be refined. Whereas the early literature on polarity did tend to collapse power bipolarity and alliance bipolarity into a single concept, Snyder and Diesing are careful to distinguish "system structure" (the number of major powers and the distribution of capabilities) from the alliance patterns in the system. However, Snyder and Diesing do see a causal connection between the two concepts; they argue that a bipolar power concentration tends to produce alignments in which the lesser powers cluster around the two largest powers.[8] The findings of this paper put a greater emphasis on the distinction between power concentration and alliance configuration than do Snyder and Diesing, who, after all, argue that the power polarity variable has a causal impact on the alliance patterns variable, while the two concepts as measured in this paper are statistically independent. Snyder and Diesing have based their argument on references to the post–World War II environment. Rapkin, Thompson, and Christopherson (1979) do find a positive correlation between bipolarity and bipolarization in the Cold War period, but one should hesitate to generalize those results to earlier eras, given the findings of the present paper.

One possible reconciliation of the findings with Snyder and Diesing would be to argue that a bipolar power concentration does produce a bipolar alliance configuration, but only when the power concentration surpasses a very high threshold, as it did in the late 1940s and early 1950s. A second possibility is that ideological fervor, having been a major cause of alliance formation after World War II, was covarying with power concentration and hence causing a portion of the correlation reported by Rapkin, Thompson, and Christopherson.[9] Certainly, the era of John Foster Dulles was a time when the U.S. formed many alliances, such as CENTO, which were appropriate to the operational code and ideology of foreign policy officials, but which may have done little to enhance the interests of the United States. Third, it is possible (indeed, likely) that future studies, based on improved measures of bipolar power concentration and bipolar alliance configuration, will yield revised findings of the relationship between the two

---

[8] Snyder and Diesing (1977), pp. 420–421. This type of alliance configuration is similar to what Rapkin, Thompson, and Christopherson (1979) have called bipolarization.

[9] See Bueno de Mesquita and Singer (1973), pp. 237–273, and especially p. 264, for a discussion of the role of ideology and other factors in alliance formation, and the need for more empirical research on the subject. For a thoughtful review of the state of the art, see Ward (1982b).

concepts.[10] At the present time, when virtually no one reports validity co-efficients for new measures of polarization, it is difficult to ascertain in what ways the alliance indicator used in the present paper would correlate with some factors from earlier efforts to measure the same thing.[11] So the debate about the above findings is by no means settled, and should continue.

For the sake of hypothesis testing in the remainder of this paper, the important fact is that the independent variables (power concentration and alliance configuration) in the following tests are indeed statistically independent of each other.

The first hypothesis, relating the amount of warfare in the system to the amount of hostility in the system, cannot be tested with the data presently available. While such a test would in all likelihood be a demonstration of the obvious, it would be useful as a way of controlling for effects that may disturb the testing of hypothesis three, as will become clear below.

The second hypothesis suggests that power bipolarity should minimize the size of any wars that might break out. The data are somewhat supportive of this hypothesis. If we classify relatively bipolar systems as ones in which the two largest powers have over fifty percent of great power capabilities, we find that the major power system was power multipolar thirty-four percent of the time, and power bipolar in the other years. The power multipolar years were, if anything, slightly less war prone. Only twenty-seven percent of the major power inter-state wars broke out in those years, and this is slightly, though insignificantly, below the thirty-four percent that would have occurred by chance. The second hypothesis contends, however, that any wars that did break out under power multipolarity would be massive conflagrations. Table 8–4 confirms this hypothesis. Three-quarters of the wars under power multipolarity were of high magnitude. These included World Wars I and II. In contrast, three-quarters of wars under power bipolarity were of low magnitude. While the size of this correlation does shrink somewhat if different cutoffs are chosen for the two dichotomies, the correlation does remain supportive of the arguments in the theoretical section of this paper. This is important because it is the opposite of what some scholars would have expected. Some scholars have argued that in a multipolar world, adjustments to the system can occur through frequent but low level warfare, whereas in a bipolar world, wars are less frequent but bigger. One of the most explicit statements of this position is made by Michael

---

[10] Indeed, as already indicated by Bueno de Mesquita's work on tightness and discreteness, alliance polarization may very well itself be a multidimensional concept, as may power concentration (which involves both the number of major powers and the distribution of power among them).

[11] On the more positive side, the correlation between two measures of power concentration—CON and TWOCON—has been reported above, and the correlations between a sample of cluster polarization measures are reported below.

Table 8–4
Power Polarization and the Magnitude of Major Power
Inter-State War, 1815–1965

	Power Polarization[a]	
War Magnitude[b]	*Power Bipolar*	*Power Multipolar*
High	27%	75%
Low	73%	25%
	N = 22	N = 8

[a] A system is treated as power bipolar if the two largest powers have at least fifty percent of major power capabilities. Otherwise it is treated as power multipolar.
[b] High war magnitude is treated as more than ten nation-months of major power inter-state war. Less than ten nation-months is considered low war magnitude.
Tau B = −.43
(Significance level = .02 for a non-directional hypothesis).

Haas (1970, p. 121): "bipolarity brings fewer but longer wars." Rosecrance (1966, p. 319) offers a more qualified assertion of the same position: "It seems highly probable that a multipolar world order will increase the number of conflicts, though it may possibly reduce their significance." Such contentions seem to be the opposite of the findings of the present paper that wars are more frequent but of lesser magnitude under power bipolarity. While Haas offers some statistical support for his position, his findings may be based upon impressionistic coding schemes that categorized, for example, all historical systems, in a dichotomous fashion, as "bipolar" or "multipolar," without clarifying whether the judgments were based on power concentration or alliance configuration. In short, the reproducible evidence seems to support proposition two.

The third hypothesis, relating the amount of war to the cluster polarization of the system, is more difficult to test wtih existing data. Because war, hostility, and even anticipated war have a *reciprocal* causal impact on alliance patterns, it is difficult to measure the causal impact of alliance bipolarity on war. Given these reciprocal causal linkages, it would be best in testing the model to have measures of variables that cause alliance patterns but not war, and other variables that cause war but not alliance patterns. Without such measures, the best evidence available is the cross-lagged correlations between war and alliance polarization (see table 8–5). The cross-lagged correlation cannot be used for causal conclusions. The autocorrelations for alliance polarization are 0.44 in the nineteenth century, 0.59 in the twentieth century, and 0.52 for the entire period 1815 to 1965; for war magnitude, the autocorrelations are 0.72 in the nineteenth century, −0.32 in the twentieth century, and −0.15 for the entire period. With such nonzero autocorrelations, the cross-lagged correlations do not have clear causal possibilities. To reduce the contaminating effect of the autocorrelations, the first differences were computed for both variables.

Table 8–5
Cross-Lagged Correlations between War (Magnitude of Major Power Inter-state War Underway) and Cluster Multipolarity[a]

Correlations of	1815–1965		Twentieth Century		Nineteenth Century	
	War Lagged before Alliance Multipolarity	*War following Alliance Multipolarity*	*War Lagged before Alliance Multipolarity*	*War following Alliance Multipolarity*	*War Lagged before Alliance Multipolarity*	*War following Alliance Multipolarity*
Static measures	.13 Sig. = .49	−.13 Sig. = .52	.18 Sig. = .52	−.14 Sig. = .64	.70 *Sig. = .006*	.43 Sig. = .12
First differences	.42 *Sig. = .03*	−.46 *Sig. = .01*	.49 Sig. = .07	−.56 *Sig. = .03*	.47 Sig. = .11	.12 Sig. = .69

[a] Pearson product-moment correlation coefficients with significance levels for non-directional hypothesis. Italicized figures show statistical significance at better than the .05 level for a directional hypothesis.

In table 8–5, war is always positively correlated with subsequent alliance multipolarity: in both centuries, war seems to lead to a dispersion of alliance blocs. In the twentieth century, this cluster multipolarity is followed by peace (see the fourth column of table 8–5), as the third hypothesis contends. In the nineteenth century, however, the opposite of the hypothesis seems to hold true, and cluster multipolarity is followed by war (see the sixth column of table 8–5). Furthermore, in the nineteenth century, an *increase* in alliance multipolarity (from t_1 to t_6) is positively correlated ($r = .31$) with the subsequent magnitude of war (the sum of nation-months from t_6 to t_{11}), indicating that prior to war alliance clusters were disintegrating. In the twentieth century, on the other hand, an increase in alliance multipolarity (from t_1 to t_6) is negatively correlated ($r = -.48$) with the subsequent magnitude of war (the sum of the nation-months from t_6 to t_{11}, indicating that prior to wars the alliance patterns were becoming more bipolarized. These differences between centuries are similar to the ones found by Singer and Small (1968) using several alliance and (cluster) bipolarity measures, all different from the ones used here.

Why are correlations from table 8–5 nonsignificant, and even in the wrong direction, in the nineteenth century? One possibility that is consistent with the theoretical structure of this paper involves the total hostility in the system. This hostility could rise to very high level in years of intense conflict between groups of states. Especially in the nineteenth century, during the balance of power era, hostility and the subsequent threat of war might induce nations to hedge their bets by dropping out of blocs to maintain maximum flexibility by cultivating many potential allies. Meanwhile (see table 8–6), the hostility could also lead to war. Even if the alliance multipolarity were itself having a pacifying effect on the system, the bivariate correlation between multipolarity and war could yield an insignificant re-

Table 8–6
Untested Explanation for Difference between the Two Centuries

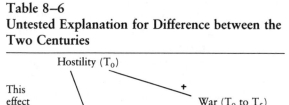
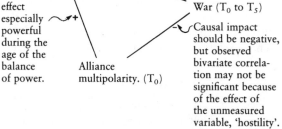

Hostility (T_0)

This effect especially powerful during the age of the balance of power.

Alliance multipolarity. (T_0)

War (T_0 to T_5)

Causal impact should be negative, but observed bivariate correlation may not be significant because of the effect of the unmeasured variable, 'hostility'.

sult. If one could control for hostility, the correlation might change enough to confirm the third hypothesis.

The statistically significant correlation supporting hypothesis three is the correlation of first differences ($r = -.56$) for the twentieth century. This correlation means that a system that has become more alliance multipolar than in the previous time period will experience significantly less war than in that earlier time period. These first differences measure velocities—the rate at which the system is becoming more warlike, and the rate at which it is becoming more cluster bipolar.

Technically, the correlation for the first difference is also significant for the entire 1815 to 1965 period (as can be seen in the second column of table 8–5). This finding considered alone would confirm proposition three for both centuries. But the separate analyses of each century indicate such disparate results that such a conclusion would appear to be an overgeneralization. The nineteenth and twentieth centuries do seem substantially different.

While this finding for twentieth century is consistent with the theoretical argument and with hypothesis three, it appears to be the opposite of the finding of Bueno de Mesquita in his analysis of the same century.[12] He computes the number of "poles" among all system members (not just major powers), and then computes the number of interaction opportunities among poles. (The number of such opportunities is found by multiplying the number of poles times that number minus once, and then dividing by two. When the system is multipolar, there will be many interaction opportunities.) He finds that the amount of war in the subsequent five years is *positively* correlated with the number of interaction opportunities (a correlation of .32) and with a shift towards more interaction opportunities than had been available five years before (a correlation of .52).

How can Bueno de Mesquita's findings be reconciled with the present findings? First, he is focusing on the polarization of the entire "system," while this paper focuses only on the major power system. Second, and related to the first point, his count of interaction opportunities swells as system size grows. For example, the present measure indicates that the 1950s were the decade of greatest alliance bipolarity since the Napoleonic Wars. His measure, which is affected by the growth in the number of independent nations, indicates that the 1950s were one of the four decades with the greatest amount of alliance multipolarity. Such disagreements about a well-known decade illustrate how two measures of alliance polarization might be weakly correlated, uncorrelated, or even negatively correlated with each other. Such correlations do not invalidate either measure, nor should

---

[12] Bueno de Mesquita (1975, p. 206). Bueno de Mesquita focuses on wars involving at least one major power, and the present study has also focused on the set of major-major and major-minor wars. The measure of alliance multipolarity in the present paper does not exactly correspond to his measures of interaction opportunities, number of clusters, tightness, and discreteness, of course.

the measures be attacked solely by appeals to face validity.[13] I have chosen major powers as the focus of measurement, however, because I remain unconvinced that the clusters of minor powers would have much causal effect on the war proneness of the major power system. For example, in 1960, Bueno de Mesquita reports a cluster made up of Finland and Mongolia. The mere existence of this cluster, in a world with ten other clusters, increases the total interaction opportunities by ten (from forty-five to fifty-five), according to Bueno de Mesquita's formula. (In contrast, the average number of interaction opportunities in the nineteenth century is about one.) According to the Bueno de Mesquita formula, the impact of the Finland-Mongolia cluster is the same as the impact of NATO. My own view of the international system, from 1815 to 1965, puts much more emphasis on power stratification; on the dominance of the core powers over the rest of the nation-members of the system; and on the tendency for major-major and even major-minor interactions to dominate over minor-minor interactions.[14] Therefore, I am very skeptical of any alleged causal implications that are based on assumptions that major and minor powers can be treated interchangeably and I have more confidence in the possible causal importance of bivariate correlations based on analyses of major-major interactions, for the period from 1815 to 1965. Until such conflicting measurement assumptions are reconciled, and until we can control for all plausible rival hypotheses, we will continue to encounter more or less plausible, but conflicting, findings in the literature.

The disagreement between this paper and the Bueno de Mesquita indicators is not unique; rather, each scholar who has attempted to measure "alliance polarization" or "cluster polarity" has developed his own idiosyncratic algorithm, and no one has documented the correlations between his indicator and others that have gone before. The resulting Tower of Babel is illustrated by Table 8–7, in which eight published indicators of cluster

---

[13] See Lee Cronbach (1970, pp. 121–124) for a discussion of construct validation and an introduction to the literature on validation.

[14] While this view originated with conservative realists, it is shared by many radicals as well. See Daniel Chirot (1977) for a summary of this perspective on the world system.

Ostrom and Aldrich (1978) have modified the Bueno de Mesquita data in a manner somewhat consistent with this view. They calculated the number of independent clusters that included at least one major power. Then they added the number of non-aligned major powers to the initial total. The resulting grand total is the sum of all the major-major and major-minor clusters and the number of non-aligned major powers. This measure will probably still be sensitive, as the underlying Bueno de Mesquita index is, to the sheer growth in the number of minor powers during the twentieth century.

Ostrom and Aldrich take the surprising but useful approach of reducing most of the literature on polarity to a set of hypotheses about the number of independent actors. While their approach produces interesting and fruitful results, it is limited by this choice they have made about how to interpret the theoretical literature. Leaving aside attempts to incorporate crosscutting cleavages, intermediary roles, divided attention, discreteness, and tightness, they find support for George Liska's conclusion that the mere number of independent actors may not matter very much.

Table 8–7
Correlations between Selected Indicators of Cluster Polarization[a]

Variable		States Included	Concept	V1	V2	V3	V4	V5	V6	V7	V8	V9
Wayman bipolarization*	(V1)	Majors	Clusters as a proportion of potential clusters	1.0								
Singer-Small bipolarization (alternate)	(V2)	Majors	Alignments as proportion of potential alignments (omits debatable targets)	.66	1.0							
Singer-Small bipolarization (initial)	(V3)	Majors	Alignments as proportion of potential alignments (includes all targets)	.62	.75	1.0						
Singer-Small alliance aggregation	(V4)	All	Alignments as proportion of possible alignments	-.06	.04	.22	1.0					
Li and Thompson cluster*	(V5)	Majors	Number of discrete clusters	.42	.50	.64	.71	1.0				
Li and Thompson alliance	(V6)	Majors	Dyads with defense pacts as proportion of possible	.35	.48	.48	.70	.89	1.0			
Bueno de Mesquita poles*	(V7)	All	Number of poles	.30	.15	.24	-.61	-.06	-.30	1.0		
Bueno de Mesquita tightness	(V8)	All	Tightness of poles	-.01	-.14	.21	.58	.46	.19	-.08	1.0	
Bueno de Mesquita discreteness	(V9)	All	Discreteness of poles	.13	-.09	.12	-.24	-.04	-.15	.47	.34	1.0

[a] Pearson product-moment correlation coefficients based on measurements at five-year intervals, 1815–1965. Correlations of .404 or greater are significant at the .05 level, and these have been indicated by italicizing. Variables marked with an asterisk have been flipped in direction, as discussed in the text, to maximize the likelihood of obtaining positive correlations. All data are from Correlates of War Project archives.

polarity (as stored in the Correlates of War Project data archives) are compared to each other and to the cluster polarization indicator used in the current paper. (In table 8–7, the sign of three indicators has been reversed in order to insure that as many correlations as possible are positive; this means that any negative correlations will point to measures of cluster polarization that have produced reversed results.) A glance at the table shows that the eight indicators by Singer and Small (1968), Li and Thompson (1978), and Bueno de Mesquita (1975) clearly are measuring (hopefully because of the different intentions of the authors) fundamentally different things. The patterns are most disconcerting for the indicators based on all nation-states. For example, the Singer and Small alliance aggregation measure is correlated, at the .01 level of statistical significance, negatively with one Bueno de Mesquita measure (number of poles) and positively with another (tightness of poles). The measures of polarization in the major power system are more convergent with each other. The Li and Thompson and Singer and Small measures are all significantly correlated, in the positive direction, to each other. The measure used in the current paper is significantly associated, in the positive direction, with all of these prior measures of polarization of the major power system except one of the Li and Thompson measures, which falls barely short of statistical significance. As a general rule, the very weak associations are those between the major power system indicators and the indicators for all nation-states; the main exception to that rule is the strong relationship of the Li and Thompson measures to the Singer-Small alliance aggregation measure. While it is beyond the scope of the present paper, in the future it would be appropriate for literature reviews to consider these correlations before reaching conclusions about the meaning of the disparate findings that have been reported. It appears that cluster multipolarity is much more of a multidimensional concept than power bipolarity, and this point needs greater attention in texts and literature reviews. Meantime, for purposes of the present paper, it can be said that the indicator used, while unrelated to measures of cluster polarization for all nation-states, is significantly correlated with the bulk of the measures of major-power system cluster polarization, and to that extent is producing reliable results. Discrepancies with studies, such as Bueno de Mesquita's, which focus on the war-proneness of the system based on polarization patterns among all nation-states, are not surprising.

To summarize my findings, with regard to the two hypotheses tested in this paper, significant correlations exist which support the power polarity hypothesis in the whole period from 1815 to 1965, and the spatial polarization hypothesis in the twentieth century. None of the correlations discovered in this paper, however, is large enough to account for over half the variance in the amount of war. Thus even the highest correlations in this study are not enough to support a monocausal explanation of warfare, and other variables besides system polarization are clearly relevant. Indeed, until these other potential causes are specified, measured, and included as control variables, causal inferences about polarization and warfare will remain only suggestive. As for the theory of polarization that has been presented, it cannot be proven by the confirmation of hypotheses derived from it. Other theoretical formulations might generate the same hypothesis. But the failure to disconfirm does lend some greater plausibility to the theory, and does raise serious questions about the contrary assertions of Haas, Bueno de Mesquita, and other authors discussed above.

Conclusions

Theoretically, this paper has contended that the Waltz thesis and the Deutsch and Singer thesis, classically juxtaposed in the literature, may both be valid. Waltz argues that bipolarity is more stable than multipolarity. It has been theorized in this paper that he is correct insofar as he refers to *power* bipolarity, which minimizes the magnitude of war, should a war break out. Deutsch and Singer argue that multipolarity is more stable. It has been theorized in this paper that they are correct insofar as they refer to *cluster* multipolarity, which is less likely to lead to war than is cluster bipolarity.

The correlational evidence analyzed above is mildly supportive of both these hypotheses, for the twentieth century. The power polarity hypothesis seems confirmed for the whole period from 1815 to 1965. The cluster, or alignment, polarity hypothesis seems confirmed for the twentieth century. Significant correlations support it for the whole 1815–1965 period. But after separate bivariate analysis of each century, it seems disconfirmed for the nineteenth century, perhaps because of the effects of hostility on the balance of power alliance structures of that era.

If the findings for the twentieth century should prove valid, and the theory should be upheld, it would follow that a combination of power bipolarity and alignment multipolarity is the formula for stability in the modern era. The implications of such a perspective for foreign policy making would include the encouragement of political diversity and multicentrism of alliance patterns, along with a discouragement of massive transfers and proliferations of weapons technologies that might destabilize the power bipolarity of the international system of our nuclear age. Whatever the empirical results may show, it is the heartening conclusion of this essay that the relevant arguments of Waltz and Deutsch and Singer were valid and consistent with each other. Students of international politics who might have concluded that the arguments were contradictory could only have been discouraged at the level of theoretical integration and agreement in this area of the literature. If the theoretical structure of the present paper is sound, this potential area of disagreement has been replaced by a consistent theoretical structure based on a clearer understanding of the wisdom of both of these earlier theories.

Editors' Commentary

Major Findings

Wayman finds that when there are only two very powerful actors in the system, wars that are fought are of less magnitude (as measured in nation-months) than when there are several powerful actors in the system (i.e., a multipolarity of capability). This is indicated in table 8–4 by the moderate tau b correlation of −.43. Of equal significance is the fact that approximately three-quarters of the wars erupting during power bipolarity remain of low magnitude, while three-quarters of the wars erupting during a multipolar distribution of power are of very high magnitude. Finally, as Wayman notes, a multipolar distribution of capability is associated with the two major world wars. All of this means that wars of low magnitude are associated with a bipolar distribution of capability, while wars of high magnitude are associated with a multipolar distribution of capability.

This does not mean, however, that a multipolar distribution of power causes world war. The lag time between a shift to a multipolar distribution and the onset of war (from 1875 to 1913 and from 1925 to 1938; see tables 8–2 and 8–3) does not suggest a direct causal connection. Instead, the multipolar condition seems to establish a foundation for making a war widespread once it is brought about by other factors. The war involves more major states, in part, simply because there are more major states to begin with.

Wars that occur in a (power) multipolar system are more apt to spread, but the mere distribution of power is probably not what makes them expand. What appears to be of more significance, at least for the twentieth century, is alliance bi(polarization). Wayman finds, in the twentieth century, a −.56 correlation (of first differences) (table 8–5) between less polarity in the system and the amount of war (i.e. bipolar alliances are correlated with large wars). This relationship does not hold for the nineteenth century ($r = .12$). Furthermore, he shows that prior to large wars in the twentieth century, alliance patterns were becoming more bipolarized.

Although Wayman does not find an association for the nineteenth century, his table 8–3 makes it clear that the (bi)polarization prior to World War I began with the slow rise of blocs after 1870. Wayman's analysis is consistent with that of Bueno de Mesquita (1978), which shows blocs tightening just before large wars. Wayman provides another piece of evidence that alliances may be associated with the expansion of war. On the basis of his study, it seems that large wars involving many actors are a function of multipolar distribution of capability and that world wars are preceded by an intense polarization of this multipolar distribution of power into two blocs. This process of actualizing a multipolar system of power into two hostile forces is probably a crucial step in turning a war into a world war. It is probably not the only process, however, that produces world wars, as is made evident by Midlarsky's study in the next chapter.

Methodological Notes

Wayman's first finding is a tau b of $-.43$. You can see in table 8–4 how the cases cluster in the lower-left and upper-right cells. In order to understand how the negative correlation supports the hypothesis, you must think in terms of predicting *less* war. Bipolarity of capability (high concentration of power) is associated with lower magnitudes of war—thus the negative relationship between bipolar power and magnitude of war.

The findings for the third hypothesis (reported in table 8–5) are somewhat complex because of the need to separate the effects of alliance polarization and war on each other. To do this, Wayman calculates cross-lagged correlations on the two variables (see the first row of table 8–5). This means that one variable is correlated with values of the other at earlier and later times to see if war is followed by alliance multipolarity or if multipolarity is followed by war. On the basis of cross-lagged correlations, Wayman can draw inferences about which levels of alliance polarity lead to peace and which lead to war. Before he can do this, however, he must check for autocorrelation.

Here it becomes important to recognize that Wayman is using a **longitudinal** research design (see the learning package in chapter 15 for the distinction between longitudinal and cross-sectional analyses). In a longitudinal study, a variable is measured over a number of time periods; this is called time series data. A plot of a college's tuition over twenty years is an example of a time series. When two time series are correlated with each other, as in the first row of table 8–5, it is possible that the level of the dependent variable is produced not only by the independent variable but by earlier values of the dependent variable itself. This phenomenon of a variable's being correlated with previous values of itself is called autocorrelation.

Wayman calculates correlations on each variable, which he mentions in the text, and finds that they are indeed autocorrelated.

When there is a correlation among values of the same variable (as Wayman says, "nonzero autocorrelations"), we cannot conclude that the dependent variable is produced solely by the independent variable. That is, even if war is correlated with later alliance multipolarity (as it is in the nineteenth century—$r = .70$), that level of alliance multipolarity is at least partly produced by previous levels of alliance multipolarity (for example, alliance multipolarity is correlated with earlier levels of itself at $r = .44$).

To reduce the effect of this autocorrelation, Wayman differenced the two series. This means that each value was subtracted from the next in order to remove the trend in the line—in other words, to remove that part of the variable that was produced by earlier levels of itself. The values that result are called the **first differences.** (If there is still a trend, one can repeat the process, producing **second differences.**) Once the trend is removed in this way, the independent and dependent variables can be correlated with each other with the assurance that the resultant correlation will not be due to the earlier values of the dependent variable itself. Thus, we can more confidently attribute any remaining correlation to the effect of the independent variable. This puts Wayman on more solid ground for drawing conclusions from the second row of table 8–5. When he refers to the correlations between the first differences, he means the correlations between these reduced values.

If these values were very low or zero, that would mean that the amount of war in the system is merely a function of previous war. As the amount of war not attributed to previous war reaches significant levels, the first differences can be seen as a measure of "velocity," indicating the extent to which there is a growing amount of war, presumably due to an independent variable. In the case of the $r = -.56$, the system has a greater magnitude of war the *fewer* the blocs (as it becomes more cluster bipolar)—hence the minus sign.

Although the autocorrelation is removed from the variables, Wayman hesitates to draw causal conclusions from the findings. Rather, he finds them to be suggestive and uses them as the basis on which to build a new explanation of the different effects of alliance multipolarity on war. This explanation gives us an idea of what the structure of a system that would be prone to high-magnitude wars would look like. Next, we would want to know what kinds of dynamics characterize such a system. Midlarsky uses a very different set of methodological tools to explore this question in the next chapter.

9
Preventing Systemic War: Crisis Decision-Making Amidst a Structure of Conflict Relationships

Manus I. Midlarsky

Editors' Introduction

Manus Midlarsky is concerned with the factors that distinguish time periods that have systematic war from those that are more peaceful. He is particularly interested in identifying the structural aspects of a conflict system that might constrain decision making in a crisis and push the system toward war. Midlarsky assumes that any system can handle a certain number of disputes. As long as the number of disputes is randomly distributed (if a new dispute begins, then another should end), the system will be stable and can be said to be in equilibrium. If disputes begin to accumulate over time, this indicates a failure of the political system to resolve conflict. As disputes accumulate and become connected with each other, they tend to become even more difficult to resolve. According to Midlarsky, such a system, by definition, is not in equilibrium; he predicts it will be unstable and break down into systematic war. Midlarsky's findings help explain why and how different actors are drawn into a war, thereby making it a world war.

Manus I. Midlarsky, "Preventing Systemic War: Crisis Decision-Making Amidst a Structure of Conflict Relationships," *Journal of Conflict Resolution,* Vol. 28, No. 4 (December 1984), pp. 563–584. Copyright © 1984 by Sage Publications, Inc. Reprinted by permission of Sage Publications, Inc. and the author.

Author's Note: An earlier draft of this article was delivered at the 1983 Annual Meeting of the Peace Science Society (International), Urbana, IL. This study was supported by NSF Grant No. SES-8309851. Professor J. David Singer graciously allowed access to the Correlates of War serious dispute data, and for this I am greatly indebted. I would like to express my appreciation to Paul Buster and Kenneth Roberts for their extremely competent efforts in, respectively, computer programming and data management.

This article examines relationships between patterns of conflict behavior and the outbreak of widespread systemic war on the order of World Wars I and II. The exclusive focus is on systemic war as a breakdown of the international system; the concerns of this inquiry are limited to wars of this magnitude.[1] Explanations of war as a generic category are found in recent prominent analyses of war (Singer et al. 1979; Bueno de Mesquita, 1981b; Organski and Kugler 1980).

Specifically, two basic questions are asked in this study: (1) Can we differentiate analytically between time periods that do not experience systemic war and those that do? (2) What are the structural contours of the conflict system that influence or at least severely constrain the decision-making process in a crisis situation? In response to the first question, an equilibrium model will be postulated for conflict systems such that departures from that equilibrium condition will be associated with the onset of systemic war. The second question will be answered by establishing an isomorphism, or at least a correspondence, between the structure of the conflict system leading to war and the decision-making process itself. The conflicts to be examined consist of all serious international disputes involving two or more major powers in the time periods under examination.

Equilibrium and Interdependence

Basic to this inquiry is the concept of equilibrium. This concept has been claimed to be central to the peaceful functioning of international systems (Fenelon 1920; Oppenheim 1974; Pollard 1923; Fay 1930; Liska 1957; Russett 1968; Stoessinger 1964; Zinnes 1967; Holsti 1976a). The type of equilibrium to be introduced shortly emerges from this fundamental theme of international relations theory and is a direct form of stochastic equilibrium that was used successfully in prior analyses of alliances and conflict behavior (Midlarsky 1981, 1982, 1983a, 1983b). This equilibrium posits an average equality in beginnings and endings of a dispute. For every dispute that begins in a certain time period, generally one must end or else there is a build-up of the simultaneous occurrence of a series of disputes. It is this accumulation of conflict behavior over time that is suggested to be destabilizing. On the other hand, if the conflicts are resolved quickly, there is little opportunity of an accumulation over time.

There are two fundamental reasons for the expectation of systemic breakdown upon the accumulation of a series of disputes. Both of these will

---

[1] In this study, the concept of systemic war is identified completely with the breakdown of the international system, or global war. However, it is possible to define a much smaller system, as in a region such as the Middle East, and carry out an analysis similar to the one found here.

be demonstrated in the later analysis of the 1914 summer crisis leading to the onset of World War I. The first is the converse of the argument used in the Deutsch and Singer (1964) treatment of the increase in number of interaction opportunities due to the increase in the number of new nation-states. In that instance, the share of attention devoted to each new protagonist is diminished because of the rapidly increasing $(N[N - 1]/2)$ number of interaction opportunities. Thus the attention devoted to an arms race between only two nation-states or other manifestations of dyadic hostility leading to war is lessened. In the present analysis, however, the share of attention devoted to each dispute by great power decision makers is diminished, thus potentially decreasing possibilities for the peaceful resolution of each crisis. If decision makers are overwhelmed by a succession of conflicts, each requiring a fair amount of attention, then possibilities for resolving each crisis peacefully are diminished accordingly.

A rough analogy to the $N(N - 1)/2$ formula for the number of interaction opportunities may exist in this case, for if several disputes exist simultaneously, each involving two or more countries, then the simple condition of being in a state of conflict may lead to the desire for allies on the part of each protagonist. This may lead to a "conflict interaction opportunity" as in the merging of two or more disputes ("the enemy of my enemy is my friend"), and a multiplicative element may be introduced for the number of dyadic disputes existing at a particular point in time.

The second basic reason for the onset of systemic war upon the accumulation of a series of disputes consists of a set of possibilities for interdependence among the disputes. These are three in number: a demonstration or diffusion effect; a widespread process occasioning similar responses by geographically separate sovereign entities; and a reinforcement effect.

A demonstration or diffusion effect exists whenever the behavior of one country, and in particular its success in aggressive conflict behavior, serves as a model or prototype for other countries. Those countries whose governments are most similar to one another (e.g., dictatorships), and therefore can identify with each other, are most likely to imitate the model or prototype. This process seemed to have occurred in the decade preceding World War II. The invasion of Manchuria by Japan in 1931, followed by the invasion of Ethiopia by Italy, may have constituted the kind of demonstration of international politics by conquest that then led Hitler (and possibly Stalin) to adopt similar tactics later in that decade. On the other hand, the rapid resolution of these conflicts, and especially the absence of gain for an aggressor, implies that there is no demonstration of success. There are no ongoing instances of aggressive behavior that can serve as a "demonstration effect" for others and consequently intensify a conflict learning spiral. The probability models to be introduced shortly assume statistical independence among all of the instances of conflict behavior.

The occasioning of similar responses by countries to a geographically widespread process may be found in the period preceding World War I. The declining power of the Ottoman Empire may have led both to expansionist tendencies by Italy in the southwestern fringes of the Empire, leading to the conquest of Libya in 1911–1912, and the desire for increased territory and population in the Balkans at Turkish expense by Bulgaria, Serbia, Greece, and Montenegro, leading to the Balkan Wars of 1912–1913. The rise to power of the Young Turks in 1908 and the subsequent deposing of the Sultan Abdul Hamid in the following year likely advertised to those interested external powers that they could gain at Turkey's expense during this period of internal instability and power interregnum. As we shall see later, both the Italo-Turkish War and the Balkan Wars are conflict events immediately preceding the onset of World War I and contributing to the instability of that period.

The last source of interdependence to be considered here—that of reinforcement—occurs when the behavior of a country is conditioned by its earlier success when it engaged in a similar type of behavior. In the approach to World War II, there very likely was a reinforcement effect operating, in that each of Hitler's successes in the late 1930s increased the probability that he would resort to a similar behavior at a later time. In the analysis of World War I, the success of the "blank check" support of Austria-Hungary by Germany, and the ultimatum to Russia in the conflict with Russia and Serbia after the annexation of Bosnia-Herzogovina by Austria-Hungary in 1908, likely increased the probability that such unconditional support of Austria-Hungary and an ultimatum to Russia would appear again in the Summer Crisis of 1914. The second time, however, the Russians would not accede to a German ultimatum essentially requiring the cessation of support for the smaller Slav ally. Thus the three forms of increased conflict interdependence as the number of disputes accumulate, and the sheer complexity and decreased attention span for each dispute, argue for an increased systemic instability as the number of disputes in existence at any one point in time increase.

The average equality between beginnings and endings of disputes can be written as

$$C_i = <D_i> av = \sum_{n=i}^{\infty} P(n)D_i \qquad (9.1)$$

where $P(n)$ is the Poisson probability that n disputes exist in any time interval t, and C_i and D_i are the respective probabilities of the creation and dissolution of disputes. With some fairly simple independence and uniformity assumptions, this equation leads to the Poisson distribution for dispute onset (C_i) and a binomial distribution for dispute resolution (D_i). These assumptions are that the various disputes (not countries)[2] do not influence each other and are therefore stochastically independent, and that time within the interval t is uniform, such that each dispute found in t is equally likely to be resolved. Equations 9.2–9.4, below, which have the structure of a Poisson combined with a binomial, then follow directly (Midlarsky 1981:273–275). P(n, n+j) is the probability of passing from the state of n disputes in existence to n+j in the interval t, while P(n, n − j) and P(n, n) have corresponding interpretations. The constant p is defined as the probability of a single dispute being resolved during the interval t, whereas μ is the mean number of disputes in existence in t. These equations, therefore, presuppose a randomness and fluidity in the conflict behavior of the international system (especially the major powers) that effectively preclude the build-up of an interdependent set of conflict events.

$$P(n, n+j) = e^{-\mu p} \sum_{i=0}^{n} \frac{n!}{i! \, (n-i)!} \, p^i \, (1-p)^{n-i} \times (\mu p)^{i+j} / \, (i+j)! \quad (9.2)$$

$$P(n, n-j) = e^{-\mu p} \sum_{i=j}^{n} \frac{n!}{i! \, (n-i)!} \, p^i \, (1-p)^{n-i} \times (\mu p)^{i-j} / \, (i-j)! \quad (9.3)$$

$$P(n, n) = e^{-\mu p} \sum_{i=0}^{n} \frac{n}{i! \, (n-i)!} \, p^i \, (1-p)^{n-i} \, \frac{(\mu p)^i}{i!} \quad (9.4)$$

Stable and Unstable Systems

The international systems to be compared are the nineteenth-century (1816–1899) system of conflict behavior and the period of 1893–1914, which is that preceding World War I. (A small amount of overlap is allowed in order to accommodate the relatively slow diplomatic change in this period, beginning with the Franco-Russian alliance in the years 1891–1894, during which the alliance solidified and formed the basis for the Triple Entente, which was soon to oppose the Dual Alliance in the Summer Crisis of 1914.)[3] The former period is well known for its historic stability; here that stability will have to be demonstrated analytically. The second of the two periods, of course, will have to demonstrate properties that are substantially different

---

[2] Obviously countries can influence each other, but if the specific terms of various disputes are kept independent of each other, then stochastic independence can be achieved for the disputes themselves (e.g., the Soviet intervention in Afghanistan being largely independent of the U.S. involvement in Central America, despite the influence the individual great powers can have on each other).

[3] The use of the 1899 ending for the nineteenth century not only conforms to standard usage but also facilitates comparison with other studies (e.g., Midlarsky 1981, 1983a).

and, in addition, that have a structural correspondence with the Summer Crisis of 1914. This crisis has been studied perhaps more than any other and therefore provides an excellent referent for the present study. A principal question is, Why was there widespread systemic warfare at the termination of one of these periods (1893–1914) but no such war in the other (1816–1899)? Also, what are the distinguishing features of each that lead to the different outcomes?

The data used are the Correlates of War militarized dispute data for the period 1816–1914. For each of the two systems, (a) disputes between two or more major powers will be examined, followed by (b) disputes between two or more powers that involve at least one central (i.e., diplomatically active minor) power as defined in Singer and Small (1968:254) and (c) the set of disputes combining both a and b.[4] Only European disputes are included because of the centrality of Europe in the onset of World War I.

Applying equations 9.2–9.4 to the 1816–1899 period for disputes involving two or more major powers yields the matrix of table 9–1. The value of p in the table was estimated by the ratio of the mean number of disputes initiated to the mean number in existence as in Midlarsky (1981:278). The observed entries in the table are the frequency of transitions from one state, n, of numbers of disputes in existence to another, k, in two successive years. The top line of each cell entry gives the observed value and the bottom line is one predicted by an equation $z(n, k) = P(n) P(n, k)$, where $k = n + j, n-j$ or n, so that the values of $P(n, k)$ are given by equations 9.2–9.4 and $P(n)$ by values of the Poisson distribution for disputes in existence as in Midlarsky (1981:276).

The table records 55 times when the system passed from 0 disputes in existence in one year to 0 in the succeeding year, with 53.09 predicted transitions of this type. Similarly, there were 8 instances where the system underwent change from 0 disputes in one year to 1 in the next, with 9.99 predicted transitions from 0 to 1. As can be seen, the chi-square goodness of

---

[4] The conflict behaviors analyzed here include all instances of serious disputes involving two or more major powers in the time periods under investigation. The major powers are Austria-Hungary, France, Germany, Great Britain, and Russia. A listing of the central powers is found in Singer and Small (1968:254) and includes countries such as Belgium, the Netherlands, Serbia, Bulgaria, and Rumania. The disputes range from minimal conflict behaviors at the lower end of a five-point hostility scale to the outbreak of war at the upper end of the scale. However, none of the time periods investigated here includes instances of international systemic war (World Wars I and II), and it is suggested here that both theoretically and empirically, systemic wars of this magnitude demonstrate fundamentally different properties from nonsystemic wars such as the Austro-Prussian or Balkan wars. Not only does the scope of the conflict in the form of the number of protagonists and duration of the war differ widely in the two instances, but the number of battle deaths in a systemic war (9 million and 15 million, respectively, in World Wars I and II) vastly exceeds that found in any of the nonsystemic variety. Removing the instances of war from the data set and repeating the analyses made no difference in the conclusions reached.

Table 9–1

Observed and Expected Frequencies of Occurrence of the Pairs (n, k) of Disputes between Two or More Major Powers, 1816–1899 (p = .6957)

n	$k = 0$	1	2
0	55[a] 53.09	8 9.99	2 .94
1	8 9.99	5 6.25	2 1.00
2	2 .94	2 1.00	0 .35

$\chi^2 = 4.576^b$, df = 3, p < .30.

[a] The top line of each entry gives the observed value and the bottom line is one predicted by the equation z (n, k) = P (n) P (n, k) where k = n + j, n − j, or n, so that the values of P (n, k) are given by equations 9.2–9.4 and P(n) by the values of the Poisson distribution for disputes in existence.

[b] For the chi-square test, predicted values less than 1.5 are combined with adjacent values until that figure is obtained as suggested in Gibbons (1971:72).

fit statistic gives a probability value suggesting that the conflict system of the major powers exclusively was stable.[5] A fit between observation and prediction will be rejected at p≤.10 in order to adopt a fairly conservative policy on the acceptance of the equilibrium model.[6]

An interesting property of equations 9.2–9.4 is the symmetry in transitions from n to k and from k to n. This, of course, is reflected in the predicted values in table 9–1 (e.g., 9.99 both for 0 to 1 and 1 to 0), but also is found in several of the observed values in that table. Thus there were eight cases of transition from 0 to 1 disputes in existence and eight from 1 to 0, and there were also two instances of transition from 0 to 2 disputes in existence and two from 2 to 0.

When we analyze disputes involving at least one central power, the results are similar. The chi-square value suggests an excellent fit between observation and prediction.

Coalescing all of the disputes into one set, that constituting the combined set of disputes, or those between major powers, and major powers involving central and European powers also yields a strong pattern of sta-

---

[5] Use of somewhat different criteria, such as a requirement that a major power exist in that state for at least half of the time period under consideration, gives a more impressive fit between observation and prediction (Midlarsky 1983a:783). However, these criteria led to the absence in the data set of certain major powers such as Italy in the latter portion of the nineteenth century, and these powers are included here.

[6] For the chi-square test, adjacent categories were combined until a minimum expected value of 1.5 was obtained. In this process of summing across rows, values greater than 1.5 were skipped in order to maximize the number of available degrees of freedom (see Gibbons 1971:72).

Table 9–2

Observed and Expected Frequencies of Occurrence of the Pairs (n, k) of Disputes between Two or More Major Powers, Involving at Least One Central Power, 1816–1899 (p = .7000)

n	$k = 0$	1	2	3
0	47	10	2	0
	46.10	11.39	1.41	.12
1	10	9	1	1
	11.39	7.70	1.55	.18
2	1	2	0	0
	1.41	1.55	.60	.10
3	1	0	0	0
	.12	.18	.10	.03

$\chi^2 = 1.060$, df = 5, p <.98.

bility.[7] This of course constitutes the entire set of nineteenth-century disputes, and no further conflicts could be added to the overall array. For purposes of comparability with the later analysis of 1893–1914, the overall 1816–1907 period was divided into 4 intervals of 22 years each (the significance of 1907 will emerge later), and each of these was analyzed separately. All of the chi-square values were nonsignificant at least at p<.50, with the highest attaining a value of $\chi^2 = 5.752$ at p<.50 and the lowest reaching a value of $\chi^2 = 1.558$ at p<.95.Thus in this nineteenth-century system all combinations of conflicts lead to a highly equilibrated system.

We now turn to an analysis of the 1893–1914 period and, as before, present the disputes solely involving two or more major powers. The pattern here is not substantially different from that shown in the earlier period and is acceptable.

The fit between observation and prediction for disputes between major powers with at least one central power also is acceptable, and in these respects the 1893–1914 system does not differ substantially from the nineteenth-century system. If anything, once again the presence of smaller powers in the disputes improves the overall fit between observation and prediction.

When we combine the disputes of tables 9–4 and 9–5 as presented in table 9–6, we find our first statistically significant departure from the equilibrium condition of equation 9.1. Substantively, we can say that the ab-

---

[7] In order to include all possible European countries, the smaller European (noncentral) countries are included here (e.g., Baden, Bavaria, Parma, Modena), although they are absent from the 1893–1914 period because these countries either became central powers later in the century or were absorbed in the unifications of Italy and Germany. The criterion governing both the nineteenth-century analysis in table 9–3 and that for 1893–1914 in table 9–6 is that all possible sovereign European entities be included.

Table 9–3
Observed and Expected Frequencies of Occurrence of the Pairs (n, k) of
Disputes between Two or More Major Powers and Those Involving Any
Other Countries in the European System, 1816–1899 (p = .7231)

n	k = 0	1	2	3	4
0	26	11	3	0	1
	22.49	12.44	3.44	.63	.09
1	11	12	3	3	0
	12.44	11.64	4.53	1.08	.18
2	2	4	1	1	0
	3.44	4.53	2.49	.78	.16
3	2	1	1	0	0
	.63	1.08	.78	.32	.09
4	0	1	0	0	1
	.09	.18	.16	.09	.03

$\chi^2 = 7.097$, df = 9, p < .70.

sence of equilibrium for this system was a consequence of the combined set
of major power disputes alone and major power disputes involving at least
one central power. (Use of the year 1913 as an endpoint for this interval also
led to the finding of instability.)

Note that there are two additional ways of analyzing the data in these
tables, representing, respectively, the simple accumulation of disputes and
evidence of interdependence. The first way is to count the number of transitions from n to k above and below the matrix diagonal. Transitions above
the diagonal (k>n) represent increases from smaller to larger numbers of
disputes in existence, while those below the diagonal (k<n) represent decreases in the number of disputes in existence. Only tables 9–5 and 9–6
demonstrate a measurable imbalance between the two, favoring an increase
in existing conflict behavior relative to the number of years included in the
analysis. Table 9–5 records six transitions from n to k where k>n and four
where k<n. Table 9–6 reports nine instances where k>n and six cases
where k<n. All of the preceding tables demonstrate either equality or at

Table 9–4
Observed and Expected Frequencies of Occurrence of the Pairs (n, k) of
Disputes between Two or More Major Powers, 1893–1914 (p = .8889)

n	k = 0	1	2
0	10	4	1
	10.51	3.65	.64
1	4	0	1
	3.65	1.73	.38
2	1	1	0
	.64	.38	.10

$\chi^2 = 3.439$, df = 2, p < .20.

Table 9–5
Observed and Expected Frequencies of Occurrence of the Pairs (n, k) of Disputes between Two or More Major Powers, Involving at Least One Central Power, 1893–1914 (p = .5429)

n	k = 0	1	2	3
0	11	4	1	0
	11.25	2.65	.31	.02
1	3	1	0	1
	2.65	2.86	.60	.07
2	0	0	0	0
	.31	.60	.36	.07
3	1	0	0	0
	.02	.07	.07	.03

$\chi^2 = 2.036$, df = 2, p < .50.

most an excess of one dispute for k>n versus k<n (22 versus 21 in table 9–3) and this for the much longer time period of 1816–1899. The equilibrium condition of equation 1, of course, specifies equality. This observation for table 9–6 is consistent with the previous finding of instability for the combined major power and major-central power disputes shown in that table. For table 9–5, it is indicative of a tendency toward some diffusion and reinforcement of individual major-central power conflicts reported elsewhere (Midlarsky 1983b).

What additionally distinguishes table 9–6 from table 9–5 and the preceding tables is the second mode of analysis, which constitutes an examination of each table for substantial numbers of abrupt transitions from one state to the next. In table 9–6, we have four instances of transitions from 0 to 2 disputes in existence and two cases of 3 to 0 disputes. Although these transitions might not be considered to be especially abrupt in a larger dimension matrix, here in this matrix, the values of n, k = 2 or 3 are the largest

Table 9–6
Observed and Expected Frequencies of Occurrence of the Pairs (n, k) of Disputes between Two or More Major Powers and Those Involving Any Other Countries in the European System, 1893–1914 (p = .9474)

n	k = 0	1	2	3
0	6	3	4	0
	4.40	3.45	1.35	.35
1	3	0	0	0
	3.45	2.89	1.21	.33
2	1	0	1	2
	1.35	1.21	.54	.16
3	2	0	0	0
	.35	.33	.16	.05

$\chi^2 = 16.505$, df = 5, p < .01.

values that these indices can assume. In a Markovian (memoryless) matrix of this type, which has Poisson initiations and exponential durations of disputes (not demonstrated here, but actually found in an analysis of alliances in 1816–1899; [Midlarsky 1983a]), the vast majority of transitions should be only from n to k = n or n + 1 or n − 1, with all other transitions having a much smaller probability of occurrence. Any appreciable number of abrupt changes as found in table 9–6, where k = n + 2 four times or k = n − 3 twice, would depart from this pattern and signify instability via the presence of memory as a form of interdependence encompassing diffusion, a common source of prior events, or reinforcement.

Aside from the finding of an unstable system and its implications for the predictability of major systemic war, the pattern of table 9–6 suggests an understanding of the onset of World War I that differs substantially from more traditional interpretations (e.g., Albertini 1967; Fay 1928). In that view, conflicts among the major powers were the principal or nomothetic causes of the war, while the conflict between Austria-Hungary and Serbia was simply the "spark" or proximal cause of the war. Here the two patterns of causation have equal status, in the sense that neither the pattern of great power conflicts involving a small power, as in table 9–5, or exclusively great power conflicts, as in table 9–4, is demonstrably unstable. Only when the two are combined in a joint set is instability demonstrated. This finding should be contrasted with that of the nineteenth century in table 9–3, where the joint set of the two conflict varieties demonstrates greater stability than that of the major powers alone. This fundamental difference will be discussed in more detail at a later point. For now, the equality of the two modes of explanation—that is, great power conflicts and great power conflicts involving central powers—suggests that both patterns existed in the period approaching World War I and contributed to its onset. This conclusion is further supported by the existence of a pattern of major-central power conflicts of at least twenty years duration prior to 1914 (Midlarsky 1983b).

Isomorphism to the Summer Crisis

When asked at the start of World War I how all this could have happened, Bethmann Hollweg, the German chancellor, is said to have replied, "Oh, if I only knew" (Nomikos and North 1976:7). Although this quote is often used in Germany to exculpate the German government from responsibility for the war's onset, there is a wider meaning to be found here. The joint occurrences of great power conflicts on the one hand, and small power–great power conflicts on the other, may be sufficiently complex so that few decision makers in a crisis could foresee the outcome. This is the first destabilizing consequence of the accumulation of disputes noted earlier. While individually each of these sets of equilibrated disputes was manageable, the simultaneous occurrence of both conflicts may have made decision makers concerned with the one type unaware of the dangers of the other. For example, although Germany and Russia could resolve their fundamental differences without reference to third powers, the escalation of the Austro-Serbian dispute introduced an element of small power–great power conflict to which decision makers concerned solely with great power differences would most likely not lend much credence. It was this complexity of the overall system of conflict that may have led decision makers either to err or to grossly underestimate the consequences of the crisis at its outset. It probably led directly to the loss of control over events in the crisis noted by Snyder and Diesing (1977). In addition, the failure to realize that the small power–great power disputes had actually formed a discernible and dangerous pattern of conflict behavior (Midlarsky 1982) also likely increased the propensity toward inadequate decision making in the crisis.

But there is a deeper sense in which the structure of the conflict process preceding the war conditioned the pattern by which the crisis unfolded. Recall that table 9–6 is the fusion or combination of sets of conflicts analyzed in tables 9–4 and 9–5. If that fusion had not taken place, then the preceding analysis implies that each of the two conflict sets could have been resolved peacefully. Thus *any decision or action that provided such unification can be cited as a principal contributor to the unstable outcome of international warfare.*

There is, in fact, one such decision that unified the two conflict sets, and that is the famous "blank check" given to the Austro-Hungarian diplomats by the Kaiser at the outset of the crisis and that had been used so successfully in the prior Bosnian Crisis of 1908. As noted earlier in this article, the preceding successful use of the blank check by Germany likely constituted a basis for the reinforcement of this type of behavior. The Kaiser, in 1914, explicitly indicated his express support for any actions Austria-Hungary might contemplate against Serbia, including the possibility that the Serbs "be disposed of *and* that right *soon*" (quoted in Nomikos and North 1976:37). This was intended as a reprimand for the German ambassador to Vienna, who was counseling restraint to the Austrians. As a result of this policy of complete support, the Austrians could be seriously emboldened in their policy toward Serbia, with consequences that we now know. From the perspective of this study, however, this was not simply an invitation to boldness by Germany, but the effecting of a juncture between two sets of disputes—those involving major powers exclusively and those that had central power (e.g., Serbian) involvement as well.

It was Germany, of course, that tended to have the greatest number of disputes with other major powers such as France, Russia, or Great Britain. Although Austria-Hungary also experienced conflict with Russia, the major share of its disputes were with the Balkan powers such as Bulgaria, Serbia, or Turkey. Thus the promise of complete support by Germany effected the union between predominantly major power disputes such as those experienced by Germany and disputes involving central powers that were the main preoccupation of Austro-Hungary (table 9–5). Without that juncture, the crisis could not have followed the pattern that did indeed evolve, and it likely would have had a peaceful outcome.

There is one further way to test this structural correspondence between precrisis conflict processes and crisis behavior. This can be done by examining a crisis similar in characteristics to that of 1914, but with a peaceful outcome: the Bosnian Crisis of 1908 (Sabrosky 1975). Here all of the initial protagonists are involved at the outset, with Russia supporting the strong Serb protest of the annexation of Bosnia-Herzegovina by Austria-Hungary and Germany fully supporting the Austro-Hungarians. A "blank check" between Germany and Austria-Hungary is found here too, and yet a war did not develop, the crisis ending peacefully. But if the structure of the conflict process is substantially different such that a conjunction between two sets of conflict events is *not* inherently unstable, then a blank check of this type would have little consequence. If the system resulting from the combination of the two forms of conflict is not an unstable system, then complete support of the type given to Austria-Hungary by Germany would have no major impact. Was such a system unstable at the time of the Bosnian Crisis?

Table 9–7 presents the analysis of the entire set of disputes (comparable to table 9–6) from 1893 until 1908. As can be seen, there is an excellent fit between observation and prediction, suggesting that a fundamental difference in the structure of conflict relationships exists between the time of the Bosnian Crisis and the time of the Summer Crisis of 1914. Thus, despite the existence of a blank check in both instances, these differences in conflict behavior preceding both crises apparently led to the different outcomes.

Table 9–7
Observed and Expected Frequencies of Occurrence of the Pairs (n, k) of Disputes between Two or More Major Powers and Those Involving Any Other Countries in the European System, 1893–1908 (p = .9167)

n	$k = 0$	1	2	3
0	4 4.14	3 2.68	2 .87	0 .19
1	3 2.68	0 1.97	0 .72	0 .17
2	1 .87	0 .72	1 .29	1 .08
3	1 .19	0 .17	0 .08	0 .02

$\chi^2 = 2.846$, df $= 3$, p $< .50$.

Implications for the Study of Crisis

The first clear implication of this study is that structure does matter for the outcome of international crisis, but it does not necessarily mean system structure as measured by alliances, polarity, or other forms of structural cohesion. Here the structure of conflict relationships has been found to be important. Thus in effect this study assumes a somewhat different position from that of those researchers who suggest that system structures (e.g., polarity, alliances) are virtually deterministic in their outcomes (Waltz 1979) and others who are now advocating that the outcome of war resides largely in the process of crisis decision making (Most and Starr 1983, 1984). By focusing on conflict relationships or, more specifically, the equilibrium or disequilibrium of the structure of conflict relationships, we can approach more closely the dynamics of the conflict process itself that will be resolved one way or another during the crisis period. This is not to say that the conflict structure is in any way deterministic, but simply that, given the instability of the set of conflict relationships, the probabilities are higher that war will be an outcome of the crisis.

The second implication is that surprise may be a less important component of the crisis than had been considered until now, at least in the World War I instance (Brecher 1980; Hermann 1972). This is simply because the juncture between the two conflict sets (table 9–6) occurred very early in the crisis; in fact, it occurred on July 4–5, only one week after the crisis had begun. The remaining four weeks of the crisis may have been the consequence of working out the implications of that early decision, and indeed the perceptual distortions—such as the excessive amount of hostility versus capability perceptions (Zinnes et al. 1961)—may actually have been a consequence not so much of the surprise element or excessive stress but of a self-justification or rationalization mechanism. After all, once the blank check had been issued and the two conflict sets joined, how else could one justify what may have been a hasty and unwarranted decision except by reference to perceptions of threat and hostility from the potential enemy? By perceiving the enemy as a monolithic hostile coalition, the decision to forge one's own coalition as an inseparable entity (the direct consequence of the blank check) becomes justified.

Seeing the opposing coalition as excessively hostile or "frustrating" in intent (Holsti et al. 1968) is attributing a nonrational set of motivations to the potential enemy, and therefore that enemy would be much less amenable to rational discourse in negotiation. This is an almost ideal way to justify and rationalize one's own behaviors that, in the instance of strong support for Austria-Hungary's aggressive behaviors toward Serbia, have a high hostility component at the outset. This excessive perception of hostility by the Dual Alliance at the beginning of the crisis is mirrored in the fact that in the first month of the crisis there were 171 perceptions of hostility on the part of the Dual Alliance decision makers, but only 40 for the Triple Entente (Holsti et al. 1968:152). The tendency for the Dual Alliance decision makers to magnify or "overperceive" the actions of the Triple Entente countries (Holsti et al. 1968:158) is consistent with this hypothetical justification of past hostile decisions. Only if the opponents are seen as truly acting in a hostile and vindictive fashion can such early hostile action be justified. Viewed from this perspective, the decision making during the crisis becomes an ex post facto process designed to provide justification for what had already occurred.

This interpretation of the crisis dynamics provides a reasonably straightforward explanation for the finding by Holsti (1972b:67) that Germany, of all of the Dual Alliance and Triple Entente protagonists, had the highest number of perceptions of "necessity" for its own actions (110), even more than Austria-Hungary (80), which, in many ways, was the single major power originator of the crisis. In addition, the chi-square comparison between "necessity" and "choice" for "self" and "enemies" for Germany was by far the highest ($\chi^2 = 85.8$, $p < .001$) of any of the protagonists. Although Austria-Hungary reacted very strongly to the assassination, it still was in the nature of a reaction, whereas Germany made the early and, in many ways, self-conscious decision to support its ally fully. Thus a decision of this kind would require more justification than a reactive one, and the concept of a necessity for action in the sense of being compelled in a certain direction would provide that justification.

At the same time, this is not to say that stress, time constraints, and perceptions of threat are not salient aspects of international crises (Holsti 1972b). Rather, the preceding analysis suggests that just as there exists an interaction process among many decision makers in which these elements indeed are induced in the interactive process, there also can exist a priori rationalization processes that can augment these properties of crisis in order to justify past hostile behavior. Indeed, both processes are likely present, but it is the hostile behavior at the outset conditioning later responses that has received little, if any, systematic attention in the crisis literature.

Comparison with crises that had been resolved peacefully reveals the absence of such a juncture of conflict relationships. The explicit rejection by the Soviet Union of any influence by Castro in the Cuban Missile Crisis (Holsti et al. 1964; Holsti 1972a) had the consequence not only of removing a potentially erratic source of decision making but also of preventing the set of conflicts between the United States and other Latin American nations from intruding into the crisis. The then fairly recent U.S. influence in the removal of Jacobo Arbenz from leadership in Guatemala or the memory of other more overt interventions in Central America such as that in Nicaragua might have provided material for Cuban propaganda and possibly excited some anti-American feeling in the form of protests or demonstrations that could have diverted the attention of American decision makers from the goal of resolving the crisis peacefully. If the Soviet Union had allowed Castro a public opportunity to declare the crisis a joint Soviet-Cuban venture against "American imperialism," then the complexity of the crisis would have increased accordingly. In the "mini-crises" between the United States and the Soviet Union at the end of both Middle East wars of 1967 and 1973, neither of the superpowers allowed their Middle East allies to influence policy unduly, thus preventing the joining of the regional conflict sets to the global ones (Brecher 1980:225, 285).

Creating Disjoint Sets

The findings here and the preceding arguments have clear implications for crisis management. The prevention of the juncture between two or more sets of conflict relationships should be a principal goal of policymakers. Similarly, creating what may, in a formal sense, be called disjoint sets of conflict relationships should also be a goal of policymakers. These would be two or more sets of conflicts in which no conflict element would be found in more than one set. The probability of a widespread systemic war resulting from a crisis is likely proportional to the extent to which such sets are created. The desirability of this strategy may not only be true of policy in the midst of crisis but also may be a vehicle for overall conflict resolution. Henry Kissinger's Middle East policy of separating the Egyptian-Israeli conflict from the remainder of the Middle East controversies had the result not only of yielding the peace treaty between the two countries but also of possibly preventing a future widespread war in the Middle East. Interestingly, Syrian support of the effort to destroy the PLO as an independent political force may have had a similar consequence, for the Palestinian conflict with Israel can now be fully controlled by Syria, thus creating to the north of Israel a single set of conflicts not joined to any others.

From this perspective, Soviet support of Cuban military activities in Africa had the opposite consequence, for it joined a regional set of African conflicts with Caribbean ones involving a great power—the United States—which potentially could have involved the Soviet Union itself in some crisis far removed from its boundaries as a result of this mixed and conjoint set of conflict relationships.

Conclusion

The analysis has demonstrated significant analytical differences between the nineteenth-century pattern of conflict behavior, which did not lead to widespread war, and the early twentieth-century pattern, which did. The finding of the presence of an overall equilibrium in conflict behavior in the former but not in the latter emerges from theories of international politics that emphasize equilibrium as a fundamental property of peaceful systems. Additionally, the absence of war as an outcome of the Bosnian Crisis but its presence after Sarajevo can be understood as a consequence of the essential instability of the pre-1914 period compared to the stability of the pre-1908 period, despite the the presence in both instances of a juncture between two sets of conflict relationships. If the 1908 system had been equally unstable, then similar decision-making processes in both instances might have had the same outcome. Perhaps it was the increased strength of the Triple Entente relative to the Dual Alliance after 1908 (Sabrosky 1975) that led to an increased willingness on the part of the Entente partners to engage the Dual Alliance in various system-destabilizing conflicts prior to 1914.[8] Whatever its source, however, the 1914 system demonstrates an instability in conflict relationships not shared by its temporal predecessors.[9]

These findings also shed a somewhat different light on the dynamics of the 1914 crisis. In addition to the consequences of interactions among decision makers, which have been studied carefully and at length, the outcome of the crisis also may have been strongly conditioned by the need for German decision makers to justify their early hostile behaviors in providing unconditional support for the proposed Austro-Hungarian action against Serbia. Later perceptions of hostility and the necessity for aggressive action may have been direct consequences of the need to justify the earlier decision.

There are clear implications of these findings for crisis management such that even if a system is unstable, decision-making procedures can minimize the probability of war as an outcome of crisis. Chief among these is the prevention of conjoint sets of conflict relationships or even, as a precrisis strategy, the creation of joint sets. In this fashion, instabilities can be localized such that widespread systemic war becomes much less likely.

---

[8] The major strengthening of the British navy occurred after 1908 with the passage of the Naval Bill in the following year. There may have been a curious and unfortunate coalescence of several events in 1908. The rise to power of the Young Turks and the consequent power interregnum, which likely invited the latter aggressive actions of Italy and the Balkan countries, the Bosnian crisis with its potential for the later reinforcement of Austria-Hungary against Russia., and the failure of the London Naval Conference to regulate conditions of naval warfare that led to the 1909 English Naval Bill all occurred in 1908. This suggests that 1908 be used as the year to date the onset of instability in this time period. However, there are insufficient data in the seven years from 1908 until 1914 to test this hypothesis. Further, the critical variable is the stability or instability evident at the end of a period rather than the choice of a year to begin it. What must be avoided is the inclusion of too many years preceding the onset of instability so that an essentially stable earlier period could mask the emergence of instability at a later point. Since this did not happen in the 1893–1914 analysis, the selection of the historically suggested year of the consummation of the Franco-Russian alliance (1893) in opposition to the Dual Alliance is an appropriate choice.

[9] The finding here of the instability of the period ending in 1914 is consistent with the theory of long cycles (Modelski 1983), which suggests a deterioration of the global political system prior to the onset of global war. For further development of the long cycle theory and its empirical testing, see Thompson and Zuk (1982) and Rasler and Thompson (1983).

Editors' Commentary

Major Findings

Midlarsky finds that, during the period prior to World War I, disputes build up, whereas for most of the time after 1816, this does not occur. In a subsequent analysis, Midlarsky (1988:150, 236) finds that the period prior to World War II also experiences an accumulation of disputes, although the fit here is not as significant as that for World War I. Midlarsky has made a major contribution by developing a mathematical analysis and statistical measure that are able to confirm the historical fact that just prior to the two world wars, crises were coming upon one another at a fast and furious pace that leaders could not handle.

What Midlarsky has uncovered that was not understood before is that this instability occurs in these years only when the disputes involving major states exclusively are combined with disputes between major states in which a central power is also involved. Disputes between major states or between major states and one central power are stable. Thus, table 9–4, which is confined to disputes between two or more major states, shows a system that is stable, and so does table 9–5, which treats the disputes between major states involving central powers. However, when the disputes represented in these two tables are combined in table 9–6, the system becomes unstable. From this series of tests, it can be inferred that instability is introduced when disputes between major states are combined with disputes between major states involving central powers.

By using this same procedure of manipulating the sample, Midlarsky pinpoints the time period where instability is introduced. For example, in table 9–1, he finds the period 1816–1899 is stable, but then, in table 9–6, he identifies 1893–1914 as unstable. Using his historical knowledge, he then sees if the 1893–1908 period will be stable and finds that it is (table 9–7). He concludes that 1908 is probably a critical year in the history of the system and cities a number of unusual events that make it a turning point.

Midlarsky's findings imply that world war is associated with the emergence of intractable disputes that are not being resolved. His statistical model shows that prior to war, disputes are connected. Statistically, this means that there is a significant relationship among disputes, indicating that previous interactions affect current ones. Such a system can be referred to as having "memory." This is not much different from Leng's conclusion (chapter

5) that behavior in one crisis affects behavior in the next. In light of Leng's findings, it can be hypothesized that one of the reasons an accumulation of disputes results in war is that as actors move from one crisis to the next, they escalate their bargaining tactics, and hostility intensifies. If a number of states are going through recurrent crises, then the probability that one of them will escalate to war increases, and if these disputes are connected with each other, as they were in 1914, the escalation of one dispute can set off a chain reaction that results in world war.

But how are these disputes combined in history? Why do major states make the disputes of minor states their own? Prior to World War I, it seems that the system of alliances built coalitions between major states and between them and central powers in a way that linked the issues and concerns of each together. The accumulation of disputes is an important process by which world war comes about, but it turns out that one of the factors that encourages the accumulation of disputes is alliances. This suspicion is partially confirmed by another analysis by Midlarsky (1986a:ch 4, 5), which finds alliances accumulating after 1871. This implies that alliance making may be responsible for entangling major and minor states and their disputes.

The combining of disputes as a result of coalition building is likely to have two effects. First, it helps reduce many of the separate issues of the system to one grand issue by linking together the individual issues of each ally. Second, the linking of issues makes resolution much less probable since it is inherently more difficult to reach an overall settlement and compromise on several linked disputes than it is on one. These two effects are likely to push actors to exhibit the kind of escalatory behavior that Leng sees as leading to war. This implies that systemic war can be prevented if the political system can resolve disputes. The article by Peter Wallensteen reprinted in the next chapter identifies some of the factors associated with periods during which disputes have been peacefully resolved.

Methodological Notes

Midlarsky illustrates how modeling can be used to study world politics. He starts by presenting a set of equations that comprise a mathematical model. The difference between a mathematical model and statistical analysis is that, while a statistical analysis measures the relationships that occur among variables in the empirical realm, a model is a mathematical description of a hypothetical world. Midlarsky uses the Poisson model (which you will recognize from the Levy article [chapter 1]) to create a mathematical description in a series of equations (9.2–9.4) of a stable equilibrium system. The point is to use the model to estimate the values that would fit in such an equilibrium system and then compare to them the corresponding values from the actual data. The idea behind modeling is to take something we understand (the model—in this case, a model of a system in equilibrium) and see if it fits the phenomenon we are trying to understand (in this case, the distribution of disputes prior to World War I). If the model fits, then the knowledge we have about equilibrium and disequilibrium systems can be used to explain what we are trying to understand.

Table 9–1 shows the comparison of the data on disputes between major powers with the values predicted by the equations. The top line of each of the three entries contains the actual data, and the bottom line shows the predicted values. The procedure now is to compare the two lines using a chi-square goodness-of-fit statistic, which measures whether the values observed in the data are close enough (as measured by a statistical significance test) to conclude that the observed data fit the model. You have seen statistical significance used to indicate whether a finding is random. A very low value for p ($p < .001$) means that there is less than one chance in a thousand that the finding is random.

In this first test, however, Midlarsky is trying to show that the observed values are *not* statistically significantly different from the predicted values, so he is looking for p values *above* .10 (like the .30 in table 9–1). If he were to find a value lower than .10, he would have observed values that were significantly different from the predicted ones. Hence, the low chi-square of 1.060 has a p value of less than .98 (a very high value), meaning that the difference between the observed and predicted values has less than a 98 percent chance (that is, a very good chance) of being random. This means that the observed data and the values predicted by the model are essentially the same. Since this chi square indicates a strong probability that the observed system is close to the model, Midlarsky concludes that the system he observed is in equilibrium—that is, the system of interactions between major states is stable (i.e., disputes are randomly distributed along a Poisson model). There is likewise no significant difference between the equilibrium model and the other models treated in tables 9–2 through 9–5, meaning that they are all stable.

The data on twentieth-century disputes involving all European states (table 9–6), on the other hand, show observed values that are significantly different from the equilibrium model. You can see that $p < .01$, indicating that there is very little chance that the difference between the observed values and the predicted values is random. Since it is different, it is not an equilibrium system; it is unstable. Through this mathematical distinction among different systems, Midlarsky is able to identify the types of conditions that have led to world war.

Midlarsky is concerned that there might be a certain structure associated with war. The next article looks at whether there is a certain structure associated with peace.

III
Peace and the Global Institutional Context

10
Universalism vs. Particularism: On the Limits of Major Power Order

Peter Wallensteen

Editors' Introduction

Peter Wallensteen's analysis shows that peace is possible. There have been long stretches of peace among major states in Western history. If we can delineate what these periods have in common, we may attain a better understanding not only of how to prevent war but also of some of the factors that cause war.

War has been studied in a scientific fashion much more extensively than peace. In order to study peace, it is necessary to demarcate unambiguously the periods of peace in global history. Once that is done it is possible to see what these periods have in common and how they differ from the periods of war. Wallensteen's research moves inquiry along these lines by identifying some of the characteristics of historical periods that are associated with peace.

Universalism vs. Particularism

Autonomy has been a most cherished value for major powers throughout history. It has been a motivating force for smaller powers to free themselves from the influence of others. Liberation has been the ambition of revolutionaries. Still, at no time has autonomy been more restrained than today,

Reprinted from the *Journal of Peace Research*, Vol. 21, No. 3 (1984), pp. 243–257, by permission of the publisher and the author.

This article is part of an ongoing project on Armed Conflicts and Durable Conflict Resolution, at the Department of Peace and Conflict Research, Uppsala University. Valuable comments have been made by many readers of an earlier draft, notably Nils Petter Gleditsch, Miroslav Nincic, Melvin Small, and Raimo Väyrynen, as well as by students in my seminar on War and World Politics, University of Michigan, winter 1984.

even for the major powers. Nuclear threats and strategic doctrines link even the most powerful to one another and restrict the space for independent action. In spite of nuclear vulnerability, major powers can pursue policies to further their particularist interest as witnessed in Eastern Europe, West Asia or Central America. Also, they may pursue policies of universalist application, taking into account legitimate interests of others as witnessed during the period of détente. In this sense, nothing is new. Similar options have always been available to major powers, and, at some period in time, universalism has been preferred to particularism. This study analyzes experiences of major power universalism as opposed to particularism: what has historically been the difference, what has been the result, why have policies shifted and which lessons can be drawn?

Universalist policies are understood to be concerted efforts among major powers to organize relations between themselves to work out acceptable rules of behavior (general standards). Particularist policies, in contrast, are understood to be policies which emphasize the special interest of a given power, even at the price of disrupting existing organizations or power relationship.[1] In the first case, the aim is order, but this is not to say that order is the result or that disorder necessarily follows from the other. On the contrary, some would argue that the pursuit of self-interest is creating more order than is altruism, as it redirects imbalances in power distribution and makes possible the voicing of grievances. Thus, it is for the historical record to decide whether universalism or particularism results in war.

This formulation of the problem is hardly novel or original, but still there have been few efforts to systematically compare the outcome of the different set of policies. Under the concept of world order fruitful incursions into the area have been made by the Institute for World Order, as well as by scholars like Stanley Hoffmann.[2] The conceptions might be different, but mostly they point in a similar direction: world order policies aim at including more than the particularistic interest of a given actor as the actor's goals. There is, in other words, a more universalistic ambition. Apart from preserving the actor itself as an actor, there is also an understanding of the demands and worries of the opponent. Obviously, the structural framework in which such globalistic policies are carried out differ; the Institute for

---

[1] Universalism and particularism as defined by Parsons focuses on norms rather than actions. Still the concepts are useful as they point to the general rather than the specific as the center of attention (see Parsons and Shils 1951, p. 82).

[2] Most definitions of world order are multidimensional. Falk and Mendlovitz find world order to be the answer to questions of worldwide economic welfare, social justice, ecological stability as well as to reduction of international violence (see Falk and Mendlovitz 1973, p. 6). A broad and most stimulating contribution is Falk (1975). Hoffmann (1980, p. 188) also gives a very broad definition of the concept of world order, as a state in which violence and economic disruptions have been "tamed", "moderation" has emerged, economies progress and collective institutions act. The concept of Common Security, introduced in the so-called Palme Commission, involved a conception similar to the one of Hoffmann (see *Common Security*, 1982).

World Order in general wants to go beyond the nation-state, and develop policies more fitting for local ("smaller") actors, whereas the Hoffmann conception clearly focuses on the role of the major powers. Here it suffices to note that the structure of the global system makes it necessary to point to the significance of the major powers and their mutual relations. It is also evident that mutual relations between these powers tend to undergo dramatic shifts and changes, swinging between more universalistic and more particularistic emphases. Thus, major powers pursuing universalistic policies would, for some, be world order policies. For others, this might still be unsatisfactory if the basic question is policies *by whom?* It is self-evident that there are limits to universalism of the major powers. Their status as major is not to be threatened. On the contrary it constitutes the postulate of their policies. Thus, at some point, the divergent definitions of world order also become incompatible, boiling down to the question of whether, in the long-run, major powers are to remain majors or not.

Individual actors can have individual orders of preference and priorities can change over time. However, we are interested in the collectivity of major powers. General standards are general only to the extend they have support from many actors. Major powers are significant in setting such standards and in achieving adherence to them. Thus, if a collectivity of major powers, tacitly or openly, sets up certain rules of behavior and applies them consistently over time, this will have an effect beyond the collectivity. If, on the contrary, there are no such agreed rules, particularism is likely to become a predominant pattern.

Here the focus is on comparing periods of collective major power universalism, and on contrasting them to periods of predominant particularism. Historical experiences of universalism can give insight into useful methods, but also into the limits of such efforts. The study of particularism might yield knowledge of legitimate dissatisfaction with existing arrangements. If a given—formal or informal—collective arrangement constantly works to the advantage of some and to the disadvantage of others, the arrangement itself becomes questioned.

Identifying Universalism and Particularism

Since the Napoleonic era, there have been several serious attempts at creating universalist relations among major powers. These attempts, initiated by major powers, have built on the consent of all or most major powers. They have sometimes been constructed around particular organizations (such as the League of Nations) or around more informal arrangements (such as the Concert of Europe). Common to them is the ambition to develop general rules of behavior among the major powers, and attempts to reconcile differences so as to maintain the consensus among the involved

Table 10–1
Universalism and Particularism, 1816–1976: Periodization of Relations among Major Powers

Analytical Classification	Historical Labelling	Time Period	No. of Years	No. of Majors
Universalist	Concert of Europe	1816–1848	33	5–6
Particularist		1849–1870	22	5–6
Universalist	Bismarck's order	1871–1895	25	6
Particularist		1896–1918	23	8
Universalist	League of Nations	1919–1932	14	7
Particularist		1933–1944	12	7
Particularist	Cold war	1945–1962	18	5
Universalist	Détente Peaceful Coexistence	1963–1976	14	5

Note: Major Power definitions follow the usual Correlates of War practice. (See Small and Singer 1982, pp. 44–45.)

powers. Thus, what historians refer to as periods of concerts, orders, or détente, is what we here label universalism. Such periods are delimited on two grounds. First, there has to be a certain consistency and continuity in the policies pursued by the major powers within the particular period. Secondly, there has to be a marked difference (qualitative break) between these policies and those in the following period. The analysis, in other words, has a double task: to find the consistent elements within a given period and to find the important factors contributing to the qualitative change in relations.

Table 10–1 reproduces eight periods of universalist and particularist policies among major powers since the Napoleonic age. The periodization is drawn from customary historical writing. The organizing principle is that of policy. The periods are separated with respect to the existence or non-existence of a consistent effort among the major powers to pursue universalist ambitions. These periods are our units of analysis in the following.[3]

Table 10–1 gives some characteristics of each of the periods, at the same time explaining the various delimitations. However, some comments are necessary. The European Concert of 1816–1848 is recognized by historians as a period of its own, centered on the activities of the Austrian Chancellor Metternich, but involving all the major European powers. The revolutions

---

[3] Thus we attempt to describe dominant traits in the major power relations during these periods. A most interesting contribution in the same direction is Rosecrance (1963). Recently, the interest in long waves has resulted in similar generalizations for particular periods, mostly focusing on economic variables. A contribution pertinent to the present discussion is Väyrynen (1983).

of 1848, rather than those of 1830, are seen to mean the ending of this period. The following period was one exhibiting many of the marks of particularism, as we have defined it. Several countries were, in this period, pursuing more limited ambitions (notably unification and aggrandizement). Thus, in the writings of historians, also this period stands out clearly.

The following two periods are more difficult to separate. Bismarck's policy had a universalist coloring, where the definition of Germany's interest was not equated with the expansion of the Reich, but rather the establishment of a workable relationship, cementing what had already been gained. Germany, then, was a central force in this attempt at universalist construction. Following the downfall of Bismarck, and the rise of a more daring political leadership in Germany, the situation changed during the 1890s. The exact dating might be hard to pinpoint, but the difference is there. Here it has been set as 1895, but that is an approximation. It should be noted that also other, non-European countries, at this time, began to pursue particularistic interests (United States and Japan).

The organization created after the First World War was a more conscious attempt to work out constructive relations among the majors, this time centering on France and Britain. However, the universalism was incomplete, a great number of countries were not involved or supportive of these attempts, and with Hitler's taking of power in 1933, the arrangement rapidly fell apart. Finally, following the Second World War, the alliance between the victors, containing a potential for universalist relations, was quickly changed into a severe confrontation. Not until after the Cuban missile crisis did a period of more constructive relations emerge.

This means that our analysis will concentrate on eight periods, four of each type. It is interesting to note, from table 10–1, that there is more consensus among historians on the labelling of periods of universalism. The particularist periods are not dominated by one overarching ambition, and consequently, the naming becomes problematic. There is, however, one exception to that, the period 1945–1962. The bipolarization of the confrontation between the United States and the Soviet Union has given it one customary label. Universalism in this bipolar world has, however, attracted two different conceptions, suggesting that there might, at this time, be more agreement about conflict than about collaboration.

The fact that the periods in general appear to become shorter, and that the universalist periods are smaller relative to the particularist ones, might be indicative of a general rise in confrontation among major powers. The development of conflict behavior in the different periods can be seen more closely in table 10–2.

Table 10–2 shows a different pattern for the two sets of policies. There are no major-major wars reported in the periods of universalism, whereas all the major-major wars are to be found in periods of particularism. This observation should be treated cautiously, however, as it could be affected by

Table 10–2
Wars and Military Confrontations Involving Major Powers,
in Universalist and Particularist Periods, 1816–1976

	Universalist Periods	Particularist Periods
Major-Major Wars	0	10
Major-Minor Wars	10	16
Major-Major Confrontations	24	49
Major-Minor Confrontations	72	84
Length, Years	86	74
Average no. of Wars and Confrontations per year	1.2	2.1
Wars to Confrontations, ratio	1:9.6	1:5.1

Source: Wars: Small and Singer (1982). Military Confrontations: Data from
the Correlates of War project, 1980.

the labelling. Historians might be quicker to find an orderly pattern in
periods without major power wars, and thus we would face a tautology. It
might, however, also suggest that universalist policies are successful, at least
with respect to major power relations. As the ambition is to develop constructive relations, and as a dominant group among the majors agree on
this, major power war could be avoided. An indication is that no periods of
universalism end with the outbreak of a major power war. Rather, such
wars come way into a period of particularism.[4]

Furthermore, it could be noted in table 10–2 that there is some conflict
behavior recorded in all other categories. One third of all major power
confrontations have taken place in periods of universalism. This might mean
that such periods have witnessed a somewhat greater ability to cope with
confrontation than have periods of particularism: none escalated into a
major war. With respect to major-minor confrontations, fewer escalated
into war in periods of universalism than in periods of particularism. The
ratio of wars to confrontations (a rough measure of escalation) for all
categories shows a lower frequency of war per confrontation in periods of
universalism. This reinforces, although does not prove, the thesis that major
power policies have a significant bearing on the chances for war. If such
relations are couched in a cooperative, constructive fashion, the danger of
war might decrease.

Many of the typical structural traits that often are pointed to in order
to explain differences will not help in discriminating between these periods;

---

[4] Such wars have come at earliest in the sixth year of particularist policy: the Crimean War in
1854, the Russo-Japanese War in 1938 (Changkufeng War) and the Korean War in 1950, all
within this range, the Russo-Japanese war of 1904 being somewhat later. This list, furthermore,
suggests that such first major-major wars occur in areas fairly distant from the main major
power area of contention (at all these times being Europe). For data, see Small and Singer
(1982).

often the same countries found themselves involved in both. The five states making up the Concert of Europe are also those involved in the following, more tumultuous period. Similarly, the countries setting up the League in 1919 are also those confronted with German challenges in the 1930s. The actors of the global competition after World War II, from 1963 onward, attempted to work out an orderly relationship. Thus, it appears more promising to relate such changes to short-term variations rather than to lasting properties of the global system.

Let us only note that as none of the four periods of universalism have lasted, but all have been transformed into periods of particularism, the inadequacies of the policies pursued need to be specified. The shifts and changes obviously give food for thought to the pessimist as well as to the optimist: no period of universalism has lasted, but neither has a period of particularism.

Universalism and Particularism in Practice

The strongly different outcomes of periods of universalism and particularism make a closer scrutiny important. Thus, we ask what the differences in policy consist of. The eight periods of major power relations differ from one another in many ways. The economic conditions, the reach of weapons, the speed of communication, the ideological framework have greatly changed over time. Thus, the periods are comparable in some respects but not in others. A comparison over time becomes less comprehensive the longer the time span applied. In this case, it means that considerable detail is lost in the search for general phenomena. Still, a general observation, such as the shifts in the predominant pattern of policy, could be expected to be associated with a general explanation. In this light we attempt to search for discriminating patterns of policies in some admittedly limited, but still crucial, areas.

First, table 10–2 suggests a difference in symmetric and asymmetric relations: major powers might approach one another differently from how they approach non-majors at the same time. Thus, we will compare the experiences of universalism and particularism in both these relationships. Second, the analysis employs a framework of four sets of policy, introduced in earlier work: *Geopolitik, Realpolitik, Idealpolitik* and *Kapitalpolitik*.[5] Geopolitik is, in particular, concerned with the geographical conditions: contiguity and ways to handle contiguity, as well as control over distant (from the point of view of core countries) territories. Realpolitik emphasizes military capability, arms build-up of particular countries and the formation of alliances. Idealpolitik concerns the handling of nationalistic or ideolog-

---

[5] This distinction, built on the basic arguments in different schools of thinking, is elaborated in Wallensteen (1981).

ical disputes, ranging from messianism to neutrality with respect to such issues, whereas Kapitalpolitik refers to the economic capabilities and interactions among states.

The difference between the two patterns in *Geopolitik* terms can be seen in the different policies pursued in the "core" areas, in territories particularly close or militarily significant to the major powers. During several periods of universalism, conscious attempts were made to separate the parties geographically, thus attempting to reduce the fear of attack or the danger of provocation. The creation of buffer zones was a particularly pronounced effort, for instance, in relation to France after 1814 or Germany after 1918. In times of particularism, policies were reversed: the buffer zones were perceived as dangerous areas of "vacuum," making majors compete for control. Examples are the Prussian expansion into Central Europe in the 1850s and the 1860s and Germany's invasion of demilitarized zones or neighboring countries during the 1930s. Also, following the Second World War, the United States as well as the Soviet Union tried to secure as much territory as possible before and after the German and Japanese capitulations. Indeed, in the 1945–1962 period, "free" territory was equally disliked on both sides, neither being willing to accept neutrality or neutralism, for instance. In the periods 1870–1895 and 1963–1976 such basic arrangements were left intact, keeping the parties at close geographical confrontation, but at the same time other measures were instituted to somewhat reduce the fear of attack from the opponent (e.g., confidence-building measures in the latter period). Compared to earlier experiences of universalism, these periods saw less of such attempts, however.[6]

Looking at the major-minor relations, the patterns are less clear-cut. Although the expectation might be for "softer" attitudes during periods of universalism, this appears not to be born out. Rather, during periods of universalism, major powers tried to establish or extend control, as in periods of particularism. Perhaps there is a discernable trend of greater major power collaboration during the former than during the latter. Thus, the colonization of Africa took place largely during a period of universalism, and partly this process was mutually agreed on by the major powers themselves (notably the Berlin Congress in 1884–1885). Similarly, British and French control were extended into Arab countries during such periods, during the 1880s as well as in the 1920s. It is, furthermore, interesting to observe that the decolonization process was initiated during a period of confrontation between the major powers. The peak year of African inde-

---

[6] The lack of disengagement in German-French relations following the war of 1871 is often pointed to by historians. The annexation of Alsace-Lorraine became a humiliating experience for the French, although the military value of the area to either party could be disputed. Thus, no buffers were created between the two, making the relations tense. A result of this was the War Scare of 1875. See Kennan (1979, pp. 11–23). For a general discussion, see Patem (1983).

pendence, 1960, coincided with particularly tense times in American-Soviet relations (e.g., the aborted Paris summit meeting and the U-2 affair).

Realpolitik concerns itself with military power and alliance patterns. In periods of universalism, we would expect less emphasis to be put on military armaments, while greater efforts would go into diplomatic means to work out major power relations. Studying the four periods, this is clearly true for three, but not for the fourth one (1963–1976). Conversely, the periods of particularist policies would exhibit a more rapid arms build-up among the majors. Again, this is true for three out of four periods, the exception being the 1849–1870 period. Partly, this might reflect an important inter-century difference: during the 19th century, the institutionalized pressures for arms build-up did not exist to the same degree that has been true for the 20th century. With respect to the nuclear age, the patterns are somewhat surprising. In terms of military expenditures, the increase seems less striking during the 1950s than during the 1960s or 1970s, for the United States and the Soviet Union. In terms of the amassing of nuclear arsenals, however, there is a continuous increase for both sides.[7] Again, the 1963–1976 period does not follow the pattern of previous universalist periods.

Most periods of universalism seem associated with a loose alliance system. The exception is the 1963–1976 period, but also in this period there are some elements of a loosening-up of the system (notably the withdrawal of France from military cooperation in NATO, and Rumania taking a special position within the Warsaw Pact). However, also particularism could go well with a loose alliance pattern, as alliances might restrain rather than give freedom to a given actor. Three periods of particularism showed fairly tight alliance patterns, but in one of these (1933–1945) not all powers were involved in the alliance configurations. In one, the 1849–1870 period, loose alliances served the particularist ambitions well.

There is an interesting trade off between alliance patterns and arms build-up. In a sense, one reason for entering into an alliance is to reduce the need for armaments. In this way, a major power can increase its military strength, at a lower cost and at a faster rate than otherwise would have been possible. This, then, favors the emergence of loose alliance patterns, and thus makes it plausible that universalism as well as particularism might be associated with such a pattern. On the other hand, if the alliances are closely knit, and the option of withdrawing or switching is not available, the only way to increase the strength for a given actor and for the alliance as a whole is through arms build-ups. Thus, in bipolarized situations with "permanent" alliances, arms races become a more likely outcome. The few exam-

---

[7] For an overview of the development of arms expenditure for these periods, see Nincic (1982). For an overview of the nuclear arsenals, drawn from several sources, see Botnen (1983) and SIPRI (1983). The total nuclear arsenals are estimated at 1000 in 1952, 23,500 in 1960, 35,500 in 1970 and 48,800 in 1975.

ples available of such situations indeed suggest this to be the case (1895–1918, 1933–1945 and the post-1945 periods).

Armaments and alliance patterns largely concern the relations between major powers. We would expect Realpolitik policies in major-minor relations to be less different for the two patterns. Thus, it is noteworthy that, in table 10–2 above, universalist periods have also been periods of extensive major power involvement in major-minor disputes. If we take into account the length of the periods and the number of majors, we find that the majors, in fact, during such periods are heavily concerned with minors.

With respect to *Idealpolitik,* universalist policies would be less chauvinistic and less messianic among majors than particularism. Earlier it has been demonstrated that Idealpolitik contradictions correlate with wars and confrontations among major powers for the entire epoch (Wallensteen 1981), but we now expect a pattern of shifting periods. It is probably enough to have one major displaying messianism in a given period to upset all relations. This expectation is well borne out: the four universalist periods show very little of either of these types of Idealpolitik, whereas, in each of the four particularist periods, there was at last one major power pursuing such a policy. Chauvinism certainly was part of the German unification policy during Bismarck, as was French renaissance during Napoleon III, both appearing in the same 1849–1870 period. The policies of Wilhelm II and of Hitler are typical examples. In the 1945–1962 period too there was a strong element of messianism, for very different reasons than previous ones, in Soviet as well as American postures.

In their relations to minor powers, the majors have often been less constrained, also in times of universalism. Thus, in the Concert of Europe period, majors did not hesitate to intervene against changes in minor countries going against the convictions held by the major. In the 1870–1895 period, this might have been less marked, as this to a large degree was a period of parallel nationalism, as well as in the period of the League of Nations. In the détente period, however, the reluctance among the majors to accept dissent within areas of their domination has drawn increasing tension, also among the majors. Thus, the Soviet invasion of Czechoslovakia significantly affected the formulation of détente policies. The American warfare in Vietnam seems to have slowed down the pace of collaboration between the two superpowers. Thus, a policy of coexistence between the majors also might require the acceptance of coexistence between different social forms in major-minor relations.

As to *Kapitalpolitik* patterns, there are some interesting divergencies, necessitating a lengthier discussion. Universalism would here refer to a policy that attempts to be more inclusive, such as setting up of a joint international regime for economic affairs, or extending trade, investment or capital flows in an equitable way among the major powers. Particularist policies, on the contrary, would be those that aim at self-reliance, autarchy or exclusion from ties with other countries. Taken in this way, there seems to be little relationship between the universalist policies described previously and economic relations. Thus, in the period of the European Concert, introvert policies or policies of exclusion seem to have been the predominant pattern. Free trade actually cannot be dated until the end of this very period, with the repeal of the Corn Laws in Britain in 1846. The following period, then, is one of a more ambitious attempt at spreading international trade, pressing for free trade. An important breakthrough was the Anglo-French Treaty of 1860, during a period which, in terms of other affairs, is most appropriately described as a particularist one. Prussia and the German Customs Union followed in this period, to return to high tariff policies only in the next period, in 1879. Thus, this universalist period is characterized by a retreat from free trade, rather than the reverse (Kindleberger 1978).

In the period of particularism leading to the First World War, the growth of international trade was strong, but it appears that it also to a larger degree took place within the colonial empires (Kindleberger 1964). Thus, in this period, there might have been a closer correspondence with particularism. The same is true for the post–World War I periods, the universalist period being one of increasing international independence, followed after the Great Depression with increasing attempts at withdrawing from the international economic exchanges.

Also, in the post–1945 periods, there is a correspondence between the economic policies and other policies. Thus, for the first particularist period, the West clearly expanded free trade within its area, but consciously tried to exclude the Soviet bloc from trade (e.g., the strategic embargo). Such policies were partially reversed with the onset of détente, symbolized by the first major grain deal between the United States and the Soviet Union in 1963. In U.S.-Soviet as well as in West European–East European relations, the development of economic relations was strongly favored by the political leadership.[8]

Thus, we find that in several of the periods there has been a close correspondence between increasing economic interaction and universalism, but that this is perhaps more pronounced for the periods after 1895 than before. In periods of particularism, however, policies of economic bloc-building or economic autarchy have been preferred. The closer correspondence between these sets of policies in the 20th century might suggest closer

---

[8] Reporting to the U.S. Congress on his visit to Moscow in 1972 Nixon summarized this policy as one of "creating a momentum of achievement in which progress in one area could contribute to progress in others," and "when the two largest economies in the world start trading with each other on a much larger scale, living standards in both nations will rise, and the stake which both have in peace will increase." Cooperation in space exploration was also part of this, resulting in a joint orbital mission in 1975. See "Address by President Nixon to a Joint Session of the Congress," June 1, 1972 in Stebbins and Adams (1976, pp. 80–81). The resulting space mission was in 1975 hailed by *Le Canard Enchaîné:* Vive La Coexistence Espacifique!

coordination of international interaction than previously was the case. Political-strategic conditions seem increasingly to have colored economic relationships.

Table 10–3 shows that the policies pursued in different areas have been designed to support one another, and on the whole, few contradictions or inconsistencies are to be reported. Thus, periods of universalism have generally involved attempts at separation of majors through buffer zone arrangements or self-imposed restraint in vital areas. Predominantly a pattern of slow arms build-ups and loose alliances has been pursued. Ideologically, a policy of coexistence has prevailed and economically, trade has been extended among the dominant countries. Taken together, this means that the concept of "universalism" summarizes consistent efforts among many major powers, working in the same direction of building constructive and multi-dimensional relations. We have already observed, in table 10–2, that in such periods the incidence of war and confrontation among major power is lower.

The patterns displayed in periods of particularism are in sharp contrast. Buffer zone arrangements have been overturned, less restraint has been exhibited in vital areas, rapid arms build-ups have occurred and solid, internationally binding alliances have been formed. Among at least some of the majors, messianism/chauvinism has been prevalent, and trade has been used as an instrument for coercion or exclusion. Again this is a pattern of internally consistent policies, all reinforcing the underlying conflict between major powers. Indeed, as we have already noted, periods of particularism are also periods with major power wars and military confrontations.

However, there are some notable inconsistencies in these patterns. Most exceptional is the 1849–1870 period: in several ways it had traits also typical for the periods immediately preceding or succeeding: loose alliance structures and little arms build-up, apart from the time immediately before a major war. Thus, in these respects, there is considerable intra-19th century

Table 10–3
Typical Policies in Periods of Universalism and Particularism, 1816–1976

	Universalism	*Particularism*
Geopolitik	Buffer zones (not 1871–1895, 1963–1976)	Elimination of vacuum
Realpolitik	Caution in vital areas	Boldness in vital areas
	Loose alliances (not 1963–1976?)	Solid alliances (not 1849–1870)
	Slow arms build-up (not 1963–1976)	Rapid arms build-up (not 1849–1870)
Idealpolitik	Coexistence among majors	Messianism also among majors
Kapitalpolitik	Extension of relations among majors (not 1816–1848, 1871–1895)	Seclusion for majors or major blocs (not 1849–1870)

Notes: Periods are the unit of analysis. In parenthesis: periods departing from the overall pattern. Few systematic differences concern direct major-minor relations.

similarity. Also, with respect to economic relations, this period was one of free trade becoming more acceptable as a general policy, and countries, in most other respects aiming at their own self-aggrandizement, embraced the concept. This, then, is in contrast to the other 19th century periods, which both were, for a considerable extent of time, markedly inner- or intra-bloc-oriented.

For the 20th century the inconsistencies are few but still obvious. First, the 1933–1944 period showed less solidification of opposing blocs than could be expected. Secondly, the period 1963–1976 saw a notable lack of the loosening of blocs that previously had been associated with universalist patterns, and most markedly, a failure to curtail the arms build-up and accept internal dissent.

Looking over the entire period, most of these inconsistencies refer to the Realpolitik domain; the alliances and the armaments do not correspond with the message from other policies. In Geopolitik terms, the consistency is fairly complete (with some exceptions as to buffer zone policies), as is also the case for Idealpolitik, and Kapitalpolitik (with the exceptions of the 19th century pointed to). In one period the Realpolitik divergence goes in a universalist direction, perhaps influencing the major wars of the period to become shorter (1849–1870). In another period the outcome might well have been the reverse, meaning the abandoning of universalist policies altogether (1963–1976).

Consistency would, in particular, have the effect of reducing uncertainty among the major powers. Given that these powers have a fairly uniform understanding of the dimensions involved, consistency would reinforce a given message. Thus, at times some inconsistency might have been less important, notably the lack of correspondence of Kapitalpolitik policies with other elements in the 19th century. In the 20th century, however, Kapitalpolitik might have been more important. With such an understanding it becomes clear that all universalist periods are highly internally consistent, with one exception, 1963–1976. Also, on the whole, all the 20th century particularist periods are highly consistent. Of the latter, two ended in world wars, and one in a crisis that might well have resulted in the third one.

Inconsistency could give rise to a demand for change, consistency being a more preferable condition. Thus, a given period could change into its opposite. But change would also have other roots and to these we now turn.

From Universalism to Particularism, and Vice-Versa

Although the universalist policies have largely been consistent and not resulted in major war, they were all abandoned. Obviously, the policies pursued were not satisfactory to all involved. This means that they were built on a foundation that was solid enough for a certain period of time, but not solid enough to handle particular changes.

Also the conditions that brought about the universalist periods in the first place should be considered, as this might suggest the outer limits of the policies. Thus, there are two particular points of change that need to be scrutinized: the change from universalism to particularism and changes in the opposite direction.

Such changes could be sought in three particular areas:

1. Changes among the majors: the composition of their relationships, relative capabilities, but also inconsistency in policy.
2. Changes involving the minors: their direct relations to the majors, degree of independence, etc.
3. Internal changes in the different actors, notably in the majors: revolutions, change of perspectives.

Altogether, there are six shifts to consider, three in each direction. In all cases, the years of change have been identified and factors mentioned by historians as influential have been collected. Some typical variables are presented in table 10–4.

Although table 10–4 indicates dates for changes, such dates of course are but symbolic; changes are always the result of long-term trends. Some of the changes, consequently, are harder to locate exactly in time. However, dates are important for understanding change; their symbolic value is highly educational.

First the transformation from *universalism to particularism* is comparatively non-violent; there are some wars recorded, but no sharp change is evident in the power relationships between the leading actors. The wars at

Table 10–4
Factors Affecting Change in Policy Pattern

	From Universalism to Particularism	From Particularism to Universalism
Identified Timepoints of Change	1848/1849, 1895/1896 1932/1933	1870/1871, 1918/1919 1962/1963
Geopolitik	End of expansionism in 1895/1896	Territorial redistribution 1870/1871, 1918/1919
Realpolitik	Entrance new actors 1895/1896	Defeat in War 1870/1871, 1918/1919
Idealpolitik	New alliances 1895/1896	Close to War 1962/1963
	Internal revolution 1848/1849, 1932/1933	Revolutions 1870/1871, 1918/1919
Kapitalpolitik	Economic crisis 1932/1933	Economic turmoil following war 1918/1919

the time were those of major powers solidifying their position by attacking minors (e.g., Prussia on Denmark, Japan on China, the United States on Spain), but such wars are hardly novel or directly related to the shifts. More interesting, and more frequently emphasized by historians, are the internal changes within major powers. The revolutions in France, Austria and Germany are related to the breakdown of the existing order. In the first two cases, revolution brought back a Napoleon and brought down a Metternich, in the third case it overthrew the Weimar Republic and created the Third Reich. These changes were not ordinary domestic shifts of power, as the internal orders were integral parts of the entire international arrangement at the time. Consequently, these revolutions were as much challenges to predominant universalism as to the internal order. With Louis Philippe and the Weimar Republic removed, not only were symbols of the previous order replaced, but something more fundamental had changed; the role of these countries as majors was redefined. The shifts in 1848/1849 and 1932/1933 could both be seen this way.

The third change away from universalism is more difficult to analyze. The shifts around the turn of the century resulting in the confrontation patterns leading to World War I were more gradual. There is no particular revolution to point to. Instead factors such as the removal of Bismarck from power in Germany, the realignment among European powers, the decreasing number of territories available to territory-seeking European countries and the emergence of non-European major states seem important.

However, the parallel between the changes in 1848/1849 and those of 1932/1933 might still permit a more general conclusion; the revolutionary changes were related to economic crisis, uneven development of industry, unemployment, and, thus, to protest and radicalism ("leftist" as well as "rightist" and in both situations "rightists" coming out on the top). The regimes that were overthrown were closely identified with the previous "world order" either in personal capacity or in (close to) legal terms. This close association between the internal and international arrangement led to the downfall of both.

Possibly, we can specify a chain of events that is potentially very destabilizing for a given international arrangement; economic mismanagement and reduced popular support for a regime whose role is highly significant for universalist policies will endanger not only these regimes, but, very likely, also upset the entire policy. In other words, a weakness of these universalist policies might have been their excessive reliance on the maintenance of a particular order in particular countries. The policies were, in a sense, not adaptive enough to handle the internal changes of leading and crucial states. Indeed, the policies of appeasement, pursued during the 1930s, rested on the assumption that adaptation was possible, and that, at a given moment, Germany's ambitions could be satisfied, preserving most of the League arrangement. The challenge to the entire Versailles construction was only understood at a very late moment. Such a policy of adaptation is, in other words, not likely to be successful if/when the entire international arrangement is the matter of dispute. The only alternative might be a policy of "pre-emptive" adaptation to defuse tensions when they are still latent. However, to change an already existing arrangement before it has become an issue will mostly not have sufficient political support. Politics seem to require much more concrete signals of warnings.

The changes in the mid-1890s followed a slightly different logic. There were no internal revolutions, but the interaction between inter-state relations and internal politics was still there. The removal of Bismarck suggested that Germany's role in the world could be seen in a different light by Germany as well as by others, notably Russia. The rapid colonization meant that there were fewer distant territories to struggle for. Together these factors might have contributed to making Germany take a stronger, less compromising stand.[9]

Turning to the transformation from *particularism to universalism*, we find more violent change, and at that, among the majors themselves. Two of the shifts are multidimensional, and relate to two major wars: 1870/1871 and 1918/1919. These changes are, however, not ordinary major power defeats; the era investigated has seen a number of such defeats (e.g., Russia in the Crimean war or in the Russo-Japanese war). In addition they involved considerable internal changes. New regimes and new constitutions were developed in France and Germany, respectively. The new orders created were not simply rearrangements of inter-state relations. Rather, the three universalist periods following a major war (including, for the sake of the argument, 1814, as well as 1871 and 1919) are parallel; they aimed not only at containing a given major power but also at reducing the perceived threat of certain types of internal policies. Thus, universalism became linked to particular regimes. In post-Napoleonic France, as well as in the Weimar Republic, these new regimes became identified with the defeat. This seems, however, not to have been the case for the post-1871 Third Republic.

As was the case with transformations away from universalism, there is one case which is less clear-cut. It is comparable to the 1895/1896 shift but the direction is the opposite one: 1962/1963. There can be no doubt that the policy of détente, introduced in the immediate aftermath of the 1962 nuclear confrontation between the United States and the Soviet Union, reflected a fear of a nuclear war between the two. Also, at this time, increased attention was given to Third World problems (the United States becoming increasingly involved in the Vietnam war, the Soviet Union extending support to liberation movements throughout the Third World). The process of decolonization created a new area for the leading majors, the year 1960 and

---

[9] Such links form some of the conclusions in Choucri and North (1975, ch. 16). On the significance of Bismarck's departure, see Kennan (1979).

the Congo crisis being symbolic. Thus, the universalism introduced and pursued until the end of the 1970s seems to have had a double origin: fear of nuclear war and focus on Third World activities.

This means that the policy of détente had a different origin than the other universalist policies encountered in this analysis; it was not a matter of victors setting up a system to be preserved against others, but rather of the competitors trying to preserve themselves against a possible catastrophe. Nuclear weapons, in other words, changed the dynamics of relations between the major powers. In one sense, this was a profound change; it meant that anticipation of devastation was brought into the calculations before devastation actually took place. In another sense, it was less profound; the consensus among the majors was less developed than was the case in earlier universalist periods. An argument could still be made in favor of confrontation, brinkmanship, in order to continue the battle between the majors. Unlike the other situations, there was no reordering of priorities; rather a policy of caution succeeded a policy of boldness. In this vein, the shift in 1962/1963 is comparable to the one of 1895/1896: no change in basic goals or basic perception of incompatibility, but a change in the means to be used. Wilhelm II grasped for vigor, Kennedy/Khrushchev for caution; Wilhelm was in a hurry to arrive at final victory, Kennedy/Khrushchev settled down to wait for the ultimate collapse of the other, either from internal contradictions or from changes in global relationships.

In 1895/1896 the lack of "empty" territory meant that the conflict had to be pursued in more vital (to the majors) areas, in 1962/1973 the "opening up" of new territory through decolonization meant that the same conflict could be pursued in less vital areas. Either way, the armament build-up received new stimuli.

This, in other words, suggests a possible link between "central" and "peripheral" areas, the one replacing the other as a forum for continued confrontation between major powers having defined themselves in incompatibility with one another. In general terms, such incompatibilities can either end in major wars (as indeed has been the outcome for two periods of particularism, as shown above) or internal revolutions (as indeed has been the outcome for two periods of universalism), or in a continuous shift between "arenas" of competition, as long as such arenas exist (as happened in the two remaining transformations). In the latter case, this means that "peripheral" areas are "outlets" for major powers, striving to gain a leverage on the other, but hoping to manage this without a direct onslaught.

A final note: 1976 is here, as a matter of convenience and availability of data, regarded as the ending of one universalist period. In retrospect, it appears correct to suggest that détente gradually thinned out beginning at approximately this time, culminating with the Soviet invasion of Afghanistan in 1979 and the election of Ronald Reagan in 1980. Seen in this light, it is interesting to relate some of our previous findings to this development.

Neither in terms of Idealpolitik nor Kapitalpolitik are there any important changes among or within the major powers. In Realpolitik terms there are some changes: a new actor entering more actively, China, during these years of transition forming new relations with the West. Also, there is a set of new challenges emerging from the Third World: the oil crisis and rising Islamic fundamentalism, the latter resulting in confrontation with both superpowers (in Iran and Afghanistan, respectively). A criterion for success for détente might have been the ability of the United States and the Soviet Union to win Third World support, but these developments were set-backs, for both. Thus, there is a parallel between this transition and the one in 1895/ 1896. Failure in promoting success in distant areas (from the point of view of the major powers) tends to result in increasing tension in the central arena. To this, then, should be added the obvious inconsistencies in the policies of détente, pointed to in the previous section, primarily the failure to control the arms race.

Limits of Major Power Universalism

Major powers have continuously tried to work out constructive relations among themselves. Such attempts have, in some periods, lasted for a considerable period of time. The record suggests that the pursuit of such universalist policies is associated with fewer wars and confrontations in general and among the major powers in particular. Such policies have served at the same time to maintain the independence of the majors and reduce the dangers of war among them. Invariably, however, they have been superceded by periods of particularism, when one or several of the majors have embarked on policies advancing the particular interest, rather than the joint interest of all. Such periods are associated with higher levels of war and confrontations among the majors. In several instances they have resulted in the dismemberment or defeat of one or several of the majors. Invariably, such periods have been followed by universalist policies.

Looking at the four concerted attempts of universalism in the 1816– 1976 period, they display some discernible common traits.

First, they have been arrangements worked out among *major powers, normally the victors* in a previous war: the Concert of Europe, Bismarck's order and the League of Nations all followed immediately on major wars. Thus, they represented attempts by the victors to handle their victory, to avoid the reemergence of threat from the losers. The détente period differs, but in some respect it could be seen as a belated attempt among the victors to agree on a set of relations, in particular for Europe. More directly, however, it attempted to stabilize the relations between the majors themselves in the face of a mutual nuclear threat. The three first examples of universalist policies, consequently, built on a much more developed common interest than did the period of détente. In the former situations, the victors had a clear actor to worry about, in the latter case, the fear came primarily from the other party of from the general threat of nuclear war. There was, consequently, less of an incentive to solve conflict in the latter case. The focus was more on avoiding escalation than on conflict settlement.

Second, all these arrangements have been *conservative* as they have tried to stabilize the status quo: maintaining the major powers as majors, keeping the existing power relationships among them and upholding the distance to non-majors. In the face of challenges, the policy has been one of adaptation, trying to make the challenges fit within the existing framework, rather than substantially alter the framework itself. The duration of some of the periods of universalism indicates that this sometimes has been possible: confrontations among majors have been resolved without escalation to war. However, the conservative nature obviously has some short-comings, as there are many challenges which are less easily accommodated.

Thirdly, the *consistency across several dimensions* of policy has been marked for most of the periods, except most notably for the détente period. This internal consistency might well have contributed to reducing uncertainty and thus to make actions and reactions more predictable. Such more predictable relations, it could be argued, would reduce the emergence of conflict in the first place. An indication of this is that the number of wars and confrontations with major powers involved per year is much lower for the periods of consistent universalism than for the period of détente.[10]

Fourthly, all universalist periods witnessed a shift in focus away from direct major-major confrontations in central areas to a *preoccupation with major-minor relations*. Most markedly this is true for the Concert of Europe, Bismarckian and détente periods. This diversion of attention could deflect some of the tension in the central areas and point to common interests in other areas. Inevitably, however, it means that the universalist policies become dependent on the degree of success in that field, resulting in interventionism. For both the Bismarckian and détente period, frustrations in these respects seem to have made the powers turn to the central area again. If that is where the origin of conflict is, this can be seen as logical within this framework. In both these cases it resulted in an intensification of arms build-ups and increasingly unpredictive major power relations.

---

[10] The average annual major power involvement in war or confrontation is 1.0 for 1816–1848, 0.9 for 1871–1895, 1.7 for 1919–1932, and 2.2 for 1963–1976. The latter figure actually puts the détente period parallel to some of the particularist periods, notably the 1896–1918 period with 2.3 and 1933–1944 with 2.2.

Fifth, the universalist policies have not simply been an arrangement built among states. There has also been a *significant internal component* to them. In the cases where victors worked out an order for the post-war period, new regimes have been installed in the defeated countries. These regimes have been the ultimate guarantors of the new order, meaning that the orders become vulnerable to the efficacy of these regimes. Internal change in such countries becomes directly relevant to international relations. Thus, French reconstruction in 1815 and the German Weimar Republic had to carry a double burden of confirming the defeat and reconstructing their countries. In the end neither succeeded. Most notable, however, is the fact that the Third Republic was not, in the same way, identified with the war defeat. In somewhat the same way, the new German governments after 1949 have been absolved of the misdeeds of their predecessors.[11]

Major power universalism has been highly constrained. Most markedly this appears true for the most recent attempt, the period of détente. It could not build on the power of united victors; it failed to be consistent across significant dimensions and ultimately internal inconsistencies brought it down. The question, then, arises if there is an alternative to such universalist policies.

This analysis suggest some principles for an alternative form of universalism, making it possible to break out of some of the historically observed constraints:

- A greater involvement of non-major powers in questions of world peace and security.

- A greater openness, on the part of the major powers, to change in non-major countries and in relations among states.

- A greater consistency in major power relations, particularly in the fields of disengagement, disarmament and dissensus.

- A greater restraint on permissible behavior of major powers in Third World conflicts.

- A greater domestic accountability for the foreign policies of major powers.

- And breaking out of the framework, a greater reliance on non-governmental organizations.

These principles would serve to make universalism truly universal, not simply the universalism of major powers.

---

[11] The significance of the German question is given an extensive and interesting treatment in DePorte (1979).

Editors' Commentary

Major Findings

Wallensteen argues that peace arises from attempts by major states to organize relations among themselves according to certain rules and norms of acceptable behavior. He calls such efforts universalist policies. When major states are successful (at some minimal level) in developing universalist policies, they are able to create a world order where issues can be resolved nonviolently, and the use of force, especially between major states, is regulated and limited.

In contrast, Wallensteen maintains, particularist policies occur when major states are unable to develop, or eschew, rules and norms. They then do whatever they feel is in their immediate self-interest and within their power. Unilateral acts and autonomy are the main characteristics of particularist policies. In universalist policies, norms and rules constrain actors' autonomy, and actions are taken in consultation with other major states or with their acquiescence.

On the basis of a careful reading of historians, Wallensteen identifies which periods between 1816 and 1976 are universalist and which are particularist (table 10–1). He predicts that when universalist policies dominate the system, wars and militarized confrontations between major states will be considerably less frequent than in particularist periods.

The findings, which are reported in table 10–2, are quite impressive for relations between major states. In universalist periods, no wars between major states were fought; whereas, in particularist periods, ten wars occurred. This result is obtained despite the fact that the total number of years in universalist periods exceeds that of particularist periods by twelve years (eighty-six versus seventy-four years). By chance alone, then, one would expect to have more wars in the universalist category. In addition, during universalist periods, the number of confrontations between major states is half that during particularist periods (twenty-four versus forty-nine).

Universalist policies have less of an impact on relations between major and minor states. They do appear to attenuate wars between majors and minors, since there are ten such wars in universalist periods and sixteen in particularist periods. There are also fewer major-minor confrontations in universalist periods (seventy-two versus eighty-four)—but just barely. Although these findings show that universalist policies do not have the same kind of impact on major-minor relations as they do on relations between major states, that does not undercut Wallensteen's analysis, since he recognizes that major states often use universalist policies to collaborate in taking advantage of weaker states.

Wallensteen's findings suggest that in systems in which there is no consensus on rules of the game and no norms to govern behavior, actors have few means to resolve issues. As a result, they rely on unilateral actions to attain their goals. Force and war then become the *ultima ratio* of politics. In this kind of system, war becomes a way of making authoritative decisions. Unless alternative ways of making decisions can be developed, war will persist. One of the merits of Wallensteen's study is that he establishes that major states have been able to employ alternative and nonviolent means of making decisions about important issues. Additional evidence that acceptance of norms is characteristic of peaceful eras is provided by Kegley and Raymond (1982, 1990; see also their historical analysis in Kegley and Raymond 1986).

Wallensteen's analysis is also interesting for its insight into the practices associated with war. Wallensteen argues that particularist periods tend to be characterized by tight alliances, rapid arms buildups, attempts to eliminate power vacuums, and messianic ideologies. His identification of the first two practices is especially significant, since this is consistent with the findings of Levy (1981) and Wallace (1982).

The major contribution of Wallensteen's study, however, is its emphasis on the role of norms and rules for establishing peace. Peace systems are usually constructed following major systemic wars (Gilpin 1981), and how they are made often determines how well they will succeed in avoiding future war (see Doran 1971). Wallensteen's analysis shows that war is not inevitable and that humanity can learn how to make peace as well as war.

Methodological Notes

In this article, Wallensteen relies almost exclusively on the examination of raw numbers. In order to learn something interesting from raw data, they must be collected and organized according to some theoretical understanding of the matter under study. An early and essential step in scientific inquiry is the construction of typologies. A **typology** organizes phenomena into categories based on a theoretically important variable. Imagine the breakthrough in biology when, instead of looking at each animal or species as unique, scientists could conceive of them as mammals, reptiles, birds, and so forth.

Wallensteen does something like this when he makes the distinction between universalist and particularist policies. He argues that when major states follow "particularist" policies, they will engage in more wars than when they follow "universalist" policies. He then sees if the time periods he has labeled as universalist and particularist are, respectively, peaceful and warlike.

Table 10–2 shows clearly that particularistic periods are more warlike. Many more wars are fought during the particularist periods than during the universalist periods. This is apparently not due to an absence of conflicts. The war-to-confrontation ratio shows that universalist periods are characterized by a greater ability to resolve confrontations peacefully. This ratio compares the number of wars to the number of confrontations. The ratio of 1:5.1, for particularistic periods, means that there are 5.1 times as many confrontations as wars. The ratio for universalist periods, 1:9.6, means that there are 9.6 times as many confrontations as wars; thus, war is proportionately rarer as a type of conflict. Although there are no further statistical findings, it is clear that a period with fewer total wars and confrontations, a complete lack of major-major war, and so many confrontations that do not result in war must be more peaceful for a reason.

One of the problems in Wallensteen's study is that the determination of a universalist or particularist period is based on historical judgment rather than precise operational criteria. This always raises the possibility that one might unconsciously see peaceful periods as more ordered and "universalist" than they actually were. Wallensteen notes this danger and indicates why he thinks he has avoided it (see footnote 4). In addition, some of the specific policies he sees associated with universalist periods (table 10–3), for example, the creation of buffer zones, could be used as variables in future research to overcome this problem. Thus, while Wallensteen's analysis is not definitive, its delineation of characteristics associated with peaceful periods provides an essential foundation for future research.

IV
The Termination and
Impact of War

11

War Power and the Willingness to Suffer

Steven Rosen

Editors' Introduction

Who will win a war and the factors associated with victory have long been a concern of military strategists, for obvious reasons. Peace researchers have also been keenly interested in these factors, particularly the role played by demographic, economic, and military variables. Little systematic work has been conducted on this question until recently, however, primarily because of the absence of data. Steven Rosen's study was among the first to address this question after the pathbreaking work of Richardson (1960a) and Klingberg (1966).

Damage and Cost-Tolerance

The United States entered the war in Indochina with what now seem very optimistic assumptions about its ability to defeat the Communists quickly and at a low cost to itself. The United States, the conventional reasoning went, is after all the most powerful nation in the history of mankind, and a decisive application of its might against a fifth-rate power like North Vietnam should quickly convince them of the futility of struggle. Even with Russian and Chinese aid they could not hope to match American forces.

Reprinted from *Peace, War, and Numbers,* edited by Bruce M. Russett (Sage Publications, 1972), pp. 167–183. Reprinted by permission of the editor.

Author's note: I wish to thank the following people for comments on parts of this work: Michael O'Leary, Julian Friedman, Robert Gregg, and William Coplin of Syracuse University; Steven Brams, NYU; and Richard Cottam, John Tyler, Robert S. Walters, Douglas White, Ray Owen, Robert Donaldson, and Michael Margolis of the University of Pittsburgh.

The North Vietnamese and the Viet Cong perhaps entered the American phase of the struggle equally confident. They did not doubt the manifest physical superiority of the United States, but rather took it for granted. The very essence of the doctrine of guerrilla struggle is that it is a form of struggle designed to combat a materially stronger opponent; the basic idea is that the regime has the guns, but the guerrillas have the hearts of the people. The guerrilla's superiority is not in his ability to harm, but in his greater willingness to be harmed. Ho Chi Minh formulated this in a classic way with his familiar prediction that "In the end, the Americans will have killed ten of us for every American soldier who died, but it is they who will tire first." This was the model of Algeria, where the vastly superior French were eventually exhausted by the cost-tolerance of the Algerians. The Algerians suffered in a ratio of perhaps 10 to 1, but valued their goal much more deeply than the French did theirs. In a sense, the Communist victory at Dienbienphu was also of this type. It did not really destroy the French forces as much as it demonstrated to France that victory could not be obtained at a price commensurate with the value of Indochina to France.

So while the strategic theory of the United States was derived from a model of war power based on the ability to harm, the strategic theory of the guerrilla is based on the willingness to suffer. Arab guerrillas recognize the critical place of cost-tolerance in war power by calling themselves "fedayeen"—the sacrificers. An Irish revolutionist said, "It is a question which can last longer, the whip or the back." Castro's victory in Cuba, the Communist victory in China, and perhaps even the revolutionists' victory in the American colonies were won by sheer persistence in the face of overwhelming odds. In each case, a highly committed party exhausted a materially stronger opponent by making the costs of victory exceed the privileged party's willingness to suffer.

So while the United States expected victory on the model of the World Wars or Greece or Malaya, where superior force prevailed, the Communists expected victory on the model of Algeria or Dienbienphu, where the willingness to suffer gave an edge to the weaker party. It appears at the time of this writing that the confident expectations of victory by both sides were wrong. The Communists have demonstrated an unexpected and incredible willingness to suffer, but the United States has arrayed against them destructive power beyond anything previously imagined in so small a country.

The history of the War from 1965 through 1971 may be summarized as the progressive disappointment of each side in the hope that its original model would prevail, but the defeat of neither side. The two have gained respect for each other, the Communists for the awesome wealth and technology of the American war machine, the Americans for the tenaciousness of the Communists' struggle. In a sense, the war power model of each side is being modified to give some effect to the theory of the other. In a very gross way, we can represent the synthesis of their theories as follows[1]:

$$\text{Power ratio} = \frac{\text{Party A}}{\text{Party B}} = \frac{\text{Cost-tolerance of A/Strength of B}}{\text{Cost-tolerance of B/Strength of A}}$$

The ratio of power between A and B consists of A's ability to tolerate the costs that B imposes, against B's ability to tolerate the costs that A imposes. There is a trade-off: one may compensate for an opponent's strength, his ability to harm, by a greater willingness to be harmed. The formal expression above highlights the fact that greater cost-tolerance is no more a guarantee of victory than is greater strength. The question might be, does my willingness to suffer exceed his by more than my ability to harm is exceeded by his?

Is this a general theory of war power? Is every war a test of each side's ability to hurt against the other side's willingness to be hurt, to establish a ratio of power in proportion to which the contested values (e.g., land, degrees of control of the state) may be allocated? Is the subjective factor in war power usually as crucial as the simple theory suggests?

Testing the validity of this theory ideally would involve assembling aggregate data about a large number of wars, and testing the potency of "strength," the ability to harm, against "cost-tolerance," the willingness to be harmed, as predictors of victory and defeat. This is not fully possible for a number of reasons. Strength is itself an aggregate of many dimly understood factors. Those listed by Morgenthau (1967:106–44) include geography, natural resources, industrial capacity, military preparedness, population, and others. Morgenthau gives none of these in terms of a single quantitative index, partly because each is again composed of a multitude of factors. Also, there is no simple formula by which we can assign an appropriate weight to each factor to develop an overall index of strength.

Cost-tolerance is even more difficult to measure as it is wholly subjective and sometimes not even an explicit or conscious property of the thinking of relevant individuals. Up to what cost in American lives should we have fought to prevent a Nazi conquest of Europe? One's cost-tolerance does have a limit, but most of the time it is not defined, and even when it is,

---

[1] This unusual double ratio is used rather than the identity:

$$\frac{\text{(Cost-tolerance of A)}}{\text{(Cost-tolerance of B)}} \qquad \frac{\text{(Strength of A)}}{\text{(Strength of B)}}$$

because the strength of A and the cost-tolerance of B are both measured in units of harm to B (e.g., B lives lost) while the strength of B and cost-tolerance of A are measured in units of harm to A (e.g., A lives taken or lost). Consequently, the double ratio compares meaningful magnitude while the simpler identity does not.

without the opportunity to conduct interviews the researcher may not be able to discover it. I have nevertheless tried to find some available means of measuring strength and cost tolerance to test their relative potency. Most of the rest of this paper will describe these operations and the reasoning behind them.

Strength

I have chosen as an available measure of strength the wealth available to the government of a nation at war. This decision is based partly on the intuitive belief that national wealth can be shown to be the strongest correlate of a nation's destructive potential, and partly on the availability of wealth data. The subject of war power has received relatively little attention from scientific students of war behavior. Most research has been devoted to the study of the etiology of war, the search for factors associated with its outbreak. The subject of war power has been mainly the realm of the strategic studies research tradition, which has a strong "how-to" bias. There are, however, a few aggregate/empirical studies of war power, and these point to wealth as the single best gauge of strength.

One example is A.F.K. Organski's (1968:189–220) development of an "index of national power." Organski first identifies the following as elements of national power on a deductive or inferential basis: size of territory, geographical location, natural resources, population size, age structure and growth rate, industrial development, urbanization, education, geographic and social mobility, family structure, innovation attitudes, religious beliefs, political development, diplomatic and propaganda skill, military strength, military and civilian morale, and political ideology. These are compressed through a process of intuitive factor reduction to the "three most important determinants of national power": population size, political development, and economic development. Political development is then excluded for lack of an adequate quantitative measure. Economic development is indexed by per capita Gross National Product (GNP). Multiplying this by population yields the GNP itself. Hence, Organski's initially quite elaborate scheme boils down to sorry old GNP. Organski then uses GNP as his sole index of national power.[2]

Another more elaborate study is that of F. Clifford German (1960), who develops measures of more than 20 factors (chosen on the basis of plausibility and what data is available), intuitively gives these factors mathematical weights, and thus develops an overall index as a "tentative evaluation of world power." For example, "working population" is corrected for

---

[2] See also Hitch and McKean (1960, ch. 1) and Russett (1965:2–3).

"technical efficiency" by multiplying the working population "by 1 if the national consumption of energy is less than 0.5 ton of coal equivalent per head per year; by 2 if between 0.5 and 1.5 tons," etc. "Morale" is measured by inflating the working population of selected nations (e.g., Japan and Germany) by an increase of ⅓ to ½, again on an intuitive basis. For possession of nuclear weapons the entire index is doubled. The ranking of 19 countries in the late 1950's that results from use of this index is fairly plausible, but the index may have been manipulated exactly to achieve this result.

Since Organski's "index of national power" ranks the power of countries by GNP, and German ranks his "tentative evaluation of world power" by using a much more complex list of economic factors, a rank-order correlation between the two may indicate whether it is necessary to use something more refined than crude wealth to measure the economic power of a state. The German and Organski indices result in power rankings that correlate with each other strongly (Spearman's rho = .89), though it should be emphasized that German ranked only the wealthiest and probably most powerful states, and that Organski considers his list more reliable at this end of the scale. Thus German's index tapped the same factors that are summarized by the GNP measure, or are highly correlated with it. This same result has occurred in a number of studies which have factor analyzed data on GNP along with many other size and capability indices (Rummel 1969; Russett 1967a:17–21, 41–46). The complexities of German's index do not seem to yield results substantially different from GNP alone, and it would be preferable not to introduce controversial assumptions of the type he suggests if nothing is gained thereby.

Recently Alcock and Newcomb (1970) have shown that GNP rankings are a good predictor of what lay subjects believe to be the relative power of states. Thirty-eight Canadian subjects were asked to indicate what they believed to be the relative power rankings of groups of nations. The researchers compared these perceptions with GNP and found a .85 rank-order correlation. Also, GNP alone explained power perceptions as well as did an index based on GNP combined with national area and population measures. A measure of military expenditures had a slightly higher correlation with power perceptions than did GNP (.92). This might suggest the desirability of using military expenditures for the present study. However, we will be studying historical wars, for which such data are generally not available. Also, Newcombe and Alcock show a correlation of .89 between military expenditures and GNP, so wealth is strongly associated with the allocation of resources to war preparations. The few quantitative studies of war power, then, as well as the best non-quantitative studies (Knorr 1970), point to GNP as the most useful simple measure of physical strength in war, though none of them has validated the GNP measure of war power by showing that it correlates with the winning of wars.

Despite the strong case to be made for GNP, we will in fact not be able to use it. The body of wars in this study begins in 1928. GNP data are a Keynesian phenomenon and are not available for most states before 1930 or later. The closest and most interesting gross economic measure is the revenue of the central government, which has been recorded by the *Statesman's Yearbook* since 1864. This is the portion of wealth that is available to the warring government itself for all purposes, including the conduct of war, so one may expect that it is both highly correlated with GNP and, perhaps, even more sensitive than GNP as a gauge of the influence of wealth on war power. For this study of 40 wars, interval comparisons were possible for the antagonists on 22 wars, ordinal comparisons ("more/less") were estimated with a high expectation of reliability for 17 others, and one case (the Russo-Turkish War of 1828) was excluded for lack of a reliable basis for estimation.

The potency of material capability in war power will hence be tested by finding the frequency with which the state with more government revenue won the war. But in doing so we must remain aware of the imperfections of this measure, not least of which are the complex ways in which the conduct of military operations far away from the center of a nation's power may diminish its capabilities (Boulding 1962; Wohlstetter 1968).

Cost-Tolerance

The second component of war power in our theory is cost-tolerance. Very little is known about the actual setting of cost-limits for goals by actors, despite the central nature of this question to utility theory. Much more research has been devoted to the identification of goals than to the question, "Up to what cost do you favor this goal?" Even for contemporary problems, there are few opinion surveys from which one might derive cost-tolerance estimates; for historical cases, the problem is much worse. An alternative might be to make inferences from existing records of opinion and values, i.e., content analysis. But content analysis in this field is extremely hazardous in that cost-limits asserted by parties engaged in struggle may be deliberately inflated as a bargaining tactic or to bolster one's own morale. It is easy and useful to assert that one will fight to the last breath, but parties seldom fulfill such promises.

Also, as noted earlier, actors may be only dimly aware of their own limits. In a recent study reported elsewhere (Rosen 1971) I administered a survey instrument seeking cost-tolerance statements from 600 student subjects who were asked to express cost-limits in human lives for a number of foreign policy goals. One finding was a great resistance to setting life-prices; 1 in 6 of my respondents appended an unsolicited comment objecting to the idea of cost-limits in human lives. As Warner Schilling (1965:389) suggested, "The objects for which statesmen contend are not easily weighed in human lives." Alden Voth (1967:438) also found this resistance in a study of Vietnam opinion. In my study the cost-tolerance limits that were given were very much lower than those professed by American policy-makers. In a scenario featuring a Communist attempt to seize West Berlin, for example, the average maximum number of American lives that the respondents would give to stop the Soviets was under 5000. Contrast this with Herman Kahn's (1960:29–30) estimate that Americans would give $\frac{1}{3}$ of their population—70 million—or with contemporary American strategic assumptions that deterrence of the Soviet Union requires an "assured destruction capability" of $\frac{1}{5}$ to $\frac{1}{4}$ of the Soviet population and $\frac{1}{2}$ to $\frac{2}{3}$ of Soviet industry (Stillman 1970). One discovers when he constructs a survey instrument of this type how complex questions become when even the simplest cost considerations are introduced. In any event, my study did not result in plausible expressions of the actual willingness to suffer. My subjects had fairly clear priorities in their foreign policy goals, but rather unclear cost-tolerance limits for these goals.

We do not, then, have a good way of gauging the cost-tolerance attitudes of parties in wars of the past. We do, however, know the cost that they actually did suffer, at least in terms of human lives. We may test our hypothesis about the importance of cost-tolerance by comparing the losses of the winner and the loser. If there is a very strong correlation between losing fewer lives and winning, then we may infer that cost-tolerance is not a major factor since the party that inflicted greater harm usually won. If on the other hand there is not a strong tendency for the party losing fewer lives to win, then the hypothesis is at least not disconfirmed. We cannot infer that it is confirmed because we are not really measuring cost-tolerance directly. One problem is that the war may have ended at the point where it is clear to the loser that he will suffer greatly in the future, his defenses having been penetrated, but he has not suffered greatly yet. If the amount of suffering that actually occurred determined the outcome, then the willingness to suffer could not have been very important. On the other hand, if the amount of suffering did not predict the outcome very well, the reason may be the endurance factor, but it may also be expectations about future suffering or another unmeasured factor.

Another problem is our measure of suffering. Life costs are not the only cost in war. There are also financial costs, the loss of common interests with the opponent, the diversion of resources from other goals to war, alliance costs, sometimes social dissolution at home (e.g., Vietnam), etc. In Algeria the main cost to France was probably political disintegration rather than the loss of life; in Angola, Mozambique, and Portuguese Guinea, the main costs to Portugal are probably inflation and economic retardation; in Vietnam some have argued that the main costs to the United States are the continued decay of American cities and the disillusionment of young people. Again, a strong correlation between loss of life and losing the war will disconfirm the hypothesis about the importance of cost-tolerance, but a lack of relation between the two may be due to the exogenous factor of other cost items rather than the cost-tolerance factor.

It might also be argued that absolute losses of life are less important than losses relative to population size. The significance of a cost relates partly to the size of the pool of resources from which it is drawn; this is the theory behind the graduated income tax. The argument on the other side is also compelling. Human lives are valued absolutely for many purposes. Even while tolerating the loss of huge numbers of lives in highway slaughter and cigarette-induced cancer, wide attention may focus on the fate of a single individual trapped in a mine. Systems which encourage thinking in terms of "tolerable" losses of life are despised by the layman, though in an unconscious way all social systems do exactly this. This factor of the absolute value of life makes it plausible that a nation of 200 million may experience the loss of 500 men quite as painfully as would a mini-state with a population in the tens of thousands.

We will try both measures of life loss, absolute and relative to population. But with all the caveats listed above, the sole aspect of cost-tolerance in this study will be lives actually lost in war. The data used include only battle deaths of military personnel; knowledge of civilian deaths would be important but the data are unreliable.

The Wars

The principle of cost-tolerance, as formulated in other language by guerrilla theorists, was intended originally as a theory of "internal" war (including colonial independence struggles). Here the control of populations is a central factor, so a willingness to suffer in resistance is an obvious asset. We are attempting to generalize the theory of cost-tolerance to all wars, civil and international, including those where population control is not a central factor. I have chosen to test the theory in a body of "international" wars, partly because these are the ones where its applicability is intuitively less clear, and partly because data are more readily obtainable for discrete national units than for struggles in which one party is not a state but a movement.

The body of cases is drawn from Singer and Small's (1972) standard list of all international wars from 1815 to 1945, which is a total of 41 wars according to their definition of "international" and "war." (One of these is excluded from the present study for lack of data, so we will have a total of 40.) For each of the 40 wars it was necessary to identify a "winner" and a "loser." Obviously these designations are crude. What is winning? If winning consists of accomplishing the general political objectives of the party, then Japan may be said to have won World War II in that many of her

"Co-Prosperity Sphere" goals in that war have been realized since 1945. For present purposes, however, we are interested in the realization of goals directly through the application of war power. In other words, which of the parties at the time of the termination of the war came closer to accomplishing its goals in the war (i.e., achieving the distribution of the contested values that it sought)?

Another methodological problem is how to count coalitions. Who are the warring parties? For present purposes coalitions are limited to partners actively participating in the dispute by the direct application of military power. What if one member of the coalition is defeated while the other members fight on to a successful conclusion? For example, France was defeated in World War II, but her allies fought on to win. Nonetheless, we will adopt the convention of ascribing the gross coalition outcome to each of its members—French population, wealth, etc. will be taken as part of the winning Allied coalition. This assignment does not materially affect the statistical results to be reported, as the latter are exclusively concerned with ordinal, more/less comparisons between winning and losing coalitions, and in every controversial case herein the magnitude of the differentials between winners and losers is such that even wholesale reassignment of dubious cases to the opposite column would not change the ordinal comparison.

The Findings

First, was there a very strong tendency for the party that suffered least in absolute terms to win the war? The answer is somewhat surprising: in only slightly more than half the cases (55 percent; 22 of 40) was the winner the party that suffered less in absolute life loss. In almost half the cases (45 percent; 18 of 40) the winner lost more lives in battle than the loser! (See figure 11–1 and table 11–1.) It definitely is not the case that the winner is usually the party who kills more of the enemy. Perhaps this finding would be even stronger if we looked at internal wars where the cost-tolerance factor is clearer.

We will turn to losses relative to population in a moment, but first it might be argued that while absolute losses are not a good predictor of victory in all wars, they are crucial in very large wars in which total societies are pitted against each other. I have tested this by correlating the size of wars against a ranking based on the winner's losses as a percentage of the loser's losses (see table 11–1, columns 2 and 3). The rank-order correlation is only .02. In other words, it definitely is not the case that absolute loss levels are more important in large wars than in small ones. The lack of relation between battle loss magnitudes and winning and losing is true throughout the size range of the sample.

Turning to battle losses relative to population, we see in table 11–1 that

Table 11-1
Does the Party Which Suffers Least Win the War?

War and Date begun (1)	Size of War (Total Battle Deaths 000) (2)	Who Lost More Lives in Battle? (Winner/Loser) (3)	Who Had More Population? (Winner/Loser) (4)	Who Lost More % of Population in Battle? (Winner/Loser) (5)	Who Had More Revenue? (6)
World War II, 1939	15443.6	210.8%	470.1%	44.8%	Winner
World War I, 1914	8557.8	156.2	352.9	44.2	Winner
Sino-Japan, 1937	1000.0	33.3	15.1	220.2	Winner
Russo-Turk, 1877	285.0	72.7	304.2	23.9	Winner
Crimean, 1853	264.2	164.2	166.4	98.2	Winner
Franco-Prus, 1870	187.5	33.9	85.2	39.7	Loser
Russo-Japan, 1904	130.0	188.9	36.2	532.3	Loser
Chaco, 1928	130.0	62.5	39.5	157.8	Loser
Russo-Turk, 1828	130.0	62.5	182.9	34.0	—
Russo-Finn, 1939	90.0	125.0	4662.6	2.6	Winner
First Balkan, 1912	82.0	173.3	39.7	439.2	Loser
Second Balkan, 1913	60.5	236.1	832.2	28.2	Winner
Sino-Japan, 1931	60.0	20.0	14.6	136.3	Winner
Greco-Turk, 1919	50.0	66.7	441.2	15.1	Winner
Austro-Prus, 1866	36.1	63.3	148.0	41.7	Winner
Italian, 1859	22.5	80.0	167.4	45.7	Winner
Mexican, 1862 (Fr.)	20.0	150.0	21.5	714.2	Loser
Italo-Turk, 1911	20.0	42.9	145.5	29.3	Winner

Italo-Ethiop, 1935	20.0	25.0	413.9	5.6	Winner
Mexican, 1846 (USA)	17.0	183.3	261.0	70.1	Winner
Sino-Japanese, 1894	15.0	50.0	10.4	600.0	Winner
Pacific, 1879	14.0	27.3	46.2	58.6	Loser
Moroccan, 1859	10.0	66.7	577.3	11.4	Winner
Spanish Amer, 1898	10.0	100.0	398.1	22.2	Winner
Moroccan, 1909	10.0	25.0	394.2	6.2	Winner
Austro-Sardin, 1848	9.0	164.7	786.7	20.5	Winner
Danish, 1848	6.0	71.4	710.0	9.7	Winner
Schleswig-Holst, 1864	4.5	50.0	2102.4	1.7	Winner
Roman, 1849	2.2	2100.0	3198.4	50.0	Winner
Persian, 1856	2.0	33.3	427.2	5.8	Winner
Greco-Turkish, 1897	2.0	233.3	1504.4	12.5	Winner
Boxer Uprising, 1900	2.0	300.0	108.7	300.0	Winner
La Plata, 1851	1.3	160.0	16.0	1100.0	Winner
Roman, 1860	1.0	42.9	700.6	4.5	Winner
Sicilian, 1860	1.0	150.0	951.1	11.7	Winner
Colombian, 1863	1.0	42.9	228.0	18.8	Winner
Spanish, 1865	1.0	233.3	30.3	1400.0	Loser
Central Amer, 1885	1.0	25.0	45.9	55.1	Loser
Central Amer, 1906	1.0	66.7	115.7	56.7	Winner
Central Amer, 1907	1.0	150.0	269.3	56.0	Winner

Sources: Battle death data from Singer and Small (1972). Government revenue sources available on request from the author.

Columns (2) and (3), Spearman's rho = .018.

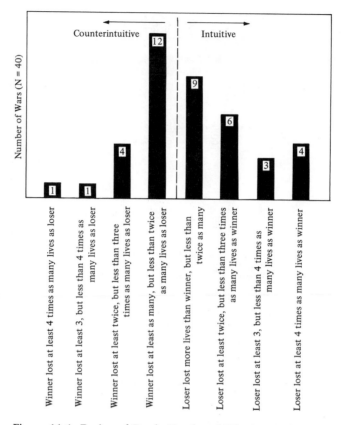

**Figure 11-1. Ratios of Battle Deaths of Winning and Losing
States in 40 International Wars, 1815-1945**

there is a stronger relationship between relative suffering and victory and
defeat; 30 of the 40 wars (75 percent) were won by the party which lost a
smaller percentage of its population. Whereas absolute losses of life compared to those of the opponent was a poor predictor of success, percentage
population loss is a fairly strong correlate of winning.

However, an analysis of these 30 cases shows that most of the effect
indicated was not produced by the loss rate, but rather by mere population
size; table 11–2 breaks down the 30 cases of parties who won by losing a
smaller percentage of their populations. This breakdown shows that population size explained 90 percent (27 of 30) of the cases in which the victor
was the party with a smaller population loss rate. The relative magnitude of
losses explained only 60 percent (18 of 30) of the cases. Putting it another
way, if a victorious party lost a smaller percentage of its population than did
the loser, chances were very good that it had a larger population, but only
a little better than even that it lost fewer men. Overall, 70 percent (28 of 40)

Table 11–2

Had More Population	Lost More Lives	
	Winner	Loser
Winner	12	15
Loser	0	3

of the wars were won by the party with a larger population. This also shows the greater potency of population size compared to the loss rate.

To summarize, it is not the case that the winner is the party who suffers less. Often the winner suffers more than the loser in terms of battle deaths. It is possible that this paradox is explained by the cost-tolerance factor.

What about our measure of wealth as an index of strength, the ability to harm? How great was the tendency for the wealthier or stronger party to win? If strength explains most of the variation in winning and losing, then the factor of cost-tolerance cannot be very important.

Our principal finding is that 79 percent (31 of 39) of the wars were won by the wealthier party. There is an impressively strong relationship between wealth and victory. Only about 1 war in 5 was won by the party with less wealth. And table 11–3 shows that there was a small tendency for wealth to be more important in large wars than small ones.

If strength predicts the outcome of 4/5 of all international wars, and is more important in large, costly wars than in small ones, then there is only a small range within which cost-tolerance factors could influence victory and defeat. On the other hand, the theory we suggested at the outset is consistent with this data. If we assume that the stronger party is as likely to have more cost-tolerance as he is to have less cost-tolerance, then the party with more strength should win 3 of 4 wars. (In half the cases he has more strength and more cost-tolerance: he is the obvious victor in these cases. In the other half, he has more strength but the opponent has more cost-tolerance; ideally, he wins half of these.) If the cost-tolerance factor indeed accounts for the unexplained 20 percent of international wars, and a somewhat higher percentage of internal wars, the findings about strength are consistent with the theory.

We can submit the theory to one further simple test. Some researchers have asked whether there is a fixed level of population loss at which point warring states concede the issue. Such a "fixed" level of cost-tolerance would be a partial disconfirmation of our theory. The present theory argues that the willingness to suffer, like the ability to impose suffering, is highly variable, and that in fact differences between two states' willingness to suffer for their goals sometimes explain why one wins a war and the other loses.

Population losses were of particular interest to two previous researchers: Lewis Richardson and Frank Klingberg. Klingberg (1966:147–148) concluded from a detailed study of a few cases that

Table 11–3
Is Wealth More Important in Large Wars?

War and Date Begun	Size of War (Total Battle Deaths, 000)	Who Had More Government Revenue (Winner/Loser) in Percentages?
World War II, 1939	15443.6	124
World War I, 1914	8557.8	355
Sino-Japanese, 1937	1000.0	2197
Russo-Turkish, 1877	285.0	4021
Franco-Prussian, 1870	187.5	46
Russo-Japanese, 1904	130.0	55
Chaco, 1928	130.0	26
Russo-Finnish, 1939	90.0	2702
First Balkan, 1912	82.0	96
Second Balkan, 1913	60.5	1005
Sino-Japanese, 1931	60.0	1097
Greco-Turkish, 1919	50.0	120
Austro-Prussian, 1866	36.1	115
Sino-Japanese, 1894	15.0	978
Pacific, 1879	14.0	37
Spanish-American, 1898	10.0	248
Greco-Turkish, 1897	2.0	513
Boxer Rebellion, 1900	2.0	671
Spanish, 1865	1.0	16
Central American, 1885	1.0	75
Central American, 1906	1.0	343
Central American, 1907	1.0	2645

Sources: Battle death data from Singer and Small (1972). Government revenue sources available on request from the author.

Spearman's rho = +.308.

> When population losses approach three or four percent, a critical period may have been reached in the nation's morale. . . . [Other factors must be considered, but] if one assumes that the given nation is losing productive power by steady attrition . . . and has lost hope of aid from other nations, then there may be a critical figure in population loss beyond which the nation will not go without surrendering.

Richardson (1960b:299) searched for such a "critical" level of population loss. He found that "Defeat would usually occur when the less populous side had lost in dead some number between 0.05 percent and 5.0 percent of its population."

To analyze the relationship between population loss and defeat, Richardson's test was replicated for the present study, enlarging his sample of 21 defeated parties greatly to 77. Richardson's upper limit is indeed confirmed: in only 2 of the 77 cases did states suffer more than 5 percent population loss in battle before yielding (see figure 11–2). On the other hand, his lower limit is definitely disconfirmed: in 23 of 77 cases the defeated party lost less

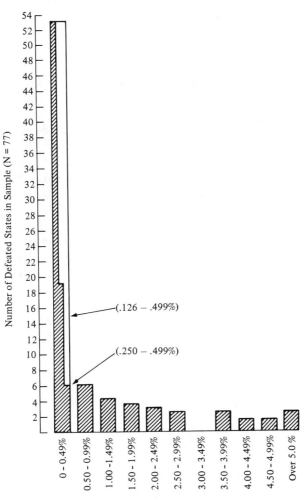

Y-axis: Number of Defeated States in Sample (N = 77)

Labels: (.126 — .499%), (.250 — .499%)

X-axis categories: 0 – 0.49%, 0.50 – 0.99%, 1.00 –1.49%, 1.50 – 1.99%, 2.00 – 2.49%, 2.50 – 2.99%, 3.00 – 3.49%, 3.50 – 3.99%, 4.00 – 4.49%, 4.50 – 4.99%, Over 5.0 %

Percentage Population Lost in Battle Deaths

Figure 11-2.

than 0.05 percent of its population in battle deaths. (An interesting implication of these figures is that war has not really functioned as a Malthusian
population-limiting device in the past.)

Cost-tolerance levels do indeed seem to have had a fairly limited range
of variance. But within this range there are great differences between individual cases. For example, the median of the highest decile of cases is 1000
times the median of the lowest decile (4.1 percent vs. .004 percent). (In
Vietnam, we may crudely estimate that the North Vietnamese and Viet
Cong have lost 800,000 men against a population base of over 20 million—
about 4 percent. The U.S. has lost under 50,000 against a population of over

200 million—less than ¼ of ¹⁄₁₀ of one percent. Their losses are 16,000 times ours in terms of population, but they are not more weary than we are.) Cost-tolerance does indeed vary greatly as measured by actual war losses.

This variation actually is not surprising, on careful theoretical consideration. There are a number of important elaborations of this simple theory that I have discussed elsewhere (Rosen 1970). Both strength and cost-tolerance, particularly the latter, are subject to large changes over time, both before a war and within the span of a single war. Also, the two factors are inter-related. Strength, the ability to impose harm, is partly a function of the willingness to commit resources, which is itself a function of cost-tolerance. A sophisticated analysis thus might look at changes in government revenues as war progresses, to tap the ability of a government to persuade its people they should tighten their belts to achieve their war aims. Indeed, any full theory must recognize that cost-tolerance is a variable for different groups within a nation as well as varying over time and between nations. In large part it will depend on the alternatives to war that are available to a government and a people; rats in corners fight especially hard (Russett 1963, 1967b). The whole question addressed in this paper also gives rise to questions concerning counter-force vs. counter-value targeting. Even for deterrent purposes, is it likely to be more useful to direct one's strength against the strength of the opponent, or to impose costs against his cost-tolerance for civilian lives?

Combinations of Factors

It is obvious that war power is composed of many factors. Ideally some operational measure could be found for each factor and multivariate techniques of analysis be used to determine the weight of each and the degree to which factors covary. In this way factors might be combined to produce a war power index explaining a very large portion of the variance in winning and losing. This small study is concerned with only a few of the relevant variables, and the number of cases is much too small to employ high-powered multivariate techniques. It is possible, however, to examine a few combinations of factors using common-sense techniques (see table 11-4).

The strongest factors of the 4 we have examined are wealth (.79 probability of victory) and lower population loss rate (.75 probability). One way to test the combined predictive power of these 2 measures is to take all the cases in which one party had both more government revenue and a lower loss of life rate. There were 31 such cases, of which 26 were won by the party favored in both respects.

What if the party has more revenue but lost a larger percentage of population? There were only 8 such cases, of which 5 resulted in victory and 3 in defeat. There were 35 cases in which the party that had more revenue

Table 11–4
Summary of Data on Correlates of War Performance

In . . . wars	One of the parties had . . .	It won in . . .	Probability
39	more government revenue	31	.79
40	more population	28	.70
40	fewer battle deaths	22	.55
40	lower population loss rate	30	.75
31	both *more* revenue *and lower* population loss rate	26	.84
8	more revenue *but a higher* population loss rate	5	.63
35	more revenue *and* more population	27	.73
4	more revenue *but less* population	4	1.00
22	more revenue and fewer deaths	18	.82
17	more revenue but *more* deaths	13	.76
36	more population and a lower population loss rate	27	.75
4	*less* population but a lower population loss rate	3	.75
20	more population *and* fewer deaths	15	.75
20	more population *but more* deaths	13	.65
24	fewer deaths *and* lower population loss rate	18	.75
16	*more* deaths *but* lower population loss rate	12	.75
31	more revenue, more population *and* lower population loss rate	26	.84
19	more revenue, more population, fewer battle deaths and a lower population loss rate	15	.79

also had more population. It won 77 percent of these (27). There were 4 other cases in which the party with more revenue had less population. It won all 4 anyway. In this sample, population is not important as a factor separate from revenue. Revenue predicts all the cases that population predicts plus some that it does not.

Revenue also predicts as well alone as it does in combination with absolute life losses. In the 22 cases in which one party had both advantages (more wealth and lower losses), it won 72 percent of the time (18 cases). The other 17 parties with more revenue but also higher losses won 76 percent of the time (13 cases). Adding the battle death factor to the revenue factor does not increase explanatory power, and of course revenue has the useful predictive quality of being knowable in advance of the war with some reliability.

The same lack of increase in explanatory power results from adding battle deaths to the rate of population loss (which is somewhat redundant anyway), and from adding population size to the population loss rate.

Given revenue data, the only other factor that seems to have a significant degree of statistical independence and to be important in predicting to victory or defeat is the population loss rate. To summarize: a party with either more revenue or a lower population loss rate is favored to win by about 3 or 4 to 1. A party favored in both respects gets odds of almost 5 to 1.

Conclusions

We have outlined a theory of war power in which the power of party A is a function both of A's ability to harm B and A's willingness to be harmed by B.[3] To validate the theory a number of attempts were made to disconfirm the importance of cost-tolerance in war power. The findings lend some credence to the theory, though they fall short of full validation: It is not the case that winners of wars were usually the parties who suffered less (in 18 of 40 international wars, the winner lost more lives than the loser). Strength alone, as measured by wealth, explained 80 percent of the victories, which is close to the theory's prediction that, assuming that each of the two parties is equally likely to have greater cost-tolerance, the stronger party should win in 75 percent of wars. Finally, there has been great variation in the level of population loss at which point defeated states conceded—cost-tolerance indeed varies greatly.

Pieces of these data reflect importantly on the strategic theories of both the United States and the Vietnamese Communists. The early confidence of the United States that it would prevail because of its vastly superior means might have been shaken by our finding that 1 of 5 international wars (and perhaps a higher percentage of internal wars) has been won by the weaker party. Also, it is significant that almost half of our international wars (18 of 40) were won by the party losing more lives in battle.

On the other side, the data show that while superior cost-tolerance may occasionally give the advantage to the weaker party, having less strength but more cost-tolerance more often results in defeat. Our crude data suggest that the party superior in strength but inferior in cost-tolerance (e.g., the United States in Vietnam) is favored, at least by the odds (60/40) to win anyway. Cost-tolerance as a single factor is no more a guarantee of victory than strength, probably less.

Research on war power may aid forms of social engineering and political policy that will reduce the need for political violence. Given a political dispute over competing claims to an important value, the actual occurrence of a war often can be attributed to erroneous judgment by at least one of the parties concerning its military power. This proposition is based on the following reasoning: if two parties are in a dispute, but they both know in advance who would win should a war occur, they could settle the dispute without violence simply by simulating the decision that both know will

---

[3] This theory is elaborated in Rosen (1970).

result from war. Most wars occur because the two parties have very different expectations of the likely outcome. "The most effective prerequisite for preventing struggle, the exact knowledge of comparative strength of the two parties, is very often obtainable only by the actual fighting out of the conflict" (Simmel 1904). Much fighting might be prevented if social scientists could devise a "yardstick of war power, some kind of measuring device that would enable parties to come to a common picture of the power situation in lieu of actual conduct of violent struggle" (Coser 1961). A useful metaphor is the picture of men fighting in a darkened room. If the lights were turned on, and some of the combatants had a clearer picture of the hopelessly superior size of their opponents, much of the fighting would end. Some would continue to fight because there was still some prospect of victory, and others would defy from desperation at the alternatives or confident hopes of a miracle, but in at least some cases a quixotic struggle would be abandoned. Research on war power just might be as useful in reducing violence as research on war causation.

Editors' Commentary

Major Findings

Rosen finds that the single most important factor in winning wars is the amount of revenue available to a government. As reported in table 11–4, 79 percent of the wars (thirty-one of thirty-nine) in his sample are won by the wealthier side. In addition, there is a slight tendency for wealth to be more important for large wars than small ones.

The second most important factor is the percentage of population lost. Rosen finds that 75 percent of wars (thirty of forty) are won by the side that lost a smaller percentage of its population. This does not mean, however, that the winner usually suffers fewer deaths. In fact, in absolute terms, Rosen finds that in 45 percent of the wars (eighteen of forty), the winner lost more people than the defeated.

To determine which is more important—revenue or percentage of population loss—Rosen attempts a controlled "experiment." He identifies those cases in which a side has more revenue but has lost a greater percentage of its population. In this situation, the variables are pushing the actor in opposite directions—more revenue toward victory and greater loss of life (in percentage) towards defeat. If revenue is more important, the actor should win; if percentage of population loss is more important, the actor should lose.

There are only eight cases to conduct this "experiment." In five instances, the side with more revenue won, and in three it lost. This finding, along with the fact that revenue alone predicts a greater percentage of victories (79 percent versus 71 percent), suggests that revenue is a more important factor.

Rosen then conducts a second "experiment" to see if the two variables together would be a better predictor than each alone. Put another way, this experiment seeks to answer the question, Would a side that had *both* more revenue and a lower percentage of its population lost have a double advantage (in other words, would it win more wars than if it just had one advantage)? There were thirty-one wars where this double advantage was present, and in twenty-six of them (84 percent), the favored side won. Taking both variables into account adds to our ability to predict the outcome of a war.

It is important to keep in mind, however, that although this success in prediction is impressive, it still means that reliance on these predictors will be erroneous anywhere from 16 percent to 21 percent of the time. There is nothing inevitable about winning a war. American efforts in Vietnam—where the United States killed probably over a million people, suffered a very small percentage loss of its population, and had a tremendous advantage in revenue at its disposal—demonstrate that. Among hawks, it is a shibboleth that the United States could have won if it had tried harder and had untied the hands of the military. Such rationalizations ignore the fact that the United States dropped more bombs on Vietnam than the combined total of bombs it dropped on Germany and Japan in World War II. Victory in war is never guaranteed by economic and demographic advantages. That does not mean, however, that the outcome is completely unpredictable. Exceptions should not be confused with the general pattern, nor should the exception be denied because of a general pattern, as hawks are wont to do with Vietnam.

Since Rosen wrote, additional evidence has supported his conclusions. Wayman, Singer, and Goertz (1983) find that the single best indicator of whether an initiator will win a war is its industrial capability rather than its prewar military capability or population size. Organski and Kugler (1978) demonstrate that some of the instances in which seemingly less capable sides (for example, those having a lower population or gross national product) win wars do so because they have a greater capacity to extract resources from their societies. They are thereby able to provide more revenue than one might surmise from looking at an aggregate measure like GNP. Rasler and Thompson (1983) argue, on the basis of historical evidence from the sixteenth through eighteenth centuries, that in the struggle for world leadership, the ability to secure long-term credit at low interest plays a key role in the ascendant powers' winning wars against their rivals. In a historical analysis of World War I, Paul Kennedy (1984) holds that it was the industrial and financial base of the Allies and the economic staying power they could manage through pooling their resources that counted the most. In part, world wars last longer than separate dyadic wars among the same belligerents would have because economically strong allies can rescue poor allies at critical junctures. Germany did this for Austria-Hungary, as did Britain for France and then the United States for Britain and France.

These analyses, along with Rosen's, suggest that it is difficult to overcome a rival's economic and demographic advantages by military strategy and prowess. This is not because these factors are unimportant; indeed, in the 16 percent to 21 percent of the wars that are exceptions to the rule, these factors may be critical. In general, however, national will and military effort have less of an impact because the two sides are so equal in these aspects that they tend to cancel each other out. In the end, structural factors are more important.

Methodological Notes

Rosen's analysis is an example of using percentages as probabilities and an illustration of how to make careful comparisons through the use of control variables. Rosen relies mostly on percentages expressed as probabilities rather than correlations. He does this because he is not trying simply to demonstrate a relationship, say, between national wealth and winning a war, but to see exactly how many times the wealthier side wins, so that he can offer a measure of the probability of winning in the presence of greater wealth.

He begins with the counterintuitive cases in figure 11–1, where the winner lost more lives than the loser. Turning to the variable of percentage of population lost, Rosen finds on the basis of table 11–1 that 75 percent of the wars were won by the party that lost a smaller percentage of its population. Such a figure can be more useful than a correlation. Using percentages, or probabilities, is akin to how gamblers assess their chances of winning a bet. If a side loses a smaller percentage of its population, its chance of winning is 75 percent; if it loses a greater percentage of its population, its chance of winning is only 25 percent.

This advantage does not guarantee victory. Table 11–2 lists only the thirty wars that were won by the side that lost a smaller percentage of its population. Of those thirty cases, fully twenty-seven had winners that had larger populations to start out with; whereas only eighteen of the thirty had losers that lost more lives. A country can lose more lives and still win if it has the sheer numbers. In only three cases was the victor able to overcome an opponent with a larger population, and that was only where the defeated lost more lives. There are no cases of a winner's losing more lives *and* having a smaller population (neither Vietnam nor Algeria is in this data set).

Nevertheless, it is possible to lose more lives and still win, provided the winner has a larger population (twelve of the thirty cases). By looking at the effects of number of lives lost and size of population, Rosen introduces the notion of control. He had already shown that loss rate was an important predictor of victory (75 percent), but when he introduced the two control variables in table 11–2, we could see that population size is also important and that number of lives lost is not very important.

Although most of the findings are in percentages, or probabilities, table 11–3 does report a correlation, but note that this is not a correlation between victory and wealth. The correlation in table 11–3, a Spearman's rho of .308, is the relationship between the ranking of the size of the wars and the wealth advantage of the winner in order to see if wealth is more important in large wars than small wars. Spearman's rho is an ordinal-level statistic, like tau b, which also compares two rank orderings to each other. The low .308 shows there is not much of a relationship. This is because wealth is important in winning large and small wars, not just large wars.

With the findings in table 11–4, Rosen attempts to assess the relative potency of various factors against each other. Remember not to interpret probabilities like correlations. While a correlation of .55 would indicate a moderate relationship, a probability of .55 (as for the fewer-battle-deaths variable) means that the variable is no more useful than flipping a coin. In other words, the side that has fewer battle deaths has a 55/45 chance of winning.

In order to assess the relative potency of the variables, Rosen uses them as controls. A **control variable** is a variable that produces different conditions under which the independent variable must perform. In a laboratory experiment on a drug, one group is given the drug, and there are two control groups: one group that receives a placebo (a sugar pill with no therapeutic effect) and another that receives no treatment at all. In this way, the researcher can identify the effects of the drug compared to the psychological effect of a placebo and compared to no treatment at all.

Rosen wishes to create some of the conditions of a laboratory experiment. He cannot manipulate the historical facts, but he can manipulate the variables, in effect, by removing the cases that have certain variables present. The way we assess control variables is to calculate a relationship or probability separately for two (or more) values of the control variable. If the results are the same for each, the control variable is not an important factor; if they are different, then it is important. Observe in table 11–4 that the side with more revenue has a 79 percent chance of winning. If percentage of population loss were not important, the probability of winning with more revenue and lower loss rate would be the same as that with more revenue but higher loss rate. That is not the case. Adding the positive factor of lower loss rate raises the probability to .84, and the negative factor of higher loss rate lowers the probability to .63, meaning that population loss rate has an impact.

Through such comparisons, Rosen provides a great deal of information on who will generally win wars and who will lose them. In the next article, A. F. K. Organski and Jacek Kugler uncover an unexpected twist in the answer to the question of what difference it makes whether one wins or loses by examining the impact of defeat on the long-term power of states.

12

The Costs of Major Wars:
The Phoenix Factor

A.F.K. Organski
Jacek Kugler

Editors' Introduction

War has been a central feature of modern life. Even as we approach the end of the century, there is little doubt that we still live in the shadow of the two world wars. Yet how much of a difference does it make who wins a war? How long does it take for winners and losers to recover from war? These are the two main questions underlying Organski and Kugler's analysis on what they call the phoenix factor.

They focus on the impact of war on the gross national product and economic growth. It would be a mistake, however, to see them as confining their study solely to the economic effects of war. They treat GNP as a simple indicator of overall national power. In another study, they justify the use of this indicator by showing that the correlation between GNP and the more complicated Singer, Bremer, and Stuckey (1972) composite index of (demographic, economic, and military) capabilities is .86 (Organski and Kugler 1980:38). For this reason, they see the implications of their study broadly, in terms of the impact of war on the overall power ranking and pecking order of the international system.

Introduction

There is no end of books and articles about war, and yet we know little of the subject that is of use. Of the three major aspects of interest in war—its

Reprinted from the *American Political Science Review*, 71:4 (1977), pp. 1347–1366. Reprinted by permission of the American Political Science Association and the authors. Abridged version approved by the authors.

causes, its outcomes, and its consequences—our concern in this paper is with consequences. These, of course, are intimately related both to beginnings and outcomes. The relationship between studies undertaken in the past and the effort in hand is useful briefly to elucidate.

Specialists and laymen alike have traditionally assumed the existence of a tie between the outbreak of major wars and the distribution of power among the major actors in an international system. In a general way, this premise postulates which power distributions went with war and which with peace. But there has been no interest in viewing the problem from the opposite angle of vision: what effects did outcomes of the conflicts have on the power distribution of the international system?

Can an inferior power reduce a superior one by means of war? Can the superior turn back the inferior by winning such a war? In short, what is "gained" and what is "lost," in power terms, by war? The overriding answer to such questions, the one accepted in the past, is that major wars and their outcomes make a tremendous difference in the international system. The future of a belligerent nation depends on victory or defeat. Regardless of other rationales advanced, this is the "logical" basis for going to war. It seems a powerful reason, and it is widely accepted. The justification of wars is rooted in such convictions.

However, we suspect that such reasoning is invalid. Hence, this investigation. A problem confronting the researcher in this area is how to ascertain the validity of the propositions that the outcomes of war either do or do not affect the power distribution in the international system. . . .

The Measurement of Power Resources

. . . Our choice of an overall yardstick of national capabilities, in preference to all others considered, is gross national product.[1] This decision may appear unwise. Might not a single economic indicator prove inadequate? Would not a more comprehensive index, composed of a number of other indicators, perform better? Unfortunately, more complicated indices do not perform so well as does this single one, and data for them are not as reliable for the period covered by this research. . . .[2]

---

[1] Alternate explicit attempts to estimate a single measure of national capacities are: Fucks (1965); German (1960); Organski (1968):207–14; Singer, Bremer, and Stuckey (1972):19–49; Knorr (1970);Cline (1975).

[2] We compared the performance of GNP over time with the measure developed by Singer, Bremer, and Stuckey (1972), the only other multidimensional measure available for the same period. Both measures are highly correlated and the similarity increases as the reliability of data improves. (R^2 of .95 was obtained for the sample of major powers for 1870–1970.) See Kugler (1973):82–96.

Estimating Consequences of War

As critical as the problem of power aggregation is the decision about the procedure to follow in estimating outcomes of war. This can be accomplished in one of three ways. First, one can simply establish suitable points before and after a conflict and compare them, with the differences regarded as the costs of war. This method is often applied, but is vulnerable to major error.

A second technique consists of calculating losses from a conflict by taking into account those changes that one estimates would have occurred had no conflict taken place. This procedure controls for normal growth, but is still based on the difference between two points. The rates of change are stipulated to be the same as those before the onset of the conflict. This procedure is clearly superior to the first, but it is weak because any comparison of the last year *before* and the first year *after* a conflict, work with times that are plainly abnormal, thus rendering difficult, if not impossible, the estimation of war costs. On the other hand, choosing points more widely separated distorts even more the measurement of war's effect. Moreover, the method produces misleading results because it maximizes the effects of different growth rates across countries and usually imputes high losses to rapidly growing nations.[3]

A third method represents a significant improvement over the others. Three steps are involved: (1) a base period prior to the war is selected, and a trend during this period is established; (2) the trend is extrapolated and serves as a moving base for comparison with actual performance; (3) differences between real behavior and the extrapolated lines are estimated. Figure 12–1 should facilitate an understanding of the mechanics of the model. The procedure we suggest permits the avoidance of distortions resulting from others proposed.

Forecasting

Our efforts to extrapolate require additional comment. The attempt to estimate changes over time by extrapolating trends from the base period is obviously a crucial factor since the quality of the projections is of paramount importance. The difference between anticipated and actual behavior rests on where we place the extrapolated line. If the selected series is well behaved with only minor fluctuations from year to year, regression techniques can be used to extrapolate from the pattern established in the base period. These techniques are particularly well suited for time series analysis, provided a variety of tests are performed guarding against violations of

---

[3] See Notestein et al. (1944: ch. 3); also Frumkin (1951).

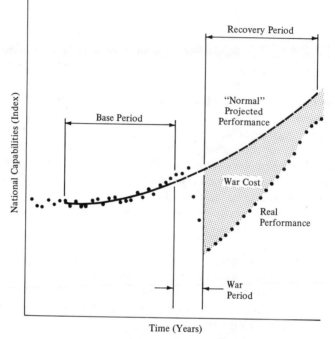

Figure 12-1. The Costs of Major Wars

assumptions and controls are introduced reducing undesirable effects of fluctuations. However, a number of interrelated questions must be answered: (1) Of what durations should the base period and the projections be? (2) How is one to deal with the abnormalities in periods serving as bases for forecasts? (3) What models should be employed in making projections?

Let us begin with the question of the lengths of base and extrapolation periods. Where a base period is said to end and a recovery period to begin are critical moments to choose. For example, Germany began to arm and mobilize long before the declaration of hostilities in World War II. Italy quit that war long before peace was declared. Such contingencies abound in wars, and adjustments become increasingly arbitrary. To avoid bias, the starting point of conflict for all contenders was judged to be the first full year of active confrontation between two sides. The beginning of the recovery period was judged to be the first full year after belligerence came to a halt.

From these two points, the official beginning of the war and the official termination, we selected a base period of 19 years and extrapolated onward for 20. Our decision was not arbitrary. We were aware that the longer the time segment available to fit the regression line, the more reliable the prediction. On the other hand, the longer the period, the less characteristic were the growth trends.[4] Our own selections were made by trial and error. Similar regressions were run for periods of 15, 20, and 25 years prior to the two conflicts in order to determine the stability of results. Those obtained for regressions using a period of 15 years were considerably less stable than those of 20, and regressions using a period of 25 years did not produce improved results. A period of 19 years seemed most suitable, because it provided as much separation as possible between the two world wars and a sample of years large enough to permit the use of at least 16 points in all estimates.

We extrapolated for 20 years. Clearly, a recovery period is difficult to isolate. Some effects of war linger. French resentment simmered for decades after their defeat by Germany in the Franco-Prussian War. German anger and revanchism, after their defeat by the Allies in World War I, produced World War II. We are primarily interested in the period when the effects of war are immediate and dominate the behavior of the international system.

Much of the analysis that follows rests on our choice of a forecasting model. We decided that linear models would not serve; they imply that yearly additions to total output are constant. They assume, therefore, a decrease in growth rates as the base expands. Such assumptions seemed invalid; the problem of underestimation is reduced with logarithmic transformations, because constant growth rates can be estimated with an ever-extending base.

To check our choice, we tested the performance of logarithmic adjustments with data unaffected by war from 1870 to 1913. In all cases, the nonlogarithmic projections consistently underestimated the real performance of the nations considered, and outliers systematically increased in the latter part of the series. In all instances better fits resulted from data which had been logarithmically transformed (Kugler 1973:116–17).

One caveat, however, should be made: there is no assurance that the patterns of growth for the period of 1900–1970 which we used for this study are identical to those of 1870–1913 used to test our model. The log model excludes all acceleration of growth rates over time. We know that national growth sometimes undergoes such acceleration.

An additional matter should be raised. Normal growth is essential if one is seeking to forecast the future through extrapolation. Periods between wars are regarded as times when normal growth takes place. This is not the case. Wars are but one kind of disturbance; depressions and revolutions can also occasion havoc with patterns of total output, as did the Great Depression of the 1930s. This economic downturn overlapped the period of recovery from the effects of World War I and the end of the era which served as the base for our projections from 1946 to 1965. No analysis could be carried out unless the effects of the depression were eliminated or at least

---

[4] Scholars have justifiably cautioned that given the deficiencies in data and models in the social sciences, projections should not exceed 20 years; see Heiss et al. (1973):107; Simon Kuznets (1971:ch. 1) demonstrates that growth rates of developed countries remained constant or increased in the last century.

substantially reduced. The simplest and most efficient way was to omit some outlying points to obtain estimates for nations affected by the cycle. It was impossible and theoretically unacceptable, however, to eliminate all of the effects of the depression, and some of the results show the distortions which originate in this disturbance in the base period.

Nor was the depression the only disturbance in the trends of our base period: two revolutions and accompanying civil wars also created major problems. The disastrous effects of the Spanish revolution and civil war on Spain's economic performance caused us to drop that country from our sample altogether, in spite of our wish not to reduce further the already small sample. The Russian revolution and civil war also had extreme effects on the economic performance of the country. Moreover, data were available only for 1895, 1899, 1913, 1920, and yearly after 1928. Nevertheless, we retained the USSR for compelling reasons: Russia was a critical actor in World War I.

Making the best of the situation, we used the data we had and maintained our procedure of estimation of consequences. Reliability measures were quite good, but it should be clear that results in the Russian case cannot be considered as stable or reliable as other projections.

Projections are not predictions. The fitting of data statistically is not equivalent to predicting how much real output there would have been in the absence of war. Moreover, even the correspondence between estimates and reality is not a final test of the validity of the estimates themselves. As Frumkin reminds us, absurd and unscientific estimates occasionally hit the mark (Frumkin 1951:17).

Standardization

Consequences of war as they affect power distribution cannot be estimated merely by the calculation of comparative national losses. Differences in size and rates of growth render meaningless comparisons of absolute losses. Total national capabilities of a country the size of Denmark are smaller than losses of a major power involved in the same great war. Again, identical absolute losses for a fast- versus a slow-growing nation imply greater absolute losses for the faster growing nation because of its expectation of greater growth. Standardization is obviously required.

We have used three methods. First we constructed an index. Theoretically, the optimal choice of a base year would have been 1930, for it stands at the halfway point in the period under analysis. This was, however, a year of general depression; thus, 1913, the base year established by Angus Maddison who provided us with the original data, was a more useful point of departure, for it was the last year of a very long period of peaceful growth.

We also held constant the size of all nations in our sample to avoid the distortions produced by any changes in boundaries rather than by human or material losses incurred during the war. We dealt with the problem by using throughout the boundaries of 1970. Maddison, whose national product data we used, had followed the same procedure. In his adjustments of his gross national product series Maddison assumed territorial changes to influence output in direct proportion to population changes (Maddison 1964:194–203; Kugler 1973:31–36).

And we chose *years* as our unit of measure in order to cope with differences in size and growth rates among nations. Our estimation however was complicated by the fact that our original index was logarithmically transformed and prevented simple evaluations of losses in time units as deviations from the original regression, because algebraic manipulations could not be applied to them. This difficulty was resolved by reversing the dependent and independent variables in the regression estimates and reducing the resulting residuals to time units.[5] For time is obviously a commodity equally available to all and one that is not affected by growth rates. Thus, when we say that one country has lost or gained 15 years, we mean only that its power resources diminish or increase relative to the performance of that nation in the base period. Because we thought it important to establish negative signs corresponding to losses and positive signs corresponding to gains, the residuals are multiplied by -1.

Independent estimates of normal performance were run for all relevant nations and included the study of each of the wars considered. In all cases, the model was:

Time = a + b log of the index of total output of each nation + error, where Time = 0, 1, 2, ... , n, where n is the length of the base period.

In this model, the slope and intercept have no significance; only the residuals are important. Two variables are used in the estimate, and goodness-of-fit measures are not affected when we once again reverse the model to the more familiar function, with total output as the dependent and time as the independent variables.

The Reliability of the Projections

As we have noted earlier, estimates of normal growth after a war depend on stable data for trends in the prewar period. A variety of interrelated statistical techniques was used to determine the reliability of the regression estimates, given the assumptions of that model. The coefficient of determination, R^2 (showing the proportion of total variance explained), was used to estimate the reliability of the trend in the base period. Average values were utilized to establish levels of tolerance for residuals central to the evaluation of costs of war.

Table 12–1 displays results of major tests conducted. It is evident from

---

[5] Thomas Sanders, Lutz Erbring, Department of Political Science, and J. Landwehr, Statistical Research Laboratory, University of Michigan, generously contributed to the solution of this difficult methodological problem. They are not responsible, of course, for any weaknesses of the final product.

Table 12–1
Measures of Goodness of Fit and Range of Residuals in Base Period

	World War I					World War II					
			Residuals for Base Period 1895–1913 (Years)						Residuals for Base Period 1921–1939		
Nation	Number of Observations	R^2	Max. Loss	Max. Gain	Last Year (1913)	Number of Observations	Depression Years Excluded	R^2	Max. Loss	Max. Gain	Last Year
United States	19	.97	-1.7	2.0	-.9	19		.30			
						16	1932–1934	.66	-6.2	4.6	2.6
West Germany	19	.99	-1.0	1.0	.7	19		.76			
						16	1931–1933	.87	-4.5	2.7	-1.9
United Kingdom	19	.80	-6.0	5.2	-.1	19		.83			
						16	1931–1933	.84	-2.9	2.3	-2.3
Japan	19	.87	-4.1	5.0	-.3	19	1931–1933	.84	-2.9	2.3	-2.3
						16		.92	-2.4	2.6	-.7
USSR	3	Special Estimate				—	None	.98	—	—	—
Italy	19	.96	-2.4	1.9	-.6	19		.98			
						16	1931–1933	.80	-1.3	1.5	.7
France	18	.92	-2.4	2.7	1.2	19		.80	-4.2	3.3	.8
						16	1931–1933	.56	-5.1	5.5	4.5

Country													
Belgium	19	Data Unavailable				19	16	1931–1933	.65	.67	−5.1	5.5	4.4
Denmark	19	.98	−1.5	1.3	.6	19	16	1931–1933	.95	.95	−2.8	2.2	.3
Sweden	19	.98	−1.8	1.5	1.4	19	16	1932–1934	.89	.93	−2.5	2.1	.1
Switzerland		Data Unavailable				19	16	1931–1933	.79	.79	−3.6	4.8	3.0
Canada	19	.97	−1.6	2.3	.6	19	16	1932–1934	.37	.59	−5.9	6.1	3.2
Australia	19	.96	−2.4	1.8	.4	19	16	1931–1933	.56	.79	−5.0	6.4	1.1
Netherlands	14	.96	−1.3	1.1	.7	19	16	1932–1934	.75	.78	−4.0	4.4	2.4
Norway	19	.95	−2.2	2.3	2.3	19	16	1931–1933	.98	.98	−1.2	2.0	.1
Czechoslovakia		Not a Nation				17	14	1933–1935	.47	.61	−6.8	3.4	n.a.
Hungary		Not a Nation				15	12	1931–1933	.65	.72	−3.4	3.7	n.a.
Yugoslavia		Not a Nation				19	16	1932–1934	.80	.83	−4.9	3.9	.1

a consideration of table 12–1 that the coefficient of determination for the period before World War I is consistently in the high nineties, and that only in the case of the United Kingdom and Japan can one obtain an R^2 figure below that level, .80 and .87 respectively. Such estimates are not unexpected, given the behavior of the series in that period. Thus, one could consider projections of normal trends after World War I to be stable and reliable.

Results of World War II, following similar criteria, are less satisfactory. Only after controls are imposed to minimize the effects of depression does the coefficient of determination for most countries rise to the levels reached for World War I. Without such controls, coefficients run as low as .04 for Austria, .30 for the United States. But in the cases of some nations considered, even after controls are established, the coefficients remain low: Austria ($R^2 = .17$), France ($R^2 = .56$), Canada ($R^2 = .59$), Czechoslovakia ($R^2 = .61$), the United States ($R^2 = .66$), and Belgium ($R^2 = .67$). Such evaluations require exegesis.

Austria's performance is explained by her troubled history in the postwar period: Austria-Hungary was dismembered after World War I; the economic depression was particularly acute; there was civil war; and finally, Austria was absorbed by the Third Reich. A stable estimate was not possible. Therefore, Austria was dropped from the sample. France also represents a special case. French growth was very slight in the interwar period, and the regression estimate, while producing a good fit, was statistically not significant because it was close to zero. The remaining low correlations show the effects of the depression of the 1930s. Although the impact of the economic catastrophe is minimized when outliers are removed from the calculations, it is plain from table 12–1 that the effects of the depression are still visible; residual values of maximum losses reach -12.3 years in the case of the United States when no controls are imposed and are cut almost in half, to -6.2 years, when three outliers are deleted.

The residuals in our table indicate three points: (1) estimated trends are more reliable for the period prior to World War I than for that before World War II; (2) we expect that the performance of nations over time in the sample will not depart more than two or three years from the projected line during the period covered; (3) the sharp improvement in values in the last year of observation suggests that the forces depressing the economies of the nations considered were being overcome.

One more important item should be noted. Because the information contained in the residuals was so crucial to this study, some additional tests were carried out. In the base period for World War II, some residuals were high when previous values were high. These traces of tracking, however, were sharply reduced when the outlying points for the depression years were eliminated. This operations considerably increased our confidence in the accuracy of the regression model designated (see Kugler 1973:ch. 4, App. III).

Choice of Test Cases

. . . The stringent theoretical and data requirements reduced to a very small number the sample of utilizable wars. Although the Napoleonic Wars and World Wars I and II meet the theoretical criteria we have established, only for the latter pair have we time series data at frequent enough intervals and of high enough quality to permit the analyses we wished to undertake. Here, therefore, we must raise the question of whether or not the analysis of two wars can be more generally representative than the examination of simply two case studies, with all the limitations this approach has on the drawing of broad inferences beyond the cases themselves.

We think that the results of this study should be considered sources of significant generalization because, although the number of wars we analyze is extremely small, the sample of 31 cases we observe is adequate. These cases are observed throughout the two most terrible wars in history and include most of the countries of the central international system. Moreover, the two great wars we examine are those which offer the best opportunity for testing our propositions. The reduction of our area of study to two wars undoubtedly has sharply restricted the nature of the inferences that one might wish to make. On the other hand, the process developed allows tests on a much enlarged sample as soon as improved theory, methodology, and data permit it.

Actors

. . . In seeking the cast of nations whose performance we should measure, it was clear that it should incorporate all belligerents in World Wars I and II, with a group of nonbelligerents serving as a control group. We began with the comprehensive list of belligerents compiled by Singer and Small (1972) in their classic data-gathering effort, *The Wages of War,* to which we added, as an initial massing for a control group, all of the nations in existence at the time of the conflict under study which had not participated in it.

The first list had to be pared. We immediately eliminated from our sample all nations that were not developed,[6] since there was no way to estimate their power satisfactorily. A number of combatants in the two wars had to be dropped from our consideration for this reason. This category is unfortunately long, including Mongolia, Bulgaria, Rumania, Ethiopia, Greece, Brazil, and Turkey. On the other hand, South Africa, New Zealand, Poland, and Finland were eliminated from the study because data were inadequate.

---

[6] Wherever more than 50 percent of the working-age males were in non-agricultural pursuits, the country was considered developed.

... This sample was further reduced when we lost Spain and Austria because reliable estimates could not be generated.

The Analytic Groups: Belligerents/Nonbelligerents; Winners/Losers; Active/Occupied

Having assembled our basic components, we divide our cast into belligerents and nonbelligerents, winners and losers, both active and occupied. . . .

Operational distinctions such as those above require definitions which clarify any ambiguities arising from the theoretical conceptions; thus the following definitions of the analytic groups:

1. Belligerent nations are those whose participation in the conflict resulted in military losses of 5000 troops.

2. Nations whose strict neutrality or symbolic participation resulted in losses of less than 5000 troops were considered nonbelligerents.

3. Nations still fighting in the final third of the conflict on the same side as at its beginning were classified as active belligerents.

4. Belligerents which in the last third of the conflict were no longer members of the coalition they had joined at the beginning were classified as occupied belligerents.

5. Nations that retained all their territories or extended them immediately after a conflict and as a direct result of that conflict were considered winners. The rational support for such a definition is plain: no victor in a major war would tolerate the loss of any territory under its jurisdiction.

6. Loss of territory would be construed as the behavior of a loser. Even transfer of territory, with full compensation made for that loss, is considered an overt sign of defeat; for no victor would submit to such terms, and only a loser would have no alternative.

The analytical groupings that we use from different combinations of our three fundamental dichotomies—belligerent/nonbelligerent, active/occupied, and winner/loser—do not exhaust all the logical combinations one could explore. They do, however, satisfy the theoretically interesting possibilities for the analysis of war. . . .

. . . The distribution of our total cast of nations into analytic groups discussed above can be seen in table 12–2. The sample of 18 nations and 31 cases respectively was the very best we could assemble given our theoretical constraints and the lack of data. It is scant, but sufficient for the research we wished to undertake.

Table 12–2
Final Sample of Nations Used in the Analysis

	Active Belligerent Winners	*Active Belligerent Losers*	*Occupied Belligerent Winners*	*Occupied Belligerent Losers*	*Nonbelligerents*
Australia	I & II[a]				
Belgium			II		
Canada	I & II				
Czechoslovakia				II	
Denmark			II		I
France*	I		II		
Germany (West)*		I & II			
Hungary		II			
Italy*	I	II			
Japan*		II			I
Netherlands			II		I
Norway			II		I
Sweden					I & II
Switzerland					II
Russia (USSR)*	II	I			
United Kingdom*	I & II				
United States*	I & II				
Yugoslavia			II		
Total WWI	6	2	—	—	5
Total WWII	5	4	6	1	2

[a] I = World War I; II = World War II.
* = Major Powers.

Theoretical and Empirical Propositions

Theoretical Propositions

To many observers, the power position of members of the international system seems obviously influenced by their choice to participate in conflict and by their fortunes in war. Most scholars and practitioners have believed that it made the greatest difference to the power of a country in the modern age whether it won or lost a war. Very few disputed this view.

In our effort to separate the long-run from the short-run consequences of war and to present, in an approximate way, the distribution of opinion, three important theoretical propositions, with different short- and long-term results, seem to emerge.

The first proposition asserts that in the short run the movement of power between winners and losers creates a pattern much like the gradual opening and then closing of a pair of scissors. J.M. Keynes maintained that the gap which developed between winners and losers as a result of war would continue to increase for a short time in the future and the losers would fall behind at an ever-growing rate. Interestingly enough, Keynes also thought that in the long run, losers laid waste by economic ills would contaminate their partners in trade and bring chaos to the entire system.

Thus, the winners would move downward to join the losers, and the gap between them would tend to disappear.[7]

A second view suggests that as a result of war all nations lose national power, but the winners do not lose as much as losers, and the gap thus created between victors and defeated nations continues for a lengthy period of time. Norman Angell was a supporter of this notion.[8]

A third proposition, advanced by A.F.K. Organski, asserts that while it is indisputable that losers suffer a good deal more than winners and are in a much worse position immediately after conflicts, levels of power distribution return reasonably soon to the patterns they would have followed had no war taken place. The mechanics of the change work in approximately the following way: After their defeat (and the plummeting of their capabilities) losers accelerate their recovery. Winners, in the wake of victory, show a rate of recovery in capabilities depleted by war which is substantially slower than that of losers. Neutrals are not affected. Within a relatively short period of time, all nations return to the levels of national capabilities they would reasonably expect to hold had there been no war. There is a convergence of winners and losers; the major reason for this seems to be the speed with which the losers recover. They appear almost literally to rise from the ashes of their defeat.[9] There is a "phoenix factor" at work.

Empirical Propositions

Let us phrase our empirical propositions in the precise operational language of this study. We have eight hypotheses: The first four represent short-range expectations; the second four represent long-range expectations. Our propositions for short-range effects are:

H_1. Belligerent countries that emerge as winners of major wars gain in power; nonbelligerent countries retain their antebellum power patterns; belligerent losers suffer substantial power losses.

H_2. In the period immediately after a war, belligerent winners and nonbelligerents retain antebellum power patterns; belligerent losers suffer substantial power losses.

H_3. After major wars, all belligerent countries suffer major losses in their power capabilities; nonbelligerents retain antebellum power patterns.

---

[7] Keynes (1920). For discussion of the short-term effects of wars on belligerents, see United States Strategic Bombing Survey (1945, 1946).

[8] Two works argue at length that there are enormous permanent losses as a result of war. See Angell (1933) and Nef (1950).

[9] For the effects of war on belligerent populations, see United Nations (1971).

Our null hypothesis is stated thus:

H_4. After major wars, the power patterns of belligerents and non-belligerents are not affected in a systematic manner.

Our propositions for long-range effects are:

H_5. All groups involved in war suffer long-range losses of power and do not regain power patterns at levels established before the onset of major conflicts.

H_6. Belligerent winners and nonbelligerents retain antebellum levels of growth; power cleavages between belligerent winners and non-belligerents, on the one hand, and belligerent losers, on the other, are rapidly erased by the accelerated recovery rate manifested by losers.

H_7. Differences which result from victories and defeats in major wars are maintained or even slowly increased; thus, the immediate postwar gap between belligerent winners and nonbelligerents, on the one hand, and losers, on the other, is maintained or possibly enlarged.

Our null hypothesis for long-range expectations is:

H_8. The postwar patterns of all groups considered are not affected in a systematic manner as a result of war.

Two final points: it should be clear that in order to test our propositions about long-range effects, the null hypothesis for short-range expectations must be disproved. Second, the two sets of hypotheses, as well as the theoretical propositions that precede them, do not represent all the logical possibilities, but do summarize the views expressed in the literature regarding the outcomes of war and the effects of these outcomes on power distribution.
Now let us turn to what we have found.

Findings

We first wish to examine the behavior of the entire sample; then, in order, that of the subset of great powers taken together; and then that of both for each war taken separately. Had our sample of countries and wars been larger, the performance of all countries taken together would have offered evidence of the kind of behavior we could expect from winners, losers, and neutrals as a consequence of even a major war. However, due to the smallness of the sample, it seemed wise to explore, as deeply and broadly as possible, how important subsets of the total sample behaved. It is important to note that while each of the partitions of the total sample is separately and discretely observed, they are not independent, since the sample is identical for all.

The first partitions permit us to see the behavior of all nations in both wars. Only three of our analytic groups (active belligerent winners, active belligerent losers, and nonbelligerents) are considered. Occupied belligerent winners and losers are excluded because, by our definition, there were no occupied countries during World War I.

The results (figure 12–2) show that in the first two postwar years, belligerent winners and nonbelligerents lose from 1.5 to 3.5 years. The devi-

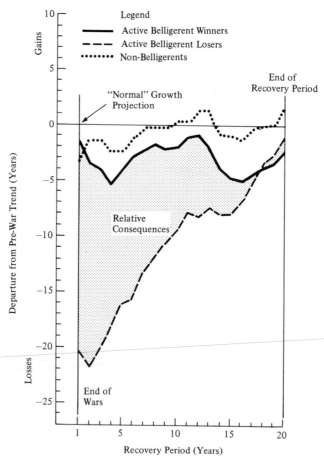

Sample: All nations, both wars.

Figure 12-2. Partition I: General Consequences

ation of both groups from expected performance is minimal. Active belligerent losers, however, suffer losses in a comparable period of 20.4 to 21.6 years. The difference between the two groups is substantial: 19 years.

In the long run, the nonbelligerent nations retain growth rates characteristic of their prewar performances. Active winners incur an average deviation of about three years from the zero line, indicating that losses suffered after postwar demobilization are maintained. Among active belligerent losers, however, the Phoenix phenomenon manifests itself. Losers begin and maintain a steady accelerating recovery rate after the war and overtake the winners in the eighteenth year of the postwar period. At the conclusion of that period, differences in power distribution among all groups have been eradicated; levels of power return to points one would have anticipated had no war occurred.

Thus, the results we obtained strongly support hypotheses two and six.

In testing the second subset of actors in our breakdown, the behavior of the great power system over two wars, the results are very much the same (see figure 12–3). Only active belligerent winners and losers are considered, for none of the great powers was neutral in World War II. Active winners begin with a two-year loss immediately after the war, then recover briefly, only to slide away once more. Overall, their performance is below expected levels and is heavily influenced by depressions in the interwar period. However, the trajectory as a whole reveals no loss in relation to prewar capabilities. The active belligerent losers, on the other hand, suffer a 20-year loss immediately after the war, but recover rapidly, overtaking the winners in the fifteenth year. After this point, both groups resume previous patterns.

Hypotheses two and six are confirmed again by a study of the composite data of the great powers for both wars. In our next four operations, we partitioned our sample to show the performance of the entire system and the subsystem of great powers for each world war.

Our third partition permits us to observe the behavior of the entire system after World War I (see figure 12–4). In the short run, nonbelligerents appear slightly affected during the first year after the war, but remain within one year of the zero line during the second. The active belligerent winners incur losses of from five to seven years right after the conflict. Active belligerent losers suffer losses of from 21 to 25 years. Winners lose, but losers suffer four times more severely. There can be no doubt that in the short run, there are serious power consequences both to winners and losers of major wars. Again, the evidence in large part supports hypothesis two, although active belligerent winners do suffer markedly.

The evaluation of long-term consequences is intimately related to the effects of economic depression. Consider first the initial 12-year period after World War I. The characteristics described in hypothesis six are supported. Active belligerent winners recover very slowly from war effects; nonbelligerents retain previous growth patterns; active belligerent losers, after the

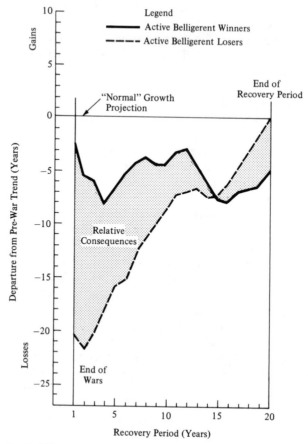

Sample: Major powers, both wars.

**Figure 12-3. Partition II: Major Power Consequences
Sample: Major Powers, Both Wars**

immediate postwar period of heavy loss, display a substantially faster rate of recovery than winners. Then the Great Depression strikes and, within two years, performances of all groups are diminished. Belligerents, however, seem to suffer more than nonbelligerents. After 1933, predepression trends reestablish themselves, but the subsequent period is too short for adequate evaluation.

The great power system during World War I behaves in much the same way described for the sample as a whole (see figure 12–5). Active belligerent winners fare slightly worse than the whole sample, but differences are so marginal that we feel secure in concluding again that the results support hypotheses two and six. We draw this conclusion despite the disruption caused by the depression. The graph shows the depression to be a major factor in

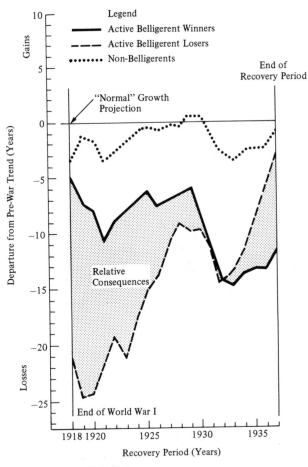

Figure 12-4. Partition III: World War I Consequences

distorting the recovery patterns of all countries taken together, not merely for World War I but for both conflicts. Moreover, the depression is also a major reason why our projections for the period following World War II are so weak, underestimating egregiously the growth trends (see figure 12–6).

In our fifth partition, all major analytic groups are represented for World War II. Some of these representations, however, are so tentative that one needs to take the information they convey with caution.

The consequences of World War II on power distribution, in its immediate aftermath, are much as expected. In the first year, active belligerent winners are slightly ahead, but move toward the zero line in the second year. Nonbelligerents are slightly below the zero line but move to points within tolerance limits (two years for this partition) in the second year. Active

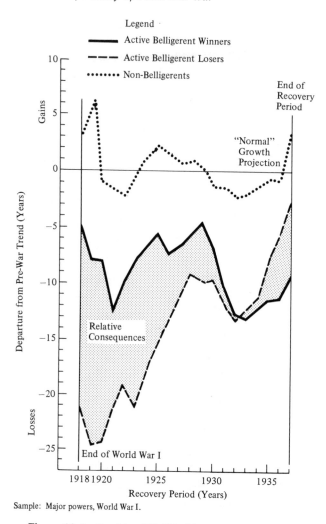

Sample: Major powers, World War I.

Figure 12-5. Partition IV: World War I Major Power Consequences

belligerent losers suffer substantial losses, between 16 and 17 years, in the first 24 months after the war, and the occupied belligerent winners lose from 11 to 14 years in the same period. The differences of loss between active winners and active losers range from 21 to 23 years in the initial period.

In the long-run analysis we find, for the first time, evidence to support the proposition that the gap between winners and losers can continue instead of closing.

A number of points should be made. The logarithmic projections seriously underestimate the growth of the system. An indication of this is to be

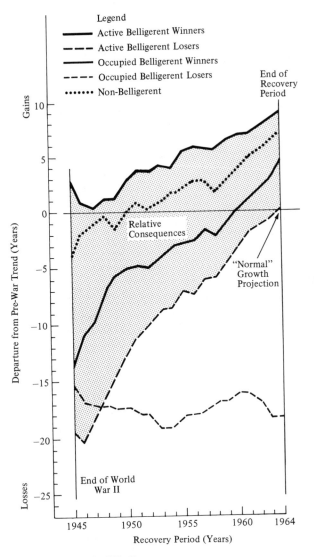

Sample: All nations, World War II.

Figure 12-6. Partition V: World War II Consequences

seen in the fact that nonbelligerents make increasing gains over time, indicating that prewar patterns distorted by the depression are not a good indicator of the behavior of the group as a whole in the period after World War II. In some part, however, as Kuznets suggests, economic growth since 1945 is due to a liberalization of trade in the industrial world and is therefore unexpected (Kuznets 1971:43). It is our impression that a more accurate projection of growth trends would place the zero line approximately where one finds the trajectory for the nonbelligerents. In any event, our main concern is with active winners and losers, and we must first establish that distortions in the pattern do not, in that respect, affect relative calculations. Over the entire period, the active belligerent winners maintain a constant but slight edge over nonbelligerents amounting to about three years. Absolute differences between winners and losers are not distorted by the acceleration of recovery rates.

One should note that here, too, active losers enjoy a sharply accelerated recovery pattern and regain the prewar level of growth within the stipulated period. They do not actually close the gap between themselves and the winners because of: (1) the acceleration of the entire system; (2) a decided deceleration in recovery in the last five years of the period, which may have caused an absolute loss of from five to eight years.

Nevertheless, a gap of roughly nine years remains at the end of the recovery period, and one might argue that we have, as a result, evidence supporting hypothesis seven, that winners maintain the advantage they gain from victory over the long-run.

The remaining analytic groups behave in interesting ways. The performance of occupied belligerent winners is somewhere between that of active winners and losers and follows closely the performance of the former. Occupied belligerent winners regain prewar rates in 15 years, surpass them, and come close to convergence with winners at the end of the recovery period.

Since only Czechoslovakia falls into the category of occupied belligerent losers, one obviously cannot refer to "findings" in observing the behavior of one country. But one should note that the matter merits investigation when sufficient data become available; for if other occupied belligerent losers behave as does Czechoslovakia, we may have identified the real losers in major wars—the nations which do not recover. It is possible that we have also identified the conditions necessary to support an alternative hypothesis to those advanced here. This may be significant. In all the analyses so far offered, we have discerned only marginal differences in the long-range consequences of victory and defeat on the power distribution of the system. However, if the case of Czechoslovakia is a true indication of what obtains for other occupied belligerent losers, it would then be clear that had the victors insisted on occupation, exploitation, and repression of defeated populations, our findings would be dramatically different. It may be that victors can delay the recovery of the vanquished by occupation and repression. For example, if Hitler, with his plans to depopulate and exploit his victims, had won the war, the vanquished might not have recovered. Had Hitler been victorious, hypothesis five might have been sustained.

Be that as it may, the results of the fifth partition should not be viewed separately, but rather must be compared with those of partition six (see figure 12–7) for the deviations disappear when one observes only the subsystem of great powers in World War II, which behaves entirely in consonance with the

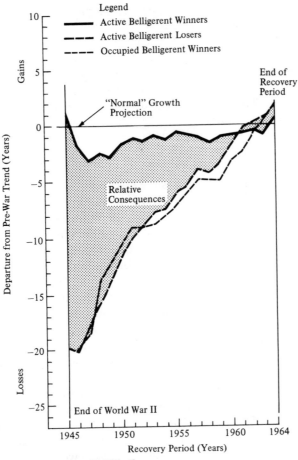

Figure 12-7. Partition VI: World War II Major Power
Consequences

expectations of hypotheses two and six. In the short term, active belligerent winners suffer no loss; occupied belligerent winners and active belligerent losers suffer a loss of 20 years of "normal" growth in the first two years after the war's end. The relative differences between active winners and the latter two categories in this period are 20.9 and 18.1 years respectively. Evidence on long-term effects fully supports hypothesis six. Active winners maintain expected growth patterns, while active losers accelerate recovery rates and overtake winners in the sixteenth postwar year.

How is one to reconcile these results with those obtained when examining the behavior of the total sample? Some explanatory points should be considered: the differences noted across the two partitions are not rooted in the behavior of all our analytic groups. The behavior of the active losers and occupied winners changes only slightly from one partition to the other. It is also plain that the logarithmic model we chose projected accurately the performance of great powers in the period after World War II. Not projected accurately, therefore, are the behaviors of the smaller winners. Their unprecedentedly rapid growth inflates the performance of the entire sample.

The Phoenix Factor

Most unexpected and interesting is the discovery that after wars the active losers catch up with winners in comparatively short order, and that the system of international power begins to behave as one would have anticipated had no war occurred. We cannot explain the phenomenon; we do not know why losers rise from the ashes as they appear to do.

We can, however, make some surmises. It is plausible to believe that structural elements may play a part. For example, favorable occupational distributions may help to accelerate recovery rates, as may the destruction of obsolescent plants and industrial equipment. It is probable that attitudinal factors may also play a significant role in increasing the pace of recovery. A defeated but economically developed population living in the midst of destruction will recall the antebellum status quo and be motivated to rebuild. So motivated a populace would have the technology to make an economic system function well. It is also plausible that the defeated population would exert a greater effort to recover than that of a victorious country—the latter more intent on enjoying the spoils of war. The necessity for work and sacrifice is evident to all members of a vanquished society. Charles Tilly found, for instance, substantially fewer strikes in Italy and Germany for a time after World War II than in England and France.[10]

These reasons are credible, but we have no assurance that any of them is accurately to be judged responsible for hastening the recovery rates of defeated nations. We do know, however, that one aspect widely believed to be influential had little if any effect. Losers do not rise from the ashes because winners pick them up and help them to their feet. Were this true, it would completely overturn the results we have obtained. For if losers could not recoup their losses without aid, the gap between them and winners would remain if an active winner refused this kind of assistance. This would support the continuing-gap proposition, one of the possibilities previously hypothesized. The point was of major concern, and we tested it with two propositions. First, we were interested to discover whether or not aid was positively associated with the recovery of the recipient and, second, whether

---

[10] Charles Tilly, personal communication to the senior author.

Table 12–3
Correlation of U.S. Aid With Recovery of Recipients, 1948–1961[a]

	Aid Years	Aid	Aid Partialed on Time	Aid Per Capita	Aid Per Capita Partialed on Time
Recovery rate	1948–1961	−.01 (N = 63)	−.17 (N = 63)	−.01 (N = 63)	−.15 (N = 63)
	1948–1953	−.33 (N = 23)	−.21 (N = 23)	−.18 (N = 23)	−.30 (N = 23)

[a] The correlation coefficient R is used to indicate positive or negative influences, but R^2 is never above .1.

or not a large-scale foreign assistance effort does start recovery on its way, as some economists believe.

Our test was simple: since the United States was the major source of aid after World War II, and since such help was dispensed annually between 1948 and 1961, we compared the amounts of aid given by the United States, in totals and per capita, with the relative growth rates of the recipients—Japan, Germany, Italy, the United Kingdom, and France.[11]

Had there been a direct relationship between aid and recovery, and if one controlled for population, growth rates would show increases as a result of aid. Had aid intensity been a factor one would also expect that growth rates would show strong gains after those years when recipients received particularly large gifts. Because we are dealing with time series data we replicated each evaluation controlling for possible linear influences of time. Table 12–3 displays the connection between United States aid and the recovery rates of the beneficiaries.

---

[11] One would expect the growth rates of aid recipients to show effects of the foreign help a year after aid has been received. We tested our assumptions of time response by lagging aid and recovery rates for 2 and 3 years and our results remained unchanged. We calculated the recovery rates of each recipient by subtracting the growth rate in the year aid was received from the growth rates posted in the following year. For example, if a nation posted − 15 years of growth in 1948 and − 13 years of growth in the following year the recovery rate was adjudged 2 years. It should be emphasized that negative numbers do not necessarily indicate a lack of growth but rather a lack of recovery.

Recovery rates were calculated as follows:

$$\text{Recovery Rate} = \text{Relative Growth}_{i+1} - \text{Relative Growth}_i$$

Where i = Recovery Years.

Data on aid were obtained from the Agency for International Development (1972:46, 68–76): population figures from Banks (1971:segment 1, pp. 3–54); our sample included only West Germany, Japan, France, and the United Kingdom as we were only interested in major power behavior. No data on Soviet aid were available.

From a consideration of the above figures, we can determine only the weakest association between external aid and recovery; the variance explained by the coefficient of determination is always below .1, indicating that growth and foreign aid, totals or per capita, are almost wholly independent of each other. Such relationship as may exist is negative: the countries that received most of the aid for the longest period performed worst. The United Kingdom received much more aid on a total and per capita basis than France; France received much more than Italy; Italy much more than Germany; and Germany much more than Japan (Kugler, 1973:196–202). Yet it was Japan that enjoyed the more rapid rate of recovery, followed by Germany, Italy, and France, with the United Kingdom bringing up the rear. It is, therefore, very hard to credit the conviction that foreign assistance and recovery are closely associated.

These particular findings are not completely unexpected.[12] Many economists have questioned the efficacy of this kind of aid.[13] What the figures underscore is that foreign assistance, as a form of investment in the economy of another country intended to incline it toward faster recovery, is not very effective. The variables truly important to recovery lie within the devastated nations themselves. Previous patterns of performance are far more significant than external aid.

Conclusions

We began this inquiry with a number of questions: Does the outcome of a major war reshape the distribution of international power? Does it make a real difference—in power terms—whether a country wins or loses a major war? How long can winners hold on to their advantages? How long do losers stay behind?

Let us begin with a simple list of what we have found.

1. Systematic patterns in the distribution of power (as measured by gross national product) are registered after major conflicts.

2. The power levels of winners and neutrals are affected only marginally by the conflict.

3. Nations defeated in war suffer intense short-term losses; the outcome makes much difference to them in the short run, especially in terms of power levels.

---

[12] The literature on aid is immense; an excellent review is available in Little and Clifford (1968). The "big push" proposition was derived from Rosenstein-Rodan (1961a:107–38; 1961b:57–66).

[13] For a classic discussion of the uses of foreign aid, see Friedman (1973) and Wolf (1973).

4. In the long run (from 15 to 20 years), the effects of war are dissipated, because losers accelerate their recovery and resume antebellum rates; they may even overtake winners. Soon, the power distribution in the system returns to levels anticipated had the war not occurred. We have evidence that this happens and we can speculate about the explanation, but we have no definitive solution. There is substantial research remaining to be done.

If one wishes to forecast the behavior of a country 15 or 20 years after the end of a war, one should not refer to the outcomes of that war, whether the country in question participated in it or not, whether it was a winner or a loser. The best indicator of the power posture of a nation less than a generation after the conclusion of a war is its performance before that conflict.

One other finding should be mentioned. It is clear that the assistance offered by winners to losers is not a significant factor in the losers' recovery rate.

We are tempted to suggest that the outcomes of war, insofar as international power is concerned, make no difference. We cannot forget, however, that we have found a tracing which indicates that we may have heard only part of the story. While winners cannot help losers to recovery by contributing aid, whatever the quantity, winners may be able to prevent or delay the recovery of losers. If the behavior of Czechoslovakia is an accurate indication, the victor may retard the recovery of the loser by occupation and exploitation. Adequate information on this aspect of the question is not available; there are merely hints on which to base speculation.

Such findings are clearly tentative. In this case, however, the tentative nature of the conclusions should be stressed once more because we have been plagued with data problems. If our findings are confirmed through comparable and more exhaustive researches, the implications for study strategies could be substantial.

If the distribution of international power and changes in that distribution are shaped by differential rates of growth across critical sectors of a nation's life and across nations of that system, and in the long term such rates cannot be altered even by the most violent international interactions, such as major wars, then what must be studied are the causes of such alterations and not the interactions of countries. Thus, independent variables in international relations are *not* found in international relations, but in the growth of the units that comprise the system. Some scholars already study international politics in this fashion, but this is still a very different conception of the field from that traditionally held.

Editors' Commentary

Major Findings

Organski and Kugler find that in the long run—about fifteen to twenty years—war does not make any difference in terms of power (as measured by GNP). At least, this has been the case for World War I and World War II for the major states. Their most important findings can be found in figures 12–5 and 12–7. Immediately following World War I, defeated belligerents are much worse off than the victors, and this gap (the shaded area in the graph) is maintained for some time. After a few years, the losers experience rapid growth, which eventually leads them to catch up to the winners and, about fifteen years later, to surpass them. A similar pattern holds for the post–World War II period when only major states are examined. Again the losers are much worse off initially but then exhibit a very sharp growth rate, which about fifteen years or so later leads them to surpass the winners.

Theoretically, the losers' surpassing the winners in about fifteen years is significant because Organski (1968:364–67) argues in his power transition thesis that war is most likely when a dissatisfied ascendent state surpasses the power of the dominant state in the system. This finding is also theoretically relevant to the realist concern that international politics is a struggle for power and that nation-states are constantly trying to maintain, increase, or demonstrate their power. Seen in this intellectual context, the implications of the findings are that war and, hence, politics do not have much of a permanent impact on the power of states. Thus, Organski and Kugler's analysis has a much wider theoretical significance than someone outside the discipline of international relations might suspect.

It should be noted that war probably does not make an eventual surpassing of the winners inevitable; that would be an incorrect interpretation of the findings. What makes more sense is that the natural growth of these particular states has been delayed by the world wars and eventually resumes a pattern that they would presumably experience if the war had never been fought. Organski and Kugler argue, on the basis of their findings, that the power of states follows an internal dynamic, and little can be done from the outside to change it.

Part of the reason for this conclusion is that they find that foreign aid given after the war seems to have little effect on recovery rates (see table 12–3). The states that received the most aid, U.S. allies, had the slowest recovery rates. The authors do, however, note that it may be possible for a victor to prevent recovery in a defeated state if it so chooses. The evidence on Czechoslovakia (occupied belligerent loser in figure 12–6) suggests that conclusion. Ancient history also offers other examples, for example, Rome's destruction of Carthage.

Organski and Kugler's analysis, along with Rosen's in chapter 11, raises disturbing normative questions. If the outcome of a war can be predicted almost 80 percent of the time by the wealth of a government and if the national power of the losers equals that of winners after about fifteen years, why fight the war in the first place? Although few are prepared to argue that war as a human institution is a desirable or efficient way of conducting world relations, many have seen it as necessary, functional, and/or rational. The findings of the last two articles raise questions about that view.

While most informed observers are prepared to question the wisdom of World War I in these terms, only a few would be prepared to see World War II in this manner. This has led some scholars to argue that Organski and Kugler conceive of power too narrowly and place too much emphasis on the struggle for power as measured by economic growth. World War II is an excellent example. Japan and Germany have recovered, but they are not the same Japan and Germany. Wars are fought not simply to keep or gain power. Power is a means to an end, and the world order of the post-1945 period has not been what it would have been had World War II turned out differently, especially in Europe.

As a result of arguments like these, some social scientists have been spurred to look more directly at the political effects of war. Siverson (1980) finds that war brings about nonconstitutional changes in governments. For example, forty-five of the 184 war participants in his sample experienced such a change. The likelihood of this occurring for losers is twice as great as for winners (35.7 percent of the losers have a change versus 17.5 percent of the winners). This is how the victorious state tries to get its way: by putting the groups it prefers into power in the defeated state.

Siverson (1980) also argues that Organski and Kugler ignore military expenditures in the post-1945 period. An examination of this indicator shows no recovery of German and Japanese status, a point that made eminent sense when Siverson was writing in 1980. Now, a decade later, the economic power of Japan and a united Germany make it seem inevitable that they will take a much more active political role in the world. Unless the course of history changes drastically, it seems probable that this new political role will give rise to a new military presence. Nevertheless, the ideological coloration of the new world order, even if it were to change (which does not seem too likely), will not revert to the overt fascist and militarist ideology of the 1930s.

Methodological Notes

Organski and Kugler use time-series analysis to investigate their claim that losers in world wars recover to the same level as, and even surpass, winners in the long term. The time series are generated by regression analysis, which is fairly complicated, but their actual presentation is fairly simple because it entails mainly the visual inspection of the graphs in figures 12–2 through 12–7.

The basis for the analysis is the use of forecasting. **Forecasting** uses data from the past to mathematically project values for future time periods by tracing the trend in the data and extrapolating it. The weakness of forecasting is that the estimation of future performance is based on the assumption that the future will be like the past. Imagine making an economic forecast for the depressed 1930s on the basis of data from the roaring twenties. Organski and Kugler run into this kind of a problem when they use the data from the 1930s, when the economy was depressed, to project hypothetically the performance to be expected in the 1940s and 1950s. Their projection, based on the depression, underestimates what historically was possible once the economy recovered. Post–World War II performance exceeds what is "normal" because it is so superior to that of the 1930s (see figure 12–6).

Their underestimation is not a serious problem for this study. What is important here methodologically is whether the authors can draw the inferences they wish to draw from data with such a problem. If a precise estimate of growth rate were essential to their conclusions, they would be in trouble. However, they are interested only in *comparing* the performance of winners to that of losers, so the absolute values are not as important (see the section on figure 12–6). It is of little consequence that in figure 12–6, the baseline ("normal" growth projection) should probably be higher; rectifying this estimation would not change the conclusions of the study.

The technique used to produce these trends is regression. The way it is used to extrapolate is that historical data (such as GNP) are plotted on the y-axis and time (usually in years) is plotted on the x-axis. A regression line is drawn such that the points are as close to the line as possible, and it is continued on the basis of the shape it took, using the regression formula $y = a + bx + e$ (see the methodological notes in chapter 2). Economic growth, however, is not linear; if one draws a straight line based on increases of a constant raw amount, the percentage of growth will be smaller each year (because of the larger base). For example, if you made $30,000 a year, would you rather get five annual raises of $1,500 ($31,500; $33,000; $34,500; $36,000; $37,500) or of 5 percent ($31,500; $33,075; $34,729; $36,465; $38,288)? In order to produce an estimate based on percentage increases (see figure 12–1), they transform the data into logarithms.

In the "Standardization" section, the authors explain how they generate the estimated curves. In this analysis, it does not matter where the regression line crosses the y-axis (the intercept) or how steep the slope is. The regression line generated by the estimates of normal growth becomes a flat, straight horizontal line with the value of zero (identified as "normal" growth projection in figures 12–2 through 12–7). Then the actual values are plotted, and what is important is the **residuals**. A **residual** is the numerical value of the distance of a point from the regression line. A common procedure is to run a regression on a time series and then, using the regression line as a new base (0) line, to plot the residuals. This shows not the absolute value of each point but the extent to which and the direction in which each point deviates from the estimated value. This is how a series can be "detrended." For this analysis, the residuals are plotted to see how far behind (or ahead) a nation is in years in terms of GNP.

Once a study has produced findings on its hypotheses, its job is essentially finished. Sometimes analysts go further and pursue tests of ad hoc explanations or hypotheses based on potential criticisms. Organski and Kugler conclude their study in this manner by asking what produces the phoenix factor. Several possible answers are suggested, and they test the proposition that foreign aid produces the losers' recovery. This is a case of drawing a new inference on the basis of one's findings in an inductive fashion and then deductively testing it. They find essentially no relationship or a weak negative relationship between the amount of foreign aid received and the rate of recovery. They conclude that foreign aid does not have this effect and, hence, are on more solid ground drawing the overall conclusion for their study: that the likelihood of recovery can be estimated by the prewar performance of the nation.

There are two important caveats to make regarding these conclusions. One is that the number of wars is very small—only two—so that it is not known whether the recovery of defeated belligerents would be as quick after other wars. Because the victors in both world wars had a liberal global market as one of their goals and the victorious allies set up liberal-style governments in many countries, including defeated ones, it may be that (a) recovery of defeated belligerents depends on the goals of the victors, and (b) when the concern of the victors is to ensure an open international market (as opposed to territorial expansion, destruction of rivals, etc.), economic recovery of defeated belligerents is in fact a goal of the war.

The other caveat is that the lack of correlation between amount of aid and rate of recovery should not be interpreted as meaning that recovery is inevitable. The authors note that the postwar order might have been quite different had Hitler won.

The Organski and Kugler study provides an example of how time-series data can be used for forecasting and to demonstrate the impact of war on the global system. The article in the next chapter also employs time-series data but to examine the impact of war on the domestic political system.

13

War Making and State Making: Governmental Expenditures, Tax Revenues, and Global Wars

Karen A. Rasler
William R. Thompson

Editors' Introduction

Karen Rasler and William Thompson argue that the growth and power of the nation-state has been a major consequence of involvement in large global wars. War poses a severe crisis for the state and requires rapid increases in military expenditures. In order to meet these obligations, new revenue must be raised, usually through increased taxation and by borrowing. While these effects on domestic political arrangements are obvious, war, they argue, may also have more subtle effects. The state bureaucratic apparatus is expanded not only to facilitate the collection of taxes but to help conduct the military effort and mobilize the economy for war production. War-related social services increase, especially in regard to veterans' benefits and pensions. More generally, states involved in war think of their people as important resources, whose health, morale, literacy, and skills can make a significant difference in developing an effective military force. All of these effects can lead to an increase in the centralization of the state and its internal political power.

This implies, as Tilly (1975:42) so aptly puts it, that "war made the state, and the state made war." What Tilly means by this is that one of the rationales of the rise of the modern Western nation-state out of medieval feudalism is to protect people from invasion and plunder. The state is created, not exclusively but to

Reprinted from the *American Political Science Review*, 79 (1985), pp. 491–507. Reprinted by permission of the American Political Science Association and the authors.
    The research reported in this article has been supported by National Science Foundation grants SES 81-06063 (Rasler) and SES 82-06062 (Thompson). An earlier version of this article was presented at the Annual Meeting of the International Studies Association, Mexico City, Mexico, April, 1983. The comments of a number of reviewers have helped clarify the presentation of our findings.

a significant degree, to make war. The actual conduct of war then helps shape the form the state takes and, in particular, increases its scope and revenue and as a consequence its control over its subjects. These ideas, along with numerous variations that Rasler and Thompson review in their discussion of the literature, are the focus of their empirical inquiry.

We live in an era in which the appropriate scope of governmental activities is a subject of intensive political debate. Conservatives complain that governmental expansion and the encroachment of the public sector on the private sector have gone too far and must be curbed. Liberals, on the other hand, complain that the process has not gone far enough to satisfy the demands of public welfare. Whatever one's ideological persuasion, it is clear that governments have expanded the scope of their activities and functions. But even if this last statement enjoys consensus agreement, it is by no means evident that we have a clear understanding of how and why states have expanded their scale of operation. Toward the end of the nineteenth century, for instance, advocates of Wagner's Law contended that governmental activities would expand in roughly linear response to the development of growth-related social problems (see Bird 1971; Wagner and Weber 1977). However, Peacock and Wiseman (1961) have argued that governmental expansion has outpaced economic growth in the twentieth century and that increasing the scope of governmental functions requires the advent of national crisis so that the popular reluctance to accept tax increases can be overwhelmed by the need to respond to the crisis. We agree that long-run governmental growth tends to be discontinuous but contend that, for certain states at least, the principal agent of change is a singular type of crisis—global war—and that the fundamental war making–state building process is much older than developments relatively unique to the twentieth century. Throughout the remainder of this article, we will attempt to provide empirical support for this longer-term view by examining the long-term pattern of changes in governmental expenditures and revenues in relation to the onset of different types of war. In the process, we hope to contribute to the overcoming of our collective underappreciation of the general significance of war (see Stein and Russett 1980) to an understanding of domestic changes and developments.

The Expenditure Displacement Hypothesis

Expressed most simply, Peacock's and Wiseman's (1961) displacement hypothesis states that governmental expenditures will increase during periods of national crisis and that although expenditures may decline in the post-crisis period, they will remain higher than pre-crisis expenditure levels. This permanent displacement effect on expenditures is attributed primarily to crisis-induced shifts in taxpayers' perceptions of what tax-burden levels are viewed as tolerable. Depending on the governmental decision makers' attitudes toward the roles of public expenditures and their willingness to take advantage of the opportunity, major crises, especially wars, work to weaken or override normal (non-crisis) resistance to increased taxes. Tax revenues therefore are easier to raise. Wars, in addition, offer excellent opportunities to revise or overhaul the prevailing tax system and to create new sources of revenue. As a result, the widened tax base facilitates greater spending after the war or crisis than before.

Peacock and Wiseman (1961) present a detailed examination of Great Britain's principally twentieth-century expenditure patterns as a test of their hypothesis. Because their central hypothesis is attitudinally based, there are of course very real constraints on the extent to which expenditure data can be used to address their thesis. Through the visual examination of a large number of spending series, however, they are able to demonstrate that World Wars I and II brought about major shifts in governmental spending that cannot be accounted for by either population growth, inflation, or economic growth. Further support for their interpretation is produced by the finding that the expenditure increases are not due solely to increases in war-related and military costs. If this had been the case, the expenditure displacement process would represent merely the periodic augmentation of military spending and the gradual accumulation of war debts and pensions. But because non-military and war-related spending increases as well, Peacock and Wiseman view this indicator as evidence of genuine governmental role expansion made possible by the involvement of a society in crisis or war.

Beyond the difficulty of tapping taxpayer attitudes with spending patterns, the Peacock-Wiseman evidence is also restricted by the small sample of one state and their exclusive reliance on the visual examination of longitudinal plots of numerous expenditure series. Yet their hypothesis has stimulated a respectably extensive literature that sometimes uses more sophisticated empirical techniques or expands the number of countries surveyed or both. Although the most popular examples remain the British and American ones, the following states have also received some expenditure displacement effect attention: Brazil, Canada, Costa Rica, Dominican Republic, France, Germany, Guyana, Haiti, Honduras, Iceland, India, Japan, Panama, Sweden, and Taiwan. Looked upon in the aggregate, the empirical outcomes represent some decidedly mixed support for the original Peacock-Wiseman assertion. Four conclusions seem to have emerged.

Crises associated with world wars:

1. Bring about permanent changes in state expenditure levels (Emi 1963; Gupta 1967).

2. Sometimes bring about permanent changes in state expenditure levels (Andre and Delorme 1978; Blondal 1969; Kaufman 1983; Tussing and Henning 1974).

3. Create, at best, only temporary, not permanent, shifts in state expenditure levels. The temporary impact may be attributed to the wartime higher priority given to military over civilian spending (Borcherding 1977a, 1977b; Musgrave 1969; Pryor 1968; Reddy 1970) or postwar increases in civilian spending presumably related to addressing war damages and reconstruction (Bonin, Finch, and Waters 1967; Rosenfeld 1973).

4. May effect expenditure growth but so do a number of other influences (Bennett and Johnson 1980; Meltzer and Richard 1978) including non–world wars (Emi 1963; Leff 1982; Nagarjan 1979), depression (Blondal 1969; Gupta 1967), and changes in governmental philosophies during peacetime (Goffman and Mahar 1971; Mahar and Rezende 1975; Reddy 1970).

Clearly, the four conclusions do not add up to anything resembling a consensus. Nor can the extent of disagreement be explained away by the variety of examined countries. For example, all four conclusions have been arrived at by different analysts of the same or similar British and American expenditure data. To be sure, some of the findings should be viewed with more skepticism than some of the others, owing to various research design problems.[1] Nevertheless, it is apparent that several questions deserve further investigation. Does the war-induced expenditure displacement phenomenon apply to Great Britain? To what extent does it apply outside of Great Britain? Alternatively, Peacock and Wiseman's explanation stresses "national crises," but their examination is restricted primarily to the effects of World Wars I and II. Yet several authors contend that some interstate wars (e.g., the 1904–1905 Russo-Japanese War for Japan, the 1962 Indo-Chinese War for India) had greater impacts on spending patterns than some of the twentieth century's world wars. Other authors find significant impacts associated with World War I but not World War II and vice versa. Do all wars influence governmental spending in idiosyncratic ways and to varying ex-

---

[1] For Peacock's and Wiseman's reactions to some of this literature's design problems, see Wiseman and Diamond (1975) and Peacock and Wiseman (1979).

tents? Or, are some kinds of warfare, such as "world wars," more likely than others to bring about permanent expenditure displacement effects?

The War Making–State Making Interpretation

The variety of specification problems raised by the empirical studies that have followed Peacock and Wiseman do not exhaust the questions that need to be raised about the asserted displacement process. The Peacock-Wiseman emphasis on the crisis-induced stretching of tax burden tolerances is not implausible, and we see no need to reject it completely. But it is very much a twentieth-century explanation in flavor, just as it is based primarily on the examination of twentieth-century data. If the displacement phenomenon, however, is much older than the twentieth-century, it is conceivable that a more general or broader and less time-bound explanation is needed.[2]

Support for our contention that the displacement process predates the twentieth century is not particularly difficult to find. Tilly's (1975, 1979) expression that "war made the state and the state made war" summarizes a number of overlapping views on the long-term contribution of war to several hundred years of European state-building (see Ames and Rapp 1977; Anderson 1974; Ardant 1975; Bean 1973; Braun 1975; Eichenberg 1983; Gilpin 1981; Gourevitch 1978; Hintze 1975; McNeill 1982; Modelski 1972; North and Thomas 1973). A primary, if not the primary, imperative of state building has been the suppression of internal rivals and the defeat of external enemies. To remain in power at home and competitive abroad, military preparations have been essential and increasingly costly as military technology has improved. To pay for these seemingly ever-rising military costs, rulers have felt compelled to extract more and more resources from their populations. To collect and manage the increasing scale of these resource extractions, rulers have been forced or encouraged to create and expand their state's bureaucratic-administration apparatus as well.

This version of the death-and-taxes cycle has not been unaffected by change. Economic growth in general, and industrial development in particular, have made tax collections easier and more remunerative, but these same developments have also contributed to the likelihood of more inten-

---

[2] We are reluctant to argue that the twentieth century is an era generally characterized by more governmental sensitivity to taxpayer preference schedules. It is true that taxpayer revolts, Proposition 13 notwithstanding, were once more common than they are currently. But whether this generalization suggests greater governmental sensitivity or greater taxpayer passivity, resignation, acquiescence, or all of the above, remains debatable. Nevertheless, we are suggesting that contemporary analysts are much more conditioned to emphasize popular constraints on governmental expansion than they were likely to before the twentieth century. In a similar vein, Wagner's Law's complete avoidance of the subject of war betrays a late-nineteenth-century flavor. As Bird (1971, p. 4) notes, Wagner's late-nineteenth-century generation did not expect wars to be very common in the future.

sive and costlier wars. The idea of national debt has been invented to overcome shortfalls in tax revenues, especially in time of war, but the institutionalization of state debts also implies long-term debt accumulation and predictable debt interest payment schedules (increasing organizational fixed costs). Much more recently, and hardly in isolation from other ongoing developments, the scope of governmental intervention in society and economy has also expanded. Yet although these developments may have modified the processes of state building and expansion, it is doubtful that they have been so radically transformed that we need to look for entirely new patterns. Interstate competition, wars, and the increasing costs of military preparations have not disappeared, nor has the need to pay for these activities. It seems reasonable to suggest, therefore, that the historical connection between war making and state making and expansion is a persistent one.

The differences between this historical perspective on the growth of the state and the Peacock-Wiseman interpretation can be viewed as a matter of degree and emphasis. Peacock and Wiseman stress an image of contemporary state decision makers, with a perceived need to expand the scope of governmental activities, taking advantage of periods of crisis and war to expand their revenue base. The longer view does not preclude this inherently opportunistic possibility, but it chooses to emphasize instead a broader conceptualization of states owing their very organizational existence and raison d'être to the need to survive, and to prevail, during the periods of warfare. Confronted with very real threats, decision makers are compelled to mobilize human and material resources at their disposal in the interest of state security and military victory. At war's end, successful and unsuccessful states demobilize, but there is no reason to assume or to expect that the demobilization will be complete, except perhaps in cases of absolute defeat. Nor is it likely that state decision makers will insist on the strict restoration of the state's prewar role in national society. To the contrary, the realities of wartime change will make turning back the political clock extremely difficult and unlikely.

New sources of revenue will have been created and old sources will have been expanded, embellished, and perhaps made more efficient.

New social problems (e.g., price controls, provision for the homeless and refugees, concerns over inadequate diets and education for the draft-eligible portions of the population, the need to suppress racial tensions at home and in combat units, reconstruction) will emerge and old problems will receive greater political attention than before.

New domestic political coalitions may emerge or have an improved opportunity to emerge as their constituencies' contribution to the war effort becomes more highly valued. The general resistance to social and political change, in any event, is more likely to be either weakened or even overwhelmed by the need to respond to the demands of the war effort.

New bureaucratic organizations will emerge to deal with novel war-related problems. Old governmental agencies will be expanded not only to deal with the increase in management problems, but also because the opportunity to invoke security-related justifications for bureaucratic expansion will be expanded as well.[3]

The significance of some of these war-induced changes may be eliminated or subsequently diminished in the postwar era, but it is most unlikely that all of the war-induced changes in expenditures, revenues, number of governmental agencies and personnel, salience of social issues and problems, and the nature and identity of political coalitions will disappear or even fade away. Wars, especially major wars, thus induce direct domestic changes in the short run and also serve as catalysts and facilitators for direct and indirect domestic changes in the long run. A respectable proportion of the war-induced growth of the state is thus a not-altogether-planned by-product of making war.

Yet there is no reason to believe that all wars will have the same impact on state-building processes. Some wars may bring about very little in the way of change, whereas others may be associated with profound and wide-ranging impacts. Modelski's (1978, 1981, 1982) long cycle of world leadership perspective is crucial in this regard because it supplies a theoretical rationale for anticipating that one category of warfare, the global war, will be more likely than others to be associated with significant societal impacts. Global wars are identified as the decisive contests fought over the issue of succession to world leadership and, therefore, demarcate the transition from one long cycle of leadership to the next. During and immediately after each global war, one state emerges in a leading capability position. The eventual erosion of this preponderance leads to leadership challenges mounted by rivals and another succession struggle to be resolved in global war.

Although global wars are not defined in terms of scope, participation, or costs, they tend to be unusually extensive in terms of geography encompassed and the number of major actors involved. Global wars tend also to be among the most costly wars in terms of both lives lost and resources expended. Consequently, it seems reasonable to hypothesize that the most important wars, the deadly turning points in modern political history for the global political system, should have the most important and significant impacts on the state-building processes of the participants. In contrast, non-global interstate wars generally tend to be much less extensive and intensive affairs and, therefore, are relatively less likely to exert significant impacts.

By focusing on the two categories of warfare as separate types of impact-

---

[3] On this point, see Porter's (1980) argument that American governmental agencies learned to use national defense rationalizations to justify expanded budgets to legislators even when they were not directly related to the ongoing World War II effort.

producing interventions, our version of the war making–state making approach differs from the Peacock and Wiseman interpretation in several respects. First, Peacock and Wiseman restrict the temporal scope of their displacement argument to late-nineteenth- and early-twentieth-century British attitudinal and philosophical shifts toward greater state involvement in social policy arenas. Alternatively expressed, the two most recent world wars facilitated the expansion of the British state into new areas of governmental intervention. However, the distinction between global and interstate war applies as far back as the initially crude emergence of the global political system in 1494, thereby encompassing nearly 500 years of state building and expansion.

Peacock and Wiseman (1961, p. 38) had noted that their emphasis on changing governmental attitudes would have been less tenable if crisis-related expenditure displacements had occurred before 1900. They then proceeded to demonstrate the absence of a permanent displacement effect on British spending after the Napoleonic Wars. If they are correct, the validity of our own historical argument is open to some question unless the British pattern is exceptional. To ascertain what is a deviation from the norm will of course require an expansion of the number of states examined. However, we also believe that Peacock and Wiseman misinterpreted the early nineteenth-century British data. In order to explore this claim and to assess better the longer view on state building, the present examination will need to develop data series that extend back in time as far as is practical. The development of reasonably lengthy time series will also facilitate the employment of impact assessment models that measure the displacement impact of war in as systematic a manner as is possible.

Although the global war making perspective expands the temporal scope of the displacement explanation, the focus on the intervention agents is being narrowed considerably. Despite the fact that their own examination was restricted to the twentieth century's two world wars, Peacock and Wiseman equated their conceptualization of the opportunities for displacement with "social disturbances" or "national crises." These broad categories imply the need to investigate the possible impacts of a relatively large list of candidate events. Non-war crises such as severe economic depressions may indeed lead to the expansion of the state but we doubt that any single type of crisis can compare over the long run to the ostensibly consistent, historical impact of global war.

Implicit in our approach is the assumption that seeking information on war impacts for all states is not likely to prove to be a very efficacious strategy. Instead, given the disparities in types of states and historical experiences, a more selective and categorically homogeneous state sample is desirable. Peacock's and Wiseman's focus on a single state, of course, could be said to represent the extreme interpretation of this preference. But there is a middle course between the extremes of single state case studies and large sample aggregations. The logic of our hypothesis development suggests an actor focus on states that have participated in both global and interstate wars. Yet all war participants do not participate fully or in the same way. For example, we might expect to find some differences in comparisons between strong and weak states or between persistent combatants and states defeated and occupied early in a war. On the other hand, we need to avoid eliminating all of the variance. Consequently, we will confine our sample construction to the premise that the hypothesized displacement effects of global war should be most noticeable in the expenditures of those states that are most acutely involved in the succession struggles as contenders for systemic power. Ideally, then, our examination would focus on the nine states that have been identified as the principal contenders (at various points in time) in the long cycle process.[4]

Unfortunately, continuous expenditure records from the sixteenth century on are not available for any state. We also need to be careful to control for the possible complications of economic growth. Moreover, we wish to determine whether tax revenues follow the same historical course as do expenditures. In spite of the explanatory emphasis on tax revenues in Peacock's and Wiseman's tax burden argument, these data are only rarely inspected vis-à-vis the displacement hypothesis. Finally, we too wish to check whether any war-induced displacement effect that is uncovered can be explained solely in terms of increased military and war-related spending. A greater emphasis on the historical significance of warfare need not preclude the expansion of non-war-related activities but the extent to which these governmental activities have expanded is probably subject to some degree of evolution.

The need for hard-to-come-by, continuous time series data on central government expenditures, tax revenues, military expenditures, and some measures of national wealth—all of which must encompass one or more global wars—forces some compromises on analysts.[5] Longitudinal data that meet the requirements outlined immediately above are readily accessible for only a very few states. Accordingly, we will concentrate our analyses on four global powers: Great Britain (1700–1980), the United States (1792–1980),

---

[4] From the long cycle perspective, global wars have taken place in 1494–1516, 1580–1608, 1688–1713, 1792–1815, and 1914–1918/1939–1945. Global powers must satisfy minimum global reach capacity (naval power) criteria. The following states qualify for consideration: Portugal (1494–1580), Spain (1494–1815), England/Great Britain (1484–1945), France (1494–1945), Netherlands (1579–1815), Russia/Soviet Union (1714–present), United States (1816–present), Germany (1871–1945), and Japan (1875–1945). Other assessments of the impacts of global wars on wholesale prices, economic growth, and public debts may be found in Thompson and Zuk (1982) and Rasler and Thompson (1983, 1985).

[5] By dividing expenditures and tax revenues by GNP, we are not overlooking the probability that government spending and the economy as a whole are likely to be subject to different rates of inflation. Specialized deflationary indexes, however are not normally available for long time series.

France (1815–1979), and Japan (1878–1980), and the sets of global and interstate wars listed in table 13–1.[6]

Time Series Problems and the Utility of Box-Tiao Impact Assessment Models.

Previous studies concerned with estimating the impact of war on various processes such as economic growth and the increase in national and social welfare expenditures can be divided into two groups. The first group basi-

Table 13–1
Interstate and Global Wars

Interstate Wars		Global Wars	
France (1815–1979)			
Franco-Spanish	1823	World War I	1914–1918
Roman Republic	1849	World War II	1939–1945
Crimean	1854–1856		
Italian unification	1859		
Franco-Mexican	1862–1867		
Franco-Prussian	1870–1871		
Sino-French	1884–1885		
Franco-Thai	1940–1941		
Korean	1951–1953		
Sinai	1956		
Great Britian (1700–1980)			
Anglo-Swedish	1715–1719	Spanish succession	1701–1713
Quadruple alliance	1718–1720	French Revolutionary	1793–1802
Anglo-Spanish	1726–1729	Napoleonic	1803–1815
Austrian succession	1739–1748	World War I	1914–1918
Seven years	1756–1763	World War II	1939–1945
American independence	1778–1783		
Anglo-American	1812–1814		
Crimean	1854–1856		
Anglo-Persian	1856–1857		
Korean	1950–1953		
Sinai	1956		
Japan (1878–1980)			
Sino-Japanese	1894–1895	World War I	1914–1918
Russo-Japanese	1904–1905	World War II	1941–1945
Manchurian	1931–1933		
Sino-Japanese	1937–1941		
United States (1792–1980)			
Anglo-American	1812–1814	World War I	1917–1918
Mexican-American	1846–1848	World War II	1941–1945
Spanish-American	1898		
Korean	1950–1953		
Vietnam	1965–1973		

cally relies on visual evaluations of the differences between pre- and post-intervention series in an attempt to assess war impact (Emi 1963; Mahar and Rezende 1975; Peacock and Wiseman 1961; Reddy 1970; Rosenfeld 1973). As a preliminary step or in instances where an impact is acutely obvious, the eyeball technique may suffice and certainly is always helpful. As the number of interventions and national series to be examined increases, however, visual plots quickly become cumbersome analytical and communication devices, especially if space is limited and if not all of the impacts are readily discernible. In general, but particularly in these circumstances, more objective tests are definitely desirable.

The second group, for the most part, uses regression techniques to estimate the changes in the level of prewar and postwar intervention series (Andre and Delorme 1978; Barbera 1973; Bonin et al. 1967; Gupta 1967; Kaufman 1983; Nagarajan 1979; Organski and Kugler 1980; Pryor 1968; Stohl 1976; Tussing and Henning 1974; Wheeler 1980). The ultimate validity of many of these regression-based findings, we feel, is handicapped by certain statistical problems related to an overemphasis on data fitting operations and an underemphasis on controlling for autocorrelation and trend.

Most of the earlier expenditure displacement analyses exclude war period data from their analyses in an effort to assess long-term effects without the results being unduly influenced by the war outliers. In the process, analysts have selected various time periods ranging anywhere from 3 to 70 years or more for the ad hoc prewar and postwar data intervals. In order to fit a least squares model to the data, prewar and postwar contortions in the original series that might reduce the degree of fit tend to be ignored.

In the presence of autocorrelation, a problem commonly encountered in time series and frequently ignored, the data will track for a period away from the equilibrium point. This tracking phenomenon results in unbiased but inefficient estimates of the parameters of a model. In linear regression,

---

[6] Gathering data on governmental expenditures and revenues is subject to a host of pitfalls—some of which, no doubt, we have failed to avoid. Whenever possible, we have attempted to use closed accounts as reported by governmental agencies or secondary and tertiary sources based on governmental abstracts. We have occasionally been forced to deviate from a reliance on official accounts in cases of overtly understated military spending figures. We have also attempted to exclude from the expenditure and revenue series spending for, and receipts from, public enterprises in order to enhance their longitudinal comparability. The data sources utilized are for France, Sudre (1883), de Kaufmann (1884), Marion (1914), Jeze (1927), Mallez (1927), Ministere des Finances (1946), Marczewski (1961), Mitchell (1975, 1981), Ministere de l'Economie (various years), OECD (1980, 1981); for Great Britain, Deane (1955), 1968), Deane and Cole (1962), Mitchell (1962, 1975, 1981), Mitchell and Jones (1971), Feinstein (1972), Central Statistical Office (various years), Cole (1981), OECD (1980, 1981); for Japan, Emi (1963, 1979), Ohkawa and Rosovsky (1973), Mitchell (1982), Japan Statistical Yearbook (various volumes); and for the United States, U.S. Department of Commerce (1975), Berry (1978), U.S. Office of the President (1982, 1983). The identification of the wars has been guided by information found in Wright (1965), Singer and Small (1972), Dupuy and Dupuy (1977), and Small and Singer (1982).

OLS [ordinary least squares] estimates of β will be unbiased while the variances of the estimators will be understated. In addition, the error variance of the regression model will be minimized and, if autocorrelation is ignored, the model will appear to provide a much better fit to the empirical data than is actually the case. Inferences based on sample t and F-statistics will be misleading owing to the deflation of the true variance of β and the regression model (Hibbs 1974).

Trend poses still another obstacle in time series analysis. It produces a systematic change in the level of the series in such a way that it is difficult to interpret the short- and long-term effects of an intervention. The conventional method of removing trend has been to subtract a least squares trend line from the data. However, it can be argued that the OLS parameters cannot be estimated with much accuracy owing to their sensitivity to outliers as well as their somewhat static dependence on the positions of the first and last observations of the observed series.[7]

Perhaps an even more central issue with OLS detrending methods is the presumption by researchers that a time series is influenced by deterministic trend when it may be characterized by stochastic drift. A time series that is modeled as a fixed function of time (deterministically) when in fact the values vary in a probabilistic manner (stochastically) will result in errors in assessing the magnitude of an intervention's impact (McCleary and Hay 1980). In addition, because a time series can drift upward or downward for long periods of time owing only to random forces, it is not always obvious whether a progressive change in the level of a series is due to deterministic trend or stochastic drift.

To address the problems of fitting, autocorrelation, and trend, we use impact assessment models developed by Box and Tiao (1975). These models avoid the fitting problem because they use all of the data in a time series to estimate parameters that are likely to have generated the series. Consequently, the analyst has the opportunity to avoid excluding selected data

---

[7] To subtract a least squares trend line from a series, a researcher regresses that Y_t series on time $(X_t = 1, 2, 3, \ldots N)$, estimates the least squares slope of the model, and then calculates the "detrended" Y_t series. In this case, the Y series is a function of the $Y_t = b_0 + b_1 \text{(time)} + e_t$ equation where b_0 is the intercept and represents the mean level of the Y_t series and b_1 (time) represents the slope of the trend line or the expected change in the level of Y_t from one observation to the next. However, b_0 and b_1 are derived by minimizing the sums of squares function

$$\Sigma (Y_t - \hat{Y}_t)^2 = \Sigma [b_0 - \hat{b}_0 + (b_1 - \hat{b}_1)]^2.$$

As the independent variable t (time) increases monotonically, the first and last observations of Y_t usually make the greatest contribution to the sums of squares function. Consequently, the OLS estimates of b_0 and b_1 are estimated so that the OLS trend line generally passes through Y_t and Y_n regardless of how well the middle observations ($Y_{t+1} \ldots Y_{n-1}$) fit. This procedure represents a rather static approach to dynamic phenomena (McCleary and Hay 1980). Moreover, studies that do not attempt to remove trend may be subject to many of the same problems in comparing pre-intervention and post-intervention slopes.

points arbitrarily. Another advantage of Box-Tiao models is that they provide a parsimonious way to control for the effects of autocorrelation. An ARIMA [autoregressive-integrated-moving average] scheme is used to model a noise component which includes the random and deterministic effects of drift, trend, and autocorrelation. A linear filter(s) is then applied to transform the observed time series into white noise before estimating the actual effect of the intervention.[8] Moreover, the Box-Tiao models neutralize the problems associated with trend and drift, without a priori distinctions, through the use of difference equation models that can be used to differentiate between trend and drift and to provide dynamic estimates of trend.[9]

Types of Intervention Effects

The intervention component of the Box-Tiao models is represented by two transfer function parameters, ω_0 and δ, which estimate the initial impact of an event (I_t) on the observed Y_t series and the rate of growth or decay in the level of the time series after the impact. While the omega parameter (ω_0) reflects the initial impact of the intervention, an estimate of the difference between the pre-intervention and postintervention levels of Y_t, the delta parameter (δ) captures the dynamic response. Delta is a rate parameter in the sense that it specifies how quickly the postintervention series level continues to change (increasing or decreasing) by smaller and smaller increments (or decrements). The size of δ, which is constrained between -1 and $+1$, indicates how quickly (or slowly) the postintervention series reaches equilibrium. When δ approximates 1, the postintervention series returns to equilibrium very slowly. Conversely, when δ approximates 0, the postintervention series returns to equilibrium very quickly.

ω_0 and δ provide the tools to assess whether an intervention has an initial abrupt or gradual effect on Y_t and whether it is associated with a temporary or permanent change in the level of Y_t. The behavior of a time series generated from the impact of an event will take the form of two basic

---

[8] A white noise series describes a set of independent and random observations that are normally distributed about a zero mean and constant variance.

[9] If a time series is the realization of an integrated process (i.e., a random walk due to drift), it can be modeled by simply differencing that Y_t series. If the differenced series has a nonzero mean, it is characterized by linear trend which is represented in the following equation as

$$Y_t = Y_{t-1} + \theta_0 + a_t,$$

where θ_0 is estimated as the mean of the differenced series. To distinguish between drift and trend, θ_0 is subjected to a t-test. If θ_0 is not statistically different from zero, the series is considered to be drifting rather than trending. Whereas OLS detrending methods estimate linear trend using a time counter as the independent variable, the difference equation model uses the values of Y_{t-1} as the independent variable. Since all of the Y_{t-1} values influence the estimate of θ_0 (the constant of the difference equation), a dynamic estimate of linear trend is produced (see Box and Jenkins 1976; McCleary and Hay 1980).

patterns, a step or pulse model of intervention. These models and their appropriate Box-Tiao intervention components are displayed in figure 13–1.

Step model A represents an abrupt, permanent impact pattern where the event (I_t) is associated with a significant shift in the level of the Y_t time series from pre-intervention to postintervention. Model B characterizes a gradual, permanent impact. The onset of an event is accompanied by a significant initial change in the level of the postintervention series. However, the full impact of the event is not realized immediately. Instead, it has a gradual effect over a number of subsequent observations (or time periods) until the postintervention series reaches a new equilibrium.

Alternatively, Model C illustrates a situation in which the event under study has a significant initial impact on a Y_t series at one period—the onset of the event—and has no residual effects on the rest of the observations. Finally, Model D represents the case when an event is associated with an abrupt but temporary change in the level of the postintervention series.

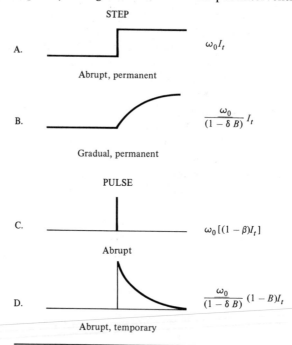

STEP

A. $\omega_0 I_t$

Abrupt, permanent

B. $\dfrac{\omega_0}{(1 - \delta B)} I_t$

Gradual, permanent

PULSE

C. $\omega_0 [(1 - \beta)I_t]$

Abrupt

D. $\dfrac{\omega_0}{(1 - \delta B)} (1 - B)I_t$

Abrupt, temporary

ω_0 = An estimate of the difference between the pre- and post-intervention process levels.

I_t = 1 during a war and 0 during nonwar years.

δ = Rate of decay or increase.

B = A backshift operator which may be interpreted as $B(Y_t) = Y_{t-1}$.

Figure 13-1. Models of Intervention and Impact

Summarily, the strategy of this approach is to identify the noise model (ARIMA structure) of the Y_t series with the pre-intervention data. Then, an intervention component from figure 13–1 is selected based on theoretical notions about the type of impact that I_t will have on the observed time series.[10] These parameters, in addition to the ARIMA parameter(s), are estimated in a full model through iterative, nonlinear estimation procedures. In most cases, parameters lacking statistical significance are removed from the equation, and the full model is reestimated. An important exception to this rule is provided by cases involving deltas with values greater than one or where the confidence intervals associated with the deltas are not constrained within the ± 1 range. This warning of model misspecifications reflects what is referred to as "explosive growth" (also known as a ramp effect) after the impact of the intervention. Intuitively, such an outcome is more likely to be interpreted as providing support for a step function, permanent change than it is for a delta-less, temporary, pulse function model.[11] In any event, an intervention model's ultimate goodness-of-fit is judged by the degree of correspondence between the observed and predicted output series values, the residual mean squared error, the statistical significance of the model parameters, and the white noise or random character of the residuals.

Data Analysis

Our principal hypothesis states that for certain states, global wars are more likely to displace governmental expenditures and revenues than are interstate wars. In the Box-Tiao context, we would then expect to find significant, permanent impacts associated with the intervention of global wars and either temporary or nonsignificant impacts registered by interstate wars. This expected outcome is very close to what is found and reported in table 13–2. All of the interstate war impacts reflect abrupt, temporary models, and only half of the omegas are significant. All of the global war omegas are

---

[10] The intervention (I_t) is represented as a discontinuous variable that ranges between zero (denoting the absence of the event) and one (denoting the presence of the event). Although the effects of war are not always restricted to the actual duration of warfare, we will code as one only those years of actual warfare. To do otherwise could easily bias the attempt to assess the impact of war by capturing other, postwar influences on expenditures and revenues and thus incorrectly exaggerating or minimizing the war impacts.

[11] McCleary and Hay (1980) suggest that when $\delta \geq 1.00$, the level of the series changes by the quantity ω_0 in each postintervention moment. In other words, before the intervention the series is trendless. After the intervention, the series follows a trend with the parameter ω_0 interpreted as the slope. Such a radical change (from a state of equilibrium to a state of growth) is more than likely due to a postintervention time series which is too short to encompass the equilibrium state of the process.

Table 13–2

The Impact of War on Logged Expenditures/GNP and Tax Revenues/GNP[a]

State	Interstate Wars[b]		Global Wars	Noise Model[c]	
	$\omega_0{}^d$	δ	ω_0	N_t	χ^2
Logged expenditures/GNP					
Great Britain (1700–1980)	.13* (4.8)	.72* (6.9)	.39* (7.8)	White noise	18.6
United States (1792–1980)	.15 (1.8)		1.01* (7.6)	White noise	20.1
France (1815–1979)	.07* (2.4)		.50* (6.7)	White noise	18.4
Japan (1879–1980)	.27* (3.4)		.65* (5.2)	White noise	12.4
Logged revenues/GNP					
Great Britain (1700–1980)	.03* (2.6)	.87* (6.2)	.08* (2.6)	White noise	12.0
United States (1792–1980)	−.06 (−1.2)		.30* (2.4)	White noise	19.4
France (1815–1979)	−.02 (−1.2)		.27*c (5.7)	White noise	12.4
Japan (1878–1980)	.05 (1.3)		.20* (2.3)	$\theta 1 = .41*$ (4.3)	15.2

Note: No statistically significant trend parameters were encountered; *t*-values are reported in parentheses.

[a] All data have been logged in order to achieve variance stationarity.

[b] The impact of interstate wars was abrupt and temporary, whereas the impact of global wars was abrupt and permanent.

[c] The first seven noise models are white noise, first differenced series (0,1,1). The Japanese revenue noise model is a first differenced, moving average process (0,1,1). $\chi^2 \le .05$ where H_o: residuals are white noise.

[d] The reported omega is based on a five-year lag for World War I.

* Statistical significance at the .05 level.

significant, and all but one are associated with abrupt, permanent models.[12] The sole exception is the Japanese expenditures GNP series, which requires the imposition of an abrupt, temporary model.

In contrast to the evident British, French, and American displacements owing to global war, World War I had no visible impact on Japanese expenditures and revenues, especially in comparison to the disturbance in the

[12] Significant deltas approximating or exceeding the value of one were estimated in each of table 13–2's global war intervention components (with the exception of the Japanese expenditure/GNP case). Substantively, this outcome may suggest that new expansionary influences were introduced in the aftermath of war. For our immediate purposes, however, the

expenditure series caused by the 1904–1905 interstate war and the temporary expenditure spike during World War II. If it is fair to dismiss the first Japanese global war as a case of marginal participation (Singer and Small 1982 report 400 Japanese battle deaths for World War I), the second case suggests that defeat and occupation may interrupt the displacement effect, or at least alter the direction of displacement. Interestingly, however, Japanese revenues/GNP are permanently displaced by World War II even though expenditures/GNP are not.

Nevertheless, in three of the four expenditure cases and in all four revenue cases, the intervention outcomes are markedly different. The intervention impact of the global wars are permanent or sustained while the impacts of the interstate wars are either insignificant or transitory. It is of course possible to be more specific about the nature of these impacts. We could, for example, translate each of the logged omega parameters into estimates of percentage change before and after the interventions. The largest omega in table 13–2, for instance, is the 1.01 parameter associated with the impact of global wars on the United States expenditure/GNP series. In percentage change terms, the 1.01 parameter can be interpreted as an approximately 175% change in the expenditures-to-gross-national-product ratio. This figure can be compared to the insignificant and temporary 16% change ($\omega_0 = .15$) associated with the expenditure/GNP impact of the United States participation in interstate wars. Yet it should be kept in mind that we are modelling multiple interventions over fairly long periods of time and that the omega parameters and percentage changes reflect average, as opposed to cumulative, effects. Calculating percentage changes in this context, therefore, does not really provide us with a more concrete numerical handle for interpreting and comparing the specific outcomes. Only the metric of the parameter is changed. Although such changes are helpful when the impact of a specific war is being analyzed, the interpretation advantage when the average impact of wars is being assessed collectively seems quite marginal.[13]

---

important thing to note is that the postwar levels in French, British, and American spending and revenue series (and the Japanese revenue series) did not return to the prewar levels, thus indicating abrupt, permanent changes. More precisely, what tends to occur is a very large temporary spike, especially in the spending series, that recedes to a level higher than that found in the prewar era. Efforts to estimate compound models (incorporating both temporary and permanent changes) were unsuccessful, we believe, due to the substantial parameter collinearity encountered and the often overwhelming size of the temporary spike. While Box-Tiao models offer certain statistical advantages, they also clearly possess some limitations in analyzing global war-induced changes.

[13] For those readers who wish to pursue the percentage change conversion procedure further, McCleary and Hay (1980, pp. 171–185) advance the following formula for translating omega parameters in log metric into percentage change intervention estimates:

$$\text{percentage change} = (e^{(\omega)} - 1)100,$$

This observation seems all the more true when the outcome is as clearcut as the findings summarized in table 13–2 indicate. The persistent effects of global war on both the expenditures and revenues of the states examined are simply of a different order of magnitude than the impacts of interstate war. The logged parameter values also permit us to point out an interesting difference between expenditure and revenue outcomes. In the aggregate, global war tends to exert similar impacts on both types of series—that is, permanent and statistically significant. But wartime displacements of revenues are far less dramatic than for expenditures. In fact, revenue increases during wartime tend to lag behind expenditure increases in terms of magnitude and timing. Revenue levels only begin to match expenditure levels toward the end, or after the end, of a war and only after expenditure levels have begun to decline.

This tendency could be viewed as somewhat contrary to what one might expect, based on Peacock's and Wiseman's argument that wars increase tax burden tolerances. Alternatively, it could be argued that dramatic expenditure increases drag revenues upwards and that the extent to which this occurs is dependent on the extent to which postwar expenditures decline and not the other way around. Unfortunately, there is only so far one can push this counter-argument with aggregate data. We need more detailed case studies of how wars bring about both temporary and permanent governmental expansion (see, for example, Burke 1982; Marwick 1974; Skowronek 1982; Stein 1980; Strickland 1983).

Several data problems prevent us from examining many pre-twentieth century global wars. Although the limited French data that are available do indicate some, but less than expected, expenditure displacement between 1688–1713 and 1792–1815, our current empirical evidence is restricted to the eighteenth- and nineteenth-century British record. Fortunately, however, these data encompass the period used by Peacock and Wiseman to reject the presence of permanent pre–twentieth-century displacements. Our analysis, whether all British global wars are lumped together or examined separately, suggests that British participation in global wars, at least since 1700, has brought about permanent displacements.[14] How then do we account for the

---

where $e(\omega)$ is the ratio of post-intervention to pre-intervention equilibrium. However, in models with significant delta parameters, the incremental post-intervention movement of the process requires the analysis to exponentiate the asymptotic change $(\omega_0/1 - \delta)$, in the process level.

[14] This statement is not entirely true. When British global wars are examined separately (as opposed to being treated as a class of warfare as in table 13–2), the impact of the 1701–1713 Spanish Succession war on expenditures/GNP is not statistically significant, even though the same war has a significant impact on revenues/GNP. We do not regard the 1701–1713 deviation as a meaningful exception, however, because we have only one year (1700) of prewar GNP data. Moreover, the 1701–1713 warfare constituted only the second phase of the 1688–1713 global war.

Table 13–3
British Expenditures, GNP, and Expenditures/GNP

	Expenditures/GNP (%)		Expenditures	GNP
	Peacock-Wiseman	Rasler-Thompson		
1700		5	4	70
1720		9	8	67
1792	11	9	16	182
1800	24	17	28	166
1814	29	29	61	209
1822	19	15	51	350
1831	16	12	48	413
1841	11	11	47	428
1850	12	10	61	596
1860	11	10	65	621
1870	9	7	65	1013
1880	10	6	84	1446
1890	9	6	113	1890

Note: British expenditures and GNP are expressed in 1913 pounds (000.000 omitted).

more general discrepancy between our findings and those of Peacock and Wiseman?

Table 13–3 lists Peacock's and Wiseman's 1792–1890 data on expenditures/GNP for selected years and contrasts it with our own corresponding data. Clearly, the numbers we are using are not exactly identical with those utilized by our predecessors, but the direction of movement is sufficiently similar to regard them as being in the same ballpark. However, there are two important differences. First, our series begins in 1700. This enables us to see a permanent displacement occurring between 1700 and 1720 (5% to 9% which roughly persists in peacetime through the rest of the century), an impact that probably would be even more impressive if our data could be extended back through the 1680s.

The second difference is seen in Peacock's and Wiseman's expenditure/GNP level returning to the 1792 level by 1841. Our series suggests that this does not occur until some 20 years later in the 1860s. Nevertheless, both series indicate an eventual return to the pre–French Revolutionary/Napoleonic Wars equilibrium level thereby suggesting a less-than-permanent effect. But how long is "permanent"?[15] The disturbance to our series does not subside for some 45 years, and even Peacock's and Wiseman's evidence indicates a 25-year effect, or nearly a generation in length. Regardless of how permanence is defined, it is equally clear that Great Britain enjoyed remarkable economic growth rates during the period in question. Between 1700 and 1792, the British economy expanded by

---

[15] The effect lasts sufficiently long to be able to model the impact of the French Revolutionary/Napoleonic wars as exerting a permanent effect on the British series.

roughly a factor of 2.5, although much of this growth was offset by population growth. In marked contrast, the size of the nineteenth-century British economy doubled approximately every 20 to 25 years. Any British government might have been hard pressed to expand their budgets at this same rate—particularly in an era consistently characterized (through the 1870s) by a conservative approach to governmental spending.

Thus, Peacock and Wiseman are not incorrect to treat the 1793–1815 displacement as less than permanent, but the nature of the evidence also requires careful consideration. In absolute terms or constant British pounds (see table 13–3), there is no doubt that British governmental expenditures were displaced upward. In relation to economic growth, this upward displacement ultimately proved to be temporary. How long the effect took to be regarded as temporary depends upon whose data are used, but it is also evident that the "temporary" status is as much, if not more, dependent upon the intervention of the Industrial Revolution as it is dependent upon austerity budgets. Considered in conjunction with the permanent impact (on revenues/GNP at least) of the second half of the 1689–1713 global war, we should be most reluctant to restrict permanent expenditure displacement to the twentieth century and the evolution of contemporary ideas about the appropriate scope of governmental activities.

Our final question centers on the extent to which the permanent expenditure/revenue impacts of global war can be traced to military spending. The long view of state making stresses the role of military and war expenditures and preparations as the primary impetus of the growth of the state organization. Yet we do not infer from this emphasis that the growth of the state is predicated solely upon the growth of military spending. On the contrary, preparing for war and interstate competition has had a number of spillover consequences, ranging from the need for a permanent bureaucracy to collect taxes in order to pay for sporadic warfare to the war-related growth of social services administered by the state. Titmuss (1969), for example, has argued for a close link between the ascending intensity of war and the evolution of British social policy. As an increasing proportion of the population has become involved in the warfare of the past few centuries, the state has been forced to expand its efforts to improve the health and morale of, initially, men available for combat, later, the next generation of recruits (especially children) and, ultimately, to the whole population as they have all become important to war efforts.

There seems little need to restrict this argument to the British experience for it is indeed a point of view that is quite compatible with what we are referring to as the broader view of the war making–state making linkage. At the same time, it also means that we have little basis—aside from the distinction about relevant crises—for expecting findings different from those advanced by Peacock and Wiseman. Global wars presumably should influence both military and nonmilitary expenditures.

In this examination, we will initially pursue a minimal definition of military spending by restricting the concept to those expenditures consumed directly by the state's armed forces. Accordingly, we will confine our empirical attention to the differential impacts of interstate and global war on military and nonmilitary expenditures/GNP, as reported in table 13–4 for the four global powers.

The outcome reported in table 13–4 is not quite as clearcut as the findings put forward in table 13–2. With the exception of the American case, both interstate and global wars exert abrupt, temporary impacts on military spending. Only in the American case is there a temporary/permanent split between the impacts of the two types of war. Further analysis, however, suggests that the categorical approach to war impacts requires some qualification, depending on which global wars are involved. When the impact of each global war is examined separately, it is the pre-1939 global wars that are associated with temporary impacts. World War II, however,

Table 13–4
The Impact of War on Logged Military and Nonmilitary Expenditures/GNP[a]

	Interstate Wars[b]		Impact Type	Global Wars			Noise Model[c]	
	ω_0	δ		ω_0	δ	ω_0	N_t	χ^2
Logged military expenditures/GNP								
Great Britain (1700–1980)	.32* (4.0)	.69* (4.9)	Abrupt, temporary	1.60* (9.6)			White noise	11.9
United States (1792–1980)	.32* (2.9)	.71* (3.7)	Abrupt, permanent	1.49* (8.3)			White noise	11.9
France (1815–1979)	.13* (2.3)		Abrupt, temporary	1.10* (8.9)	.47* (5.8)		White noise	28.8
Japan (1878–1980)	.30* (2.1)		Abrupt, temporary	2.32* (8.0)			White noise	29.9
Logged nonmilitary expenditures/GNP								
Great Britain (1700–1980)	.00 (−.5)		Abrupt, permanent	.33* (4.7)			$\theta_1 = .50*$ (10.0)	15.7
United States (1792–1980)	−.04 (1.8)		Abrupt, permanent	.52* (4.7)			White noise	18.4
France (1815–1979)	−.03 (−.6)		Abrupt, permanent	.27* (3.2)			$\theta_1 = −.11*$ (2.2)	21.0
Japan (1878–1980)	.08 (1.9)		Gradual permanent	.35* (3.5)		.86* (9.5)	$\phi = −.35*$ (−3.5)	32.8

Note: No statistically significant trend parameters were encountered; *t*-values are reported in parentheses.

[a] All data have been logged in order to achieve variance stationarity.

[b] The impact of the interstate was abrupt and temporary.

[c] Five of the first six noise models are white noise, first differenced series (0,1,0). The British and French nonmilitary noise models are first differenced, moving average processes (0,1,1) whereas the Japanese nonmilitary noise model is a first differenced, autoregressive process (1,1,0).

* Statistical significance at the .05 level.

led to significant and permanent increases in British, American, and French military expenditures/GNP. Not too surprisingly, the Japanese experience requires the construction of a more complicated model—a temporary pulse model for war years followed by an abrupt, permanent model for the dramatic postwar decrease.

In contrast, the war-type distinction is operative for nonmilitary expenditures/GNP. The impact of interstate wars is nonsignificant for all four countries, whereas abrupt, permanent models are found to be applicable in the British, American, and French global war cases. The unusual Japanese case takes a gradual, permanent model in this instance, reflecting increases in nonmilitary spending after both twentieth-century world wars. Ironically then, it is nonmilitary, and not military, spending that is more systematically influenced by periodic global warfare. Nor is this phenomenon an innovation of the twentieth century.

Still, dividing expenditures into military and nonmilitary spending categories constitutes a limited test of the extent to which global war expands nonwar-related allocations. We can take this analysis one step further by removing some more of the war-related expenditures from the nonmilitary side of the ledger. Two prime budgetary candidates for removal as explicitly war-related are interest payments on the national debt and veteran pensions. Series pertaining to the first item are relatively available for all four global powers. Data concerning veteran pensions, unfortunately, are somewhat less accessible for our long periods of time, but we were able to extract them for the Japanese and American cases.

Table 13–5 reports selected observations on two proportional series: 1) nonmilitary expenditures/GNP (nonmilitary expenditures equal total expenditures minus military expenditures, as analyzed in table 13–4) and 2) nonwar expenditures/GNP (nonwar expenditures equal total expenditures minus (military expenditures plus debt interest payments plus veteran pensions) for the United States and Japan and minus (military expenditures plus debt interest payments) for Great Britain and France). The point of the exercise is not to compare the magnitude of the two sets of observations (the nonwar proportions must be smaller than the nonmilitary ones, by definition) but rather to check whether the global war changes in the nonwar series appear to behave much differently from the previously analyzed nonmilitary series.

The nonwar spending series do seem to exhibit the same patterns of discontinuous growth and permanent changes before and after global wars observed in the more broadly defined nonmilitary spending series. Equally worth noting is the 1790–1820 doubling of the proportions of GNP devoted to nonwar purposes in the British case. The proportions admittedly are quite small, in accordance with pre–twentieth century austerity policies, and decline between 1820 and 1840 but, unlike the nonmilitary series, the upward shift in the nonwar proportion reflects a permanent change. Thus,

Table 13–5
Selected Data on Nonmilitary and Nonwar Expenditures as a Proportion of GNP

	Great Britain		France		United States		Japan	
	Non-military	Nonwar	Non-military	Nonwar	Non-military	Nonwar	Non-military	Nonwar
1780	.057	.013						
1790	.070	.013						
1820	.110	.027						
1830	.088	.021						
1840	.071	.019						
1850	.076	.022						
1860	.064	.023						
1870	.045	.019						
1880	.040	.020						
1890	.038	.023	.096	.047	.019	.008	.063	.049
1900	.035	.024	.085	.046	.018	.008	.074	.062
1913	.042	.035	.061	.037	.010	.005	.083	.052
1920	.145	.092	.150		.045	.031	.054	.038
1930	.147	.084	.112	.055	.027	.018	.081	.051
1938	.132	.094	.174	.136	.065	.050	.173	.058
1950	.192	.155	.219	.207	.104	.076	.160	.158
1960	.175	.141	.181	.168	.096	.071	.108	.099
1970	.227	.202	.235	.212	.119	.094	.103	.096
1980	.285	.247	.272[a]	.234[a]	.172	.143	.176	.146

The United States and Japan nonwar proportions exclude veteran pensions, whereas the British and French nonwar proportions are restricted to the common base (total expenditures − (military + debt interest spending)/GNP).

[a] 1979 values.

table 13–5 reinforces the support for the contention that the displacement phenomenon should not be dismissed simply as an artifact of postwar increases in war-related spending.

Conclusion

We have attempted to achieve several goals in the present study. First, we have sought to reduce some of the empirical ambiguities about, and disputes over, the existence of a war-induced expenditure displacement phenomenon. In contrast to the divergence of opinion in the literature, the relationship between global war and permanent spending shifts in some of the world system's most important states (Great Britain, the United States, France, and Japan) is statistically and substantively significant. Moreover, the displacement that takes place is only partially a function of war-related expenditures. Nonwar-related spending is affected as well. Global war must therefore be considered one of the more important sources of the growth and expansion of the modern state.

Second, we have also attempted to make a distinction between Peacock's and Wiseman's hypothesized displacement effect and their tax tolerance explanation of the relationship. Demonstrating the existence of the displacements does little to confirm, or to disconfirm for that matter, the relatively independent idea that national crises provide opportunities for overcoming taxpayer resistance to greater revenue extraction efforts. Rather than seeking ways to compare taxpayer attitudes during war and peacetime, something about which we know very little (see Goetz 1977), our own interpretive preferences are to stress the broader, historical context of the reciprocal interactions between war and state-building processes. For the older and most powerful states at least, an appreciation for the persistent role of war is central to explaining the growth and expansion of the state, whether or not governmental leaders choose to pay much attention to citizen preferences on tax burdens.

Last but not necessarily least, the outcomes of the data analyses underscore the theoretical significance of a special category of warfare—the global war—that is far less appreciated than it deserves. There is no need to overstate our case by insisting that global wars are the only external events to have significant internal impacts. Other types of events, including the more frequent nonglobal wars, can and do have domestic repercussions,[16] but we have been able to demonstrate that the spending and tax revenue patterns and, more generally, the organizational expansion of some of the system's leading states are more likely to be displaced and displaced permanently by global wars than they are by interstate wars. We suspect that we are only beginning to tap, in a systematic way, the domestic implications of the global war as both a catalyst and as an agent of socioeconomic and political change.[17]

---

[16] Intensive civil wars may also have a permanent impact on expenditures and revenues that is comparable to global war as occurred in the United States in the nineteenth century.

[17] Although an emphasis on global wars may not tell us much about the growth of states made independent since 1945, our findings should at least encourage other analysts of the ongoing expansion of public expenditures and revenues in industrialized states (e.g., Cameron 1978; Gould 1983; Kohl 1983; Schmidt 1983; and Taylor 1981) to consider incorporating the effects of global wars in their models. In the 1983 conference version of this article, we extended our global war impact analysis to the twentieth-century expenditure and revenue experience of 22 states other than those examined here. Although these data are characterized by a number of missing values that hamper serial examination, the permanent impacts of global war do not appear to be restricted to the major or global contenders for systemic power. The expenditures and revenues of other war participants (including minor power active belligerents and occupied states) as well as some nonparticipating states that were located near the combat theaters appear to have been affected as well. However, the examination of these data introduces several analytical complications that cannot be discussed adequately in the space presently available and will have to be postponed for separate treatment in the future.

Editors' Commentary

Major Findings

Rasler and Thompson seek to establish the impact of war on increases in a state's revenues and expenditures. They find that the impact varies depending on the type of war. Global wars (like World War II) have a permanent impact on the ability of the state to extract greater revenue from its people. This is true for all four countries in their study: Great Britain, United States, France, and Japan (see the bottom of table 13–2). Simple interstate wars typically do not have this effect; when they do have an impact, it is only temporary. Furthermore, global wars tend to increase permanently the overall expenditures of a state (see the top of table 13–2). The impact of interstate wars on expenditures tends to be temporary and of a weaker order of magnitude than the strong impact of global wars. Interestingly, Rasler and Thompson also find that the growth in expenditures occurs before the increase in revenues, indicating that revenues must catch up with expenditures.

According to Rasler and Thompson, global wars produce increases in taxation and expenditures as part of the war effort, but once the war ends, taxes and expenditures do not return to prewar levels. This is sometimes referred to as a **ratchet effect.** Thus, global wars can be seen as bringing about a permanent expansion and growth of the state, whereas interstate wars tend not to have this effect. Interstate wars are more likely to produce increases in expenditures than taxation, but whatever the impact, it is temporary.

The last part of the analysis addresses the question of whether the increase in expenditures is due to just an increase in military expenditures or a more general increase in spending. The authors find that both military and nonmilitary expenditures are significantly affected by global war (table 13–4). Surprisingly, however, nonmilitary expenditures tend to be permanently increased after global wars, whereas the impact on military expenditures tends to be abrupt but temporary. The major exception to this is the United States, which has an abrupt and permanent increase in military expenditures after global war. This exception is consistent with Russett's (1970) finding that war has a ratchet effect on U.S. military expenditures.

Rasler and Thompson conclude that global war is one of the more important sources of the expansion of the modern state. Their study suggests that war can have profound effects on the internal political economy of states. Evidence in other studies (for example, Goldstein 1985) can be used to show that war and the preparation for it may have a profound effect on the nature of the global political economy as well by producing certain kinds of long-term global price upswings (called *Kondratieff waves* in economics). These studies and that of Rasler and Thompson suggest that the unanticipated consequences of global war have played a more crucial role in the historical development of the global system than previously thought. If this is so, it implies that some of the most important choices in history have been made inadvertently, which does not say much for the rational nature of human choice in history.

Methodological Notes

Rasler and Thompson demonstrate how advances in statistical tools—in this case, the development of Box-Jenkins and Box-Tiao models—have allowed them to conduct new research and resolve some earlier inconsistent findings. **Box-Tiao technique** is based on economic forecasting models applied to time-series data. It measures the impact of events on changes in data at different times and is thus often referred to as *impact assessment.*

There are two major sets of methodological issues you need to grapple with in this article. The first is the question of why the authors chose to use Box-Tiao technique. Their rationale is comprised of a critique of earlier analyses and justification of their method. Their methodological discussion is difficult, and readers should not be daunted if they are unable to grasp all of the points. Far more important is the second set of questions: those that deal with what Box-Tiao technique can tell us about the hypotheses under study. The findings on the hypotheses presented in the "Data Analysis" section deserve close scrutiny but are fairly straightforward.

You have already encountered time-series data and autocorrelation in the commentary on Wayman (in chapter 8) so you are on the way. The main methodological contribution that Rasler and Thompson make is to use the impact assessment technique developed by Box and Tiao to measure the impact that global war has on revenue and expenditure levels in four major states. Their choice of method is based on three critiques of earlier methods. Previous studies have used simple "eyeball technique" or ordinary-least-squares (OLS) regression analysis, but Rasler and Thompson argue that once more than one country is examined, it becomes necessary to measure precisely the extent of the impact of the independent variable, and OLS is inadequate to this task. Regression mathematically averages in **outliers,** which are cases that have values that are either much higher or much lower than most other cases. For example, in a set of data on GNP per capita, the United States is an outlier; in data on population of nations, China is an outlier. Since outliers pull a regression line toward them, the overall trend in the data will not be described accurately by regression. When the researcher suspects that an outside variable such as war is causing the outliers, then a technique is needed that can assess the significance of the outlier, not just average it in. This is Rasler and Thompson's first critique: OLS regression analysis relies too heavily on the goodness of fit of a regression line.

The other two critiques refer to autocorrelation and trend. When one point in a series is correlated with the previous point (autocorrelation), OLS still underestimate the amount of error, producing stronger findings than are justified. Rasler and Thompson show how Box-Tiao technique removes that type of error. Often time series appear to trend upward. Sometimes, however, they are not really trending (systematically increasing with each time period) but rather drifting more randomly. In order to assess the impact of some event, the trend must be removed. In Box-Tiao technique, the series is differenced (see the methodological notes on Wayman in chapter 8).

Having offered these critiques and justifications, the authors now introduce Box-Tiao technique. Applying this technique involves modifying and modelling a series in such a way that one can determine where it will head in the future. It is essentially univariate, the series is modeled in terms of itself to see how the end point came about.

ARIMA is an acronym for autoregressive-integrated-moving average, three processes that either exist in or can be performed on series data. Usually not all three are involved in any one series, but the beauty of a Box-Jenkins model is that it can account for any combination of the three processes in a given series. The autoregressive component measures the extent to which each point (y_t) is a function of itself in the past $(y_t - 1)$, addressing the problem of autocorrelation. The moving averages component is used for a series that is a function of itself in the past *plus* error or shocks, which are outside events (such as war). The integrated process describes a series in which each value is equal to the previous value, *plus* a constant increase, *plus* stochastic error (for example, a series of governmental expenditures that increases over time and increases even more after a war).

All you need to know here about Box-Jenkins technique, or

ARIMA modelling, is that this step is used to remove the trend or drift in the series and the autocorrelation referred to earlier. Once this is accomplished statistically, the series is said to be *white noise* (no more trend or autocorrelation). Only when we achieve white noise can we proceed to test a hypothesis to explain the remaining variance not accounted for by the previous pattern. Then we can proceed to the second and more interesting and important step: Box-Tiao technique, or impact assessment analysis.

Rasler and Thompson observed series of revenues and expenditures and saw that they increase over time but could not determine simply by looking at them why the increases occurred. Peacock and Wiseman said it was war that caused them, but other research found that wars were not always so important. Rasler and Thompson have made the theoretical argument that global wars have the effect Peacock and Wiseman observed but interstate wars do not. Testing this is fairly easy once the white noise series is achieved. War is coded as a simple nominal variable, where O = no war and 1 = war, and the findings for interstate wars are compared with the findings for global wars. Two aspects of the impact of war are measured. Omega (ω), which measures the strength of the impact, and delta (δ), which measures its duration. The findings can be assessed on the basis of the strength of these two measures.

Table 13–2 reports the omegas for the impact of interstate wars and global wars on expenditures and revenues. If the omegas were the same for the two types of war, Rasler and Thompson's hypothesis would be falsified. You can see, however, that the only statistically significant omegas for interstate wars are of small magnitude (ranging from .03 to .27), while the omegas for global war are all statistically significant and, except for revenues for Great Britain (.08), much larger (.20 to 1.01). These findings support the contention that global wars have the hypothesized displacement effect and interstate wars do not. Table 13–4 offers further evidence using military and nonmilitary expenditures as the dependent variables. Again, only four of the omegas for interstate war are statistically significant, and they are of small magnitude (.13 to .32). The omegas for global wars are all statistically significant and generally higher (.27 to 2.32).

In summary, Rasler and Thompson have employed a previously underutilized technique to give a high level of precision to their findings on the displacement effects of global war. Their precision of measurement allows them to show in which types of wars this effect is most significant and on which economic indicators.

As progress is made in the scientific study of peace and war it becomes possible to piece the findings together into a comprehensive explanation of war. In the next selection, John Vasquez begins the task by synthesizing the extant findings into an analysis of The Steps to War.

V
Conclusion

14

The Steps to War:
Toward a Scientific Explanation of
Correlates of War Findings

John A. Vasquez

Editors' Introduction

Despite the fact that a large percentage of the quantitative work on war uses the same data, that is, Correlates of War data, there is not as much integration of the findings as one might expect. Sometimes the findings are contradictory, or two sets of findings exist independently without any attention given to how they relate to each other. This can be expected in a field still in its infancy, but, the lack of integration is also due to the absence of theoretical consensus and the inability of the dominant realist approach to easily pass empirical tests. Many international relations scholars accept the tenets of the dominant paradigm of realism, but others argue that realism is a faulty guide to knowledge, and only when the field finds a more useful paradigm will substantial progress be made. One assumes that this is not a problem in the long run for science. As findings contradict some arguments and evidence accumulates for others, the field will move forward. As part of this process, John Vasquez reviews the quantitative findings on war in order to weave them into a coherent explanation.

Introduction

The scientific study of war began with the hope and promise that the collection of reproducible evidence and its systematic analysis would result in

Reprinted from *World Politics* XL (October 1987), pp. 108–145. Copyright © 1984 by Princeton University Press. Reprinted by permission of Princeton University Press and the author. Abridged.

Support for this study has been provided by a Fulbright research grant, a Rutgers Competitive Fellowship, and the Rutgers University Research Council. My thanks to Marie T. Henehan for suggestions. The responsibility for the paper is mine alone.

343

a major breakthrough in our understanding of general factors associated with war and peace. That breakthrough has not yet occurred; the task has been more intractable than was thought. Nevertheless, during the last fifteen years an increase in statistical findings on war has contributed a new body of evidence and insight separate from those provided by history, traditional discourse, and political philosophy.

These findings and the testing process itself have exposed some long-held beliefs as erroneous or confused. What is of greater significance is that these analyses may constitute the critical mass of evidence that could provide a turning point in the long effort to discover the causes of war. If that turning point occurs, a large part of the credit will have to go to the Correlates of War project and its director, J. David Singer, for it is in the research of the project and in the secondary analysis of its data that the main relationship and patterns are being uncovered. . . .

If cumulation is to occur, however, there must be more explicit attempts at explanation through the integration of findings. The present review is an initial attempt, by someone outside the Correlates of War project, to piece existing clues together and build upon various theoretical suggestions within the project in order to construct a scientific explanation of war.[1] The analysis will begin by examining the overall picture of the factors that lead to war that is suggested by the project's findings. An explanation of war will then be constructed by looking at (1) how security issues arise; (2) how alliances are a response to the rise of security issues, and how they affect the onset and expansion of war; (3) the effect of alliances on polarization and changes in power, and how these factors influence the probability of world war; (4) how differences in findings for the 19th and 20th centuries can be explained by looking at differences in alliances and the role of arms races; (5) how arms races are a response to security issues; and (6) why some crises escalate to war and others do not.

Explaining War as a Series of Steps

If we piece together some of the findings and theoretical suggestions made within the Correlates of War project, we get the following picture of the process that leads two or more actors to war, a process best characterized as

---

[1] It should be pointed out that the Correlates of War project has not yet produced an integrated explanation. For Singer's view of what, in principle, would constitute an adequate explanation of war, see Singer (1973:161–63). For his own review and assessment of Correlates of War findings, see Singer (1981). For an early survey of a variety of studies on war, see Deutsch and Senghaas (1973).

steps to war.[2] As a situation develops that might portend the use of force, leaders and various policy influencers become concerned primarily with security goals and/or the use of force to gain stakes that they have been unable to attain up to this point (Singer 1982:40). In order to test their rival and to demonstrate resolve, leaders rely on threats and coercive tactics, which involves them in crises (or serious disputes) (Rummel 1979:186; Maoz 1983). Leaders respond to a crisis and to security issues that are perceived as posing a long-term threat by attempting to increase their military power through alliances and/or a military build-up (Wallace 1972; Diehl 1985a:331–32). In a tense environment, military build-ups lead to arms races, and alliance-making may result in a polarization (of blocs), both of which increase insecurity. In serious disputes between equals, actors employ realpolitik tactics (Leng 1983). Eventually a dispute arises that escalates to war. Disputes or crises are most likely to escalate if there is an ongoing arms race (Wallace 1979), and if (1) they are triggered by physical threats to vital issues (Gochman and Leng 1983); (2) they are the second or third crisis with the same rival (with realpolitik tactics becoming more coercive and hostile in each succeeding crisis) (Leng 1983); (3) a hostile interaction spiral emerges during the crisis (Holsti, North, and Brody 1968); and (4) hard-liners dominate the leadership of at least one side (see Vasquez 1987).

This process assumes that war results from a series of steps taken by each side. Each step produces, in succession, a situation that encourages the adoption of foreign policy practices which set the stage for the involved parties' taking another step that is closer to war. This assumption suggests that those explanations that see war as a "rational" response to changes in power are, at best, incomplete; at times, they distort the nature of the underlying process by making it appear simpler and more deterministic than it is. Bueno de Mesquita (1981b:4–5), for example, argues that his rational expected-utility theory delineates only the necessary conditions of war, not the sufficient conditions. While his theory tells us something about last-minute calculations and who is likely to initiate and win wars, it does not tell us why actors resort to force and war in the first place. In a different way, many of the power-cycle theories, such as those of Organski/Kugler (1980), Gilpin (1981), Modelski (1978), and Thompson (1983b) simply state that fundamental shifts in power will result in war; they leave out the details.[3] It is in the presence of these theoretical hedgehogs that the empirical foxes of the Correlates of War project make their most important contribution. For it is precisely the details that they have patiently, over the years, tried to sniff out.

---

[2] Singer (1980:xxiv–xxx) has suggested that conflict be seen as an unfolding escalatory process involving different stages.

[3] For an attempt to get at some of the details, see Doran and Parsons (1980). For a thoughtful review of this type of explanation, see Levy (1985b).

The Rise of Security Issues

The beginnings of wars can be traced to those situations in which some leaders believe that their state's security is threatened and start to take measures to protect themselves. Contrary to realist assertions, however, not all actors, particularly states, are always engaged in a struggle for power. It seems more accurate to assume that security issues and the power-politics behavior associated with them only occur at certain stages in inter-state relationships and predominate only in certain periods of history.[4]

If realists have been generally too alarmist in their assumptions about the pervasiveness of war and threats to security, they have been more accurate in *describing* the kinds of behavior associated with the rise of security issues. Such issues are usually raised by one actor testing another's willingness to use its capability (diplomatic, economic, or military) to maintain a given distribution of political stakes. In such a situation, actors believe that victory is most likely to be associated with some demonstration of resolve; that is, making it credible that they are more willing than the other side to use force, and risk escalation and war, either to defend or to advance their position (Maoz 1983; Leng 1980; 1983).

It is logical to assume that only after such threats appear, and especially if they are perceived as long-term threats, will actors seek allies or build up their military. The research on this question and on the factors that preceded alliance-making and military build-ups has been neither extensive nor conclusive, however.[5] Most research within the Correlates of War project has centered, instead, on the effects of alliances, capabilities, and arms races; it is in these areas that the project has made its contributions.

Responding to Security Issues: Alliances

Research on alliances has produced two major conclusions. First, alliances do not prevent war or promote peace; instead, they are associated with war, although they are probably not a cause of war. Second, the major consequence of alliances is to expand the war once it has started; in this way, alliances are important in accounting for the magnitude and severity of war.

---

[4] War is a relatively rare event. Only 67 inter-state and 51 other wars (involving at least one nation-state against a nonrecognized state) were fought between 1816 and 1980 (Small and Singer 1982:59–60). According to these data, war is even a rarer event in the history of specific inter-state relations. Wallensteen (1984:245–46) shows that some periods of history—namely 1816–1848, 1871–1895, 1919–1932, 1963–1976—are devoid of major-power wars and have few military confrontations.

[5] Within the project, the work most relevant to these questions is by Wallace (1972). For the factors that lead actors to become involved in disputes, see Gochman (1980) and Maoz (1982:ch. 4–5).

The major evidence that alliances do not prevent war, but are associated with it, is presented in an article by Jack Levy (1981), who supplements his own data on alliances and war in the 16th through 18th centuries with Correlates of War data on the 19th and 20th.[6] The longer perspective provides a critical insight: Levy finds that, except for the 19th century, the majority of alliances (56 to 100 percent, depending on type) have been followed, within five years of their formation, by war involving at least one of the allies. Moreover, *all* great-power alliances in the 16th, 17th, and 20th centuries have been followed, within five years, by a war involving a great power. These findings do not hold for the 19th century, during which only 44 percent of all alliances were followed by war (compared with 89 percent, 73 percent, and 81 percent in the 17th, 18th, and 20th centuries), and *none* of the great-power alliances were followed by a great-power war within five years of their initiation (Levy 1981:597–98 esp. table 7).

The data on the 19th century show that wars do not always have to result from alliances, but that in the other centuries they often did. Levy also finds that alliances are not a necessary element in war, in that most wars occur without an alliance preceding them. (From the 16th to the 20th century, only 26 percent of wars, on average, were preceded by an alliance involving one of the war participants).[7] Clearly, such evidence goes a long way in dispelling the notion that alliances promote peace; nevertheless, how much of a factor they play in causing war is difficult to discern, since actors may join alliances because they anticipate war.

Further evidence that alliances are associated with war is provided by Ostrom and Hoole. In a reformulation of some of the propositions on alliance aggregation and war examined by Singer and Small, they compare the number of dyads experiencing inter-state war with the number of dyads having defense alliances. They find that within the first three years of alliance formation, as the number of alliance dyads increases, so does the number of war dyads. After three years, this positive correlation is reversed, and the more alliance commitments, the fewer war dyads. After twelve years, there is no relationship. This suggests that soon after alliances are made, there is a danger of war, but four to twelve years later there is not. After twelve years, it is probably a new game in which old alliances are irrelevant to questions of war and peace (Ostrom and Hoole, 1978:228–29; see also Singer and Small 1966c, 1968).

Since the making of alliances often does not produce the results that were desired, it is unlikely that those who enter alliances can accurately

---

[6] A similar conclusion had been reached earlier by Singer and Small (1966c, 1974) on the basis of more limited tests.

[7] But note that 60% of the wars of the 20th century were preceded by alliances, compared to 18%, 14%, 35%, and 25% of the wars in the 16th, 17th, and 18th, and 19th centuries, respectively. Levy (1981:599, table 8).

anticipate their consequences. For example, a major purpose of entering alliances is to increase relative military power; but this outcome often does not occur, because the making of an alliance usually leads to the creation of a counteralliance. This makes for greater insecurity, and usually greater uncertainty, because of the possibility that one or more allies will not honor their commitments.[8] More importantly, alliances not only fail to prevent wars, but make it likely that wars that do occur will expand.

Two major studies provide evidence that alliances expand wars. The more important one is by Randolph Siverson and Joel King (1979:45; 1980), both of whom are outside the project. The authors hypothesize that a war between two states that do not have allies has a much lower probability of spreading than a war between states that do have allies. Using Correlates of War data on inter-state wars from 1815 to 1965, they identify 188 instances in which an actor participated in war (note that 50 inter-state wars generated these 188 participations). In 112 of these incidents an actor fought in coalition with others, and in 76 it fought alone. What determines whether a war will involve a coalition and not just dyadic combat? Of the 112 participants who fought war in a coalition, 76 had prewar alliance bonds and 35 did not. Conversely, of the 76 participants who fought the war alone, 52 had made no prewar alliances and only 24 had (Yule's Q = .64). This means that when a war breaks out among states that have alliances with nonbelligerents, these nonbelligerents are likely to be drawn in. In this way, alliances act as a contagion mechanism by which war spreads and expands. Hence, it might be expected that a system with extensive alliances will tend to have wars with many participants, whereas a system with few alliances will tend to have small wars. Siverson and King found that in 19 (38 percent) of the 50 inter-state wars that took place between 1815 and 1965, neither party had a prewar alliance. These wars tended to have few participants, with all but three being dyadic, and those three involving only three parties. Alliances, then, not only fail to prevent wars, but by making wars spread, they encourage more dangerous, complex (multilateral) wars. Siverson and King (1979:48) point out that in 1870, France had no alliances and fought alone, but in 1914 it had plenty of allies.

Indirect support for the hypothesis that alliances are associated with the expansion of war is provided by Yamamoto and Bremer (1980:216–17), who examine three probability models to see which best explains (fits) the decision of a major power to enter an ongoing war. The three models they examine are an independent choice model, which assumes that the decision

---

[8] Sabrosky (1980:176, 196) shows that even at the most fundamental level—whether an ally will fight on your side in a war—expectations are not fulfilled. More often than not, allies remain neutral. In addition, some alliances, like neutrality pacts (especially those between major and minor powers) are more likely to be violated than honored; i.e., if one party (especially a major power) enters the war, it will enter against its ally (particularly if the ally is a minor power).

of one actor has no effect on the decision of another; a one-way conditional choice model, which assumes that a decision to enter the war has a great impact on what others do, but that a decision to remain neutral has no effect; and a two-way conditional choice model, which assumes that whatever an actor decides encourages the other actors to make the same decision. Of the fifty inter-state wars between 1816 and 1965, only eight involve major-power intervention, so the sample is small. Nevertheless, the authors are able to show that the two-way conditional choice model fits the data better than the one-way conditional choice model, and much better than the independent choice model, which does not fit at all. This means that if a state intervenes in an ongoing war, it increases the probability of others intervening; if it remains neutral, it increases the probability of others being neutral.[9] Yamamoto and Bremer do not investigate the role of alliances, but simply find that, when faced with an ongoing war, major powers will do what other major powers do. Thus, once there is an intervention, the probability of other major powers intervening will increase. In light of Siverson and King's findings, one may infer that the presence of alliance bonds increases the likelihood of an initial intervention; once this occurs, other major powers eventually follow suit, whether they have alliance bonds or not.

All the above suggests that alliances are a key factor in the expansion of wars, but that they are not the only factor. Siverson and King point out that the three largest wars in terms of participants (the two World Wars and the Korean War) contain intervening participants who do not have previous alliances—two in World War I, eight in World War II, and six in Korea. Very large wars may involve other contagion factors (Siverson and King 1979:46–47). One of these factors is contiguous territory. For example, Most and Starr (1980) show that a state with a warring nation on its border has an increased probability of becoming involved in a war in the next five years. Contiguity certainly was a contagion factor in World War I, World War II, and the Korean War.

As a war spreads, especially through alliances, it is likely to become longer and more severe to the extent that intervention makes each side equal to the other.[10] In this way, alliances are probably more responsible for the severity, magnitude, and duration of war than for its onset. Since there is

---

[9] Although the two-way conditional model holds for both the 19th and 20th centuries, the finding is stronger for the 20th. Major powers in the 20th century were more likely to intervene in ongoing wars, and were more affected by what others did (Yamamoto and Bremer 1980:218–21). While this inference is based on a very small number of cases, it suggests that alliances in the 20th century were more dangerous than in the 19th.

[10] Yamamoto and Bremer (1980:226) find that, when only one side is joined by major powers, the war is usually brought to a rapid close (the chief exception being the Crimean War); but when major powers join opposite sides, as has often happened in the 20th century, the war is more severe.

often an interval between the alliances and the outbreak of war, it is a legitimate inference that alliances do not directly cause war, but help to aggravate a situation that makes war more likely. They may do this in two ways: by promoting an atmosphere that polarizes the system and by encouraging arms races.

The Effect of Alliances on Polarization and Power

The work on polarity has been extensive, with the findings exceedingly complicated and sometimes inconsistent (see Singer 1981:8–9). The reason is that different definitions of polarity have been employed: some studies are based on the number of blocs (sometimes called polarization or cluster polarity), some on the distribution of power, and some—most notably that of Wallace (1985)—on a combination of the two.[11] Differences in definitions have been further aggravated by differences in the measurement of both the independent and dependent variables and by differences in research design. Some, like Bueno de Mesquita (1978), examine the entire system, while others, like Frank Wayman (1984a) and Jack Levy (1985a), look only at major powers. Although it is far from obvious how the various findings fit together, a number of important clues have surfaced about the effect of alliances on system structure.

The most obvious effect of widespread alliance-making is that it decreases the number of independent actors, resulting in a reduction of what Deutsch and Singer (1964) call interaction opportunities. Wallace (1973a) and Bueno de Mesquita (1978) have conducted the most sophisticated studies of the reduction of interaction opportunities. Wallace finds no linear relationship between such polarization and nation-months of war and battle deaths (indicators most valid for the magnitude and severity of war), but does uncover a curvilinear relationship. The wars of the highest magnitude and severity are apt to occur when the system is highly polarized (maximum polarization would be two blocs) or had no polarization at all (minimum polarization would be no blocs); a moderate amount of war, or no war, is associated with moderate polarization (Wallace 1973a).[12] This finding can be interpreted as meaning that when there are no alliances, the weak fall victim to the strong, but when most actors are bonded into two blocs, intense rivalry and preparation for war develop. One would suspect that the findings produced by very low or no polarization would be the result of many

---

[11] Wayman (1984a:74–75) shows that polarity based on the number of blocs and polarity based on the distribution of power are two uncorrelated and empirically separate dimensions.

[12] Kegley and Raymond (1982:585–89) find that when alliance structures are either extremely flexible or extremely rigid, the magnitude and severity of war are high.

wars not directly connected,[13] while the finding on high polarization would be the result of large, multilateral (complex) wars, like the two World Wars.

Wallace also finds a moderate curvilinear relationship between cross-cutting (links across blocs) and the magnitude and severity of war, with moderate cross-cutting reducing the intensity of war, and very low and very high cross-cutting increasing it. This is consistent with the earlier results and is of interest primarily because it means that systems that are very polarized and have no cross-cutting will be subject to wars of high magnitude and severity. The findings on both polarization and cross-cutting are consistent with the findings of Siverson and King that alliances serve to expand wars. Wallace's results also make clear that a polarized alliance structure can give rise to multilateral (complex) wars immediately and not simply expand dyadic wars—a possibility that was not examined by Siverson and King.

Bueno de Mesquita's (1978) analysis takes us a step further: he finds that it is not so much the mere existence of polarity that is important, but the change in tightness and, to a lesser extent, the change in interaction opportunities. These relationships, however, are found only in the 20th century. Here, increasing tightness (polarization) is associated with the occurrence of war (probit correlation = .29 for all interstate wars and .47 for wars involving only major powers); decreasing tightness is associated with the absence of war. After periods of declining tightness, war almost never occurs: 89 percent of these periods are followed by peace. Conversely, 84 percent of the wars that do begin in the 20th century follow a rise in systemic tightness, making this an almost necessary condition for war. For the 20th century, Bueno de Mesquita also finds one significant correlation (.33) between the occurrence of war and change (increase) in the number of interaction opportunities.[14] Each of these findings indicates that it is change itself which is a predictor of war, since no relationship is found between the number of poles, discreteness, or tightness and the onset of war. Since the

---

[13] The correlation between an increase in interaction opportunities and the occurrence of war is probably a function of the rise of new actors rather than of a reduction in blocs. Wayman (1984a) makes a similar point against Bueno de Mesquita (1978). The sheer increase in interaction opportunities increases conflict and war—contrary to what Deutsch and Singer (1964) expected—because new states often raise fundamental issues that challenge the given order; they must also create a (territorial) place for themselves in the system. For evidence on the latter, see Maoz (1989). Evidence that an increase in the number of states is associated with an increase in wars and serious disputes is provided, respectively, in Small and Singer (1982:130, 135, 141) and in Gochman and Maoz (1984:591–94).

[14] Since creation of alliances leads to a reduction of interaction opportunities, one would expect a negative correlation between change in interaction opportunities and war. This relationship may not have been uncovered by Bueno de Mesquita (1978) because such a reduction would have been wiped out by the rise of new actors, especially in the post-1945 period. It is suggestive, therefore, that he does find a slight (but statistically insignificant − .25) relationship between a reduction of interaction opportunities and the onset of wars involving major powers in the 19th century (see Bueno de Mesquita, 1978:table 2). The positive .33 for the 20th century may be explained away as a function of system size.

most drastic change in the number of interaction opportunities and systemic tightness comes with the initial making of alliances, one could hypothesize that alliance-making upsets relations between actors and increases the likelihood of war. This is consistent with Ostrom and Hoole's (1978:229) finding that war follows (in a statistically significant sense) within three years of the formation of alliances. At minimum, these findings show that alliances, at least in the 20th century, do not prevent war, but are a way of preparing for war, and in that manner bring states one step closer to war.

The other major effect of a change in polarization is that it encourages each side to make better preparations for war—so that, when a war comes, it is longer. Bueno de Mesquita finds that in the 19th and 20th centuries a change (increase) in the number of poles is associated with longer wars involving major powers (but not related to longer wars in general). He infers that an increase in poles produces uncertainty and encourages nations to be prepared for war. This probably results, in my view, in arms races and attempts to secure commitments from allies, thereby also producing greater tightness and discreteness (i.e., more polarization). Although Bueno de Mesquita (1978) does not examine the effects of an increase in poles on changes in tightness and discreteness of blocs, he does find that, in the 20th century, increases in systemic tightness and discreteness do produce longer wars (both interstate wars and wars involving major powers). Since increasing discreteness (few bonds across blocs) means little cross-cutting, this finding is consistent with Wallace's (1973a) that the absence of cross-cutting is associated with severe wars.[15]

Increasing tightness probably produces longer wars because it reflects each side's ability to get it own house in order by firming up commitments and pooling resources, which means that alliances that work result in longer wars. Since Steven Rosen (1972) has shown that the outcome (and probably the length) of war is a function of the comparative amount of revenue available and the percentage of population loss, allies that can effectively pool resources will have a "larger aggregate of capabilities" to sustain longer wars than they would if they fought dyadically (see also Wayman, Singer, and Goertz 1983). Also, the pooling of resources permits wealthier allies to sustain weaker allies who do not have the revenues for longer wars (Kennedy 1984).

Finally, Bueno de Mesquita (1978) concludes that increasing tightness is a factor in making wars spread, since no multilateral (complex) wars occur following a decline in systemic tightness at any time between 1815 and 1965, and nearly 80 percent of the complex wars occur in periods of

---

[15] On the importance of cross-cutting (*per se*) for reducing conflict, see Deutsch and Singer (1964); Dean and Vasquez (1976:24–27); and Levy (1981:608).

rising tightness. This is another piece of evidence that alliances are associated with the expansion of war.

Sabrosky (1985:148, 151, 181) uncovers some additional details on the kinds of wars that are likely to enlarge, and the role alliances play in that process. He finds that of the 50 inter-state wars between 1816 and 1965, 40 remained localized. None of the wars that initially involved major powers on each side expanded; they remained dyadic. Major powers that were neutral at the beginning of these wars remained neutral. The probability of other wars expanding was also not very high (only 5 out of 24 wars between a major and a minor power, and 5 out of 22 wars between minor powers, expanded).

However, *if* major-minor wars expanded, it was highly likely that they would be enlarged in such a way that there would be a major power on each side. Of the five major-minor wars that expanded, four were enlarged in this manner; of the five minor-minor wars that expanded, only one was enlarged to include a major power on each side. Although the number of cases is small, the major-minor wars that enlarged were the Crimean War, the War of Italian Unification, World War I, and World War II; this indicates that the main complex wars among major powers began through intervention to help a minor power. Sabrosky is unable to retrodict which wars remained localized; but by analyzing whether there was a higher concentration of military capabilities in the major powers, a high level of alliance aggregation in the system, and an increase in both these factors during the preceding five years, he has some success in classifying the wars that expanded and enlarged.

The findings of Wallace, Bueno de Mesquita, and Sabrosky suggest that alliance-making that leads to polarization produces wars of the highest magnitude, severity, and duration—i.e., complex and total wars.[16] The reason for this is not fully explained in the literature, but it seems plausible that in a protracted conflict between equals that becomes a rivalry, the making of an alliance by one side will lead to the making of a counter-alliance as well as a competition for allies. This will polarize the system and produce a number of effects which increase the perceived threat and lead to behavior that is more conflictual. First, polarization increases the perceived threat by increasing the power of each side and enlarging the possible theater of war. This leads each side to prepare for a worst-case scenario and to increase its military expenditures. Second, polarization focuses the attention of both sides on the main issues that divide them and reduces the salience of cross-cutting issues. This promotes persistent disagreement; makes all minor stakes symbolic of large ones (thereby collapsing all issues between the main

---

[16] For an elaboration of these distinctions, see Vasquez (1986), where wars are classified on the basis of three dimensions: capability (wars between equals vs. wars between unequals), the number of participants (dyadic vs. complex), and the goals and means (limited vs. total war).

rivals into one overarching issue); and greatly accentuates rivalry and hostility. Third, complete polarization removes the possibility of any major powers' acting as mediators; it also reflects the fact that no one is committed to rules and norms (from the last peace) to resolve disputes, but all are relying on measures of self-help—therefore indicating that violence is a legitimate and perhaps the only effective means for resolving the fundamental issues at hand.[17] Further, the bringing in of allies along with their particular issues makes it more difficult to reach any compromise; it prevents the war from being limited and encourages total war. The reason is that the war becomes an opportunity to resolve all major differences between all major parties. The increase in military expenditures and the competition for allies is also likely to make each side relatively equal; therefore, once it comes, the war is severe, long, and widespread.

One may conclude that the making of alliances has two different effects. First, it leads to a polarization, which is a step to war in that it produces behavior that increases the probability of war. Second, the increasing tightness of blocs indicates that each side is making last-minute preparations for war, which are usually successful, leading wars to be longer and probably of greater magnitude and severity.

Another area in which alliances are seen as having important consequences is the distribution of power, which has traditionally been seen as crucial for preserving peace. Although there has been little research on mapping the actual impact that alliances have on the distribution of power, a great deal of effort has been expended on examining the effect of the distribution of power on war. The thrust of this research, like other work on alliances, suggests that the distribution of power is unrelated to the preservation of peace, but associated with the types of war that are fought.

In the major study on this question, Singer, Bremer, and Stuckey (1972) uncover an important anomaly. They find that a balance-of-power system (parity) is associated with less war in the 19th century but with more war in the 20th, while a preponderance of power is associated with more war in the 19th and less war in the 20th. Because the dependent variable in this study is based on nation-months of war rather than on war/no war, the findings are relevant primarily for explaining the magnitude of war rather than its onset. In this sense, the finding does not mean that peace is associated in one century with a balance and in the next with a preponderance of power, as is sometimes implied; instead, preponderance of power is associated with one type of war in the 19th century, and balance of power with another type in the 20th. As I have shown in detail elsewhere, this interpretation best fits the evidence (Vasquez 1986). The wars of the 19th century after 1815 were simply different from the wars of the 20th. In the

---

[17] On the relationship between norms justifying violence and the use of force, see Gurr (1970:170); Maoz (1982:96, 98–100).

former, a preponderance of power was associated with the Crimean War and the state-building wars of Germany and Italy and, to a lesser extent, with imperial wars of conquest. All of these wars were limited in magnitude, severity, and duration, compared to the major wars of the 20th century, which were associated with a relative balance of power. This means that, although neither a balance of power nor a preponderance of power will prevent or give rise to a war, *if* a war occurs, the distribution of power will have a major (but probably not the only) influence on the kind of war that is fought. Evidence to support the first part of this conclusion is provided by Bueno de Mesquita (1981a): in a re-analysis of the Singer, Bremer, and Stuckey study, he employs war/no war as the dependent variable and finds no relationship between the distribution of capability and the onset of war in either century, thereby eliminating the anomaly.[18]

The finding that the major wars of the 20th century are associated with a relative balance of power is consistent with the hypothesis that, when war occurs between two sides that are relatively equal, war will be severe and long. But it is not clear that such wars need to be widespread and of high magnitude. Singer, Bremer, and Stuckey may have found the latter relationship because they do not attempt to separate the effects of capability from those of coalition-making. In view of the earlier findings on polarization, one might hypothesize that alliances are associated with the expansion and magnitude of war, while equal capability is associated with severity, with duration increasing when an increase in the tightness of blocs just prior to the war makes both sides equal and highly committed to their allies.

Any association between national capability and the severity and duration of a war will be affected by the objectives of the war and the extent to which one or both sides commit their resources; that is, whether participants see themselves as fighting a limited or a total war. Total wars will always be more severe than limited wars; but within this context, one may hypothesize that when two sides are relatively equal in capability, any given (limited *or* total) war will be longer and more severe for both sides than when the sides are not equal.

The fact that severe and long wars did not occur in the 19th century when there was a relative balance of power provides an opportunity for determining why and how such wars were avoided even though the capability for them existed. As we shall see, the reason this type of war did not occur in the 19th century may be that those periods of balance of power coincided with periods in which norms and rules were more widely accepted as constraints than they were in the 20th century. That would also explain why Bueno de Mesquita (1978:table 4) finds no relationship between change

---

[18] Likewise, Wayman et al. (1983:506, 509) show that, among major powers, the stronger are as likely as the comparatively weaker to initiate wars and disputes; compare Tables 3 and 5.

in tightness and war in the 19th century, but does find this relationship in the 20th.

Further and more recent evidence that the structural distribution of capability is associated with the type of war is provided by Jack Levy and by Frank Wayman. Levy's (1985a:50–59) analysis is useful primarily because it extends the purview of inquiry from two centuries to five. His major finding is that periods of bipolar distributions of power are more stable than multipolar periods. Bipolar periods have more frequent wars, but these are less severe and of lower magnitude than the wars of multipolar periods. That is the exact opposite of what had earlier been believed to be the case.

According to Levy, unipolar periods are very unstable; they have the wars of the highest magnitude and duration. Unipolar periods also have most of the general or hegemonic wars that involve the leading powers, while bipolar periods have none of these. Multipolar periods are associated with extremely severe wars. Since war occurs frequently in all periods, none can be credited with producing peace and avoiding war, but unipolar periods are by far the most war-prone.

While these findings are suggestive, the classification of periods as unipolar, bipolar, and multipolar is based on historical judgment rather than on precise and replicable measures.[19] That is not to say that the classifications are wrong or arbitrary—only that one must proceed cautiously until there is more evidence. In this context, Frank Wayman's (1984a) study proves to be very interesting.

Wayman's analysis is the most thorough to date employing measures of polarity based on both the distribution of power (power polarity) and the number of blocs (cluster polarity, or polarization). Utilizing a variation of Singer, Bremer, and Stuckey's capabilities index, Wayman (1984a:71–72) examines the percentage of system capabilities of the two most powerful states for each half-decade from 1815 to 1965. With a cut-off point of over 50 percent for bipolarity, he finds (like Levy [1985a], but contrary to Rosecrance [1966] and Michael Haas [1970]) that a bipolar distribution of capability has wars of a lower magnitude (fewer nation-months) than a multipolar distribution of capability, which is associated with the great world wars. Seventy-five percent of the *high*-magnitude wars occur in power multipolarity; 73 percent of the *low*-magnitude wars occur in power bipolarity.

This makes sense in that multiple nations will draw in more participants; and, if they are fairly equal in capability, their pooled resources

---

[19] For example, Wayman (1984) measures shifts in polarity within the 19th and 20th centuries, while Levy codes the entire 1815–1945 period as multipolar. Compare Levy (1985a:49, table 4.1), with Wayman (1984a, 69, table II). Nevertheless, Levy can make a plausible argument that the 1815–1945 period is relatively multipolar when compared to other periods between 1495 and 1975. Levy's classification of unipolar periods is more controversial: Michael Wallace (1985:108–9), in the same volume, takes sharp exception to it.

should make the war not only longer, but more severe. In this sense, one could expect the most disastrous wars to occur when a multipolar distribution of power produces a fairly equal distribution of capability between two polarized blocs. We know from the Singer, Bremer, and Stuckey study that relative equality of capability in the 20th century is associated with severe wars of great magnitude. Now Wayman (1984a:73) shows that in the 20th century, alliance patterns prior to wars were also becoming more (bi)polarized; he thereby adds an important piece to help solve this puzzle. He finds that an increase in polarization among major powers in the 20th century is associated with an increase in the subsequent magnitude of war ($r = -.48$ between many blocs and nation-months of war). This is compatible with and extends Bueno de Mesquita's (1978) finding that increasing systemic tightness in the 20th century is associated with the duration of war.

A close inspection of Wayman's (1984a:69, table II) data shows how this occurs. He measures cluster polarity by the ratio of actual poles to potential poles among major powers; his scale ranges from 1.00 for no blocs or complete depolarization and the absence of major power alliances to scores that would approach 0.00 when there is cluster bipolarity or complete polarization. Beginning in 1870 (which has no blocs; score of 1.00), the system gradually develops more alliances until it is polarized at .50 in 1905, where it remains until the end of World War I. The system then experiences a rapid disintegration of blocs (score of .80 for 1920, 1.00 from 1925 to 1935); they build up against just before the war (with a score of .86 in 1938) and disintegrate at the end of the war (score of 1.00). Although there is a movement toward polarization just before World War I and World War II (as well as the Korean War), the score of .86 for 1938 is too high.

In part, this score reflects Hitler's initial success in neutralizing the Soviet Union and then avoiding war with the United States. This success fell apart in 1941, when Hitler and Japan polarized the system by attacking the U.S.S.R. and the U.S., respectively. These two expansions of the war account for much of its magnitude, severity, and duration. By examining the alliance structure between 1939 and 1942, then, the evidence becomes more consistent with that for World War I.

In terms of the previous analyses we can now hypothesize as follows: an increase in polarization as measured by tightness is associated with an increase in the duration of wars (Bueno de Mesquita (1978); and a multipolar distribution of power is associated with wars of greater magnitude (Wayman 1984a). If that distribution is polarized into two blocs, as was the case in World Wars I and II (Wayman 1984a), and there is a relative equality of power between the belligerents (Singer, Bremer, and Stuckey 1972), the war will also be severe. All other factors being equal, we can conclude that increasing polarization of blocs makes for longer wars, multipolar distribution of power makes for wars of a greater magnitude, and equal capability between blocs increases the severity of wars. Because alliance-making can affect each of these variables, it has the peculiar consequence of bringing all of these factors together in their most disastrous and explosive combination, so that a war that occurs in this context is most likely to become a general war, eventually encompassing all leading states. We know from Sabrosky (1985:181) that the situation that is most likely to trigger such a general war is a war between a major power and a minor power, in which another major power intervenes to come to the aid of the minor power.[20]

Differences Between the 19th and the 20th Century: Alliances and Arms Races

One reason why Correlates of War findings differ for the 19th and 20th centuries is that in the 19th century after 1815, there are no general wars. It may be that these general wars are absent in the so-called 100 years of peace (1815–1913) because alliance-making did not produce the explosive mixture of polarization of blocs, multipolar distribution of power, and equal distribution of power between blocs. This absence may help to explain why the 19th-century wars between major powers—the Crimean, Seven Weeks', and Franco-Prussian wars—were comparatively limited. In addition, general wars may have been avoided because 19th-century alliances, unlike those of the 20th century, did not fuel arms races. Michael Wallace (1985), trying to account for his previous research, which found a strong relationship between polarization and the magnitude and severity of war in the 20th century but only a weak relationship in the 19th, notes that after 1903, major power alliances that were aimed at another major power always produced a sharp increase in the rate of growth of the target's military expenditures. Prior to 1903, this effect did not occur; Wallace (1985:110–11) speculates that, in the 20th century, alliances were formed to build winning coalitions, whereas in the 19th century they were equilibrium mechanisms in the classic balance-of-power fashion.[21]

---

[20] Further evidence of the importance of minor powers in the occurrence of world wars is provided by Manus Midlarsky (1984, 1986b), who is outside the project. He finds that such systemic wars occur when serious disputes in the system begin to accumulate and are no longer stable (i.e., they are no longer randomly distributed in the sense that there is a balance in the number of disputes that are begun and ended in a given period). He finds that if only the disputes between major powers are examined, the periods prior to the two World Wars, 1893–1914 and 1919–1939, are stable. However, if the disputes involving "mid-range powers" (like Serbia, Rumania, or Belgium) are included, the system becomes very unstable.

[21] In my view, it is not the balance-of-power aspect that is the significant difference: in the 19th century, alliances more frequently aimed to prevent war by coming to an understanding about how to deal with major issues; failing that, they aimed to keep any war that did occur limited. Bismarck was particularly adept at using alliances in this manner. After his departure, the approach of Kaiser Wilhelm II made alliances more threatening and therefore more likely to give rise to counter-alliances and arms races. The notion that a balance of power in and of itself

The kinds of alliances that are formed will make a big difference in whether wars will be limited or become general wars. For research to progress, there is a need to create more theoretical typologies of alliances. Despite the variety of purposes served by alliances in different historical contexts, the critical distinction in terms of a comparative analysis of the causes of war seems to be whether an alliance was aimed at forming a winning coalition.

The immediate effect of alliances that seek to form a winning coalition is to intensify military expenditures and to embroil actors in arms races. It is through the creation of these arms races that alliances are linked to the onset of war. Direct evidence to support this argument comes from an early path analysis of Wallace's (1972:64) in which he finds that alliance aggregation in the system leads to arms expenditures, but not the reverse: arms expenditures do not lead to alliances. He maintains that major power alliances after 1903 *always* led those who were targeted by the alliance to increase the rate of growth of their armed forces; in turn, this *always* produced a counter-response which led to an arms race (Wallace 1985:110–11). This suggests that alliances that do not produce arms races will not lead to war, explaining why Levy (1981) and Wayman (1984a) find that, while many alliances are associated with war, not *all* are, and especially not those in the 19th century. Wallace's (1985) research also suggests part of what might be going on during the typical three-year (or so) time lag between the formation of alliances and the onset of war.

This raises the question why some alliances do not lead to arms races. The answer may lie with the level of hostility between rivals preceding and following the formation of an alliance. Alliances that attempt to build a winning coalition are born in a hostile environment and pose a new threat that increases the level of hostility and the sense of insecurity. Alliances that do not seek a winning coalition pose less of a threat, and thus do not add to existing hostility. Alliances and arms races may thus be critical intervening variables that increase the level of hostility until it is sufficient to generate the kinds of disputes that escalate to war. On the basis of this analysis, we can hypothesize that hostility is produced by dramatic changes in relations between actors, and that the presence of hostility produces a step-level effect in subsequent behavior, making states more sensitive to negative acts and leading them to discount positive ones.[22] If this hypothesis were confirmed, it would identify the operating force that gets actors from one step to war to the next: it shows that the taking of one step, instead of reducing threat, leads to a permanent increase in hostility, which leads to the taking

---

can prevent war appears to be incorrect; see Levy (1981:608, esp. n. 19) and Vasquez (1986). On the differences in alliances in different centuries, see Levy (1981:604–7).

[22] Testing a complex interaction model originally offered by Mansbach and Vasquez (1981): Wayman (1984b:180–82) finds considerable support for this hypothesis explaining up to 88% of the variance.

of more threatening steps by the other side, which in turn are matched by the first. Such a hypothesis helps to explain how alliances lead to arms races and underlines the fact that alliances, like most practices associated with war, are important as part of a dynamic reciprocal process.

Responding to Security Issues: Arms Races

Most of the threads of an explanation of why arms races begin have long been part of the literature (see Richardson 1960a; Singer 1958, 1970c, 1984:ch. 7). There is a consensus that arms races presuppose rivalry, at least at some level, and intensify that rivalry once they are under way. In terms of the steps outlined here, the key motivation for arms races is the insecurity resulting from perceived threat and hostility. This general insecurity, which is awakened whenever a situation occurs that might portend force, becomes a specific fear whenever a rival state is perceived as having a larger military capacity, as building arms, or as increasing its capability by making an alliance (see Singer 1958:33–34).

While such factors may lead decision makers to seek a military build-up, decision makers are unlikely to get domestic support without some concrete manifestation of the threat posed by the rival. This usually comes in the form of an international crisis although the formation of an alliance itself can so alarm leaders that it may be seen (by them and the public) as a crisis. One can hypothesize that the greater the number of crises between two rivals, the harder it is to avoid an arms race.

In order to generate the necessary domestic mobilization for arms races, such as increased taxes, a shift in resources and spending, and the adoption of some form of conscription, leaders often exaggerate the external threat (Singer 1958:36–37; 1970a [1979:73]; Lowi 1967:320–23; Wayman et al. 1983:498). In turn, this increases the fear in the other side, extends the influence of hard-liners in both camps, and helps to produce an arms-race spiral.[23]

In such an atmosphere, war is likely but not inevitable. The trigger that is needed to explode the various elements that have been put in place is an international crisis, and the mere presence of an ongoing arms race makes it more probable that such a crisis is the kind that will escalate to war. The first systematic evidence that arms races are, in themselves, a major factor in the onset of war was published by Michael Wallace (1979). He examines 99 serious disputes between 1816 and 1965, which he divides into those that

---

[23] For Singer's views on the role of the military and other bureaucratic and domestic groups in sustaining arms races, see Singer (1970a [1979:77–78]; 1970c [1979:151–52]; 1984:259–60; 1985:247–48, 254, 257–59).

escalated to war and those that did not. He then asks whether the presence of an ongoing arms race is what distinguishes the relatively few serious disputes that escalate from the many that do not. Of the 28 serious disputes that occurred in the presence of an ongoing arms race, 23 escalated to war; of the 71 serious disputes that occurred where there was no arms race, only 3 escalated to war. This is impressive evidence that arms races are a crucial factor in determining whether serious disputes will escalate to war; it is confirmed by Yule's Q of .96.[24]

A challenge to these findings comes from the "peace-through-strength" counter-hypothesis, which maintains that it is not the *presence* of arms race but who *is winning* the arms race that is the key factor. If this logic were coupled with Organski's (1958:325–33) distinction between satisfied and dissatisfied states (or revisionist and status quo actors), then it could be expected that serious disputes would be likely to escalate to war only if revisionist states were winning the arms race. Wallace (1982) examines this claim by comparing the relative adequacy of this "peace-through-strength" approach with his own and Singer's (1958) "armament-tension spiral" approach; he produces several interesting results.

In a number of tests, Wallace (1982:41–44) finds no statistically significant relationship (and hardly any strength of association) between whether arms races favor (or are won by) revisionist actors and whether serious disputes escalate. It can be concluded that spending more on arms than one's rival is not related to the escalation of serious disputes—which

---

[24] Erich Weede (1980:285–87) has criticized Wallace for treating *each* arms race and serious dispute as a dyadic case rather than counting all disputes and wars involving the same set of participants as a single case, regardless of the number of dyads. This is particularly important for World War I and World War II, both of which Wallace treats as several discrete cases. Wallace has re-analyzed the data and eliminated all cases in which two or more allies simultaneously entered the war against a common foe, thereby reducing the 28 cases of serious disputes having arms races to 15. Nevertheless, the relationship still holds; 11 of the 15 serious disputes escalate to war while only 4 do not. Conversely, only 2 of the 65 serious disputes escalate when there is no ongoing arms race (see Wallace 1982:46).

Paul F. Diehl (1983:205–12) manages to eliminate most of the relationship Wallace establishes; but to do so, he must remove 17 cases from the sample. Ten cases are eliminated because they are connected with ongoing wars and 7 more are deleted because they are connected with the First and Second World Wars (Diehl 1983:210). In addition, some new cases are added and changes are made in the arms-race index. These manipulations are too extensive to support a conclusion that arms races are unrelated to the escalation of serious disputes. Diehl's (1983) main contribution is to suggest that much of Wallace's finding depends on the presence of ongoing wars and on World War I and World War II. (On the latter, see Houweling and Siccama [1981:161, n. 13].) This suggests that, while arms races may escalate disputes between rivals (relative equals), they may not be a factor in other types of wars. This hypothesis would also help to account for Diehl's (1983:209) finding that 77% of the wars that occur are not preceded by an arms race, since many of these wars are wars between unequals. Finally, the connection between arms races, escalation of disputes, and ongoing wars may provide a clue about how wars spread to become world wars. The presence of a series of disputes that might escalate to war may encourage others to arm because of the threatening environment, and thereby encourage war, when it comes, to enlarge.

means that strength of arms neither prevents war nor leads to war. Wallace (1982:47–51) goes on to demonstrate that the peace-through-strength hypothesis has nowhere near the accuracy of the armament-tension spiral hypothesis by showing that, whether a revisionist state is "superior" or "weaker," arms races still lead to escalation. Of the 10 serious disputes that occur when there is an ongoing arms race while the revisionist state is "superior," 8 escalate and 2 do not. Conversely, of the 18 disputes that occur when there is *no* arms race and the revisionist state is "superior," only one dispute escalates, and 17 do not. The cases involving "weaker" revisionist states exhibit the same pattern. In the 18 disputes that occur when there is an ongoing arms race while the revisionist state is "weaker," 15 escalate to war and only three do not. Conversely, of the 53 disputes that occur when there is *no* arms race and the revisionist state is "weaker," only 2 escalate, and 51 do not. In light of such consistent findings, it must be concluded that arms races or military build-ups do in fact, by their mere presence, make it more likely that a serious dispute will escalate to war.[25]

These findings imply that, in the absence of serious disputes, war can still be avoided during an arms race. Although this inference is plausible, there has been no test of whether this factor distinguishes arms races that lead to war from those that do not.[26] It is more difficult to discern whether arms races encourage actors to become involved in the kinds of serious disputes that are apt to escalate. The mere *presence* of arms races may not be what leads disputes to escalate; it may just be that arms races introduce greater insecurity and hostility in political relationships and therefore make it likely that actors will become involved in the *kinds* of serious disputes that

---

[25] Also relevant to evaluating the peace-through-strength argument are two studies by Stuart Bremer (1980a, 1980b), which show that stronger nations tend to be involved in wars more often. In a related study, Wolf-Dieter Eberwein (1982) finds that the more powerful a nation, the more likely it is to initiate or join a(n ongoing) serious dispute.

Paul Diehl (1985a:343) also finds the peace-through-strength hypothesis deficient. Although Diehl questions the importance of arms races, *per se*, in the escalation of disputes, he does show that both arms races and military build-ups can be critical *indirect* factors in the escalation of disputes between states that have become rivals (i.e., have already experienced two disputes). His reservations about Wallace's finding on arms races, however, stem primarily from the fact that he has removed a number of cases associated with the two World Wars and has included 42 (out of 104) cases involving rivalries where at least one party has nuclear capacity (Diehl 1983:table 1, p. 335). Among the latter are a large number of cases that have not resulted in the escalation of disputes to war; this should not be interpreted as undercutting Wallace's (1982) finding, which is primarily a product of the prenuclear era. On the whole, the Correlates of War project has not treated the post-1945 period in a way that permits an assessment of the impact of nuclear weapons; for an initial attempt by someone outside the project, see Altfeld (1985).

[26] See Singer (1970c:147–53). What is known is that many wars grow out of serious disputes and that it is difficult to avoid war when there is a pattern of repeated military confrontations. Peter Wallensteen (1981:74–75, 84), in a study of major power pairs, found that 75% (12 of 16) of the pairs of nations that had repeated confrontations also experienced war. See also Houweling and Siccama (1981:157–97).

are likely to escalate. The research on crisis escalation has identified a number of characteristics besides arms racing which distinguish serious disputes that escalate to war from those that do not.

Crisis Escalation

While arms races could be regarded as a critical background factor, most of the other characteristics related to crisis escalation are internal to the crisis itself. One set of factors that has received a great deal of attention consists of the bargaining tactics and strategy employed by the participants, especially the initiators. Another set is the perceptual response on leaders to the tactics employed, especially the effect of these perceptions on hostility. A third set consists of the personal characteristics of leaders and the domestic political context in which they operate. Finally, the characteristics of the issues at stake in the dispute and the overall foreign policy of the actor that provoked the crisis in the first place must be considered.

Within the Correlates of War project, the work of Russell Leng has been devoted to analyzing the role of bargaining in the escalation of serious disputes. In a series of studies, which usually employ a small random or representative sample, he has uncovered a number of suggestive findings. At the most basic level, Leng and Wheeler (1979) found that a bullying strategy is usually associated with disputes escalating to war, and that a reciprocating strategy provides the best overall outcome while avoiding war (see also Leng with Goodsell 1974). More significantly, in a later study on realpolitik tactics he finds that threats—especially negative inducements that are highly credible—are apt to produce extreme responses, either outright compliance or defiance (in terms of counterthreats or punishments). Defiant responses, however, are most likely to occur when the disputants are relatively equal in capability. There is also some indirect evidence that defiant responses are associated with war. These results suggest that, while decision makers may behave in crises in ways that conform to the description of realists like Morgenthau (1960) and conflict strategists like Schelling (1960), this behavior often leads (among equals) to war, rather than to diplomatic success (Leng 1980).[27]

Apparently, the key to understanding how realpolitik tactics lead to the escalation of disputes lies in the way in which leaders change their behavior toward a rival from one dispute to the next. In a review of six pairs of evenly matched states that were involved in three successive disputes, Leng uncovers a definite learning pattern. He finds that the loser of the previous dispute attributes the loss to a failure to demonstrate sufficient resolve (i.e., com-

---

[27] For an attempt to create a model that predicts which disputes will escalate on the basis of interstate interactions, see Maoz (1984).

mitment to force), and is likely to initiate the second dispute. As a result, both participants tend to escalate the level of coercion in each successive crisis (a finding that holds true for 17 of 24 cases), with war becoming increasingly likely by the third dispute, if it has not occurred earlier. This suggests that, as the underlying issue fails to be resolved, bargaining techniques in successive disputes will become more coercive and more likely to escalate (Leng 1983:398–99; 1984).

Charles Gochman and Russell Leng (1983) find that disputes between equals that pose a physical threat to vital issues are more apt to escalate than disputes involving other issues or triggered by other events (see also James and Wilkenfeld 1984). They define vital issues as involving questions of political independence or control of one's own or contiguous territory.[28] It might be hypothesized that because such issues are difficult to resolve, actors employ increasingly coercive tactics to get the other side to give in. Among equals, these tactics meet with defiant responses and lead to successive crises. By the third crisis, if not before, all the characteristics associated with escalation (initiation by physical threat, vital issues, previous learning, and more coercive tactics) are in place, and war breaks out. In addition, the presence of arms races probably increases the likelihood that disputes with these explosive characteristics will emerge.

It is encouraging to note that Leng's findings are compatible with the earlier findings of Richard Barringer (1972:102–12), who is outside the project. Barringer employs a cluster analysis of 300 characteristics of 18 disputes. He finds that one of the main distinctions between non-military and military disputes is the way the issues at stake are perceived. Barringer also suggests that domestic mobilization is associated with the militarization of disputes. He finds that both sides tend to equalize their military manpower just prior to the war, whereas they had earlier been unequal.[29] Often any shift in the military balance is seized upon to gain an immediate advantage. Attitudes among the public of each side are more supportive of hostilities, and ideological differences which had been previously mild are now extreme. Finally, Barringer finds that military hostilities tend to erupt after a crisis and a change in the leadership of one side.

Barringer's (1972) analysis suggest that, to get a sense of why leaders take the actions they do, a complete understanding of escalation must go beyond the bargaining factors that arise within a crisis and examine the nature of the leadership (and the domestic political context within which it oper-

---

[28] It is probably the territorial aspect of issues that is particularly explosive. See Most and Starr (1980); Singer (1982:40; and Diehl (1985b). However, it seems that issues that involve several parties are also explosive, since an intervention by a third party into an ongoing dyadic dispute will increase the likelihood of escalation to war. See Cusack and Eberwein (1982).

[29] Singer (1982:40) hypothesizes that the more equal the protagonists are militarily, the more likely an escalation to war.

ates).[30] Singer recognized long ago that there is an interaction between the international and domestic political contexts that encourages leaders to take escalatory actions and makes it difficult to initiate conciliatory moves within a dispute. Domestically, in the attempt to mobilize the public and gain support for military expenditures, leaders paint a picture of a hostile enemy and create a climate that is responsive to hard-line and jingoistic appeals. This tendency is reinforced by traditional realist notions that one must show firmness (and resolve) in the struggle for power. Both domestic and global factors interact to produce self-aggravating propensities that increase hostility and make compromise more difficult (Singer 1970a:72–78; 1982:40).

Such factors affect decision makers' perceptions, encouraging both sides to develop not only mirror-images, but a shared intellectual context that sees power politics as a legitimate and useful means for dealing with the adversary (Vasquez 1987). In this climate it is not surprising that perceived hostility is correlated with violent behavior, and that crisis interactions generate a hostile interaction spiral in which each side overreacts to the other while thinking its own policy is less hostile than that of the other (Holsti, North, and Brody 1968:146, 148, 152–57). The development of a hostile spiral is the final step to war. If the spiraling effect can be avoided through diplomatic skill and bold leadership, the crisis can be successfully managed and war averted.[31] This is difficult, however, because of the weight of all the previous decisions (steps) that have been taken and have brought the parties to where they now stand.

This suggests that, while the decisions taken in crises are crucial, they are not the fundamental causes of war. Psychological stress, selective inattention, and poor decision making may make it hard to avoid war at the last minute; but, even if a particular crisis is successfully managed, another will inevitably come along (and will be more intense and more difficult to manage) if there is no fundamental change in policy (goals and means). It is not the dynamics of decision making that produce war, but a set of foreign policy goals and a sequence of practices which create a political relationship and an atmosphere that is apt to result in war given the right set of triggers.

Conclusion: Conditions of Peace

Although much of the research supports realist descriptions of what actors are likely to do when faced with threats, the adoption of common realist

---

[30] Little quantitative work has been conducted on the effect of the domestic political context, and especially the role of hard-liners, on the decision of leaders to go to war or use force. For a set of hypotheses that seek to identify general patterns, see Vasquez (1987).

[31] For an attempt to model different hostile spirals so as to distinguish those that will escalate to war from those that will not, see Zinnes and Muncaster (1984).

practices, such as alliance-making, military build-ups, balancing of power, and realpolitik tactics, does not produce peace, but leads to war.[32] Elsewhere (Vasquez 1983:215–23) I have argued that power politics is not so much an explanation of behavior as it is a type of behavior found in the global political system that must itself be explained. A more comprehensive nonrealist analysis would explain when decision makers exhibit power-politics behavior and when they do not, and how a system that is dominated by power-politics images and behavior could be transformed into one that is not. Only the hints of broader nonrealist analysis that draws on the insight of social psychology are present in the work of the Correlates of War project, and these are mainly, though not exclusively, in the more policy-oriented analyses of Singer (1979:ch. 2, 4, 6, 7, 15, and Singer 1984, epilogue).

Throughout Singer's work one finds a steadfast commitment to develop a scientific analysis of war that is motivated by a normative concern for building a more peaceful world. This concern is reflected not only in his policy essays, but also in his efforts to encourage other scholars to develop policy-relevant, quantitative indicators that can be used to improve understanding and to provide warnings of harmful trends (see Singer 1984:299; Singer and Wallace 1979; Singer and Stoll 1984). Eschewing conspiratorial or highly rational explanations of elite behavior, Singer has long maintained that most foreign policy decisions are made in ignorance, and that even modest improvements in the scientific cumulation of knowledge can be policy-relevant (see Singer 1979:131–32; Singer and Small 1974 [1979:328–29]).

The idea that the correlates of war can be explained as a series of steps certainly fulfills this expectation and belies the early criticism that quantitative analysis could succeed in discovering only the obvious and the trivial. Although the steps to war must be seen as a working outline of a scientific explanation of war that needs to be further tested, refined, and fitted to specific historical cases, its propositions provide the kind of precision and nonobvious findings that make scholarly work policy-relevant. The findings of the Correlates of War project suggest that the implementation of common realist practices against equals produces neither peace nor victory (as realists imply by their prescriptions), but increased insecurity, coercion, and entanglement in a process that may lead to war. Each step leads decision makers further and further into a trap (both globally and domestically) where they have little choice but to fight. The relevancy of delineating these steps is that it highlights what must be done to avoid the next step, and

---

[32] Singer would probably find this statement too strong; but see Singer (1982:42–43). It should also be kept in mind that this statement does not mean that those who have advocated such realist practices are necessarily in favor of war. No one familiar with the political life of Hans Morgenthau or Reinhold Niebuhr would make such an assertion.

warns leaders of the negative and unanticipated consequences of taking the steps. Although a discussion of the policy implications of each step would take a separate paper of its own, suffice it to say that, in the early 20th century, decision makers did not understand, nor really anticipate, how alliance formation could lead to world war. The findings suggest that alliances formed in response to threats can lead to polarization. If complete enough, and in a world where power is equally distributed around more than two poles, such polarization can produce world wars. If the initial step had not been taken, the issues might have been resolved dyadically through limited war.

In this way the findings suggest how war might be mitigated and controlled. Can it ever be avoided, or is humankind condemned, as realists would have us believe, to a history of war and a struggle for power? Although the project has not been directly concerned with the correlates of *peace,* there are some interesting findings that suggest that the frequency of war varies in different periods and systems; there are cases where actors do not always exhibit the kind of power-politics behavior involved in the steps to war.

Peter Wallensteen (1984:246, table 2) marshals evidence to show that when major powers make concerted efforts to work out a set of rules to guide their relations (what he calls "universalist policies"), no wars among major powers are fought, military confrontations are drastically reduced, and even wars and confrontations between major and minor powers are somewhat attenuated. Conversely, when major powers do not (or are unable to) make an effort to create an order based on acceptable rules, but fall back on "particularist policies" based on unilateral actions, wars break out among them, and confrontations increase two-fold. A full understanding of the conditions of peace requires discovering the factors that encourage states (and other political actors) to create rules.

In a series of articles, Charles Kegley and Gregory Raymond have provided evidence that when states accept norms, the incidence of war is reduced. They find that, when global cultural norms consider alliance commitments binding and regard the unilateral abrogation of commitments and treaties as illegitimate, then war (particularly in the major power system) is less frequent and of less severity, magnitude, and intensity.[33] A similar relationship is found when all serious disputes are examined (Kegley and Raymond 1984). While alliance norms may be important, it is unlikely that, in and of themselves, they would have such an impact on the onset of war; rather, the presence of such norms is an

---

[33] Specifically, they find that war occurs in every half-decade (from 1820–1914) among great powers when commitments are not considered binding (*clausa rebus sic stantibus*) in the international legal culture, but only in 50% of the half-decades when they are considered binding (*pacta sunt servanda*). See Kegley and Raymond (1982:586).

indicator of broader consensus (on rules of the game) that prevents unilateral actions.[34]

Since war and force can be regarded as a way of making political decisions under conditions of anarchy, the creation of a system of rules by which to make political decisions can serve as the functional equivalent of war. It does this when rules provide for an allocation mechanism[35] other than force for resolving issues, and actors accept the outcomes of using those mechanisms, even if it means they will lose a particular contest. This acceptance, in turn, is probably a function of their ability to avoid raising fundamental issues that are questions of life and death.

If we assume that war avoidance at the domestic, regional, or global level involves the creation of a political system or regime capable of making decisions, then how long the peaces that end major wars will last depends upon their success in creating an order that institutionalizes procedures for the resolution of political demands. How successful a peace will be depends on its ability to set the agenda so that certain issues are avoided, and to assimilate new and/or recovered major powers (Doran 1971) so that they do not take actions outside the system.[36]

Such an explanation will need to be more fully elaborated and tested; it is consistent, however, with the early finding by Singer and Wallace (1970) that war produces an increase in the number of intergovernmental organizations. It is also consistent with Wallace's (1972:65–66) intriguing finding that the absence of status inconsistency in the system is associated with formation of (and presumably the effectiveness of) intergovernmental organizations. Formation of intergovernmental organizations, in turn, is negatively associated with arms build-ups (which have a strong correlation with the onset of war).[37] All this suggests not only that power-politics

---

[34] Because serious disputes (including wars) also decrease when there is a moderate degree of alliance flexibility (as opposed to rigid, polarized, or extremely fluid alliance structure), these findings (fn. 110, esp. p. 210) can also be explained by a deterrence logic. The deterrence explanation seems less compelling than the one offered here because the explanation that the creation of a consensus on the rules of the game is an independent factor producing peace is consistent not only with the evidence presented by Kegley and Raymond, but also with the other evidence presented in this section. In addition, Kegley and Raymond (1986:217–24) use the notion of rules to account in detail for actual historical practices.

[35] An allocation mechanism is a set of rules and procedures, no matter how informal, for making and implementing political decisions, thereby providing a way for the disposition of stakes, see Mansbach and Vasquez (1981: 282–87).

[36] A stable peace also reduces the number of major-minor wars and confrontations (see Wallensteen [1984:246]); but such a peace does not imply justice, since it may be used by major states to divide or control minor states or other territories, as was done in the 19th century.

[37] Skjelsbaek's (1971) finding that shared membership in intergovernmental organizations decreases prior to the outbreak of war is consistent with Wallace's (1972) findings. So, too, is the elaboration and re-test of the Singer and Wallace (1970) study by Faber and Weaver

behavior has been avoided at certain times of global history, but also that, when actors have taken a more Grotian approach, they have succeeded in avoiding war among themselves.

Through the careful collection of scientific data and the systematic analysis of wars since 1815, the Correlates of War project has provided a body of findings that are beginning to cumulate into a number of insights. These suggest what factors are, and are not, associated with war, what factors are associated with the severity, magnitude, and duration of war, and what actions may have produced past periods of peace. Much remains to be done, but it is heartening, as Singer (1981:14) states, that after literally centuries of inconclusive theorizing and philosophizing on the causes of war, real progress in our knowledge is beginning to be made.

Editors' Commentary

Major Findings

By reviewing and comparing the various findings associated with the Correlates of War project, Vasquez attempts to come up with a description of some of the major patterns that precede certain types of war. He finds that wars between major states tend to be preceded by the making of alliances, military buildups, the use of realpolitik bargaining that becomes increasingly coercive, and a series of crises, one of which eventually erupts into war. Crises that escalate to war also have discernible characteristics. Escalation is associated with physical attacks, disputes involving territorial contiguity, the second or third crisis with the same rival, a hostile interaction spiral, and hard liners in the leadership of at least one side.

To this empirical description Vasquez adds a theoretical analysis that suggests that war breaks out by rivals taking one action (like the making of an alliance), which increases the probability that it will take another action (like involvement in a crisis or a military buildup) that moves each party closer to war. The analysis implies that most practices associated with war, such as alliances, are part of a dynamic reciprocal process that increases hostility and brings about a situation in which it becomes more and more difficult for decision makers not to opt for war. For

---

(1984), which provides evidence for the notion that the presence of effective rules of the game reduces the need to go to war. For an interpretation of Wallace's (1972) findings along these lines, see Mansbach and Vasquez (1981:304–13). This evidence is also consistent with much of what Gilpin (1981) has to say about the outcome of hegemonic struggles.

Vasquez, the practices of power politics do not lead to peace but increase the likelihood of war.

In a later book, Vasquez (forthcoming) extends his analysis to findings outside the Correlates of War project and develops a more comprehensive framework that examines not only how interstate interactions lead to war but also the role of domestic politics and the global institutional context in the onset of war and the conditions associated with the expansion of war to world war.

Methodological Notes

Vasquez's article is an exercise in inductive scientific theory construction. What makes it inductive is that he looks at the findings that exist and then attempts to explain them. Once such an explanation exists, it does not constitute knowledge in the scientific sense—it has yet to be tested. The research agenda suggested by this work is to derive propositions from the explanation and then test them, a design that would be deductive. What makes this effort scientific is that the author is concerned at every turn that what he proposes in the way of explanation involves generalizable propositions composed of concepts that are operationalizable. He strives to propose explanations that are testable (falsifiable), nonobvious, and nontautological.

The need to construct a generalizable explanation has led Vasquez to identify different types of war, each having its own set of factors associated with it. It has certainly become clear that most scholars who study war do not try to look at all kinds of wars simultaneously. Notice that none of the articles in this book treats civil wars or revolutions. Many articles look only at wars involving major states. Elsewhere Vasquez (forthcoming) argues that in order to make progress in understanding war, we need to distinguish wars between equals from wars between unequals. Wars between two equal sides he calls wars of rivalry, and it is these wars that he has tried to explain in "The Steps to War."

Appendix
Applying the Scientific Method to the Study of War

15
The Scientific Study of War: A Learning Package

Stuart A. Bremer
Cynthia Cannizzo
Charles W. Kegley, Jr.
James Lee Ray
(adapted by *Marie T. Henehan*)

This learning package is designed to introduce students to the scientific study of war. We have two goals in this regard: (1) to teach the student some basic principles of the scientific method and (2) to teach the student the application of these principles to the study of war. To accomplish this dual aim, the package is structured in four major sections.

The first section, Introduction to the Scientific Study of War, was primarily authored by Charles Kegley and serves as an introduction to major quantitative research projects on war. This gives the students a feel for the rationale, history, and orientation of such studies, as well as serving as the literature review with which normal scholarly papers begin. Part II, What Is a War? was primarily authored by James Ray and introduces students to the problems and procedures of variable definition and operationalization, data coding and collection—the next steps in conducting research after statement of the problem and literature review. In part III, Data Analysis, primarily authored by Stuart Bremer and Cynthia Cannizzo, the learning package proceeds with the next stages of a basically inductive research design: description and presentation of data, plus a discussion of inductive versus deductive strategies. Using the information gained on national war involvement from the description-presentation phase, the student is introduced to hypothesis formulation. Taking a simple hypothesis on the relationship between the number of years a nation-state has existed and the number of

Editors' note: A discussion of the limits of Yule's Q and exercises 15–11 and 15–15 have been added.

interstate war involvements, the learning package teaches students the technique of cross-tabulation and the computation of Yule's Q. Part IV, also authored by Stuart Bremer and Cynthia Cannizzo, presents an important design refinement, cross-national versus longitudinal research. In addition, this section contains an exercise that necessitates the student's performing an analysis more or less on his or her own, starting with literature survey, proceeding through variable definition/operationalization, data coding, description, analysis, and finally interpretation. Thus, by using data on national war involvement, we present in a logical, scientific manner both the basics of inductive research and the manner in which such techniques have been and can be used to study the causes of war.

We have tried to make this package as self-contained as possible, especially with regard to the learning of concepts and techniques. To further that end, the answers to short-answer exercises are given in appendix D. Realizing, however, that scientific study is not a solo flight, several of the exercises are designed to be done by the student on his or her own and then discussed in the classroom. Such exercises as 15–1, 15–2, 15–3, 15–5, 15–8, 15–9, 15–12, 15–13, 15–14, and 15–15 ask students to compare their work and explore the implications and interpretations of their results. Although some students will be able to do the entire package completely alone, we feel that the exchange of ideas and information in a small group setting greatly enhances the acquisition of knowledge.

I. Introduction to the Scientific Study of War

War between groups of people has been a recurrent phenomenon throughout recorded history. The danger that war poses to humanity today is dramatically expressed by one scholar:

> Partly as a consequence of . . . technological developments, and partly as an independent result of political change, the number of deaths from war has increased.
>
> . . . Less than 2 million people died in wars between 1820 and 1863. From 1964 to 1907 about 4.5 million died in wars, and over 40 million in the final period. Very roughly this is equivalent to a tenfold increase ever 50 years. . . . If this growth rate of tenfold about every 50 years were to continue, wars by around the end of this century would kill the equivalent of the present population of the globe. (Russett 1965: 12–13)

Traditional and Scientific Approaches to the Study of War

The pernicious consequences of war have led modern scholars and statesmen alike to attempt to understand the sources of violent behavior and thereby obtain the knowledge necessary to control it. Most of the effort thus far has taken the traditional approach to the study of war (i.e., speculation and detailed study of particular wars). As a result, the heritage of impressionistic and propagandist investigation of war has produced a large number of intuitively pleasing, equally plausible, but often contradictory hypotheses about the determinants of international war.

The lack of scientific studies prevents the attainment of confirmed knowledge, based on evidence, about the origins of war among nations. Most information about war only relates what happened at a particular time, in a particular place, and under particular circumstances; such information is practically useless in anticipating the outbreak and devising strategies for preventing future wars. For that goal, what is needed is a general theory of war containing an interrelated set of generalizations which specify the causal connections between the factors which are related to the initiation of war. The occurrence of war, therefore, will not be controllable until a large number of wars are compared in order to understand what they share in common, in order to ascertain what behavioral changes will make war less likely. In order to do this, generalizations are needed which describe what is patterned (i.e., regular and characteristic) about wars. Such a strategy cannot guarantee that humanity will eventually be able to control war, only that the possibility of such control is increased by using scientific methods to understand the causes of war.

Dissatisfied with the state of knowledge about war and its determinants, a number of researchers began to inquire if the methods of science might be applicable to the study of war and prove more successful in increasing our understanding of the ways that form of behavior might be controlled. After all, it was reasoned, science is first and foremost a generalizing activity, and a scientific analysis of the determinants of war offered the prospect, in principle, of discovering the conditional uniformities most commonly associated with it. Historical records of past wars, it was further contended, could serve as a data source, and these data of past wars could be quantitatively analyzed through statistical procedures in order to ascertain which generalizations about the determinants of war make the most sense, on the basis of the accumulated scientific evidence.

Three monumental research projects dedicated to the proposition that war can be meaningfully studied in a scientific fashion pioneered this endeavor.[1] These are:

1. Quincy Wright, A Study of War (Chicago: University of Chicago Press, 1942).

---

[1] Actually, efforts to use sophisticated scientific techniques to study war have a long and reputable history. A significant example of such work on the frontiers of knowledge which paved the way for subsequent projects was Sorokin (1937), but space precludes a description here.

2. Lewis Fry Richardson, *Arms and Insecurity* (Chicago: Quadrangle Press, 1960) and *Statistics of Deadly Quarrels* (Chicago: Quadrangle Press, 1960).

3. Melvin Small and J. David Singer, *Resort to Arms* (Beverly Hills: Sage, 1982).

Let us review the major characteristics of these research efforts.

Three Perspectives on Scientific Studies of War

Quincy Wright. Professor Wright had a long and distinguished career as a scholar trained initially in the field of international law. A prolific writer, Dr. Wright authored over 1,100 scholarly articles and numerous books during a lifetime spanning 80 years. By far his most important contribution was *A Study of War*, published in 1942 and subsequently updated in 1965. This magnum opus of almost encyclopedic proportions summarized and inventoried a large body of research and thought about the study of war and its causes; moreover, it demonstrated to the discipline of international relations that complex social phenomena such as war could be subjected to systematic inquiry by methodologically sophisticated techniques.

The prime objective Wright hoped to achieve through his research project, started in 1926 at the University of Chicago, was to find the means for bringing war under control. His research was guided by humanitarian concern for human welfare and the sanctity of life; and he believed that while "the problem of war has become more exigent and more difficult to solve, . . . a solution must be found" (Wright 1942:3).

If Wright was convinced that a solution to the problem of war had to be found, he was equally convinced about the appropriate research procedure to employ to discover that solution. He felt this substantive phenomenon should be addressed by the methods of science. Wright's study of war was derived from an inductive analysis of 278 "Wars of Modern Civilization" he identified in the period from 1480 to 1940. Wright sought to compare a large number of wars so that he could discover their similarities and differences and derive generalizations about their commonalities.

Using explicit rules of observation, he based his findings on a statistical examination of his population of wars, each coded in terms of (1) opening and termination dates (i.e., duration), (2) the treaty which brought the war to an end, (3) the nations which participated in the wars and when they entered them, and (4) which nations were involved in the wars as initiators as contrasted with those playing a defensive position. Moreover, Wright classified wars in terms of the proportion of states involved in a given war out of the set of all states existing at the time of the war, in terms of the number of battles each war entailed, and in terms of the type of war each was (balance of power, civil, defensive, or imperialistic). While he did not collect data on casualty figures for the participants in each war, he did provide estimates of casualties and number of combatants for some of the major powers during several time periods. When subjected to comparative analysis by quantitative procedures, the study was able to uncover a number of empirical regularities about the nature of war hitherto unsuspected to be present.

The findings emergent from this data collection and analysis approach were many and are too numerous to be described here. But they were integrated into a general picture of the components of war and the conditions which give rise to its occurrence, and this vision was stated in the form of a "factor theory." Karl Deutsch has summarized its major features:

> Quincy Wright has done more than pile up information about war. He has developed a basic theory of war. Summarized and in drastically oversimplified form, it might be called in effect a four-factor model of the origins of war. Put most simply, his four factors are (1) technology, particularly as it applies to military matters; (2) law, particularly as it pertains to war and its initiation; (3) social organization, particularly in regard to such general-purpose political units as tribes, nations, empires, and international organizations; and (4) the distribution of opinions and attitudes concerning basic values. (Deutsch in Wright 1965 xiii–xiv)

In summary, then, Wright engaged in pathfinding efforts to bring the field of peace research from its polemical and normative foundations to its present empirical and quantitative emphasis. The consequence of this effort was the growth and emergence of the modern peace research movement, comprised of an exponentially growing number of scholars who emulate Wright's example by conceiving of international relations as a subject which can be studied by empirical procedures and who believe that such study may provide answers to the problem of abolishing war as a recurrent human institution.

Lewis Fry Richardson. In 1881, Lewis Fry Richardson was born to a staunch Quaker family in Great Britain. His professional career began in the field of mathematical physics and meteorology, where his research received wide recognition as a contribution to its field. With the advent of World War I, Richardson elected to serve in the Friends' Ambulance Unit in a motor convoy attached to the 16th French Infantry Division. His experiences in that capacity, and the loss of two brothers-in-law in combat, intensified his feelings that war was a morally repugnant social disease. After spending the first part of his professional life in the physical sciences, in the 1920s he undertook study in psychology and received a doctorate in that field in 1929. By 1940, Richardson retired to do research on wars, at just about the time that Wright was completing his monumental *Study of War*. Richardson's work resulted in a manuscript which was published after his death as two books, *Arms and Insecurity* and *Statistics of Deadly Quarrels*.

Richardson felt that it was necessary to clear away the myth and cant about the causes of war if the means to control it were ever to be found. This objective could be attained, he submitted, by obtaining empirical data regarding war with which hypotheses regarding the dynamics of interstate interaction which lead to war could be quantitatively verified. He suspected that such hypotheses, if confronted with and confirmed by data, would be of immediate use to the policymaker and hence directly applicable to the management of conflict. Thus, like Wright, Richardson strongly believed that scientific knowledge could be used to prevent the threat to humanity which war posed and continues to pose.

In order to gather data with which to acquire this knowledge, Richardson turned, like Wright, to the body of recorded history of warfare, covering the period from 1820 to 1949, from which he identified and classified *all* "deadly quarrels" (interactions between people resulting in death to one or more parties to a conflict). His total data set included all fatal interactions, such as "gangsterism," "feuds," "banditry," and "homicides," as well as wars, thereby recording in a single collection an inventory of all incidents where the number of deaths ranged from one to over 10 million. Included in this inventory were over 300 *wars*, which he defined as interactions resulting in 317 or more deaths.

With respect to wars, Richardson sought as well to measure conditions surrounding and associated with their occurrence. These attributes included such things as (1) a listing and classification of the nation-participants to the wars, (2) the number of deaths each war was responsible for (classified according to the logarithm of the number of estimated deaths they caused), (3) the intentions of the parties to each international war, and (4) the duration of each war (measured from date of initiation to date of termination). The result of this labor was a rich mine of quantitative material for the comparative analysis of warfare and its related phenomena.

In addition to collecting information on "deadly quarrels," Richardson was ingenious in his creation of mathematical models[2] for the analysis of the data, and the resultant equations that emerged have since become known as "Richardson Processes." Richardson's application of mathematical methods to his data enabled him to extract a large number of conclusions, in the form of differential equations, which express the relations over time among variables (e.g., arms race and alliance formation); the equations enable the researcher to evaluate the relative potency of various factors in contributing to the outbreak of war and to estimate the probabilities with which war will

---

[2] By "mathematical model" we mean an attempt to describe a process in the real world by means of mathematically defined terms and relationships.

occur under given circumstances. Illustrative of the kind of propositions emerging from his analysis are the following:

1. Wars are randomly distributed across time and do not appear to be becoming more or less frequent; however, large wars tend to be increasingly frequent while small wars tend to become less frequent.
2. Increases in world population do not seem to be associated with increases in the loss of life from war.
3. Cultural factors such as similarity of religious convictions do not appear to reduce the likelihood of war between interacting parties.
4. Sea powers seem in general to be less belligerent than land powers.
5. All nations are not equally likely to engage in war; geographical location exerts great influence on war involvement.

And, with respect to the dynamics of internation interaction,

6. The amounts of armaments in arms races tend either to constant equilibrium or to increase to infinity with time (depending on interaction among socioeconomic and psychological factors); in the latter case, war will eventually break out.
7. Nations which engage in arms buildups are more likely to experience war than nations which do not.

The significance of Richardson's attempts to study war scientifically is that, like Wright, he set a precedent for scientific empirical investigation of the causes of war.

J. David Singer and Melvin Small. The legacy of Wright and Richardson's scientific studies of war serves as a precursor to a major contemporary effort to continue the study of war which has been undertaken by J. David Singer, a political scientist at the University of Michigan, and Melvin Small, a historian at Wayne State University. They are explicit in their intellectual indebtedness to others, as well as their motives in undertaking the investigation:

> Without belittling the efforts of earlier generations, it is only within the past several decades that any intellectual assault of promise has been launched against this organized tribal slaughter. That is, until war has been systematically *described*, it cannot be adequately *understood*, and with such understanding comes the first meaningful possibility of controlling it, eliminating it, or finding less reprehensible substitutes for it. In our judgment, the most important turning point is marked by the rise of scientific (and therefore quantitative) analyses of war, manifested primarily in the

work of Quincy Wright and Lewis Richardson in the 1930's. (Singer and Small 1972:4)

The scope of the Singer-Small (1972:4) study, called the Correlates of War project, is

> to identify the variables that are most frequently associated with the onset of war. . . . More specifically, we hope to ascertain which factors characterize those conflicts which terminate in war, and which ones accompany those which find a less violent resolution. One of the first requirements in such a study is to discover the trends and fluctuations in the frequency, magnitude, severity, and intensity of war . . . ; once our data are gathered for these variables, a systematic search for the most potent independent and intervening variables may begin.

The Correlates of War project shares much in common with its predecessors in concept and motive. Several similarities as well as differences, however, may be noted:

1. Data collection procedures: The Correlates of War (COW) project improves on the observation procedures employed by the Wright and Richardson studies in the collection of data stage. Both those previous efforts, while thorough and innovative, left something to be desired in providing clear criteria for determining the existence of and objectively defining in an intersubjectively transmissible manner (i.e., in a manner which permits shared common meaning), what is meant by war (a problem which will be addressed in part II of this package).

2. Like their predecessors, Singer and Small approach the study of war in what is essentially an inductive fashion. Rather than attempting to construct formal deductive theories of warfare, the COW project is directing its initial efforts toward "mapping" the domain of violent behavior between nations in order to understand its empirical attributes. Given what is patently a meager level of verified knowledge about the characteristics and causes of war, this is a defensible strategy. We simply do not know enough about war to postulate assumptions about it from which deductive theories might be derived.

3. The COW project differs from its predecessors with respect to time periods and variables included in analysis. Singer and Small use the 1816–1965 period for their era of observation of war. Moreover, the criteria for identifying and measuring the salient characteristics of war (i.e., their frequency, magnitude, severity and intensity) are carefully specified by rules somewhat different from those of Wright and Richardson, as are the procedures for defining the population (number) of states in the globe at any given time. These rules are illustrated in part

II of this learning package and result in a somewhat reduced set of ninety-three events that can be considered wars.

4. Like Richardson and especially Wright, Singer and Small rely to some extent on historical insight and intuition for clues as to which factors are most likely to promote or deter war under varying conditions. Such pretheoretical hunches assist the search for causal patterns in a systematic fashion by suggesting a multitude of variables which can be subjected to data analysis. For instance, the traditional literature suggests that it is reasonable to inquire if there is any association between the number of international organizations or alliances formed between states and the frequency of war, inquiries which have now been conducted with the COW data. To some, such work may appear as "barefoot empiricism" in which everything is correlated against everything in a bivariate (correlation between two variables) fashion. Such an approach may appear mindless to those who forget that the approach represents merely preliminary attempts at analysis. Singer and Small and others who employ this strategy have carefully avoided the tendency to confuse correlation with causation but have quite accurately seen bivariate correlational knowledge as useful in searching for causality prior to multivariate statistical analysis and causal modeling of the sort which can eventually generate the kinds of multifactor theories which Wright articulated.

5. Singer and Small share with their predecessors an underlying rationale for undertaking this type of scientific investigation. Their work, like that of both Wright and Richardson, is based on the expectation that the effort will eventually produce the knowledge necessary to control and perhaps eliminate war as a human institution. The prospects for realizing such a goal may appear dim at the moment to anyone but the most convinced idealist. There is no way of estimating whether such efforts will eventually succeed, but it seems reasonable to grant those involved in the effort the benefit of the doubt and remain patient in permitting them to demonstrate the fruitfulness of the endeavor. When it is recalled that systematic quantitative inquiry into the determinants of war is still in its infancy (the movement is really less than three decades old) and that modern physics required three centuries to mature into a truly predictive science, it becomes apparent that to regard the effort as a lost cause is both premature and unwarranted.

To test your understanding of the information presented in part I, do the exercises which follow. If you are uncertain about the appropriate responses to these questions, it is recommended that you reread the material carefully before proceeding to part II.

Exercise 15–1

According to your understanding of "scientific" as opposed to "traditional" approaches to the study of war, classify the following statements according to the approach they most reflect by putting a "T" for traditional or "S" for scientific in the space provided.

_____ a. The higher the level of civil disturbance a nation experiences, the greater will be the extent of its foreign conflict behavior.

_____ b. The assassination of Archduke Ferdinand led to the outbreak of World War I.

_____ c. The American naval blockade of Cuba during the Cuban missile crisis violated the international law principle of freedom of the sea.

_____ d. The United States should get out of Europe.

_____ e. Increases in military expenditures increase in proportion to the number of threats a country receives from other states.

_____ f. The CIA was responsible for the Bay of Pigs fiasco.

_____ g. President Truman elected to use the atomic bomb at Hiroshima in order to impress the Soviets with American military capabilities.

_____ h. The more states a nation shares a common border with, the higher the probability that it will become involved in war.

_____ i. Bismarck was a warmonger.

_____ j. The incidence of war co-varies with the number of nations in the global system.

_____ k. The election of Teddy Roosevelt to the presidency marked a turning point in the foreign policy of the United States.

_____ l. The wealth of a nation is correlated with the probability of its becoming involved in foreign conflict.

_____ m. The best way to obtain international peace is to create a world government.

Exercise 15–2

How do the Wright, Richardson, and Small and Singer studies appear to differ from other treatments of war with which you are familiar? Identify at least three respects in which they differ from each of the following:

1. Treatment in diplomatic history books.

2. Treatment in books such as Stephen Crane's *The Red Badge of Courage* and Ernest Hemingway's *For Whom the Bell Tolls* or in such movies as *Gone with the Wind*, *Glory*, and *Born on the Fourth of July*.

II. Variable Operationalization and Data Collection: What Is a War?

Before you can begin to study war scientifically, it is important that you understand (1) some of the basic principles of measuring variables relevant to war and (2) the procedures by which information contained in historical narrative material may be coded through the application of specific decision criteria. It is to that objective that we turn in this part of the learning package. In reading the subsequent material, you will note that the illustrations are drawn from the operational rules of the Correlates of War project. Because of the prominence of that project, most of our comments will refer to it, unless otherwise noted, since the characteristics and data of this project are generally typical of, and illustrative of, the problems involved in contemporary quantitative approaches to the study of war.

Exercise 15–3

Since wars are spectacular, violent, and quite visible, it might seem that identifying them would be no problem. However, the task is not trivial. Some of the problems that arise will become apparent as you read the following list of events and try to decide which are wars.

[Although this is called an exercise, you should not think of the answers as being right or wrong. Remember that the way we use language is fairly arbitrary. For certain uses, the term *war* is useful to describe a wide variety of phenomena. For the purposes of the quantitative study of war, we must use a definition that includes all phenomena with certain characteristics and excludes all others. This exercise gives you an idea of how to begin that process.—Eds.]

1. Check which of the events below you consider to be a war.

_____ a. Palestinian attacks on Israeli athletes at the 1972 Olympics.

_____ b. "Cod War" over fishing rights between Iceland and the United Kingdom in 1973.

_____ c. Soviet invasion of Czechoslovakia in 1968.

_____ d. "Liberal" coup in Portugal in 1974.

_____ e. Soviet invasion of Hungary in 1956.

_____ f. U.S. "War" between the States, 1861–1865.

_____ g. "War" declared by the Symbionese Liberation Army against the United States in 1974.

_____ h. Italian invasion of Ethiopia in 1936.

_____ i. Overthrow of the Allende government in Chile in 1973.

_____ j. Sino-Soviet border clashes in 1969.

_____ k. Seizure of the U.S. *Pueblo,* by North Korea in 1968.

_____ l. Conflict between Nigeria and Biafra, 1967–1970.

_____ m. "World War II."

_____ n. 1973 "Yom Kippur War" in the Middle East.

_____ o. Spanish Civil "War," 1936–   _____ p. "Cold War" between the U.S.
1939.   and the U.S.S.R.

2. Consider what criteria you used in deciding whether each of these events was, or was not, a war. Express those criteria in completing the following sentence: A war is _____

3. Compare your selection of wars and your definition of war with others in the class.

Undoubtedly, there is some disagreement among you as to which of the events above were international wars. Imagine for a moment that each member of the class started a research project aimed at discovering the causes of war. Some of you might decide that all the events in the list above are relevant to your project. Others would include only a few for their projects, and still others might exclude nearly all of the events in the list. Obviously, if there is no agreement among different researchers about what a war is, the findings of all of them will be different, and possibly contradictory, but certainly not easily comparable. Instead of *cumulative* scientific progress toward the discovery of the causes of war, there would be endless confusion.

Therefore, it is important that any scientific enterprise begin with an operational definition of the phenomenon to be investigated. Here, we need a definition of the concept "war" that is so clear and precise that any person basing decisions on it would include exactly the same conflicts in a list of wars.

Operationally Defining War

Let us begin to construct such a definition. A sensible way to begin is by deciding which kind of events we do *not* want to include. There are many kinds of intergroup conflicts, of course, and we do not want to analyze all of these kinds, at least not immediately. One of the characteristics of the kind of conflicts we know as "wars" that makes them different from other kinds of conflicts is that in wars, people get killed. Thus, if we stipulate that an event must involve deaths, we have already begun to delimit the class of events we are going to study. In the list above, the Cod War and the Cold War do not meet even this preliminary criterion.

We must, of course, be more specific; we cannot define a war as any conflict in which people die. Murders, and some robberies and kidnappings, involve deaths, but they are certainly different from wars and almost certainly have different causes. And even some international conflicts, such as border clashes, or isolated terrorist attacks, involve so few deaths that we do not think of them as wars. It therefore makes good sense to adopt a "threshold of violence" over which an event must cross before we will consider it to be a war. In choosing this threshold, we must keep in mind that we do not want it to be so small that unimportant, perhaps accidental clashes between forces will be included as wars; on the other hand, we do not want it to be so large that really important conflicts between states are excluded. We must also keep in mind, purely as a practical matter, that the threshold must be large enough so that (1) it is an event to which historians will have paid attention, and therefore have recorded the requisite information, and (2) enough people are killed that somebody thinks it is worthwhile to count them. In the final analysis, the selection of an *exact* threshold must be somewhat arbitrary, but, keeping the considerations discussed above in mind, Singer and Small stipulate in their study that no conflict qualifies as an international war unless it leads to a minimum of 1,000 battle-connected fatalities. They further stipulate that these must be the deaths of military personnel.

If we adopt this criterion, we can see that it excludes more of the events in the list in exercise 15–3 from our study. To be more specific, the Palestinian attacks on the Israeli athletes at the 1973 Olympics, the Soviet invasion of Czechosloakia in 1968, the coup in Portugal in 1974, the war declared by the Symbionese Liberation Army against the United States, the Allende overthrow, the Sino-Soviet border clashes, and the *Pueblo* incident all resulted in casualties, but none resulted in 1,000 battle deaths. Therefore, none of them qualifies, by our definition, as a war.

Even with the criteria we have up to this point, we still have in our list widely different kinds of conflicts, some of which we would not want included in a study of *international* war. Consider, for example, the U.S. War between the States, the conflict between Nigeria and Biafra, and the Spanish Civil War. All of these involved at least 1,000 battle deaths, and yet we would not consider them *international* wars. The reason, obviously enough, is that they all involved conflict *within*, and not *between*, nations. If we want to exclude *civil* wars from our focus, then we must specify that an international war is one fought between two different political entities, or *nation-states*.

Having done this, we have certainly moved closer to an operational definition of international war. There is at least one further step we must take, however. There are may nationlike entities that are so small and/or so obscure (at least to the historians whose writings are available today) that we must exclude them from our study. There are at least two good reasons for this. The first is that such entities as American Indian tribes, African tribes, and even very small European states such as Monaco are so different from entities we usually think of as sovereign states that it is safe to assume that the process through which they get into wars is probably quite different from the process in which larger and more modern entities become involved in such conflicts. Since we are mainly interested in the larger and more modern entities and the wars they fight, it makes sense to exclude from our study of war tribes of American Indians, for example, even though this certainly does not mean we consider the deaths of American Indians less significant or regrettable. Second, the plain fact is that many small and/or obscure entities are not within our grasp historically; that is, for most of these entities, no records were kept, or whatever historical information might have been recorded has by now been lost forever. Therefore, it is impossible for us to find out when such entities became involved in wars, with whom they became involved, or how large their wars were. Obviously, we could not get very far in any empirical attempt to discover why these wars were fought.

We can avoid these difficulties by stipulating that an international war is one that involves at least one *state*. (We use *state*, *nation*, and *nation-state* interchangeably in this package.) And to qualify as a state, we will further stipulate that a political entity must be "large enough in population or other resources to play a moderately active role in world politics, to be a player more than a pawn, and to generate more signal than noise in the system" (Singer and Small 1972:19). Naturally, to identify such entities in an operational manner, we will have to use more specific criteria. The first criterion adopted by Singer and Small is a population threshold. That is, a political entity is not a state, according to Singer and Small, unless it has a population of at least 500,000. This criterion alone will allow us to eliminate from our consideration such small entities as Monaco, Andorra, Lichtenstein, and San Marino.

However, many political entities with a population over 500,000 are not full-fledged states because they lack independence. In a preliminary step toward determining which political entities qualify as states, Singer and Small focused on the number of states in the international system that established diplomatic missions in a given entity, reasoning that states are likely to establish diplomatic missions in nations that they consider independent. They discovered while performing this preliminary step that it was not entirely necessary, especially in the time period up to World War I. Up to that time, they discovered that if Great Britain and France established diplomatic missions in a given entity, at least a majority of the states in the system would follow suit. (Up to World War I, the international system was dominated by European states, and throughout the years from 1815 to 1914, Great Britain and France were two of the most powerful and influential European states. Thus, it is not surprising that their decisions about where to send diplomatic missions made such an impact on the rest of the states in the system.) Therefore, Singer and Small adopted a simpler criterion than the original one based on the establishment of missions by majority of states in the system; they decided that a political entity could safely be considered independent if it had received diplomatic missions from Britain and France and if it met the population threshold mentioned above.

Unfortunately, these rules do not work as well for the period following World War I. By that time, Britain and France were no longer so dominant and influential. Furthermore, after World War I, the League of Nations and the United Nations provided states in the international system with an institution through which they could officially decide whether a political entity is a state. Therefore, for the time period beginning with the end of World War I and running until 1965, Singer and Small use a slightly different set of criteria for determining whether a political entity qualifies as a state. First, any member of the League of Nations or the United Nations is considered a state. If an entity does not meet this criterion, it can still qualify as a state if (1) it has a population of at least 500,000, *and* (2) if it receives diplomatic missions from any two "major powers."

This last criterion brings up an obvious question: "What is a major power?" This, it turns out, is not an easy question to answer. Singer and Small decided to rely on the opinions of historians and other scholars of international relations as to which states were particularly important and powerful during the time period from 1816 to 1965. Fortunately, they found that most experts agree with the following list:

Nation-State	Years of Major Power Status
Austria-Hungary	1816–1918
Prussia/Germany	1816–1918, 1925–1945
Russia/U.S.S.R.	1816–1917, 1922–1965
France	1816–1940, 1945–1965
Great Britain	1816–1965
Italy	1860–1943
Japan	1895–1945
United States	1898–1965
China	1949–1965

Using the coding rules discussed earlier and the major power list above, Singer and Small identified 144 different entities that qualified as states sometime between 1816 and 1965.

We are now ready to define, fully and operationally, what we mean by an international war: *An international war is a military conflict waged between (or among) national entities, at least one of which is a state, that results in at least 1,000 battle deaths of military personnel.*

We can also delineate two different categories of international war. One of these categories contains only wars in which at least one participant on each side of the conflict is a *nation-state*. Such wars are called *interstate* wars. Wars involving a nation-state on only one side of the conflict are called *extrasystemic* wars, since they are waged by states against national entities that fall outside the interstate system. Only interstate wars are used in the data set in the next sections of this learning package, but you should remember the distinction since it has implications for one's data base.

Let us now return to the list of international events in exercise 15–3. Relying upon our operational definition, we should all be able to agree that only the following qualify as international wars, and all of these are also interstate wars: (1) the Soviet invasion of Hungary in 1956, (2) the Italian invasion of Ethiopia in 1936, (3) World War II, and (4) the 1973 Yom Kippur War in the Middle East.

Singer and Small have compiled a list of international wars (interstate wars plus extrasystemic wars) that occurred between 1816 and 1980. This list, divided into interstate and extrasystemic wars, is presented in table 15–1.

III. Data Analysis: Describing and Examining National War Involvement

Now that you are acquainted with operational definitions and data collection procedures, you are ready to move on to the next steps in the scientific study of war: presentation and description of data and the scientific evaluation of hypotheses. We will use as our data set some of the information collected by Singer and Small on national involvement in interstate wars between 1816 and 1965. You are already aware of the way in which Singer and Small operationalized war and collected their data. Using data on the number of interstate wars in which each nation-state has been involved, the number of wars each initiated, and the number of years each entity has been a nation-state, you will learn the following: presenting and describing data, framing scientific questions, and evaluating hypotheses.

Presenting and Describing Data

How to Read and Interpret a Table of Data. Table 15–2 presents Singer and Small's data on national war involvement in the period 1816–1965. Four *columns* of information appear in this table. The first column contains the names of the nations; the second column contains the number of years each of these nations qualified as nation-states between 1816 and 1965; the third column contains the number of wars each of the nations was involved in during the years indicated in column 2; and the fourth column contains the number of wars that each nation initiated. Each *row* thus contains a particular nation's *score* on these different variables, and each nation is considered to constitute one *case*.

In addition to the above information, table 15–2 contains information for the major powers. For the nine nation-states identified as major powers during the period 1816–1965, the following data are given in brackets following the entries in columns 2, 3, and 4, respectively: the number of years as a major power, the number of interstate war involvements while a major power, and the number of interstate war initiations while a major power.

By way of review, let us take the case of the United States, which is the first case listed in table 15–2. The first column, which is labeled "Years as Nation-State," indicates that the United States had the necessary attributes

Table 15–1
International Wars between 1816 and 1980 Identified by Singer and Small*

Interstate Wars (N = 67)	Extrasystemic Wars (N = 51)**	
Franco-Spanish (1823)	British-Maharattan (1817–1818) I	Mahdist (1882–1885) C
Russo-Turkish (1828–1829)	Greek (1821–1828) I	Serbo-Bulgarian (1885) I
Mexican-American (1846–1848)	First Anglo-Burmese (1823–1826) I	Franco-Madagascan (1894–1895) I
Austro-Sardinian (1848–1849)	Javanese (1825–1830) C	Cuban (1895–1898) C
First Schleswig-Holstein (1848–1849)	Russo-Persian (1826–1828) I	Italo-Ethiopian (1895–1896) I
Roman Republic (1849)	First Polish (1831) C	First Philippine (1896–1898) C
La Plata (1851–1852)	First Syrian (1831–1832) C	Second Philippine (1899–1902) C
Crimean (1853–1856)	Texan (1835–1836) C	Boer (1899–1902) C
Anglo-Persian (1856–1857)	First British-Afghan (1838–1842) I	Ilinden (1903) C
Italian Unification (1859)	Second Syrian (1839–1840) C	Russian Nationalities (1917–1921) C
Spanish-Moroccan (1859–1860)	Franco-Algerian (1839–1847) I	Riffan (1921–1926) C
Italo-Roman (1860)	Peruvian-Bolivian (1841) I	Druze (1925–1927) C
Italo-Sicilian (1860–1861)	First British-Sikh (1845–1846) I	Indonesian (1945–1946) C
Franco-Mexican (1862–1867)	Hungarian (1848–1849) C	Indochinese (1945–1954) C
Ecuadorian-Colombian (1863)	Second British-Sikh (1848–1849) I	Madagascan (1947–1948) C
Second Schleswig-Holstein (1864)	First Turco-Montenegran (1852–1853) I	First Kashmir (1947–1949) I
Lopez (1864–1870)	Sepoy (1857–1859) C	Hyderabad (1948) I
Spanish-Chilean (1865–1866)	Second Turco-Montenegran (1858–1859) I	Algerian (1954–1962) C
Seven Weeks (1866)	Second Polish (1863–1864) C	Tibetan (1956–1959) C
Franco-Prussian (1870–1871)	Spanish-Santo Dominican (1863–1865) I	Philippine-MNLF (1972–)C
Russo-Turkish (1877–1878)	Ten Years (1868–1878) C	Ethiopian-Eritrean (1974–) C
Pacific (1879–1883)	Dutch-Achinese (1873–1878) C	Timor (1975–) C
Sino-French (1884–1885)	Balkan (1875–1877) C	Saharan (1975–) C
Central American (1885)	Bosnian (1878) C	Ogaden (1976–) C
Sino-Japanese (1894–1895)	Second British-Afghan (1878–1880) I	
Greco-Turkish (1897)	British-Zulu (1879) I	
Spanish-American (1898)	Franco-Indochinese (1882–1884) I	
Boxer Rebellion (1900)		
Russo-Japanese (1904–1905)		
Central American (1906)		
Central American (1907)		
Spanish-Moroccan (1909–1910)		
Italo-Turkish (1911–1912)		
First Balkan (1912–1913)		
Second Balkan (1913)		
World War I (1914–1918)		
Russo-Polish (1919–1920)		
Hungarian-Allies (1919)		
Greco-Turkish (1919–1922)		
Sino-Soviet (1929)		
Manchurian (1931–1933)		
Chaco (1932–1935)		
Italo-Ethiopian (1935–1936)		
Sino-Japanese (1937–1941)		
Changkufeng (1938)		
Nomohan (1939)		
World War II (1939–1945)		
Russo-Finnish (1939–1940)		
Franco-Thai (1940–1941)		
Palestine (1948–1949)		
Korean (1950–1953)		
Russo-Hungarian (1956)		
Sinai (1956)		
Sino-Indian (1962)		
Vietnamese (1965–1975)		
Second Kashmir (1965)		
Six Day (1967)		
Israeli-Egyptian (1969–1970)		
Football (1969)		
Bangladesh (1971)		
Yom Kippur (1973)		
Turco-Cypriot (1974)		
Vietnamese-Cambodian (1975–)		
Ugandan-Tanzanian (1978–1979)		
Sino-Vietnamese (1979)		
Russo-Afghan (1979–)		
Irani-Iraqi (1980–)		

* This list has been updated to include wars between 1965 and 1980. However, the data discussed and analyzed in this package go up to only 1965.

** I = imperial war—between a member of the international system and a non-member. C = colonial war—between a member of the international system and a colony or protectorate.

Table 15–2
National War Involvement in Interstate War, 1816–1965

Nation-State	Years as Nation-State (1816–1965)	Interstate War Involvements	Interstate War Initiations
Western Hemisphere			
United States	150 [68][a]	5 [4][b]	2 [1][c]
Canada	46	2	0
Cuba	64	0	0
Haiti	107	0	0
Dominican Republic	79	0	0
Jamaica	4	0	0
Trinidad-Tobago	4	0	0
Mexico	135	2	0
Guatemala	117	2	1
Honduras	67	2	0
Salvador	91	3	1
Nicaragua	66	1	1
Costa Rica	46	0	0
Panama	46	0	0
Colombia/New Granada	135	2	1
Venezuela	125	0	0
Ecuador	112	1	0
Peru	128	2	0
Brazil	140	2	1
Bolivia	118	2	0
Paraguay	70	1	1
Chile	127	2	1
Argentina	125	1	0
Uruguay	84	0	0
Europe			
United Kingdom	150 [150]	7 [7]	1 [1]
Ireland	44	0	0
Netherlands	145	2	0
Belgium	131	3	0
Luxembourg	42	0	0
France	148 [146]	12 [12]	5 [5]
Switzerland	150	0	0
Spain	150	5	3
Portugal	150	1	0
Hanover	29	1	0
Bavaria	55	2	0
Prussia/Germany	130 [124]	6 [6]	4 [4]
German Federal Republic	11	0	0
German Democratic Republic	12	0	0
Baden	55	2	0
Saxony	52	1	0
Wurttemberg	55	2	0
Hesse Electoral	51	1	0
Hesse Grand Ducal	52	1	0
Mecklenburg-Schwerin	25	1	0
Poland	41	1	0
Austria-Hungary	103 [103]	6 [6]	2 [2]

[a] Years as a major power.

[b] Interstate war involvements while a major power.

[c] Interstate war initations while a major power.

Table 15–2 continued

Nation-State	Years as Nation-State (1816–1965)	Interstate War Involvements	Interstate War Initiations
Austria	30	0	0
Hungary	47	3	0
Czechoslovakia	42	1	0
Sardinia/Italy	150 [84]	11 [6]	5 [2]
Vatican/Papal States	45	2	0
Two Sicilies	46	2	0
Modena	19	0	0
Parma	10	0	0
Tuscany	45	0	0
Malta	2	0	0
Albania	47	0	0
Serbia/Yugoslavia	85	4	1
Greece	134	7	2
Cyprus	6	0	0
Bulgaria	53	5	1
Rumania	88	5	1
Russia/U.S.S.R.	150 [146]	10 [10]	4 [4]
Estonia	23	0	0
Latvia	23	0	0
Lithuania	23	0	0
Finland	47	2	0
Sweden	150	0	0
Norway	56	1	0
Denmark	145	2	0
Iceland	22	0	0
Africa			
Gambia	1	0	0
Mali	6	0	0
Senegal	6	0	0
Dahomey	6	0	0
Mauritania	6	0	0
Niger	6	0	0
Ivory Coast	6	0	0
Guinea	8	0	0
Upper Volta	6	0	0
Liberia	46	0	0
Sierra Leone	5	0	0
Ghana	9	0	0
Togo	6	0	0
Cameroun	6	0	0
Nigeria	6	0	0
Gabon	6	0	0
Central African Republic	6	0	0
Chad	6	0	0
Congo	6	0	0
Zaire	6	0	0
Uganda	4	0	0
Kenya	3	0	0
Tanzania	5	0	0
Zanzibar	2	0	0
Burundi	4	0	0
Rwanda	4	0	0

Table 15–2 continued

Nation-State	Years as Nation-State (1816–1965)	Interstate War Involvements	Interstate War Initiations
Somalia	6	0	0
Ethiopia	63	3	0
Zambia	2	0	0
Malawi	2	0	0
South Africa	46	1	0
Malagasy	6	0	0
Middle East			
Morocco	74	2	0
Algeria	4	0	0
Tunisia	10	0	0
Libya	14	0	0
Sudan	10	0	0
Iran	111	1	0
Ottoman Empire/Turkey	150	11	2
Iraq	34	1	1
Egypt/U.A.R.	29	2	1
Syria	17	1	1
Lebanon	20	1	1
Jordan	20	1	1
Israel	18	2	1
Saudia Arabia	39	0	0
Yemen Arab Republic	40	0	0
Kuwait	5	0	0
Asia			
Afghanistan	46	0	0
China	106 [17]	7 [2]	1 [1]
Mongolia	45	2	0
Taiwan	17	0	0
Korea	18	0	0
Korea, Democratic Peoples' Republic of	18	1	1
Korea, Republic of	17	1	0
Japan	99 [51]	7 [6]	5 [4]
India	19	2	1
Pakistan	19	1	0
Burma	18	0	0
Ceylon/Sri Lanka	18	0	0
Maldive Islands	1	0	0
Nepal	46	0	0
Thailand	79	1	0
Khmer Republic	13	0	0
Laos	12	0	0
Vietnam, Democratic Republic of	12	0	0
Vietnam, South	12	0	0
Malaysia	9	0	0
Singapore	1	0	0
Philippines	20	1	0
Indonesia	17	0	0
Australia	46	2	0
New Zealand	46	1	0

of a nation-state for all of the 150 years in the century and a half under study. The bracketed number tells us that for 68 of those 150 years, the United States is classified as a major power. In the second column, labeled "Interstate War Involvements," we find that the United States was involved in five interstate wars during the time it was a nation-state and the number in brackets tells us that four of these five war involvements occurred while the United States was a major power. The third column, labeled "Interstate War Initiations," reveals that the United States initiated two wars during the 150 years, with one of these initiations occurring during the time it was a major power. As you will discover in the following exercise, additional information can be derived from the table through arithmetic operations with the data.

Exercise 15–4: Reading and Interpreting a Table

The best way to know if you understand how a table presents information is for you to find specific pieces of information; this exercise is designed for this purpose. Examine table 15–2, and answer the following questions.

1. How many years did Brazil qualify as a nation-state?_____
2. How many interstate wars was Portugal involved in during the years it qualified as a nation-state?_____
3. How many interstate wars did the United Kingdom initiate?_____
4. Of the total number of interstate wars in which Japan was involved, how many occurred while it was a major power?_____
5. How many interstate wars did China initiate while a major power?_____

In the next set of questions, you are to derive certain additional pieces of information from the data given in the table.

6. How many interstate wars did the United States fight when it was *not* a major power?_____
7. How many interstate wars did Italy initiate when it was not a major power?_____
8. How many interstate war involvements by all states did Singer and Small identify between 1816 and 1965?_____
9. How many of these interstate war involvements were by major powers while they were major powers?_____
10. How many interstate war involvements have the nations in the Western Hemisphere experienced?_____
11. How many major power war involvements have the major powers in Asia experienced?_____

If you were able to answer all of the above questions correctly, you clearly understand that a great deal of information can be contained in just a few columns of data. Although the information given explicitly in the table is very important, you should always be aware of how much additional information may be obtained by simple subtraction (e.g., questions 6 and 7) or by aggregating (adding up) information (questions 8–11). Having mastered the table, you are ready to proceed to the preparation of a frequency distribution.

Preparing a Frequency Distribution. Look at table 15–2 and determine which nation had the most war involvements. You should conclude that it is France, with a total of twelve war involvements. Count the number of countries that were not involved in any wars while they qualified as nation-states. It takes a little time to do this since there are so many, but you should end up with seventy-seven. Now count the number of nation-states that were involved in only one war. Your answer in this case should be twenty-five. If you did this for the entire range of values (zero wars, one to twelve wars) and constructed a table presenting your results, it would look like table 15–3.

If you're still uncertain about where these numbers came from, turn again to table 15–2 and answer the question, "How many nations had exactly (no more and no less than) two war involvements?" If you are counting correctly, you should conclude that the answer is twenty-three, which, as you an see, is the number in the third row of the second column in table 15–3.

The type of table we have constructed below is known as a *frequency distribution*; this one is the frequency distribution of war involvements by nation-states, since it tells us how frequently we observe a certain number of war involvements by nation-states.

Table 15–3
Frequency Distribution of War Involvement

Number of War Involvements	Number of nations
0	77
1	25
2	23
3	4
4	1
5	4
6	2
7	4
8	0
9	0
10	1
11	2
12	1
	Total 144

Exercise 15–5: Preparing a Frequency Distribution

Prepare a frequency distribution of war initiation using the data in table 15–2.

Number of War Initiations	Number of Nations
0	_____
1	_____
2	_____
3	_____
4	_____
5	_____

As you can tell, a frequency distribution is slightly different from a table of raw data, such as table 15–2. We lost information on *particular* nation-states, but we gain the type of information upon which *generalizations* about war can be made; such generalizations are, you will recall, one of the primary reasons for the scientific study of war. One generalization that could be made on the basis of table 15–3 is that only 67/144 = .47, or 47 percent of all the nation-states that existed between 1816 and 1965 are responsible for 100 percent of the interstate wars. Such a finding raises the possibility that we are perhaps dealing with two types of nation-states: war-prone nations and non-war-prone, or peaceful, nations. Similarly, from exercise 15–5, you can determine that thirty nations are responsible for all the war initiations during our time period. Combining this information with the fact from table 15–3 that only sixty-seven nations have ever been involved in war, we would have 30/67 = .45, or 45 percent of the nations involved in interstate wars between 1816 and 1965 initiating 100 percent of those wars.

Constructing a Histogram. Once a frequency distribution has been tabulated, it is often useful to construct a diagram that summarizes in graphic form the nature of this distribution. Such a diagram is called a histogram, although you may know it as a bar graph.

One of the easiest ways to understand how a histogram is made is to look at one. Figure 15–1 is a histogram of the frequency distribution found in table 15–3. At the bottom of the graph, we see a line divided into thirteen intervals of equal width and labeled "Number of War Involvements." This line is called the *horizontal axis* of the graph, and numbers underneath the intervals correspond to the values listed in the left-hand column of table 15–3. This line is joined on the left-hand side of the graph by a line divided into intervals of five and labeled "Number of Nations." This is referred to as the *vertical axis* of the histogram.

Looking at the body of the graph itself, we see bars of varying height

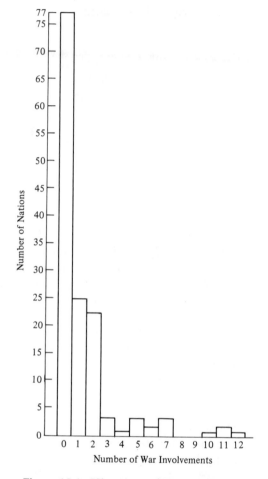

Figure 15.1. Histogram of War Involvement

and equal width. The first bar corresponds to the number of nations having zero war involvements, and, according to table 15–3, 77 of our 144 nations were not involved in an interstate war between 1816 and 1965. Thus, the first bar is 77 units tall. The next bar indicates the number of nations having exactly one war involvement, and since there are 25 of these, this bar is 25 units tall. The last bar on the right represents the number of nations having exactly 12 war involvements, and, since France is the only nation that qualifies, the bar is only 1 unit tall.

Sometimes it is useful to assign a range of values to each bar rather than a specific value. Suppose, for example, we were interested in looking at the number of nations with no war involvements, as opposed to those with few (one or two) war involvements and those with several (three or more) war involvements (figure 15–2). The horizontal axis would be divided into three parts: one corresponding to no war involvements, one corresponding to few

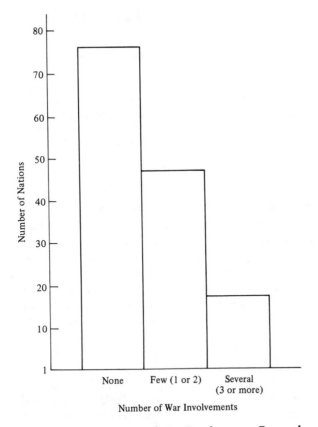

Number of War Involvements

Figure 15.2. Histogram of War Involvement, Grouped Data

(one or two) war involvements, and one to several (three or more) war involvements. We know from table 15–3 that 77 nations had zero war involvements. We can then add the number of nations having one war involvement, 25, to the number having two war involvements, 23, for a total of 48 nations with "few" war involvements. Rather than add the remaining nations with 3, 4, 5 up to 12 war involvements to get the "several" total, we can simply add 77 + 48 = 125 nations and then subtract that number from 144, the total number of nations in our data set. This procedure gives us 144 − 125 = 19 nations with "several" war involvements. We can use this subtraction shortcut because our groups (none, few, several) are *mutually exclusive* and *exhaustive*; that is, a nation can be in only *one* group, and *every* nation belongs in one of the three groups.

Again, the height of the bars is proportional to the number of nations that have zero, few, or several war involvements, and the bars are of equal width. We could make the bars wider or narrower, and the graph would look essentially the same. It is important, however, that the bars be of equal width.

Exercise 15–6: Constructing a Histogram

1. Using the frequency distribution you prepared in exercise 15–5, construct a histogram for 0, 1, 2, 3, 4, or 5 war initiations.

2. Now group your data in some fashion, such as we did for none, few, or several war involvements. Note that you may not necessarily want to group war initiations exactly the same way as we grouped war involvements, since the *range* (the difference between the highest and lowest scores) is different. Construct a histogram of your grouped data of interstate war initiations.

Looking at the two histograms you have just constructed, you can see how easy it is to get a good idea of the distribution of data from a histogram. A person can readily tell if one group is larger than another by the height of the bars, as well as roughly *how much* larger by the *relative* heights of the bars. With the variables we used, war involvements and initiations, the task of constructing informative frequency distributions and histograms was fairly easy because we were able to group our data into meaningful groups. In the next section, you'll learn how to construct histograms on data that do not group as easily as war involvement and war initiation do.

Histograms for More Complex Data. If we look carefully at the numbers in column 2 of table 15–2, "Years as Nation-State," we see that the values are quite diverse, ranging from 1 year to 150 years. If we wanted to depict in histogram form the distribution of this variable, we could follow the procedure already outlined. The vertical axis would be number of nations, as before, but what about the horizontal axis? We could make each bar correspond to a specific value of the variable. The minimum value would be 1, since an entity that qualifies as a nation-state for zero years would be impossible, and the maximum value would be 150, since that is how many years separate January 1, 1816, and December 31, 1965. If we did this, however, our graph would not be very informative since it would look something like figure 15–3.

What we do in a situation like this is to assign a range of values to a horizontal unit instead of a single value. This was what we did when we switched from number of war involvements (zero through twelve) to none, few, or several (zero; one or two; three or more) war involvements. The range of values that is selected is arbitrary, and often one tries a variety of intervals until a satisfactory one is obtained. In this particular case, suppose we differentiate between political entities that have been around for more than fifty years and political entities that qualify as a nation-state for fifty years or less.

If you looked at each of the 144 cases in table 15–2, you would find that 94 of the 144 nations existed for fifty years or less. The remaining 50 nations qualified as nation-states for more than fifty years. Thus, the frequency distribution for this variable would look like this:

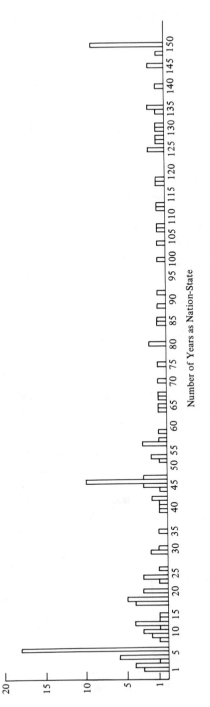

Number of Years as Nation-State

Figure 15–3. Histogram of Years as Nation-State

Years as Nation-State	Number of Nation-States
50 or less	94
More than 50	50
Total	144

Exercise 15–7: Constructing More Histograms

1. Using the frequency distribution of years as a nation-state, construct a histogram of years as a nation-state, differentiating between those nations that existed for fifty years or less and those that existed for more than fifty years.

2. Since dividing "years as nation-state" into two groups provides little information and no grouping provides "too much," one usually would try some intermediary groupings, such as dividing the data into four or five groups. One often divides the range of values into equal intervals. For example, if you wanted five groups, each group would represent 150/5 = 30 years; thus, your intervals would be 1–30 years, 31–60 years, 61–90 years, 91–120 years, and 121–150 years.

   a. On a separate sheet of paper, prepare a frequency distribution and construct a histogram for the five intervals given above from the data in table 15–3.

   b. Choose one other grouping and prepare a frequency distribution and histogram for that grouping of the data.

   c. Compare your histograms with each other and with those constructed by other students who chose a different grouping than you did. Discuss how much information is lost for deciding on the "best" grouping method in terms of the amount of information conveyed by the histogram.

What do we know about war after constructing frequency distributions and histograms? One substantive conclusion that stemmed from our visual inspection of the various data displays that we have constructed is that nations vary a great deal in the number of wars they become involved in. The obvious question is, Why is this so? What factors lead some nations to become involved in many wars while other nations are able to avoid war altogether?

Framing Scientific Questions

Implicit in the framing of our question about why some nations are involved in more wars than other nations is the assumption that those nations that are frequently involved in wars are *systematically* different from those nations that are infrequently involved. That is, we assume that there is a set of general factors (for example, military power, industrial power, alliance bonds) that, if known, would enable us to predict successfully the number of war involvements of each particular nation based on its standing on these more general factors. Our task, clearly, is identifying these more general factors.

Unacceptable Answers. If we approach the question of what leads some nations into war from a scientific point of view, several different types of answers would *not* be acceptable.

First, we would reject any explanations based upon metaphysical or mythical grounds. For example, the assertion that nations go to war when the planet Mars stands in a particular relation to the planet Venus (an astrological explanation) would not be acceptable as a scientific explanation.

A second and similar type of unacceptable explanation is one that rests on assumptions that are *in principle* untestable. An example of this would be the notion that nations are driven to war by unobservable forces, such as a collective, subconscious death wish.

Tautological explanations, such as "Some nations fight more wars than others because that's the way nations are," would be a third type of unacceptable explanation from a scientific viewpoint.

A fourth type of explanation that the scientist would reject is one that rests on ad hoc and idiosyncratic (particular) factors. For example, one might argue that England has many war involvements because it is an island, while Russia has been war prone due to the fact that it did not have a warm water port. Germany, on the other hand, has been war prone (an ad hoc explanation would continue) because it is in the center of Europe, while Turkey's war proneness stems from its location on the periphery of Europe. We could go on indefinitely giving reasons why each particular nation was or was not involved in war frequently, but from a scientific standpoint, these kinds of explanations are inadequate. Offering a unique explanation for each case is equivalent to not providing any explanation at all. That is, from the scientific point of view, explanations for why something is the way it is must be sufficiently general as to allow the scientist to explain why other phenomena are similar or different. You will recall from part I of this package that one of the primary reasons that Richardson, Wright, and Singer and Small began investigating war "scientifically" was to provide *generalized* statements on the causes and consequences of war.

Asking Questions. You now know what types of explanations are unacceptable from a scientific point of view. The question remains, however, How do we arrive at scientifically acceptable answers to appropriate questions?

In general, there are two strategies available to us to generate potential answers to our questions. We can choose to approach the subject *deductively*, which entails beginning with a few basic, highly abstract assumptions. From these assumptions we logically derive what we should observe in the real world if the assumptions are true, and then we subject our *deductions* or expectations to empirical testing. The second strategy is to proceed *inductively*. Following this strategy, we begin with our empirical observations, rather than with abstract assumptions, and by *summarizing* and synthesizing the discrete observations we try to detect patterns, or what are often called *empirical regularities*.

Let us take a simple example—when and why do flowers bloom? If you were a deductivist, you would start with the abstract assumption that flowers blossom when the plant undergoes certain chemical changes. Your "theory" would further specify that the chemical changes producing blossoms are triggered by increases in air temperature, sunlight, and moisture. From climatological studies we know that spring is usually warmer, sunnier, and rainier than winter. Thus, you would conclude that flowers should bloom in the spring due to the change in weather. The last step in your analysis would be to observe the frequency of flowers blooming in different seasons to see if your prediction is confirmed.

On the other hand, if you were an inductivist, you would begin with data collection. You would gather data on the frequency of flowers blooming in different seasons, as well as data on other "relevant" variables. You suspect that temperature, sunshine, and rainfall are important, so data must also be assembled for those variables. Once you have your data, you would go through a variety of statistical techniques, attempting to discover patterns of association. If you did your analysis properly, you should discover that the frequency of blooming increases in the spring, as do the air temperature and amount of sun and rain. You would therefore *generalize* that flowers bloom when the weather changes to warm, sunny, and humid.

Briefly then, with a deductive research strategy we move from the abstract to the concrete and from the general to the specific. An inductive research strategy leads one to move in the opposite direction, that is, from the concrete to the abstract and from the specific to the general. In practice, most research rests on a blend of inductive and deductive approaches. Our strategy in this learning package has a slightly heavier emphasis on the inductive approach.

To return to our query of why nations become involved in war, we have already noted two characteristics of our data set. First, nations vary greatly in their war involvements, and, second, they vary greatly in the length of time that they exist as nations. Under what circumstances would we expect these two characteristics to be associated? If we think of wars as akin to natural disasters like tornadoes, hurricanes, and earthquakes, then it becomes obvious that the longer we observe a particular place, the more such natural disasters we can expect to witness at that location. Thus, we might deduce that if wars are like natural disasters, the longer a nation exists, the more wars we would expect it to become involved in. The last statement is a *hypothesis*, that is, a contingent statement about what should be observed in the empirical world if the assumptions are correct. In this particular case, the hypothesis is not particularly earthshaking, but it will enable us to demonstrate how we go about evaluating such hypotheses and determine the degree to which we must take this association into account in other studies.

To review and test your knowledge on inductive versus deductive strategies and scientific hypotheses, complete exercise 15–8.

Exercise 15–8: Identifying Hypotheses

Indicate which of the following statements are scientific hypotheses, and tell why or why not.

1. If God can do anything, then He can create a stone He cannot lift.
2. George Washington was the first president of the United States.
3. If a nation has a high GNP, then it is more likely to give foreign aid.
4. The U.S. defense budget is $140 billion.
5. If the Soviet Union gives weapons to Syria and Egypt, the United States will give weapons to Israel.
6. Democracies are more peaceful than dictatorships.

Evaluating Hypotheses

Let us restate the hypothesis that we are examining in this part of the learning package: *the longer a nation exists, the more wars it will become involved in.*

This hypothesis has two aspects that are especially noteworthy. First, it is what is referred to as a bivariate hypothesis; that is, it specifies an association between two variables—length of national existence and number of war involvements. This distinguishes it from univariate hypotheses, such as: "Nations differ greatly in the number of war involvements they experience," which deals with only one variable, number of war involvements. We also have a third type of hypothesis—*multivariate*—which specifies a relationship among three or more variables, such as: "The more powerful a nation is, *and* the longer a nation exists, the more war involvements it will experience." Multivariate hypotheses are more difficult to evaluate than bivariate hypotheses, and we will focus only on the latter in the remainder of this learning package.

A second important characteristic of the bivariate hypothesis is the *direction* of the association between the two variables. In this case, a *positive* association is predicted since the hypothesis specifies that as one variable increases, the other increases also. Hypotheses predict *negative* associations when they specify that as one variable increases, the other decreases. An example of a negative association might be, "The more alliances a nation has, the fewer wars it will be involved in." Finally, hypotheses may stipulate that there is no relationship between the two variables; such hypotheses are commonly referred to as *null* hypotheses. A null hypothesis regarding war involvement might be, "A nation's domestic standard of living does not affect the number of war involvements."

When we evaluate empirical evidence with regard to a hypothesis, we need to look at both aspects of hypotheses we noted above: the existence of a relationship between the two variables and the direction of that relationship. In terms of the existence of a relationship, we will be concerned with assessing the *strength of association*. By strength of association, we mean how well one variable predicts to another or how often the presence of one is associated with the presence (or absence) of the other variable. The *direction of the relationship* is concerned with common increases and decreases. That is, if nations have high scores on one variable, do they have high scores on the other, indicating a *positive* relationship, or do high scores on one variable predict to low scores on the other, indicating a *negative* relationship? Thus, we want to know the "how" (direction) and the "how much" (strength) of the hypothesized relationship.

Often, an investigation of a bivariate hypothesis begins with the preparation of a cross-tabulation, and it is to this technique that we now turn.

Preparing a Cross-Tabulation. A cross-tabulation is a visual representation of data on two variables that enables us to examine our cases and determine whether the presence of one characteristic tends to predict, or be associated with, the presence or absence of the other. To take a simple example, suppose we selected a sample of 100 nations from the contemporary world and determined for each its geographical location and level of economic development. In this preliminary analysis we will call a nation rich if it has a gross national product (GNP) per capita of more than $500 per year; otherwise we will designate it as poor. As to geographical location, we will be concerned only with whether the bulk of a nation's territory is in the Northern or Southern Hemisphere.

Suppose the data on the 100 nations broke down as follows:

Variable 1, economic development: 60 were poor, and 40 were rich.

Variable 2, geographical location: 55 were in the Northern Hemisphere, and 45 were in the Southern Hemisphere.

Here we have information about two different characteristics of our 100 nations: development and location. Suppose we want to know whether countries in the Northern or Southern Hemisphere are more (or less) likely to be poor. According to our coding scheme, there are only four possibilities: poor Northern Hemisphere, rich Northern Hemisphere, poor Southern Hemisphere, rich Southern Hemisphere. We would need to consult our records and determine how many of each type we had in our sample. Suppose the results of this tabulation were as follows:

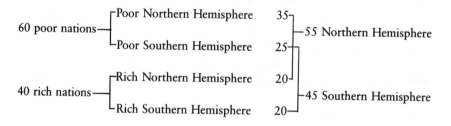

Table 15–4
Cross-Tabulation of Economic Development and Geographic Location

| Economic Development | Geographic Location | | Total |
	Northern Hemisphere	Southern Hemisphere	
Poor	35	25	60
Rich	20	20	40
Total	55	45	100

You will notice that our 60 poor nations split into 35 Northern Hemisphere nations and 25 Southern Hemisphere nations; our 40 rich nations are composed of 20 Northern Hemisphere nations and 20 Southern Hemisphere nations. This gives us a total of 35 + 20 = 55 Northern Hemisphere nations and 25 + 20 = 45 Southern Hemisphere nations.

Table 15–4 is a much simpler way of presenting the same information. From this cross-tabulation we can quickly see that our total sample is 100 nations, 60 of which are "poor" and 40 of which are "rich." In addition, we can see that 55 are located in the Northern Hemisphere and 45 in the Southern Hemisphere. These subtotals of each category are called the *marginal totals*, which is easy to remember if you think of them as being on the margin of the table.

It is also clear from this table that 35 of the 60 poor nations are located in the Northern Hemisphere, and the remaining 25 are in the Southern Hemisphere. The corresponding distribution for the 40 rich nations is 20 nations located in each hemisphere. The table we have just constructed is called a *cross-tabulation*, since it "crosses" the "tabulation" of data on two variables.

Now let us return to the question we were concerned with: Do nation-states with longer life spans experience more wars than nation-states with short life spans? Let us review what we know at present about these two characteristics, using the frequency distributions we constructed earlier:

	Totals
Nations with no war involvements	77 ⎤
	├─ 144
Nations with one or more war involvements	67 ⎦
Nations existing for fifty years or less	94 ⎤
	├─ 144
Nations existing for more than fifty years	50 ⎦

Inserting these marginal totals into a cross-tabulation would yield table 15–5.

Having thus specified the marginal totals, we can now turn to filling in the remaining cells. Looking at the cell in the upper-left-hand corner of table

Table 15–5
Preliminary Cross-Tabulation of Years as
Nation-State and War Involvement

War Involvements	Years as Nation-State		Total
	50 or Less	More Than 50	
None			77
1 or more			67
Total	94	50	144

15–5, we find we need to count the number of nations that existed for fifty years or less *and* had no war involvements. In order to do this, we would need to look at the data in table 15–2 and ascertain the number of cases that satisfy these conditions. If you performed this counting operation correctly, you would find that 70 of the 144 nations existed for fifty years or less *and* experienced no war. This value would then be inserted in the upper-left-hand cell.

We could follow a similar procedure for the upper-right-hand cell, but as it turns out we have all the information we need to fill in the rest of the cells. We know that 77 of our 144 nations had no war involvements and 70 of these existed for 50 years or less. How many of these 77 un-involved nations existed for more than fifty years? Obviously, the answer is (77 − 70 =) 7 nations that avoided war and existed for more than fifty years.

Turning to the lower left-hand cell, we notice that 94 of our 144 nations existed for fifty years or less and 70 of these 94 had no war involvements. How many existed for fifty years or less and had one or more war involvements? Obviously (94 − 70 =) 24 nations qualify.

The remaining cell in the lower right-hand corner can be determined in the same manner as the previous two cells. We can either subtract 24 from 67 and get 43 or subtract 7 from 50 and get 43 again. Table 15–6 shows the completed cross-tabulation.

Table 15–6
Completed Cross-Tabulation of Years as
Nation-State and War Involvement

War Involvements	Years as Nation-State		Total
	50 or Less	More Than 50	
None	70	7	77
1 or more	24	43	67
Total	94	50	144

Exercise 15–9: Preparing a Cross-Tabulation

Construct a cross-tabulation of war initiation and years as nation-state using this partially completed exercise table:

War Initiations	Years as Nation-State		
	50 or Less	More Than 50	Total
None			
1 or more			
Total	94	50	144

1. Fill in the marginal totals for war initiations (third column, rows 1 and 2) from the frequency distribution you tabulated in exercise 15–5.

2. Count the number of nations in table 15–2 that have no war initiations *and* have existed as nation-states for fifty years or less. This number goes in the upper left-hand cell (first row, first column).

3. Fill in the remaining three internal cells by the subtraction method. For example, to obtain the number of nations with no war initiations that have existed for more than fifty years, subtract the number of nations counted in step 2 from the marginal total of no war initiations.

4. Check your work by counting the number of nations in table 15–2 that fall in the lower-right internal cell—those nations with at least one war initiation and that have existed for more than fifty years.

If the number of nations you counted in step 4 is the same as the number of nations you computed in step 3, you understand the essentials of a *contingency table*, as a cross-tabulation is sometimes called. Although cross-tabulations are basically a visual representation of two variables—or their *joint frequency distribution* (still another name for the same old thing)—it is the beginning step in analysis and hypothesis evaluation. You will learn how to use and interpret a contingency table in the next section.

Computing a Contingency Coefficient. The cross-tabulation we constructed in the previous section was in response to the question of whether a nation that exists for a longer period of time can expect to be involved in more wars than one that is in existence for a shorter period of time.

Looking back at table 15–6, it would appear that the data support the conclusion that the longer a nation exists, the more wars it can expect to be involved in. A large number of the nations having no war involvements (77) existed for less than fifty years (70), while most of those nations with one or more war involvements (67) existed for more than fifty years (43).

There are several ways in which we can better evaluate the evidence with regard to this question, and one of the simplest of these is the statistic

Table 15–7
Partial Cross-Tabulation of Years as
Nation-State and War Involvement

War Involvements	Years as Nation-State	
	50 or Less	More Than 50
None	a 70	b 7
1 or more	c 24	d 43

known as Yule's Q. This statistic is one member of a whole family of statistics that are called collectively *contingency coefficients*. Such statistics provide us with a single number representing the direction and strength of association between two variables.

To compute a Yule's Q we do not need the marginal totals in table 15–6, so we cut our table down to four cells, labeled a–d, as shown in table 15–7.

The formula for Yule's Q is as follows:

$$Q = \frac{(a \times d) - (b \times c)}{(a \times d) + (b \times c)}$$

If we substitute into this equation the values corresponding to the a, b, c, and d cells, we would get the following.

$$Q = \frac{(70 \times 43) - (7 \times 24)}{(70 \times 43) + (7 \times 24)} = \frac{3010 - 168}{3010 + 168} = \frac{2842}{3178} = +.89$$

Interpreting a Contingency Coefficient. What does a Q of +.89 mean? Consider for a moment a hypothetical (for example only, not necessarily real) case where nations in existence for more than fifty years accounted for *all* war involvements and nation-states that existed for fifty years or less had *no* involvements. This hypothetical situation would provide the strongest evidence for the proposition that the longer a nation exists, the more war involvements it can expect. The internal cells in the cross-tabulation of this hypothetical data would look like table 15–8.

If we computed the Yule's Q for table 15–8, it would be:

$$Q = \frac{(77 \times 67) - (0 \times 0)}{(77 \times 67) + (0 \times 0)} = \frac{5159}{5159} = +1.00$$

Thus, if it were true that no nations that existed for less than fifty years were involved in any wars and all wars involved nations that existed for more than

Table 15–8
Hypothetical Values for Years as Nation-State
and War Involvement, Set 1

War Involvements	Years as Nation-State	
	50 or Less	More Than 50
None	a 77	b 0
1 or more	c 0	d 67

50 years, then the Q statistic would reach its *maximum value of +1.00.*

Now suppose that the opposite were true; pretend this time that all our wars involved nations that existed for fifty years or less. Such data would be evidence for the exact opposite of our hypothesis; the cross-tabulation for this contrary set of hypothetical numbers would look like table 15–9.

If we computed Yule's Q according to the formula, we would get:

$$Q = \frac{(0 \times 0) - (77 \times 67)}{(0 \times 0) + (77 \times 67)} = \frac{-5159}{5159} = -1.00$$

From this hypothetical example, we can see that the lowest value for our Q statistic is -1.00, indicating that the presence of one characteristic is associated with the absence of the second characteristic.

Finally, let us consider the case where the results are very mixed, as in table 15–10, which presents a third set of example numbers; again, these values are purely arbitrary. The corresponding Q statistic would be:

$$Q = \frac{(39 \times 34) - (38 \times 33)}{(39 \times 34) + (38 \times 33)} = \frac{1326 - 1254}{1326 + 1254} = \frac{72}{2580} = +.03$$

As you can see, the resulting value is quite close to zero. What this would tell us is that the number of wars that a nation is involved in is not connected with the number of years that it exists.

Table 15–9
Hypothetical Values for Years as Nation-State
and War Involvement, Set 2

War Involvements	Years as Nation-State	
	50 or Less	More Than 50
None	a 0	b 77
1 or more	c 67	d 0

Table 15–10
Hypothetical Values for Years as Nation-State
and War Involvement, Set 3

War Involvements	Years as Nation-State	
	50 or Less	More Than 50
None	a 39	b 38
1 or more	c 33	d 34

As we have seen with our three sets of imaginary data, a *high positive* value of our Q statistic indicates that a substantial number of the cases are found in the *upper left-hand and the lower right-hand* corner cells. A *low negative* Q value indicates that most of our cases are in the *upper right-hand and lower left-hand* cells. A value close to zero indicates a relatively even distribution of cases among the four cells, hence, no relationship.

Now that you understand that the Q statistic varies between $+1.00$ and -1.00, what interpretation should you give to the finding that the relationship between the number of war involvements and the length of time as a nation-state is $+.89$? Since this value is close to $+1.00$, we would interpret the evidence as strongly supporting the conclusion that the longer a nation-state exists, the more wars it can expect to be involved in. Hence, our hypothesis that variations in war involvement by nation-states are partially explained by the fact that they exist for different lengths of time is confirmed.

Exercise 15–10: Computing a Contingency Coefficient and Interpreting the Result

Using the data you compiled in exercise 15–9, compute the Yule's Q statistic, and evaluate the results in light of what you have learned by answering the questions in this exercise.

Exercise Table
Partial Cross-Tabulation of Years as Nation-State
and War Initiation

War Initiations	Years as Nation-State	
	50 or Less	More Than 50
None	a	b
1 or more	c	d

Computation of Yule's Q:
    Formula: $Q =$
    Numbers: $Q =$

1. Are "years as nation-state" and "war initiation" positively or negatively associated? _____ How do you know this (a) based on the value of the Q and (b) based on the distribution of cases in the cells?
    Explain in words what the direction of the relationship between these two variables means.

2. Would you say that life span of a nation-state and frequency of war initiation are strongly or weakly related? _____. Explain your answer in terms of the values Q can assume; for example, how does the Q you computed compare with the highest possible value of Q and with the lowest value of Q?

Editors' Commentary

Methodological Notes: Uses and Limitations of Yule's Q

As is true of all other statistics, Yule's Q is appropriate in some instances and not in others, and there are limits to how much information it can provide. First, it is appropriate only for what are called two-by-two contingency tables. This is obvious from the fact that the formula calls for values corresponding to cells a, b, c, and d, but it bears explicit mention. This means that each variable can have only two values. When we want to use variables with more values, we must use different statistics.

For example, you may have noticed when you did the histogram in part 2 of exercise 15–6 that you were asked to create a measure of war initiation with three values: no wars, few wars, and several wars. This measure is ordinal; each successive value of the variable indicates more of that variable. For an analysis of ordinal variables, you could use statistics such as tau b (as Levy does), Spearman's rho (of which Rosen computes one), or gamma. If you want your variables to be even more precise and capture more information, you can use an interval-level measure. In Part I of exercise 15–6, you saw that the variable "war initiation" had six values: zero to five. This was an interval-level measure.

When a researcher wants to measure the relationship between war initiation and number of years as a nation-state using all of the richness that interval-level data provide, he or she uses interval-level measures and interval-level statistics. Such a procedure would produce a contingency table that would have six rows (0–5 initiations) and 150 columns (150 being the oldest age of a nation in this data set). Clearly, this is not the kind of contingency table you would want to draw or for which anyone would want to compute a statistic by hand. Computers are used to compute statistics for this type of analysis (for instance, Pearson's *r*; see Singer, Bremer, and Stuckey [chapter 2] and Wayman [chapter 8]), but the principle of computing a statistic to describe the relationship between two variables is the same as for Yule's Q.

Second, there is a mathematical limitation to Yule's Q that renders it invalid when there is a zero in just one cell. As you observed earlier, if there are zeros in two *diagonal* cells, Yule's Q is either 1.0 or −1.0. The perfect association corresponds to a visual inspection of the cells because we can see that the association is perfect.

Suppose, however, you have the following hypothetical set of data:

War Initiations	Years as Nation-State	
	50 or Fewer	*More Than 50*
None	3	0
1 or more	8	2

How many cases support the hypothesis that older nations initiate war and younger ones do not? There are five. How many cases do *not* support the hypothesis? Eight. Based on this observation, one would expect a slight negative association, since there are so many cases of young states that have initiated war. However, look what happens when you calculate Yule's Q:

$$\frac{(3)(2) - (8)(0)}{(3)(2) + (8)(0)} = \frac{6 - 0}{6 + 0} = \frac{6}{6} = 1.0$$

Five minus 8 times something would normally be a negative number and be much smaller than 5 plus 8 times something, producing a small negative association, but because multiplying a number by zero produces zero, the numerator and denominator come out to be equal. Mathematically, this produces a 1.0, but this is clearly not a valid representation of the relationship shown in the contingency table.

This means that it is not valid to use Yule's Q when one cell has a zero in it. The preferred solution is to use a different statistic; however, when you complete part IV, you will not have this option. Instead, statisticians have made the argument that it is permissible to insert a 1 in place of the zero—1 is a small enough increase over zero that we can justify this mechanism in order to get an idea of what the actual relationship is.

Note that if we insert a 1 in the example, we would get:

$$\frac{(3)(2) - (8)(1)}{(3)(2) + (8)(1)} = \frac{6 - 8}{6 + 8} = \frac{-2}{14} = -.142$$

This is a much more accurate result on two counts. First, the sign is negative, as we would expect when the younger states initiate more wars. Second and more important, the Yule's Q is very weak, and this corresponds with a case distribution that has five cases supporting the hypothesis and eight cases refuting it. In other words, there is not much of relationship here. Putting in a 1 clearly gives a more accurate representation of the relationship.

Each researcher must decide whether to use another statistic or insert a 1. Keep in mind that inserting a 1 is more justifiable the larger the number of cases. When the cell entries are large, substituting a 1 for a zero is not so significant, but when the cell entries are small, the difference a 1 makes is more substantial. Furthermore, when the number of cases is very small, calculating a measure of association of any sort may not be valid. Statistics of this sort are useful only for generalization, and it is dangerous to generalize from a small number of cases.

Third is a general point about Yule's Q. It is useful for this learning package because it is so simple to compute. The price we pay for this simplicity is some loss in what it can tell us. When there is a very large number of cases in just one cell, the Q can be quite high. However, a hypothesis generally predicts that cases will fall in two diagonal cells. A high Yule's Q may not necessarily mean that the hypothesis is correct for both cells. For example, suppose again that we hypothesize that older nation-states experience more war, and we find results as follows:

War Initiations	Years as Nation-State	
	50 or Less	More Than 50
None	75	2
1 or more	4	2

There are only two cases of older countries going to war, and there are six cases that deviate from the hypothesis, yet the Yule's Q is .92. We would have to interpret such a finding with great care. (There is an example of such an uneven distribution in the article by Siverson and King in chapter 7.) Likewise, when just one cell is very low, for example,

100	1
100	100

Yule's Q comes out very high. Although there are many cases in a and d, as predicted, the Yule's Q is .999, a very high value for a set of data with 101 deviant cases out of 301.

In sum, Yule's Q gives a useful, valid, and accurate description of the relationship when there are two diagonal zeros (perfect relationship), when there are high values in two diagonal cells (moderate to strong relationship), or when there are relatively equal values in each cell (low to no relationship). As long as there is balance between each diagonal pair, for example,

75	3	or	6	356
4	80		432	8

Yule's Q will overstate the relationship. When one cell is zero, Yule's Q is invalid.

Do not let this list of caveats discourage you from appreciating the utility of statistics. First, there are many other statistics that are sophisticated enough to over come these problems. For example, Wallace (chapter 3) reports an occasional Yule's Q but uses the more conservative phi throughout his analysis. Bueno de Mesquita (chapter 6) computes both Yule's Q and lambda for his two-by-two contingency tables. Second, and more important, the point is not to find a statistic that has no problems; the point is to understand the limits of statistics so that we can make intelligent use of them.

Exercise 15–11

For each of the following sets of data, indicate whether Yule's Q would be valid or invalid, and explain why. Then compute Yule's Q for each of the valid cases. (Number 1 has two possible answers).

1.	60	50	2.	60	40	3.	30	40	20
	40	0		10	20		20	750	30

4.	60	0	5.	20	70
	0	50		90	10

IV. Research Design Refinement: Testing a Hypothesis on Your Own

The analyses that you undertook in the previous section were chiefly designed to introduce you to some elementary analytical methods. As you shall see, these methods can be used to address a number of interesting questions once some additional refinements in research design are mastered. You have already been introduced to one major aspect of research design: inductive versus deductive strategies. We have been basically inductively oriented in this learning package, although a number of hypotheses on the causes of war are to be found in the literature that can be used in a more deductive fashion. We will use one of the more famous hypotheses to present another major aspect of research design. You will be introduced to the concepts of cross-sectional and longitudinal research designs. Once you have mastered this distinction, you will read a discussion of the major hypothesis relating national power and war involvement. Next, the data you will use to test the hypothesis will be discussed, and finally you will learn how to use the data to undertake a study of your own.

Research Design: Cross-National and Cross-Temporal

A research design is essentially a scientist's plan of attack on a particular empirical question. It usually specifies where he or she will get data, how they will be organized, and how they will be analyzed. Constructing good research designs is not easy, but it is very important. More than a few scientists have completed a piece of research only to find in the end that, due to faulty research design, they have arrived at answers to questions they did not ask and cannot answer the questions they were originally interested in.

Although an elaborate specification of what constitutes a good research design is clearly beyond the scope of this learning package, there is one aspect of this topic we want to discuss at length: the difference between cross-national and cross-temporal (longitudinal) research designs. Consider for a moment the following hypothesis:

> The more powerful a nation is, the more likely it is to become involved in war.

This is a bivariate hypothesis that posits that war involvement is related positively to national power. This hypothesis has been frequently put forth in one form or another by international relations scholars as early as Thucydides. Leaving aside for the moment the problems of measuring national power, how might we approach this hypothesis?

If you reread the hypothesis carefully, you should see that there are really two different interpretations as to its meaning:

1. The more powerful a nation is (in comparison to other nations at a particular point in time), the more likely it is to become involved in war.
2. The more powerful a nation is (in comparison to some standard at some point in its history), the more likely it is to become involved in war.

The first version states that during any given time period, say a decade, nations that are more powerful than the other nations are expected to be involved in more wars than the less powerful nations. In testing this kind of hypothesis, we would be comparing *many nations* at a *single time point*. Thus, this would be referred to as a *cross-national* research design since our comparison would be made *across nations*.

The second version of the hypothesis posits that as a particular nation rises and falls in power, its war involvement should also rise and fall accordingly. Obviously, since this would involve examining *many time periods for a single nation*, it should be apparent why this is referred to as a *cross-temporal* or *longitudinal* research design.

To test your understanding of the difference between cross-national and cross-temporal research designs, complete exercise 15–12.

Exercise 15–12: Differentiating Cross-National and Cross-Temporal Research Designs

The following hypotheses are from exercise 15–1; restate each general hypothesis as a cross-national hypothesis and a cross-temporal hypothesis:

1. Increases in military expenditures increase in proportion to the number of threats a nation receives from other states.
2. The higher the level of civil disturbance a nation experiences, the higher the level of its foreign conflict behavior.
3. The more states a nation shares a common border with, the higher the probability that it will become involved in war.

The preceding exercise should have given you a good basic understanding of the differences between cross-national and longitudinal studies. Before proceeding further, however, let us investigate in more detail the dual nature of general, conceptual hypotheses by examining the different types of analyses resulting from different designs.

Historically, the need for "living space" has often been advanced by statesmen as a reason for territorial aggression. Both Germany and Japan in the years preceding World War II claimed that their population was too crowded on the land. Thus, let us use the following hypothesis as an example:

The higher the population density of a nation, the more likely it will initiate a war.

The cross-national version of this hypothesis would read:

Nations that have high population density relative to other nations at a given point in time, are more likely to initiate wars than the less population-dense nations.

You would need to formulate an operational definition of population density and of war initiation and then specify the nations to be studied (the *spatial domain*) and the time period to be covered (the *temporal domain*). For example, you might use the nations in Asia 1890–1900 as your spatial-temporal domain. Next you would collect data on the two variables for the specified nations and time period, coding each nation as being "high" or "low" on population density and as having "none" or "one or more" war initiations. Your resulting cross-tabulation would look like this:

	Number of Nations with		
Number of Nations with:	No War Initiations	One or More War Initiations	Total
Low population density			
High population density			
Total			

You could then compute a Yule Q and see if your hypothesis was confirmed or disconfirmed by the empirical evidence.

Alternatively, you could do a longitudinal analysis. The cross-temporal version of the population density–war initiation hypothesis would be:

At those times when a nation's population density is high relative to other times in its history, the nation is more likely to initiate a war.

In this case you would still need to define operationally your two variables of population density and war initiation; then you would specify your spatial-temporal domain. Here, the spatial-temporal domain would be *one nation over many time periods*; for example, you might choose Germany during the years 1816–1965. This time, rather than code each nation on your variables, you would have to code each *time unit* because you want to know if the times when German population density is high are the same times it initiates wars. Just as we collapsed data for histogram construction, you would probably want to collapse the time units somewhat; rather than code data for each year, you might code every five-year period from 1816 to 1965 as being high or low on your two variables. Following this strategy, your cross-tabulation would be:

Number of Half-Decades with:	Number of Half-Decades with		
	No War Initiations	One or More War Initiations	Total
Low population density			
High population density			
Total			

Again, you would compute a Yule's Q to see if your hypothesis was confirmed or disconfirmed.

Exercise 15–13: Analyzing Results of Cross-National and Cross-Temporal Studies

Suppose you tested the population density–war initiation hypothesis and obtained a Yule's Q of $+.80$ for both the cross-national and the cross-temporal studies. What conclusions could you draw from each study? How are these conclusions different? How are they similar? Which strategy do you think is better for this particular hypothesis, and why? (Both a cross-national and a longitudinal study of the population density hypothesis have been done by the Correlates of War project; see Bremer, Singer and Luterbacher [1973].

We have now gone through a number of aspects and implications of the differences and similarities in cross-national and cross-temporal research designs. Now try to put all that you have learned in the foregoing pages together in the next exercise.

Exercise 15–14: Preparing a Research Design

Using the hypothesis below, decide whether you would prefer to use a cross-national or longitudinal design in investigating the relationship posited. Give a rationale for your choice, and restate the hypothesis in the proper form. Next, indicate what spatial-temporal domain you would want to use, giving your reasons for the choice. Briefly indicate how the variables involved in the hypothesis might be operationalized, and briefly describe the coding procedure you would have to perform. Then construct the outline of a cross-tabulation (as we did in the text for population density and war initiation). Discuss what inferences you might draw if you obtained a Q of $-.40$.

Hypothesis: The more severe a war involvement is, the longer it will be before a nation is involved in another war.

Exercise 15–15: Testing the Powerful and the War-Prone Hypothesis

If you had no trouble with the preceding exercise, you are ready to go through a complete analysis, pretty much on your own from start to finish. Your ability to finish the last exercise will depend on how well you have learned the material in the learning package and will give you an indication of what doing "real" research is all about. To save time and trouble, we have structured the exercise a good deal, but most of the hard thinking has been left for you. In the exercise, you are to test a version of the powerful and war-prone hypothesis.

Editors' Adaption: Hypothesis Testing Paper

For this paper you will go through the basic steps of the scientific method. You will develop a proposition, specify how it can be tested, operationalize your concepts, marshal data (provided in appendix 15A), analyze the data using Yule's Q, and then accept or reject your hypothesis on the basis of the evidence you have examined.

The paper you write can be anywhere from five to ten pages, depending on how many tests you conduct. The paper should have four sections: I. Theoretical Rationale, II. Research Design, III. Findings, and IV. Interpretation and Conclusion.

1. Develop a proposition that you think is true about the relationship between the power of states and their proneness to war. Some people think that strong states are aggressive and prone to war and would tend to *initiate* more wars. Others think that weak states would be more *involved* in wars than strong states because they are easy targets. Notice these are two different propositions: one is about war *initiation* and the other about war *involvement*. Both of these propositions are cross-sectional in their theoretical rationale; they compare nations to each other.

Propositions that are longitudinal in character look at whether states initiate or become involved in war at those times in their history when they are stronger (or larger). Here a rationale might make reference to the role of militarism in a society (for example, the influence of a military-industrial complex) or to factors promoting expansion, like overpopulation.

After some reflection, state a proposition specifying a relationship between power and war and indicate why you think it is true or false.

2. In appendix 15A you will find data for European states in five-year intervals from 1816 to 1965 on war involvements and war initiations (table 15A–1). You will also find data on military personnel (table 15A–2) and total population (table 15A–3). In your research design, indicate how you will use these empirical observations to "test" your proposition cross-nationally and longitudinally. In other words, indicate (by use of a contingency table, if you wish) the evidence that would support your proposition and the evidence that would lead you to reject your proposition.

3. The notes to tables 15A–2 and 15A–3 contain the operational definitions Singer and Small used for the military personnel and population variables. Choose military personnel, total population, or some combination of the two as your indicator of power. Conclude by discussing

the strengths and weaknesses of your measure(s) in terms of whether it is a **valid** indicator of power.

4. Convert your proposition into a testable hypothesis by operationalizing power and war with the data you have been given. Formulate a cross-national and a longitudinal hypothesis, and indicate how each hypothesis is different from and similar to the other, especially in terms of theoretical rationale.

5. For the cross-national study, analyze the data for the entire period for all relevant states. Begin by copying the appropriate war data in table 15A–1 to a coding sheet. (A blank coding sheet is provided in appendix 15C.) The last column of the table shows the total number of war involvements and initiations for each state.

6. Calculate average (modal) capability scores for each country over the entire time using the data in table 15A–2 or 15A–3, depending on which indicator you use. For the cross-national study, compare the score each state has in a half-decade with the average score for all states given at the bottom of the table (15A–2 or 15A–3). Then score that state's half-decade as either above or below the European average. For example, in table 15A–2, Prussia in 1860 has a 20, while the average for all states is 21.8. Thus, Prussia is below average. By 1865, however, Prussia has gone up to 22, and the system average has gone down to 19.8; therefore Prussia would be scored as above average. Once you have scored each half-decade in this manner, count the most frequent score to determine the mode. For Prussia, the mode is above average. As you use the data coding sheets for the cross-national study, you may find it useful to place the name of each state in a contingency table like the following one:

	War Involvements	
Population	None	One or More
Low		
High		Prussia

7. Follow the directions in appendix 15B to fill out the analysis form and calculate the Yule's Q. (A blank analysis form is provided in appendix 15C.)

8. After completing the cross-national study, select at least five states, and test your hypothesis longitudinally. In order to calculate the power score for your longitudinal design, compare the half-decade score of a state with its own overall average given at the far right of the table. Determine the mode, and follow the steps given in the longitudinal analysis form (Figure 15B–2). This will produce five sets of findings (five Yule's Qs).

9. For those wishing to do a more sophisticated paper, control for century by doing separate tests of the nineteenth and twentieth centuries once you have completed the tests for the entire period.

10. After completing the tests, decide whether you should accept or reject your hypothesis. Indicate whether you think your findings reflect "reality" or flaws in your test design or measures. Outline the implications of your tests for future research.

After completing your paper, you may want to read Bremer (1980a, 1980b) and Bremer, Singer, and Luterbacher (1973) to see how similar propositions have been tested in the literature and how their results compare to yours.

Alternate Paper

For those wishing to test their own hypotheses, additional data can be found in the articles reprinted in this book. See in particular Singer *et al.*, table 2–1 (capability concentration, war underway), Wallace, Appendix 3A (disputes, arms expenditures index); Bueno de Mesquita, appendix 6A (expected utility scores, war initiations and outcomes); Wayman, tables 8–2 and 8–3 (power polarization, alliance polarization), Wallensteen, table 10–1 (universalist/particularist periods), Rosen, tables 11–1 and 11–3 (battle deaths by war, winner/loser ratios); Rasler and Thompson tables 13–1 and 13–5 (selected wars and expenditures 1700–1980 for the United Kingdom, France, the United States, and Japan). The last paragraph of the bibliographical essay in this volume cites additional sources of data.

Conclusion

What have you accomplished in this package? If you have carefully read the material in the learning package and faithfully performed all the exercises, you have mastered some very basic and important aspects of conducting scientific research, as well as learned a good deal about the manner in which the causes of war are and can be studied scientifically. With regard to conducting research, you have learned the basic steps in a primarily inductive research strategy.

In part I you learned of the need for scientific investigations and the three major research projects that pioneered the peace research movement. Using the coding rules of the Correlates of War project as an example, in part II you learned of the difficulties in defining and operationalizing war, as well as how to apply coding rules to historical narratives such as provide the raw data for the scientific investigation of war. Then in part III, using Correlates of War data, you examined the relationship between war involvement and the length of time a nation exists, finding a relatively strong positive association. Last, in part IV, you conducted a piece of research to examine one of the most prominent hypotheses on the causes of war. Exercise 15–15 should have made clear to you the importance of stating explicitly your rationale and procedures at each stage in hypothesis testing; different variable operationalizations, different designs, and/or different spatial-temporal domains can lead to different conclusions. Thus, for scientific study to be cumulative and enable future scholars to carry on where others have ended, we must always strive for clarity and replicability in our research. You have learned the basic skills necessary for beginning such research. A great deal of the basic type of investigation we have performed in this learning package, as well as much more sophisticated analyses, remain to be done before we have developed and tested a general theory of the causes of war that would help humanity avoid war in the future.

Appendix 15A:
Data for Exercise 15–15

Table 15A–1
Number of War Involvements and War Initiations for Major European Nation-States, 1816–1965

Nation-State	1820	1825	1830	1835	1840	1845	1850	1855	1860	1865	1870	1875	1880	1885
England	0	0	1/0	0	0	0	0	1/0	1/1	0	0	0	0	0
Ireland	X	X	X	X	X	X	X	X	X	X	X	X	X	X
Holland	X	0	0	0	0	0	0	0	0	0	0	0	0	0
Belgium	X	X	0	0	0	0	0	0	0	0	0	0	0	0
Luxembourg	X	X	X	X	X	X	X	X	X	X	X	X	X	X
France	0	1/1	1/0	0	0	0	1/1	1/0	1/0	1/1	1/1	0	0	1/1
Switzerland	0	0	0	0	0	0	0	0	0	0	0	0	0	0
Spain	0	1/0	0	0	0	0	0	0	1/1	1/1	0	0	0	0
Portugal	0	0	0	0	0	0	0	0	0	0	0	0	0	0
Prussia/Germany	0	0	0	0	0	0	1/1	0	0	1/1	2/1	0	0	0
German Federal Republic	X	X	X	X	X	X	X	X	X	X	X	X	X	X
German Democratic Republic	X	X	X	X	X	X	X	X	X	X	X	X	X	X
Poland	X	X	X	X	X	X	X	X	X	X	X	X	X	X
Austria-Hungary	0	0	0	0	0	0	2/0	0	1/1	1/0	1/0	0	0	0
Austria	X	X	X	X	X	X	X	X	X	X	X	X	X	X
Hungary	X	X	X	X	X	X	X	X	X	X	X	X	X	X
Czechoslovakia	X	X	X	X	X	X	X	X	X	X	X	X	X	X
Italy	0	0	0	0	0	0	1/1	1/0	3/2	0	1/0	0	0	0
Albania	X	X	X	X	X	X	X	X	X	X	X	X	X	X
Serbia/Yugoslavia	X	X	X	X	X	X	X	X	X	X	X	X	0	0
Greece	X	X	0	0	0	0	0	0	0	0	0	0	0	0
Bulgaria	X	X	X	X	X	X	X	X	X	X	X	X	X	X
Rumania	X	X	X	X	X	X	X	X	X	X	X	0	0	0
Russia/U.S.S.R.	0	0	2/1	0	0	0	0	1/0	0	0	0	0	1/1	0
Estonia	X	X	X	X	X	X	X	X	X	X	X	X	X	X
Latvia	X	X	X	X	X	X	X	X	X	X	X	X	X	X
Lithuania	X	X	X	X	X	X	X	X	X	X	X	X	X	X
Finland	X	X	X	X	X	X	X	X	X	X	X	X	X	X
Sweden	0	0	0	0	0	0	0	0	0	0	0	0	0	0
Norway	X	X	X	X	X	X	X	X	X	X	X	X	X	X
Denmark	0	0	0	0	0	0	1/0	0	0	1/0	0	0	0	0
Iceland	X	X	X	X	X	X	X	X	X	X	X	X	X	X
Total	0	2/1*	4/1	0	0	0	6/3	4/0	7/5	5/3	5/2	0	1/1	1/1

Source: Singer and Small (1972: Tables 2.1, 4.2).

Notes: Entries are the total number of wars in which the nation was involved in the (usually) five-year period ending in the year given at the top of each column; following the slash is a number representing the number of those war involvements that the nation initiated.

Table 15A–1 continued

1890	1895	1900	1905	1910	1913	1920	1925	1930	1935	1938	1946	1950	1955	1960	1965	TOTAL
0	0	0	0	0	0	1/0	0	0	0	0	1/0	1/0	0	1/0	0	7/1*
X	X	X	X	X	X	X	0	0	0	0	0	0	0	0	0	0/0
0	0	0	0	0	0	0	0	0	0	0	1/0	1/0	0	0	0	2/0
0	0	0	0	0	0	1/0	0	0	0	0	1/0	1/0	0	0	0	3/0
X	X	X	X	X	X	0	0	0	0	0	0	0	0	0	0	0/0
0	0	0	0	0	0	1/0	0	0	0	0	1/0	1/0	0	1/0	0	12/5
0	0	0	0	0	0	0	0	0	0	0	0	0	0	0	0	0/0
0	0	1/0	0	1/1	0	0	0	0	0	0	0	0	0	0	0	5/3
0	0	0	0	0	0	1/0	0	0	0	0	0	0	0	0	0	1/0
0	0	0	0	0	0	1/0	0	0	0	0	1/1	X	X	X	X	6/4
X	X	X	X	X	X	X	X	X	X	X	X	X	0	0	0	0/0
X	X	X	X	X	X	X	X	X	X	X	X	X	0	0	0	0/0
X	X	X	X	X	X	0	0	0	0	0	1/0	0	0	0	0	1/0
0	0	0	0	0	0	1/1	X	X	X	X	X	X	X	X	X	6/2
X	X	X	X	X	X	0	0	0	0	0	0	0	0	0	0	0/0
X	X	X	X	X	X	1/0	0	0	0	0	1/0	0	0	1/0	0	3/0
X	X	X	X	X	X	1/0	0	0	0	0	0	0	0	0	0	1/0
0	0	0	0	0	1/1	1/0	0	0	1/1	0	2/0	0	0	0	0	11/5
X	X	X	X	X	X	0	0	0	0	0	0	0	0	0	0	0/0
0	0	0	0	0	2/1	1/0	0	0	0	0	1/0	0	0	0	0	4/1
0	0	1/1	0	0	2/0	2/1	0	0	0	0	1/0	1/0	0	0	0	7/2
X	X	X	X	0	2/1	1/0	0	0	0	0	2/0	0	0	0	0	5/1
0	0	0	0	0	1/0	2/1	0	0	0	0	2/0	0	0	0	0	5/1
0	0	0	1/0	0	0	1/0	0	0	0	0	3/1	0	0	1/1	0	10/4
X	X	X	X	X	X	0	0	0	0	0	X	X	X	X	X	0/0
X	X	X	X	X	X	0	0	0	0	0	X	X	X	X	X	0/0
X	X	X	X	X	X	0	0	0	0	0	X	X	X	X	X	0/0
X	X	X	X	X	X	0	0	0	0	0	2/0	0	0	0	0	2/0
0	0	0	0	0	0	0	0	0	0	0	0	0	0	0	0	0/0
X	X	X	X	0	0	0	0	0	0	0	1/0	0	0	0	0	1/0
0	0	0	0	0	0	0	0	0	0	0	0	0	0	0	0	2/0
X	X	X	X	X	X	X	X	X	X	X	X	0	0	0	0	0/0
0	0	2/1	1/0	1/1	8/3	16/3	0	0	1/1	0	21/2	5/0	0	4/1	0	94/29

* The total number of war involvements/initiations for each nation is given at the end of each nation's row in the table; similarly, the total number of war involvements/initiations that occurred in each half-decade is given at the bottom of each column.

An X in a cell of the table indicates that the political entity in the row was not a member of the interstate system during that half-decade.

Table 15A–2
Military Personnel of Major European Nation-States, 1816–1965 (10,000s of Men)

Nation	1820	1825	1830	1835	1840	1845	1850	1855	1860	1865	1870	1875	1880	1885
England	14	13	14	14	17	18	20	33	35	30	26	25	25	26
Ireland	X	X	X	X	X	X	X	X	X	X	X	X	X	X
Holland	5	5	5	5	5	5	4	3	3	3	3	3	3	4
Belgium	X	X	6	3	5	3	4	4	4	4	4	4	5	5
Luxembourg	X	X	X	X	X	X	X	X	X	X	X	X	X	X
France	21	24	26	29	45	36	44	65	61	48	45	49	54	52
Switzerland	0	0	0	0	0	0	0	0	0	0	0	0	0	0
Spain	15	9	8	10	8	11	12	9	13	12	12	11	16	13
Portugal	2	3	4	5	3	3	2	2	2	2	3	4	3	4
Prussia/Germany	13	13	13	13	14	14	13	14	20	22	32	43	43	46
German Federal Republic	X	X	X	X	X	X	X	X	X	X	X	X	X	X
German Democratic Republic	X	X	X	X	X	X	X	X	X	X	X	X	X	X
Poland	X	X	X	X	X	X	X	X	X	X	X	X	X	X
Austria-Hungary	26	27	27	26	27	32	43	43	31	30	25	30	27	30
Austria	X	X	X	X	X	X	X	X	X	X	X	X	X	X
Hungary	X	X	X	X	X	X	X	X	X	X	X	X	X	X
Czechoslovakia	X	X	X	X	X	X	X	X	X	X	X	X	X	X
Italy	4	3	3	4	4	3	4	5	18	21	16	18	17	23
Albania	X	X	X	X	X	X	X	X	X	X	X	X	X	X
Serbia/Yugoslavia	X	X	X	X	X	X	X	X	X	X	X	X	1	1
Greece	X	X	1	1	1	1	1	1	1	1	1	2	1	3
Bulgaria	X	X	X	X	X	X	X	X	X	X	X	X	X	X
Rumania	X	X	X	X	X	X	X	X	X	X	X	X	2	3
Russia/U.S.S.R.	77	86	83	67	62	71	87	78	86	73	74	84	91	78
Estonia	X	X	X	X	X	X	X	X	X	X	X	X	X	X
Latvia	X	X	X	X	X	X	X	X	X	X	X	X	X	X
Lithuania	X	X	X	X	X	X	X	X	X	X	X	X	X	X
Finland	X	X	X	X	X	X	X	X	X	X	X	X	X	X
Sweden	5	5	5	5	5	5	5	5	6	7	6	6	6	6
Norway	X	X	X	X	X	X	X	X	X	X	X	X	X	X
Denmark	3	4	4	4	5	3	3	3	3	4	4	2	1	1
Iceland	X	X	X	X	X	X	X	X	X	X	X	X	X	X
Half-decade average	16.8	17.5	15.3	14.3	15.5	15.8	18.6	20.4	21.8	19.8	19.3	21.6	19.7	20.0

Source: Data are from the holdings of the Correlates of War Project by the kind permission of J. David Singer.

Notes: "Military personnel" is defined as the total number of men (and women if applicable) in the standing armed forces (army, navy, and later air force). This variable does *not* include reservists or paramilitary personnel such as the U.S. National Guard, unless the latter were known (from historical records) to constitute *de facto* the standing armed forces of the nation under consideration. The figure reported represents the best estimate, based on national records and international yearbooks such as

Table 15A–2 continued

1890	1895	1900	1905	1910	1913	1920	1925	1930	1935	1938	1946	1950	1955	1960	1965	Nation Average
28	31	49	39	37	53	60	34	32	32	38	205	83	91	48	42	40.4
X	X	X	X	X	X	X	2	1	1	1	1	1	1	1	1	1.1
3	3	4	5	5	4	2	2	1	2	2	20	21	17	14	10	5.6
5	5	5	4	5	5	16	9	7	7	9	8	7	9	11	11	6.0
X	X	X	X	X	X	0	0	0	0	0	.2	.3	.3	.3	.3	.3
60	59	62	63	65	63	146	48	41	55	58	58	60	80	103	56	55.9
0	0	0	0	0	0	0	0	0	0	0	1	1	2	2	2	1.6
14	15	11	11	14	15	24	15	13	14	55	46	49	51	37	33	18.9
3	3	4	4	4	4	4	4	4	4	4	7	7	8	8	16	4.2
51	60	62	65	67	86	11	11	11	46	78	X	X	X	X	X	34.4
X	X	X	X	X	X	X	X	X	X	X	X	X		31	41	36.0
X	X	X	X	X	X	X	X	X	X	X	X	X		11	12	11.5
X	X	X	X	X	X	96	27	27	27	31	13	33	30	20	28	33.7
33	31	31	31	32	36	X	X	X	X	X	X	X	X	X	X	30.9
X	X	X	X	X	X	3	3	2	3	6	X	X	2	4	4	3.4
X	X	X	X	X	X	3	4	3	4	4		11	20	8	14	7.4
X	X	X	X	X	X	15	13	13	12	16	25	25	25	30	24	19.4
26	23	26	27	28	36	30	41	32	33	33	X	20	23	34	45	20.9
X	X	X	X	X	X		1	1	1	1	6	6	4	3	4	3.0
1	2	2	3	4	3	21	15	11	12	14	16	25	37	37	25	12.8
3	3	3	3	3	3	7	8	7	6	10	12	19	14	16	16	5.3
X	X	X	X	6	6	2	2	2	2	2	11	21	21	12	17	8.6
4	5	6	7	9	11	25	14	19	14	17	11	22	27	23	26	13.6
85	82	91	116	138	129	305	56	56	130	157	600	430	590	360	293	156.7
X	X	X	X	X	X	2	2	1	1	1	X	X	X	X	X	1.4
X	X	X	X	X	X	2	2	2	3	3	X	X	X	X	X	2.4
X	X	X	X	X	X	5	2	2	2	2	X	X	X	X	X	2.8
X	X	X	X	X	X	4	3	3	3	4	4	4	4	4	4	3.7
6	6	6	4	7	8	9	6	3	4	5		7		4	2	5.6
X	X	X	1	1	1	1	1	.4	.4	.4	3	3	3	4	3	1.7
2	1	1	1	2	2	2	1	1	1	1	1	2	3	3	5	2.4
X	X	X	X	X	X	X	X	X	X	X	0	0	0	0	0	0
21.6	21.9	24.2	24.0	25.1	27.4	33.1	12.6	11.8	16.8		57.8	39.0	47.9	33.1	27.2	

the *Almanac de Gotha* and *Statesmen's Yearbook*, of the actual number of persons under arms on January 1 of the last year of the half-decade.

An X in any cell of the table indicates that the political entity was not a member of the international system during the half-decade under which the X is located.

A blank cell indicates that no estimate could be found of the size of the nation's armed forces in the given half-decade.

Table 15A–3
Total Population of Major European Nation-States, 1816–1965
(millions of persons)

Nation-State	1820	1825	1830	1835	1840	1845
England	21.40	22.30	24.27	25.00	26.33	27.00
Ireland	X	X	X	X	X	X
Holland	5.58	5.93	2.64	2.70	2.86	3.00
Belgium	X	X	3.53	4.20	4.23	4.26
Luxembourg	X	X	X	X	X	X
France	31.22	31.86	32.50	33.54	34.14	35.40
Switzerland	1.66	2.04	2.10	2.19	2.20	2.30
Spain	10.61	11.70	12.00	12.29	12.80	13.40
Portugal	3.60	3.60	3.70	3.70	3.80	3.80
Prussia/Germany	11.64	12.55	12.78	14.00	14.93	15.45
German Federal Republic	X	X	X	X	X	X
German Democratic Republic	X	X	X	X	X	X
Poland	X	X	X	X	X	X
Austria-Hungary	30.00	31.90	32.50	33.00	33.50	34.20
Austria	X	X	X	X	X	X
Hungary	X	X	X	X	X	X
Czechoslovakia	X	X	X	X	X	X
Italy	3.97	4.17	4.10	4.40	4.65	4.80
Albania	X	X	X	X	X	X
Serbia/Yugoslavia	X	X	X	X	X	X
Greece	X	X	.64	.85	.96	.98
Bulgaria	X	X	X	X	X	X
Rumania	X	X	X	X	X	X
Russia/U.S.S.R.	49.00	52.00	56.00	59.11	63.00	65.90
Estonia	X	X	X	X	X	X
Latvia	X	X	X	X	X	X
Lithuania	X	X	X	X	X	X
Finland	X	X	X	X	X	X
Sweden	3.73	3.92	4.20	4.20	4.40	4.65
Norway	X	X	X	X	X	X
Denmark	1.75	2.00	2.06	2.13	2.20	2.36
Iceland	X	X	X	X	X	X
Half-decade average	14.515	15.331	13.780	15.420	16.080	16.648

Source: Data are from the holdings of the Correlates of War Project by the kind permission of J. David Singer.

Notes: "Total population" is defined as the number of men, women, and children residing within the legal boundaries of the territory under the sovereign jurisdiction of that nation as reported in various national censuses, international yearbooks, and compilations of demographic statistics by international organizations such as the League of Nations and the United

Table 15–A3 continued

1850	1855	1860	1865	1870	1875	1880	1885	1890	1895
27.45	29.00	30.00	31.00	31.63	32.75	34.62	36.02	38.10	39.11
X	X	X	X	X	X	X	X	X	X
3.24	3.45	3.57	3.60	3.69	3.81	4.06	4.34	4.51	4.93
4.38	4.51	4.73	4.83	5.09	5.40	5.52	5.85	6.07	6.41
X	X	X	X	X	X	X	X	X	X
35.71	36.04	37.47	38.07	39.00	36.50	37.62	38.22	38.34	38.52
2.40	2.45	2.51	2.60	2.67	2.70	2.85	2.90	3.00	3.20
14.22	15.45	16.30	16.30	16.79	16.63	16.84	17.55	18.00	18.13
3.90	3.90	4.00	4.20	4.30	4.40	4.60	4.80	5.05	5.20
16.35	17.20	18.50	23.58	38.30	42.73	45.00	47.00	49.43	52.25
X	X	X	X	X	X	X	X	X	X
X	X	X	X	X	X	X	X	X	X
X	X	X	X	X	X	X	X	X	X
34.40	35.00	34.50	35.53	36.00	37.50	39.11	39.22	41.17	43.00
X	X	X	X	X	X	X	X	X	X
X	X	X	X	X	X	X	X	X	X
X	X	X	X	X	X	X	X	X	X
4.92	5.17	21.92	22.29	26.72	27.48	28.45	29.70	30.35	31.29
X	X	X	X	X	X	X	X	X	X
X	X	X	X	X	X	1.70	1.94	2.16	2.31
1.00	1.14	1.20	1.35	1.46	1.60	1.68	2.00	2.19	2.30
X	X	X	X	X	X	X	X	X	X
X	X	X	X	X	X	5.29	5.38	5.50	5.60
69.00	71.24	74.14	79.00	85.69	91.00	91.50	108.31	118.00	125.00
X	X	X	X	X	X	X	X	X	X
X	X	X	X	X	X	X	X	X	X
X	X	X	X	X	X	X	X	X	X
X	X	X	X	X	X	X	X	X	X
4.90	5.20	5.46	5.70	5.90	6.10	6.40	6.60	6.80	7.10
X	X	X	X	X	X	X	X	X	X
2.30	2.47	2.69	1.72	1.79	1.87	1.98	2.10	2.19	2.30
X	X	X	X	X	X	X	X	X	X
16.012	16.591	18.356	19.269	21.359	22.176	20.859	22.026	23.179	24.167

Nations. The figure reported represents the best estimate of the actual population in the last year of the half-decade.

An "X" indicates that the political entity was not a member of the international system during the half-decade indicated.

A blank cell indicates that no estimate could be found of the size of the nation's population in the given half-decade.

Table 15A–3 continued

	1900	1905	1910	1913	1920	1925	1930	1935
Eng	41.98	43.22	45.99	46.18	46.94	45.00	45.80	46.87
Ire	X	X	X	X	X	3.16	2.99	2.97
Hol	5.18	5.59	5.95	6.11	6.84	7.42	7.94	8.48
Bel	6.69	7.16	7.52	7.57	7.46	7.81	8.00	8.30
Lux	X	X	X	X	.26	.27	.30	.30
Fr.	38.90	39.23	40.00	41.00	39.21	40.74	41.84	41.91
Swi	3.32	3.51	3.77	3.80	3.88	4.00	4.07	4.16
Sp	18.62	19.05	18.59	20.36	21.30	22.00	23.56	24.58
Por	5.40	5.70	6.00	6.20	6.50	6.80	7.10	7.40
Ger	56.37	60.64	64.78	67.00	59.85	62.41	65.29	66.87
FRG	X	X	X	X	X	X	X	X
GDR	X	X	X	X	X	X	X	X
Pol	X	X	X	X	26.70	27.30	31.50	33.60
A–H	45.41	47.32	51.34	53.00	X	X	X	X
Aus	X	X	X	X	6.41	6.53	6.72	6.76
Hun	X	X	X	X	7.98	8.37	8.76	8.98
Czech	X	X	X	X	13.00	13.50	14.00	14.34
It	32.00	33.36	34.69	35.24	38.45	40.13	40.76	42.62
Alb	X	X	X	X	.82	.83	1.00	1.00
Yugo	2.49	2.69	2.92	4.50	11.90	12.80	13.80	14.77
Gr	2.50	2.60	2.67	2.70	5.50	5.80	6.21	6.83
Bul	X	X	4.34	4.77	4.85	5.48	5.70	6.10
Rum	6.05	6.48	6.97	7.09	16.00	17.00	18.03	19.09
USSR	132.00	143.00	154.00	162.00	137.00	141.00	156.00	161.00
Est	X	X	X	X	1.11	1.11	1.12	1.13
Lat	X	X	X	X	1.60	1.85	1.90	1.95
Lith	X	X	X	X	2.00	2.23	2.40	2.48
Fin	X	X	X	X	3.37	3.53	3.67	3.79
Swe	7.40	5.34	5.52	5.64	5.85	6.00	6.14	6.25
Nor	X	2.31	2.46	2.50	2.65	2.76	2.82	2.88
Den	2.43	2.57	2.80	2.90	3.27	3.44	3.55	3.71
Ice	X	X	X	X	X	X	X	X
Avg.	25.421	25.281	25.628	26.587	17.804	17.902	18.963	19.611

Table 15A–3 continued

1938	1946	1950	1955	1960	1965	Nation Average
47.49	49.20	50.78	51.36	52.49	54.53	38.077
2.94	2.96	2.97	2.92	2.83	2.88	2.960
8.73	9.42	10.11	10.75	11.48	12.29	5.572
8.39	8.37	8.64	8.87	9.15	9.46	6.519
.30	.29	.30	.31	.31	.33	.297
41.10	39.00	41.74	43.79	45.68	48.76	38.552
4.19	4.47	4.69	4.98	5.36	5.95	3.330
25.28	27.01	27.87	29.06	30.30	32.06	19.319
7.51	8.12	8.41	8.61	8.83	9.20	5.614
71.79	X	X	X	X	X	40.549
X	X	X	50.17	53.22	56.84	53.410
X	X	X	17.95	17.24	17.03	17.407
34.93	23.96	24.82	27.28	29.70	30.65	29.244
X	X	X	X	X	X	38.380
6.75	X	X	6.95	7.05	7.25	6.803
9.17	9.04	9.34	9.83	9.98	10.13	9.153
14.60	12.92	12.39	13.09	13.65	14.16	13.565
43.60	X	46.77	48.20	49.64	51.58	27.290
1.05	1.13	1.22	1.38	1.61	1.87	1.191
15.38	14.80	16.35	17.52	18.40	19.43	9.770
7.10	7.42	7.55	7.97	8.33	8.55	3.932
6.24	7.00	7.25	7.50	7.87	8.20	6.275
19.75	15.79	16.31	17.33	18.40	19.03	12.505
170.42	160.00	180.00	196.20	214.20	230.94	120.092
1.14	X	X	X	X	X	1.122
1.97	X	X	X	X	X	1.854
2.55	X	X	X	X	X	2.332
3.86	3.81	4.01	4.24	4.43	4.61	3.932
6.29	6.72	7.01	7.26	7.48	7.73	5.857
2.92	3.13	3.27	3.43	3.58	3.72	2.956
3.78	4.15	4.27	4.44	4.58	4.76	2.819
X	.13	.14	.16	.18	.19	.160
20.581	18.210	20.675	22.261	22.734	24.894	

Appendix 15B:
Instructions for and Samples of Data Coding Sheet and Analysis Form

The steps for filling out a data coding sheet and an analysis form are given below. Following the instructions are partial samples of completed data sheets and analysis forms for both a cross-national and a longitudinal study (figures 15B–1 and 15B–2). You should examine the sample sheets in conjunction with the data matrices in Appendix 15A to make sure you understand the procedures.

DATA CODING SHEET   Coder   *C. Cannizzo*   Date   *9/1/75*

Cross-National   Study of War   *Involvement*   and   *Total Population*

Spatial-Temporal Domain: *Major European Nations, 1816-1825*

I *Nation-State*	II Number of War *Involvements*	III Power Score: High or Low on *Total* *Population*
England	0	*Hi*
*France	1	*Hi*
Switzerland	0	*Lo*
Spain	1	*Lo*
Portugal	0	*Lo*
Prussia	0	*Hi*
Austria-Hungary	0	*Hi*
Italy	0	*Lo*
Sweden	0	*Lo*
Denmark	0	*Lo*

*Countries not in the international system have been omitted from analysis.

Figure 15B–1. Sample Data Coding Sheets

Data Coding Sheet Instructions (see Figure 15B–1)

1. Fill in "cross-national" or "cross-temporal" and the appropriate variable and spatial-temporal domain information at the top of the page.

2. Fill in the title of the first column—"Nation-State" for a cross-national study and "Decade" (or half-decade) for a longitudinal study; then fill in the appropriate nation names or years in column one.

3. Turn to Table 15A–1 in Appendix 15A and copy the appropriate war data from the last column of the table to the data coding sheet. For a cross-national study, transfer the information from the designated *year columns* for the nations in Europe to the corresponding *rows* in column 2 of the data coding sheet. For a longitudinal analysis, transfer the information in the particular nation's *row* to the corresponding entries in column 2 of the data coding sheet.

4. Turn to Table 15A–2 or 15A–3 in Appendix 15A, depending on the variable you have chosen to measure "power," and follow the instructions in steps 6 and 8 in exercise 15–15.

DATA CODING SHEET   Coder   *C. Cannizzo*   Date   *9/1/75*

Longitudinal   Study of War   *Initiations*   and   *Military Personnel*

Spatial-Temporal Domain: *Greece, 20th century (by half-decades)*

I	II	III
Half-Decade Ending in	*Number of War Initiations*	Power Score: High or Low on *Military Personnel*
1905	*0*	*Lo*
1910	*0*	*Lo*
1913	*0*	*Lo*
1920	*1*	*Hi*
1925	*0*	*Hi*
1930	*0*	*Hi*
1935	*0*	*Hi*
1938	*0*	*Hi*
1946	*0*	*Hi*
1950	*0*	*Hi*
⋮	⋮	⋮

Figure 15B–1. cont.

Analysis Form Instructions (see Figure 15B–2)

Once you have filled in the data coding sheet properly, you should have no trouble with the analysis. If you have difficulty, go back to the section on constructing a cross-tabulation in part III.

1. Fill in the information at the top of the page as for the data coding sheet.
2. State your hypothesis clearly.
3. Fill in the frequency for each variable for each category in the frequency distribution tables.
4. Transfer the frequencies from the tables in step 3 to the marginals of the contingency table. Go to your data coding sheet and count the number of cases that have some combination of two characteristics (e.g., below-average power scores *and* no war involvements); then compute the remaining cell entries by the subtraction method. (You might wish to count one other combination from the data coding sheet to check your work.)
5. Compute Yule's Q.

ANALYSIS FORM   Researcher *C. Cannizzo*   Date *9/1/75*

Cross-National   Study of War *Involvement*   and *Total Population*

Spatial-Temporal Domain: *Major European Nations 1816 – 1825*
Operational Hypothesis:

European nations that have larger than the

average population of European nations are more

likely to be involved in interstate war.

FREQUENCY DISTRIBUTIONS

War Involvements	Number of Nations	Power Score on Total Population	Number of Nations
None	*8*	Low	*4*
One or More	*2*	High	*6*
Total	*10*	Total	*10*

CROSS-TABULATION

War *Involvements*

Power Score on Total Population		None	One or More	Total
	Low	*a* 5	*b* 1	4
	High	*c* 3	*d* 1	6
	Total	8	2	10

COMPUTATION OF YULE'S Q

Formula: $Q = \dfrac{ad - bc}{ad + bc}$ Numbers: $Q = \dfrac{(5)(1) - (1)(3) = 5 - 3 = 2}{(5)(1) + (1)(3) = 5 + 3 = 8} = .25$

Figure 15B–2. Sample Analysis Forms

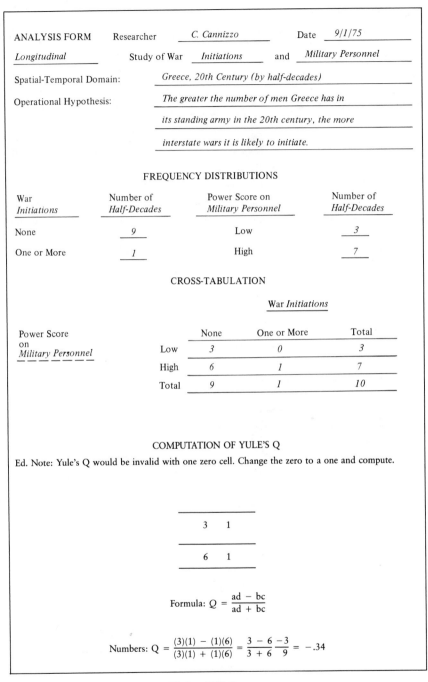

ANALYSIS FORM   Researcher   *C. Cannizzo*   Date   *9/1/75*

Longitudinal   Study of War   *Initiations*   and   *Military Personnel*

Spatial-Temporal Domain: *Greece, 20th Century (by half-decades)*

Operational Hypothesis: *The greater the number of men Greece has in*

its standing army in the 20th century, the more

interstate wars it is likely to initiate.

FREQUENCY DISTRIBUTIONS

War Initiations	Number of Half-Decades	Power Score on Military Personnel	Number of Half-Decades
None	9	Low	3
One or More	1	High	7

CROSS-TABULATION

War *Initiations*

Power Score on Military Personnel	None	One or More	Total
Low	3	0	3
High	6	1	7
Total	9	1	10

COMPUTATION OF YULE'S Q

Ed. Note: Yule's Q would be invalid with one zero cell. Change the zero to a one and compute.

3	1
6	1

Formula: $Q = \dfrac{ad - bc}{ad + bc}$

Numbers: $Q = \dfrac{(3)(1) - (1)(6)}{(3)(1) + (1)(6)} = \dfrac{3 - 6}{3 + 6} \dfrac{-3}{9} = -.34$

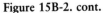

Figure 15B-2. cont.

Appendix 15C:
Data Coding Sheets and Analysis Forms

DATA CODING SHEET   Coder_____ Date_____

_____ Study of War _____

                         and _____

Spatial-Temporal Domain: _____

I	II Number of War _____	III Power Score: High or Low on _____
_____	_____	_____
_____	_____	_____
_____	_____	_____
_____	_____	_____
_____	_____	_____
_____	_____	_____
_____	_____	_____
_____	_____	_____
_____	_____	_____
_____	_____	_____
_____	_____	_____
_____	_____	_____
_____	_____	_____
_____	_____	_____
_____	_____	_____
_____	_____	_____
_____	_____	_____
_____	_____	_____
_____	_____	_____
_____	_____	_____
_____	_____	_____
_____	_____	_____
_____	_____	_____
_____	_____	_____
_____	_____	_____
_____	_____	_____

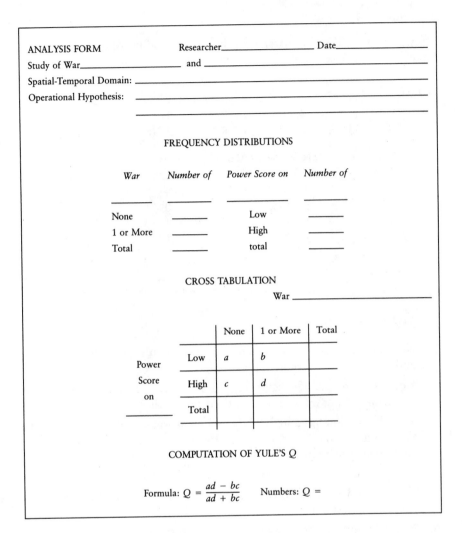

Appendix 15D:
Answers to Exercises

Answers are not given for exercises that are to be discussed in class.

Exercise 15–1

a. S b. T c. T d. T e. S f. T g. T h. S i. T j. S k. T l. S m. T

A class discussion might also be helpful to explain the answers.

Exercise 15–3

Only e, h, m, and n are wars according to the coding rules of Singer and Small. This exercise should be discussed at length in class.

Exercise 15–4

1. 140 3. 1 5. 1 7. 3 9. 59 11. 8
2. 1 4. 6 6. 1 8. 191 10. 30

Number of War Initiations	Number of Nations
0	114
1	20
2	4
3	1
4	2
5	3
Total	144

Exercise 15–8

1. Not a hypothesis. The statement is based on an untestable assumption and is a logical contradiction as well.
2. Not a hypothesis. The sentence is a statement of fact; no contingent predictions from explicit assumptions are made by the statement.
3. Yes. "If a nation has a high GNP" is a measurable and testable assumption, and "then it is more likely to give foreign aid" is a testable, contingent prediction.
4. No, for the same reasons as 2.
5. Yes. Again we have an observable assumption and a contingent prediction that is testable.
6. Not a hypothesis as it stands. The statement is an *assertion* of fact, which may or may not be true. However, it does contain an *implicit* (indirect, not stated outright) hypothesis. Rephrase the sentence using an "if—then" format such as in 3, to make it an *explicit* hypothesis.

Exercise 15–9

Number of War	Years as Nation-State		
Initiations	50 or Less	More Than 50	Total
Zero	86	28	114
1 or more	8	22	30
Total	94	50	144

Exercise 15–10

$$Q = \frac{(86)(22) - (28)(8)}{(86)(22) + (28)(8)} = \frac{1892 - 224}{1892 + 224} = \frac{1668}{2116} = +.79$$

Exercise 15–11

1. Invalid, because of 0 in cell d; cannot compute Yule's Q. Or valid if one changes the 0 to 1; Yule's $Q = -.94$.
2. Valid; Yule's $Q = .5$.
3. Invalid, because it is not a two-by-two table.
4. Valid; Yule's $Q = 1.0$.
5. Valid; Yule's $Q = -.94$.

Bibliographical Essay

The two seminal works in the scientific study of war are Lewis F. Richardson, *Statistics of Deadly Quarrels* (Boxwood Press, 1960), and Quincy Wright, *A Study of War,* 2d ed. (University of Chicago Press, 1965). Although both are dated, they are still worth reading. Also of interest is Pitirim A. Sorokin, *Social and Cultural Dynamics,* vol. 3: *Fluctuations of Social Relations, War and Revolution* (American Book Co., 1937).

Recent scientific studies have centered around the Correlates of War project, directed by J. David Singer. *Resort to Arms: International and Civil Wars, 1816–1980,* by Melvin Small and J. David Singer (Sage, 1982), contains the best data and listing of wars available, as well as a plethora of related information. Some of the main studies of the project have been collected in five volumes. *The Correlates of War: I* (Free Press, 1979) and *Models, Methods, and Progress: A Peace Research Odyssey* (Westview, 1990), both edited by J. David Singer, provide an overview of the theoretical rationale and research origins of the project. *Explaining War,* by Singer and associates (Sage, 1979); *The Correlates of War: II,* edited by Singer (Free Press, 1980); and *Measuring the Correlates of War,* edited by Singer and P. Diehl (University of Michigan Press, 1990), are collections of the major research.

An overview of the field is provided in Manus I. Midlarsky, ed., *Handbook of War Studies* (Unwin Hyman, 1989). Jack S. Levy provides a comprehensive discussion of some of the theories of war that have guided those taking a scientific approach in "The Causes of War: A Review of Theories and Evidence," pp. 209–333 in P. Tetlock et al., eds., *Behavior, Society, and Nuclear War,* vol. 1 (Oxford University Press, 1989). A perceptive discussion of some of the conceptual problems in doing research on war can be found in Benjamin A. Most and Harvey Starr, *Inquiry, Logic, and International Politics* (University of South Carolina Press, 1989). A critique of the scientific study of international relations, with attention to peace research, is provided in Dina A. Zinnes, *Contemporary Research in International Relations* (Free Press, 1976).

439

The major scholarly journals in which ongoing research on the scientific study of peace and war can regularly be found include: *The Journal of Conflict Resolution, International Interactions, Journal of Peace Research, International Studies Quarterly,* and *Conflict Management and Peace Science.* Edited volumes, such as the recent *Prisoners of War? Nation-States in the Modern Era,* edited by Charles S. Gochman and Alan N. Sabrosky (Lexington Books, 1990), have also been an important vehicle for scholarly publications of peace research.

Students and other readers who are looking for a clear discussion of how the scientific approach can be applied to test commonsense notions about war and peace should consult J. David Singer and Melvin Small. "Foreign Policy Indicators: Predictors of War in History and in the State of the World Message," *Policy Sciences* 5 (1974): 271–96, reprinted in *The Correlates of War: I.*

The various sources of conflict that might give rise to war are analyzed in Peter Wallensteen, "Incompatibility, Confrontation and War," *Journal of Peace Research* 18 (1981): 57–90. Zeev Maoz, "Joining the Club of Nations: Political Development and International Conflict 1816–1976," *International Studies Quarterly* 33 (1989): 199–231, presents major findings on the sources of conflict. Charles S. Gochman, "Status, Capabilities, and Major Power Conflict," pp. 82–123 in *The Correlates of War: II,* tests three models on the initiation of disputes. R. Paul Shaw and Yuwa Wong, *Genetic Seeds of Warfare: Evolution, Nationalism, and Patriotism* (Unwin Hyman, 1989), examine the biological basis of war. A classic and still essential study on the origins of war as a human institution is Margaret Mead, "Warfare Is Only an Invention—Not a Biological Necessity," *Asia* 40/8 (1940): 402–405, reprinted in J. Vasquez, ed., *Classics of International Relations* (1986), 1990).

The role of alliances has been a major focus of research. A very early and still highly informative analysis is J. David Singer and Melvin Small, "National Alliance Commitments and War Involvement, 1815–1965," *Peace Research Society (International) Papers* (1966): 109–40. A study that identifies the characteristics of alliances most associated with war is Randolph M. Siverson and Joel King, "Attributes of National Alliance Membership and War Participation, 1815–1965," *American Journal of Political Science* 24 (1980): 1–15. Additional findings on alliances are presented in Charles Ostrom and Francis Hoole, "Alliances and War Revisited," *International Studies Quarterly* 22 (1978): 215–36, and in Patrick McGowan and Robert M. Rood, "Alliance Behavior in Balance of Power Systems: Applying a Poisson Model to Nineteenth-Century Europe," *American Political Science Review* 69 (1975): 859–70. A nice review of the literature is Michael D. Ward, *Research Gaps in Alliance Dynamics* (Monograph Series in World Affairs, Graduate School of International Studies, University of Denver, 1982).

Alliances are more related to the expansion of war than to its onset. The role that alliances and territorial contiguity play in the expansion of war is carefully examined in a key book by Randolph M. Siverson and Harvey Starr, *The Diffusion of War: A Study of Opportunity and Willingness* (University of Michigan Press, 1991). Relevant to the general question of expansion are Yoshinobu Yamamoto and Stuart A. Bremer, "Wider Wars and Restless Nights: Major Power Intervention in Ongoing War," pp. 199–229 in *The Correlates of War: II,* and Henk Houweling and Jan G. Siccama, "The Epidemiology of War, 1816–1980," *Journal of Conflict Resolution* 29 (1985): 641–63. The role the accumulation of disputes and alliances plays in the onset of world war is reported in Manus I. Midlarsky, *The Onset of World War* (Allen and Unwin, 1988). Three other works that have uncovered important factors associated with the expansion, magnitude, and severity of war in light of the polarity debate are Bruce Bueno de Mesquita, "Systemic Polarization and the Occurrence and Duration of War," *Journal of Conflict Resolution* 28 (1978): 563–84; Jack S. Levy and T. Clifton Morgan, "The Frequency and Seriousness of War: An Inverse Relationship?" *Journal of Conflict Resolution* 28 (1984): 731–49; and Alan N. Sabrosky, "Alliance Aggregation, Capability Distribution, and the Expansion of Interstate War," pp. 145–89 in A. Sabrosky, ed., *Polarity and War* (Westview, 1985).

Much theoretical discussion in the past has centered on the role of the balance of power in the onset of war. The concept of the balance of power has many problems, as pointed out by Ernst B. Haas, "The Balance of Power: Prescription, Concept, or Propaganda?" *World Politics* 5 (1953): 442–77. Randolph M. Siverson and Michael P. Sullivan, "The Distribution of Power and the Onset of War," *Journal of Conflict Resolution* 27 (1983): 473–94, provides an illuminating discussion and review of how to test correctly hypotheses about capability and the onset of war, as does Dina A. Zinnes, "An Analytical Study of the Balance of Power Theories," *Journal of Peace Research* 4 (1967): 270–88. One of the most important tests and theoretical discussions of the balance of power is Bruce Bueno de Mesquita "Risk, Power Distributions, and the Likelihood of War," *International Studies Quarterly* 25 (1981): 541–68.

A number of studies have examined what role, if any, capability or changes in power play in the onset of war. Robert Gilpin, *War and Change in World Politics* (Cambridge University Press, 1981), is a traditional and neorealist statement on power and war that has attracted wide attention for its use of rational cost-benefit explanations and is sometimes referred to as the hegemonic theory of war. It has not been widely tested because it does not make as precise predictions as does the power transition thesis. Nevertheless, Raimo Vayrynen, "Economic Cycles, Power Transitions, Political Management and Wars between Major Powers," *International Studies Quarterly* 27 (1983): 389–418, provides a partial test. Stuart A. Bremer,

"National Capabilities and War Proneness," pp. 57–82 in *The Correlates of War: II*, studies whether more powerful nations are more involved in war. A data-based critique of the realist paradigm as an adequate guide for scientific inquiry is given in John A. Vasquez, *The Power of Power Politics: A Critique* (Rutgers University Press, 1983).

Organski's power transition thesis has been widely discussed and debated. The first major test on the power transition thesis was provided by A. F. K. Organski and Jacek Kugler in *The War Ledger* (University of Chicago Press, 1980), chap. 1. Additional tests and important critiques are provided by Henk Houweling and Jan G. Siccama, "Power Transition as a Cause of War," *Journal of Conflict Resolution* 32 (1988): 87–102, and by William R. Thompson, "Succession Crises in the Global Political System: A Test of the Transition Model," pp. 93–116 in A. Bergesen, ed., *Crises in the World System* (Sage, 1983).

Two other approaches to capability and the onset of war are Doran's power cycle theory and the long cycle approach of Modelski and Thompson. On the former, the key works are Charles F. Doran and Wes Parsons, "War and the Cycle of Relative Power," *American Political Science Review* 74 (1980): 947–65, and Charles F. Doran, *Systems in Crisis* (Cambridge University Press, 1991). On the latter, see George Modelski, "The Long Cycle of Global Politics and the Nation-State," *Comparative Studies in Society and History* 20 (1978): 214–35, and William R. Thompson, *On Global War* (University of South Carolina Press, 1988).

Arms races have been the focus of much debate. On the theoretical relationship between arms races and war, two key works are J. David Singer, "Threat-Perception and the Armament-Tension Dilemma," *Journal of Conflict Resolution* 2 (1958): 90–105, reprinted in *The Correlates of War: I*, and Samuel P. Huntington, "Arms Races: Prerequisites and Results," *Public Policy* 8 (1958): 41–86. Wallace's work has been at the center of much of the debate. Critiques of his work by Erich Weede, "Arms Races and Escalation: Some Persisting Doubts," *Journal of Conflict Resolution* 24 (1980): 285–87, and by Michael Altfeld, "Arms Races?—and Escalation? A Comment on Wallace," *International Studies Quarterly* 27 (1983): 225–31, and Wallace's replies are worth reading, as is Wallace's reply to Diehl in "Racing Redux: The Arms Race–Escalation Debate Revisited," pp. 115–22 in Gochman and Sabrosky's, eds., *Prisoners of War?* (1990). Additional research of significance is Henk Houweling and Jan G. Siccama, "The Arms Race–War Relationship: Why Serious Disputes Matter," *Arms Control* 2 (1981): 157–97, and James D. Morrow, "A Twist of Truth: A Reexamination of the Effects of Arms Races on the Occurrence of War," *Journal of Conflict Resolution* 33 (1989): 500–529. Also of relevance is the historical work of Paul Kennedy, "Arms Races and the Causes of War, 1870–1945," pp. 163–77 in P. Kennedy, *Strategy and Diplomacy, 1870–1945* (Allen and Unwin, 1983).

A number of studies have examined the dynamics of arms races. The seminal work is Lewis F. Richardson, *Arms and Insecurity* (Boxwood Press, 1960). Several studies have extended the work of Richardson. Among the most prominent has been the work of Dina Zinnes; see her previously cited *Contemporary Research in International Relations* (1976) and D. Zinnes, J. Gillespie, and R. Rubison, "A Reinterpretation of the Richardson Arms Race Model," pp. 189–217 in D. Zinnes and J. Gillespie, eds., *Mathematical Models in International Relations Research* (Praeger, 1976). A great deal of research has also been carried out on whether specific arms races follow a Richardson process or a bureaucratic politics model. Probably the most important work on this question is Michael D. Ward, "Differential Paths to Parity: A Study of the Contemporary Arms Race," *American Political Science Review* 78 (1984): 297–317. An enlightening review of this problem is Bruce M. Russett, "International Interactions and Processes," pp. 541–53 in A. Finifter, ed., *Political Science: The State of the Discipline* (American Political Science Association, 1983).

The role of territorial contiguity in crisis escalation, which has recently received new attention, has given rise to some strong findings. An early important work is Benjamin A. Most and Harvey Starr, "Diffusion, Reinforcement, Geopolitics, and the Spread of War," *American Political Science Review* 74 (1980): 932–46. Two essential studies to read are Paul F. Diehl, "Contiguity and Military Escalation in Major Power Rivalries, 1816–1980," *Journal of Politics* 47 (1985): 1203–11, and Stuart A. Bremer, "Dangerous Dyads: Conditions Affecting the Likelihood of Interstate War, 1816–1965" *Journal of Conflict Resolution* (Forthcoming). Major findings are also reported in two recent books: the previously cited Siverson and Starr, *The Diffusion of War,* and Gary Goertz and Paul F. Diehl, *Territorial Changes and International Conflict* (Routledge, 1992).

Crisis escalation has been a critical area of investigation that has produced a number of findings. The role of perception of threat has been analyzed by Ole R. Holsti, Robert C. North, and Richard A. Brody, "Perception and Action in the 1914 Crisis," pp. 123–58 in J. David Singer, ed., *Quantitative International Politics* (Free Press, 1968), and by D. Zinnes, R. North, and H. Koch, "Capability, Threat, and the Outbreak of War," pp. 469–82 in J. Rosenau, ed., *International Politics and Foreign Policy,* 1st ed. (Free Press, 1961). Russell Leng's various studies on crisis bargaining are integrated and extended in his *Risky Realpolitik* (Cambridge University Press, forthcoming). For an insightful application of game theory to the study of bargaining in specific historical crises, see Glenn H. Snyder and Paul Diesing, *Conflict Among Nations: Bargaining, Decision Making, and System Structure* (Princeton University Press, 1977). An important general model of crisis bargaining is developed in T. Clifton Morgan, "A Spatial Model of Crisis Bargaining," *International Studies Quarterly* 28 (1984): 407–26.

Major empirical analyses of the dynamics of crisis behavior, especially as it relates to war and peace, may be found in Michael Brecher and Jonathan Wilkenfeld et al., *Crisis, Conflict, and Instability* (Pergamon Press, 1989), Patrick James, *Crisis and War* (McGill–Queen's University Press, 1988), and Charles S. Gochman and Zeev Maoz, "Militarized Interstate Disputes, 1816–1976: Procedures, Patterns, and Insights," *Journal of Conflict Resolution* 28 (1984): 585–616. See also the early work of Richard Barringer, *War: Patterns of Conflict* (MIT Press, 1972), and Charles F. Hermann, ed., *International Crises: Insights from Behavioral Research* (Free Press, 1972).

The role of domestic factors has not received wide treatment. A good review and significant discussion of the role of internal conflict is provided in Jack S. Levy, "The Diversionary Theory of War: A Critique," pp. 259–88 in M. Midlarsky, ed., *Handbook of War Studies* (Unwin Hyman, 1989). The allegedly peaceful nature of democratic states is studied in R. J. Rummel, "Libertarianism and International Violence," *Journal of Conflict Resolution* 27 (1983): 27–71, and in Zeev Maoz and Nasrin Abdolali, "Regime Types and International Conflict, 1816–1976," *Journal of Conflict Resolution* 33 (1989): 3–36. See also the philosophical discussion in Michael Doyle, "Liberalism and World Politics," *American Political Science Review* 80 (1986): 1151–70. Some of the more important studies that look at the domestic political factors promoting the use of external force by democracies are Frank L. Klingberg, "The Historical Alternation of Moods in American Foreign Policy," *World Politics* 4 (1952): 239–73; Jack E. Holmes, *The Mood/Interest Theory of American Foreign Policy* (University of Kentucky Press, 1985); Richard J. Stoll, "The Guns of November: Presidential Reelections and the Use of Force, 1947–1982," *Journal of Conflict Resolution* (1984): 231–46; Charles W. Ostrom and Brian L. Job, "The President and the Political Use of Force," *American Political Science Review* 80 (1986): 541–66; and Bruce Russett, "Economic Decline, Electoral Pressure, and the Initiation of Interstate Conflict," pp. 123–140 in C. Gochman and A. Sabrosky, eds. *Prisoners of War?* (1990). An aggregate data analysis of the associations among domestic political structure, trade, and war proneness is given in William K. Domke, *War and the Changing Global System* (Yale University Press, 1988).

The role of nuclear weapons and of deterrence in crisis escalation is treated in Paul K. Huth and Bruce M. Russett, "What Makes Deterrence Work? Cases from 1900–1980," *World Politics* 36 (1984): 496–526; Paul K. Huth, *Extended Deterrence and the Prevention of War* (Yale University Press, 1988); Jacek Kugler, "Terror without Deterrence: Reassessing the Role of Nuclear Weapons," *Journal of Conflict Resolution* 28 (1984): 470–506; and Daniel S. Geller, "Nuclear Weapons, Deterrence and Crisis Escalation," *Journal of Conflict Resolution* 34 (1990): 291–310. See also the important theoretical discussion in John Mueller, *Retreat from Doomsday: The Obsolescence of Major War* (Basic Books, 1989), on the irrelevance of nuclear weapons.

Whether personal characteristics are related to the use of violence has been the subject of only a few scientific studies. Among the more notable are Lloyd S. Etheredge, *A World of Men: The Private Sources of American Foreign Policy* (MIT Press, 1978), and Margaret G. Hermann, "Explaining Foreign Policy Behavior Using the Personal Characteristics of Political Leaders," *International Studies Quarterly* 24 (1980): 7–46. A suggestive comparison of wars and the role played by images is Ralph White, *Nobody Wanted War* (Doubleday, 1970). See also the comprehensive review of simulation findings in Harold Guetzkow and Joseph J. Valadez, eds., *Simulated International Processes* (Sage, 1981), esp. chaps. 7, 8.

A number of scholars have attempted to develop theoretical models of war in light of data analyses. Michael D. Wallace, "Status, Formal Organization, and Arms Levels as Factors Leading to the Onset of War, 1820–1964," pp. 49–69 in Bruce Russett, ed., *Peace, War, and Numbers* (Sage, 1972), is important for delineating the paths to war and the paths to peace. Nazli Choucri and Robert C. North, *Nations in Conflict* (W.H. Freeman, 1975), provide one of the few systematic theories of the causes of war with an emphasis on domestic determinants and interstate interactions. In a very important book, R.J. Rummel, *War, Power, Peace,* vol. 4 of *Understanding Conflict and War* (Sage, 1979), constructs a set of testable hypotheses about the causes of war and evaluates them in light of existing evidence. Zeev Maoz, *Paradoxes of War: On the Art of Self-Entrapment* (Unwin Hyman, 1990), examines some anomalies in theory, research, and common sense expectations to advance our understanding of the causes of war, its dynamics, and its consequences. John A. Vasquez, *The War Puzzle* (Cambridge University Press, forthcoming), attempts to integrate various findings into a scientific explanation of war with emphasis on the foreign policy practices that lead to war.

Significant work has been conducted on the victors of wars and on the long-term effects of war. On predicting the outcome of war, the following are important and not very difficult: John E. Mueller, "Trends in Popular Support for the Wars in Korea and Vietnam," *American Political Science Review* 65 (1971): 358–75; Organski and Kugler, *The War Ledger,* chap. 2; and Paul Kennedy "The First World War and the International Power System," *International Security* 9 (Summer 1984): 7–40. On the impact of war, see Arthur A. Stein, *The Nation at War* (Johns Hopkins University Press, 1978): Karen A. Rasler and William R. Thompson, *War and State Making* (Unwin Hyman, 1989); and Joshua S. Goldstein, "Kondratieff Waves as War Cycles," *International Studies Quarterly* 29 (1985): 411–44. See also Joshua S. Goldstein, *Long Cycles: Prosperity and War in the Modern Age* (Yale University Press, 1988).

Not much work has been conducted on the characteristics of global systems at peace. Charles W. Kegley, Jr., and Gregory A. Raymond, "Alliance Norms and War: A New Piece in an Old Puzzle," *International Studies Quarterly* 26 (1982): 572–95, and Kegley and Raymond, *When Trust*

Breaks Down (University of South Carolina, 1990), provide evidence on the importance of binding norms. Charles F. Doran, *The Politics of Assimilation* (Johns Hopkins University Press, 1971), and Robert F. Randle, *Issues in the History of International Relations* (Praeger, 1987), give useful historical and theoretical accounts about the nature and characteristics of peaceful global systems. An overview of peace research is offered in Peter Wallensteen, ed., *Peace Research: Achievements and Challenges* (Westview Press, 1988).

Data relevant to the study of peace and war that can be used for term papers can be located in several handbooks. Data on war are contained in Small and Singer, *Resort to Arms*. Data on earlier wars (from 1495) are listed in Jack S. Levy, *War in the Modern Great Power System* (University of Kentucky, 1983). Recently a number of data sets have been completed and/or updated to include data on serious disputes, material capabilities, and wars between major and minor states since 1495. These data are described in Claudio Cioffi-Revilla, *The Scientific Measurement of International Conflict: Data Sets on Crises and Wars, 1495–1990* (Lynne Rienner, 1990). Data on crises are compiled in Michael Brecher et al., *Crises in the Twentieth Century*, vol. 1, *Handbook of International Crises*, and Jonathan Wilkenfeld et al., *Crises in the Twentieth Century*, vol. 2, *Handbook of Foreign Policy Crises* (Pergamon, 1988). See also Gochman and Maoz, "Militarized Interstate Disputes, 1816–1976," *Journal of Conflict Resolution* 28: (December 1984): 585–615. It should also be noted that original data that are analyzed in a study are often reproduced in tables or appendices. Data on the attributes of nations may be located in *World Handbook of Political and Social Indicators*, 3rd ed., C. Taylor and D. Jodice, eds. (Yale University Press, 1983).

References

Agency for International Development. Office of Statistics and Reports. 1972. *U.S. Economic Assistance Programs Administered by the Agency for International Development and Predecessor Agencies, April 3, 1942–June 30, 1971.* Washington, D.C.: AID.

Albertini, L. 1967. *The Origins of the War of 1914.* 3 vols. Translated and edited by I. Massey. London: Oxford University Press.

Albrecht-Carrié, R. 1958. *A Diplomatic History of Europe.* New York: Harper & Row.

———. 1975. "European Diplomacy and Wars (c. 1500–1914)." *Encyclopedia Britannica,* 6: 1081–1115.

Alcock, N., and A. Newcombe. 1970. "The Perception of National Power." *Journal of Conflict Resolution* 14 (3):335–43.

Alker, H.R., Jr., and B. Russett. 1964. "On Measuring Inequality." *Behavioral Science* 9 (July):207–18.

Allan, P. 1982. "From Crisis to Crisis: A Dynamic Model of Inter-nation Interaction." Presented at the annual meeting of the American Political Science Association, Denver, September 2–5.

Allison, G. 1971. *Essence of Decision: Explaining the Cuban Missile Crisis.* Boston: Little, Brown.

Altfeld, M. 1979. "The Reaction of Third States toward Wars." Ph.D. dissertation, University of Rochester.

———. 1983. "Arms Races?—and Escalation? A Comment on Wallace." *International Studies Quarterly* 27 (June): 225–31.

———. 1985. "Nuclear Weapons and War-Choice Decisions." In A. Sabrosky, ed., *Polarity and War,* pp. 191–207. Boulder, Colo.: Westview.

Altfeld, M., and B. Bueno de Mesquita. 1979. "Choosing Sides in Wars." *International Studies Quarterly* 23 (March): 87–112.

Ames, E., and R.T. Rapp. 1977. "The Birth and Death of Taxes: A Hypothesis." *Journal of Economic History* 37: 161–78.

Anderson, P. 1974. *Lineages of the Absolutist State.* London: New Left Books.

André, C., and R. Delorme. 1978. "The Long-Run Growth of Public Expenditure in France." *Public Finance* 33:42–67.

Angell, N. 1933. *The Great Illusion.* New York: Putnam.

Ardant, G. 1975. "Financial Policy and Economic Infrastructure of Modern

States and Nations." In C. Tilly, ed., *The Formation of National States in Western Europe*, pp. 164–242. Princeton, N.J.: Princeton University Press.

Ashley, R. 1981. "Political Realism and Human Interests." *International Studies Quarterly* 25:204–36.

Banks, A. 1971. *Cross-Polity Time-Series Data*. Cambridge, Mass.: MIT Press.

Barbera, H. 1973. *Rich Nations and Poor in Peace and War*. Lexington, Mass.: Lexington Books.

Barringer, R. 1972. *War: Patterns of Conflict*. Cambridge, Mass.: MIT Press.

Bean, R. 1973. "War and the Birth of the Nation State." *Journal of Economic History* 33:203–21.

Beer, F.A. 1981. *Peace against War*. San Francisco: W.H. Freeman.

Bell, C. 1971. *The Conventions of Crisis: A Study in Diplomatic Management*. London: Oxford University Press.

Bennett, J.T., and M.H. Johnson. 1980. *The Political Economy of Federal Government Growth: 1959–1978*. College Station, Texas: Center for Education and Research in Free Enterprise, Texas A&M University.

Berry, T.S. 1978. *Revised Annual Estimates of American Gross National Product*. Richmond, Va.: Bostwick Press.

Bird, R.M. 1971. "Wagner's 'Law' of Expanding State Activity." *Public Finance* 26:1–26.

Blainey, G. 1973. *The Causes of War*. New York: Free Press.

Blalock, H.M., Jr. 1960. *Social Statistics*. New York: McGraw-Hill.

———. 1961. "Evaluating the Relative Importance of Variables." *American Sociological Review* 26 (December): 866–74.

———. 1965. "Theory Building and the Statistical Concept of Interaction." *American Sociological Review* 30 (June): 374–80.

Bleicher, S. 1971. "Intergovernmental Organization and the Preservation of Peace: A Comment on the Abuse of Methodology." *International Organization* 25 (Spring): 298–305.

Blondal, G. 1969. "The Growth of Public Expenditure in Iceland." *Scandinavian Economic History Review* 17:1–22.

Bodart, G. 1916. *Losses of Life in Modern Wars*. Oxford: Clarendon.

Bonin, J.M., B.W. Finch, and J.B. Waters. 1967. "Alternative Tests of the 'Displacement Effect' Hypothesis." *Public Finance* 24:440–56.

Borcherding, T.E. 1977a. "One Hundred Years of Public Spending, 1870–1970." In T.E. Borcherding, ed., *Budgets and Bureaucrats: The Sources of Government Growth*. Durham, N.C.: Duke University Press.

———. 1977b. "The Sources of Growth of Public Expenditures in the United States, 1902–1970." In T.E. Borcherding, ed., *Budgets and Bureaucrats: The Sources of Government Growth*. Durham, N.C.: Duke University Press.

Botnen, I., ed. 1983. *Fakta om Krig og Fred*. Oslo: Pax.

Boulding, K. 1962. *Conflict and Defense: A General Theory*. New York: Harper & Row.

Box, G.E.P., and G.M. Jenkins. 1976. *Time Series Analysis: Forecasting and Control*. Rev. ed. San Francisco: Holden-Day.

Box, G.E.P., and G.C. Tiao. 1975. "Intervention Analysis with Applications to Economic and Environmental Problems." *Journal of the American Statistical Association* 70 (March): 70–92.

Brams, S. 1968. "Measuring the Concentration of Power in Political Systems." *American Political Science Review* 62 (June):461–75.

Braudel, F. 1973. *The Mediterranean and the Mediterranean World in the Age of Philip II.* New York: Harper & Row.

Braun, R. 1975. "Taxation, Socio-Political Structure, and State-Building: Great Britain and Brandenburg-Prussia." In C. Tilly, ed., *The Formation of National States in Western Europe*, pp. 243–327. Princeton, N.J.: Princeton University Press.

Brecher, M. 1980. *Decisions in Crisis: Israel, 1967 and 1973.* Berkeley: University of California Press.

Bremer, S.A. 1972. "Formal Alliance Clusters in the Interstate System: 1816–1965." Presented at the annual meeting of the American Political Science Association.

———. 1980a. "National Capabilities and War Proneness." In J.D. Singer, ed., *The Correlates of War: II, Testing Some Realpolitik Models*, pp. 57–82. New York: Free Press.

———. 1980b. "The Trials of Nations: An Improbable Application of Probability Theory." In J.D. Singer, ed., *The Correlates of War: II, Testing Some Realpolitik Models*, pp. 3–35. New York: Free Press.

———. Forthcoming. "Dangerous Dyads: Conditions Affecting the Likelihood of Interstate War, 1816–1965." *Journal of Conflict Resolution.*

Bremer, S.A., J.D. Singer, and U. Luterbacher. 1973. "The Population Density and War Proneness of European Nations, 1816–1965." *Comparative Political Studies* 6 (October): 329–48.

Bueno de Mesquita, B. 1975. "Measuring Systemic Polarity." *Journal of Conflict Resolution* 19 (June): 187–216.

———. 1978. "Systemic Polarization and the Occurrence and Duration of War." *Journal of Conflict Resolution* 22 (June): 241–67.

———. 1981a. "Risk, Power Distributions, and the Likelihood of War." *International Studies Quarterly* 25 (December): 541–68.

———. 1981b. *The War Trap.* New Haven: Yale University Press.

Bueno de Mesquito, B., and J. D. Singer. 1973. "Alliances, Capabilities, and War: A Review and Synthesis. In C. Cotter, ed., *Political Science Annual: An International Review* 4:237–80. Indianapolis: Bobbs-Merrill.

Bull, H. 1966. "International Theory: The Case for a Classical Approach." *World Politics* 18 (April): 361–77.

Burgess, P.M., and D.W. Moore. 1972. "Inter-Nation Alliances: An Inventory and Appraisal of Propositions." In J.A. Robinson, ed., *Political Science Annual* 3:339–84. Indianapolis: Bobbs-Merrill.

Burke, K., ed. 1982. *War and the State: The Transformation of British Government, 1914–1919.* London: George Allen and Unwin.

Burke, S.M. 1974. *Mainsprings of Indian and Pakistani Foreign Policies.* Minneapolis: University of Minnesota.

Busch, P.C. 1970. "Mathematical Models of Arms Races." In B.M. Russett, ed., *What Price Vigilance?* pp. 193–233. New Haven: Yale University Press.

Cameron, D.R. 1978. "The Expansion of the Public Economy: A Comparative Analysis." *American Political Science Review* 72 (December): 1243–61.

Campbell, D.T. 1958. "Common Fate, Similarity, and Other Indices of the Status of

Aggregates of Persons as Social Entities." *Behavioral Science* 3 (January): 14–25.

Carr, E.H. 1939. *The Twenty Years' Crisis.* 1964 ed. New York: Harper & Row.

Central Statistical Office. *Annual Abstract of Statistics.* London: HMSO.

Chaterjee, P. 1975. *Arms, Alliances, and Stability.* Delhi: Macmillan.

Chirot, D. 1977. *Social Change in the Twentieth Century.* New York: Harcourt Brace Jovanovich.

Choucri, N., and R.C. North. 1975. *Nations in Conflict: National Growth and International Violence.* San Francisco: W.H. Freeman.

Claude, I.L., Jr. 1962. *Power and International Relations.* New York: Random House.

Cline, R. 1975. *World Power Assessment.* Washington, D.C.: Georgetown University.

Cole, W.A. 1981. "Factors in Demand, 1700–80." In R. Floud and D. McCloskey, eds., *The Economic History of Britain since 1700, vol. 1: 1700–1860.* London: Cambridge University Press.

Coleman, J.S. 1964. *Introduction to Mathematical Sociology.* New York: Free Press.

Common Security. A Programme for Disarmament. 1982. Report of the Independent Commission on Disarmament and Security. London: Pan.

Coser, L. 1961. "The Termination of Social Conflict." *Journal of Conflict Resolution* 5 (December): 347–53.

Cronbach, L. 1970. *Essentials of Psychological Testing.* New York: Harper & Row.

Cusack T., and W. Eberwein. 1982. "Prelude to War: Incidence, Escalation and Intervention in International Disputes, 1900–1976." *International Interactions* 9 (1):9–28.

Dahl, R. 1970. *Modern Political Analysis.* 2d ed. rev. Englewood Cliffs, N.J.: Prentice-Hall.

Dahrendorf, R. 1959. *Class and Class Conflict in Industrial Society.* Palo Alto: Stanford University Press.

Davis, J.A. 1971. *Elementary Survey Analysis.* Englewood Cliffs, N.J.: Prentice-Hall.

Davis, W. W., G.T. Duncan, and R.M. Siverson. 1978. "The Dynamics of Warfare, 1816–1965." *American Journal of Political Science* 22 (November): 772–92.

Dean, P.D., and J. Vasquez. 1976. "From Power Politics to Issue Politics: Bipolarity and Multipolarity in Light of a New Paradigm." *Western Political Quarterly* 29 (March): 7–28.

Deane, P. 1955. "The Implications of Early National Income Estimates for the Measurement of Long-term Economic Growth in the United Kingdom." *Economic Development and Cultural Change* 4:3–38.

———. 1968. "New Estimates of GNP for the United Kingdom, 1830–1914." *Review of Income and Wealth* 14:95–112.

———, and W.A. Cole. 1962. *British Economic Growth, 1688–1959.* London: Cambridge University Press.

Dehio, L. 1962. *The Precarious Balance.* New York: Vintage.

Denton, F.H. 1966. "Some Regularities in International Conflict, 1820–1949." *Background* 9 (February): 283–96.

DePorte, A.W. 1979. *Europe between the Superpowers.* New Haven: Yale University Press.

Deutsch, K.W., et al. 1957. *Political Community and the North Atlantic Area.* Princeton: Princeton University Press.

Deutsch, K.W., and D. Senghaas. 1973. "The Steps to War: A Survey of System Levels, Decision Stages, and Research Results." In P.J. McGowan, ed., *Sage International Yearbook of Foreign Policy Studies* 1:275–329. Beverly Hills, Calif.: Sage.

Deutsch, K.W., and J.D. Singer. 1964. "Multipolar Power Systems and International Stability." *World Politics* 16 (April): 390–406.

Deutsch, K.W., J.D. Singer, and K. Smith. 1965. "The Organizing Efficiency of Theories: The N/V Ratio as a Crude Rank Order Measure." *American Behavioral Scientist* 9 (October): 30–33.

Diehl, P. 1983. "Arms Races and Escalation: A Closer Look." *Journal of Peace Research* 20 (5):205–12. Reprinted herein (chapter 4).

———. 1985a. "Arms Races to War: Testing Some Empirical Linkages. *Sociological Quarterly* 26 (3): 331–49.

———. 1985b. "Contiguity and Military Escalation in Major Power Rivalries, 1816–1980." *Journal of Politics* 47 (4):1203–11.

Doran, C. 1971. *The Politics of Assimilation.* Baltimore: Johns Hopkins University Press.

Doran, C., and W. Parsons. 1980. "War and the Cycle of Relative Power." *American Political Science Review* 74 (December): 947–65.

Dumas, S., and K.O. Vedel-Petersen. 1923. *Losses of Life Caused by War.* Oxford: Clarendon.

Dupuy, R.E., and T.N. Dupuy. 1977. *The Encyclopedia of Military History.* New York: Harper & Row.

East, M.A. 1969. "Stratification and International Politics." Ph.D. dissertation, Princeton University.

Eberwein, W.D. 1982. "The Seduction of Power: Serious International Disputes and the Power of Nations, 1900–1976." *International Interactions* 9 (1): 57–74.

Eichenberg, R.C. 1983. "Problems in Using Public Employment Data." In C.L. Taylor, ed., *Why Governments Grow.* Beverly Hills, Calif.: Sage.

Emi, K. 1963. *Government Fiscal Activity and Economic Growth in Japan, 1868–1960.* Tokyo: Kinokuniya.

———. 1979. "Expenditure." In K. Ohkawa and M. Shinohara with L. Meissner, eds., *Patterns of Japanese Economic Development: A Quantitative Appraisal.* New Haven: Yale University Press.

Ezekiel, M., and K.A. Fox. 1959. *Methods of Correlation and Regression Analysis.* New York: Wiley.

Faber, J., and R. Weaver. 1984. "Participation in Conferences: Treaties and Warfare in the European System, 1816–1915." *Journal of Conflict Resolution* 28 (September): 522–34.

Falk, R. 1975. *A Study of Future Worlds.* New York: Free Press.

Falk, R., and S. Mendlovitz. 1973. *Regional Politics and World Order.* San Francisco: Freeman.

Fay, S.B. 1928. *The Origins of the World War.* New York: Macmillan.

———. 1930. "Balance of Power." In E.R.A. Seligman and A. Johnson, eds., *Encyclopedia of the Social Sciences* 2:395–99. New York: Macmillan.

Feinstein, C.H. 1972. *National Income Expenditure and Output of the United Kingdom, 1855–1965*. London: Cambridge University Press.

Fenelon, F. 1920. *Ecrits et Lettres Politiques*. Paris: Editions Bossard.

Feinberg, S.E. 1977. *The Analysis of Cross-Classified Categorical Data*. Cambridge: MIT Press.

Freeman, L.C. 1965. *Elementary Applied Statistics*. New York: Wiley.

Friedman, M. 1973. "Foreign Economic Aid: Means and Objectives." In G. Ranis, ed., *The United States and the Developing Economies*. Rev. ed. pp. 250–63. New York: Norton.

Frumkin, G. 1951. *Population Changes in Europe since 1939*. New York: Augustus M. Kelley.

Fucks, W. 1965. *Formeln zur Macht*. Stuttgart: Deutsch Verlagsanfalt.

Gamson, W. 1975. *The Strategy of Social Protest*. Homewood, Ill.: Dorsey.

George, A. 1979. "The 'Operational Code': A Neglected Approach to the Study of Political Leaders and Decision-making." *International Studies Quarterly* 13 (June): 190-222.

George, A., D. Hall, and W. Simons. 1971. *The Limits of Coercive Diplomacy*. Boston: Little Brown.

George, A., and R. Smoke. 1974. *Deterrence in American Foreign Policy: Theory and Practice*. New York: Columbia University Press.

German, F.C. 1960. "A Tentative Evaluation of World Power." *Journal of Conflict Resolution* 4 (March): 138–44.

Gibbons, J.D. 1971. *Nonparametric Statistical Inference*. New York: McGraw-Hill.

Gilpin, R. 1981. *War and Change in World Politics*. Cambridge: Cambridge University Press.

Gleditsch, N.P., and J.D. Singer. 1972. *Spatial Predictors of National War-Proneness, 1816–1965*. Oslo: Peace Research Institute.

Gochman, C.S. 1975. "Status, Conflict and War." Ph. D. dissentation. University of Michigan.

———. 1980. "Status, Capabilities, and Major Power Conflict." In J.D Singer, ed., *The Correlates of War: II*, pp. 83–123. New York: Free Press.

Gochman, C.S., and R.J. Leng. 1983. "Realpolitik and the Road to War." *International Studies Quarterly* 27 (March): 97–120.

Gochman, C.S., and Z. Maoz. 1984. "Militarized Interstate Disputes, 1816–1976: Procedures, Patterns, Insights." *Journal of Conflict Resolution* 28 (December): 585–616.

Goetz, C.J. 1977. "Fiscal Illusion in State and Local Finance." In T.E. Borcherding, ed., *Budgets and Bureaucrats: The Sources of Government Growth*. Durham, N.C.: Duke University Press.

Goffman, I.J., and D.J. Mahar. 1971. "The Growth of Public Expenditures in Selected Developing Nations: Six Caribbean Countries, 1940–65." *Public Finance* 26:57–74.

Goldberger, A.S. 1964. *Econometric Theory*. New York: John Wiley.

Goldmann, K. 1974. *Tension and Détente in Bipolar Europe*. Stockholm: Esselte Studium.

Goldstein, J.S. 1985. "Kondratieff Waves as War Cycles." *International Studies Quarterly* 29 (December): 411–44.

Gould, G. 1983. "The Growth of Public Expenditures: Theory and Evidence from

Six Advanced Democracies." In C.L. Taylor, ed., *Why Governments Grow.* Beverly Hills, Calif.: Sage.

Gourevitch, P. 1978. "The Second Image Reversed: The International Sources of Domestic Politics." *International Organization* 32 (Autumn): 881–911.

Gray, C.S. 1971. "The Arms Race Phenomenon." *World Politics* 24 (October): 39–79.

Grenville, J.A.S. 1974. *The Major International Treaties, 1914–1973.* London: Methuen.

Gulick, E.V. 1955. *Europe's Classical Balance of Power.* New York: W.W. Norton.

Gupta, S.P. 1967. "Public Expenditure and Economic Growth: A Time Series Analysis." *Public Finance* 22:423–61.

Gurr, T.R. 1970. *Why Men Rebel.* Princeton, N.J.: Princeton University Press.

Haas, E.B. 1953. "The Balance of Power: Prescription, Concept, or Propaganda?" *World Politics* 5 (April): 442–77.

Haas, E.B., and A.S. Whiting. 1956. *Dynamics of International Relations.* New York: McGraw-Hill.

Haas, M. 1970. "International Subsystems: Stability and Polarity." *American Political Science Review* 64 (March): 98–123.

Harris, C., ed. 1963. *Problems in Measuring Change.* Madison: University of Wisconsin Press.

Hayes, W.L., and R.L. Winkler. 1970. *Statistics.* New York: Holt, Rinehart, and Winston.

Heiss, K.P., K. Knorr, and O. Morgenstern. 1973. *Long-Term Projections of Political and Military Power.* Princeton, N.J.: Mathematica.

Helmreich, E.C. 1938. *The Diplomacy of the Balkan Wars, 1912–1913.* New York: Russell and Russell.

Hermann, C.F. 1972. "Threat, Time, and Surprise: A Simulation of International Crisis." In C.F. Hermann, ed., *International Crises: Insights from Behavioral Research*, pp. 187–211. New York: Free Press.

Hibbs, D.A., Jr. 1974. "Problems of Statistical Estimation and Causal Inference in Time Series Regression Models." In H.L. Costner, ed., *Sociological Methodology.* San Francisco: Jossey-Bass.

Hill, D.J. 1914. *A History of Diplomacy in the International Development of Europe.* 3 vols. London: Longman's.

Hintze, O. 1906. "Military Organization and the Organization of the State." In F. Gilbert, ed., *The Historical Essays of Otto Hintze.* 1975 ed., pp. 178–215. New York: Oxford University Press.

Hitch, C.J., and D. McKean. 1960. *The Economics of Defense in the Nuclear Age.* Cambridge, Mass.: Harvard University Press.

Hoffmann, S. 1980. *Primacy or World Order. American Foreign Policy since the Cold War.* New York: McGraw-Hill.

Hollist, W.L., ed. 1978. *Exploring Competitive Arms Processes.* New York: Marcel-Dekker.

Holsti, O.R. 1972a. *Crisis, Escalation, War.* Montreal: McGill–Queens University Press.

———. 1972b. "Time, Alternatives, and Communications: The 1914 and Cuban Missile Crises." In C.F. Hermann, ed., *International Crises: Insights from Behavioral Research*, pp. 58–80. New York: Free Press.

———. 1976a. "Alliance and Coalition Diplomacy." In J.N. Rosenau et al., eds., *World Politics: An Introduction*, pp. 337–72. New York: Free Press.

———. 1976b. "Foreign Policy Formation Viewed Cognitively." In R. Axelrod, ed., *Structure of Decision*, pp. 18–54. Princeton: Princeton University Press.

Holsti, O.R., R.A. Brody, and R.C. North. 1964. "Measuring Affect and Action in International Reaction Models." *Journal of Peace Research* 1 (3–4):170–90.

Holsti, O.R., P.T. Hopmann, and J.D. Sullivan. 1973. *Unity and Disintegration in International Alliances*. New York: Wiley.

Holsti, O.R., R.C. North, and R.A. Brody. 1968. "Perception and Action in the 1914 Crisis." In J.D. Singer, ed., *Quantitative International Politics*, pp. 123–58. New York: Free Press.

Houweling, H.W., and J.G. Siccama. 1981. "The Arms Race–War Relationship: Why Serious Disputes Matter." *Arms Control* 2 (September): 157–97.

Howard, M. 1976. *War in European History*. Oxford: Oxford University Press.

Huelshof, M., and L. Soltvedt. 1981. "Economic Interdependence and the Escalation of Serious Disputes." Mimeo. Correlates of War Project.

Huntington, S.P. 1958. "Arms Races: Prerequisites and Results." *Public Policy* 8:41–46.

James, P., and J. Wilkenfeld. 1984. "Structural Factors and International Crisis Behavior." *Conflict Management and Peace Science* 7 (Spring): 33–53.

Japan Statistical Yearbook. Tokyo: Executive Office of the Statistics Commission and Statistics Bureau of the Prime Minister's Office.

Jervis, R. 1976. *Perception and Misperception in International Politics*. Princeton, N.J.: Princeton University Press.

Jeze, G. 1927. *Les Dépenses de Guerre de la France*. Paris: Les Presses Universitaires de France.

Johnston, J. 1972. *Econometric Methods*. New York: McGraw-Hill.

Kagan, D. 1969. *The Outbreak of the Peloponnesian War*. Ithaca, N.Y.: Cornell University Press.

Kahn, H. 1960. *On Thermonuclear War*. Princeton: Princeton University Press.

Kaplan, M.A. 1957. *System and Process in International Politics*. New York: John Wiley.

Kaufman, J.P. 1983. "The Social Consequences of War: The Social Development of Four Nations." *Armed Forces and Society* 9:245–64.

de Kaufmann, R. 1884. *Les Finances de la France*. Paris: Guillaumin et Cie.

Keesing's. 1974. *Treaties and Alliances of the World*. New York: Scribner's.

Kegley, C.W., Jr., and G.A. Raymond. 1982. "Alliance Norms and War: A New Piece in an Old Puzzle." *International Studies Quarterly* 26 (December): 572–95.

———. 1984. "Alliance Norms and the Management of Interstate Disputes." In J. D. Singer and R. J. Stoll, eds., *Quantitative Indicators in World Politics*, pp. 199–220. New York: Praeger.

———. 1986. "Normative Constraints on the Use of Force Short of War." *Journal of Peace Research* 23 (3):213–27.

———. 1990. *When Trust Breaks Down: Alliance Norms and World Politics*. Columbia: University of South Carolina Press.

Kennan, G. 1979. *The Decline of Bismarck's European Order*. Princeton: Princeton University Press.

Kennedy, P. 1984. "The First World War and the International Power System." *International Security* 9 (Summer): 7–40.

Keohane, R., and J. Nye. 1977. *Power and Interdependence: World Politics in Transition*. Boston: Little, Brown.

Keynes, J. 1920. *The Economic Consequences of the Peace*. New York: Harcourt.

Kindleberger, C.P. 1964. *Economic Growth in France and Britain, 1851–1950*. Cambridge, Mass.: Harvard University Press.

———. 1978. *Economic Response: Comparative Studies in Trade, Finance and Growth*. Cambridge, Mass.: Harvard University Press.

Kissinger, H. 1957. *A World Restored*. Boston: Houghton Mifflin.

———. 1979. *White House Years*. Boston: Little, Brown.

Klingberg, F. 1941. "Studies in the Measurement of the Relations among Sovereign States." *Psychometrica* 6 (6): 335–52.

———. 1966. "Predicting the Termination of War." *Journal of Conflict Resolution* 10 (June): 129–71.

Knorr, K. 1956. *The War Potential of Nations*. Princeton: Princeton University Press.

———. 1970. *Military Power and Potential*. Lexington, Mass.: Lexington Books.

Kohl, J. 1983. "The Functional Structure of Public Expenditures: Long-Term Changes." In C.L. Taylor, ed., *Why Governments Grow*. Beverly Hills, Calif.: Sage.

Kugler, J. 1973. "The Consequences of War." Ph.D. dissertation, University of Michigan.

Kuznets, S. 1971. *Economic Growth of Nations*. Cambridge, Mass.: Harvard University Press, Belknap Press.

Lambelet, J. 1975. "Do Arms Races Lead to War?" *Journal of Peace Research* 12 (2):23–28.

Langer, W.L. 1931. *European Alliances and Alignments, 1871–1890*. New York: Vintage.

———. 1968, 1972. *An Encyclopedia of World History*. Boston: Houghton Mifflin.

Leff, N.H. 1982. *Underdevelopment and Development in Brazil*. Vol 2. London: George Allen and Unwin.

Leng, R.J. 1980. "Influence Strategies and Interstate Conflict." In J.D. Singer, ed., *The Correlates of War: II*, pp. 124–157. New York: Free Press.

———. 1983. "When Will They Ever Learn? Coercive Bargaining in Recurrent Crises." *Journal of Conflict Resolution* 27 (September): 379–419. Reprinted herein (chapter 5).

———. 1984. "Reagan and the Russians: Crisis Bargaining Beliefs and the Historical Record." *American Political Science Review* 78 (September):338–55.

———. 1986. "Realism and Crisis Bargaining: A Report on Five Empirical Studies." In J. Vasquez, ed., *Evaluating U.S. Foreign Policy*, pp. 39–57. New York: Praeger.

Leng, R.J., and C. Gochman. 1982. "Dangerous Disputes: A Study of Conflict Behavior and War." *American Journal of Political Science* 26 (November): 664–87.

Leng, R.J., with R. Goodsell. 1974. "Behavioral Indicators of War Proneness in Bilateral Conflicts." In P.J. McGowan, ed., *Sage International Yearbook of Foreign Policy Studies*, 2:191–226. Beverly Hills, Calif.: Sage.

Leng, R.J., and J.D. Singer. 1970. "Toward a Multi-Theoretical Typology of International Behavior." Ann Arbor: Mental Health Research Institute, April.

———. 1977. "Toward a Multi-Theoretical Typology of International Behavior." In M. Bunge et al., eds., *Mathematical Approaches to International Politics*, pp. 71–93. Bucharest: Romanian Academy of Social and Political Sciences.

Leng, R.J., and H. Wheeler. 1979. "Influence Strategies, Success, and War." *Journal of Conflict Resolution* 23 (December): 655–84.

Levy, J.S. 1981. "Alliance Formation and War Behavior: An Analysis of the Great Powers, 1495–1975." *Journal of Conflict Resolution* 25 (December): 581–613. Reprinted herein (chapter 1).

———. 1983. *War in the Modern Great Power System, 1495–1975*. Lexington: University Press of Kentucky.

———. 1985a. "The Polarity of the System and International Stability: An Empirical Analysis." In A.N. Sabrosky, ed., *Polarity and War*, pp. 41–66. Boulder, Colo.: Westview.

———. 1985b. "Theories of General War." *World Politics* 37 (April): 344–74.

Li, R.P.Y., and W.R. Thompson. 1978. "The Stochastic Process of Alliance Formation: A Time-Series Analysis." *American Political Science Review* 72 (December): 1288–1303.

Liska, G. 1957. *International Equilibrium: A Theoretical Essay on the Politics and Organization of Security*. Cambridge, Mass.: Harvard University Press.

———. 1962. *Nations in Alliance*. Baltimore: Johns Hopkins University Press.

Little, I.M.D., and J.M. Clifford. 1968. *International Aid*. London: Allen and Unwin.

Lockhart, C. 1979. *Bargaining in International Conflicts*. New York: Columbia University Press.

Lowi, T. 1967. "Making Democracy Safe for the World: National Politics and Foreign Policy." In J. Rosenau, ed., *Domestic Sources of Foreign Policy*, pp. 295–331. New York: Free Press.

Luterbacher, U. 1975. *Dimensions Historiques des Modèles Dynamiques de Conflit*. Leiden: A.W. Sythoff.

McCleary, R., and R.A. Hay. 1980. *Applied Time Series Analysis for the Social Sciences*. Beverly Hills, Calif.: Sage.

McClelland, C.A. 1961. "The Acute International Crisis." *World Politics* 14 (October): 182–204.

McNeill, W.H. 1982. *The Pursuit of Power*. Chicago: University of Chicago Press.

Maddison, A. 1964. *Economic Growth in the West*. New York: Twentieth Century Fund.

Mahar, D.J. and R.A. Rezende. 1975. "The Growth and Pattern of Public Expenditure in Brazil, 1920–1969." *Public Finance Quarterly* 3:380–99.

Mallez, P. 1927. *La Restauration des Finances Françaises après 1814*. Paris: Librairie Delloz.

Mansbach, R.W., and J.A. Vasquez. 1981. *In Search of Theory: A New Paradigm for Global Politics*. New York: Columbia University Press.

Maoz, Z. 1982. *Paths to Conflict: International Dispute Initiation, 1816–1976*. Boulder, Colo.: Westview.

———. 1983. "Resolve, Capabilities, and the Outcomes of Interstate Disputes, 1816–1976." *Journal of Conflict Resolution* 27 (June): 195–229.

———. 1984. "A Behavioral Model of Dispute Escalation: The Major Powers, 1816–1976." *International Interactions* 10 (3–4): 373–99.

———. 1989. "Joining the Club of Nations: Political Development and International Conflict, 1816–1976." *International Studies Quarterly* 33 (June): 199–231.

———. 1990. *Paradoxes of War: On the Art of National Self-Entrapment.* Boston: Unwin Hyman.

Marczewski, J. 1961. "Some Aspects of the Economic Growth of France, 1660–1958." *Economic Development and Cultural Change* 9:369–86.

Marion, M. 1914. *Histoire Financière de la France depuis 1715.* 6 vols. Paris: Arthur Rousseau.

Marwick, A. 1974. *War and Social Change in the Twentieth Century: A Comparative Study of Britain, France, Germany, Russia and the United States.* New York: St. Martin's Press.

Mattingly, G. 1955. *Renaissance Diplomacy.* Baltimore: Penguin.

Meltzer, A.H., and S.F. Richard. 1978. "Why Government Grows (and Grows) in a Democracy." *Public Interest* 52:111–18.

Midlarsky, M.I. 1969. "Status Inconsistency and the Onset of International Warfare." Ph.D. dissertation, Northwestern University.

———. 1981. "Equilibria in the Nineteenth-Century Balance-of-Power System." *American Journal of Political Science* 25 (May): 270–96.

———. 1982. "The Coming of World War I: Conflict Reinforcement in the Period 1871–1914." Presented at the annual meeting of the American Political Science Association, Denver.

———. 1983a. "Absence of Memory in the Nineteenth-Century Alliance System: Perspectives from Queuing Theory and Bivariate Probability Distributions." *American Journal of Political Science* 27 (November): 762–84.

———. 1983b. "Alliance Behavior and the Approach of World War I: The Use of Bivariate Negative Binomial Distributions." In Dina Zinnes, ed., *Conflict Processes and the Breakdown of International Systems*, pp. 61–80. University of Denver Monograph Series in World Affairs, Vol. 20.

———. 1984. "Preventing Systemic War." *Journal of Conflict Resolution* 28 (December): 563–84. Reprinted herein (chapter 9).

———. 1986a. *The Disintegration of Political Systems: War and Revolution in Comparative Perspective.* Columbia: University of South Carolina Press.

———. 1986b. "A Hierarchical Equilibrium Theory of Systemic War." *International Studies Quarterly* 30 (March): 77–105.

———. 1988. *The Onset of World War.* Boston: Unwin Hyman.

Ministère de l'Economie. Various years. *Annuaire Statistique de la France.* Paris: Republique Française.

Ministère des Finances. 1946. *Inventaire de la Situation Financière (1913–1946).* Paris: Imprimerie Nationale.

Mitchell, B.R. 1962. *Abstract of British Historical Statistics.* London: Cambridge University Press.

———. 1975. *European Historical Statistics, 1750–1970.* New York: Columbia University Press.

———. 1981. *European Historical Statistics, 1750–1975.* 2d rev. ed. New York: Facts on File.

————. 1982. *International Historical Statistics, Africa and Asia.* New York: New York University Press.

Mitchell, B.R., and H.G. Jones. 1971. *Second Abstract of British Historical Statistics.* London: Cambridge University Press.

Modelski, G. 1972. *Principles of World Politics.* New York: Free Press.

————. 1978. "The Long Cycle of Global Politics and the Nation-State." *Comparative Studies in Society and History* 20 (April): 214–35.

————. 1981. "Long Cycles, Kondratieffs, and Alternating Innovations: Implications for U.S. Foreign Policy." In C.W. Kegley, Jr., and P.J. McGowan, eds., *The Political Economy of Foreign Policy*, pp. 63–83. Beverly Hills, Calif.: Sage.

————. 1982. "Long Cycles and the Strategy of U.S. International Economic Policy." In W.P. Avery and D.P. Rapkin, eds., *America in a Changing World Political Economy*, pp. 97–116. New York: Longman.

————. 1983. "Long Cycles of World Leadership." In W.R. Thompson, ed., *Contending Approaches to World System Analysis*, pp. 115–39. Beverly Hills, Calif.: Sage.

Morgenthau, H.J. 1960, 1967, 1978. *Politics among Nations: The Struggle for Power and Peace.* New York: Knopf.

Morrow, J.D. 1989. "A Twist of Truth: A Reexamination of the Effects of Arms Races on the Occurrence of War." *Journal of Conflict Resolution* 33 (September): 500–29.

Most, B.A., and H. Starr. 1980. "Diffusion, Reinforcement, Geopolitics, and the Spread of War." *American Political Science Review* 74 (December): 932–46.

————. 1983. "Conceptualizing 'War': Consequences for Theory and Research." *Journal of Conflict Resolution* 27 (March): 137–59.

————. 1984. "International Relations Theory, Foreign Policy Substitutibility, and Nice Laws." *World Politics* 36 (April): 383–406.

Mostecky, V., ed. 1965. *Index to Multilateral Treaties.* Cambridge, Mass.: Harvard Law School Library.

Moul, W.B. 1980. "Great Powers and War." Ph.D. dissertation, University of British Columbia.

Mowat, R.B. 1928. *A History of European Diplomacy.* London: Edward Arnold.

Moyal, S.E. 1949. "The Distribution of Wars in Time." *Journal of the Royal Statistical Society*, ser. A 112–4:446–49.

Musgrave, R.A. 1969. *Fiscal Systems.* New Haven: Yale University Press.

Nagarajan, P. 1979. "Econometric Testing of the 'Displacement Effect' Associated with a 'Non-Global' Social Disturbance in India." *Public Finance* 34:100–113.

Nef, J. 1950. *War and Human Progress.* Cambridge, Mass.: Harvard University Press.

Nincic, M. 1982. *The Arms Race.* New York: Praeger.

Nomikos, E.V., and R.C. North. 1976. *International Crisis: The Outbreak of World War I.* Montreal: McGill–Queens University Press.

North, D.C., and R.P. Thomas. 1973. *The Rise of the Western World.* Cambridge: Cambridge University Press.

North, R., R. Brody, and O. Holsti. 1964. "Some Empirical Data on the Conflict Spiral." *Peace Research Society (International) Papers* 1: 1–14.

Notestein, F., I. Taeuber, D. Kirk, A. Coale, and L. Kiser. 1944. *The Future Popu-*

lation of Europe and the Soviet Union: Population Projection, 1940–1970. Geneva: League of Nations.

OECD. 1980. *Main Economic Indicators: Historical Statistics, 1960–1979.* Paris: Organization for Economic Cooperation and Development.

———. 1981. *National Accounts of OECD Countries: Detailed Tables, 1963–1980.* Paris: Organization for Economic Cooperation and Development.

Official Airline Guide. 1978. Oak Brook, Ill.: Reuben H. Donnelley.

Ohkawa, K., and H. Rosovsky. 1973. *Japanese Economic Growth.* Palo Alto, Calif.: Stanford University Press.

Oman, C. 1936. *The Sixteenth Century.* New York: E.P. Dutton.

Oppenheim, L.F. 1947. *International Law: A Treatise.* 6th ed., vol. 1. Edited by H. Lauterpacht. London: Longmans, Green.

Organski, A.F.K. 1958, 1968. *World Politics.* New York: Knopf.

Organski, A.F.K., and J. Kugler. 1978. "Davids and Goliaths: Predicting the Outcomes of International Wars." *Comparative Political Studies* 11 (July): 141–80.

———. 1980. *The War Ledger.* Chicago: University of Chicago Press.

Osgood, R.E., and R.W. Tucker. 1967. *Force, Order, and Justice.* Baltimore: Johns Hopkins University Press.

Ostrom, C.W., Jr. 1978. *Time Series Analysis.* Beverly Hills, Calif.: Sage.

Ostrom, C.W., Jr., and J. Aldrich. 1979. "The Relationship between Size and Stability in the Major Power International System." *American Journal of Political Science* 84 (August): 743–71.

Ostrom, C.W., Jr., and F.W. Hoole. 1978. "Alliances and War Revisited: A Research Note." *International Studies Quarterly* 22 (June): 215–36.

Parry, C., and C. Hopkins. 1970. *An Index of British Treaties, 1101–1968.* London: George Allen and Unwin.

Parsons, T., and E.A. Shils, eds. 1951. *Towards a General Theory of Action.* Cambridge, Mass.: Harvard University Press.

Patem, M.G. 1983. "The Buffer System in International Relations." *Journal of Conflict Resolution* 27 (March): 3–26.

Peacock, A.T., and J. Wiseman. 1961. *The Growth of Public Expenditures in the United Kingdom.* Princeton, N.J.: Princeton University Press.

———. 1979. Approaches to the Analysis of Government Expenditure Growth." *Public Finance Quarterly* 7:3–23.

Petrie, C. 1947. *Earlier Diplomatic History.* London: Hollis and Carter.

Pollard, A.F. 1923. "The Balance of Power." *Journal of the British Institute of International Affairs* 2 (March): 53–64.

Popper, K.R. 1959. *The Logic of Scientific Discovery.* New York: Science Editions.

Porter, B.D. 1980. "Parkinson's Law Revised: War and the Growth of American Government." *Public Interest* 60: 50–68.

Pryor, F.L. 1968. *Public Expenditures in Communist and Capitalist Nations.* Homewood, Ill.: Richard D. Irwin.

Rae, D., and M. Taylor. 1970. *The Analysis of Political Cleavages.* New Haven: Yale University Press.

Rapkin, D., W. Thompson, and J. Christopherson. 1979. "Bipolarity and Bipolarization in the Cold War Era." *Journal of Conflict Resolution* 23 (June): 261–95.

Rapoport, A. 1970. "Is Peace Research Applicable?" *Journal of Conflict Resolution* 14 (June): 277–86.

Rapoport, A., and A. Chammah. 1965. *Prisoner's Dilemma: A Study in Conflict and Cooperation.* Ann Arbor: University of Michigan Press.

Rasler, K.A., and W.R. Thompson. 1983. "Global Wars, Public Debts, and the Long Cycle." *World Politics* 35 (July): 489–516.

———. 1985. "War and the Economic Growth of Major Powers." *American Journal of Political Science* 29 (August): 513–38.

Ray, J.L., and A. Vural. 1986. "Power Disparities and Paradoxical Conflict Outcomes." *International Interactions* 12 (4):315–42.

Reddy, K.N. 1970. "Growth of Government Expenditure and National Income in India: 1872–1966." *Public Finance* 25:81–97.

Richardson, L.F. 1960a. *Arms and Insecurity.* Pacific Grove, Calif.: Boxwood Press.

———. 1960b. *Statistics of Deadly Quarrels.* Pacific Grove, Calif.: Boxwood Press.

Riker, W. 1962. *The Theory of Political Coalitions.* New Haven: Yale University Press.

———. 1969. "Some Ambiguities in the Notion of Power." In R. Bell, ed., *Political Power.* pp. 110–19. New York: Free Press.

Rohn, P.H., ed. 1974. *World Treaty Index.* Santa Barbara, Calif.: ABC-Clio.

Rosecrance, R.N. 1963. *Action and Reaction in World Politics.* Boston: Little, Brown.

———. 1966. "Bipolarity, Multipolarity and the Future." *Journal of Conflict Resolution* 10 (September) : 314–27.

Rosen, S. 1970. "A Rational Actor Model of War and Alliance." In J. Friedman, C. Bladen, and S. Rosen, eds., *Alliance in International Politics*, pp. 215–37. Boston: Allyn and Bacon.

———. 1971. "Cost-Tolerance in Human Lives for Foreign Policy Goals." *Peace Research Society (International) Papers* 15.

———. 1972. "War Power and the Willingness to Suffer." In B.M. Russett, ed., *Peace, War, and Numbers*, pp. 167–83. Beverly Hills, Calif.: Sage. Reprinted herein (chapter 11).

Rosenfeld, B.D. 1973. "The Displacement-Effect in the Growth of Canadian Government Expenditure." *Public Finance* 28:301–14.

Rosenstein-Rodan, P. 1943. "Problems of Industrialization of Eastern and South Eastern Europe." *The Economic Journal* 53 (June):204–207.

———. 1961a. "International Aid for Underdeveloped Countries." *Review of Economics and Statistics* 43 (May): 107–38.

———. 1961b. "Notes on the Theory of the 'Big Push'." In H. Willis, ed., *Economic Development for Latin America*, pp. 57–66. New York: St. Martin's Press.

Rubin, T., and G. Hill. 1973. *Experiments in the Scaling and Weighting of International Events Data.* Arlington, Va.: Consolidated Analysis Center.

Rummel, R.J. 1969. "Indicators of Cross-National and International Patterns." *American Political Science Review* 68 (March): 127–47.

———. 1979. *War, Power, Peace: Understanding Conflict and War*, vol. 4. Beverly Hills, Calif.: Sage.

Russett, B.M. 1963. "The Calculus of Deterrence." *Journal of Conflict Resolution* 7 (June): 97–109.

———. 1965. *Trends in World Politics.* New York: Macmillan.

———. 1967a. *International Regions and the International System.* Chicago: Rand McNally.

————. 1967b. "Pearl Harbor: Deterrence Theory and Decision Theory." *Journal of Peace Research*, no. 2: 89–105.

————. 1968. "Components of an Operational Theory of International Alliance Formation." *Journal of Conflict Resolution* 12 (September): 285–301.

————. 1970. *What Price Vigilance?* New Haven: Yale University Press.

————. 1971. "An Empirical Typology of International Military Alliances." *Midwest Journal of Political Science* 15 (May): 262–89.

Russett, B.M., J.D. Singer, and M. Small. 1968. "National Political Units in the 20th Century: A Standardized List." *American Political Science Review* 62 (September): 385–90.

Russett, B.M., et al. 1964. *World Handbook of Political and Social Indicators*. New Haven: Yale University Press.

Sabrosky, A.N. 1975. "From Bosnia to Sarajevo: A Comparative Discussion of Interstate Crises." *Journal of Conflict Resolution* 19 (March): 3–24.

————. 1980. "Interstate Alliances: Their Reliability and the Expansion of War." In J.D. Singer, ed., *The Correlates of War: II*, pp. 161–98. New York: Free Press.

————. 1985. "Alliance Aggregation, Capability Distribution, and the Expansion of Interstate War." In A.N. Sabrosky, ed., *Polarity and War*, pp. 145–89. Boulder, Colo.: Westview.

Sarbin, T., and V. Allen. 1968. "Role Theory." In G. Lindsay and E. Aronson, *The Handbook of Social Psychology*, vol. 1. Reading, Mass.: Addison-Wesley.

Schelling, T. 1960. *The Strategy of Conflict*. Cambridge, Mass.: Harvard University Press.

Schilling, W. 1965. "Surprise Attack, Death, and War." *Journal of Conflict Resolution* 9 (September): 385–90.

Schlesinger, A.M., Jr., 1965. *A Thousand Days: John F. Kennedy in the White House*. New York: Houghton Mifflin.

Schmidt, M.G. 1983. "The Growth of the Tax State: The Industrial Democracies, 1950–1978." In C.L. Taylor, ed., *Why Governments Grow*. Beverly Hills, Calif.: Sage.

Schwartzenberger, G. 1951. *Power Politics*. New York: Praeger.

Scott, A.M. 1967. *The Functioning of the International System*. New York: Macmillan.

Simmel, G. 1904. "The Sociology of Conflict." *American Journal of Sociology* 9 (January): 490–525.

Singer, J.D. 1958. "Threat-Perception and the Armament-Tension Dilemma." *Journal of Conflict Resolution* 1 (September): 249–99.

————. 1963. "Inter-Nation Influence: A Formal Model." *American Political Science Review* 57 (June): 420–30.

————. 1970a. "Escalation and Control in International Conflict: A Simple Feedback Model." *General Systems Yearbook* 15:163–73. Reprinted in Singer, 1979: 68–88.

————. 1970b. "Knowledge, Practice, and the Social Sciences in International Politics." In N. Palmer, ed., *A Design for International Relations Research*, pp. 137–49. Monograph 10. Philadelphia: American Academy of Political and Social Science.

————. 1970c. "The Outcome of Arms Races: A Policy Problem and a Research

Approach." *Proceedings of the International Peace Research Association* 2:137–46. Reprinted in Singer, 1979: 145–54.

———. 1972. "The Correlates of War Project: Interim Report and Rationale." *World Politics* 24 (January): 243–70.

———. 1973. "Peace Research and Foreign Policy Prediction." Presidential address. *Peace Science Society (International) Papers* 21:1–13. Reprinted in Singer, 1979: 155–71.

———, ed. 1979. *The Correlates of War: I.* New York: Free Press.

———, ed. 1980. *The Correlates of War: II.* New York: Free Press.

———. 1981. "Accounting for International War: The State of the Discipline." *Journal of Peace Research* 18 (1):1–18.

———. 1982. "Confrontational Behavior and Escalation to War 1816–1980: A Research Plan." *Journal of Peace Research* 19 (1):37–48.

———. 1984. *Deterrence, Arms Control, and Disarmament.* 2d ed. Latham, Mass.: University Press of America.

———. 1985. "The Responsibilities of Competence in the Global Village." Presidential address to the International Studies Association. *International Studies Quarterly* 29 (September): 245–62.

Singer, J.D., and associates. 1979. *Explaining War: Selected Papers from the Correlates of War Project.* Beverly Hills, Calif.: Sage.

Singer, J.D., S.A. Bremer, and J. Stuckey. 1972. "Capability Distribution, Uncertainty, and Major Power War, 1820–1965." In B. Russett, ed., *Peace, War, and Numbers*, pp. 19–48. Beverly Hills, Calif.: Sage. Reprinted herein (chapter 2).

Singer, J.D., and J.L. Ray. 1972. "Measuring Distributions in Macro-Social Systems." Ann Arbor: Mental Health Research Institute.

Singer, J.D., and M. Small. 1966a. "The Composition and Status Ordering of the International System, 1815–1940." *World Politics* 18 (January): 236–82.

———. 1966b. "Formal Alliances, 1815–1939." *Journal of Peace Research* 3:1–32.

———. 1966c. "National Alliance Commitments and War Involvement, 1815–1945." *Peace Research Society (International) Papers* 5:109–40.

———. 1968. "Alliance Aggregation and the Onset of War, 1815–1945." In J.D. Singer, ed., *Quantitative International Politics*, pp. 247–86. New York: Free Press.

———. 1972. *The Wages of War, 1816–1965: A Statistical Handbook.* New York: John Wiley.

———. 1974. "Foreign Policy Indicators: Predictors of War in History and in the State of the World Message." *Policy Sciences* 5 (September): 271–96.

Singer, J.D., and R. Stoll, eds. 1984. *Quantitative Indicators in World Politics: Timely Assurance and Early Warning.* New York: Praeger.

Singer, J.D., and M.D. Wallace. 1970. "Inter-Governmental Organization and the Preservation of Peace, 1816–1965: Some Bivariate Relationships." *International Organization* 24 (Summer): 520–47.

———, eds. 1979. *To Augur Well: Early Warning Indicators in World Politics.* Beverly Hills, Calif.: Sage.

SIPRI. 1983. *World Armaments and Disarmament.* London: Taylor and Francis.

Siverson, R.M. 1980. "War and Change in the International System." In O. Holsti, R. Siverson, and A. George, eds., *Change in the International System*, pp. 211–29. Boulder, Colo.: Westview.

Siverson, R.M., and P.F. Diehl. 1989. "Arms Races, the Conflict Spiral, and the

Onset of War." In M. Midlarsky, ed., *Handbook of War Studies*, pp. 195–218. Boston: Unwin Hyman.

Siverson, R.M., and J. King. 1979. "Alliances and the Expansion of War." In J.D. Singer and M. Wallace, eds., *To Augur Well*, pp. 37–49. Beverly Hills, Calif.: Sage. Reprinted herein (chapter 7).

———. 1980. "Attributes of National Alliance Membership and War Participation, 1815–1965." *American Journal of Political Science* 24 (February): 1–15.

Siverson, R.M., and H. Starr. 1990. "Opportunity, Willingness, and the Diffusion of War." *American Political Science Review* 84 (March): 47–67.

Skjelsbaek, K. 1971. "Shared Membership in Intergovernmental Organizations and Dyadic War, 1865–1964." In E. Fedder, ed., *The United Nations: Problems and Prospects*, pp. 31–61. St. Louis: Center for International Studies, University of Missouri.

Skowronek, S. 1982. *Building a New American State: The Expansion of National Administrative Capacities, 1877–1920*. Cambridge, Mass.: Harvard University Press.

Small, M., and J.D. Singer. 1969. "Formal Alliances, 1816–1965: An Extension of the Basic Data." *Journal of Peace Research* 6 (3):257–82.

———. 1970. "Patterns in International Warfare, 1816–1965." *Annals of the American Academy of Political and Social Science* (September): 145–55.

———. 1982. *Resort to Arms: International and Civil Wars, 1816–1980*. Beverly Hills, Calif.: Sage.

Smith, T.C. 1980. "Arms Race Instability and War." *Journal of Conflict Resolution* 24 (June): 253–84.

Snyder, G., and P. Diesing. 1977. *Conflict among Nations: Bargaining, Decision Making, and System Structure in International Crises*. Princeton: Princeton University Press.

Sorokin, P.A. 1937. *Social and Cultural Dynamics*, vol. 3: *Fluctuation of Social Relationships, War, and Revolution*. New York: American Book Co.

Starr, H. 1972. *The War Coalitions*. Lexington, Mass.: Lexington Books.

Starr, H., and B.A. Most. 1976. "The Substance and Study of Borders in International Relations Research." *International Studies Quarterly* 20 (December): 581–620.

Stebbins, R.P., and E.P. Adams, eds. 1976. *American Foreign Relations 1972: A Documentary Record*. New York: New York University Press.

Stein, A.A. 1980. *The Nation at War*. Baltimore: Johns Hopkins University Press.

Stein, A.A., and B.M. Russett. 1980. "Evaluating War: Outcomes and Consequences." In T.R. Gurr, ed., *Handbook of Political Conflict: Theory and Research*, pp. 399–422. New York: Free Press.

Stillman, E.O. 1970. "Civilian Sanctuary and Target Avoidance Policy in Thermonuclear War." *Annals of the American Academy of Political and Social Science* 329 (November): 119.

Stoessinger, J.G. 1964. *The Might of Nations: World Politics in Our Time*. New York: Random House.

Stohl, M. 1976. *War and Domestic Political Violence: The American Capacity for Repression and Reaction*. Beverly Hills, Calif.: Sage.

Strickland, J. 1983. " 'The Second Image Reversed' Revisited." Presented to the annual meeting of the International Studies Association, Mexico City.

Sudre, F.C. 1883. *Les Finances de la France au XIXe Siècle*, vol. 1. Paris: Librairie E. Plon et Cie.

Taylor, A.J.P. 1971. *The Struggle for the Mastery of Europe, 1848–1918*. London: Oxford University Press.

Taylor, C.L. 1981. "Limits to Governmental Growth." In R.L. Merritt and B. Russett, eds., *From National Development to Global Community*, pp. 96–114. London: George Allen and Unwin.

Thompson, W.R. 1983a. "Cycles, Capabilities, and War: An Ecumenical View." In W. Thompson, ed., *Contending Approaches to World Systems Analysis,* pp. 141–62. Beverly Hills, Calif.: Sage.

———. 1983b. "Succession Crises in the Global Political System: A Test of the Transition Model." In A. Bergesen, ed., *Crises in the World System*, pp. 93–116. Beverly Hills, Calif.: Sage.

Thompson, W.R., and G. Zuk. 1982. "War, Inflation, and Kondratieff's Waves." *Journal of Conflict Resolution* 26 (December): 621–44.

Thucydides. 1954. *History of the Peloponnesian War*. Translated by Rex Warner. Baltimore: Penguin.

Tilly, C. 1975. "Reflections on the History of European Statemaking." In C. Tilly, ed., *The Formation of National States in Western Europe*, pp. 3–83. Princeton: Princeton University Press.

———. 1979. "Sinews of War." Presented at the annual meeting of the Council of European Studies Conference of Europeanists, Washington, D.C., March.

Titmuss, R.M. 1969. *Essays on the Welfare State*. 2d ed. Boston: Beacon Press.

Tussing, A.D., and J.A. Henning. 1974. "Long-Run Growth of Non-Defense Government Expenditures in the United States." *Public Finance Quarterly* 2:202–22.

United Nations. 1971. *The World Population Situation in 1970*. Population Studies No. 49. New York: United Nations.

U.S. Department of Commerce. 1975. *Historical Statistics of the United States: Colonial Times to 1970*. Washington, D.C.: Government Printing Office.

U.S. Navy. Oceanographic Office. 1965. *Distance between Ports*. Washington, D.C.: Government Printing Office.

U.S. Office of the President. 1982. *Economic Report of the President*. Washington, D.C.: Government Printing Office.

———. 1983. *The Budget of the United States*. Washington, D.C.: Government Printing Office.

United States Strategic Bombing Survey. 1945. *The Effects of Strategic Bombing on the German War Economy*. Washington, D.C.: Government Printing Office.

———. 1946. *The Effects of Strategic Bombing on Japan's War Economy*. Washington, D.C.: Government Printing Office.

Vasquez, J.A. 1983. *The Power of Power Politics: A Critique*. New Brunswick, N.J.: Rutgers University Press.

———. 1986. "Capability, Types of War, Peace." *Western Political Quarterly* 39 (June): 313–27.

———. 1987. "Foreign Policy, Learning, and War." In C. Hermann, C. Kegley, Jr., and J. Rosenau, eds., *New Directions in the Study of Foreign Policy*, pp. 366–83. Winchester, Mass.: Allen & Unwin.

———. Forthcoming. *The War Puzzle*. Cambridge: Cambridge University Press.

Vayrynen, R. 1983. "Economic Cycles, Power Transitions, Political Management and Wars between Major Powers." *International Studies Quarterly* 27 (December): 389–418.

Voth, A. 1967. "Vietnam: Studying a Major Controversy." *Journal of Conflict Resolution* 9 (December): 428–48.

Wagner, R.E., and W.E. Weber. 1977. "Wagner's Law, Fiscal Institutions and the Growth of Government." *National Tax Journal* 30:59–67.

Walker, S. 1977. "The Interface between Beliefs and Behavior: Henry Kissinger's Operational Code and the Vietnam War." *Journal of Conflict Resolution* 21 (March): 129–68.

Wall, G.R. 1972. *Bipolarization and the International System: 1946–1970*. Stockholm: Swedish Institute of International Affairs.

Wallace, M.D. 1971. "Power, Status and International War." *Journal of Peace Research* 8 (1): 23–35.

———. 1972. "Status, Formal Organization, and Arms Levels as Factors Leading to the Onset of War." In Bruce Russett, ed., *Peace, War, and Numbers*, pp. 49–69. Beverly Hills, Calif.: Sage.

———. 1973a. "Alliance Polarization, Cross-Cutting and International War, 1815–1964." *Journal of Conflict Resolution* 17 (December): 576–604.

———. 1973b. *War and Rank among Nations*. Lexington, Mass.: Lexington Books.

———. 1976. "Arms Races and the Balance of Power: A Preliminary Model." *Applied Mathematical Modelling* 1 (September): 83–92.

———. 1979. "Arms Races and Escalation: Some New Evidence." *Journal of Conflict Resolution* 23 (March): 3–16.

———. 1980. "Some Persisting Findings: A Reply to Professor Weede." *Journal of Conflict Resolution* 24 (June): 289–92.

———. 1982. "Armaments and Escalation: Two Competing Hypotheses." *International Studies Quarterly* 26 (March): 37–51. Reprinted herein (chapter 3).

———. 1985. "Polarization: Towards a Scientific Conception." In A. Sabrosky, ed., *Polarity and War*, pp. 95–113. Boulder, Colo.: Westview.

———. 1990. "Racing Redux: The Arms Race–Escalation Debate Revisited." In C. Gochman and A. Sabrosky, eds., *Prisoners of War? Nation-States in the Modern Era*, pp. 115–22. Lexington, Mass.: Lexington Books.

Wallace, M.D., and J.D. Singer. 1970. "Inter-Governmental Organization in the Global System, 1816–1964: A Quantitative Description." *International Organization* 24 (Spring): 239–87.

Wallensteen, P. 1981. "Incompatibility, Confrontation and War: Four Models and Three Historical Systems, 1816–1976." *Journal of Peace Research* 18 (1):57–90.

———. 1984. "Universalism vs. Particularism: On the Limits of Major Power Order." *Journal of Peace Research* 21 (3): 243–57. Reprinted herein (chapter 10).

Wallerstein, I. 1976. *The Modern World System*. New York: Academic Press.

Waltz, K.N. 1964. "The Stability of a Bipolar World." *Daedalus* 93 (Summer): 881–909.

———. 1967. "International Structure, National Force, and the Balance of World Power. *Journal of International Affairs* 21 (2):215–31.

———. 1979. *Theory of International Politics*. Reading, Mass.: Addison-Wesley.

Ward, M.D. 1982a. "Cooperation and Conflict in Foreign Policy Behavior: Reaction and Memory." *International Studies Quarterly* 26 (March): 87–126.

———. 1982b. *Research Gaps in Alliance Dynamics*. Denver: University of Denver Monograph Series in World Affairs.

Wayman, F.W. 1984a. "Bipolarity and War: The Role of Capability Concentration and Alliance Patterns among Major Powers, 1816–1965." *Journal of Peace Research* 21 (1):61–78. Reprinted herein (chapter 8).

———. 1984b. "Voices Prophesying War: Events and Perceptions as Indicators of Conflict Potential in the Middle East." In J.D. Singer and R.J. Stoll, eds., *Quantitative Indicators in World Politics: Timely Assurance and Early Warning*, pp. 153–85. New York: Praeger.

Wayman, F.W., J.D. Singer, and G. Goertz. 1983. "Capabilities, Allocations, and Success in Militarized Disputes and Wars, 1816–1976." *International Studies Quarterly* 27 (December): 497–514.

Weede, E. 1980. "Arms Races and Escalation: Some Persisting Doubts." *Journal of Conflict Resolution* 24 (June): 285–87.

Wesley, J.P. 1962. "Frequency of Wars and Geographical Opportunity." *Journal of Conflict Resolution* 6 (September): 387–89.

Wheeler, H.G. 1980. "Postwar Industrial Growth." In J.D. Singer, ed., *The Correlates of War: II*, pp. 258–84. New York: Free Press.

Winch, R., and D. Campbell. 1969. "Proof? No. Evidence? Yes. The Significance of Tests of Significance." *American Sociologist* 4 (February): 140–43.

Wiseman, J., and J. Diamond. 1975. "Comment: On Long-run Growth of Nondefense Government Expenditures in the United States." *Public Finance Quarterly* 3:411–14.

Wohlstetter, A. 1968. "Illusions of Distance." *Foreign Affairs* 46 (January): 242–56.

Wolf, C., Jr. 1973. "Economic Aid Reconsidered." In G. Ranis, ed., *The United States and the Developing Economies*, pp. 250–78. Rev. ed. New York: Norton.

Woods, F.A., and A. Baltzly. 1915. *Is War Diminishing?* Boston: Houghton Mifflin.

Wright, Q. 1942, 1965. *A Study of War*. Chicago: University of Chicago Press.

Yamamoto, Y., and S.A. Bremer. 1980. "Wider Wars and Restless Nights: Major Power Intervention in Ongoing War." In J. D. Singer, ed., *The Correlates of War: II*, pp. 199–229. New York: Free Press.

Young, H.D. 1962. *Statistical Treatment of Experimental Data*. New York: McGraw-Hill.

Young, O. 1967. *The Intermediaries*. Princeton: Princeton University Press.

Zinnes, D.A. 1967. "An Analytical Study of the Balance of Power Theories." *Journal of Peace Research* 4 (3):270–88.

Zinnes, D., and R. Muncaster. 1984. "The Dynamics of Hostile Activity and the Prediction of War." *Journal of Conflict Resolution* 28 (June): 187–229.

Zinnes, D., R.C. North, and H.E. Koch, Jr. 1961. "Capability, Threat, and the Outbreak of War." In J. Rosenau, ed., *International Politics and Foreign Policy*, pp. 469–82. 1st ed. New York: Free Press.

Author Index

467

Subject Index

About the Editors

John A. Vasquez is professor of political science at Rutgers University. He is the author of *The Power of Power Politics*, coauthor (with Richard Mansbach) of *In Search of Theory*, and editor of the reader, *Classics of International Relations*. His forthcoming book, *The War Puzzle*, builds on many of the findings reported in this volume.

Marie T. Henehan is assistant professor of political science at the University of Scranton. She received her Ph.D. in political science from Rutgers University in 1989. She is currently working on a project on critical issues, Congress, and foreign policy.